CAS PROFESSIONAL STANDARDS FOR HIGHER EDUCATION

Eighth Edition
2012

Dorothy I. Mitstifer, PhD
CAS Publications Editor
Executive Director, Association of College Honor Societies

Council for the Advancement of Standards in Higher Education

Washington, DC

CAS Professional Standards for Higher Education
8th Edition

© Copyright 2012 by the Council for the Advancement of Standards in Higher Education

Library of Congress Cataloging-in-Publication Data
Mitstifer, Dorothy
CAS Professional Standards for Higher Education
Includes bibliographic references.

ISBN: 978-0-9858819-0-0
1. Student Affairs, 2. Student Services, 3. Professional Standards, 4. Advising,
5. Counseling, 6. Higher Education, 7. Learning Assistance

This book is a revision of *CAS Professional Standards* previously published in 1986, 1997, 1999, 2001, 2003, and 2006, and 2009.

Appropriate citation format:
Council for the Advancement of Standards in Higher Education. (2012). *CAS professional standards for higher education* (8th ed.). Washington, DC: Author.

Council for the Advancement of Standards in Higher Education

CAS Professional Standards for Higher Education (8th ed.)

Table of Contents

New or revised since 2009 edition

Appendices

CAS

CAS President's Letter to the Profession

Thirty-three years, eight editions, six presidents, three editors. An increase from 17 sets of standards published in the first edition in 1986 to 43 sets in this edition. Evolution from copies in three ring binders to CDs and electronic downloads. Growth from 11 member associations, all representing traditional student affairs functional areas, at the time CAS was chartered to 42 current members reflecting areas across higher education. Development from a little-recognized entity to an internationally known organization with a Facebook presence and an office at the National Center for Higher Education at One Dupont Circle in Washington, DC. Over more than three decades, CAS has changed significantly, but much of the foundation on which it was built remains the same.

The CAS Guiding Principles, outlined in the CAS Context that follows, reflect the values that inform the standards. A focus on the student as a whole person, the concept that the total environment is educational and should engender health, the importance of diversity and multiculturalism, the necessity of strong leadership and well-managed organizations, and the obligation to practice ethically—these are some of the ideas that undergird the standards. CAS is rooted in a belief in self-regulation, with confidence that professionals can and will use standards to assure quality in their work. Finally, CAS continues to be grounded in the conviction that strong programs and services lead to positive outcomes for students. These ideas are as relevant today as they were over thirty years ago.

It is my privilege and pleasure, as President of CAS, to present this 8th edition of CAS Professional Standards for Higher Education. This edition includes a number of changes from previous editions: the General Standards that are embedded in every set of functional area standards have been updated; standards related to distance learning have been incorporated into the General Standards rather than appearing separately; and five new functional areas have been added since the 7th edition. These new functional areas reflect a variety of issues facing our institutions today; CAS now offers standards for Campus Police and Security Programs, Parent and Family Programs, Sexual Assault and Relationship Violence Prevention Programs, Transfer Student Programs and Services, and Veterans and Military Programs and Services. These topics echo some of the very real challenges that professionals confront, and I am proud that CAS continues to be in the forefront of identifying such needs and offering resources to help practitioners address them in positive and productive ways.

As a former CAS Editor, I am fully acquainted with what it takes to produce this volume. My appreciation goes out to the CAS Executive Committee, the CAS Board of Directors, the expert reviewers, and the member organizations who worked to ensure that these standards are informed by multiple perspectives and represent the very best thinking across higher education today. I particularly want to extend my thanks to Dorothy Mitstifer, CAS Editor, and to her Editorial Assistant, Jen Wells. Their work, attention to detail, and dedication to the task are exemplary, and we are all indebted to them.

Finally, I would be remiss if I were not to recognize the many contributions to CAS by Phyllis Mable—founder, past president, and first Executive Director. For over three decades, Phyllis was a guiding force in CAS, and a constant presence across both meeting rooms and dinner tables. Although we keenly feel her recent loss, her legacy will live on in the work that we do.

It is my hope that this 8th edition of CAS Professional Standards for Higher Education continues to serve practitioners, preparation program faculty, and graduate students across higher education as we work together to create high quality programs and services for the benefit of our institutions and, ultimately, our students.

As Phyllis would remind us, live, love, learn, and leave a legacy,

Laura A. Dean
CAS President
Associate Professor, University of Georgia

Editor's Note

Standard: example of something measured; a principle of propriety, honesty, and integrity; level of quality or excellence . . .

Standards Committees, the Executive Committee, the Board of Directors, and external experts, without whom this publication would not have been possible, have supported my work as editor. Board members as well as the respective associations have been helpful; some have had a greater role in this publication because some of the standards were revised for this edition. Other board members updated the contextual statements to reflect the current status of programs. I am proud that this edition has a new set of General Standards that is incorporated in every functional standard. This was not an easy task, but the voices and perspectives of the CAS membership came together to create a revision that found consensus. We can be proud that there are some new standards: Campus Police and Security Programs, Parent and Family Programs, Sexual Assault and Relationship Violence Prevention Programs, Transfer Student Programs and Services, and Veterans and Military Programs and Services. Certainly, over time, the CAS standards have not only been expanded and updated but improved in clarity and function.

As an outsider to student affairs, I have appreciated the opportunities to learn more about the functional areas of the academy. Coming from the academic side, I shared an interest in standards for learning and development as well as for operational domains in programs and services, but now I have been able to expand my knowledge as well as contributions. And I must say that I'm a little jealous that academic programs, for the most part, are not as advanced in setting standards and in measuring outcomes. I have shared some CAS approaches, but it takes a community to initiate change. CAS is such a community.

From my perspective as an educator, the CAS approach of voluntary self-regulation of student outcome assessment is beneficial. But the trend toward more accountability, demanded by the public and accrediting associations, may mean that the functional areas of higher education risk external mandates for assessment systems. It is better to be proactive than reactive, so CAS must continue its outreach to provide leadership. It is my hope that this publication serves that purpose.

I am grateful to prior editors for establishing the general content and process for communicating the latest professional standards and especially Laura Dean for her guidance and support. Certainly this publication depended upon the skills of Jen Wells for the technical aspects of production. Although I have developed my skills of editing and publishing over time, this was a new arena. It was reassuring that both had my back. Thank you Laura and Jen. Thank you, too, Karen Agee for your eagle eye.

The Association of College Honor Societies (ACHS) has supported me in this undertaking. Certainly ACHS has profited from CAS membership and the CAS focus on student learning and development. College honor societies will prosper with more focus on measuring outcomes of chapter membership. The support of the functional areas of the academy to assist in changing the culture of student organizations to one of professional development and lifelong learning could be a great legacy for CAS.

It took a great many people working behind the scenes to bring this book to life. My thanks to you all.

Dorothy I. Mitstifer, PhD
CAS Publications Editor
Executive Director, Association of College Honor Societies

Introduction
CAS Professional Standards for Higher Education

This 2012 edition of *CAS Professional Standards for Higher Education,* often referred to as the *CAS Blue Book* or the *CAS Book of Standards,* is the eighth iteration of professional standards generated and promulgated by the Council for the Advancement of Standards in Higher Education (CAS). This edition contains 31 previously published functional area standards, along with 7 standards that have recently undergone major revision and 5 new standards that appear for the first time in this edition. This brings the total number of functional area standards to 43, including the standard for Masters-Level Student Affairs Professional Preparation Programs. CAS continues to attract interest from professionals across higher education, whether they are seeking to use existing professional standards or to develop new ones.

As institutions of higher learning face new challenges, faculty and staff members often find it necessary to implement their responsibilities in new and different ways. Approaches and strategies that were previously successful may need to be amended as institutions and programs evolve and student populations and characteristics change. As institutions and their constituents change, so too must the vehicles that guide practice within the shifting culture. As new developments result in previously unrecognized or newly identified student needs, programs and services must change as well. In light of these factors, each CAS standard must be viewed as a living document that will shift over time as it reflects an evolving function.

The standards that have been revised since the 2009 edition include those focused on Campus Information and Visitor Services; Career Services; Lesbian, Gay, Bisexual, and Transgender Programs and Services; Undergraduate Admissions Programs and Services; Counseling Services; and Conference and Event Programs. As the field changes, so does our language, and several of these have been renamed to reflect more current philosophy and practice. Additionally, new standards have been developed in the areas of Parent and Family Programs, Veterans and Military Programs and Services, Sexual Assault and Relationship Violence Prevention Programs, Campus Police and Security Programs, and Transfer Student Programs. Again, the development of new standards reflects the evolving nature of our work in higher education. As has been increasingly true in previous editions, the breadth of CAS standards focuses attention not only on functions that comprise the traditional student affairs areas and directly support student learning and development but also on other educational functions essential to institutional effectiveness that may be less focused on direct work with students. This expanded CAS vision reflects an increased emphasis on developing standards to guide professional practice throughout the whole of higher education.

In addition to the inclusion of new standards and revision of existing ones, every set of standards has been embedded with the updated General Standards, which were revised in 2011. The General Standards appear within every set of standards and represent areas of practice that are essential regardless of functional area. CAS periodically reviews and updates the General Standards to ensure currency. This revision has combined parts and reduced the number for each set of standards to 12. Finally, it aligns the General Standards with the essentials of professional practice today.

Also included in this edition are two documents: the *CAS Characteristics of Individual Excellence* and the *CAS Statement of Shared Ethical Principles.* Both were the result of extended work within CAS, these materials expand the work of CAS to the consideration of the hallmarks of high quality professional practice and of the ethical values that are held in common across functional areas.

Rationale and Evolution

As appears obvious in retrospect, CAS was created as a direct response to the emerging profession's need to establish standards to guide both practice and preparation. By the 1960s, the felt need for a profession-wide entity to speak as one voice for all was very apparent. An initial attempt to establish such a group, the Council of Student Personnel Associations in Higher Education (COSPA), was mounted in the late 1960s by 10 student affairs associations. This consortium is best remembered for its promotion of an enlightened approach to student affairs practice reflected in a statement published in 1972 by its Commission of Professional Development entitled "Student Development Services in Post-Secondary Education" (Rentz, 1994). Unfortunately, COSPA was dissolved in 1976, largely as a result of member disillusionment resulting from unresolved political issues.

CAS was established as a consortium comparable to COSPA for an equally important, though less ambitious, purpose. Whereas COSPA was intended to function on a full range of professional issues, CAS from the outset sought to avoid politicization and to be driven by shared values rather than special interests. Consequently, the purposes and objectives of CAS are highly focused, which tends to protect the Council from internal strife resulting from member disagreement about its designated purpose and the processes used to accomplish its mission.

Although some professional associations or inter-association collectives may work to establish standards of good practice for specific student support services, their products and models are unlikely to become part of the educational culture unless they are viewed as an enhancement to the broad educational interests of students and institutions. In other words, credibility within the whole of higher education is more effectively gained through collective action than through narrowly defined initiatives of individuals or associations. For standards of professional practice to be truly viable, they must reflect the interests and values of multiple professional organizations and the functional areas they champion. CAS strives to provide this collaborative avenue to establishing thoughtful, balanced, and achievable standards upon which all can rely.

A Legacy of Collaboration

CAS was established over thirty years ago for purposes of developing and promulgating standards of professional practice to guide higher education practitioners and their institutions, especially in regard to work with college students. The Council for the Advancement of Standards in Higher Education, a name adopted in 1992 to reflect the expanded context of the Council's higher education focus, was originally established in 1979 as a not-for-profit corporation called the Council for the Advancement of Standards for Student Services/Development Programs. Impetus for its existence was encouraged by a movement on the part of several national associations to develop accreditation standards for academic programs that prepare counselors and counselor educators. This movement, which culminated in the establishment of the Council for the Accreditation of Counseling and Related Educational Programs (CACREP) in 1980, provided the American College Personnel Association (ACPA) with impetus to create a set of preparation standards for use in master's level college student affairs administration programs. Rather than promulgating these standards as its own, ACPA sought out other professional associations interested in the development of standards for student affairs preparation and practice. The National Association of Student Personnel Administrators (NASPA) indicated an interest in the project, and the two associations jointly issued invitations to a meeting of interested professional associations. Seven student affairs-oriented organizations sent representatives to the exploratory meeting held in Alexandria, Virginia in June 1979. This meeting resulted in the creation of an inter-association consortium for purposes of developing and promulgating professional standards to guide both student affairs practice and academic preparation of those who administer student support programs and services. A subsequent organizational meeting in September 1979 resulted in the establishment of CAS as a not-for-profit corporate consortium of 11 charter member associations (see Appendix A).

Today, after nearly three decades of collaboration and a name change to reflect its expanded interests, the Council for the Advancement of Standards in Higher Education is composed of 36 member associations from the U.S. and Canada, and has generated and promulgated 42 sets of functional area standards and guidelines, one set of master's level academic preparation program standards for college student affairs administration, statements regarding characteristics of individual excellence for professionals in higher education and the ethical principles that are held in common across the many areas of professional practice represented at CAS, and a learning and development outcomes model that reflects the most current thought on the intended results of quality practice.

Considering the history of CAS, it now seems certain that without CAS working collaboratively and speaking collectively on behalf of practitioners and their functional area specialties, there would be no profession-wide criteria of good practice such as the CAS standards. In effect, CAS desires to represent every college and university educator and functional area specialist who believes the learning and development of all students to be the essence of higher education.

A Mission of Quality Enhancement

CAS was founded to implement several profession-wide initiatives, with emphasis on the development and promulgation of professional standards. As CAS has evolved, its *raison d'être* has shifted as well. The following reflects the contemporary CAS mission, as revised in 2008:

> The mission of the Council for the Advancement of Standards in Higher Education (CAS) is to promote the improvement of programs and services to enhance the quality of student learning and development. CAS is a consortium of professional associations who work collaboratively to develop and promulgate standards and guidelines and to encourage self-assessment.

As the mission implies, CAS exists to accomplish several complementary tasks. A primary purpose is to provide a forum in which representatives from higher education organizations can meet and interact for purposes of seeking consensus on the fundamental principles of "best practice" that can lead to enhanced professional standards. The CAS initiative provides a forum where all voices can be heard in the creation of current and useful standards to guide contemporary practice. This approach encourages the establishment of viable linkages among professional associations, most of which focus on highly specialized functions. This professional collaboration results in the creation of standards that represent a profession-wide perspective rather than a narrow and limited viewpoint.

Not only does the CAS initiative provide a vehicle for the development of functional area and academic preparation standards, but it also provides a well recognized and credible profession-wide entity to publish and promulgate standards and related materials and to encourage and educate practitioners to apply the standards effectively in their work with students. Further, and of special significance, the CAS consortium speaks with a single voice that bridges numerous specialty areas and can represent the profession-at-large on matters concerning professional standards and quality assurance.

Foundations for Standards and Guidelines

The initial full CAS publication, *CAS Standards and Guidelines* (CAS, 1986), was based on the premise that practitioners needed access to a comprehensive and valid set of criteria by which to judge program quality and effectiveness. Further, it was viewed as essential that those standards represent quality practices that any college or university program could reasonably achieve.

From the CAS perspective, virtually all functional areas of practice, no matter how specialized, have identifiable commonalties with other functions. For example, an institution's admission, academic advising, campus activities, and career services programs, although established to accomplish clearly different purposes, will each benefit from establishing a written mission statement that is compatible with the mission of the institution. Likewise, the same is true for human, fiscal, physical, and technological resources; legal responsibilities; campus and community relations; ethical considerations; and assessment, among others. Consequently, CAS developed and has incorporated a number of common criteria that have relevance for each and every functional area, no matter what its primary focus. These common criteria are referred to as "general standards" and are embedded in all functional area standards. These general standards are designed to overcome the "silo effect" so common throughout higher education in which autonomous administrative units, programs, and services function independently and sometimes inconsistently. In effect, the general standards make the CAS standards highly utilitarian and promote inter-departmental, inter-program, and inter-service cooperation and collaboration. Users are encouraged to view the CAS standards and guidelines as vehicles that interconnect administrative units. Because what these various functional units have in common (e.g., educational purpose, student learning and development) often exceeds their differences, the effective practitioner will find that collaboration between and among units will enhance the educational environment in many important ways.

Another use of the general standards is in those offices or areas for which no CAS standards have been developed. Although the general standards do not offer the specialty standards designed to address specifically the particular functional area, they do offer essential standards of practice that are applicable to all areas and so can be used where no other standards exist. The general standards are also useful in conducting an assessment of an office that has multiple functional responsibilities (e.g., activities, leadership, and orientation). By identifying the general standards that are the same in each of the relevant sets of standards, practitioners can recognize the parts of the standards that overlap and the parts that speak to the various functions, thereby creating one non-repetitive set of standards that reflects the complex nature of the office.

The CAS standards and guidelines are written using similar language to clearly reflect the intent of the statements. All CAS standards use the auxiliary verbs "**must**" and "**shall**" and appear in **bold print** so that users can quickly identify them. As previously noted, all functional areas have specialty standards in addition to the general standards. Specialty standards are essential to accomplishing a support program's purpose and appear in **bold print** as do the general standards.

CAS standards are constructed to represent criteria that every higher education institution and its student support programs should be expected and able to meet with the application of reasonable effort and diligence. Although the standards are carefully worded, it is sometimes helpful to amplify them by providing additional information to facilitate the user's ability to interpret them accurately. Also, when programs are organizationally mature, there is need to provide users with additional criteria that may be used to make good programs even better. Consequently, as a supplement to its standards, CAS has established "guidelines" designed to clarify and amplify the standards. Guidelines may be used to guide enhanced practice when a program has previously achieved high levels of effectiveness. Guidelines use the auxiliary verbs "should" and "may" and are printed in lightface type to distinguish them from the standards.

In summary, CAS functional area standards and guidelines are basic statements that should be achievable by any program in any higher education institution when adequate and appropriate effort, energy, and resources are applied. Further, standards reflect a level of good practice generally agreed upon by the profession-at-large. In addition to the standards, guidelines are incorporated into each functional area to amplify and explain the standards and to guide enhanced practice. This dual presentation is helpful because functional area programs in both early and advanced stages of development can use the CAS standards effectively. Most important is the fact that the CAS standards have been conceived and developed via a profession-wide process that can ensure continuity and consistency of practice among all higher education institutions. In addition, each set of standards is reviewed regularly to assess currency and determine need for revision.

In considering the CAS standards and guidelines, it is important to note and understand that they are not value-neutral. As discussed further in the next section (see CAS Context), there is a clear set of values that serves as the underpinning for the standards. The values are derived from the theories and models that inform our work and from the historical documents that have guided the development of our field; they serve today as important touchstones for the ideas that shape our approaches and that have shaped these standards. Although these ideas have been consistently incorporated in the development of the standards to date, there has been some criticism that they are too reflective of the democratic culture of U.S. higher education and therefore not inclusive enough for application to a global higher education environment. As users of CAS standards broaden to an international arena, so does the geo-political environment that increasingly connects us. These new situations and voices may inform future development of the standards, but they remain grounded in American ideals.

Influence of CAS on Practice

The CAS standards and guidelines were established for institutions' student support programs and services to use for program development, program self-study, and staff development purposes. Although the standards have utility for institutional and program accreditation purposes, CAS has not sought to establish its own accrediting process. Rather, CAS takes the position that individualized institutional and program "self-regulation" is the preferred route to program quality and effectiveness. CAS views its profession-wide role as that of developing and promulgating professional standards to guide practice and of educating practitioners in the appropriate use of those standards.

The professional role of the Council for the Advancement of Standards in Higher Education has become increasingly important during the past three decades. The first order of business for CAS was to develop and promulgate professional standards of practice and preparation for student affairs and student support programs and services. However, CAS is now viewed by many as an important professional development vehicle as well. Results of CAS user surveys designed to determine how CAS influences professional practice and how CAS materials are used have been revealing.

Many practitioners indicated that CAS standards are important because they speak to issues of institutional change as practitioners struggle to meet the needs of ever-changing student bodies, not only in numbers but in age, gender, race, ethnicity, ability, sexual orientation, and long-term goals as well. One respondent shared the perspective that

. . . as each campus has examined its own situation, and looked to its peers for ideas, the CAS standards have guided not only implementation but review and evaluation. Most of this work was done in expansionary times. Now as we regroup, downsize, retrench, whatever institutions name it, we need to have some means by which to measure what we do. The CAS standards, in all of the functional areas, serve as an excellent tool to begin that process. They are flexible without being vague, broad without being limitless, and ideal for what we constantly face in higher education, change.

This comment reflected the value of the CAS initiative for entry-level professionals:

I can easily imagine that the standards would provide indispensable guidance for some of our younger or less experienced colleagues in graduate education. It must be like having a consultant's report at your finger tips that attests, "Do at least this much well, and you will find success in your program."

The CAS enterprise has led to a number of spin-offs in that some professional groups have expanded on the standards to meet sometimes highly specific professional needs. One example is in the area of learning assistance. As one respondent noted,

No sooner than the first *Learning Assistance Program Standards* were published, we were already talking about how to build upon that work. Whereas the CAS standards addressed broad basic elements that are essential to a comprehensive learning assistance program, practitioners in the field expressed interest in obtaining similar statements that addressed pedagogical components as well.

Consequently, the National Association for Developmental Education [NADE] responded to the challenge by creating "NADE Guides." These documents emulated the CAS standards assessment model and addressed the specific functions of tutoring services, adjunct instructional programs, developmental coursework, and the teaching/learning process. This developmental activity led to inter-association cooperation among learning assistance and developmental education organizations and paved a path for communication and collaboration in subsequent revisions of the *CAS Learning Assistance Program Standards* that follow in Part 2 of this volume. A related comment was made by a close observer of CAS initiatives.

I have two general observations. First, CAS has filled a void that no other organization could accomplish. A network has been established to mutually equip the student affairs profession with standards of performance. Second, the CAS effort has attracted increased attention and offered increased value over the years. A genuine service has been provided to the academy by helping and guiding all students toward achieving holistic development.

Another CAS-sponsored survey was initiated in Spring 2000 and directed by Jan L. Arminio at Shippensburg University (Arminio & Gochenaur, 2004). CAS surveyed over 5,000 individual members from 22 CAS member associations. Of those responding, 62.5 percent had heard of CAS (i.e., 85% of responding vice presidents; 67% of functional area directors, 66% of new professionals, and 31% of faculty members). Of those who stated that CAS has positively influenced their programs, 27 percent believed CAS positively influenced programs through assessing current programs, 22 percent in expanding current programs, 13 percent through clarifying mission and goals, 10 percent by justifying current programs, 8 percent by emphasizing student and staff training, 5 percent as a guide for new programs, and 4 percent to influence budget programs. Eighty-two percent of vice presidents and associate vice presidents for student affairs stated that CAS standards were positively associated with learning outcomes. A member of NACA noted, "CAS has closed the loop in student activities advising to see if student leaders learn or do not."

Additional research is needed to answer other important questions about the influence of CAS and its initiatives. In an article published in the *College Student Affairs Journal* (2003), Don G. Creamer, a past president of CAS, offers several CAS-related research questions that need to be addressed:

1. What is the level of use of CAS Standards by functional area and geographic area?
2. What is the type and frequency of use of CAS Standards and Guidelines?
3. How do CAS Standards shape professional practice?
4. What is the role of CAS in shaping educational programs and services?
5. Do practitioners perceive that the use of CAS Standards and Guidelines improves their performance?
6. Does CAS benefit professionals' learning and development?
7. Are programs and services that meet CAS Standards and Guidelines more effective in meeting learning goals than those that do not?
8. How does professional practice that is influenced by CAS in turn influence student learning?

The recently created CAS research grant program is intended to provide support for researchers interested in pursuing these and related questions.

There can be little doubt that the CAS initiative has been fruitful during its thirty-plus year existence. Although there is much work yet to do, the Council for the Advancement of Standards in Higher Education has made a professional difference and is prepared to continue its important efforts toward professionalizing programs and services in higher education.

Recent Developments

While continuing to develop and revise functional area standards, CAS has also continued to explore ways to improve and enhance its work. One of the most significant and potentially influential CAS initiatives was the 2003 revision of the CAS general standards, along with the subsequent 2008 and 2011 revisions. The 2003 revision included a new, major emphasis on student learning and development, which is evident primarily in the Program component (Part Two of each functional area standard). This section included a table of 16 student learning and development outcome domains designed to guide practitioners in their attempts to both emphasize and assess student learning and development.

The 2008 revision built on this work, maintaining the focus on student learning and development, but reconceptualizing the structure and expression of the outcome domains. Rather than the previous 16 areas, the new revision was comprised of 6 broad categories which are then further defined into narrower dimensions to assist practitioners in implementing them. As described more fully in the contextual statement that introduces the General Standards later in this book, the revision resulted from the observation that the many sets of outcomes existing in the field were confusing for practitioners and the subsequent decision to convene a "think tank" of experts to consider how best to integrate and build upon the previous approaches. The result, later amended and approved by the CAS Board of Directors, is the CAS Learning and Development Outcomes statement and chart, which also appears later in this volume. This process and its outcome are good examples of the CAS role in higher education—that of creating collaborative strategies to address challenges to good practice and then disseminating the results with the intention of helping practitioners and bringing coherence to the field.

In 2006, in conjunction with the previous edition of this book, CAS published a companion book to the Standards. The Frameworks for Assessing Learning and Development Outcomes (FALDOs) were created to assist practitioners in developing sound and effective strategies for assessing outcomes. Because they were based on the previous 16 student learning and development outcome domains, the FALDOs have not been reprinted with this edition; however, they still provide useful insight into the process of understanding and designing ways to assess intended learning and development outcomes.

CAS has also used its collective voice and inter-association collaboration to develop two statements related to the work of individual professionals in higher education. The first, the *CAS Characteristics of Individual Excellence for Professional Practice in Higher Education*, is designed to define a list of necessary attributes for professionals in higher education that is broader than competencies and includes other markers of professionalism. Although CAS has historically focused on quality assurance with regard to programs and services, the *characteristics* were created to suggest the hallmarks of quality on an individual basis. The second statement, the *CAS Statement of Shared Ethical Principles*, articulates those values which underlie the ethics statements of CAS member associations. By identifying the themes, the statement is designed to highlight the beliefs shared by professionals working across the range of functional areas in higher education. Like the standards themselves, the Characteristics of Individual Excellence and the Statement of Shared Ethical Principles seek to identify, articulate, and promulgate quality practices in the work we do.

Finally, because it is part of the CAS mission to promote improvement of programs and services and to encourage self-assessment, CAS also educates practitioners in a more direct way. Individual member associations typically offer CAS-related training and workshops at conferences and other professional development venues, and CAS offered two national symposiums, timed to coincide with the publication of new editions of *CAS Professional Standards for Higher Education*. CAS is now exploring alternatives for practitioners to learn from experts in the field and network with others engaged in the process of using CAS standards on their campuses to enhance student learning and development across campuses. From the earliest conversations, that is the thread that has been constant throughout the development, discussions, and initiatives of the Council for the Advancement of Standards, and that is the goal that will continue to inform our work into the future.

References

Arminio, J. & Gochenaur, P. (2004). After 16 years of publishing standards, do CAS standards make a difference? College Student Affairs Journal, 23, 51-65.

Council for the Advancement of Standards (CAS). (1986). CAS standards and guidelines for student service/development programs. Iowa City: American College Testing Program.

Council of Student Personnel Associations in Higher Education. (1994; 1972). Student development services in post-secondary education (pp. 428-447). In A. L. Rentz (Ed.), *Student affairs: A profession's heritage*. Washington, DC: American College Personnel Association.

Creamer, D. G. (2003). Research needed on the use of CAS standards and guidelines. *College Student Affairs Journal, 22*(2), 109-124.

CAS Context
CAS Professional Standards for Higher Education

A standard to guide practice is an essential characteristic of any established profession. It is vital during the evolution of a mature profession that a relevant set of standards be developed and promulgated by and for those working in that arena. The Council for the Advancement of Standards in Higher Education (CAS) was founded in 1979 as a profession-wide entity to establish standards to guide practice by student affairs, student development, and student support service providers employed by institutions of higher learning. Currently, 41 professional associations hold membership in CAS, representing nearly 100,000 higher education service providers. This book provides 43 functional area standards for use by the profession at large, as well as statements related to individual characteristics of excellence and to ethical principles. This edition of *CAS Professional Standards* represents the eighth major iteration of CAS standards, the first having been published under the auspices of the American College Testing Program (CAS, 1986).

During the twentieth century, college and university student support programs evolved from a few faculty members being assigned part-time to attend to students' needs beyond the classroom to institutional divisions designed to complement the educational goals of academic affairs. Further, contemporary student support programs employ many full-time, well-qualified staff members, most with highly specialized knowledge and skills and with advanced degrees. There is little doubt that the complexity of student support services has increased as organizational structures have expanded. It is largely in response to the increasing complexity of role, function, and purpose that the CAS standards were developed. As the field matured and the responsibilities of its practitioners expanded, a complementary need for accountability increased. It is no longer feasible, let alone desirable, for practitioners to function on the basis of best guesses or intuition when creating environments conducive to student learning and development. Likewise, practitioners have demanded that standards be developed to guide the quality of practice. The CAS functional area standards and guidelines have been developed to meet these important professional needs. CAS was created as a bellwether for the profession at large. To ensure cross-fertilization of theories, research, and application strategies from the field as a whole, knowledgeable representatives from member associations bring to the table the most current thinking in the functional areas they represent and champion. This commitment to collaboration among functional area specialties ensures that no single perspective will dominate the foundations that underlie the generation, revision, and presentation of each CAS standard. Although the standards reflect a broad range of interests, they are clearly values-driven. Underlying them is a set of fundamental principles upon which CAS was founded and by which it continues to be guided.

CAS Guiding Principles

The fundamental principles that undergird the work of CAS and guide its initiatives are organized into five categories. They were derived from theories and conceptual models implicit within human development, group dynamics, student learning, organizational management, and higher education administration that inform the work of student affairs administrators, student development educators, and student support service providers. Further, CAS was developed in the U.S., and while the membership includes Canadian representation, the guiding principles are grounded in a Western, and specifically American, perspective. There is interest in CAS and in professional standards in a number of other countries; however, as the CAS standards are considered for adaptation to different cultures, professionals must identify those underlying assumptions and aspects that need to be adjusted to better reflect the values of that new context.

Students and Their Institutions

These initial eight principles are concerned with how students learn and the environmental conditions that institutions need to emphasize for learning and development to occur. The first four principles were derived from the 1938 and 1949 editions of the Student Personnel Point of View (Miller & Prince, 1976, p. 4) and reflect fundamental "truths" upon which the CAS standards and guidelines are based. Principles five through eight reflect institutional perspectives that complement the student-focused viewpoint. When combined, these principles represent the presuppositions upon which student support programs and services are founded.

- The student must be considered as a whole person.
- Each student is a unique person and must be treated as such.
- The student's total environment is educational and must be used to achieve full development.
- Students seek higher education in responsible ways and will, when encouraged to do so, access appropriate educational resources when they are provided, made known, and relevant to students' felt educational and developmental needs.
- Institutions of higher learning are purposeful and function as social and cultural resources to provide opportunities for students to learn and develop in holistic ways.
- The primary responsibility for learning and development rests with the student.

- Institutions of higher learning reflect the diversity of the societies and cultures in which they exist.
- Institutions are responsible for creating learning environments that provide a choice of educational opportunities and challenge students to learn and develop while providing support to nurture their development.

Each CAS functional area standard was created to inform practitioners about the criteria that represent fundamental levels of programmatic and organizational quality that must be met if institutions are to be effective in facilitating student learning and development.

In effect, when a college or university provides programs and services that meet or exceed the CAS criteria, the institution will have effectively implemented an intentional educational environment conducive to the learning and development of its students. It is important to note that the CAS standards do not dictate that students, individually or collectively, must conform to a prescribed standard of involvement or behavior. Rather, they call for institutions and student support programs to meet a standard of programmatic and organizational efficiency and effectiveness sufficient to provide opportunity and encouragement for students to grow, develop, and achieve individual potentials. They further call upon institutions and their programs and services to identify the outcomes that they intend students to achieve and to assess those outcomes to determine the extent to which they have been accomplished. The institution and its educational programs are social resources that provide citizens opportunities to expand their horizons and capacities to serve society. The CAS standards have been developed and promulgated from a profession-wide point of view to provide institutions with a relevant, reasonable, and achievable set of voluntary professional standards.

Diversity and Multiculturalism
Issues of diversity in institutions of higher education can be fraught with dissension and discord. The CAS standards assert the importance of affirming the existence of diversity and considering its influence when creating and implementing educational and developmental initiatives. In an increasingly complex and shrinking global environment, it is essential that students learn to function effectively and justly when exposed to ideas, beliefs, values, physical and mental abilities, sexual orientations, gender expressions, and cultures that differ from their own. Two principles in this regard are embedded in the CAS standards.
- Recognizing the ubiquitous nature of human diversity, institutions are committed to eliminating barriers that impede student learning and development, attending especially to establishing and maintaining diverse human relationships essential to survival in a global society.
- Justice and respect for differences bond individuals to community; thus education for multicultural awareness and positive regard for differences is essential to the development and maintenance of a health engendering society.

The CAS standards call for institutions and their student support programs to recognize the increasingly diverse cultures to be served and the importance of enhancing students' capacities to function effectively within the context of constantly shifting environments and opinions. CAS recognizes that the spirit of affirmative action is inherent in the delivery of effective student support services and that discrimination against any student population or employment category is antithetical to belief in the dignity of the individual. This proposition is fundamental to student development theory and its applications to practice. The CAS standards reinforce the fact that those responsible for creating educational environments need to be open to and accepting of differences, and that they must recognize that such environments are important for enhancing the quality of the education provided and the learning achieved. Further, the standards consistently call for staffing with personnel whose demographic characteristics reflect those of the institution's constituencies. In addition, all students must have access to the educational and co-curricular resources available to the academic community at large; no student, for any reason, should be denied access to them.

Organization, Leadership, and Human Resources
The CAS standards reflect the belief that form follows function; consequently, the structure of an organization should mirror the purposes for which it was established. It is essential that institutions, programs, and services be based on a mutually determined, clearly and publicly stated, and well-understood purpose. Without a clearly defined mission, an institution and its programs are virtually rudderless and will ultimately founder. Unmistakably defined lines of authority must be drawn, detailed duties and job responsibilities described, and policies and procedures established to guide the desired processes. Those who lead and administer programs of student support must remember that because theory without practice is empty and practice without theory is blind, it is essential that the theory embraced be connected to the purposes sought, in pursuit of quality practice. Three basic principles concerned with these factors also underlie the CAS standards:
- Capable, credible, knowledgeable, and experienced leadership is essential for institutional success; organizational units are most successful when their missions and outcome expectations are effectively documented and understood by all concerned.
- Effective programs and services require well-qualified staff members who understand and support the student

learning and development outcomes the programs are intended to promote.
- Student learning and personal development will be enhanced when staff members at all levels of responsibility possess appropriate, relevant, and adequate educational preparation and practical experience.

CAS standards do not prescribe organizational or administrative structures to which institutions and programs are expected to adhere. CAS is guided by the belief that every institution is unique and must establish the frame of administrative reference most appropriate to its particular mission. Consequently, the standards do not prescribe specific requirements, but rather provide fundamental criteria that practitioners can use to judge the effectiveness of their current or projected structures. For example, certain elements clearly are essential to functional success, including employing leaders who possess viable visions of how and what is to be achieved and are suitably positioned for access to the highest administrative levels. Leaders and staff members alike must possess effective managerial skills, be properly titled, and be well qualified by both education and experience. Under-educated and under-experienced staff members, good intentions notwithstanding, will virtually always fail to accomplish the program's objectives over the long term.

Health-Engendering Environments
Institutional environments of quality combine educational philosophies and values in conjunction with adequate physical facilities, human resources, and fiscal support to create positive influence on the education and development of students. The establishment of effective, health-generating environments is an important aspect of the CAS standards.
- Student support and developmental programs and services prosper in benevolent environments that provide students with appropriate levels of challenge and support.

The primary purpose of education has always been to promote change, both in individuals and in society. College and university student support programs are primarily educational enterprises. Clearly, the Student Learning Imperative (ACPA, 1996) prevails throughout each CAS functional area standard because an important purpose of the standards is to provide criteria that can be used to judge a program's capacity and effectiveness in creating learning and development opportunities. The establishment of educational environments conducive to student learning and development is essential if an institution of higher learning is to achieve its educational purposes.

Ethical Considerations
A major component in each CAS standard incorporates the fundamental ethical expectations to which all student support practitioners must adhere to ensure fair and equitable practice. Just as a mission statement is essential to provide programs with direction, ethical standards are essential to guide the behavior of staff members in ways that enhance the overall integrity of both the program and the institution.
- Because special mentoring relationships exist between students and those who facilitate their learning and development, support service providers must exemplify impeccable ethical behavior in both their professional relationships and their personal lives.

As an essential task of every profession's emergence, it establishes and codifies ethical standards to guide the behavior of its members. The CAS standards provide the essential ethical foundations upon which to build humane, ethical practice. Without a clearly defined code of ethics, staff members would have little or no guidance for establishing and maintaining a reasonable level of effective moral and ethical behavior. The best of intentions are insufficient if they are not founded on a solid ethical base that can be understood and acknowledged by all concerned. Practitioners can be informed by their own association's ethical codes, the relevant criteria in the CAS standards, and the CAS Statement of Shared Ethical Principles.

Putting CAS Standards to Work
CAS standards and guidelines are conceived and crafted with care to be instructive and useful to practitioners and educational leaders. Based upon professional judgment and societal expectations, they include principles that are fundamental to student learning and development and guidelines for practice for particular functional areas.

Because CAS believes in the importance of self-assessment, the standards and guidelines, as well as other CAS-related materials, are offered as criteria that can be used in multiple ways toward the goal of assuring and enhancing quality practice. As noted in the CAS Preamble, they can be used for design of new programs and services, for determining the efficacy of programs, for staff development, or for programmatic assessment as part of an institutional self-study. CAS does not prescribe or proscribe ways of using the standards; rather, they are intended to be tools for practitioners to improve practice.

The development of an assessment process is a task that many practitioners are facing today. Although CAS can be an important tool for part of the plan, it is important to think about the larger picture. Upcraft and Schuh (1996, pp. 27-30), in describing a comprehensive assessment model, asserted that it should include

- keeping track of who uses student services, programs, and facilities
- assessing of student and other clientele needs
- assessing clientele satisfaction
- assessing campus environments and student cultures
- assessing outcomes
- conducting comparable institutions assessment (i.e., benchmarking)
- using nationally accepted standards to assess

An institution, division, program, or service with an assessment plan that incorporates all of these elements will have abundant documentation with which to complete a CAS self-study. Assessing the separate elements of the program or service supplies the evidence with which to support ratings in the self-study process.

Self-Study for Program Evaluation

The most thorough and, perhaps, productive use of the standards involves a self-study process for program evaluation. This process involves others at the institution in examining evidence to determine collectively whether the program is in compliance with the standards. Involvement of others serves several purposes; it ensures a broader and more objective perspective, increases knowledge and awareness of the program across the institution, and develops support for implementation of identified improvements.

For each set of standards and guidelines, CAS provides a Self-Assessment Guide (SAG) that includes a recommended comprehensive self-study process for program evaluation. Seven basic steps to using a SAG are suggested for implementing a functional area self-study. The following, in summary form, is the recommended self-study process.

1. Establish and Prepare the Self-Assessment Team

Division and functional area leaders need first to determine the functional area or areas to be evaluated and the reason for the project. This may be dictated by institutional program review cycles or planning for accreditation processes, or it may result from internal divisional goals and needs.

It is desirable to involve the full functional area staff in the initial planning stage of the self-study process, including support staff members and knowledgeable students and faculty members when feasible. This approach provides opportunity for shared ownership in the evaluation. For a self-study of a single functional area, a representative group of three to five members, including one or more knowledgeable individuals from outside the area under review, should be selected to compose the primary self-study team.

Initially, the team should familiarize itself with the relevant CAS functional area standard by examining it carefully before making individual or group judgments. It is important that all members come to understand and interpret the standard in similar fashion. Team training should be conducted to ensure that members' interpretive differences are resolved before initiating the study. Likewise, ground rules for the study should be established and agreed upon. Team members should realize and accept that disagreement is natural, healthy, and probably inevitable, but the resulting debates will usually strengthen the team's understanding and ultimate consensus on the matter. Finally, the team should discuss whether any of the guidelines (included with the standards to indicate areas where practice can be enhanced beyond the minimum expectations) should be treated as a standard for self-study purposes. For example, a functional area guideline might include the statement "facilities should include a private office where individual consultations can be held." The study team may decide that this guideline statement, which is not a CAS standard compliance requirement, is imperative at the institution and should therefore be treated as a standard for purposes of their self-study. If so decided, a criterion measure statement such as "private office space is available for staff members to use for consultation purposes" would be inserted as a criterion measure to be rated along with the other criterion measures included in the SAG and evaluated accordingly.

It is helpful to have relevant documents and evidence collected prior to initiating the self-study. Although the team may identify additional information that is needed to complete the review, having basic documents from the functional area available at the outset will assist them in making progress in their work (see further detail in 3. below).

2. Beginning the Self-Study

It is suggested that team members use the CAS Functional Area Self-Assessment Guide (SAG) to implement the self-study. When used, the initial steps are for members to review available documentation, to rate the criterion measures individually and then collectively to make judgments about how well the program meets the criteria. The SAG provides a 5-point scale from Does Not Meet to Exemplary for rating the criterion measures, which reflect the essence of the standards.

3. Identify and Summarize Evaluative Evidence

Judging the program by rating it against the standard's criterion measures and identifying program strengths and weaknesses does not represent a completed self-study. Rather, the process requires documentation of the evidence that supports each criterion measure rating. The nature of such documentary evidence may be quantitative, qualitative, or, most typically, a combination of the two. For example, quantitative measures might include the staff-to-student ratio for a given activity, an analysis of the cost-effectiveness of a given activity, or the results of a developmental task assessment of student outcome achievement. Qualitative documentation, on the other hand, might include notes on the process used to develop the program's mission or outcome objectives or structured interviews with students. Essential documentation includes relevant publications (e.g., student and staff handbooks), program descriptions (e.g., career decision-making workshop outlines), program evaluation data (e.g., program assessment results), institutional data (e.g., student profiles), and research initiated for the self-study (e.g., student survey or focus group results). No self-study can be considered complete without relevant data and related documentation to support and validate the team's judgments. These data can be collected over time and stored in a database for self-study purposes. Such data also have utility for preparing annual reports.

The Program section of the CAS standards for every functional area includes learning and development outcome domains for which programs must demonstrate outcomes. It is particularly important that outcomes assessment information be available for review, since assessing the results of our work is a crucial part of determining the effectiveness of the program or service.

Following the rating and review procedure, it is desirable for the study team to invite the full staff to review and discuss the team's interim assessment of program compliance with the standards. This approach provides opportunity to inform all staff members of the team's evaluation and permits all staff members to explore together how well the program appears to be accomplishing its stated purpose. Through this process, team members may be exposed to alternative interpretations of the study results-to-date and obtain additional insight into the program from the perspective of others.

4. Identify Discrepancies

Study team members should compare their ratings and interpretations of program characteristics, accomplishments, strengths, and shortcomings against the criteria expressed in the standard. Further, the study team should carefully review each criterion measure and related practice that study team members rated as Does Not Apply, Insufficient Evidence/Unable to Rate, or Does Not Meet, or where rater differences of two or more were noted. A specific rationale should be prepared for each shortcoming identified.

When discrepancies are noted between the assessment criteria and actual practice, the team can then identify existing operational problems that need resolution. For example, each standard calls for the existence of a program mission statement consistent with the nature and goals of the institution. If the program has no written mission statement or an outdated one, then the discrepancy between the standard and actual program practice clearly calls for the creation of a current, relevant program mission statement that is consistent with the institution's mission.

5. Determine Appropriate Corrective Action

The self-study team should describe in detail the adjustments that need to be implemented for the program to achieve the quality and effectiveness to which it aspires. For example, returning to the example of the program mission, the action required would call for program staff members to draft a statement delineating the elements they believe are agreed upon, circulate them for review and comment, and then prepare and disseminate a final program mission statement to guide the program and its services.

An important point to note in regard to corrective action is the importance of subdividing the overall task into manageable parts. Trying to revise a total functional area in one step is neither a desirable nor an effective approach to program development. It is important that the study team list specific actions identified in the self-study that require implementation. It is also desirable to set priorities on the list by order of importance, need, feasibility, and achievability of the desired change.

6. Recommend Steps for Program Enhancement

Even excellent programs can be further refined to provide more desirable and effective outcomes. Unless staff members are satisfied with meeting basic standards only, additional initiatives can be implemented to enhance program quality and effectiveness. This can be accomplished by listing each specific action identified in the self-study that would enhance and strengthen services and by setting priorities among them for follow-up purposes. The guidelines provide possibilities for identifying enhanced practice.

7. Prepare an Action Plan

As the self-study process comes to closure, it is important for staff members to identify and establish priorities to influence the program's future direction. This represents a process of comparing past performance with desired outcomes and can best be accomplished by carefully reviewing the actual self-study process that was conducted to ensure that all relevant program issues are addressed. The post-self-assessment action plan should acknowledge the program's strengths as well as its shortcomings as it moves toward establishing a strategic approach for correcting deficiencies and initiating enhancements. The primary goal of this final step is to identify and set priorities for future actions and directions after comparing the results of the self-study with the outcomes to which the program aspires.

This process consists of preparing a comprehensive action plan for implementing program changes, identifying resources (i.e., human, fiscal, physical) that are essential to program enhancement, establishing dates by which specific actions are to be completed, identifying responsible parties to complete the action steps, and setting a tentative start-up date for initiating a subsequent self-study.

Other Uses of the CAS Standards

In addition to the model presented for program evaluation, the CAS standards are a resource that can be used for a number of other purposes. The uses outlined below are representative; because the standards and guidelines are tools to be used by practitioners, there are not really "wrong" ways to use them, as long as the values and spirit underlying them are honored.

Design of New Programs and Services

As student and institutional needs change, the opportunity may arise to develop a new program or service on campus, or to expand or restructure existing areas. In doing so, it is helpful to have criteria to serve as an outline to guide and ground planning. The functional area standards and guidelines can serve as a helpful resource when such planning is needed. The mission and program sections are particularly helpful in specifying important goals and components relevant to the functional area being developed.

Staff Development

Staff members can study the various criteria to determine how well they and their colleagues are implementing the standards in their daily work with students. The relevant functional area standards can be used as an orientation device to assist new professionals in understanding and reviewing their areas, as a point of discussion for supervisors and staff to discuss program strengths and weaknesses, as a resource for educating others at the institution about what is involved in a sound program, or as the format by which annual program reports are prepared. The more the CAS standards are used within a division or institution, the more it will lead to a common language and shared perception of the elements of good practice.

A comprehensive staff development program, using one of the functional area standards and guidelines, or the General Standards, as a training device, may require from several hours to a full day of meeting time during which staff members share responsibility for leading discussions about the standard's various components. This approach is particularly valuable when a program or division self-study is in the offing. In such an instance, staff members can both learn how CAS standards can be used to guide and influence good practice and how they can provide a vehicle for implementing a self-study. Training staff members before conducting a self-study typically produces a more comprehensive and valuable program evaluation.

Academic Preparation

The CAS standards have another valuable educational function when used as a resource in formal academic preparation programs, especially in an introductory course concerned with student support functions common to institutions of higher learning. The 43 CAS functional area standards and their accompanying contextual statements, as well as the statements regarding individual characteristics, shared ethical principles, and learning and development outcomes, all presented in Part 2 of this book, provide an excellent primer for those entering the fields of student affairs and higher education administration. The contextual statements summarize the roles and functions of key program and service units, their primary purposes, historical perspectives, and relevant resources available to explore the areas in greater detail. These succinct summary statements provide an introduction for those unfamiliar with the areas under study. The CAS standards provide an in-depth description of the characteristics common to and expected of the various functional areas.

For students who desire to examine a given functional area in greater detail or participate in a practicum, internship, or other field-based experience, the CAS Self-Assessment Guide (SAG) provides a unique resource for obtaining a comprehensive understanding. Each functional area SAG includes the standards, guidelines, and criterion measures that can be used to judge the level of compliance a program exhibits in regard to the standards. Using a SAG, students can readily identify a program's strengths and shortcomings. Further, the SAG has utility as a vehicle for both students and supervisors for examining together and discussing the various components of the area under study. For learning the basics of student support functions, there is no better information available than that provided by the CAS standards and the complementary Self-Assessment Guides.

Credibility and Accountability

Any profession, along with its practitioners, must exhibit a reasonable level of credibility if it is to survive. Professional entities lacking user confidence will be at best under-utilized and may ultimately disappear. In effect, credibility is essential to the existence of all service agencies, including those associated with higher education. Through adherence to standards of professional practice, institutions seek to assure potential student users and the general public of their competence and credibility. Both laypersons and professionals alike attribute credibility to programs, professions, and institutions that meet stringent standards; compliance with such standards demonstrates that quality is present.

Various means have been established to ensure accountability and quality assurance. Institutional and academic program credibility is typically established through accreditation, a voluntary process by which agencies encourage and assist institutions and their sub-units (e.g., colleges, schools, departments, and programs) to evaluate and improve their programs and services (Eaton, 2001). Information about the institutions and programs that voluntarily meet or exceed acceptable standards of quality and effectiveness is made public by the accrediting body. It is not uncommon for institutions lacking accreditation to be denied federal aid or other resources available to accredited institutions. Graduates of non-accredited institutions may be denied admission to graduate schools or certain employment opportunities. Accreditation is intended to assure the public that an institution and its programs do indeed provide quality education.

However, the general public cannot be assured that individuals who have diplomas, certificates, or degrees from accredited institutions and programs are, in fact, effective practitioners. Consequently, various structures have been established by professional and governmental oversight agencies to judge the professional qualifications of service providers in education, health, and social service areas.

Three primary methods have been established to enable individuals to document their professional qualifications: registry, certification, and licensure. CAS, which is a consortium of higher education professional associations, focuses minimal attention on these credentialing options, although some have encouraged CAS to expand its focus into registry or certification, which are often initiated by non-governmental professional bodies. Licensure, on the other hand, is largely the province of governments. For instance, licenses based on generally comparable criteria are required of physicians, psychologists, and lawyers in all states; counselors and engineers, on the other hand, may be judged by diverse criteria from state to state.

As demand for accountability in higher education increases, so too does demand for practitioner accountability. CAS endorses self-regulation as the most viable approach to program accountability, calling for each institution to initiate a program of self-assessment for its student support programs, services, and personnel. Whether student support units are administratively assigned to student affairs, academic affairs, business affairs, or elsewhere in the organizational hierarchy, CAS encourages program review and evaluation on a continuing basis using the CAS standards. From this perspective, self-regulation becomes a preferred strategy to establish and maintain credibility.

When deemed appropriate and desirable, the various functional areas could invite representatives from peer institutions, or professionals with particular expertise in the areas being studied, to review their self-assessment reports as part of the validation process. Self-regulation requires institutions and their leaders to establish their own policies and procedures for institutional assessment and evaluation and to adhere to them when evaluating quality and effectiveness. Thus, through continuing assessment, institutions can compile and maintain in databases the internal documentation required by regional accrediting bodies and governmental oversight agencies. Self-regulation provides institutions and their student support programs with tools to achieve and demonstrate quality assurance. In effect, if institutions accept responsibility for initiating meaningful and well considered assessment processes and procedures, there is less likelihood that external oversight agencies, governmental or otherwise, will seek to do so.

Example Applications

The following is a summary of examples of how CAS standards have been applied in practice and for purposes of professional staff development.

Institutional Program Review

From an institutional perspective, many practitioners view the CAS standards as a staple for conducting comprehensive program reviews. One institution's policy requires that a standard external to the institution be used to implement periodic comprehensive program reviews. Because CAS standards are readily available, easily understood, consistent across functional areas, and simple to use, they are often the standard of choice for administrative unit reviews. The fact that operational versions of the standards in the form of CAS Self-Assessment Guides (SAGs) are also available has increased the ease with which the standards can be used for program review purposes. In addition, the existence of the CAS standards typically informs practitioners that professional practice is not based simply on instinct or history. Rather, it consists of the application of the collective wisdom of the profession and is subject to assessment and regulation.

Program Development and Advocacy

From a programmatic perspective, the CAS standards have special utility for emerging student support areas. For example, educators responsible for guiding programs of learning assistance and developmental education tend to exhibit strong commitment to promoting the use of professional standards in their ranks. Many leaders in this arena literally "invented" their programs and learned from each other what worked best to produce quality outcomes. During the past two decades, the CAS Learning Assistance Programs Standards and Guidelines has become a shared document among learning assistance practitioners. Leaders in this arena have indicated that the CAS standards provided a common ground to unite those responsible for ensuring that students receive the special attention and support they need to be successful.

Two important uses of the standards in addition to the self-assessment function were identified from another program-specific perspective: one as a guide for initiating new programs and the other for advocacy. The National Clearinghouse for Commuter Programs (NCCP) frequently receives requests from institutions desiring to establish on-campus commuter programs. Most practitioners interested in such initiatives fail initially to comprehend the scope of the functions essential to a comprehensive program. Often, the initiator is interested in establishing a particular type of program (e.g., peer mentoring or orientation for commuters) or service (e.g., off-campus housing referral, commuter newsletter). When such requests are made, the CAS standards are readily available as a professionally sanctioned tool that provides guidance to those interested in providing support for such populations.

Advocacy was a second use noted, because it is often helpful when consulting with colleagues about student support programs to make a case for broadening the administrators' understanding of what is required to meet the basic essentials. All too often, campus administrators tend to limit their initial thinking about a new program to relatively basic issues such as access, and not to think in terms of how a new program could help students become better integrated into the campus community or enhance their learning and development. The CAS standards have great utility for opening institutional leaders' eyes to the importance of comprehensive programming and helping them to grasp a broader view.

From another professional association perspective, the Association of Fraternity/Sorority Advisors (AFA) discovered that standards can be extremely beneficial in relating association purpose to the broader mission of higher education and those of various institutions. Association leaders determined that when colleagues utilized the CAS standards to establish or reorganize various student support services, those program changes were typically not challenged because the standards provided a recognized level of credibility that did not exist prior to the availability of the CAS standards.

Professional Preparation

From the vantage point of graduate education, many student affairs preparation programs have integrated the CAS standards into their curricula. Often, the concept of quality assurance is quite vague to graduate students, especially at the master's level. However, the idea of applying standards to practice is more concrete and students can quickly come to understand the role, function, and utility of professional standards. Thus, students from the outset can begin to internalize the professional interests of self-regulation and improvement. Many college student affairs academic programs have incorporated the CAS standards into their practicum and internship experiential components. Students may complete a "mini-self-study" of the functional areas to which they are assigned as part of their practical field-work experiences. This not only ensures that future practitioners know about the existence of the CAS standards, but also provides them with direct experience that enhances their ability to put the standards into practice as they move into entry level positions.

CAS Initiatives

The Council for the Advancement of Standards in Higher Education was established as a profession-wide collaborative body to develop and promulgate professional standards and to inform those responsible for providing higher education with information about how to use standards effectively. CAS functional area standards were created as living, evolving documents. The Council established a periodic review program to ensure that each standard undergoes regular review and updating. Protocols to guide the development of new and the revision of existing standards are in place and appear in Appendix B. These protocols identify the processes, participants, and procedures used by CAS to create and review its standards. Completion of a typical standard review takes approximately one year from initiation to Board adoption. It may take slightly longer to complete a new standard because an initial draft must be written before the CAS review process can be initiated. Historically, by the time a functional area standard has undergone the long and arduous development and review, the CAS Board of Directors has nearly always been unanimous in its decision to adopt a new or revised standard, and in fact, the Board review process is designed to lead to consensus.

In the rich discussions that emerge around the Board table, other issues or needs are sometimes identified. When ideas emerge that are found to be within the scope and purpose of CAS, projects to support and enhance the work of CAS are undertaken. This is the genesis of the projects that have developed into the SAGs, the FALDOs, the Characteristics of Individual Excellence, the Statement of Shared Ethical Principles, and the CAS National Symposium.

In addition to its primary purpose to develop and promulgate professional standards, CAS takes seriously its responsibility to inform and educate the higher education community and the public about the importance of professional standards and their utility for institutional and program self-assessment. Over the years, CAS Board members have represented the Council in numerous conferences, workshops, and instructional activities designed to inform members of the higher education community in the U.S. and abroad about CAS initiatives and instruct practitioners in using the standards. Most of the CAS member associations include CAS-related presentations and training workshops in their conference programs. CAS representatives have made presentations at national assessment institutes, and CAS has been represented internationally at the European Association of Institutional Research in Prague, through an invited series of seminars in South Africa, and at conferences in Qatar and China. In 2006 and 2009, CAS held two CAS National Symposia to further educate participants on the implementation of the CAS approach and materials. At the time of this publication, CAS is exploring ways to use technology and social media to further the opportunities for training and for developing communities of CAS users.

The CAS standards provide an important tool that expresses to students, faculty, and administrators alike the complex and vital nature of student support programs and services and their relationship to student learning and development. Within higher education, there is sometimes a lack of appreciation for the importance of creating supportive, health-engendering environments for students as an important condition that enhances their experiences. Over the years, those providing students with basic educational support services have often been viewed as secondary or supplemental participants in achieving the academic mission, rather than integral to it. The creation of clearly articulated professional standards has deepened the understanding of faculty and administrative colleagues and increased their confidence in the valuable educational and developmental role that student support service providers offer students.

Note: *The preceding section was adapted from previous editions; originally authored by Ted K. Miller, it was edited by Laura A. Dean for the 6th, 7th, and 8th editions.*

References

American College Personnel Associaiton (ACPA). (March/April 1996). Special issue: The student learning imperative. *Journal of college Student Development, 37*(2).

Council for the Advancement of Standards (CAS). (1996). *CAS standards and guidelines for student service/development programs.* Iowa City: American College Testing Program.

Eaton, J. S. (March/April 2001_. Regional accreditation reform: Who is served? *Change Magazine,* 39-45.

Miller, T. K., & Prince, J. S. (1976). *The future of student affairs: A guide to student development for tomorrow/s higher education.* San Francisco: Jossey-Bass.

Upcraft, M. L., & Schuh, J. H. (1996). *Assessment in student affairs: A guide for practitioners.* San Francisco: Jossey-Bass.

CAS Preamble
Approved by CAS Board of Directors
November 18, 1994
Washington, DC

Let us raise a standard to which the wise and honest can repair.
- George Washington, 1787

The CAS Purpose

The Council for the Advancement of Standards in Higher Education (CAS) develops and promulgates standards that enhance the quality of a student's total learning experience in higher education. CAS is a consortium of associations in higher education whose representatives achieve consensus on the nature and application of standards that guide the work of practitioners. CAS derives its authority from the prestige and traditional influence of its member associations and from the consensus of those members in establishing requirements for high-quality practice.

The CAS philosophy is grounded in beliefs about excellence in higher education, collaboration between teacher and learner, ethics in educational practice, student development as a major goal of higher education, and student responsibility for learning. Taken together, these beliefs about practice shape the vision for all CAS endeavors.

- The beliefs about excellence require that all programs and services in institutions of higher education function at optimum level.

- The beliefs about collaboration require that learning be accomplished in concert by students and educators.

- The beliefs about ethics require that all programs and services be carried out in an environment of integrity and high ideals.

- The beliefs about student development require that the student be considered as a whole person in the context of a diverse population and a diversity of institutions, that outcomes of education be comprehensive, and that the total environment be structured to create opportunities for student involvement and learning.

- The beliefs about responsibility require that the institution recognize the rights and responsibilities of students as its citizens and that it provide an array of resources and learning opportunities that enable students to exercise their responsibility to take full advantage of them.

CAS collectively develops, examines, and endorses standards and guidelines for program and service areas in higher education. The CAS approach to ensuring quality educational experiences is anchored in the assumption that its standards and guidelines can be used in a variety of ways to enhance institutional quality. They can, for example, be used for design of programs and services, for determination of the efficacy of programs, for staff development designed to enhance the skills of those providing professional services, for programmatic self-assessment to assure institutional effectiveness, and for self-regulation purposes.

Background

The Council for the Advancement of Standards in Higher Education was established in 1979 as the Council for the Advancement of Standards for Student Services/Development Programs, a consortium of professional associations representing student affairs practitioners committed to assuring quality programs and services for students. Members of 32 established professional associations directed their interests, talents, and resources to develop and promulgate professional standards and guidelines based on state-of-the-art thinking about educational programs and services. From the beginning, CAS employed an open process of consensus-building among the representatives of member associations as the primary tool for producing its standards and guidelines.

The Council published the original set of 16 functional area standards and the academic preparation standards in 1986, with a grant from American College Testing (ACT). In 1988, CAS developed a Self-Assessment Guide (SAG) for each set of functional area standards to facilitate program assessment and evaluation. Each SAG is an operational version of a functional area standard designed to provide practitioners with a detailed instrument for self-assessment.

The Council's current name and expanded mission were adopted in 1992, to be inclusive of all programs for students in higher education, including those serving undergraduate, graduate, traditional, and nontraditional students. CAS now oversees the development of standards for new service areas and the systematic review and periodic revision of existing standards and guidelines.

The CAS Approach to Self-Regulation and Self-Assessment

Self-regulation is an internally motivated and directed institutional process devoted to the creation, maintenance, and enhancement of high-quality programs and services. CAS believes this approach is preferable to externally motivated regulation, because those within an institution generally have the clearest perceptions of its mission, goals, resources, and capabilities. The essential elements of self-regulation include

- institutional culture that values involvement of all its members in decision making
- quality indicators that are determined by the institution
- standards and guidelines in quality assurance
- collection and analysis of data on institutional performance
- commitment to continuing improvement that presupposes freedom to explore and develop alternative directions for the future

The success of self-regulation depends on mutual respect between an institution and its members. Within the self-regulated institution, individual accomplishments are valued, goals are based on shared vision, systems are open and interactive, processes are carried out in a climate of mutual trust and caring, conflicts are mediated in the best interests of the entire community, and achievements are recognized and rewarded. Such an environment stimulates individual and group initiatives and fosters self-determination of goals. In a self-regulating environment, members identify quality indicators in consultation with a variety of internal and external constituencies and stakeholders, including professional associations.

These indicators may include professionally derived standards, such as those of CAS, which comprise the views of many professional practitioners and professional associations. Self-regulation relies on the willingness and capacity of the organization to examine itself meticulously, faithfully, and reliably, and then to assemble the pertinent results of that examination into coherent reports that constituents can comprehend and use. Such reports are essential for recording the evidence assembled in self-study, for displaying synthesis and analysis of information, for fostering the broad participation of members in the self-regulation process, and for registering benchmark results and conclusions for future reference.

Finally, the self-regulation process relies on the institution's capacity to modify its own practices as needed. A culture that supports self-regulation must operate in a climate that permits members to make independent choices among reasonable alternatives. These choices constitute a commitment to constant improvement of educational practices and of the health of the organization.

References

American College Personnel Association (ACPA). (March/April 1996). Special issue: The student learning imperative. *Journal of College Student Development, 37*(2).

Council for the Advancement of Standards (CAS). (1986). *CAS standards and guidelines for student service/development programs*. Iowa City: American College Testing Program.

Eaton, J. S. (March/April 2001). Regional accreditation reform: Who Is served? *Change Magazine*, 39-45.

Miller, T. K., & Prince, J. S. (1976). *The future of student affairs: A guide to student development for tomorrow's higher education*. San Francisco: Jossey-Bass.

CAS Characteristics of Individual Excellence for Professional Practice in Higher Education
CAS Contextual Statement

Defining competencies of student affairs and other professionals in higher education who plan, implement, and offer programs and services is the mark of a maturing profession. A number of authors and organizations have framed competencies in several broad areas. For example, Pope, Reynolds, and Mueller (2004) identified competencies in the areas of a) administration and management, b) multicultural awareness, knowledge, and skills, c) helping and advising, d) assessment and research, e) teaching and training, f) ethics and professional standards, and g) translation and use of theory to guide practice. This document seeks to define a list of necessary attributes for professionals in higher education that is broader than competencies and includes other markers of professionalism. These characteristics of excellence can be used in an evaluative format, both self-evaluation and in the context of "360 degree" (Tornow, London, & Associates, 1998) or supervisory format.

There are numerous purposes for the creation and use of this document. One purpose is to move the student affairs profession and other professionals within the higher education context to more concrete, concise, and agreed upon characteristics that are expected of professionals who provide, implement, and facilitate programs and services in higher education. Another purpose is to assist in the enculturation of new professionals into the profession by defining what it means to be a professional in higher education. This document also seeks to clarify the context within which people are choosing to work. In response to the literature on supervision that indicates that supervision in higher education is often irregular and when it does occur stresses operational tasks rather than professional development (Arminio & Creamer, 2001; Saunders, Cooper, Winston, & Chernow, 2000; Winston & Creamer, 1997), this document was created to provide aspirational expectations for higher education professionals (Carpenter, 2003).

Because it is the intent of this document to honor individual differences that people bring to their practice, when perceived differences from the expected characteristics are identified these differences need to be discussed. It is through these discussions with supervisors and colleagues that such differences can be acknowledged and their implications explored.

This document offers direction for professional development whether prompted by self-evaluation or from supervisory evaluation. In either case, this document is intended to be used in collaboration and discussion with a supervisor, supervisees, students, and/or colleagues. From these discussions an individual professional development plan can be created and accomplishment of that plan can be evaluated.

References

Arminio, J. & Creamer, D. G. (2001). What quality supervisors say about quality supervision. *College Student Affairs Journal, 21*, 35-44.

Carpenter, D. S. (2003). Professionalism. In S. R. Komives & D. Woodard Jr (Eds.). *Student services: A handbook for the profession* (4th edition; pp. 573-592). San Francisco: Jossey-Bass.

Pope, R. L., Reynolds, A. L., & Mueller, J. A. (2004). *Multicultural competence in student affairs*. San Francisco: Jossey-Bass.

Saunders, S. A., Cooper, D. L. Winston, R. B. Jr., & Chernow, E. (2000). Supervising staff in student affairs: Exploration of the synergistic approach. *Journal of College Student Development, 41*, 1281-191.

Tornow, W. W., London, M., & Associates (1998). *Maximizing the value of 360-degree feedback*. San Francisco: Jossey bass.

Winston, R. B., Jr., & Creamer, D. G. (1997). *Improving staffing practices in student affairs*. San Francisco: Jossey-Bass.

CAS Characteristics of Individual Excellence for Professional Practice in Higher Education

Evaluating individual professional practice in higher education requires the identification of ideal performance characteristics that describe excellence in professional practice. This document has evolved from multi-faceted professional competencies that are inherent in the purpose, development, and application of the CAS Standards and Guidelines. It assumes a philosophy and practice of life-long learning and professional development shared by individual practitioners and their institutions. Characteristics are grouped into **General Knowledge and Skills**, **Interactive Competencies**, and **Self Mastery.**

General Knowledge and Skills
General Knowledge
1. Understands and supports the broad responsibility of the institution for enhancing the collegiate experience for all students

2. Possesses appropriate knowledge of relevant theories, literature, and philosophies on which to base informed professional practice

3. Knows values, historical context, and current issues of one's profession

4. Has developed, can articulate, and acts consistently with a sound educational philosophy consistent with the institution's mission

5. Understands and respects similarities and differences of people in the institutional environment

6. Understands relevant legal issues

General Skills
7. Manages and influences campus environments that promote student success

8. Works to create campus and related educational environments that are safe and secure

9. Effectively utilizes language through speaking, writing, and other means of communication

10. Engages disparate audiences effectively

11. Teaches effectively directly or through example

12. Thinks critically about complex issues

13. Works collaboratively

14. Is trustworthy and maintains confidentiality

15. Exercises responsible stewardship of resources

16. Engages in evaluation and assessment to determine outcomes and identify areas for improvement

17. Uses technology effectively for educational and institutional purposes

18. Bases decisions on appropriate data

19. Models effective leadership

Interactive Competencies
With students:
20. Counsels, advises, supervises, and leads individuals and groups effectively

21. Knows the developmental effects of college on students

22. Knows characteristics of students attending institutions of higher education

23. Knows students who attend the institution, use services, and participants in programs

24. Interacts effectively with a diverse range of students

25. Provides fair treatment to all students and works to change aspects of the environment that do not promote fair treatment

26. Values differences among groups of students and between individuals; helps students understand the interdependence among people both locally and globally

27. Actively and continually pursues insight into the cultural heritage of students

28. Encourages student learning through successful experiences as well as failures

With Colleagues and the Institution

29. Supervises others effectively

30. Manages fiscal, physical, and human resources responsibly and effectively

31. Judges the performance of self and others fairly

32. Contributes productively in partnerships and team efforts

33. Demonstrates loyalty and support of the institution where employed

34. Behaves in ways that reflect integrity, responsibility, honesty, and with accurate representation of self, others, and program

35. Creates and maintains campus relationships characterized by integrity and responsibility

36. Effectively creates and maintains networks among colleagues locally, regionally, nationally, and internationally

37. Contributes to campus life and supports activities that promote campus community

Self Mastery

38. Commits to excellence in all work

39. Intentionally employs self reflection to improve practice and gain insight

40. Responds to the duties of one's role and also to the spirit of one's responsibilities

41. Views his or her professional life as an important element of personal identity

42. Strives to maintain personal wellness and a healthy lifestyle

43. Maintains position-appropriate appearance

44. Stays professionally current by reading literature, building skills, attending conferences, enhancing technological literacy, and engaging in other professional development activities

45. Manages personal life so that overall professional effectiveness is maintained

46. Belongs to and contributes to activities of relevant professional associations

47. Assumes proper accountability for individual and organizational mistakes

48. Espouses and follows a written code of professional ethical standards

49. Abides by laws and institutional policies and works to change policies that are incongruent with personal and professional principles

50. Re-evaluates continued employment when personal, professional, and institutional goals and values are incompatible and inhibit the pursuit of excellence

CAS Statement of Shared Ethical Principles

The Council for the Advancement of Standards in Higher Education (CAS) has served as a voice for quality assurance and promulgation of standards in higher education for thirty years. CAS was established to promote inter-association efforts to address quality assurance, student learning, and professional integrity. It was believed that a single voice would have greater impact on the evaluation and improvement of services and programs than would many voices speaking for special interests by individual practitioners or by single-interest organizations.

CAS includes membership of over 35 active professional associations and has established standards in 40 functional areas. It has succeeded in providing a platform through which representatives from across higher education can jointly develop and promulgate standards of good practice that are endorsed not just by those working in a particular area, but by representatives of higher education association.

CAS often cites George Washington, who said, "Let us raise a standard to which the wise and honest can repair." CAS has raised standards; it is now time to focus on the attributes, such as wisdom and honesty, of those professionals who would use the standards. Professionals working to provide services in higher education share more than a commitment to quality assurance and standards of practice. A review of the ethical statements of member associations demonstrates clearly that there are elements of ethical principles and values that are shared across the professions in higher education.

Most of the member associations represented in CAS are guided by ethical codes of professional practice enforced through the prescribed channels of its association. CAS acknowledges and respects the individual codes and standards of ethical conduct of their organizations. From these codes, CAS has created a statement of shared ethical principles that focuses on seven basic principles that form the foundation for CAS member association codes: autonomy, non-malfeasance, beneficence, justice, fidelity, veracity, and affiliation. This statement is not intended to replace or supplant the code of ethics of any professional association; rather, it is intended to articulate those shared ethical principles. It is our hope that by articulating those shared beliefs, CAS can promulgate a better understanding of the professions of those in service to students and higher education.

Principle I - Autonomy

We take responsibility for our actions and both support and empower an individual's and group's freedom of choice.
- We strive for quality and excellence in the work that we do
- We respect one's freedom of choice
- We believe that individuals, ourselves and others, are responsible for their own behavior and learning
- We promote positive change in individuals and in society through education
- We foster an environment where people feel empowered to make decisions
- We hold ourselves and others accountable
- We study, discuss, investigate, teach, conduct research, and publish freely within the academic community
- We engage in continuing education and professional development

Principle II – Non-Malfeasance

We pledge to do no harm.
- We collaborate with others for the good of those whom we serve
- We interact in ways that promote positive outcomes
- We create environments that are educational and supportive of the growth and development of the whole person
- We exercise role responsibilities in a manner that respects the rights and property of others without exploiting or abusing power

Principle III - Beneficence

We engage in altruistic attitudes and actions that promote goodness and contribute to the health and welfare of others.
- We treat others courteously
- We consider the thoughts and feelings of others
- We work toward positive and beneficial outcomes

Principle IV - Justice

We actively promote human dignity and endorse equality and fairness for everyone.
- We treat others with respect and fairness, preserving their dignity, honoring their differences, promoting their welfare
- We recognize diversity and embrace a cross-cultural approach in support of the worth, dignity, potential, and uniqueness of people within their social and cultural contexts

- We eliminate barriers that impede student learning and development or discriminate against full participation by all students
- We extend fundamental fairness to all persons
- We operate within the framework of laws and policies
- We respect the rights of individuals and groups to express their opinions
- We assess students in a valid, open, and fair manner and one consistent with learning objectives
- We examine the influence of power on the experience of diversity to reduce marginalization and foster community

Principle V - Fidelity

We are faithful to an obligation, trust, or duty.
- We maintain confidentiality of interactions, student records, and information related to legal and private matters
- We avoid conflicts of interest or the appearance thereof
- We honor commitments made within the guidelines of established policies and procedures
- We demonstrate loyalty and commitment to institutions that employ us
- We exercise good stewardship of resources

Principle VI - Veracity

We seek and convey the truth in our words and actions.
- We act with integrity and honesty in all endeavors and interactions
- We relay information accurately
- We communicate all relevant facts and information while respecting privacy and confidentiality

Principle VII - Affiliation

We actively promote connected relationships among all people and foster community.
- We create environments that promote connectivity
- We promote authenticity, mutual empathy, and engagement within human interactions

When professionals act in accordance with ethical principles, program quality and excellence are enhanced and ultimately students are better served.   As professionals providing services in higher education, we are committed to upholding these shared ethical principles, for the benefit of our students, our professions, and higher education.

Some concepts for this code were adopted from
Kitchner, K. 1985). Ethical principles and ethical decisions in student affairs. In H. Canon & R. Brown (Eds.), *Applied ethics in student services* (New Directions in Student Services, No. 30, pp. 17-30). San Francisco: Jossey-Bass.

CAS Learning and Development Outcomes
CAS Contextual Statement

The Council for the Advancement of Standards in Higher Education (CAS) promotes standards to enhance opportunities for student learning and development from higher education programs and services. In 2003 CAS articulated sixteen domains of learning outcomes in response to the increased shift in attention being paid by educators and their stakeholders from higher education inputs (i.e., standards and benchmarks) to the outcomes of students attending higher education. However, in 2008 after the publication of *Learning Reconsidered 2* (2006), CAS reviewed the learning outcomes it had promoted and decided an integration of both learning outcome documents would enhance the profession's efforts in promoting student learning and development. Consequently, CAS hosted a "think tank" involving writers of *Learning Considered 2*, CAS directors, and prominent practitioners and faculty members in student affairs to make recommendations for a revised learning outcomes document.

Upon recommendations of the think tank, CAS revised the student learning and development outcomes into six broad categories (called domains): knowledge acquisition, construction, integration and application; cognitive complexity; intrapersonal development; interpersonal competence; humanitarianism and civic engagement; and practical competence. To comply with CAS standards, institutional programs and services must identify relevant and desirable learning from these domains, assess relevant and desirable learning, and articulate how their programs and services contribute to domains not specifically assessed. For each of the domains, CAS offers examples illustrating achievement of the student learning outcomes.

This learning outcomes model further defines or clarifies each of the six domains by identifying learning outcome dimensions. Offering dimensions of learning within corresponding domains allows for a more focused assessment approach based on institutional mission and priorities. The revised CAS learning outcomes document a) heightens the differentiation of interpersonal competence and interpersonal development (though certainly the two influence each other), b) highlights the integration of humanitarianism and civic engagement, and c) adds the dimensions of global perspective and technological competence to important learning outcomes.

The CAS Board of Directors reviewed and approved the six domains, learning outcome dimensions, and examples of learning and development outcomes at its October 2008 meeting. The domains and learning outcome dimensions were embedded in each functional area standard. Examples were referenced in each functional area standard and appear in the chart that follows.

Reference

Keeling, R. (Ed.). (2006). *Learning reconsidered 2: Implementing a campus-wide focus on the student experience.* American College Personnel Association, Association of College and University Housing Officers-International, Association of College Unions-International, National Academic Advising Association, National Association for Campus Activities, National Association of Student Personnel Administrators, National Intramural-Recreational Sports Association.

Contributor: Jan Arminio, Shippensburg University, NACA

CAS Learning and Development Outcomes[1]

Student Outcome Domain[2]	Dimensions of Outcome Domains	Examples of Learning and Development Outcomes
Knowledge acquisition, construction, integration, and application	Understanding knowledge from a range of disciplines	Possesses knowledge of human cultures and the physical world; possesses knowledge of [a specific] one or more subjects
	Connecting knowledge to other knowledge, ideas, and experiences	Uses multiple sources of information and their synthesis to solve problems; knows how to access diverse sources of information such as the internet, text observations, and data bases
	Constructing knowledge	Personalizes learning; makes meaning from text, instruction, and experience; uses experience and other sources of information to create new insights; generates new problem-solving approaches based on new insights; recognizes one's own capacity to create new understandings from learning activities and dialogue with others
	Relating knowledge to daily life	Seeks new information to solve problems; relates knowledge to major and career decisions; makes connections between classroom and out-of-classroom learning; articulates career choices based on assessment of interests, values, skills, and abilities; provides evidence of knowledge, skills, and accomplishments resulting from formal education, work experience, community service, and volunteer experiences, for example in resumes and portfolios
Cognitive complexity	Critical thinking	Identifies important problems, questions, and issues; analyzes, interprets, and makes judgments of the relevance and quality of information; assesses assumptions and considers alternative perspectives and solutions[3]
	Reflective thinking	Applies previously understood information, concepts, and experiences to a new situation or setting; rethinks previous assumptions
	Effective reasoning	Uses complex information from a variety of sources including personal experience and observation to form a decision or opinion; is open to new ideas and perspectives
	Creativity	Integrates mental, emotional, and creative processes for increased insight; formulates a new approach to a particular problem
Intrapersonal development	Realistic self-appraisal, self-understanding, and self-respect	Assesses, articulates, and acknowledges personal skills, abilities, and growth areas; uses self-knowledge to make decisions such as those related to career choices; articulates rationale for personal behavior; seeks and considers feedback from others; critiques and subsequently learns from past experiences; employs self-reflection to gain insight; functions without need for constant reassurance from others; balances needs of self with needs of others
	Identity development	Integrates multiple aspects of identity into a coherent whole; recognizes and exhibits interdependence in accordance with environmental, cultural, and personal values; identifies and commits to important aspects of self

	Commitment to ethics and integrity	Incorporates ethical reasoning into action; explores and articulates the values and principles involved in personal decision-making; acts in congruence with personal values and beliefs; exemplifies dependability, honesty, and trustworthiness; accepts personal accountability
	Spiritual awareness	Develops and articulates personal belief system; understands roles of spirituality in personal and group values and behaviors; critiques, compares, and contrasts various belief systems; explores issues of purpose, meaning, and faith
Interpersonal competence	Meaningful relationships	Establishes healthy, mutually beneficial relationships with others; treats others with respect; manages interpersonal conflicts effectively; demonstrates appropriately assertive behavior
	Interdependence	Seeks help from others when needed and offers assistance to others; shares a group or organizational goal and works with others to achieve it; learns from the contributions and involvement of others; accepts supervision and direction as needed
	Collaboration	Works cooperatively with others, including people different from self and/or with different points of view; seeks and values the involvement of others; listens to and considers others' points of view
	Effective leadership	Demonstrates skill in guiding and assisting a group, organization, or community in meeting its goals; identifies and understands the dynamics of a group; exhibits democratic principles as a leader or group member; communicates a vision, mission, or purpose that encourages commitment and action in others
	Understanding and appreciation of cultural and human differences	Understands one's own identity and culture; seeks involvement with people different from oneself; articulates the advantages and impact of a diverse society; identifies systematic barriers to equality and inclusiveness, then advocates and justifies means for dismantling them; in interactions with others, exhibits respect and preserves the dignity of others
	Global perspective	Understands and analyzes the interconnectedness of societies worldwide; demonstrates effective stewardship of human, economic, and environmental resources
	Social responsibility	Recognizes social systems and their influence on people; appropriately challenges the unfair, unjust, or uncivil behavior of other individuals or groups; participates in service/volunteer activities that are characterized by reciprocity; articulates the values and principles involved in personal decision-making; affirms and values the worth of individuals and communities
	Sense of civic responsibility	Demonstrates consideration of the welfare of others in decision-making; engages in critical reflection and principled dissent; understands and participates in relevant governance systems; educates and facilitates the civic engagement of others
Practical competence	Pursuing goals	Sets and pursues individual goals; articulates rationale for personal and educational goals and objectives; articulates and makes plans to achieve long-term goals and objectives; identifies and works to overcome obstacles that hamper goal achievement

	Communicating effectively	Conveys meaning in a way that others understand by writing and speaking coherently and effectively; writes and speaks after reflection; influences others through writing, speaking or artistic expression; effectively articulates abstract ideas; uses appropriate syntax and grammar; makes and evaluates presentations or performances; listens attentively to others and responds appropriately
	Technological competence	Demonstrates technological literacy and skills; demonstrates the ethical application of intellectual property and privacy; uses technology ethically and effectively to communicate, solve problems, and complete tasks; stays current with technological innovations
	Managing personal affairs	Exhibits self-reliant behaviors; manages time effectively; develops strategies for managing finances
	Managing career development	Takes steps to initiate a job search or seek advanced education; constructs a resume based on clear job objectives and with evidence of knowledge, skills, and abilities; recognizes the importance of transferrable skills
	Demonstrating professionalism	Accepts supervision and direction as needed; values the contributions of others; holds self accountable for obligations; shows initiative; assesses, critiques, and then improves the quality of one's work and one's work environment
	Maintaining health and wellness	Engages in behaviors and contributes to environments that promote health and reduce risk; articulates the relationship between health and wellness in accomplishing goals; exhibits behaviors that advance the health of communities
	Living a purposeful and satisfying life	Makes purposeful decisions regarding balance among education, work, and leisure time; acts in congruence with personal identity, ethical, spiritual, and moral values

[1] This document is an adaptation of *Learning Reconsidered* and the CAS Learning Outcomes
[2] Categories adapted from *Learning Reconsidered (2004)* and Kuh, Douglas, Lund, & Ramin Gyurmek (1994)
[3] These examples are adopted from the George Mason University *Critical Thinking Assessment Report* (2006)

References

Council for the Advancement of Standards in Higher Education. (2006). *CAS professional standards for higher education* (6th ed.). Washington, DC: Author.
George Mason University (2006). *Critical Thinking Assessment Report.* Retrieved September 8, 2008 from https:assessment.gmu.edu/StudentLearningCompetencies/Critical/AssessProposal.html
Keeling, R. P. (2006). *Learning reconsidered 2: Implementing a campus-wide focus on the student experience.* American College Personnel Association (ACPA), Association of College and University Housing Officers-International (ACUHO-I), Association of College Unions-International (ACUI), National Academic Advising Association (NACADA), National Association for Campus Activities (NACA), National Association of Student Personnel Administrators (NASPA), and National Intramural-Recreational Sports Association (NIRSA).
Kuh, G. D., Douglas, K. B., Lund, J. P., & Ramin Gyurmek, J. (1994). *Student learning outside the classroom: Transcending artificial boundaries.* (ASHE-ERIC Higher Education Report No. 8.). Washington, D.C.: The George Washington University, Graduate School of Education and Human Development.
NASPA/ACPA (2004). *Learning reconsidered: A campus-wide focus on the student experience.* Washington, DC: National Association of Student Personnel Administrators and the American College Personnel Association.

Approved as revised by CAS Board of Directors, October 19, 2008

The Role of the CAS General Standards
CAS Standards Contextual Statement

The Council for the Advancement of Standards in Higher Education (CAS) was established in 1979 as a consortium of professional associations whose members championed student learning and development in a variety of functional areas within student support programs and services. From the outset, CAS identified its primary mission as the development and promulgation of professional standards that higher education practitioners could use to guide, develop, and assess programs and services. By 1986, with a repayable grant from the American College Testing Program (ACT), CAS created 16 sets of functional area standards and published them in the first CAS "blue book." It was clear by the time of the initial publication that a number of characteristics were common to all functional areas, commonalities that demanded inclusion in all current and future CAS standards. As a result, general standards were devised that CAS Board members unanimously agreed were relevant to all the functional areas within student support programs and services championed by CAS member associations. As the CAS General Standards evolved over the years, the Council consistently held to two principles: that the commonalities underlying the functional areas are indispensable and must be incorporated in all CAS standards and that student learning and development are fundamental to mission and program.

The 2002 revision of the General Standards is notable for its increased emphasis on achievable, observable, and assessable outcomes associated with student learning and development. Earlier versions of the CAS General Standards included a list of developmental domains (e.g., intellectual growth, effective communication, realistic self-appraisal, clarified values, career choices, leadership, and meaningful interpersonal relationships) for functional area programs to consider in their educational efforts. The 2002 revision, however, reaffirmed and reinforced the importance of the specified outcome domains by building into the General Standards a stated expectation that all functional area programs must place emphasis on identifying relevant learning outcomes and assessing their achievement by students. To underscore the importance of the various outcome domains for all functional areas and to facilitate assessment of outcome domains by the functional areas, the 2002 revision of the General Standards included a table listing 16 domains (intellectual growth, effective communication, enhanced self-esteem, realistic self-appraisal, clarified values, career choices, leadership development, healthy behavior, meaningful interpersonal relationships, independence, collaboration, social responsibility, satisfying and productive lifestyles, appreciating diversity, spiritual awareness, and personal and educational goals) along with examples of achievement indicators that could be used to guide the assessment process. The indicators represented examples of observable student behaviors that practitioners could use to judge learning and development achievement. CAS published the *Frameworks for Assessing Learning and Development Outcomes* (Strayhorn, 2006) to further assist practitioners in implementing outcomes assessment activities. In effect, the 2002 revision of the General Standards recognized the potential educational impact that functional area programs can have upon student learning and development and required programs to consider student learning their primary mission.

With the publication of *Learning Reconsidered* (NASPA/ACPA, 2004), CAS decided that an integration of the learning outcomes from the General Standards and from *Learning Reconsidered* would enhance efforts in promoting student learning and development. Consequently, CAS hosted a "think tank" involving writers of *Learning Reconsidered*, CAS directors, and prominent practitioners and faculty members in student affairs to recommend revisions to the CAS student learning and development domains. Simultaneously, CAS commenced the review and revision of the General Standards document.

In 2008 the CAS Board of Directors adopted revisions to the student learning and development outcomes and the General Standards that require institutional programs and services to identify relevant and desirable learning from six broad categories (called domains), assess relevant and desirable learning, and articulate how their programs and services contribute to student learning and development in domains not specifically assessed. The six domains are knowledge acquisition, construction, integration and application; cognitive complexity; intrapersonal development; interpersonal competence; humanitarianism and civic engagement; and practical competence. Each domain was further defined or clarified by learning outcome dimensions, which allow for a more focused program development and assessment approach based on institutional mission and priorities. The domains and learning outcome dimensions were embedded in each functional area standard. Examples illustrating achievement of the student learning outcomes for each of the domains appear in the CAS Learning and Development Outcomes Chart.

The 2008 revision of the CAS General Standards also recognized the pervasive use of technologies in programs and services by creating a new section on Technology. In 2008 new standards were adopted addressing sustainability practices, emergency and crisis response, and prevention efforts.

The CAS General Standards are reviewed and revised

prior to the publication of each new edition of the *CAS Professional Standards for Higher Education*. In 2011 the CAS Board of Directors adopted significant revisions to the General Standards. In support of *ACPA/NASPA Professional Competency Areas for Student Affairs Practitioners* (Bresciani & Todd, 2010), CAS revised its required competencies for professionals to align where appropriate with the ACPA/NASPA competencies. These changes are most evident in the section on Organization and Leadership. The 2011 revision also recognizes the pervasiveness of distance learning and the need for all functional areas to include service delivery methods for distance education students (SLOAN-C, 2011). For the first time, the 2011 General Standards include family education history (e.g., first generation to attend college) in its standard on discrimination. Major revisions made to the structure of the General Standards reduced the 14 sections to 12 by combining and renaming sections where common or related elements existed (i.e., a new section, Organization and Leadership, replaced two sections, Leadership & Organization and Management; Legal Responsibilities became Law, Policy, and Governance; and two sections, Diversity and Equity & Access, were combined).

Although the CAS General Standards were not designed to stand alone, they are presented here to remind and inform educators about the commonalities that exist among the many student support programs and services throughout higher education. It is anticipated that the focus on the whole student experience and its impact on learning and development will grow and that student support programs will become equal partners with formal academic programs in contributing to student learning and development. There can be little doubt that if those who lead and practice in such programs combine their collective powers to make an educational difference in the lives of the students they serve, the resulting educational trust will carry student support programs and services to new heights of achievement for all concerned.

References, Readings, and Resources

Bresciani, M. J., & Todd, D. K. (Eds.). (2010). *ACPA/NASPA professional competency areas for student affairs practitioners.* American College Personnel Association, National Association of Student Personnel Administrators.

NASPA/ACPA. (2004). *Learning reconsidered: A campus-wide focus on the student experience.* Washington, DC: National Association of Student Personnel Administrators and the American College Personnel Association.

SLOAN-C: A Consortium of Institutions and Organizations Committed to Quality Online Education. (2011). *A quality scorecard for the administration of online education programs.* Retrieved from http://sloanconsortium.org/quality_scoreboard_online_program

Strayhorn, T. (2006). *Frameworks for assessing learning and development outcomes.* Washington, DC: Council for the Advancement of Standards in Higher Education.

Contextual Statement Contributors

Current Edition:
Patricia Carretta, George Mason University, NACE

Previous Editions:
Jan Arminio, Shippensburg University, NACA
Laura A. Dean, University of Georgia, ACCA
Ted K. Miller, University of Georgia, ACPA/CAS

CAS General Standards
CAS Standards and Guidelines

Part 1. MISSION

Programs and services must develop, disseminate, implement, and regularly review their missions. The mission must be consistent with the mission of the institution and with professional standards. The mission must be appropriate for the institution's student populations and community settings. Mission statements must reference student learning and development.

Part 2. PROGRAM

The formal education of students, consisting of the curriculum and the co-curriculum, must promote student learning and development outcomes that are purposeful, contribute to students' realization of their potential, and prepare students for satisfying and productive lives.

Programs and services must collaborate with colleagues and departments across the institution to promote student learning and development, persistence, and success.

Consistent with the institutional mission, programs and services must identify relevant and desirable student learning and development outcomes from among the six domains and related dimensions:

Domain: knowledge acquisition, integration, construction, and application

- Dimensions: understanding knowledge from a range of disciplines; connecting knowledge to other knowledge, ideas, and experiences; constructing knowledge; and relating knowledge to daily life

Domain: cognitive complexity

- Dimensions: critical thinking, reflective thinking, effective reasoning, and creativity

Domain: intrapersonal development

- Dimensions: realistic self-appraisal, self-understanding, and self-respect; identity development; commitment to ethics and integrity; and spiritual awareness

Domain: interpersonal competence

- Dimensions: meaningful relationships, interdependence, collaboration, and effective leadership.

Domain: humanitarianism and civic engagement

- Dimensions: understanding and appreciation of cultural and human differences, social responsibility, global perspective, and sense of civic responsibility

Domain: practical competence

- Dimensions: pursuing goals, communicating effectively, technical competence, managing personal affairs, managing career development, demonstrating professionalism, maintaining health and wellness, and living a purposeful and satisfying life

[LD Outcomes: See *The Council for the Advancement of Standards Learning and Developmental Outcomes* statement for examples of outcomes related to these domains and dimensions.]

Programs and services must
- assess relevant and desirable student learning and development
- provide evidence of impact on outcomes
- articulate contributions to or support of student learning and development in the domains not specifically assessed
- articulate contributions to or support of student persistence and success
- use evidence gathered through this process to create strategies for improvement of programs and services

Programs and services must be
- intentionally designed
- guided by theories and knowledge of learning and development
- integrated into the life of the institution
- reflective of developmental and demographic profiles of the student population
- responsive to needs of individuals, populations with distinct needs, and relevant constituencies
- delivered using multiple formats, strategies, and contexts

Where institutions provide distance education, programs and services must assist distance learners to achieve their educational goals by providing access to information about programs and services, to staff members who can address questions and concerns, and to counseling, advising, or other forms of assistance.

Part 3. ORGANIZATION AND LEADERSHIP

To achieve student and program outcomes, programs

and services must be structured purposefully and organized effectively. Programs and services must have

- clearly stated goals
- current and accessible policies and procedures
- written performance expectations for employees
- functional work flow graphics or organizational charts demonstrating clear channels of authority

Leaders with organizational authority for the programs and services must provide strategic planning, supervision, and management; advance the organization; and maintain integrity through the following functions:

Strategic Planning

- articulate a vision and mission that drive short- and long-term planning
- set goals and objectives based on the needs of the population served and desired student learning or development and program outcomes
- facilitate continuous development, implementation, and assessment of goal attainment congruent with institutional mission and strategic plans
- promote environments that provide meaningful opportunities for student learning, development, and engagement
- develop and continuously improve programs and services in response to the changing needs of students served and evolving institutional priorities
- intentionally include diverse perspectives to inform decision making

Supervising

- manage human resource processes including recruitment, selection, development, supervision, performance planning, evaluation, recognition, and reward
- influence others to contribute to the effectiveness and success of the unit
- empower professional, support, and student staff to accept leadership opportunities
- offer appropriate feedback to colleagues and students on skills needed to become more effective leaders
- encourage and support professional development, collaboration with colleagues and departments across the institution, and scholarly contribution to the profession

Managing

- identify and address individual, organizational, and environmental conditions

that foster or inhibit mission achievement

- plan, allocate, and monitor the use of fiscal, physical, human, intellectual, and technological resources
- use current and valid evidence to inform decisions
- incorporate sustainability practices in the management and design of programs, services, and facilities
- understand appropriate technologies and integrate them into programs and services
- be knowledgeable about codes and laws relevant to programs and services and ensure that staff members understand their responsibilities through appropriate training
- assess potential risks and take action to mitigate them

Advancing the Organization

- communicate effectively in writing, speaking, and electronic venues
- advocate for programs and services
- advocate for representation in strategic planning initiatives at appropriate divisional and institutional levels
- initiate collaborative interactions with internal and external stakeholders who have legitimate concerns about and interests in the functional area
- facilitate processes to reach consensus where wide support is needed
- inform other areas within the institution about issues affecting practice

Maintaining Integrity

- model ethical behavior and institutional citizenship
- share data used to inform key decisions in transparent and accessible ways
- monitor media used for distributing information about programs and services to ensure the content is current, accurate, appropriately referenced, and accessible

Part 4. HUMAN RESOURCES

Programs and services must be staffed adequately by individuals qualified to accomplish mission and goals.

Within institutional guidelines, programs and services must

- establish procedures for staff recruitment and selection, training, performance planning, and evaluation
- set expectations for supervision and performance
- assess the performance of employees

individually and as a team
- provide access to continuing and advanced education and appropriate professional development opportunities to improve the leadership ability, competence, and skills of all employees.

Programs and services must maintain position descriptions for all staff members.

To create a diverse staff, programs and services must institute recruitment and hiring strategies that encourage individuals from under-represented populations to apply for positions.

Programs and services must develop promotion practices that are fair, inclusive, proactive, and non-discriminatory.

To further the recruitment and retention of staff, programs and services must consider work life initiatives, such as compressed work schedules, flextime, job sharing, remote work, or telework.

Professional staff members must hold an earned graduate or professional degree in a field relevant to the position they hold or must possess an appropriate combination of educational credentials and related work experience.

Professional staff members must engage in continuing professional development activities to keep abreast of the research, theories, legislation, policies, and developments that affect their programs and services.

Programs and services must have technical and support staff members adequate to accomplish their mission. All members of the staff must be technologically proficient and qualified to perform their job functions, be knowledgeable about ethical and legal uses of technology, and have access to training and resources to support the performance of their assigned responsibilities.

Degree- or credential-seeking interns or graduate assistants must be qualified by enrollment in an appropriate field of study and by relevant experience. These individuals must be trained and supervised adequately by professional staff members holding educational credentials and related work experience appropriate for supervision. Supervisors must be cognizant of the roles of interns and graduate assistants as both student and employee and closely adhere to all parameters of their job descriptions, work hours, and schedules. Supervisors and the interns or graduate assistants must agree to compensatory time or other appropriate compensation if circumstances necessitate additional hours.

Student employees and volunteers must be carefully selected, trained, supervised, and evaluated. They must be educated on how and when to refer those in need of additional assistance to qualified staff members and must have access to a supervisor for assistance in making these judgments. Student employees and volunteers must be provided clear job descriptions, pre-service training based on assessed needs, and continuing development.

All staff members, including student employees and volunteers, must receive specific training on institutional policies pertaining to functions or activities they support and to privacy and confidentiality policies and laws regarding access to student records and other sensitive institutional information.

All staff members must receive training on policies and procedures related to the use of technology to store or access student records and institutional data.

Programs and services must ensure that staff members are knowledgeable about and trained in emergency procedures, crisis response, and prevention efforts. Prevention efforts must address identification of threatening conduct or behavior of students, faculty and staff members, and others and must incorporate a system for responding and reporting.

Programs and services must ensure that staff members are knowledgeable of and trained in safety and emergency procedures for securing and vacating facilities.

Part 5. ETHICS

Programs and services must review relevant professional ethical standards and must adopt or develop and implement appropriate statements of ethical practice.

Programs and services must publish and adhere to statements of ethical practice and ensure their periodic review by relevant constituencies.

Programs and services must orient new staff members to relevant ethical standards and statements of ethical practice and related institutional policies.

Statements of ethical standards must specify that staff members respect privacy and maintain confidentiality in all communications and records to the extent that such communications and records are protected under relevant privacy laws.

Statements of ethical standards must specify limits on disclosure of information contained in students' educational records as well as requirements to disclose to appropriate authorities.

Statements of ethical standards must address personal and economic conflicts of interest, or appearance thereof, by staff members in the performance of their work.

Statements of ethical standards must reflect the responsibility of staff members to be fair, objective, and impartial in their interactions with others.

Statements of ethical standards must reference management of institutional funds.

Statements of ethical standards must reference appropriate behavior regarding research and assessment with human participants, confidentiality of research and assessment data, and students' rights and responsibilities.

Statements of ethical standards must include the expectation that staff members confront and hold accountable other staff members who exhibit unethical behavior.

Statements of ethical standards must address issues surrounding scholarly integrity.

As appropriate, staff members must inform users of programs and services of ethical obligations and limitations emanating from codes and laws or from licensure requirements.

Staff members must recognize and avoid conflicts of interest that could adversely influence their judgment or objectivity and, when unavoidable, recuse themselves from the situation.

Staff members must perform their duties within the limits of their position, training, expertise, and competence.

When these limits are exceeded, individuals in need of further assistance must be referred to persons possessing appropriate qualifications.

Promotional and descriptive information must be accurate and free of deception.

Programs and services must adhere to institutional policies regarding ethical and legal use of software and technology.

Part 6. LAW, POLICY, AND GOVERNANCE

Programs and services must be in compliance with laws, regulations, and policies that relate to their respective responsibilities and that pose legal obligations, limitations, risks, and liabilities for the institution as a whole. Examples include constitutional, statutory, regulatory, and case law;

relevant law and orders emanating from codes and laws; and the institution's policies.

Programs and services must inform staff members, appropriate officials, and users of programs and services about existing and changing legal obligations, risks and liabilities, and limitations.

Programs and services must have written policies on all relevant operations, transactions, or tasks that have legal implications.

Programs and services must regularly review policies. The revision and creation of policies must be informed by best practices, available evidence, and policy issues in higher education.

Staff members must use reasonable and informed practices to limit the liability exposure of the institution and its officers, employees, and agents. Staff members must be informed about institutional policies regarding risk management, personal liability, and related insurance coverage options and must be referred to external sources if the institution does not provide coverage.

The institution must provide access to legal advice for staff members as needed to carry out assigned responsibilities.

Programs and services must have procedures and guidelines consistent with institutional policy for responding to threats, emergencies, and crisis situations. Systems and procedures must be in place to disseminate timely and accurate information to students, other members of the institutional community, and appropriate external organizations during emergency situations.

Staff members must neither participate in nor condone any form of harassment or activity that demeans persons or creates an intimidating, hostile, or offensive environment.

Programs and services must obtain permission to use copyrighted materials and instruments. Programs and services must purchase the materials and instruments from legally compliant sources or seek alternative permission from the publisher or owner. References to copyrighted materials and instruments must include appropriate citations.

Staff members must be knowledgeable about internal and external governance systems that affect programs and services.

Part 7. DIVERSITY, EQUITY, AND ACCESS

Within the context of each institution's unique mission and in accordance with institutional polices and all applicable codes and laws, programs and services must create and maintain educational and work environments that are

- welcoming, accessible, and inclusive to persons of diverse backgrounds
- equitable and non-discriminatory
- free from harassment

Programs and services must not discriminate on the basis of ability; age; cultural identity; ethnicity; family educational history (e.g., first generation to attend college); gender identity and expression; nationality; political affiliation; race; religious affiliation; sex; sexual orientation; economic, marital, social, or veteran status; or any other basis included in institutional policies and codes and laws.

Programs and services must

- advocate for greater sensitivity to multicultural and social justice concerns by the institution and its personnel
- modify or remove policies, practices, facilities, structures, systems, and technologies that limit access, discriminate, or produce inequities
- include diversity, equity, and access initiatives within their strategic plans
- foster communication that deepens understanding of identity, culture, self-expression, and heritage
- promote respect about commonalities and differences among people within their historical and cultural contexts
- address the characteristics and needs of a diverse population when establishing and implementing culturally relevant and inclusive programs, services, policies, procedures, and practices
- provide staff members with access to multicultural training and hold staff members accountable for integrating the training into their work
- respond to the needs of all students and other populations served when establishing hours of operation and developing methods of delivering programs, services, and resources
- ensure physical, program, and resource access for persons with disabilities
- recognize the needs of distance learning students by providing appropriate and accessible services and resources or by assisting them in gaining access to other appropriate services and resources in their geographic region

Part 8. INSTITUTIONAL AND EXTERNAL RELATIONS

Programs and services must reach out to relevant individuals, groups, communities, and organizations internal and external to the institution to

- establish, maintain, and promote understanding and effective relations with those that have a significant interest in or potential effect on the students or other constituents served by the programs and services
- garner support and resources for programs and services as defined by the mission statement
- disseminate information about the programs and services
- collaborate, where appropriate, to assist in offering or improving programs and services to meet the needs of students and other constituents and to achieve program and student outcomes
- engage diverse individuals, groups, communities, and organizations to enrich the educational environment and experiences of students and other constituents

Programs and services must have procedures and guidelines consistent with institutional policy for

- communicating with the media
- contracting with external organizations for delivery of programs and services
- cultivating, soliciting, and managing gifts
- applying to and managing funds from grants

Part 9. FINANCIAL RESOURCES

Programs and services must have funding to accomplish the mission and goals. In establishing funding priorities and making significant changes, a comprehensive analysis must be conducted to determine the following elements: unmet needs of the unit, relevant expenditures, external and internal resources, and impact on students and the institution. Programs and services must demonstrate efficient and effective use and responsible stewardship of fiscal resources consistent with institutional protocols.

Part 10. TECHNOLOGY

Programs and services must have adequate technology to support the achievement of their mission and goals. The technology and its use must comply with institutional policies and procedures and be evaluated for compliance with relevant codes and laws.

Programs and services must use current technology to provide updated information regarding mission, location, staffing, programs, services, and official contacts to students and designated clients.

Programs and services must explore the use of

technology to enhance delivery of programs and services, especially for students at a distance or external constituencies.

When technology is used to facilitate student learning and development, programs and services must select technology that reflects intended outcomes.

Programs and services must
- maintain policies and procedures that address the security, confidentiality, and backup of data, as well as compliance with privacy laws
- have clearly articulated plans in place for protecting confidentiality and security of information when using Internet-based technologies
- develop plans for replacing and updating existing hardware and software as well as plans for integrating new technically-based or supported programs, including systems developed internally by the institution, systems available through professional associations, or private vendor-based systems

Technology, as well as workstations or computer labs maintained by programs and services for student use, must be accessible to all designated clients and must meet established technology standards for delivery to persons with disabilities.

When providing student access to technology, programs and services must
- have policies on the use of technology that are clear, easy to understand, and available to all students
- provide assistance, information, or referral to appropriate support services to those needing help accessing or using technology
- provide instruction or training on how to use the technology
- inform students on the legal and ethical implications of misuse as it pertains to intellectual property, harassment, privacy, and social networks

Student violations of technology policies must follow established institutional student disciplinary procedures.

Students who experience negative emotional or psychological consequences from the use of technology must be referred to support services provided by the institution.

Part 11. FACILITIES AND EQUIPMENT

Programs and services must have adequate, accessible, and suitably located facilities and equipment to support the mission and goals. If acquiring capital equipment as defined by the institution, programs and services must take into account expenses related to regular maintenance and life cycle costs. Facilities and equipment must be evaluated on an established cycle, including consideration of sustainability, and be in compliance with codes and laws to provide for access, health, safety, and security.

Staff members must have workspace that is well equipped, adequate in size, and designed to support their work and responsibilities. For conversations requiring privacy, staff members must have access to a private space.

Staff members who share workspace must be able to secure their own work.

The design of the facilities must guarantee the security and privacy of records and ensure the confidentiality of sensitive information.

The location and layout of the facilities must be sensitive to the needs of persons with disabilities as well as the needs of other constituencies.

Part 12. ASSESSMENT AND EVALUATION

Programs and services must have a clearly articulated assessment plan to document achievement of stated goals and learning outcomes, demonstrate accountability, provide evidence of improvement, and describe resulting changes in programs and services.

Programs and services must have adequate fiscal, human, professional development, and technological resources to develop and implement assessment plans.

Assessments must include direct and indirect evaluation and use qualitative and quantitative methodologies and existing evidence, as appropriate, to determine whether and to what degree the stated mission, goals, and intended outcomes are being met as effectively and efficiently as possible. The process must employ sufficient and sound measures to ensure comprehensiveness. Data collected must include responses from students and other constituencies, and aggregated results must be shared with those groups. Results of assessments must be shared appropriately with multiple constituents.

Results of assessments and evaluations must be used to identify needs and interests in revising and improving programs and services, recognizing staff performance, maximizing resource efficiency and effectiveness, improving student achievement of learning and development outcomes, and improving

student persistence and success. Changes resulting from the use of assessments and evaluation must be shared with stakeholders.

Revision approved November 2011

The Role of Academic Advising Programs
CAS Standards Contextual Statement

Academic advising is an essential element in the success and persistence of postsecondary students. "Through academic advising, students learn to become members of their higher education community, to think critically about their roles and responsibilities as students, and to prepare to be educated citizens of a democratic society and a global community. Academic advising engages students beyond their own worldviews, while acknowledging their individual characteristics, values, and motivations as they enter, move through, and exit the institution. Regardless of the diversity of our institutions, our students, our advisors, and our organizational structures, academic advising has three components: curriculum (what advising deals with), pedagogy (how advising does what it does), and student learning outcomes (the result of academic advising)" (NACADA, 2006a, ¶ 7).

Advising evolves from an institution's culture, values, and practices and is delivered in accordance with these factors. Advising practice draws from various theories and strategies in the social sciences, humanities, and education. "Good academic advising also provides perhaps the only opportunity for all students to develop a personal, consistent relationship with someone in the institution who cares about them" (Drake, 2011, p. 10). "In fact, the developmental advisor makes the establishment of the relationship the first order of business with the student" (Crookston, 1994, p. 8). As higher education curricula become increasingly complex and constituents intensify their demands for accountability, pressure to make students' academic experience more meaningful has increased. Higher education, in turn, has responded with renewed attention to the need for high-quality academic advising.

"Once almost exclusively a faculty function, today academic advising has come forward as a specialization within the higher education community. Although remaining a role that faculty members play, academic advising has emerged as an area of expertise in and of itself" (NACADA, 2006b, p. 3) and "this fact is a source of its tremendous potential" (p. 4). Faculty, professionals, graduate students, and peers now engage students in academic advising.

The establishment of the National Academic Advising Association (NACADA) followed the first national conference on advising in 1977. The creation of NACADA marked a significant turning point in according recognition to higher education academic advisors who consider their work to be purposeful and unique. Today NACADA flourishes with more than 10,000 members in over 20 countries, making NACADA truly the global community for academic advising. Each year NACADA conferences, institutes, and webcasts attract more than 14,000 participants from around the globe (NACADA, 2011). The NACADA Statement of Core Values (2005) provides the ethical principles that guide advising practice. The Core Values, along with the NACADA Concept of Academic Advising (2006) and the CAS Standards, serve as a framework all academic advisors can use to examine their professional interactions.

Academic advising became a significant category within professional literature during the 1980s and is still studied with great interest for its role in student retention and graduation. NACADA promotes research in the discipline through its research agenda, funding of research grants, and publication of the *NACADA Journal,* the juried research journal in the field. The *NACADA Journal* as well as *Academic Advising Today*, the association's electronic quarterly, feature articles that unite research, theory, and practice within the field. Rich and varied professional development resources include books, monographs, CDs, DVDs, and webcasts that examine various aspects of advising. Some of the most referenced resources in the profession include *Academic Advising: A Comprehensive Handbook* (2nd ed., 2008), *The New Advisor Guidebook: Mastering the Art of Advising through the First Year and Beyond* (2007), *Scholarly Inquiry in Academic Advising* (2010), *Guide to Assessment in Academic Advising* (2nd ed., 2010), and the resources found in the web-based *NACADA Clearinghouse of Academic Advising Resources*. Information about NACADA's resources can be located at www.nacada.ksu.edu/. Lowenstein (2006) declared that "an excellent advisor does for students' entire education what the excellent teacher does for a course: helps them order the pieces, put them together to make a coherent whole, so that the student experiences the curriculum not as a checklist of discrete, isolated pieces but instead as a unity, a composition of interrelated parts with multiple connections and relationships" (¶ 5). Thus, many within the field define academic advising as a teaching and learning process focused on the achievement of student learning outcomes. As NACADA's *Concept of Academic Advising* (NACADA, 2006a) delineated, these outcomes differ among institutions, with each institution establishing its own learning outcomes based upon its mission, goals, curriculum, co-curriculum, and assessment methods (White, 2000). The *Concept* does, however, suggest as a representative sample of learning outcomes for advising that students will

- craft a coherent educational plan based on assessment of abilities, aspirations, interests, and values
- use complex information from various sources to set goals, reach decisions, and achieve those goals
- assume responsibility for meeting academic program requirements

- articulate the meaning of higher education and the intent of the institution's curriculum
- cultivate the intellectual habits that lead to a lifetime of learning
- behave as citizens who engage in the wider world around them (NACADA, 2006, ¶ 10).

Academic advising is a crucial component of all students' experiences in higher education. Through advising, students can find meaning in their lives, make significant decisions about their futures, and access all that higher education has to offer. When practiced with competence and dedication, academic advising is integral to student success, persistence, and retention. In an age often characterized by impersonal detachment, academic advising provides a vital personal connection students need in order to persist and succeed.

References, Readings, and Resources

Aiken-Wisniewski, S. (Ed.). (2010). *Guide to assessment in academic advising* (2nd ed., Monograph No. 23). Manhattan, KS: National Academic Advising Association.

Drake, J. K. (2011, July-August). The role of academic advising in student retention and persistence. *About Campus, 16*(3), 8-12. doi:10.1002/abc.20062

Crookston, B. B. (1994). A developmental view of academic advising as teaching. *NACADA Journal, 14*(2), 5-9.

Folsom, P. (Ed.). (2007). *The new advisor guidebook: Mastering the art of advising through the first year and beyond* (NACADA Monograph No. 16). Manhattan, KS: National Academic Advising Association.

Gordon, V. M., Habley, W. R., & Grites, T. J. (Eds.). (2008). *Academic advising: A comprehensive handbook* (2nd ed.). San Francisco, CA: Jossey-Bass.

Hagen, P. L., Kuhn, T. L., & Padak, G. M. (Eds.). (2010). *Scholarly inquiry in academic advising* (Monograph No. 20). Manhattan, KS: National Academic Advising Association.

Lowenstein, M. (2006). A learning-centered view of teaching as advising. *Proceedings from the Fifth Annual Professional Development Conference on Academic Advising*. Retrieved from www.psu.edu/dus/mentor/proc01ml.htm

NACADA. (2005). *Statement of core values.* Retrieved from http://www.nacada.ksu.edu/Clearinghouse/AdvisingIssues/Core-Values.htm

NACADA. (2006a). *Concept of academic advising.* Retrieved from http://www.nacada.ksu.edu/Clearinghouse/AdvisingIssues/Concept-Advising.htm

NACADA. (2006b). The history and definitions of academic advising. In *What is academic advising: Foundation of academic advising.* (Pocket Guide No. 1). Manhattan, KS: Author.

NACADA. (2011). *NACADA member demographic information.* Retrieved from http://www.nacada.ksu.edu/forleaders/ExecOffice/Reports/documents/MY2011demographics.pdf

White, E. R. (2000). Developing mission, goals, and objectives for the advising program. In V. N. Gordon & W. R. Habley (Eds.), *Academic advising: A comprehensive handbook* (pp. 180-191). San Francisco, CA: Jossey-Bass.

Contextual Statement Contributors
Current Edition:
Marsha A. Miller, Kansas State University, NACADA Assistant Director, Resources & Services
Eric R. White, The Pennsylvania State University, Past NACADA President
Charlie Nutt, Kansas State University, NACADA Executive Director
Jayne K. Drake, Temple University, Past NACADA President

Previous Editions:
Linda C. Higginson, The Pennsylvania State University

Academic Advising Programs
CAS Standards and Guidelines

Part 1. MISSION

The primary purpose of Academic Advising Programs (AAP) is to assist students in the development of meaningful educational plans.

AAP must develop, disseminate, implement, and regularly review their missions. The mission must be consistent with the mission of the institution and with professional standards. The mission must be appropriate for the institution's student populations and community settings. Mission statements must reference student learning and development.

The institution must have a clearly written mission statement pertaining to academic advising that must include program goals and expectations of advisors and advisees.

Part 2. PROGRAM

The formal education of students, consisting of the curriculum and the co-curriculum, must promote student learning and development outcomes that are purposeful, contribute to students' realization of their potential, and prepare students for satisfying and productive lives.

Academic Advising Programs (AAP) must collaborate with colleagues and departments across the institution to promote student learning and development, persistence, and success.

Consistent with the institutional mission, AAP must identify relevant and desirable student learning and development outcomes from among the six domains and related dimensions:

Domain: knowledge acquisition, integration, construction, and application

- Dimensions: understanding knowledge from a range of disciplines; connecting knowledge to other knowledge, ideas, and experiences; constructing knowledge; and relating knowledge to daily life

Domain: cognitive complexity

- Dimensions: critical thinking, reflective thinking, effective reasoning, and creativity

Domain: intrapersonal development

- Dimensions: realistic self-appraisal, self-understanding, and self-respect; identity development; commitment to ethics and integrity; and spiritual awareness

Domain: interpersonal competence

- Dimensions: meaningful relationships, interdependence, collaboration, and effective leadership.

Domain: humanitarianism and civic engagement

- Dimensions: understanding and appreciation of cultural and human differences, social responsibility, global perspective, and sense of civic responsibility

Domain: practical competence

- Dimensions: pursuing goals, communicating effectively, technical competence, managing personal affairs, managing career development, demonstrating professionalism, maintaining health and wellness, and living a purposeful and satisfying life

[LD Outcomes: See *The Council for the Advancement of Standards Learning and Developmental Outcomes* statement for examples of outcomes related to these domains and dimensions.]

AAP must
- assess relevant and desirable student learning and development
- provide evidence of impact on outcomes
- articulate contributions to or support of student learning and development in the domains not specifically assessed
- articulate contributions to or support of student persistence and success
- use evidence gathered through this process to create strategies for improvement of programs and services

AAP must be
- intentionally designed
- guided by theories and knowledge of learning and development
- integrated into the life of the institution
- reflective of developmental and demographic profiles of the student population
- responsive to needs of individuals, populations with distinct needs, and relevant constituencies
- delivered using multiple formats, strategies, and contexts

Where institutions provide distance education, AAP must assist distance learners to achieve their

educational goals by providing access to information about programs and services, to staff members who can address questions and concerns, and to counseling, advising, or other forms of assistance.

Both students and advisors must assume shared responsibility in the advising process.   AAP must assist students to make the best academic decisions possible by encouraging identification and assessment of alternatives and consideration of the consequences of their decisions.

The ultimate responsibility for making decisions about educational plans and life goals should rest with the individual student.

AAP must be guided by a set of written goals and objectives that are directly related to its stated mission.

AAP must

- promote student growth and development
- assist students in assessing their interests and abilities, examining their educational goals, making decisions and developing short-term and long-term plans to meet their objectives
- discuss and clarify educational, career, and life goals
- provide accurate and timely information and interpret institutional, general education, and major requirements
- assist students to understand the educational context within which they are enrolled
- advise on the selection of appropriate courses and other educational experiences
- clarify institutional policies and procedures
- evaluate and monitor student academic progress and the impact on achievement of goals
- reinforce student self-direction and self-sufficiency
- direct students with educational, career, or personal concerns, or skill/learning deficiencies, to other resources and programs on the campus when necessary
- make students aware of and refer to educational, institutional, and community resources and services (e.g., internship, study abroad, honors, service-learning, research opportunities)
- collect and distribute relevant data about student needs, preferences, and performance for use in institutional decisions and policy

AAP should provide information about student experiences and concerns regarding their academic program to appropriate decision makers.

AAP should make available to academic advisors all pertinent research (e.g., about students, the academic advising program, and perceptions of the institution).

The academic advisor must review and use available data about students' academic and educational needs, performance, and aspirations.

AAP must identify environmental conditions that may positively or negatively influence student academic achievement and propose interventions that may neutralize negative conditions.

AAP must provide current and accurate advising information to students and academic advisors.

AAP should employ the latest technologies for delivery of advising information.

Academic advising conferences must be available to students each academic term.

Academic advisors should offer conferences in a format that is convenient to the student, i.e., in person, by telephone, or online. Advising conferences may be carried out individually or in groups.

Academic advising caseloads must be consistent with the time required for the effective performance of this activity.

The academic status of the student being advised should be taken into consideration when determining caseloads. For example, first year, undecided, under-prepared, and honors students may require more advising time than upper-division students who have declared their majors.

Academic advisors should allow an appropriate amount of time for students to discuss plans, programs, courses, academic progress, and other subjects related to their educational programs.

When determining workloads it should be recognized that advisors may work with students not officially assigned to them and that contacts regarding advising may extend beyond direct contact with the student.

Part 3. ORGANIZATION AND LEADERSHIP

To achieve student and program outcomes, Academic Advising Programs (AAP) must be structured purposefully and organized effectively. AAP must have

- clearly stated goals
- current and accessible policies and procedures
- written performance expectations for employees
- functional work flow graphics or organizational charts demonstrating clear channels of authority

Leaders with organizational authority for the

programs and services must provide strategic planning, supervision, and management; advance the organization; and maintain integrity through the following functions:

Strategic Planning
- articulate a vision and mission that drive short- and long-term planning
- set goals and objectives based on the needs of the population served and desired student learning or development and program outcomes
- facilitate continuous development, implementation, and assessment of goal attainment congruent with institutional mission and strategic plans
- promote environments that provide meaningful opportunities for student learning, development, and engagement
- develop and continuously improve programs and services in response to the changing needs of students served and evolving institutional priorities
- intentionally include diverse perspectives to inform decision making

Supervising
- manage human resource processes including recruitment, selection, development, supervision, performance planning, evaluation, recognition, and reward
- influence others to contribute to the effectiveness and success of the unit
- empower professional, support, and student staff to accept leadership opportunities
- offer appropriate feedback to colleagues and students on skills needed to become more effective leaders
- encourage and support professional development, collaboration with colleagues and departments across the institution, and scholarly contribution to the profession

Managing
- identify and address individual, organizational, and environmental conditions that foster or inhibit mission achievement
- plan, allocate, and monitor the use of fiscal, physical, human, intellectual, and technological resources
- use current and valid evidence to inform decisions
- incorporate sustainability practices in the management and design of programs, services, and facilities
- understand appropriate technologies and integrate them into programs and services

- be knowledgeable about codes and laws relevant to programs and services and ensure that staff members understand their responsibilities through appropriate training
- assess potential risks and take action to mitigate them

Advancing the Organization
- communicate effectively in writing, speaking, and electronic venues
- advocate for programs and services
- advocate for representation in strategic planning initiatives at appropriate divisional and institutional levels
- initiate collaborative interactions with internal and external stakeholders who have legitimate concerns about and interests in the functional area
- facilitate processes to reach consensus where wide support is needed
- inform other areas within the institution about issues affecting practice

Maintaining Integrity
- model ethical behavior and institutional citizenship
- share data used to inform key decisions in transparent and accessible ways
- monitor media used for distributing information about programs and services to ensure the content is current, accurate, appropriately referenced, and accessible

The design of AAP must be compatible with the institution's organizational structure and its students' needs. Specific advisor responsibilities must be clearly delineated, published, and disseminated to both advisors and advisees.

Students, faculty advisors, and professional staff must be informed of their respective advising responsibilities.

AAP may be a centralized or decentralized function within an institution, with a variety of people throughout the institution assuming responsibilities.

AAP must provide the same services to distance learners as it does to students on campus. The distance education advising must provide for appropriate real time or delayed interaction between advisors and students.

Part 4. HUMAN RESOURCES

Academic Advising Programs (AAP) must be staffed adequately by individuals qualified to accomplish mission and goals.

Within institutional guidelines, AAP must

- establish procedures for staff recruitment and selection, training, performance planning, and evaluation
- set expectations for supervision and performance
- assess the performance of employees individually and as a team
- provide access to continuing and advanced education and appropriate professional development opportunities to improve the leadership ability, competence, and skills of all employees.

AAP must maintain position descriptions for all staff members.

To create a diverse staff, AAP must institute recruitment and hiring strategies that encourage individuals from under-represented populations to apply for positions.

AAP must develop promotion practices that are fair, inclusive, proactive, and non-discriminatory.

To further the recruitment and retention of staff, AAP must consider work life initiatives, such as compressed work schedules, flextime, job sharing, remote work, or telework.

AAP professional staff members must hold an earned graduate or professional degree in a field relevant to the position they hold or must possess an appropriate combination of educational credentials and related work experience.

Academic advising personnel may be full-time or part-time professionals who have advising as their primary function or may be faculty whose responsibilities include academic advising. Paraprofessionals (e.g., graduate students, interns, or assistants) or peer advisors may also assist advisors.

AAP professional staff members must engage in continuing professional development activities to keep abreast of the research, theories, legislation, policies, and developments that affect their programs and services.

Academic advisors should have an understanding of student development, student learning, career development, and other relevant theories in education, social sciences, and humanities.

Academic advisors should have a comprehensive knowledge of the institution's programs, academic requirements, policies and procedures, majors, minors, and support services.

Academic advisors should demonstrate an interest and effectiveness in working with and assisting students and a willingness to participate in professional activities.

Sufficient personnel must be available to address students' advising needs without unreasonable delay.

AAP must have technical and support staff members adequate to accomplish their mission. All members of the staff must be technologically proficient and qualified to perform their job functions, be knowledgeable about ethical and legal uses of technology, and have access to training and resources to support the performance of their assigned responsibilities.

Degree- or credential-seeking interns or graduate assistants must be qualified by enrollment in an appropriate field of study and by relevant experience. These individuals must be trained and supervised adequately by professional staff members holding educational credentials and related work experience appropriate for supervision. Supervisors must be cognizant of the roles of interns and graduate assistants as both student and employee and closely adhere to all parameters of their job descriptions, work hours, and schedules. Supervisors and the interns or graduate assistants must agree to compensatory time or other appropriate compensation if circumstances necessitate additional hours.

Student employees and volunteers must be carefully selected, trained, supervised, and evaluated. They must be educated on how and when to refer those in need of additional assistance to qualified staff members and must have access to a supervisor for assistance in making these judgments. Student employees and volunteers must be provided clear job descriptions, pre-service training based on assessed needs, and continuing development.

All AAP staff members, including student employees and volunteers, must receive specific training on institutional policies pertaining to functions or activities they support and to privacy and confidentiality policies and laws regarding access to student records and other sensitive institutional information.

All AAP staff members must receive training on policies and procedures related to the use of technology to store or access student records and institutional data.

Support personnel should maintain student records, organize resource materials, receive students, make appointments, and handle correspondence and other operational needs. Technical staff may be used in research, data collection, systems development, and special projects.

AAP must ensure that staff members are knowledgeable about and trained in emergency procedures, crisis response, and prevention efforts. Prevention efforts must address identification of threatening conduct or behavior of students, faculty and staff members, and others and must incorporate a system for responding and reporting.

AAP must ensure that staff members are knowledgeable of and trained in safety and emergency procedures for securing and vacating facilities.

AAP must strive to improve the professional competence and skills of all personnel it employs.

Continued professional development should include areas such as the following and how they relate to academic advising:

- theories of student development, student learning, career development, and other relevant theories in education, social sciences, and humanities
- academic policies and procedures, including institutional transfer policies and curricular changes
- legal issues including U.S. Family Education and Records Privacy Act (FERPA)/Canadian Freedom Of Information and Protection of Privacy (FOIPP) and other privacy laws and policies
- technology and software training (e.g., degree audit, web registration)
- institutional resources (e.g., research opportunities, career services, internship opportunities, counseling and health services, tutorial services)
- ADA (disability-related accommodations) compliance issues

Part 5. ETHICS

Academic Advising Programs (AAP) must review relevant professional ethical standards and must adopt or develop and implement appropriate statements of ethical practice.

Advisors must uphold policies, procedures, and values of their departments and institutions.

AAP must publish and adhere to statements of ethical practice and ensure their periodic review by relevant constituencies.

AAP must orient new staff members to relevant ethical standards and statements of ethical practice and related institutional policies.

Statements of ethical standards must specify that staff members respect privacy and maintain confidentiality in all communications and records to the extent that such communications and records are protected under relevant privacy laws.

Statements of ethical standards must specify limits on disclosure of information contained in students' educational records as well as requirements to disclose to appropriate authorities.

Statements of ethical standards must address personal and economic conflicts of interest, or appearance thereof, by staff members in the performance of their work.

Statements of ethical standards must reflect the responsibility of staff members to be fair, objective, and impartial in their interactions with others.

Statements of ethical standards must reference management of institutional funds.

Statements of ethical standards must reference appropriate behavior regarding research and assessment with human participants, confidentiality of research and assessment data, and students' rights and responsibilities.

Statements of ethical standards must include the expectation that AAP staff members confront and hold accountable other staff members who exhibit unethical behavior.

Statements of ethical standards must address issues surrounding scholarly integrity.

As appropriate, AAP staff members must inform users of programs and services of ethical obligations and limitations emanating from codes and laws or from licensure requirements.

AAP staff members must recognize and avoid conflicts of interest that could adversely influence their judgment or objectivity and, when unavoidable, recuse themselves from the situation.

AAP staff members must perform their duties within the limits of their position, training, expertise, and competence.

When these limits are exceeded, individuals in need of further assistance must be referred to persons possessing appropriate qualifications.

Promotional and descriptive information must be accurate and free of deception.

AAP must adhere to institutional policies regarding ethical and legal use of software and technology.

Part 6. LAW, POLICY, AND GOVERNANCE

Academic Advising Programs (AAP) must be in compliance with laws, regulations, and policies that relate to their respective responsibilities and that pose legal obligations, limitations, risks, and liabilities for the institution as a whole. Examples include constitutional, statutory, regulatory, and case law; relevant law and orders emanating from codes and laws; and the institution's policies.

AAP must inform staff members, appropriate officials, and users of programs and services about existing and changing legal obligations, risks and liabilities, and limitations.

AAP must have written policies on all relevant operations, transactions, or tasks that have legal implications.

AAP must regularly review policies. The revision and creation of policies must be informed by best practices, available evidence, and policy issues in higher education.

AAP staff members must use reasonable and informed practices to limit the liability exposure of the institution and its officers, employees, and agents. AAP staff members must be informed about institutional policies regarding risk management, personal liability, and related insurance coverage options and must be referred to external sources if the institution does not provide coverage.

The institution must provide access to legal advice for staff members as needed to carry out assigned responsibilities.

AAP must have procedures and guidelines consistent with institutional policy for responding to threats, emergencies, and crisis situations. Systems and procedures must be in place to disseminate timely and accurate information to students, other members of the institutional community, and appropriate external organizations during emergency situations.

AAP staff members must neither participate in nor condone any form of harassment or activity that demeans persons or creates an intimidating, hostile, or offensive environment.

AAP must obtain permission to use copyrighted materials and instruments. AAP must purchase the materials and instruments from legally compliant sources or seek alternative permission from the publisher or owner. References to copyrighted materials and instruments must include appropriate citations.

AAP staff members must be knowledgeable about internal and external governance systems that affect programs and services.

Part 7. DIVERSITY, EQUITY, AND ACCESS

Within the context of each institution's unique mission and in accordance with institutional polices and all applicable codes and laws, Academic Advising Programs (AAP) must create and maintain educational and work environments that are
- welcoming, accessible, and inclusive to persons of diverse backgrounds
- equitable and non-discriminatory
- free from harassment

AAP must not discriminate on the basis of ability; age; cultural identity; ethnicity; family educational history (e.g., first generation to attend college); gender identity and expression; nationality; political affiliation; race; religious affiliation; sex; sexual orientation; economic, marital, social, or veteran status; or any other basis included in institutional policies and codes and laws.

AAP must
- advocate for greater sensitivity to multicultural and social justice concerns by the institution and its personnel
- modify or remove policies, practices, facilities, structures, systems, and technologies that limit access, discriminate, or produce inequities
- include diversity, equity, and access initiatives within their strategic plans
- foster communication that deepens understanding of identity, culture, self-expression, and heritage
- promote respect about commonalities and differences among people within their historical and cultural contexts
- address the characteristics and needs of a diverse population when establishing and implementing culturally relevant and inclusive programs, services, policies, procedures, and practices
- provide staff members with access to multicultural training and hold staff members accountable for integrating the training into their work
- respond to the needs of all students and other populations served when establishing hours of operation and developing methods of delivering programs, services, and resources
- ensure physical, program, and resource access for persons with disabilities
- recognize the needs of distance learning students by providing appropriate and accessible services and resources or by assisting them in gaining access to other appropriate services and resources in their geographic region

Part 8. INSTITUTIONAL AND EXTERNAL RELATIONS

Academic Advising Programs (AAP) must reach out to relevant individuals, groups, communities, and organizations internal and external to the institution to
- establish, maintain, and promote

understanding and effective relations with those that have a significant interest in or potential effect on the students or other constituents served by the programs and services

- garner support and resources for programs and services as defined by the mission statement
- disseminate information about the programs and services
- collaborate, where appropriate, to assist in offering or improving programs and services to meet the needs of students and other constituents and to achieve program and student outcomes
- engage diverse individuals, groups, communities, and organizations to enrich the educational environment and experiences of students and other constituents

AAP must have procedures and guidelines consistent with institutional policy for
- communicating with the media
- contracting with external organizations for delivery of programs and services
- cultivating, soliciting, and managing gifts
- applying to and managing funds from grants

Academic advising is integral to the educational process and depends upon close working relationships with other institutional agencies and the administration. AAP should be fully integrated into other processes of the institution. Academic advisors should be consulted when there are modifications to or closures of academic programs.

For referral purposes, AAP should provide academic advisors a comprehensive list of relevant external agencies, campus offices, and opportunities.

Part 9. FINANCIAL RESOURCES

Academic Advising Programs (AAP) must have funding to accomplish the mission and goals. In establishing funding priorities and making significant changes, a comprehensive analysis must be conducted to determine the following elements: unmet needs of the unit, relevant expenditures, external and internal resources, and impact on students and the institution.

AAP must demonstrate efficient and effective use and responsible stewardship of fiscal resources consistent with institutional protocols.

Special consideration should be given to providing funding for the professional development of advisors.

Financial resources should be sufficient to provide high-quality print and web-based information for students and training materials for advisors. Sufficient financial resources

should be provided to promote the academic advising program.

Part 10. TECHNOLOGY

Academic Advising Programs (AAP) must have adequate technology to support the achievement of their mission and goals. The technology and its use must comply with institutional policies and procedures and be evaluated for compliance with relevant codes and laws.

AAP must use current technology to provide updated information regarding mission, location, staffing, programs, services, and official contacts to students and designated clients.

AAP must explore the use of technology to enhance delivery of programs and services, especially for students at a distance or external constituencies.

When technology is used to facilitate student learning and development, AAP must select technology that reflects intended outcomes.

AAP must
- maintain policies and procedures that address the security, confidentiality, and backup of data, as well as compliance with privacy laws
- have clearly articulated plans in place for protecting confidentiality and security of information when using Internet-based technologies
- develop plans for replacing and updating existing hardware and software as well as plans for integrating new technically-based or supported programs, including systems developed internally by the institution, systems available through professional associations, or private vendor-based systems

Technology, as well as workstations or computer labs maintained by programs and services for student use, must be accessible to all designated clients and must meet established technology standards for delivery to persons with disabilities.

When providing student access to technology, AAP must
- have policies on the use of technology that are clear, easy to understand, and available to all students
- provide assistance, information, or referral to appropriate support services to those needing help accessing or using technology
- provide instruction or training on how to use the technology
- inform students on the legal and ethical

implications of misuse as it pertains to intellectual property, harassment, privacy, and social networks

Student violations of technology policies must follow established institutional student disciplinary procedures.

Students who experience negative emotional or psychological consequences from the use of technology must be referred to support services provided by the institution.

AAP must ensure that on-line and technology-assisted advising includes appropriate mechanisms for obtaining approvals, consultations, and referrals.

Part 11. FACILITIES AND EQUIPMENT

Academic Advising Programs (AAP) must have adequate, accessible, and suitably located facilities and equipment to support the mission and goals. If acquiring capital equipment as defined by the institution, AAP must take into account expenses related to regular maintenance and life cycle costs. Facilities and equipment must be evaluated on an established cycle, including consideration of sustainability, and be in compliance with codes and laws to provide for access, health, safety, and security.

AAP staff members must have workspace that is well equipped, adequate in size, and designed to support their work and responsibilities. For conversations requiring privacy, staff members must have access to a private space.

AAP staff members who share workspace must be able to secure their own work.

The design of the facilities must guarantee the security and privacy of records and ensure the confidentiality of sensitive information.

The location and layout of the facilities must be sensitive to the needs of persons with disabilities as well as the needs of other constituencies.

Privacy and freedom from visual and auditory distractions must be considered in designing appropriate facilities.

Part 12. ASSESSMENT and EVALUATION

Academic Advising Programs (AAP) must have a clearly articulated assessment plan to document achievement of stated goals and learning outcomes, demonstrate accountability, provide evidence of improvement, and describe resulting changes in programs and services.

AAP must have adequate fiscal, human, professional development, and technological resources to develop and implement assessment plans.

Assessments must include direct and indirect evaluation and use qualitative and quantitative methodologies and existing evidence, as appropriate, to determine whether and to what degree the stated mission, goals, and intended outcomes are being met as effectively and efficiently as possible. The process must employ sufficient and sound measures to ensure comprehensiveness. Data collected must include responses from students and other constituencies, and aggregated results must be shared with those groups. Results of assessments must be shared appropriately with multiple constituents.

Results of assessments and evaluations must be used to identify needs and interests in revising and improving programs and services, recognizing staff performance, maximizing resource efficiency and effectiveness, improving student achievement of learning and development outcomes, and improving student persistence and success. Changes resulting from the use of assessments and evaluation must be shared with stakeholders.

General Standards revised in 2011;
AAP content developed/revised in 1986, 1997, & 2005

The Role of Adult Learners Programs and Services
CAS Standards Contextual Statement

Adult learners constitute approximately 45 percent of enrolled college students. Rather than being evenly enrolled throughout higher education, adults are much more likely to be enrolled in community colleges and in institutions designed specifically for them than in major research universities and state universities. Further, in institutions whose admissions criteria and practices are highly tailored to traditional-age applicants, adult learners may be disproportionately represented in the non-degree seeking and provisionally admitted ranks of students.

Although institutional definitions of an adult learner vary, they often include age 24 and older, veteran's status, a hiatus in learning, and the performance of multiple adult roles regardless of age. Included within the ranks of adult learners are full- and part-time employees, recently discharged veterans, unemployed workers, single parents, career changers, and retirees. They may live on campus, in local communities, commute some distance, or study at a distance. They turn to higher education for many reasons such as earning degrees, certificates, or other credentials; taking courses for work-enhancement purposes; positioning themselves for new opportunities in order to increase earning power; and seeking enrichment. Despite the diversity of adult learners and their motivations for enrollment, they seek from higher education an understanding of both their needs and their attributes. They also seek an institution that has a desire to be responsive and interested in enrolling them. It is also critical that higher education institutions offer adults the academic programs they want when they are available to take them.

Given higher education's long-standing focus on traditional-age and residential students, adult learners often have been seen as the purview of ancillary units such as continuing and distance education units in land grant universities, evening and weekend colleges in urban universities, and community colleges that are relative newcomers to the higher education landscape. Faculty in student personnel preparation programs have conducted much of their research on and written about the young, residential students who have been easier to access than adult learners. As a consequence, new professionals may think of college student development solely from the perspective of 17- to 23-year olds. Although the numbers of traditional-age high school graduates have fallen periodically, some institutions including private colleges have changed their practices and policies to serve the adult learner

more effectively.

In the meantime, the dislocation of the nation's manufacturing economy has called for the re-education of hundreds of furloughed workers. The knowledge economy has called for adults with high school diplomas, some college, or associate degrees to earn bachelors and advanced degrees. Divorce, separation, and the death of a spouse have triggered a return to learning by many eager to increase their earning power to improve not only their own standard of living but that of their children. Longer life spans have caused persons to turn to higher education for second careers and for intellectual stimulation in their retirement. As these social and economic changes have occurred, adults have sought access to and responsiveness from colleges, academic departments, and support services beyond the units that served them previously.

As adults encountered and began to complain about difficulties with gaining admission to "mainstream" academic programs and access to financial aid, with faculty unwilling to consider awarding credit for prior college-level learning, and with a college environment that they sometimes characterized as lonely, if not hostile, the Adult Learner Programs and Services (ALPS) units began to appear. Other ALPS units were created because college and university faculty and staff realized the social and economic trends as well as the attributes that adult learners brought to higher education and wanted to increase their enrollment; or they learned that adult graduation rates were less than the overall institution's graduation rate and wanted to increase adult learner success.

Many factors, including institutional type, structure, and history as well as the rationale for founding Adult Learner Programs and Services units, have influenced the placement of ALPS in the institutional structure, the mission of ALPS, and the activities and expertise of ALPS staff. For example, ALPS units have been placed in student affairs, continuing and distance education, affirmative action, and academic support divisions. In turn, the ALPS mission may focus more on student access, on supporting enrolled student success, and on select populations of adult learners, or the focus may be more comprehensive. The CAS standards and guidelines provide a basis for institutional self-assessment and program development as institutional leaders seek to respond to projected increases in the number and diversity of adult learners and as they wish to provide a standard of program and service excellence to those whom they currently recruit and enroll.

References, Readings, and Resources

Adult learners in higher education: Barriers to success and strategies to improve results. (March 2007). Report prepared for the U.S. Department of Labor, Employment and Training Administration, Office of Policy Development and Research by Jobs for the Future.   http://www.doleta.gov/reports/searcheta/occ/

Aslanian, C. B. (2001). *Adult students today.* New York: The College Board.

Aslanian, C. B., & Brickell, H. M. (1988). *How Americans in transition study for college credit.* New York: The College Board.

Aslanian, C. B., & Brickell, H. M. (1980). *Americans in transition: Life changes as reasons for adult learning.* New York: The College Entrance Examination Board.

Bash, L. (2003). Adult learners: Why they are important to the 21st century college or university. *The Journal of Continuing Higher Education, 51*(3), 18-26.

Harrison, C. H. (2000, May). T*he adult learner: Not a student yet.* A thesis in Adult Education, Penn State University.

Kasworm, C. (2003). What is collegiate involvement for adult undergraduates?   Paper presented at the *Annual Meeting of the American Educational Research Association*, Chicago, IL. ERIC Document Reproduction Service No. ED 481 228.

Kasworm, C. E., & Blowers, S. S. (1994). Adult undergraduate students: Patterns of learning involvement.   *Final Research Report, University of Tennessee, Knoxville, TN.* Washington, DC: Office of Educational Research and Improvement.   Retrieved from ERIC database. (ED 376 321)

Kasworm, C. E., Polson, C. J., & Fishback, S. J. (2002). *Responding to adult learners in higher education.* Malabar, FL: Krieger Publishing Company.

Kilgore, D., & Rice, P. J. (2003). *New directions for student services: Meeting the special needs of adult students.* San Francisco: Jossey-Bass.

Pusser, B., Breneman, D. W., Gansneder, B. M., Kohl, K. J., Levin, J. S., Milam, J. H., & Turner, S. E. (2007, March). *Returning to learning: Adults' success in college is key to America's future.*   Report of the Lumina Foundation for Education, Indianapolis, IN.

Schlossberg, N. K., Lynch, A. Q., & Chickering, A. W. (1989). *Improving higher education environments for adults.* San Francisco: Jossey Bass Publishers.

Sissel, P. A., Hansman, C. A., & Kasworm, C. E. (2001). The politics of neglect: Adult learners in higher education. *New Directions for Adult and Continuing Education, 91,* 17-27.

Contextual Statement Contributors

Current Edition:
Melissa Mahan, Northeastern State University, NCCP

Previous Editions:
Charlene H. Harrison, Penn State University

Adult Learner Programs and Services
CAS Standards and Guidelines

Part 1. MISSION

The mission of Adult Learner Programs and Services (ALPS) is to ensure that adult learners gain equitable access to all relevant curricular and co-curricular opportunities of the institution. ALPS must ensure that programs and services support adult learner success and advocate for adult learners to ensure that they are treated fairly and justly.

Equitable access may be differentiated based upon degree status, course load, fee payment status, or other criteria.

ALPS must develop, disseminate, implement, and regularly review their missions. The mission must be consistent with the mission of the institution and with professional standards. The mission must be appropriate for the institution's student populations and community settings. Mission statements must reference student learning and development.

Part 2. PROGRAM

Adult Learner Programs and Services (ALPS) must provide direct delivery of programs and services and work collaboratively with other essential institutional units to ensure that adult learners gain full access to and support from all curricular and co-curricular opportunities offered by the institution.

Institutions must clarify the availability of programs and services based upon the student's status.

ALPS must help adult learners gain access to the institution and its academic and financial aid programs.

To assist adult learners in gaining access to the institution and its enrollment, academic, and financial aid programs, ALPS staff members should
- be available to meet and/or communicate one-on-one with prospective adult learners
- articulate admissions, transfer enrollment, re-enrollment, non-degree registration, and financial aid procedures and provide information about topics such as academic refresher resources, child and elder care, and application deadlines
- conduct programs for prospective adult learners on applying for admission, re-enrollment, and financial aid, and on relating careers to academic programs
- monitor the progress of adult learner applicants, re-enrollees, and registrants through the application, acceptance, and registration process and through the financial aid application process
- ensure that recruitment literature, websites, list

serves, and other outreach efforts are created that target adult learners and contain messages relevant to their needs and concerns
- represent the institution in the community at workplaces and community centers to help bring prospective adults to the institution
- ensure that institutional resources are available at convenient hours for adult learners

ALPS must provide programs and services that assist in increasing the retention of adult learners.

To increase the success of adult learners, the ALPS staff members should
- plan, deliver, and evaluate (either independently or in collaboration with others) orientation and other programs that acquaint adult learners and their families/support networks (a) with the institution's academic and out-of-class resources that enhance their likelihood of success and (b) with others like themselves
- inform adult learners of the availability of emergency funds, short-term loans, and scholarships
- initiate and advise adult learner honor societies and student organizations
- initiate and conduct recognition programs for adult learners that bring together both the learners and those who support them

ALPS staff members must collect data and conduct research on the institution's adult learners and on policies and practices that disproportionately impact them.

ALPS staff members may engage in these efforts either independently or in collaboration with others.

ALPS staff members must educate others about the characteristics, needs, and contributions of adult learners.

For ALPS staff members to educate others in the institution to adult learners' needs and attributes, they should
- be familiar with literature and research about adult learners
- establish relationships with faculty in adult education and other relevant academic disciplines and with staff members in the institutional research office
- meet with academic advisors, admissions, financial aid and student affairs staff members, and other staff and faculty members
- collaborate and network with colleagues to offer training, provide data, and share research in order to inform decision making and practice

- write articles and reports and deliver programs to campus and community audiences

ALPS staff members must advocate for curricular and co-curricular policies, procedures, and programs that are responsive to the needs and concerns of adult learners.

To advocate for adult learners, ALPS staff members should
- assess and monitor adult learners' needs and the degree to which the institution is meeting them
- understand and be able to articulate the diverse nature of the institution's adult learners
- support individual adult learners and adult student organizations in their self-advocacy
- promote life experiences as criteria for membership in student organizations, including honor societies and for major awards

ALPS staff members must create affirming environments where prospective and enrolled adult learners may interact with one another.

The formal education of students, consisting of the curriculum and the co-curriculum, must promote student learning and development outcomes that are purposeful, contribute to students' realization of their potential, and prepare students for satisfying and productive lives.

ALPS must collaborate with colleagues and departments across the institution to promote student learning and development, persistence, and success.

Consistent with the institutional mission, ALPS must identify relevant and desirable student learning and development outcomes from among the six domains and related dimensions:

Domain: knowledge acquisition, integration, construction, and application

- **Dimensions: understanding knowledge from a range of disciplines; connecting knowledge to other knowledge, ideas, and experiences; constructing knowledge; and relating knowledge to daily life**

Domain: cognitive complexity

- **Dimensions: critical thinking, reflective thinking, effective reasoning, and creativity**

Domain: intrapersonal development

- **Dimensions: realistic self-appraisal, self-understanding, and self-respect; identity development; commitment to ethics and integrity; and spiritual awareness**

Domain: interpersonal competence

- **Dimensions: meaningful relationships, interdependence, collaboration, and effective leadership.**

Domain: humanitarianism and civic engagement

- **Dimensions: understanding and appreciation of cultural and human differences, social responsibility, global perspective, and sense of civic responsibility**

Domain: practical competence

- **Dimensions: pursuing goals, communicating effectively, technical competence, managing personal affairs, managing career development, demonstrating professionalism, maintaining health and wellness, and living a purposeful and satisfying life**

[LD Outcomes: See *The Council for the Advancement of Standards Learning and Developmental Outcomes* statement for examples of outcomes related to these domains and dimensions.]

ALPS must
- **assess relevant and desirable student learning and development**
- **provide evidence of impact on outcomes**
- **articulate contributions to or support of student learning and development in the domains not specifically assessed**
- **articulate contributions to or support of student persistence and success**
- **use evidence gathered through this process to create strategies for improvement of programs and services**

ALPS must be
- **intentionally designed**
- **guided by theories and knowledge of learning and development**
- **integrated into the life of the institution**
- **reflective of developmental and demographic profiles of the student population**
- **responsive to needs of individuals, populations with distinct needs, and relevant constituencies**
- **delivered using multiple formats, strategies, and contexts**

Where institutions provide distance education, ALPS must assist distance learners to achieve their educational goals by providing access to information about programs and services, to staff members who can address questions and concerns, and to counseling, advising, or other forms of assistance.

ALPS staff members should be familiar with the CAS Standards and Guidelines for Distance Education Programs and with the CAS Commuter and Off-Campus Living Programs

Standards and Guidelines.

Part 3. ORGANIZATION AND LEADERSHIP

To achieve student and program outcomes, Adult Learner Programs and Services (ALPS) must be structured purposefully and organized effectively. ALPS must have

- clearly stated goals
- current and accessible policies and procedures
- written performance expectations for employees
- functional work flow graphics or organizational charts demonstrating clear channels of authority

Leaders with organizational authority for the programs and services must provide strategic planning, supervision, and management; advance the organization; and maintain integrity through the following functions:

Strategic Planning

- articulate a vision and mission that drive short- and long-term planning
- set goals and objectives based on the needs of the population served and desired student learning or development and program outcomes
- facilitate continuous development, implementation, and assessment of goal attainment congruent with institutional mission and strategic plans
- promote environments that provide meaningful opportunities for student learning, development, and engagement
- develop and continuously improve programs and services in response to the changing needs of students served and evolving institutional priorities
- intentionally include diverse perspectives to inform decision making

Supervising

- manage human resource processes including recruitment, selection, development, supervision, performance planning, evaluation, recognition, and reward
- influence others to contribute to the effectiveness and success of the unit
- empower professional, support, and student staff to accept leadership opportunities
- offer appropriate feedback to colleagues and students on skills needed to become more effective leaders
- encourage and support professional development, collaboration with colleagues and departments across the institution, and

scholarly contribution to the profession

Managing

- identify and address individual, organizational, and environmental conditions that foster or inhibit mission achievement
- plan, allocate, and monitor the use of fiscal, physical, human, intellectual, and technological resources
- use current and valid evidence to inform decisions
- incorporate sustainability practices in the management and design of programs, services, and facilities
- understand appropriate technologies and integrate them into programs and services
- be knowledgeable about codes and laws relevant to programs and services and ensure that staff members understand their responsibilities through appropriate training
- assess potential risks and take action to mitigate them

Advancing the Organization

- communicate effectively in writing, speaking, and electronic venues
- advocate for programs and services
- advocate for representation in strategic planning initiatives at appropriate divisional and institutional levels
- initiate collaborative interactions with internal and external stakeholders who have legitimate concerns about and interests in the functional area
- facilitate processes to reach consensus where wide support is needed
- inform other areas within the institution about issues affecting practice

Maintaining Integrity

- model ethical behavior and institutional citizenship
- share data used to inform key decisions in transparent and accessible ways
- monitor media used for distributing information about programs and services to ensure the content is current, accurate, appropriately referenced, and accessible

ALPS leaders must inform themselves about program and service approaches that are successful in other higher education or professional settings and establish working relationships with a network of colleagues who are dedicated to serving adult learners optimally.

ALPS must inform institutional leaders of its role in creating, reviewing, and implementing institutional policies and procedures that are responsive to the assessed needs of adult learners.

Part 4. HUMAN RESOURCES

Adult Learner Programs and Services (ALPS) must be staffed adequately by individuals qualified to accomplish mission and goals.

Within institutional guidelines, ALPS must
- establish procedures for staff recruitment and selection, training, performance planning, and evaluation
- set expectations for supervision and performance
- assess the performance of employees individually and as a team
- provide access to continuing and advanced education and appropriate professional development opportunities to improve the leadership ability, competence, and skills of all employees.

ALPS must maintain position descriptions for all staff members.

To create a diverse staff, ALPS must institute recruitment and hiring strategies that encourage individuals from under-represented populations to apply for positions.

ALPS must develop promotion practices that are fair, inclusive, proactive, and non-discriminatory.

To further the recruitment and retention of staff, ALPS must consider work life initiatives, such as compressed work schedules, flextime, job sharing, remote work, or telework.

ALPS professional staff members must hold an earned graduate or professional degree in a field relevant to the position they hold or must possess an appropriate combination of educational credentials and related work experience.

ALPS professional staff members must engage in continuing professional development activities to keep abreast of the research, theories, legislation, policies, and developments that affect their programs and services.

ALPS must have technical and support staff members adequate to accomplish their mission. All members of the staff must be technologically proficient and qualified to perform their job functions, be knowledgeable about ethical and legal uses of technology, and have access to training and resources to support the performance of their assigned responsibilities.

Degree- or credential-seeking interns or graduate assistants must be qualified by enrollment in an appropriate field of study and by relevant experience. These individuals must be trained and supervised adequately by professional staff members holding educational credentials and related work experience appropriate for supervision. Supervisors must be cognizant of the roles of interns and graduate assistants as both student and employee and closely adhere to all parameters of their job descriptions, work hours, and schedules. Supervisors and the interns or graduate assistants must agree to compensatory time or other appropriate compensation if circumstances necessitate additional hours.

Student employees and volunteers must be carefully selected, trained, supervised, and evaluated. They must be educated on how and when to refer those in need of additional assistance to qualified staff members and must have access to a supervisor for assistance in making these judgments. Student employees and volunteers must be provided clear job descriptions, pre-service training based on assessed needs, and continuing development.

All ALPS staff members, including student employees and volunteers, must receive specific training on institutional policies pertaining to functions or activities they support and to privacy and confidentiality policies and laws regarding access to student records and other sensitive institutional information.

All ALPS staff members must receive training on policies and procedures related to the use of technology to store or access student records and institutional data.

ALPS must ensure that staff members are knowledgeable about and trained in emergency procedures, crisis response, and prevention efforts. Prevention efforts must address identification of threatening conduct or behavior of students, faculty and staff members, and others and must incorporate a system for responding and reporting.

ALPS must ensure that staff members are knowledgeable of and trained in safety and emergency procedures for securing and vacating facilities.

Part 5. ETHICS

Adult Learner Programs and Services (ALPS) must review relevant professional ethical standards and must adopt or develop and implement appropriate statements of ethical practice.

ALPS must publish and adhere to statements of ethical practice and ensure their periodic review by relevant constituencies.

ALPS must orient new staff members to relevant ethical standards and statements of ethical practice and related institutional policies.

Statements of ethical standards must specify that staff members respect privacy and maintain confidentiality in all communications and records to the extent that such communications and records are protected under relevant privacy laws.

Statements of ethical standards must specify limits on disclosure of information contained in students' educational records as well as requirements to disclose to appropriate authorities.

Statements of ethical standards must address personal and economic conflicts of interest, or appearance thereof, by staff members in the performance of their work.

Statements of ethical standards must reflect the responsibility of staff members to be fair, objective, and impartial in their interactions with others.

Statements of ethical standards must reference management of institutional funds.

Statements of ethical standards must reference appropriate behavior regarding research and assessment with human participants, confidentiality of research and assessment data, and students' rights and responsibilities.

Statements of ethical standards must include the expectation that ALPS staff members confront and hold accountable other staff members who exhibit unethical behavior.

Statements of ethical standards must address issues surrounding scholarly integrity.

As appropriate, ALPS staff members must inform users of programs and services of ethical obligations and limitations emanating from codes and laws or from licensure requirements.

ALPS staff members must recognize and avoid conflicts of interest that could adversely influence their judgment or objectivity and, when unavoidable, recuse themselves from the situation.

ALPS staff members must perform their duties within the limits of their position, training, expertise, and competence.

When these limits are exceeded, individuals in need of further assistance must be referred to persons possessing appropriate qualifications.

Promotional and descriptive information must be accurate and free of deception.

ALPS must adhere to institutional policies regarding ethical and legal use of software and technology.

Part 6. LAW, POLICY, AND GOVERNANCE

Adult Learner Programs and Services (ALPS) must be in compliance with laws, regulations, and policies that relate to their respective responsibilities and that pose legal obligations, limitations, risks, and liabilities for the institution as a whole. Examples include constitutional, statutory, regulatory, and case law; relevant law and orders emanating from codes and laws; and the institution's policies.

ALPS must inform staff members, appropriate officials, and users of programs and services about existing and changing legal obligations, risks and liabilities, and limitations.

ALPS must have written policies on all relevant operations, transactions, or tasks that have legal implications.

ALPS must regularly review policies. The revision and creation of policies must be informed by best practices, available evidence, and policy issues in higher education.

ALPS staff members must use reasonable and informed practices to limit the liability exposure of the institution and its officers, employees, and agents. ALPS staff members must be informed about institutional policies regarding risk management, personal liability, and related insurance coverage options and must be referred to external sources if the institution does not provide coverage.

The institution must provide access to legal advice for staff members as needed to carry out assigned responsibilities.

ALPS must have procedures and guidelines consistent with institutional policy for responding to threats, emergencies, and crisis situations. Systems and procedures must be in place to disseminate timely and accurate information to students, other members of the institutional community, and appropriate external organizations during emergency situations.

ALPS staff members must neither participate in nor condone any form of harassment or activity that demeans persons or creates an intimidating, hostile, or offensive environment.

ALPS must obtain permission to use copyrighted materials and instruments. ALPS must purchase the materials and instruments from legally compliant sources or seek alternative permission from the publisher or owner. References to copyrighted materials and instruments must include appropriate citations.

ALPS staff members must be knowledgeable about internal and external governance systems that affect programs and services.

Part 7. DIVERSITY, EQUITY, AND ACCESS

Within the context of each institution's unique mission and in accordance with institutional polices and all applicable codes and laws, Adult Learner Programs and Services (ALPS) must create and maintain educational and work environments that are

- welcoming, accessible, and inclusive to persons of diverse backgrounds
- equitable and non-discriminatory
- free from harassment

ALPS must not discriminate on the basis of ability; age; cultural identity; ethnicity; family educational history (e.g., first generation to attend college); gender identity and expression; nationality; political affiliation; race; religious affiliation; sex; sexual orientation; economic, marital, social, or veteran status; or any other basis included in institutional policies and codes and laws.

ALPS must

- advocate for greater sensitivity to multicultural and social justice concerns by the institution and its personnel
- modify or remove policies, practices, facilities, structures, systems, and technologies that limit access, discriminate, or produce inequities
- include diversity, equity, and access initiatives within their strategic plans
- foster communication that deepens understanding of identity, culture, self-expression, and heritage
- promote respect about commonalities and differences among people within their historical and cultural contexts
- address the characteristics and needs of a diverse population when establishing and implementing culturally relevant and inclusive programs, services, policies, procedures, and practices
- provide staff members with access to multicultural training and hold staff members accountable for integrating the training into their work
- respond to the needs of all students and other populations served when establishing hours of operation and developing methods of delivering programs, services, and resources

- ensure physical, program, and resource access for persons with disabilities
- recognize the needs of distance learning students by providing appropriate and accessible services and resources or by assisting them in gaining access to other appropriate services and resources in their geographic region

On campuses where adult learners constitute a distinct minority and under-served population, they should be considered an under-represented population. Means for serving this under-represented population could include a task force on adult learner recruitment and retention and/or an adult learner commission with faculty, staff, and student membership.

Part 8. INSTITUTIONAL AND EXTERNAL RELATIONS

Adult Learner Programs and Services (ALPS) must reach out to relevant individuals, groups, communities, and organizations internal and external to the institution to

- establish, maintain, and promote understanding and effective relations with those that have a significant interest in or potential effect on the students or other constituents served by the programs and services
- garner support and resources for programs and services as defined by the mission statement
- disseminate information about the programs and services
- collaborate, where appropriate, to assist in offering or improving programs and services to meet the needs of students and other constituents and to achieve program and student outcomes
- engage diverse individuals, groups, communities, and organizations to enrich the educational environment and experiences of students and other constituents

ALPS staff members should serve on committees that address policies and procedures that affect adult learners.

If there is more than one campus unit whose clientele are principally adult learners, ALPS should share information and collaborate with those offices. Examples of on-campus units with which ALPS staff members should collaborate include continuing and distance education, commuter and off-campus living programs, campus information and visitor services programs, graduate and professional student services, veterans' programs, child care center(s), and critical access and service-providing units such as admissions, financial aid, the registrar's office, the library, career services, and learning and advising centers. This collaboration also should ensure that students enrolled at off-site locations are provided with equitable access to institutional resources.

The community agencies with which ALPS staff members should have a working relationship include local community education and literacy programs, TRIO and other equal opportunity programs, community libraries, retiree programs, veterans' programs, vocational rehabilitation offices, and social service agencies.

ALPS must have procedures and guidelines consistent with institutional policy for
- **communicating with the media**
- **contracting with external organizations for delivery of programs and services**
- **cultivating, soliciting, and managing gifts**
- **applying to and managing funds from grants**

Part 9. FINANCIAL RESOURCES

Adult Learner Programs and Services (ALPS) must have funding to accomplish the mission and goals. In establishing funding priorities and making significant changes, a comprehensive analysis must be conducted to determine the following elements: unmet needs of the unit, relevant expenditures, external and internal resources, and impact on students and the institution.

ALPS must demonstrate efficient and effective use and responsible stewardship of fiscal resources consistent with institutional protocols.

Adult learners should benefit equitably from fee-supported programs and services, including the establishment of programs and services that address their unique needs.

Part 10. TECHNOLOGY

Adult Learner Programs and Services (ALPS) must have adequate technology to support the achievement of their mission and goals. The technology and its use must comply with institutional policies and procedures and be evaluated for compliance with relevant codes and laws.

ALPS must use current technology to provide updated information regarding mission, location, staffing, programs, services, and official contacts to students and designated clients.

ALPS must explore the use of technology to enhance delivery of programs and services, especially for students at a distance or external constituencies.

When technology is used to facilitate student learning and development, ALPS must select technology that reflects intended outcomes.

ALPS must

- **maintain policies and procedures that address the security, confidentiality, and backup of data, as well as compliance with privacy laws**
- **have clearly articulated plans in place for protecting confidentiality and security of information when using Internet-based technologies**
- **develop plans for replacing and updating existing hardware and software as well as plans for integrating new technically-based or supported programs, including systems developed internally by the institution, systems available through professional associations, or private vendor-based systems**

Technology, as well as workstations or computer labs maintained by programs and services for student use, must be accessible to all designated clients and must meet established technology standards for delivery to persons with disabilities.

ALPS should be responsive to adult learner differences in competencies, knowledge, and comfort levels with technology.

When providing student access to technology, ALPS must
- **have policies on the use of technology that are clear, easy to understand, and available to all students**
- **provide assistance, information, or referral to appropriate support services to those needing help accessing or using technology**
- **provide instruction or training on how to use the technology**
- **inform students on the legal and ethical implications of misuse as it pertains to intellectual property, harassment, privacy, and social networks**

Student violations of technology policies must follow established institutional student disciplinary procedures.

Students who experience negative emotional or psychological consequences from the use of technology must be referred to support services provided by the institution.

Part 11. FACILITIES AND EQUIPMENT

Adult Learner Programs and Services (ALPS) must have adequate, accessible, and suitably located facilities and equipment to support the mission and goals. If acquiring capital equipment as defined by the institution, ALPS must take into account expenses related to regular maintenance and life cycle costs. Facilities and equipment must be evaluated on

an established cycle, including consideration of sustainability, and be in compliance with codes and laws to provide for access, health, safety, and security.

ALPS staff should advocate for access to facilities that are physically close to campus programs to enable adult learners to engage with staff and faculty members and to interact with prospective and enrolled students.

To create an affirming environment in which prospective and enrolled adult learners may interact with one another and the ALPS staff members, ALPS should advocate for access to facilities that include

- lounge and reception areas that are welcoming and comfortable
- kitchenette space to prepare and store meals
- locker facilities
- study area which permits the consumption of food and beverages
- computers and printers
- use of traditional and electronic means of communication, including display racks, bulletin boards, websites, and on-line portals
- traditional and/or electronic library of books, articles, videos, and other resources about adult learners and on topics useful to them such as study skills, financing one's education, and managing multiple roles
- toys, games, and other items for the use of children who accompany their parents/guardians to campus

ALPS staff members should work with other units such as commuter and off-campus living programs, continuing and distance education, and child care programs to assure the availability of facilities that meet adult learners' needs.
Adult learner student organizations should have access to facilities that support successful operations.

ALPS staff members must have workspace that is well equipped, adequate in size, and designed to support their work and responsibilities. For conversations requiring privacy, staff members must have access to a private space.

ALPS staff members who share workspace must be able to secure their own work.

The design of the facilities must guarantee the security and privacy of records and ensure the confidentiality of sensitive information.

The location and layout of the facilities must be sensitive to the needs of persons with disabilities as well as the needs of other constituencies.

Part 12. ASSESSMENT AND EVALUATION

Adult Learner Programs and Services (ALPS) must have a clearly articulated assessment plan to document achievement of stated goals and learning outcomes, demonstrate accountability, provide evidence of improvement, and describe resulting changes in programs and services.

ALPS must have adequate fiscal, human, professional development, and technological resources to develop and implement assessment plans.

Assessments must include direct and indirect evaluation and use qualitative and quantitative methodologies and existing evidence, as appropriate, to determine whether and to what degree the stated mission, goals, and intended outcomes are being met as effectively and efficiently as possible. The process must employ sufficient and sound measures to ensure comprehensiveness. Data collected must include responses from students and other constituencies, and aggregated results must be shared with those groups. Results of assessments must be shared appropriately with multiple constituents.

Results of assessments and evaluations must be used to identify needs and interests in revising and improving programs and services, recognizing staff performance, maximizing resource efficiency and effectiveness, improving student achievement of learning and development outcomes, and improving student persistence and success. Changes resulting from the use of assessments and evaluation must be shared with stakeholders.

ALPS assessment activities should include a focus on demographics of adult applicants and enrollees, academic performance variables, retention studies, use of and satisfaction with campus programs and services, the impact on adult learners of institutional policies and practices, access to and receipt of financial aid, and student use of the institution's prior learning assessment options, e.g., College Level Examination Program (CLEP).

General Standards revised in 2011;
ALPS content developed in 2008

The Role of Alcohol, Tobacco, and Other Drug Programs
CAS Standards Contextual Statement

Abuse of alcohol, tobacco, and other drugs has been a major concern for institutions of higher education. Many colleges and universities have employed a variety of approaches over the years to address alcohol, tobacco, and other drug (ATOD) abuse and associated problems. Serious research started to document the prevalence of alcohol and other drug use on America's college campuses during the mid-twentieth century. This newfound interest in an age-old problem may have been precipitated by the death of two students during drinking parties in 1949 and by a third incident that year in which a student almost died while being initiated into a drinking club (Strauss & Bacon, 1953). Unfortunately, it seems that such needless and senseless tragedies are still the primary impetus for action in the early part of the twenty-first century.

A little over 50 years ago, a landmark study conducted at Yale University was arguably the first formal research-based indication of substance use on college campuses in the United States. By analyzing the responses to a self-administered questionnaire completed by more than 15,000 students at 27 colleges, researchers identified specific rates of alcohol use by college students and their rationale for drinking (Strauss & Bacon, 1953). Yale researchers conducted their survey concentrating on two key pieces of information: how frequently students drank and how much alcohol they consumed. This was an area that generated further research studies and shaped ATOD programs, both in the areas of prevention and intervention, for the next twenty or more years.

In 1975, the Monitoring the Future project was established to study changes in the attitudes and behaviors of America's youth (Johnston, O'Malley, Bachman, & Schulenberg, 2004). From these studies, trends began to emerge that documented the prevalence of alcohol and other drug abuse among college students and the negative consequences that students experienced as a result of their substance use (Lucey, 2006). Research in the 1990s identified not only how much alcohol and other drugs college students were using but also why they used various substances and the negative consequences suffered as a result of such use (Core Institute, 2000). This broadening of scope of research brought much needed attention to the consequences of use, abuse, and high-risk behavior.

As the field continued to become more organized and scientific in its approach to understanding the scope of the problem, a majority of the national research on college-based alcohol and other drug abuse began to originate from one of two places: the Core Institute, located at Southern Illinois University at Carbondale, and the Harvard School of Public Health. Although these remain two of the major organizations for data collection, a number of other survey instruments are used to varying degrees by colleges and universities. These include surveys developed by the American College Health Association (i.e., National College Health Assessment) and the Cooperative Institutional Research Program (i.e., College Student Survey), each of which goes beyond looking solely at substance abuse issues by examining broader health-related and campus life issues (Lucey, 2006).

In 1999, the National Institute on Alcohol Abuse and Alcoholism (NIAAA) convened a blue-ribbon panel of leading researchers, college and university presidents, and students to review research and engage in a series of discussions to address the serious problem of college student alcohol use. Over the course of three years, this task force developed a groundbreaking report outlining the extent of the problem and its many manifestations and provided a guiding framework upon which to develop sound and effective campus alcohol programs. The 2002 report, "A Call to Action: Changing the Culture of Drinking at U.S. Colleges," outlined for the first time the troubling dimensions of the college alcohol problem in terms so stark, no college administrator, alumnus, or student could deny its deadly and damaging ramifications. However compelling the information, many prevention practitioners argue the most important contribution of the report was its recommendations for effective alcohol prevention in the college population. This included the call for an overarching comprehensive program framework and the delineation of four tiers of effectiveness. This information changed how to look at and choose programs for campuses and helped to emphasize the importance of program evaluation and assessment.

With the continued scientific focus on prevention work, we see more clearly that alcohol remains the primary substance of abuse, and we continue to see a rise in the abuse of other substances, most notably marijuana and prescription and over-the-counter medications. According to one large study, the nonmedical use of prescription medications is second only to marijuana as the most com on form of illicit drug use; in addition, the percentage of students reporting the abuse of prescription stimulants can be as high as 25 on some campuses (McCabe, Knight, Teter, & Wechsler, 2005). These drugs are being abused not only in isolation but in combination with each other and with alcohol as well as other drugs. With the rise of prescription drugs in circulation and the ease of access through Internet pharmacies, this is a fast growing challenge facing the prevention field and ATOD programs. Not only has there been a rise in the abuse of prescription medication but a rise in the abuse of over-the-counter medications such as cold and cough medications containing DMX (e.g., Robitussin, Alka-Seltzer), which is used for its dissociative and psychedelic properties. There is a belief held by students that there is no real danger or abuse potential in using these drugs as they are, after all, medications. As this behavior increases, the field is faced with the task of looking for new strategies and modifying existing programs to focus on this emerging epidemic.

The rise in abuse of these substances combined with the continued heavy use of alcohol, tobacco, marijuana, and other drugs continues to stretch ATOD prevention and intervention program resources. Adding to the stress of existing resources is the tightening of campus prevention budgets and the limited availability of local, state/provincial, and federal funding. Along with this trend the field continues to see the challenge of inadequate staffing to fully address the expanding range of ATOD program issues.

Although there is more for the field of prevention and ATOD programs to address and resources seem to be drying up, there has been progress in the practice of prevention as the field continues to look to evidence-based programming with a heavy focus on comprehensive strategies and environmental management practices. Elements of many of these approaches have been highlighted and deconstructed in "Experiences in Effective Prevention: The U.S. Department of Education's Alcohol and Other Drug Prevention Models on College Campuses Grants," published in 2007 by the U.S. Department of Education's Higher Education Center for Alcohol and Other Drug Abuse and Violence Prevention.

One element of the aforementioned comprehensive strategy is screening and brief interventions. Over the last decade, studies have shown effectiveness in getting students to move forward in making changes in their alcohol and drug use by using screenings and brief interventions that follow specific protocol (Wil, Jensen, & Havighurst, 1997). One brief intervention model/protocol that has become a mainstay on many college and university campuses over the last decade is the Brief Alcohol Screening and Intervention for College Students (BASICS), used in a variety of campus settings and with diverse practitioners. A model that is newer to higher education but has shown effectiveness in a variety of medical care venues, recommended by the Substance Abuse and Mental Health Services Administration (SAMHSA), is the Screening Brief Intervention Treatment (SBIRT) that is designed to be administered specifically in Student Health Services/Centers.

One area of the field that continues to receive a great deal of attention in recent years is assessment, whether that be in the assessment of student behavior as we saw in the 1990s or the assessment of the effectiveness of ATOD education, prevention, and intervention programs that have grown in the last decade. Programming now being offered and assessed on many campuses includes motivational interviewing, policies restricting access, individual counseling, support groups, recovery houses, social norms marketing, campus-community task forces, peer education, brief interventions, curriculum infusion, educational sanctions, policy promotion, medical amnesty policies, and the list goes on. Not every program is right for each campus; but through intentional programming and thorough assessment, ineffective programs can be discarded, effective ones retained, and new programs added. The CAS standards offer guidance for ATOD program development and evaluation, necessary components in the pursuit of effective practice.

There are also a growing number of campus and community stakeholders getting involved in the work of prevention, including law enforcement and campus security, faculty, parents, and community and professional agencies/associations. Evidence of this growth can be seen in NASPA's Alcohol and Other Drug Knowledge Community and the reorganization of The Network Addressing Collegiate Alcohol and Other Drug Issues, both allowing for a broad range of student affairs professionals to become involved in prevention and programming efforts and to gain access to a wealth of knowledge through regional trainings and technical assistance from other professionals. In addition, federal agencies are demonstrating a greater commitment to addressing ATOD issues in, and partnering with, higher education. This is most recently and prominently evidenced in a joint letter from Gil Kerlikowske of the White House Office of National Drug Control Policy and Arne Duncan, dated September 23, 2011, inviting leaders in higher education to join with other Federal agency partners to work collaboratively to prevent illegal drug use and high-risk drinking in our Nation's college and university communities. (www.whitehouse.gov/blog/2011/09/23/)

References, Readings, and Resources

A Call to Action: Changing the Culture of Drinking at U.S. Colleges: www.collegedrinkingprevention.gov/media/TaskForceReport.pdf

AMA Office of Alcohol & Other Drug Abuse: www.ama-assn.org/ama/pub/category/3337.html

American College Health Associations ATOD Coalition: http://www.acha.org/about_acha/ctfs/coalition_atd.cfm

Amethyst Initiative. (2008). *Initiative description.* Retrieved from http://www.amethystinitiative.org

Anderson, D. S., & Milgram, G. G. (1996). *Promising practices: Campus alcohol strategies sourcebook.* Fairfax, VA: George Mason University.

BACCHUS and GAMMA Peer Education Network: www.bacchusgamma.org

Califano, Jr., J. A. (2007). *Accompanying statement.* Retrieved from National Center on Addiction and Substance Abuse at Columbia University (CASA). *You've Got Drugs: IV: Prescription Drug Pushers on the Internet* (New York, 2007).

Coombs, R. H., & Ziedonis, D. (1995). *Handbook on drug abuse prevention: A comprehensive strategy to prevent the abuse of alcohol and other drugs.* Boston, MA: Allyn & Bacon.

Core Institute. (2000). *1999 statistics on alcohol and other drug use on American campuses, Carbondale, IL:* Core Institute. Retrieved from http:.siu.edu/departments/coreinst/public_html/recent.html

Johnston, L. D., O'Malley, P. M., Bachman, J. G., & Schulenberg, J. E. (2004). *National survey results on drug use for the monitoring the future study, 1975-2003.* Rockville, MD: National Institute on Drug Abuse.

Journal of Drug Education. Amityville, New York, NY: Baywood Publishing Co.

Lucey, R. (2006). Substance abuse on campus: A brief history. In R. Chapman (Ed.), *When they drink: Practitioner views and lessons learned.* Glassboro, NJ: Rowan University Press.

McCabe, S. E., Knight, J. R., Teter, C. J., & Wechsler, H. (2005). Nonmedical use of prescription stimulants among U.S. college students: Prevalence and correlates from a national survey. *Addiction, 99,* 96–106.

National Clearinghouse for Alcohol and Drug Information (NCADI): www.health.org

National Institute of Drug Abuse (NIDA): www.drugabuse.gov

National Institute on Alcohol Abuse and Alcoholism (NIAAA): www.collegedrinkingprevention.gov

NIAAA Report (2005). *Call to action information.* Retrieved from http://www.campushealthandsafety.org/niaaa/

Strauss, R., & Bacon, S. D. (1953). *Drinking in college.* New Haven, CT: Yale University Press.

Substance Abuse and Mental Health Services Administration (SAMHSA): www.samhsa.gov/

The Network Addressing Collegiate Alcohol and Other Drug Issues: www.thenetwork.ws/

U.S. Department of Education's Higher Education Center publications: www.edc.org/hec

Wechsler, H., Dowdall, G., Davenport, A., & Castillo, S. (1995). Correlates of college student binge drinking. *American Journal of Public Health, 85,* 7.

Wilk A. I., Jensen N. M., Havighurst, T. C. (1977). Meta-analysis of randomized control trials addressing brief interventions in heavy alcohol drinkers. *Journal of General Internal Medicine, 12,* 274–283.

Contextual Statement Contributors

Current Edition:
John Watson, Drexel University, The Network

Previous Editions:
Carole Middlebrooks, University of Georgia, The Network

Alcohol, Tobacco, and Other Drug Programs
CAS Standards and Guidelines

For the purpose of this document, the term "alcohol, tobacco, and other drug use or abuse" includes: (1) the illegal use of alcohol, tobacco, prescription medications, and other drugs, and (2) the high-risk use and/or abuse of alcohol, tobacco, prescription medications, over-the-counter medications, and nutritional supplements.

Part 1. MISSION

Alcohol, Tobacco, and Other Drug Programs (ATODP) must develop, disseminate, implement, and regularly review their missions. The mission must be consistent with the mission of the institution and with professional standards. The mission must be appropriate for the institution's student populations and community settings. Mission statements must reference student learning and development.

The goals of ATODP must
- acknowledge and mitigate the inherent risks to the total community associated with alcohol, tobacco, and other drug use
- develop, disseminate, interpret, and support the enforcement of campus regulations that are consistent with institutional policies and local, state/provincial, and federal law
- promote healthy choices concerning the use of alcohol, tobacco, and other drugs, emphasizing the elimination of illegal use, high-risk behavior, harmful use, and related violence
- promote a safe, healthy, and learning-conducive environment
- define ATODP policies and practices for prevention, education, training, intervention, evaluation, referral, and treatment
- develop shared ownership of the issue by involving all entities of the campus community including governing boards, administrators, faculty and staff members, students, and community leaders
- protect the legal rights of students

Part 2. PROGRAM

The formal education of students, consisting of the curriculum and the co-curriculum, must promote student learning and development outcomes that are purposeful, contribute to students' realization of their potential, and prepare students for satisfying and productive lives.

Alcohol, Tobacco, and Other Drug Programs (ATODP) must collaborate with colleagues and departments across the institution to promote student learning and development, persistence, and success.

Consistent with the institutional mission, ATODP must identify relevant and desirable student learning and development outcomes from among the six domains and related dimensions:

  Domain: knowledge acquisition, integration, construction, and application
  - Dimensions: understanding knowledge from a range of disciplines; connecting knowledge to other knowledge, ideas, and experiences; constructing knowledge; and relating knowledge to daily life

  Domain: cognitive complexity
  - Dimensions: critical thinking, reflective thinking, effective reasoning, and creativity

  Domain: intrapersonal development
  - Dimensions: realistic self-appraisal, self-understanding, and self-respect; identity development; commitment to ethics and integrity; and spiritual awareness

  Domain: interpersonal competence
  - Dimensions: meaningful relationships, interdependence, collaboration, and effective leadership.

  Domain: humanitarianism and civic engagement
  - Dimensions: understanding and appreciation of cultural and human differences, social responsibility, global perspective, and sense of civic responsibility

  Domain: practical competence
  - Dimensions: pursuing goals, communicating effectively, technical competence, managing personal affairs, managing career development, demonstrating professionalism, maintaining health and wellness, and living a purposeful and satisfying life

[LD Outcomes: See *The Council for the Advancement of Standards Learning and Developmental Outcomes* statement for examples of outcomes related to these domains and dimensions.]

ATODP must
- assess relevant and desirable student learning and development

- provide evidence of impact on outcomes
- articulate contributions to or support of student learning and development in the domains not specifically assessed
- articulate contributions to or support of student persistence and success
- use evidence gathered through this process to create strategies for improvement of programs and services

ATODP must be
- intentionally designed
- guided by theories and knowledge of learning and development
- integrated into the life of the institution
- reflective of developmental and demographic profiles of the student population
- responsive to needs of individuals, populations with distinct needs, and relevant constituencies
- delivered using multiple formats, strategies, and contexts

Where institutions provide distance education, ATODP must assist distance learners to achieve their educational goals by providing access to information about programs and services, to staff members who can address questions and concerns, and to counseling, advising, or other forms of assistance.

ATODP must involve students, faculty members, staff, and community constituents to reduce heavy and high-risk use of alcohol, tobacco, prescription medication, and other drugs.

ATODP must include
- environmental management strategies
- institutional policies
- enforcement strategies
- bi-annual review
- community collaboration
- training and education
- assistance and referral
- student leadership

ATODP staff must serve as positive role models for ethical and healthy behaviors.

Because faculty and staff members' behaviors often serve as models for students, resources should be available on-campus to assist supervisors in dealing with employees who exhibit high-risk behavior related to alcohol, tobacco, and other drugs.

ATODP must develop and provide education on policies, laws, prevention, intervention and treatment resources, and training for students, including student organizations.

ATODP education and training programs should address the cultural and economic context in which society promotes and condones alcohol, tobacco, and other drug use, including traditions and rituals conducive to high-risk drinking. Other topics may include: legal, physiological, psychological, and social aspects and effects of alcohol, tobacco, and other drug use, abuse, and dependency; high-risk uses of alcohol; risk factors for groups, including risk factors for groups as identified through assessment; differences between actual student use and perceptions of student use; and the impact of alcohol, tobacco, and other drug use related to physiological and behavioral differences linked with gender. Techniques and protocols for identifying and referring students with problems to appropriate campus entities should also be included.

ATODP should develop, provide, and advocate strategies that model practical applications of prevention theories and research results, including environmental approaches, risk reduction approaches, social norms approaches, student assistance programs, curricular infusion projects, development of on-campus task forces, and the development of campus and community coalitions.

ATODP should provide training for faculty and staff members in identifying, intervening, and referring students with alcohol, tobacco, and other drug problems.

ATODP should use public health prevention strategies that are evidenced-based and have demonstrated effectiveness in reducing heavy and high-risk drinking and other drug use in college populations.

ATODP should advocate for incorporating alcohol, tobacco, and other drugs information within relevant courses and expanding campus library holdings.

ATODP must provide access to support services for students with alcohol or other drug-related concerns.

Student involvement in assistance services may be voluntary upon self-initiation or referral, or mandatory upon referral by judicial authorities or other entities.

The student assistance services program should include confidential individual assessment for students to explore and evaluate their attitudes, perceptions, and behaviors; explore and evaluate the consequences, risk factors, and relationship to alcohol or other drugs; and make decisions based on the student's individual situation.

Student assistance services should provide, with peer involvement, a coordinated system across the campus for intervention and referral services for students. This system should include training programs on alcohol abuse and other drug use and on referral skills.

Student assistance services should identify and maintain contacts with campus and community entities that offer effective treatment, education, and support to students, family members, and friends. Such services may include structured education and counseling sessions for individuals and groups; community service work; disability support services; self-help groups such as Alcoholics Anonymous, Narcotics Anonymous, Al-Anon and Adult Children of Alcoholics; support groups; and detoxification and in-patient therapy.

Part 3. ORGANIZATION AND LEADERSHIP

To achieve student and program outcomes, Alcohol, Tobacco, and Other Drug Programs (ATODP) must be structured purposefully and organized effectively. Programs and services must have

- clearly stated goals
- current and accessible policies and procedures
- written performance expectations for employees
- functional work flow graphics or organizational charts demonstrating clear channels of authority

Leaders with organizational authority for the programs and services must provide strategic planning, supervision, and management; advance the organization; and maintain integrity through the following functions:

Strategic Planning

- articulate a vision and mission that drive short- and long-term planning
- set goals and objectives based on the needs of the population served and desired student learning or development and program outcomes
- facilitate continuous development, implementation, and assessment of goal attainment congruent with institutional mission and strategic plans
- promote environments that provide meaningful opportunities for student learning, development, and engagement
- develop and continuously improve programs and services in response to the changing needs of students served and evolving institutional priorities
- intentionally include diverse perspectives to inform decision making

Supervising

- manage human resource processes including recruitment, selection, development, supervision, performance planning, evaluation, recognition, and reward
- influence others to contribute to the effectiveness and success of the unit
- empower professional, support, and student staff to accept leadership opportunities

- offer appropriate feedback to colleagues and students on skills needed to become more effective leaders
- encourage and support professional development, collaboration with colleagues and departments across the institution, and scholarly contribution to the profession

Managing

- identify and address individual, organizational, and environmental conditions that foster or inhibit mission achievement
- plan, allocate, and monitor the use of fiscal, physical, human, intellectual, and technological resources
- use current and valid evidence to inform decisions
- incorporate sustainability practices in the management and design of programs, services, and facilities
- understand appropriate technologies and integrate them into programs and services
- be knowledgeable about codes and laws relevant to programs and services and ensure that staff members understand their responsibilities through appropriate training
- assess potential risks and take action to mitigate them

Advancing the Organization

- communicate effectively in writing, speaking, and electronic venues
- advocate for programs and services
- advocate for representation in strategic planning initiatives at appropriate divisional and institutional levels
- initiate collaborative interactions with internal and external stakeholders who have legitimate concerns about and interests in the functional area
- facilitate processes to reach consensus where wide support is needed
- inform other areas within the institution about issues affecting practice

Maintaining Integrity

- model ethical behavior and institutional citizenship
- share data used to inform key decisions in transparent and accessible ways
- monitor media used for distributing information about programs and services to ensure the content is current, accurate, appropriately referenced, and accessible

ATODP leaders should provide institutional leaders with information on ATODP issues on their campus to engender support.

The ATODP director or coordinator must be placed within the institution's organizational structures so as to be able to promote cooperative interaction with appropriate campus and community entities and to develop the support of high-level administrators.

The scope and structure of ATODP should be defined by the size, nature, complexity, and philosophy of the institution.

ATODP should maintain an advisory board, preferably appointed by the executive officer, comprised of knowledge members of the campus and community, for advice and support on policies and programs.

ATODP must collaborate in the development of policies to

- maintain consistency with federal, state/provincial, and local laws and regulations
- promote an educational, social, and living environment free from the abuse of alcohol, tobacco, and legal drugs, and the use of illegal drugs
- define geographic jurisdictions and demographic characteristics of populations to whom policies pertain
- define individual and group behaviors and group activities that are prohibited both on campus property and at off-campus events controlled by the institution
- specify the potential consequences for using or possessing, distributing, or manufacturing different amounts and/or categories of alcohol, tobacco, and other drugs
- establish protocols and procedures for the involvement of campus law enforcement, campus judicial programs, and other campus entities
- establish protocols and procedures for referring individuals with alcohol, tobacco, or other drug problems to appropriate sources for assistance
- define campus procedures on the availability and marketing of alcoholic beverages, if permitted
- define appropriate procedures for any permitted use of alcohol or tobacco

Part 4. HUMAN RESOURCES

Alcohol, Tobacco, and Other Drug Programs (ATODP) must be staffed adequately by individuals qualified to accomplish mission and goals.

Within institutional guidelines, ATODP must

- establish procedures for staff recruitment and selection, training, performance planning, and evaluation
- set expectations for supervision and performance
- assess the performance of employees individually and as a team
- provide access to continuing and advanced education and appropriate professional development opportunities to improve the leadership ability, competence, and skills of all employees.

ATODP must maintain position descriptions for all staff members.

To create a diverse staff, ATODP must institute recruitment and hiring strategies that encourage individuals from under-represented populations to apply for positions.

ATODP must develop promotion practices that are fair, inclusive, proactive, and non-discriminatory.

To further the recruitment and retention of staff, ATODP must consider work life initiatives, such as compressed work schedules, flextime, job sharing, remote work, or telework.

ATODP professional staff members must hold an earned graduate or professional degree in a field relevant to the position they hold or must possess an appropriate combination of educational credentials and related work experience.

ATODP should be supervised by professional staff members who have earned a master's degree from an accredited institution in fields of study such as health education, student services/development, psychology, social work, counseling, education, public health, or other appropriate health-related area, and who have relevant training and experience. Such training and experience should include prevention and intervention, assessment and treatment issues and strategies, and supervised work with older adolescents and adults of all ages.

ATODP prevention specialists must hold a minimum of a bachelor's degree in a related field and have relevant training and experience.

Training and experience should include an understanding of prevention and intervention strategies as well as work experience with college students.

ATODP professional staff members must engage in continuing professional development activities to keep abreast of the research, theories, legislation, policies, and developments that affect their programs and services.

ATODP must have technical and support staff members adequate to accomplish their mission. All members of the staff must be technologically proficient and qualified to perform their job functions, be knowledgeable about ethical and legal uses of technology, and have access to training and resources to support the performance of their assigned responsibilities.

Degree- or credential-seeking interns or graduate assistants must be qualified by enrollment in an appropriate field of study and by relevant experience. These individuals must be trained and supervised adequately by professional staff members holding educational credentials and related work experience appropriate for supervision. Supervisors must be cognizant of the roles of interns and graduate assistants as both student and employee and closely adhere to all parameters of their job descriptions, work hours, and schedules. Supervisors and the interns or graduate assistants must agree to compensatory time or other appropriate compensation if circumstances necessitate additional hours.

Student employees and volunteers must be carefully selected, trained, supervised, and evaluated. They must be educated on how and when to refer those in need of additional assistance to qualified staff members and must have access to a supervisor for assistance in making these judgments. Student employees and volunteers must be provided clear job descriptions, pre-service training based on assessed needs, and continuing development.

All ATODP staff members, including student employees and volunteers, must receive specific training on institutional policies pertaining to functions or activities they support and to privacy and confidentiality policies and laws regarding access to student records and other sensitive institutional information.

All ATODP staff members must receive training on policies and procedures related to the use of technology to store or access student records and institutional data.

ATODP must ensure that staff members are knowledgeable about and trained in emergency procedures, crisis response, and prevention efforts. Prevention efforts must address identification of threatening conduct or behavior of students, faculty and staff members, and others and must incorporate a system for responding and reporting.

ATODP must ensure that staff members are knowledgeable of and trained in safety and emergency procedures for securing and vacating facilities.

ATODP should provide training on problem recognition and referral procedures for professional and support staff, pre-professionals, and paraprofessionals.

Part 5. ETHICS

Alcohol, Tobacco, and Other Drug Programs (ATODP) must review relevant professional ethical standards and must adopt or develop and implement appropriate statements of ethical practice.

ATODP must publish and adhere to statements of ethical practice and ensure their periodic review by relevant constituencies.

ATODP must orient new staff members to relevant ethical standards and statements of ethical practice and related institutional policies.

Statements of ethical standards must specify that staff members respect privacy and maintain confidentiality in all communications and records to the extent that such communications and records are protected under relevant privacy laws.

Statements of ethical standards must specify limits on disclosure of information contained in students' educational records as well as requirements to disclose to appropriate authorities.

Statements of ethical standards must address personal and economic conflicts of interest, or appearance thereof, by staff members in the performance of their work.

Statements of ethical standards must reflect the responsibility of staff members to be fair, objective, and impartial in their interactions with others.

Statements of ethical standards must reference management of institutional funds.

Statements of ethical standards must reference appropriate behavior regarding research and assessment with human participants, confidentiality of research and assessment data, and students' rights and responsibilities.

Statements of ethical standards must include the expectation that ATODP staff members confront and hold accountable other staff members who exhibit unethical behavior.

Statements of ethical standards must address issues surrounding scholarly integrity.

As appropriate, ATODP staff members must inform users of programs and services of ethical obligations and limitations emanating from codes and laws or from licensure requirements.

ATODP staff members must recognize and avoid conflicts of interest that could adversely influence their judgment or objectivity and, when unavoidable, recuse themselves from the situation.

ATODP staff members must perform their duties within the limits of their position, training, expertise, and competence.

When these limits are exceeded, individuals in need of further assistance must be referred to persons possessing appropriate qualifications.

Promotional and descriptive information must be accurate and free of deception.

ATODP must adhere to institutional policies regarding ethical and legal use of software and technology.

Part 6. LAW, POLICY, AND GOVERNANCE

Alcohol, Tobacco, and Other Drug Programs (ATODP) must be in compliance with laws, regulations, and policies that relate to their respective responsibilities and that pose legal obligations, limitations, risks, and liabilities for the institution as a whole. Examples include constitutional, statutory, regulatory, and case law; relevant law and orders emanating from codes and laws; and the institution's policies.

ATODP must inform staff members, appropriate officials, and users of programs and services about existing and changing legal obligations, risks and liabilities, and limitations.

ATODP must have written policies on all relevant operations, transactions, or tasks that have legal implications.

ATODP must regularly review policies. The revision and creation of policies must be informed by best practices, available evidence, and policy issues in higher education.

ATODP staff members must use reasonable and informed practices to limit the liability exposure of the institution and its officers, employees, and agents. Staff members must be informed about institutional policies regarding risk management, personal liability, and related insurance coverage options and must be referred to external sources if the institution does not provide coverage.

The institution must provide access to legal advice for staff members as needed to carry out assigned responsibilities.

ATODP must have procedures and guidelines consistent with institutional policy for responding to threats, emergencies, and crisis situations. Systems and procedures must be in place to disseminate timely and accurate information to students, other members of the institutional community, and appropriate external organizations during emergency situations.

ATODP staff members must neither participate in nor condone any form of harassment or activity that demeans persons or creates an intimidating, hostile, or offensive environment.

ATODP must obtain permission to use copyrighted materials and instruments. ATODP must purchase the materials and instruments from legally compliant sources or seek alternative permission from the publisher or owner. References to copyrighted materials and instruments must include appropriate citations.

ATODP staff members must be knowledgeable about internal and external governance systems that affect programs and services.

ATODP staff members must be aware of and seek advice from the institution's legal counsel on privacy and disclosure of student information and parental notification.

Part 7. DIVERSITY, EQUITY, AND ACCESS

Within the context of each institution's unique mission and in accordance with institutional polices and all applicable codes and laws, Alcohol, Tobacco, and Other Drug Programs (ATODP) must create and maintain educational and work environments that are
- welcoming, accessible, and inclusive to persons of diverse backgrounds
- equitable and non-discriminatory
- free from harassment

ATODP must not discriminate on the basis of ability; age; cultural identity; ethnicity; family educational history (e.g., first generation to attend college); gender identity and expression; nationality; political affiliation; race; religious affiliation; sex; sexual orientation; economic, marital, social, or veteran status; or any other basis included in institutional policies and codes and laws.

ATODP must
- advocate for greater sensitivity to multicultural and social justice concerns by the institution and its personnel
- modify or remove policies, practices, facilities, structures, systems, and technologies that limit access, discriminate, or produce inequities
- include diversity, equity, and access initiatives within their strategic plans
- foster communication that deepens understanding of identity, culture, self-expression, and heritage
- promote respect about commonalities and differences among people within their

historical and cultural contexts
- address the characteristics and needs of a diverse population when establishing and implementing culturally relevant and inclusive programs, services, policies, procedures, and practices
- provide staff members with access to multicultural training and hold staff members accountable for integrating the training into their work
- respond to the needs of all students and other populations served when establishing hours of operation and developing methods of delivering programs, services, and resources
- ensure physical, program, and resource access for persons with disabilities
- recognize the needs of distance learning students by providing appropriate and accessible services and resources or by assisting them in gaining access to other appropriate services and resources in their geographic region

Part 8. INSTITUTIONAL AND EXTERNAL RELATIONS

Alcohol, Tobacco, and Other Drug Programs (ATODP) must reach out to relevant individuals, groups, communities, and organizations internal and external to the institution to
- establish, maintain, and promote understanding and effective relations with those that have a significant interest in or potential effect on the students or other constituents served by the programs and services
- garner support and resources for programs and services as defined by the mission statement
- disseminate information about the programs and services
- collaborate, where appropriate, to assist in offering or improving programs and services to meet the needs of students and other constituents and to achieve program and student outcomes
- engage diverse individuals, groups, communities, and organizations to enrich the educational environment and experiences of students and other constituents

ATODP must have procedures and guidelines consistent with institutional policy for
- communicating with the media
- contracting with external organizations for delivery of programs and services
- cultivating, soliciting, and managing gifts
- applying to and managing funds from grants

ATODP must gather and disseminate information to the campus community, including students, their parents, staff, and faculty members on alcohol, tobacco, and other drug problems, risk reduction strategies, resources, and related topics.

ATODP must maintain effective working relationships with various campus offices and community groups and agencies to promote a healthy environment in which the use or abuse of alcohol and use of other drugs does not interfere with the learning, performance, or social aspects of college life,

These campus offices may include senior administrators; medical services; health promotion and prevention services; counseling; law enforcement and safety; judicial programs; residential life; campus information and visitor services; fraternity and sorority life; athletics; student and other campus media; disability support services, student activities offices and student organizations; academic departments; personnel services; and community relations and public affairs. Community agencies may include relevant local, state/provincial, and federal agencies and authorities such as the state liquor store control authority, state alcohol agency, the office of highway traffic safety, mayor and council, neighborhood associations, faith community, family, parents or guardians, school systems, area health care and treatment providers, support groups, as well as representatives from the local chamber of commerce and the hospitality industry.

ATODP should engage the campus and community in the issues of access and availability of alcohol, tobacco, and other drugs, and in the enforcement of the law.

ATODP must work with campus and community resources to encourage staff members to utilize appropriate screening protocols.

Part 9. FINANCIAL RESOURCES

Alcohol, Tobacco, and Other Drug Programs (ATODP) must have funding to accomplish the mission and goals. In establishing funding priorities and making significant changes, a comprehensive analysis must be conducted to determine the following elements: unmet needs of the unit, relevant expenditures, external and internal resources, and impact on students and the institution.

ATODP must demonstrate efficient and effective use and responsible stewardship of fiscal resources consistent with institutional protocols.

The institution should provide sufficient baseline funding for ATODP so that staff members may spend the majority of their time on planning, programming, providing services, and evaluation rather than on seeking new or continuing funding sources.

Part 10. TECHNOLOGY

Alcohol, Tobacco, and Other Drug Programs (ATODP) must have adequate technology to support the achievement of their mission and goals. The technology and its use must comply with institutional policies and procedures and be evaluated for compliance with relevant codes and laws.

ATODP must use current technology to provide updated information regarding mission, location, staffing, programs, services, and official contacts to students and designated clients.

ATODP must explore the use of technology to enhance delivery of programs and services, especially for students at a distance or external constituencies.

When technology is used to facilitate student learning and development, ATODP must select technology that reflects intended outcomes.

ATODP must
- maintain policies and procedures that address the security, confidentiality, and backup of data, as well as compliance with privacy laws
- have clearly articulated plans in place for protecting confidentiality and security of information when using Internet-based technologies
- develop plans for replacing and updating existing hardware and software as well as plans for integrating new technically-based or supported programs, including systems developed internally by the institution, systems available through professional associations, or private vendor-based systems

Technology, as well as workstations or computer labs maintained by programs and services for student use, must be accessible to all designated clients and must meet established technology standards for delivery to persons with disabilities.

When providing student access to technology, ATODP must
- have policies on the use of technology that are clear, easy to understand, and available to all students
- provide assistance, information, or referral to appropriate support services to those needing help accessing or using technology
- provide instruction or training on how to use the technology
- inform students on the legal and ethical implications of misuse as it pertains to intellectual property, harassment, privacy, and social networks

Student violations of technology policies must follow established institutional student disciplinary procedures.

Students who experience negative emotional or psychological consequences from the use of technology must be referred to support services provided by the institution.

Part 11. FACILITIES AND EQUIPMENT

Alcohol, Tobacco, and Other Drug Programs (ATODP) must have adequate, accessible, and suitably located facilities and equipment to support the mission and goals. If acquiring capital equipment as defined by the institution, ATODP must take into account expenses related to regular maintenance and life cycle costs. Facilities and equipment must be evaluated on an established cycle, including consideration of sustainability, and be in compliance with codes and laws to provide for access, health, safety, and security.

ATODP staff members must have workspace that is well equipped, adequate in size, and designed to support their work and responsibilities. For conversations requiring privacy, staff members must have access to a private space.

ATODP staff members who share workspace must be able to secure their own work.
The design of the facilities must guarantee the security and privacy of records and ensure the confidentiality of sensitive information.

The location and layout of the facilities must be sensitive to the needs of persons with disabilities as well as the needs of other constituencies.

Facilities for ATODP should support a range of services, including prevention, education, assessment, intervention, programming, and a resource center.

Office space should be physically separate from human resources, campus security, and judicial programs.

ATODP should be provided facilities that ensure confidentiality and a location in which students, faculty members, and staff might access and read information on alcohol, tobacco, and other drugs.

Part 12. ASSESSMENT AND EVALUATION

Alcohol, Tobacco, and Other Drug Programs (ATODP) must have a clearly articulated assessment plan to document achievement of stated goals and learning outcomes, demonstrate accountability, provide evidence of improvement, and describe resulting changes in programs and services.

ATODP must have adequate fiscal, human, professional development, and technological resources to develop and implement assessment plans.

Assessments must include direct and indirect evaluation and use qualitative and quantitative methodologies and existing evidence, as appropriate, to determine whether and to what degree the stated mission, goals, and intended outcomes are being met as effectively and efficiently as possible. The process must employ sufficient and sound measures to ensure comprehensiveness. Data collected must include responses from students and other constituencies, and aggregated results must be shared with those groups. Results of assessments must be shared appropriately with multiple constituents.

Results of assessments and evaluations must be used to identify needs and interests in revising and improving programs and services, recognizing staff performance, maximizing resource efficiency and effectiveness, improving student achievement of learning and development outcomes, and improving student persistence and success. Changes resulting from the use of assessments and evaluation must be shared with stakeholders.

ATODP must assess systematically the following campus factors:
- attitudes, beliefs, and behaviors regarding alcohol, tobacco, and other drug use, abuse, and dependency
- consequences of alcohol, tobacco, or other drug use or abuse upon social skills; academic and work performance; property damage; policy violations; health, counseling, and disciplinary caseloads; and other indicators of problems
- perceptions of campus alcohol, tobacco, and other drug use norms
- features of the environment that abet high-risk alcohol use, tobacco, and other drug use; marketing and promotion that promotes heavy or underage consumption of alcohol; inconsistent enforcement of campus policy and community law; lack of availability of alcohol-free social and recreational options on campus and in the surrounding community

ATODP should assess the norms, behaviors, and behavioral consequences of specific focus populations.

ATODP and other campus entities must exchange general and non-confidential assessment results of mutual application and benefit.

General Standards revised in 2011;
ATODP content developed/revised in 1990, 1997, & 2003

The Role of Assessment Services
CAS Standards Contextual Statement

Assessment was an important element in higher education well before the founding of higher education in the United States; juried reviews were used to demonstrate student learning at the University of Bologna as early as 1063 CE (Bresciani, Moore Gardner, & Hickmott, 2009). Although the need for assessment and program evaluation in American higher education has long been acknowledged, it remains a pressing need today. With fiscal restraints and calls for accountability coming from multiple constituents (from parents to regional accrediting bodies), the ability to document and evaluate the impact of our programs and services is a critical responsibility.

Early proponents of outcomes assessment included William Rainey Harper, President of the University of Chicago. In 1889, he called on colleges and universities to adopt a program of research with the college student as the subject "in order that the student may receive the assistance so essential to his [sic] highest success, another step in the onward evolution will take place. This step will be the scientific study of the student" (as cited in Rentz, 1996, p. 28).

Responding to Harper's vision, the *Student Personnel Point of View* (American Council of Education, 1937) challenged the field of student services to employ "studies designed to improve these functions and services" (p. 42). Later in the document, four specific kinds of studies were identified: student out-of-class life and its connection to the educational mission, faculty and student out-of-class relationships, financial aid to students, and after-college studies to ascertain the effects of college on careers and personal adjustment.

The 1949 revision of the *Student Personnel Point of View* (American Council of Education) stated that the "principal responsibility of personnel workers lies in the area of progressive program development . . . this means that each worker must devote a large part of time to the formulation of new plans and to the continuous evaluation and improvement of current programs (p. 34). This document also stressed the importance of personnel workers being "thoroughly trained in research methods as a part of their professional preparation" (p. 35). Ultimately, the standard for student affairs programs, according to the 1949 document, is in "the difference it makes in the development of individual students" (p. 34).

Historical and foundational documents in the field give clear evidence that the role of assessment and program evaluation in higher education and student affairs is important in the education of the "whole" student. Although most agree about the importance of conducting research on students and programs, still relatively few student affairs divisions have considered it a vital part of their operations. Of the 4100 colleges and universities in the United States, approximately 100 have student affairs assessment offices (G. Henning, personal communication).

In the past decade, student affairs documents have continued the call for assessment and accountability of program effectiveness as it relates to student learning and development. *The Student Learning Imperative* (1996) charged student affairs staff to "participate in efforts to assess student learning . . . and periodically audit institutional environments to reinforce those factors that enhance, and eliminate those that inhibit student involvement in educationally-purposeful activities" (p. 6). The *Principles of Good Practice for Student Affairs* (1996) asserted the need to use systematic inquiry to improve student and institutional performance. Specifically, "student affairs educators who are skilled in using assessment methods acquire high-quality information; effective application of this information to practice results in programs and change strategies . . . [that] improve student achievement" (p. 3). In *Learning Reconsidered* (2004), the language of assessment and student learning was more comprehensive. "Student Affairs must lead broad, collaborative institutional efforts to assess overall student learning and to track, document, and evaluate the role of diverse learning experiences . . . assessment should be a way of life—part of the institutional culture" (p. 26). According to *Assessment Reconsidered*, the companion to *Learning Reconsidered*, assessment is a collaborative exercise influenced by external forces but "more importantly emerges from the desire of faculty members, student affairs professionals, parents, students, and institutional administrators to know, and improve, the quality and effectiveness of higher education (Keeling, Wall, Underhile, & Dung, 2008, p. 1).

Assessment is a process with dual purposes: accountability and continuous improvement. According to Bresciani (2006),

> . . . in assessment faculty and staff articulate what the program intends to accomplish in regard to its services, research, student learning, and faculty/staff development programs. The faculty and/or professionals then purposefully plan the program so that the intended results (e.g., outcomes) can be achieved; implement methods to systematically—over time—identify whether end results have been achieved; and, finally, use the results to plan improvements or make recommendations for policy considerations, recruitment, retention, resource allocation, or new resource requests. (p. 14)

The terms assessment, research, and evaluation are often used interchangeably, but there are distinctions.

Briefly, research concerns theory: forming it, confirming it, and disconfirming it. Research assumes broader implications than one institution or program. Assessment, on the other hand, is more focused on the outcomes of participant programs, though this can be very broad to include an entire institution. It does not infer individual student outcomes. The purpose of assessment is to guide practice rather than to relate practice to theory. Evaluation is even more particular to a specific program and is concerned with the satisfaction, organization, and attendance of a program. (Jones, Torres, & Arminio, 2006, p. 30)

Recently, student affairs literature focused on enabling practitioners to implement assessment. These "how-to" guides provide information about the assessment planning process, writing outcomes, designing instruments, and performing qualitative as well as quantitative assessments (Bresciani, Zelna, & Anderson, 2004). These resources include the self-assessment guides published by CAS, Schuh and Associates' *Assessment Methods for Student Affairs* (2009), Suskie's *Assessing Student Learning: A Common Sense Guide* (2009), and *Demonstrating Student Success* (2009) by Bresciani, Moore Gardner, and Hickmott. In addition, professional associations have begun to provide their members with assessment tools, as have numerous for-profit companies. Campuses today should have a comprehensive assessment plan that includes consideration of learning outcomes, student needs and inputs, campus environments, student motivation, student use and satisfaction, and cost effectiveness (Schuh & Upcraft, 2001).

Bresciani, Zelna, & Anderson (2004) offered reasons and uses for conducting assessment in student affairs, based on a compilation of other works, including those by the American Association for Higher Education (1994), Bresciani (2003), Ewell (1997a), Maki (2004), Palomba and Banta (1999), and Upcraft and Schuh (1996). These sources noted the multiple reasons for carrying out assessment: reinforcing or emphasizing unit missions; improving a program's quality or performance; comparing a program's quality or value to the program's previously defined principles; informing planning, decision-making, and policy discussions at the local, state, regional, and national levels; evaluating programs and personnel; assisting in the request for additional funds from the college or university and external community; assisting in the reallocation of resources; assisting in meeting accreditation requirements; identifying models of best practices and national benchmarks; celebrating successes while reflecting on the attitudes and approaches taken in improving learning and development; and creating a culture of continuous improvement—a culture of accountability, learning, and improvement.

Assessment efforts may take many forms. Assessment can employ both qualitative and quantitative data collection methods such as interviews, focus groups, observations, rubrics, portfolios, surveys, and questionnaires. On-line survey software is used frequently in creating customized assessments.

Assessment is a process that can be used to discover an institution's best practices and to bring about continual improvement within the unique context of each institution. Student affairs divisions undertaking assessment efforts should not be discouraged by the seeming enormity of the task. The important consideration is to be purposeful and systematic and to use sound assessment methods that improve operations incrementally. The assessment process can be disaggregated into its component parts for easier implementation.

Assessment Services (AS) as a functional area is sometimes organized as a single unit, while at other institutions it is a collective of institutional or departmental assessment bodies. In any case, collaboration and consultation is imperative between and within the AS and various individuals and departments as well as with institutional leadership. For a discussion of specific skills necessary to work in the AS in addition to those discussed in the attached CAS standards, the ACPA Assessment Skills and Knowledge (ASK) standards and the ACPA/NASPA Assessment, Evaluation, and Research professional competencies may be informative. The standards articulated here offer principles for assessment that are valuable for those working in or directing an assessment office as well as for those conducting assessments as a part of their position responsibilities in another functional area.

References, Readings, and Resources

American Association of Higher Education (1994). *Nine principles of good practice for assessing student learning* [On-line]. Retrieved from http://www.iuk.edu/%7Ekoctla/assessment/9principles.shtml

American College Personnel Association (1996). *The student learning imperative: Implications for student affairs* [On-line]. Retrieved from http://www.acpa.nche.edu/sli/sli.htm

American College Personnel Association. (2006). *ASK standards: Assessment skills and knowledge content standards for student affairs practitioners and scholars.* Washington, DC. Author.

American College Personnel Association & National Association of Student Personnel Administrators. (2010). *Professional competency areas for student affairs practitioners.* Washington, D.C.: Authors.

American Council of Education. (1937). *The student personnel point of view: A report of a conference on the philosophy and development of student personnel work in colleges and universities* [On-line]. Retrieved from http://www.myacpa.org/pub/documents/1937.pdf

American Council of Education. (1949). *The student personnel point of view: A report of a conference on the philosophy and development of student personnel work in colleges and universities* [On-line]. Retrieved from http://www.myacpa.org/pub/documents/1949.pdf

Angelo, T. A., & Cross, K. P. (1993). *Classroom assessment techniques: A handbook for college teachers (2nd Ed).* San

Francisco, CA: Jossey-Bass.

Banta, T. W., Lund, J. P., Black, K. E., & Oblander, F. W. (Eds.). (1996). *Assessment in practice: Putting principles to work on college campuses.* San Francisco, CA: Jossey-Bass.

Banta, T. W., & Kuh, G. D. (1998, March/April). A missing link in assessment: Collaboration between academic and student affairs professionals. *Change,* 40-48.

Blimling, G. S., & Whitt, E. J. (1999). *Good practices in student affairs: Principles to foster student learning.* San Francisco, CA: Jossey-Bass.

Bresciani, M. J. (2003). *An updated outline for assessment plans.* NetResults [On-line]. Retrieved from http://www.naspa.org/

Bresciani, M. J., Zelna, C. L., & Anderson, J. A. (2004). *Assessing student learning and development.* Washington, DC: NASPA.

Bresciani, M. J. (2006). *Outcomes-based academic and co-curricular program review: A compilation of institutional good practices.* Sterling, VA: Stylus.

Bresciani, M. J., Moore Gardner, M., & Hickmott, J. (2009). *Demonstrating student success: A practical guide to outcomes-based assessment of learning and development in student affairs.* Sterling, VA: Stylus.

Driscoll, A., & Wood, S. (2007). *Developing outcomes-based assessment for learner-centered education.* Sterling, VA: Stylus.

Ewell, P. T. (1997a). From the states: Putting it all on the line—South Carolina's performance funding initiative. *Assessment Update, 9*(1), 9-11.

Huba, M. E., & Freed, J. E. (2000). *Learner-centered assessment on college campuses: Shifting the focus from teaching to learning.* Boston: Allyn and Bacon.

Jones, W. R., Torres, W., & Arminio, J. (2006). *Negotiating the complexities of qualitative research.* New York: Routledge.

Keeling, R. P. (Ed.). (2004). *Learning reconsidered. A campus-wide focus on the student experience.* Washington, D.C.: National Association of Student Personnel Administrators & American College Personnel Association.

Keeling, R. P. (2006). *Learning reconsidered 2: Implementing a campus-wide focus on the student experience.* American College Personnel Association, Association of College and University Housing Officers-International, Association of College Unions-International, National Academic Advising Association, National Association for Campus Activities, National Association of Student Personnel Administrators, National Intramural-Recreational Sports Association.

Keeling, R. P., Wall, A. F., Underhile, R., & Dungy, G. J. (2008). *Assessment reconsidered: Institutional effectiveness for student success.* International Center for Student Success and Institutional Accountability.

Maki, P. (2010). *Assessing for learning (2nd Ed).* Sterling, VA: Stylus.

National Association of Student Personnel Administrators & American College Personnel Association. (2004) *Learning reconsidered: A campus-wide focus on the student experience.* Washington, DC: NASPA & ACPA. Retrieved from http://www.myacpa.org/pub/documents/LearningReconsidered.doc

Palomba, C. A., & Banta, T. W. (1999). *Assessment essentials:*

Planning, implementing and improving assessment in higher education. San Francisco, CA: Jossey-Bass.

Rentz, A. L. (1996). A history of student affairs. In A. L. Rentz (Ed.), Student affairs practice in higher education (pp. 28-55). Springfield, IL: Thomas.

Shuch, J. & Associates. (2009). *Assessment methods in student affairs.* San Francisco, CA: Jossey-Bass.

Schuh, J., & Upcraft, M. L. (1998, Nov/Dec). Facts and myths about assessment in student affairs. *About Campus,* 2-8.

Schuh, J. H., Upcraft, M. L., & Associates, (2001). *Assessment practice in student affairs: An application manual.* San Francisco: Jossey-Bass.

Suskie, L. (2009). *Assessing student learning: A common sense guide (2nd Ed.).* Bolton, MA: Anker.

Strayhorn, T. L. (2006). *Frameworks for assessing learning development outcomes.* Washington, DC: Council for the Advancement of Standards in Higher Education.

U.S. Department of Education. (2006). *A test of leadership:Charting the future of U.S. Higher Education.* Jessup, MD: Ed Pubs.

Upcraft, M. L., & Schuh, J. H. (1996). *Assessment in student affairs: A guide for practitioners.* San Francisco, CA: Jossey-Bass.

Walvoord, B. E. (2004). *Assessment clear and simple: A practical guide for institutions, departments, and general education.* San Francisco, CA: Jossey-Bass.

Wehlburg, C. M. (2008). *Promoting integrated and transformative assessment: A deeper focus on student learning.* San Francisco, CA: Jossey-Bass.

Williamson, E. G., & Biggs, D. A. (1975). *Student personnel work: A program of development relationships.* New York, NY: John Wiley & Sons.

Contextual Statement Contributors

Current Edition:

Gavin Henning, Dartmouth College

Jan Arminio, Shippensburg University

Previous Editions:

Jan Arminio, Shippensburg University (2009)

Joel H. Scott, University of Georgia (Baylor University) (2006)

Cara Skeat Ray, Gainesville State College/University of Georgia (2006)

Roger B. Winston, Jr., University of Georgia

Assessment Services
CAS Standards and Guidelines

Part 1. MISSION

The mission of Assessment Services (AS) is to develop a comprehensive assessment program to increase the institution's knowledge about students, the educational environment, and institutional effectiveness to continuously improve student programs and services and to enhance student learning.

AS must develop, disseminate, implement, and regularly review their missions. The mission must be consistent with the mission of the institution and with professional standards. The mission must be appropriate for the institution's student populations and community settings. Mission statements must reference student learning and development.

Part 2. PROGRAM

The formal education of students, consisting of the curriculum and the co-curriculum, must promote student learning and development outcomes that are purposeful, contribute to students' realization of their potential, and prepare students for satisfying and productive lives.

Assessment Services (AS) must collaborate with colleagues and departments across the institution to promote student learning and development, persistence, and success.

Consistent with the institutional mission, AS must identify relevant and desirable student learning and development outcomes from among the six domains and related dimensions:

Domain: knowledge acquisition, integration, construction, and application

- Dimensions: understanding knowledge from a range of disciplines; connecting knowledge to other knowledge, ideas, and experiences; constructing knowledge; and relating knowledge to daily life

Domain: cognitive complexity

- Dimensions: critical thinking, reflective thinking, effective reasoning, and creativity

Domain: intrapersonal development

- Dimensions: realistic self-appraisal, self-understanding, and self-respect; identity development; commitment to ethics and integrity; and spiritual awareness

Domain: interpersonal competence

- Dimensions: meaningful relationships, interdependence, collaboration, and effective leadership.

Domain: humanitarianism and civic engagement

- Dimensions: understanding and appreciation of cultural and human differences, social responsibility, global perspective, and sense of civic responsibility

Domain: practical competence

- Dimensions: pursuing goals, communicating effectively, technical competence, managing personal affairs, managing career development, demonstrating professionalism, maintaining health and wellness, and living a purposeful and satisfying life

[LD Outcomes: See *The Council for the Advancement of Standards Learning and Developmental Outcomes* statement for examples of outcomes related to these domains and dimensions.]

AS must
- assess relevant and desirable student learning and development
- provide evidence of impact on outcomes
- articulate contributions to or support of student learning and development in the domains not specifically assessed
- articulate contributions to or support of student persistence and success
- use evidence gathered through this process to create strategies for improvement of programs and services

AS must be
- intentionally designed
- guided by theories and knowledge of learning and development
- integrated into the life of the institution
- reflective of developmental and demographic profiles of the student population
- responsive to needs of individuals, populations with distinct needs, and relevant constituencies
- delivered using multiple formats, strategies, and contexts

Where institutions provide distance education, AS must assist distance learners to achieve their educational goals by providing access to information about programs and services, to staff members who can address questions and concerns, and to counseling, advising, or other forms of assistance.

Regardless of its structure, AS must collaborate and consult with institutional research or various departments to ensure that assessment efforts address institutional needs.

AS may be organized as a functional area or be a collective body of assessment initiatives across an institution.

Whenever there are both AS and an institutional research function in an institution, there should be clear delineation of responsibilities.

In institutions that do not have AS, a senior officer must be an advocate for assessment and program evaluation and must collaborate and consult with, and otherwise provide support to, institutional assessment efforts.

AS must include activities that assess student needs and student learning and development outcomes, assess whether goals are being achieved, describe student characteristics, determine whether professional standards are being met, and determine effectiveness of programs and services for students. Results of these studies must be disseminated to appropriate personnel and students in the institution.

AS must

- describe the demographics, personal characteristics, and behaviors of students
- conduct regular assessments of student needs
- review and use available literature about the characteristics and developmental changes of post-secondary students
- assess whether the work of AS is consistent with and achieves stated objectives
- use appropriate professional standards, tools, and instruments for assessment
- study the extent to which students, programs, departments, and institutions meet their overall educational goals and determine conditions that enhance or hamper goal achievement
- study the impact of the college experience on students and alumni
- examine retention and graduation rates
- compare institutional practices against professional standards
- investigate the impact of campus culture
- assist others in the effective use of assessment to inform decisions and guide the development and improvement of services, programs, and policies

AS should examine cost effectiveness and the level of student

satisfaction with programs and services.

AS practices must be conducted in the context of existing and developing strategic initiatives.

AS should provide assessment and evaluation support for other institutional offices and institutional decision makers.

AS should

- collect and analyze student data beginning with pre-enrollment characteristics and continuing through follow-up studies of graduates and other former students
- plan, coordinate, or conduct regular studies of various programs, facilities, services, classes, and student sub-groups
- describe students' intellectual, emotional, social, moral, spiritual, vocational, and physical development and behavior; such data should be regularly collected, updated, and disseminated
- analyze data to identify trends in student behavior and attitudes to consider the implications for institutional policies and practices
- analyze data to identify retention trends to consider the implications for institutional policies and practices
- collect and analyze data, including cost effectiveness data, to be used for making decisions about the continuation, modification, or termination of programs and services
- compare institutional practices against benchmarks
- coordinate assessment plans across units and act as a resource to faculty and staff regarding assessment and evaluation efforts
- disseminate information about assessment and evaluation findings to members of the campus community
- guide and evaluate research and assessment efforts conducted by students
- track campus studies, for example in theses and dissertations, in which campus students are participants

Part 3. ORGANIZATION AND LEADERSHIP

To achieve student and program outcomes, Assessment Services (AS) must be structured purposefully and organized effectively. AS must have

- clearly stated goals
- current and accessible policies and procedures
- written performance expectations for employees
- functional work flow graphics or organizational charts demonstrating clear channels of authority

Leaders with organizational authority for the programs and services must provide strategic planning, supervision, and management; advance the organization; and maintain integrity through the following functions:

Strategic Planning

- articulate a vision and mission that drive short- and long-term planning
- set goals and objectives based on the needs of the population served and desired student learning or development and program outcomes
- facilitate continuous development, implementation, and assessment of goal attainment congruent with institutional mission and strategic plans
- promote environments that provide meaningful opportunities for student learning, development, and engagement
- develop and continuously improve programs and services in response to the changing needs of students served and evolving institutional priorities
- intentionally include diverse perspectives to inform decision making

Supervising

- manage human resource processes including recruitment, selection, development, supervision, performance planning, evaluation, recognition, and reward
- influence others to contribute to the effectiveness and success of the unit
- empower professional, support, and student staff to accept leadership opportunities
- offer appropriate feedback to colleagues and students on skills needed to become more effective leaders
- encourage and support professional development, collaboration with colleagues and departments across the institution, and scholarly contribution to the profession

Managing

- identify and address individual, organizational, and environmental conditions that foster or inhibit mission achievement
- plan, allocate, and monitor the use of fiscal, physical, human, intellectual, and technological resources
- use current and valid evidence to inform decisions
- incorporate sustainability practices in the management and design of programs, services, and facilities
- understand appropriate technologies and integrate them into programs and services
- be knowledgeable about codes and laws relevant to programs and services and

ensure that staff members understand their responsibilities through appropriate training
- assess potential risks and take action to mitigate them

Advancing the Organization

- communicate effectively in writing, speaking, and electronic venues
- advocate for programs and services
- advocate for representation in strategic planning initiatives at appropriate divisional and institutional levels
- initiate collaborative interactions with internal and external stakeholders who have legitimate concerns about and interests in the functional area
- facilitate processes to reach consensus where wide support is needed
- inform other areas within the institution about issues affecting practice

Maintaining Integrity

- model ethical behavior and institutional citizenship
- share data used to inform key decisions in transparent and accessible ways
- monitor media used for distributing information about programs and services to ensure the content is current, accurate, appropriately referenced, and accessible

AS leaders must

- understand the foundations of higher education
- understand the educational value and objectives of programs and services
- interpret assessment results to guide educational practice
- advocate for institutional response to assessment findings
- serve as an expert in administering effective and efficient assessment programs
- stay current about trends in assessment
- work to ensure that students are not over-assessed
- understand and be able to use various research and assessment methodologies and methods

Because outcomes assessment and program evaluation efforts are conducted on most campuses in cooperation with other institutional research and evaluation efforts, a staff member must be designated to manage specific assessment activities, priorities, and timelines.

Assessment goals should result from a collaborative effort between leaders of AS, those responsible for the various programs and services being assessed, and others responsible for institutional research efforts.

Part 4. HUMAN RESOURCES

Assessment Services (AS) must be staffed adequately by individuals qualified to accomplish mission and goals.

Within institutional guidelines, AS must
- establish procedures for staff recruitment and selection, training, performance planning, and evaluation
- set expectations for supervision and performance
- assess the performance of employees individually and as a team
- provide access to continuing and advanced education and appropriate professional development opportunities to improve the leadership ability, competence, and skills of all employees.

AS must maintain position descriptions for all staff members.

To create a diverse staff, AS must institute recruitment and hiring strategies that encourage individuals from under-represented populations to apply for positions.

AS must develop promotion practices that are fair, inclusive, proactive, and non-discriminatory.

To further the recruitment and retention of staff, AS must consider work life initiatives, such as compressed work schedules, flextime, job sharing, remote work, or telework.

AS professional staff members must hold an earned graduate or professional degree in a field relevant to the position they hold or must possess an appropriate combination of educational credentials and related work experience.

AS professional staff members must engage in continuing professional development activities to keep abreast of the research, theories, legislation, policies, and developments that affect their programs and services.

AS must have technical and support staff members adequate to accomplish their mission. All members of the staff must be technologically proficient and qualified to perform their job functions, be knowledgeable about ethical and legal uses of technology, and have access to training and resources to support the performance of their assigned responsibilities.

Degree- or credential-seeking interns or graduate assistants must be qualified by enrollment in an appropriate field of study and by relevant experience. These individuals must be trained and supervised adequately by professional staff members holding educational credentials and related work experience appropriate for supervision. Supervisors must be cognizant of the roles of interns and graduate assistants as both student and employee and closely adhere to all parameters of their job descriptions, work hours, and schedules. Supervisors and the interns or graduate assistants must agree to compensatory time or other appropriate compensation if circumstances necessitate additional hours.

Student employees and volunteers must be carefully selected, trained, supervised, and evaluated. They must be educated on how and when to refer those in need of additional assistance to qualified staff members and must have access to a supervisor for assistance in making these judgments. Student employees and volunteers must be provided clear job descriptions, pre-service training based on assessed needs, and continuing development.

All AS staff members, including student employees and volunteers, must receive specific training on institutional policies pertaining to functions or activities they support and to privacy and confidentiality policies and laws regarding access to student records and other sensitive institutional information.

All AS staff members must receive training on policies and procedures related to the use of technology to store or access student records and institutional data.

AS must ensure that staff members are knowledgeable about and trained in emergency procedures, crisis response, and prevention efforts. Prevention efforts must address identification of threatening conduct or behavior of students, faculty and staff members, and others and must incorporate a system for responding and reporting.

AS must ensure that staff members are knowledgeable of and trained in safety and emergency procedures for securing and vacating facilities.

Within the institution, a qualified professional AS staff member must be designated to coordinate the assessment efforts and must work closely with or be responsive to leaders of programs and services.

The number of staff members assigned to assessment efforts should be a function of the size, complexity, and purpose of the institution. Institutions unable to assign a full-time professional staff member should devote a portion of their institutional research program's resources to this effort.

Staff assigned responsibility for assessment should possess effective communication and consultation skills and have an appropriate combination of coursework, training, and experience in the following areas: research methodology, design, and analysis; computer literacy; program planning implementation and evaluation; and human development theory, including the study of student sub-group cultures. When staff members lack adequate knowledge in any of these critical areas, they should seek expertise from appropriate resources.

Part 5. ETHICS

Assessment Services (AS) must review relevant professional ethical standards and must adopt or develop and implement appropriate statements of ethical practice.

AS must publish and adhere to statements of ethical practice and ensure their periodic review by relevant constituencies.

AS must orient new staff members to relevant ethical standards and statements of ethical practice and related institutional policies.

Statements of ethical standards must specify that staff members respect privacy and maintain confidentiality in all communications and records to the extent that such communications and records are protected under relevant privacy laws.

Statements of ethical standards must specify limits on disclosure of information contained in students' educational records as well as requirements to disclose to appropriate authorities.

AS must seek from the institutional review board approval to study human subjects for studies whose findings will be published beyond internal review of the institution. AS must know and adhere to the human subjects policies and procedures of the institution.

AS should seek approval to conduct assessment studies through the institution's human subjects review process.

Statements of ethical standards must address personal and economic conflicts of interest, or appearance thereof, by staff members in the performance of their work.

Statements of ethical standards must reflect the responsibility of staff members to be fair, objective, and impartial in their interactions with others.

Statements of ethical standards must reference management of institutional funds.

Statements of ethical standards must reference appropriate behavior regarding research and assessment with human participants, confidentiality of research and assessment data, and students' rights and responsibilities.

Statements of ethical standards must include the expectation that AS staff members confront and hold accountable other staff members who exhibit unethical behavior.

Statements of ethical standards must address issues surrounding scholarly integrity.

As appropriate, AS staff members must inform users of programs and services of ethical obligations and limitations emanating from codes and laws or from licensure requirements.

AS staff members must recognize and avoid conflicts of interest that could adversely influence their judgment or objectivity and, when unavoidable, recuse themselves from the situation.

AS staff members must perform their duties within the limits of their position, training, expertise, and competence.

When these limits are exceeded, individuals in need of further assistance must be referred to persons possessing appropriate qualifications.

Promotional and descriptive information must be accurate and free of deception.

AS must adhere to institutional policies regarding ethical and legal use of software and technology.

AS must ensure that the privacy or anonymity of study participants and the confidential nature of data are not breached.

AS must regularly purge identifiable information collected about students and other participants to protect their privacy, consistent with institutional policies and federal guidelines.

AS should maintain raw data for a number of years, based on applicable policy, after the study's written report is completed to respond to subsequent questions. Instances involving research on sensitive topics may require protections such as a Certificate of Confidentiality.

AS must acknowledge methodological limitations of assessment studies.

These limitations could include unrepresentative samples, low response rate, or errors in trying to make decisions from ungeneralizable qualitative findings.

Part 6. LAW, POLICY, AND GOVERNANCE

Assessment Services (AS) must be in compliance with laws, regulations, and policies that relate to their respective responsibilities and that pose legal obligations, limitations, risks, and liabilities for the institution as a whole. Examples include constitutional, statutory, regulatory, and case law; relevant law and orders emanating from codes and laws; and the institution's policies.

AS must inform staff members, appropriate officials, and users of programs and services about existing and changing legal obligations, risks and liabilities, and limitations.

AS must have written policies on all relevant operations, transactions, or tasks that have legal implications.

AS must regularly review policies. The revision and creation of policies must be informed by best practices, available evidence, and policy issues in higher education.

AS staff members must use reasonable and informed practices to limit the liability exposure of the institution and its officers, employees, and agents. AS staff members must be informed about institutional policies regarding risk management, personal liability, and related insurance coverage options and must be referred to external sources if the institution does not provide coverage.

The institution must provide access to legal advice for staff members as needed to carry out assigned responsibilities.

AS must have procedures and guidelines consistent with institutional policy for responding to threats, emergencies, and crisis situations. Systems and procedures must be in place to disseminate timely and accurate information to students, other members of the institutional community, and appropriate external organizations during emergency situations.

AS staff members must neither participate in nor condone any form of harassment or activity that demeans persons or creates an intimidating, hostile, or offensive environment.

AS must obtain permission to use copyrighted materials and instruments. AS must purchase the materials and instruments from legally compliant sources or seek alternative permission from the publisher or owner. References to copyrighted materials and instruments must include appropriate citations.

AS staff members must be knowledgeable about internal and external governance systems that affect programs and services.

Part 7. DIVERSITY, EQUITY, AND ACCESS

Within the context of each institution's unique mission and in accordance with institutional polices and all applicable codes and laws, Assessment Services (AS) must create and maintain educational and work environments that are
- welcoming, accessible, and inclusive to persons of diverse backgrounds
- equitable and non-discriminatory
- free from harassment

AS must not discriminate on the basis of ability; age; cultural identity; ethnicity; family educational history (e.g., first generation to attend college); gender identity and expression; nationality; political affiliation; race; religious affiliation; sex; sexual orientation; economic, marital, social, or veteran status; or any other basis included in institutional policies and codes and laws.

AS must
- advocate for greater sensitivity to multicultural and social justice concerns by the institution and its personnel
- modify or remove policies, practices, facilities, structures, systems, and technologies that limit access, discriminate, or produce inequities
- include diversity, equity, and access initiatives within their strategic plans
- foster communication that deepens understanding of identity, culture, self-expression, and heritage
- promote respect about commonalities and differences among people within their historical and cultural contexts
- address the characteristics and needs of a diverse population when establishing and implementing culturally relevant and inclusive programs, services, policies, procedures, and practices
- provide staff members with access to multicultural training and hold staff members accountable for integrating the training into their work
- respond to the needs of all students and other populations served when establishing hours of operation and developing methods of delivering programs, services, and resources
- ensure physical, program, and resource access for persons with disabilities
- recognize the needs of distance learning students by providing appropriate and accessible services and resources or by assisting them in gaining access to other appropriate services and resources in their

geographic region

AS must ensure inclusion of persons with disabilities in data collection efforts in compliance with local, state/provincial, and federal guidelines.

AS must design studies and collect data so that potential differential outcomes based on diversity among sub-groups can be explored.

Part 8. INSTITUTIONAL AND EXTERNAL RELATIONS

Assessment Services (AS) must reach out to relevant individuals, groups, communities, and organizations internal and external to the institution to
- establish, maintain, and promote understanding and effective relations with those that have a significant interest in or potential effect on the students or other constituents served by the programs and services
- garner support and resources for programs and services as defined by the mission statement
- disseminate information about the programs and services
- collaborate, where appropriate, to assist in offering or improving programs and services to meet the needs of students and other constituents and to achieve program and student outcomes
- engage diverse individuals, groups, communities, and organizations to enrich the educational environment and experiences of students and other constituents

AS must have procedures and guidelines consistent with institutional policy for
- communicating with the media
- contracting with external organizations for delivery of programs and services
- cultivating, soliciting, and managing gifts
- applying to and managing funds from grants

AS must adhere to all institutional policies with respect to the communication of student data.

Regular and effective communication systems for the dissemination of results must be established and maintained with academic and administrative offices, institutional governance bodies, and other appropriate constituencies.

Part 9. FINANCIAL RESOURCES

Assessment Services (AS) must have funding to accomplish the mission and goals. In establishing funding priorities and making significant changes, a comprehensive analysis must be conducted to determine the following elements: unmet needs of the unit, relevant expenditures, external and internal resources, and impact on students and the institution.

AS must demonstrate efficient and effective use and responsible stewardship of fiscal resources consistent with institutional protocols.

Financial resources should be sufficient to support study conceptualization, data collection, data entry and analysis, and the dissemination of assessment and research findings, as well as methodological training for staff.

Part 10. TECHNOLOGY

Assessment Services (AS) must have adequate technology to support the achievement of their mission and goals. The technology and its use must comply with institutional policies and procedures and be evaluated for compliance with relevant codes and laws.

AS must use current technology to provide updated information regarding mission, location, staffing, programs, services, and official contacts to students and designated clients.

AS must explore the use of technology to enhance delivery of programs and services, especially for students at a distance or external constituencies.

When technology is used to facilitate student learning and development, AS must select technology that reflects intended outcomes.

AS must
- maintain policies and procedures that address the security, confidentiality, and backup of data, as well as compliance with privacy laws
- have clearly articulated plans in place for protecting confidentiality and security of information when using Internet-based technologies
- develop plans for replacing and updating existing hardware and software as well as plans for integrating new technically-based or supported programs, including systems developed internally by the institution, systems available through professional associations, or private vendor-based systems

Technology, as well as workstations or computer labs maintained by programs and services for student use, must be accessible to all designated clients and must meet established technology standards for delivery to persons with disabilities.

When providing student access to technology, AS must
- have policies on the use of technology that

- are clear, easy to understand, and available to all students
- provide assistance, information, or referral to appropriate support services to those needing help accessing or using technology
- provide instruction or training on how to use the technology
- inform students on the legal and ethical implications of misuse as it pertains to intellectual property, harassment, privacy, and social networks

Student violations of technology policies must follow established institutional student disciplinary procedures.

Students who experience negative emotional or psychological consequences from the use of technology must be referred to support services provided by the institution.

AS must have access to sufficient data analysis software for efficient data collection, storage, retrieval, and analysis.

Both statistical analysis software and qualitative analysis software should be available.

AS must have timely access to appropriate institutional records.

AS should advocate for integration of institutional databases.

Part 11. FACILITIES AND EQUIPMENT

Assessment Services (AS) must have adequate, accessible, and suitably located facilities and equipment to support the mission and goals. If acquiring capital equipment as defined by the institution, AS must take into account expenses related to regular maintenance and life cycle costs. Facilities and equipment must be evaluated on an established cycle, including consideration of sustainability, and be in compliance with codes and laws to provide for access, health, safety, and security.

AS staff members must have workspace that is well equipped, adequate in size, and designed to support their work and responsibilities. For conversations requiring privacy, staff members must have access to a private space.

AS staff members who share workspace must be able to secure their own work.

The design of the facilities must guarantee the security and privacy of records and ensure the confidentiality of sensitive information.

AS must have sufficient secure storage facilities to maintain materials related to studies.

The location and layout of the facilities must be sensitive to the needs of persons with disabilities as well as the needs of other constituencies.

Part 12. ASSESSMENT AND EVALUATION

Assessment Services (AS) must have a clearly articulated assessment plan to document achievement of stated goals and learning outcomes, demonstrate accountability, provide evidence of improvement, and describe resulting changes in programs and services.

AS must have adequate fiscal, human, professional development, and technological resources to develop and implement assessment plans.

Assessments must include direct and indirect evaluation and use qualitative and quantitative methodologies and existing evidence, as appropriate, to determine whether and to what degree the stated mission, goals, and intended outcomes are being met as effectively and efficiently as possible. The process must employ sufficient and sound measures to ensure comprehensiveness. Data collected must include responses from students and other constituencies, and aggregated results must be shared with those groups. Results of assessments must be shared appropriately with multiple constituents.

AS should model good assessment practices related to its own operations as well as when assisting other entities within the institution.

Results of assessments and evaluations must be used to identify needs and interests in revising and improving programs and services, recognizing staff performance, maximizing resource efficiency and effectiveness, improving student achievement of learning and development outcomes, and improving student persistence and success. Changes resulting from the use of assessments and evaluation must be shared with stakeholders.

General Standards revised in 2011;
AS (formerly Outcomes Assessment and Program Evaluation) content developed/revised in 1986, 1997, & 2008

The Role of Auxiliary Services Functional Areas
CAS Standards Contextual Statement

Student affairs and auxiliary services are names used to describe multi-functional umbrella organizations that, through a variety of means, address the out-of-classroom needs of students, faculty, staff, and visitors on college and university campuses. Auxiliary services typically encompass functional areas that follow business practices and principles in their service design and provision. Student affairs functional areas are more likely to focus upon student life, personal development, student learning, and well-being. This distinction will vary from campus to campus, and each campus determines the heading under which each student service functional area will exist.

Over the past thirty years, several business processes and structures have been introduced to auxiliary services at colleges and universities and to describe the Auxiliary Services Functional Areas (ASFA). The following terms are among those commonly used:

Vendor. A service provider that has permission to deliver a service, using its own resources, consistent with conditions and parameters set forth by the institution. Examples may include ice cream/hot dog trucks, dry cleaning services, and pizza deliverers.

Outsourced Provider. A service provider that is hired by the institution to fill a specific need. Examples may include transportation services, travel offices, and copy services.

Contracted Provider. An entity contractually assigned to provide a continuous service, usually over multiple years, within detailed specifications, on the premises of the institution. Examples may include bookstores and food services.

Licensor. A branded provider of services who contractually sells rights to the institution for use of their name, products, and/or processes, consistent with the institution's and the licensor's guidelines and standards for providing the service. Examples may include fast food outlets and mail packaging/service shops.

Auxiliary (Ancillary) Service. A service wholly owned by the institution, either directly or through a 501(c) 3 subsidiary, which exists solely to serve the institution's students, faculty, staff, and visitors. Examples may include institutionally operated stores and dining programs.

Self-supporting Service. An institutional service that functions net-neutral, under normal circumstances, but may be called upon from time to time to fill an institutional funding need. Examples may be found within any of the aforementioned classifications of service.

Auxiliary services may include but are not limited to housing, student unions, bookstores, dining services, food courts with nationally recognized brands, conference services, health services, campus card programs, parking/transportation, mail services, telecommunications, cable and internet services, student athletics, campus recreation centers, retail outlets, convenience stores, banking services, computer kiosks, other retail outlets, and contracted services. As with all campus services, the ASFA, through its quality, reliability, and ease of use, is expected to positively impact student recruitment and retention and enhance the life experience of students. Organizationally, although many campuses include the ASFA within student life, it may also report through administrative officers or be structured as a separate division of the institution. ASFA may also be structured independently as a 501(c) 3 auxiliary services corporation. When outsourced companies provide services, the auxiliary services role may be as intermediary between private service providers and the institution.

Today's institutions face decreasing state and federal support, pressure to minimize tuition increases, the need to find alternative sources of revenue, an increasingly diverse student population, and calls to improve undergraduate student learning. Within this context are students and parents who want sophisticated and varied campus services. In general, the ASFA faces declining institutional funding and is expected to generate revenue, offer new services, provide excellent customer service, give exceptional value, and use the best technology to deliver services. In addition to following general standards of practice germane to all functional areas in higher education, it is necessary also that the ASFA follows the best business enterprise standards and guidelines to accomplish its mission.

Although ASFA professionals are concerned with providing quality campus services and funding those services, they are equally concerned with supporting the academic mission of their institutions. Among their many roles, ASFA gives students places to live, eat, buy their textbooks and supplies, recreate, meet, study, attend campus events, socialize, and work on campus. As a major source of on-campus student employment, the ASFA plays an important role in promoting individual student success (Indiana University, 1999).

The CAS Standards and Guidelines for ASFA may be used to assess a multi-functional auxiliary service organization, or they may be used to augment the CAS General Standards in development and revision of standards and guidelines for individual functional areas that are structured as auxiliary services.

Reference

Indiana University Center for Postsecondary Research. (1999).
    National Survey of Student Engagement. Bloomington. IN,
    Author.

Contextual Statement Contributors

Jeffrey Pittman, Regent University
Pat Perfetto, University of Maryland
Bob Hassmiller, NACAS CEO

Auxiliary Services Functional Areas
CAS Standards and Guidelines

Part 1. MISSION

Auxiliary Services Functional Areas (ASFA) are multi-functional organizations that address many of the out-of-classroom needs of students, faculty, staff, and visitors on college and university campuses. Typical ASFA follow business practices and principles in their service design, and they operate enterprises that provide goods and services on campus.

ASFA must adhere to ethical, effective, efficient, and sustainable business practices in the provision of relevant, quality, on-campus services that support and enhance the campus environment for students, faculty, staff, and visitors, and provide opportunities for student development.

ASFA must develop, disseminate, implement, and regularly review their missions. The mission must be consistent with the mission of the institution and with professional standards. The mission must be appropriate for the institution's student populations and community settings. Mission statements must reference student learning and development.

Part 2. PROGRAM

The formal education of students, consisting of the curriculum and the co-curriculum, must promote student learning and development outcomes that are purposeful, contribute to students' realization of their potential, and prepare students for satisfying and productive lives.

Auxiliary Services Functional Areas (ASFA) must collaborate with colleagues and departments across the institution to promote student learning and development, persistence, and success.

Consistent with the institutional mission, ASFA must identify relevant and desirable student learning and development outcomes from among the six domains and related dimensions:

Domain: knowledge acquisition, integration, construction, and application

- Dimensions: understanding knowledge from a range of disciplines; connecting knowledge to other knowledge, ideas, and experiences; constructing knowledge; and relating knowledge to daily life

Domain: cognitive complexity

- Dimensions: critical thinking, reflective thinking, effective reasoning, and creativity

Domain: intrapersonal development

- Dimensions: realistic self-appraisal, self-understanding, and self-respect; identity development; commitment to ethics and integrity; and spiritual awareness

Domain: interpersonal competence

- Dimensions: meaningful relationships, interdependence, collaboration, and effective leadership.

Domain: humanitarianism and civic engagement

- Dimensions: understanding and appreciation of cultural and human differences, social responsibility, global perspective, and sense of civic responsibility

Domain: practical competence

- Dimensions: pursuing goals, communicating effectively, technical competence, managing personal affairs, managing career development, demonstrating professionalism, maintaining health and wellness, and living a purposeful and satisfying life

[LD Outcomes: See The Council for the Advancement of Standards Learning and Developmental Outcomes statement for examples of outcomes related to these domains and dimensions.]

ASFA must
- assess relevant and desirable student learning and development
- provide evidence of impact on outcomes
- articulate contributions to or support of student learning and development in the domains not specifically assessed
- articulate contributions to or support of student persistence and success
- use evidence gathered through this process to create strategies for improvement of programs and services

ASFA must be
- intentionally designed
- guided by theories and knowledge of learning and development
- integrated into the life of the institution
- reflective of developmental and demographic profiles of the student population
- responsive to needs of individuals, populations with distinct needs, and relevant

constituencies
- delivered using multiple formats, strategies, and contexts

Where institutions provide distance education, ASFA must assist distance learners to achieve their educational goals by providing access to information about programs and services, to staff members who can address questions and concerns, and to counseling, advising, or other forms of assistance.

Auxiliary Services Functional Areas (ASFA) are expected to provide programs that target specific needs; facilities; items for sale that the ASFA and institution consider appropriate to the campus community; support services for students, faculty members, staff, and visitors; administration; information; clearly stated schedules and hours of operation; value; efficiency; and a fair cost structure.

ASFA, in conjunction with appropriate partners, must
- introduce and orient students to facilities, services, staff members, and functions
- educate students on relevant safety, security, and emergency concerns
- clearly explain policies, procedures, and expectations
- develop an atmosphere conducive to educational pursuits, community, and interpersonal growth, in a safe and non-threatening environment
- provide a balanced variety of social, cultural, and intellectual options that is reflective of the diversity of the campus
- remain transparent and open to dialogue with customers and stakeholders

ASFA, in conjunction with appropriate partners, may be expected to
- establish formal relationships and agreements with other campus service units
- collaborate with specific academic and campus units in design and provision of ASFA services
- provide opportunities for student employment, management training, and leadership development
- contribute to the socialization of students
- be self-funding (self-supporting) and contribute financially to the institution
- adhere to generally accepted practices of accounting, audit, and business records management
- function as an ancillary enterprise (separate but in concert with the academic enterprise)
- supervise contract-managed functional areas and services

Part 3. ORGANIZATION AND LEADERSHIP

To achieve student and program outcomes, Auxiliary Services Functional Areas (ASFA) must be structured purposefully and organized effectively. ASFA must

have
- clearly stated goals
- current and accessible policies and procedures
- written performance expectations for employees
- functional work flow graphics or organizational charts demonstrating clear channels of authority

Leaders with organizational authority for the programs and services must provide strategic planning, supervision, and management; advance the organization; and maintain integrity through the following functions:

Strategic Planning
- articulate a vision and mission that drive short- and long-term planning
- set goals and objectives based on the needs of the population served and desired student learning or development and program outcomes
- facilitate continuous development, implementation, and assessment of goal attainment congruent with institutional mission and strategic plans
- promote environments that provide meaningful opportunities for student learning, development, and engagement
- develop and continuously improve programs and services in response to the changing needs of students served and evolving institutional priorities
- intentionally include diverse perspectives to inform decision making

Supervising
- manage human resource processes including recruitment, selection, development, supervision, performance planning, evaluation, recognition, and reward
- influence others to contribute to the effectiveness and success of the unit
- empower professional, support, and student staff to accept leadership opportunities
- offer appropriate feedback to colleagues and students on skills needed to become more effective leaders
- encourage and support professional development, collaboration with colleagues and departments across the institution, and scholarly contribution to the profession

Managing
- identify and address individual, organizational, and environmental conditions that foster or inhibit mission achievement
- plan, allocate, and monitor the use of

fiscal, physical, human, intellectual, and technological resources
- use current and valid evidence to inform decisions
- incorporate sustainability practices in the management and design of programs, services, and facilities
- understand appropriate technologies and integrate them into programs and services
- be knowledgeable about codes and laws relevant to programs and services and ensure that staff members understand their responsibilities through appropriate training
- assess potential risks and take action to mitigate them

Advancing the Organization
- communicate effectively in writing, speaking, and electronic venues
- advocate for programs and services
- advocate for representation in strategic planning initiatives at appropriate divisional and institutional levels
- initiate collaborative interactions with internal and external stakeholders who have legitimate concerns about and interests in the functional area
- facilitate processes to reach consensus where wide support is needed
- inform other areas within the institution about issues affecting practice

Maintaining Integrity
- model ethical behavior and institutional citizenship
- share data used to inform key decisions in transparent and accessible ways
- monitor media used for distributing information about programs and services to ensure the content is current, accurate, appropriately referenced, and accessible

ASFA leaders should provide all employees with guidance on
- using effective and appropriate strategies for communicating with customers and stakeholders
- staying current with student needs, issues, perspectives, and desires
- cultivating and perpetuating relations with all campus departments
- working with student, campus, and academic leaders and organizations
- exercising safety and the safe provision of ASFA programs, goods, and services
- facility maintenance and efficient use of campus facilities, equipment, and financial and human resources
- employing standards, best practices, and processes

for budgeting, contracting, purchasing, accounting, reporting, auditing, personnel administration, and record keeping
- establishing and maintaining effective relations with community and business agencies and offices
- promoting equal access to services, programs, and facilities for all students, faculty members, staff, and other customers
- implementing effective practices and responses to trends in the respective ASFA functional area community or industry

ASFA must maintain accurate and current documentation on
- operational policies and procedures
- agreements (e.g., contracts, leases) with outsourced service providers and vendors including good faith agreements and amendments
- memoranda of understanding with campus service providers
- standards of performance and other expectations of service providers
- access provisions for clients and employees with disabilities
- day-to-day operations such as fiscal controls, maintenance of physical plant and equipment, provision of services, supervision of personnel, and customer relations

ASFA must consult with members of the campus community regarding its operations, governance, and programming structure, and the formulation of ASFA policies and procedures.

ASFA, in consultation with students, faculty members, staff, administration, and other constituents, must determine and document facility operating polices, budgets, allocations of funds, employment policies, space allocation, products and services to be offered, and hours of operation.

When these areas of consideration are part of a contractual agreement, it may be necessary to address them within pre-determined review or renewal time frames.

ASFA should be organized to
- deliver successful programs, goods, and services that are supportive of the institution's mission
- operate its business enterprises effectively and efficiently
- conduct satisfaction surveys, learning outcomes evaluations, and other assessment
- meet or exceed fiscal expectations, consistent with its organizational structure
- maintain its physical plant resources
- exercise enterprising and entrepreneurial leadership

in a manner that does not detract from the core mission of the institution

Involvement of the campus community may include students, faculty members, staff, visitors, alumni, and other constituents and stakeholders, as appropriate. Typically such involvement is through advisory, governing, and program boards, committees, or through feedback via surveys and focus groups.

Additional areas for consideration in determining structure and management of the ASFA may include:
- availability and characteristics of facilities
- size, nature, and mission of the institution
- size, scope, proximity, and availability of services in the surrounding community
- ratio of residential to commuter/off-campus student populations
- budget and finance expectations
- institutional philosophy, policies, and preferences concerning outsourcing and privatization
- variety of delivery methods being employed or available to the institution
- degree of integration with academic disciplines and academic service units
- goals of ASFA and its partners

Part 4. HUMAN RESOURCES

Auxiliary Services Functional Areas (ASFA) must be staffed adequately by individuals qualified to accomplish mission and goals.

Within institutional guidelines, ASFA must
- establish procedures for staff recruitment and selection, training, performance planning, and evaluation
- set expectations for supervision and performance
- assess the performance of employees individually and as a team
- provide access to continuing and advanced education and appropriate professional development opportunities to improve the leadership ability, competence, and skills of all employees.

ASFA must maintain position descriptions for all staff members.

To create a diverse staff, ASFA must institute recruitment and hiring strategies that encourage individuals from under-represented populations to apply for positions.

ASFA must develop promotion practices that are fair, inclusive, proactive, and non-discriminatory.

To further the recruitment and retention of staff, ASFA must consider work life initiatives, such as compressed work schedules, flextime, job sharing, remote work, or telework.

ASFA professional staff members must hold an earned graduate or professional degree in a field relevant to the position they hold or must possess an appropriate combination of educational credentials and related work experience.

ASFA professional staff members must engage in continuing professional development activities to keep abreast of the research, theories, legislation, policies, and developments that affect their programs and services.

ASFA must have technical and support staff members adequate to accomplish their mission. All members of the staff must be technologically proficient and qualified to perform their job functions, be knowledgeable about ethical and legal uses of technology, and have access to training and resources to support the performance of their assigned responsibilities.

Degree- or credential-seeking interns or graduate assistants must be qualified by enrollment in an appropriate field of study and by relevant experience. These individuals must be trained and supervised adequately by professional staff members holding educational credentials and related work experience appropriate for supervision. Supervisors must be cognizant of the roles of interns and graduate assistants as both student and employee and closely adhere to all parameters of their job descriptions, work hours, and schedules. Supervisors and the interns or graduate assistants must agree to compensatory time or other appropriate compensation if circumstances necessitate additional hours.

Student employees and volunteers must be carefully selected, trained, supervised, and evaluated. They must be educated on how and when to refer those in need of additional assistance to qualified staff members and must have access to a supervisor for assistance in making these judgments. Student employees and volunteers must be provided clear job descriptions, pre-service training based on assessed needs, and continuing development.

All ASFA staff members, including student employees and volunteers, must receive specific training on institutional policies pertaining to functions or activities they support and to privacy and confidentiality policies and laws regarding access to student records and other sensitive institutional information.

All ASFA staff members must receive training on policies and procedures related to the use of technology to store or access student records and institutional data.

ASFA must ensure that staff members are knowledgeable about and trained in emergency procedures, crisis response, and prevention efforts. Prevention efforts must address identification of threatening conduct or behavior of students, faculty and staff members, and others and must incorporate a system for responding and reporting.

ASFA must ensure that staff members are knowledgeable of and trained in safety and emergency procedures for securing and vacating facilities.

Staff must include persons reasonably capable of providing temporary oversight for entire units as well as their specialty, should the need require it.

Staff members must have technical skills, training, and experience pertinent to their work.

All ASFA staff members must understand and comply with financial, legal, personnel, and safety laws, regulations, and policies, as they relate to the core function of their unit.

Administrators in charge of ASFA and facilities must have appropriate education, experience, and credentials to adequately and safely provide a level of management consistent with industry standards and institutional expectations.

ASFA staff members must be knowledgeable about programs, goods, and services offered directly.

ASFA staff members should be familiar with related services offered by other campus agencies.

In addition to providing fair wages, ASFA should treat student employment as an important part of a student's education and intentionally incorporate career-related skills, training, and professional responsibilities into the employment experience.

ASFA should provide living wages to all employees.

A thorough job training program should be provided for all employees and volunteers and should include leadership and personal development opportunities.

ASFA staff members should strive to develop and maintain staff relations in a climate of mutual respect, support, trust, and interdependence. Recognizing the strengths and limitations of each professional staff member, professional development opportunities should be regularly made available, consistent with needs and budgets.

Relationships between ASFA and their shareholders will depend heavily on the effectiveness, cooperation, support,

and behavior of front line service personnel. Training should be closely supervised and monitored, and current industry practices should be evident in service processes, standards, and evaluation.

Desirable qualities of ASFA staff members should include
- knowledge of and ability to use management and leadership principles
- ability to train, influence, supervise, and evaluate student employees and volunteers, particularly at entry levels
- experience in assessment and planning
- interpersonal skills applicable to a variety of cultures
- ability to explain the ASFA mission and articulate the program's relationship to the mission of the institution
- knowledge of and ability to apply student development and learning theories

Desirable qualities of staff members may include
- technical proficiency certification
- knowledge of environmental and industry trends
- effective professional communication and presentation skills
- attributes necessary to meet job-related physical requirements

Part 5. ETHICS

Auxiliary Services Functional Areas (ASFA) must review relevant professional ethical standards and must adopt or develop and implement appropriate statements of ethical practice.

ASFA must publish and adhere to statements of ethical practice and ensure their periodic review by relevant constituencies.

ASFA must orient new staff members to relevant ethical standards and statements of ethical practice and related institutional policies.

Statements of ethical standards must specify that staff members respect privacy and maintain confidentiality in all communications and records to the extent that such communications and records are protected under relevant privacy laws.

Statements of ethical standards must specify limits on disclosure of information contained in students' educational records as well as requirements to disclose to appropriate authorities.

Statements of ethical standards must address personal and economic conflicts of interest, or appearance thereof, by staff members in the performance of their work.

Statements of ethical standards must reflect the responsibility of staff members to be fair, objective, and impartial in their interactions with others.

Statements of ethical standards must reference management of institutional funds.

Statements of ethical standards must reference appropriate behavior regarding research and assessment with human participants, confidentiality of research and assessment data, and students' rights and responsibilities.

Statements of ethical standards must include the expectation that ASFA staff members confront and hold accountable other staff members who exhibit unethical behavior.

Statements of ethical standards must address issues surrounding scholarly integrity.

As appropriate, ASFA staff members must inform users of programs and services of ethical obligations and limitations emanating from codes and laws or from licensure requirements.

ASFA staff members must recognize and avoid conflicts of interest that could adversely influence their judgment or objectivity and, when unavoidable, recuse themselves from the situation.

ASFA staff members must perform their duties within the limits of their position, training, expertise, and competence.

When these limits are exceeded, individuals in need of further assistance must be referred to persons possessing appropriate qualifications.

Promotional and descriptive information must be accurate and free of deception.

ASFA must adhere to institutional policies regarding ethical and legal use of software and technology. Marketing and advertising, when conducted, must be informative, accurate, respectful, non-deceptive, and useful to students, faculty members, staff, and visitors.

Private information disclosed by clients, students, faculty members, staff, and visitors in the course of conducting business (e.g., credit card information, medical conditions) must be treated as confidential unless clearly indicated otherwise by the person providing it.

ASFA representatives must not accept gifts from those who seek to do business or who intend to bid on contracts.

They should avoid activities that give the appearance of favoritism or advantage to any entity seeking to do business with ASFA.

Ethical standards of relevant professional associations should be considered.

ASFA should consider the ethical standards and expectations of suppliers and contractors with whom they do business.

Each ASFA staff member should respect students as individuals, each with rights and responsibilities, each with goals and needs, and with this in mind, should seek to create and maintain environments that enhance learning and personal development.

ASFA should exercise professionalism, expertise, and care in the development and handling of requests for proposals, bids, and contracts related to purchases, lease agreements, contractual service agreements, and any agreement that affects students and/or the institution.

Part 6. LAW, POLICY, AND GOVERNANCE

Auxiliary Services Functional Areas (ASFA) must be in compliance with laws, regulations, and policies that relate to their respective responsibilities and that pose legal obligations, limitations, risks, and liabilities for the institution as a whole. Examples include constitutional, statutory, regulatory, and case law; relevant law and orders emanating from codes and laws; and the institution's policies.

ASFA must inform staff members, appropriate officials, and users of programs and services about existing and changing legal obligations, risks and liabilities, and limitations.

ASFA must have written policies on all relevant operations, transactions, or tasks that have legal implications.

ASFA must regularly review policies. The revision and creation of policies must be informed by best practices, available evidence, and policy issues in higher education.

ASFA staff members must use reasonable and informed practices to limit the liability exposure of the institution and its officers, employees, and agents. ASFA staff members must be informed about institutional policies regarding risk management, personal liability, and related insurance coverage options and must be referred to external sources if the institution does not provide coverage.

The institution must provide access to legal advice for staff members as needed to carry out assigned responsibilities.

ASFA must have procedures and guidelines consistent with institutional policy for responding to threats, emergencies, and crisis situations. Systems and procedures must be in place to disseminate timely and accurate information to students, other members of the institutional community, and appropriate external organizations during emergency situations.

ASFA staff members must neither participate in nor condone any form of harassment or activity that demeans persons or creates an intimidating, hostile, or offensive environment.

ASFA must obtain permission to use copyrighted materials and instruments. ASFA must purchase the materials and instruments from legally compliant sources or seek alternative permission from the publisher or owner. References to copyrighted materials and instruments must include appropriate citations.

ASFA staff members must be knowledgeable about internal and external governance systems that affect programs and services.

ASFA leaders must have specific knowledge of legal issues and requirements that apply to functional areas under their control.

ASFA must continually monitor liability for potentially harmful, wrongful, or negligent activities and situations.

ASFA professionals must be aware of and understand due process, employment procedures, equal opportunity, civil rights, and liberties.

ASFA may be required to carry insurance if not sufficiently covered under the institution's policy.

Part 7. DIVERSITY, EQUITY, AND ACCESS

Within the context of each institution's unique mission and in accordance with institutional polices and all applicable codes and laws, Auxiliary Services Functional Areas (ASFA) must create and maintain educational and work environments that are
- welcoming, accessible, and inclusive to persons of diverse backgrounds
- equitable and non-discriminatory
- free from harassment

ASFA must not discriminate on the basis of ability; age; cultural identity; ethnicity; family educational history (e.g., first generation to attend college); gender identity and expression; nationality; political affiliation; race; religious affiliation; sex; sexual orientation; economic, marital, social, or veteran status; or any other basis included in institutional policies and codes and laws.

ASFA must
- advocate for greater sensitivity to multicultural and social justice concerns by the institution and its personnel
- modify or remove policies, practices, facilities,

structures, systems, and technologies that limit access, discriminate, or produce inequities
- include diversity, equity, and access initiatives within their strategic plans
- foster communication that deepens understanding of identity, culture, self-expression, and heritage
- promote respect about commonalities and differences among people within their historical and cultural contexts
- address the characteristics and needs of a diverse population when establishing and implementing culturally relevant and inclusive programs, services, policies, procedures, and practices
- provide staff members with access to multicultural training and hold staff members accountable for integrating the training into their work
- respond to the needs of all students and other populations served when establishing hours of operation and developing methods of delivering programs, services, and resources
- ensure physical, program, and resource access for persons with disabilities
- recognize the needs of distance learning students by providing appropriate and accessible services and resources or by assisting them in gaining access to other appropriate services and resources in their geographic region

ASFA should provide services and information through a variety of appropriate formats including web sites, e-mail, walk-ins during office hours, telephone, individual appointments, and customer service systems.

ASFA should ensure that services provided through third parties are offered on a fair and equitable basis and in a manner consistent with the mission of the institution.

ASFA may provide manuals, instructions, policies, signs, and training, in one or more languages in addition to English for predominant groups of employees who speak a language other than English.

All institutional units and contractors that provide services to students must share responsibility for meeting the needs of the wide variety of students on campus. Coordinated efforts to promote multicultural sensitivity and the elimination of prejudicial behaviors in all functional areas on campus must be encouraged.

ASFA should make reasonable effort to address and educate the campus community concerning cultural, religious, racial, socioeconomic, and other aspects of identity that are unique to ASFA services, such as food, holiday recognition, and products offered for sale.

Outsourced programs and services are accountable to the institution. As such, a diversity liaison should exist within each outsourced ASFA to help ensure that a diverse workplace and environment exist, consistent with the goals of the institution.

Part 8. INSTITUTIONAL AND EXTERNAL RELATIONS

Auxiliary Services Functional Areas (ASFA) must reach out to relevant individuals, groups, communities, and organizations internal and external to the institution to

- **establish, maintain, and promote understanding and effective relations with those that have a significant interest in or potential effect on the students or other constituents served by the programs and services**
- **garner support and resources for programs and services as defined by the mission statement**
- **disseminate information about the programs and services**
- **collaborate, where appropriate, to assist in offering or improving programs and services to meet the needs of students and other constituents and to achieve program and student outcomes**
- **engage diverse individuals, groups, communities, and organizations to enrich the educational environment and experiences of students and other constituents**

ASFA must have procedures and guidelines consistent with institutional policy for
- **communicating with the media**
- **contracting with external organizations for delivery of programs and services**
- **cultivating, soliciting, and managing gifts**
- **applying to and managing funds from grants**

When services are managed by outside contractors, processes must be in place to ensure that administration of the services remains the responsibility of the institution.

ASFA should share information, initiate and promote program opportunities, encourage staff development, and enhance ASFA program visibility by
- establishing cooperative relationships with procurement, student affairs, and academic departments, and direct service providers such as campus programs, alumni, parking, visitor services, libraries, bookstore, enrollment management, athletics, institutional advancement, campus information, and visitor services
- encouraging staff participation in civic and community organizations such as Rotary, Kiwanis, and Chamber of Commerce as well as involvement in ASFA professional associations
- nurturing cooperative relationships with local, state/provincial, and federal governmental entities

ASFA should adhere to institution-wide processes that systematically involve academic affairs, student affairs, and administrative units such as police, physical plant, and business offices.

ASFA should collaborate with campus agencies, as appropriate, and meet regularly with other service providers to coordinate schedules and facility use and to review services and activities under development.

ASFA should serve as a resource to the campus and community by providing professional advice on market demand, development of new auxiliary services, related business issues, and current industry activities.

ASFA should value marketing as a core function for education about, and promotion of, equal access to ASFA products and services by all constituent groups.

ASFA should provide quality customer service to all constituents and ensure they are fairly represented on ASFA governing and advisory boards.

Students should be the principal beneficiaries of ASFA, although outreach should include all constituents, including faculty members, staff, alumni, visitors, members of the community, and others.

Student government and similar groups should have ongoing involvement with ASFA and their operations.

Student publications and electronic media should be used for communicating information about ASFA.

Relationships among campus administrative staff and employees/representatives of outside contractors should be cultivated and supervised carefully.

Relations with contract service providers should receive close and frequent attention and review. Assessment of these services should be collaborative and continuous.

ASFA should foster partnerships that engage and involve campus and contract service providers in all segments of the campus community.

ASFA should foster initiatives that ensure all service providers become stakeholders in advancing the mission of the institution.

Part 9. FINANCIAL RESOURCES

Auxiliary Services Functional Areas (ASFA) must have funding to accomplish the mission and goals. In

establishing funding priorities and making significant changes, a comprehensive analysis must be conducted to determine the following elements: unmet needs of the unit, relevant expenditures, external and internal resources, and impact on students and the institution.

ASFA must demonstrate efficient and effective use and responsible stewardship of fiscal resources consistent with institutional protocols.

Funds to support the ASFA, insofar as it is possible and desirable, should be generated from pricing set at fair market rates.

For self-support programs
- when net operating income is achieved, ASFA should establish operating reserve funds as a buffer against future shortfalls and capital reserve funds for facilities renewal
- when lower than expected revenue in any one-year results in a deficit, ASFA should access reserve funds to offset the deficit

Financial planning and projections should include budget data for both current and long-term expenditures, including capital expenditures and deferred maintenance costs.

A program of asset management should be in place so that resources are adequate for meeting future repair and replacement requirements for key equipment and facilities.

ASFA should underwrite a fair proportion of overhead costs associated with shared services that support the entire campus.

The institution's budget commitment to ASFA should be sufficient to achieve its mission and to provide appropriate services, facilities, and programs deemed necessary to maintain standards and diversity of programs, goods, and services, commensurate with the organizational structure, aspirations, image, and the reputation of the institution.

ASFA should maintain adequate financial resources to ensure reasonable pricing of services, adequate programming, staffing, proper maintenance, and professional development.

ASFA may be expected to fund specific campus needs and contribute to the general fund.

Part 10. TECHNOLOGY

Auxiliary Services Functional Areas (ASFA) must have adequate technology to support the achievement of their mission and goals. The technology and its use must comply with institutional policies and procedures and be evaluated for compliance with relevant codes and laws.

ASFA should use current and appropriate technology to facilitate, improve, assess, and extend access to its programs, products, services, and facilities.

ASFA must use current technology to provide updated information regarding mission, location, staffing, programs, services, and official contacts to students and designated clients.

ASFA must explore the use of technology to enhance delivery of programs and services, especially for students at a distance or external constituencies.

When technology is used to facilitate student learning and development, ASFA must select technology that reflects intended outcomes.

ASFA must
- **maintain policies and procedures that address the security, confidentiality, and backup of data, as well as compliance with privacy laws**
- **have clearly articulated plans in place for protecting confidentiality and security of information when using Internet-based technologies**
- **develop plans for replacing and updating existing hardware and software as well as plans for integrating new technically-based or supported programs, including systems developed internally by the institution, systems available through professional associations, or private vendor-based systems**

Technology, as well as workstations or computer labs maintained by programs and services for student use, must be accessible to all designated clients and must meet established technology standards for delivery to persons with disabilities.

When providing student access to technology, ASFA must
- **have policies on the use of technology that are clear, easy to understand, and available to all students**
- **provide assistance, information, or referral to appropriate support services to those needing help accessing or using technology**
- **provide instruction or training on how to use the technology**
- **inform students on the legal and ethical implications of misuse as it pertains to intellectual property, harassment, privacy, and social networks**

Student violations of technology policies must follow established institutional student disciplinary procedures.

Students who experience negative emotional or psychological consequences from the use of

technology must be referred to support services provided by the institution.

Part 11. FACILITIES AND EQUIPMENT

Auxiliary Services Functional Areas (ASFA) must have adequate, accessible, and suitably located facilities and equipment to support the mission and goals. If acquiring capital equipment as defined by the institution, ASFA must take into account expenses related to regular maintenance and life cycle costs. Facilities and equipment must be evaluated on an established cycle, including consideration of sustainability, and be in compliance with codes and laws to provide for access, health, safety, and security.

ASFA staff members must have workspace that is well equipped, adequate in size, and designed to support their work and responsibilities. For conversations requiring privacy, staff members must have access to a private space.

ASFA staff members who share workspace must be able to secure their own work.

The design of the facilities must guarantee the security and privacy of records and ensure the confidentiality of sensitive information.

The location and layout of the facilities must be sensitive to the needs of persons with disabilities as well as the needs of other constituencies.

ASFA must periodically review and evaluate equipment and facilities to assess current and future needs.

Regularly scheduled cleaning of public areas must be provided, and grounds associated with ASFA facilities, which may include streets, paved walks, and parking lots, must be clean and well maintained.

Recycling, energy conservation, and sustainability efforts must be implemented throughout the ASFA and be compliant with institutional guidelines, government regulations, and contractual agreements.

ASFA facilities may include retail outlets; dining centers; vending operations; restaurants; residences; recreation and athletic facilities; event venues; office buildings; parking lots and transportation structures; manufacturing and production operations; maintenance shops; and shipping, receiving, and storage centers.

ASFA facilities should be sufficient to meet the needs of the program, consistent with agreements among institutional and community agencies and with students.

Size of facilities should comply with minimum effective service standards established by appropriate professional organizations for each functional area.

Facilities should be accessible, clean, reasonably priced, appropriately designed, well maintained, and have adequate safety and security features.

Facilities with multi-use capability, such as dining rooms and lounges, should be available for campus events and programs at times when they are not needed to support ASFA functions.

New construction projects should be responsive to the current and future needs of the campus community. Decisions about new construction should be based upon clearly defined needs and consistent with the mission of the institution, which may include adherence to institutional standards for sustainability.

Maintenance and renovation programs should be implemented in all operations and should include:
- preventive maintenance and audit procedures to ensure physical safety
- replacement reserves
- timely repair of equipment, vehicles, facilities, and building systems
- modifications to facilities and systems to keep them attractive, effective, efficient, and safe
- sustainable designs and practices whenever feasible

Systematically planned replacement cycles should exist for furnishings, mechanical and electrical systems, maintenance equipment, floor/wall/window treatments, and serving/point of service equipment.

The institution should be reimbursed for campus services, facilities, technology, and equipment that are used to support ASFA.

ASFA should monitor their impact on the community surrounding the campus and should work to maintain amicable relationships with affected non-university entities.

Part 12. ASSESSMENT AND EVALUATION

Auxiliary Services Functional Areas (ASFA) must have a clearly articulated assessment plan to document achievement of stated goals and learning outcomes, demonstrate accountability, provide evidence of improvement, and describe resulting changes in programs and services.

ASFA must have adequate fiscal, human, professional development, and technological resources to develop and implement assessment plans.

Assessments must include direct and indirect evaluation and use qualitative and quantitative methodologies and existing evidence, as appropriate, to determine whether and to what degree the stated mission, goals, and intended outcomes are being met as effectively and efficiently as possible. The process

must employ sufficient and sound measures to ensure comprehensiveness. Data collected must include responses from students and other constituencies, and aggregated results must be shared with those groups. Results of assessments must be shared appropriately with multiple constituents.

Results of assessments and evaluations must be used to identify needs and interests in revising and improving programs and services, recognizing staff performance, maximizing resource efficiency and effectiveness, improving student achievement of learning and development outcomes, and improving student persistence and success. Changes resulting from the use of assessments and evaluation must be shared with stakeholders.

Cost analysis and market research must be conducted at least annually when setting fees for goods and services to be offered to students, faculty members, and staff.

ASFA must maintain accurate and current documentation on program data such as usage rates, peak times of usage, learning outcomes, sales and revenue, student satisfaction, and value contribution.

Both internal and external evaluations and assessments should be encouraged.

Periodic reports, statistically valid research, outside reviews, and other tools measuring student needs and opinions should be utilized.

ASFA should collaborate with institutional research units to generate data that could be useful, such as in projecting contributions to the local economy, increasing student enrollment, or stimulating research.

A representative cross-section of qualified people from campus communities should be involved in reviewing ASFA.

ASFA should generate and disseminate an annual report identifying overall goals, program data, changes in services provided, financial contributions, regular feedback from participants, and opportunities that contribute to the overall effectiveness and quality of the institution.

General Standards revised in 2011;
ASFA content developed in 2007

The Role of Campus Activities Programs
CAS Standards Contextual Statement

One of the first noted formal campus organizations established for the purpose of bringing students together (primarily for debating important issues of the day) was the Oxford Union founded in 1823. The Union's clubs also provided educational opportunities beyond the classroom through such group activities as discussions of literature and poetry and involvement in hobbies and recreational activities. Today, numerous clubs and organizations (hundreds on some campuses) offer students opportunities to learn through their involvement in campus life. There is little debate now that the collegiate experience involves what occurs outside the classroom and that a college education includes more than what goes on in the classroom.

Campus activities describes in part the combined efforts of clubs and organizations established for and/or by students, including, but not limited to, governance, leadership, service, cultural, social, diversity, recreational, artistic, political and religious activities. Many of these efforts focus on programs that serve to educate, develop, or entertain club, organization, or group members, their guests, and the campus community.

Theory of involvement contends that the amount of energy—both physical and psychological—that students expend at their institution positively affects their development during college. Studies indicate that students who are involved in campus life devote considerable energy to their academic programs, spend considerable time on campus, participate actively in student organizations, and interact frequently with other students (Astin, 1996; Kuh, Douglas, Lund, Ramin-Gyurmek, 1994). The campus activities program is one of the vehicles for involving students with the institution.

Although students' efforts are the backbone of campus activities, campus activity advisors serve as the catalysts for these efforts. They plan and implement training for student leaders and group members to assist them in attaining their goals, primarily regarding working with others; provide continuity for student clubs and organizations from year to year; educate students about institution policy, related legal matters, and fiscal responsibility; mediate conflicts between individuals and groups; encourage innovation and responsibility in program implementation; provide opportunities to practice leadership and organizational skills; integrate knowledge gained in the classroom with actual practice; and instruct about ethics, diversity, and other critical values.

The role of campus activity advisors is certainly linked to the quality of a student's involvement experience and thus a student's development. The CAS Standards and Guidelines that follow offer direction for campus activity advisors to create quality campus activity programs that are engaging, developmental, and experiential.

References, Readings, and Resources

American College Personnel Association, College Student Educators International. One Dupont Circle, N.W., Suite 300, Washington, DC 20036-1110. (202) 835-2272; Webpage: http://www.myacpa.org

Association of College Unions International (ACUI), One City Center. 120 W. Seventh Street, Suite 200, Bloomington, IN 47404-3925; Webpage: www.acui.org

Astin, A. W. (1996a). Involvement in learning revisited: Lessons we have learned. *Journal of College Student Development, 37,* 123-134.

Boatman, S. (1997). Leadership programs in campus activities. *The management of campus activities.* Columbia, SC: National Association of Campus Activities Education Foundation.

Cuyjet, M. J. (1996). Program development and group advising. In S. R. Komives & D. B. Woodward, Jr. (Eds.), *Student services: A handbook for the profession* (3rd ed., pp. 397-414). San Francisco: Jossey-Bass.

Julian, F. (1997). Law and campus life. T*he management of student activities.* Columbia, SC: National Association for Campus Activities.

Kuh, G. D., Douglas, K. B., Lund, J. P., & Ramin-Gyurmek, J. (1994). *Student learning outside the classroom: Transcending artificial boundaries.* ASHE-ERIC Higher Education Report No. 8, Washington, DC: The George Washington University, Graduate School of Education and Human Development.

Meabon, D., Krehbiel, L., & Suddick, D. (1996). Financing campus activities. *The management of student activities.* Columbia, SC: National Association for Campus Activities.

Metz, N. D. (1996). *Student development in college unions and student activities.* Bloomington, IN: Association of College Unions International.

National Association for College Activities. 13 Harbison Way, Columbia, SC 29212-3401. (803) 732-6222; Web Page: www.naca.org

Nejman, M. R. (1995). *Diversity, student activities, and their roles in community colleges: Developing an effective program to achieve unity through diversity.* Columbia, SC: National Association for Campus Activities.

Roberts, D. C. (2003). Community building and programming. In S. R. Komives & D. B. Woodard (Eds.), *Student Services: A handbook for the profession* (4th ed.) (pp. 539-554). San Francisco: Jossey Bass.

Skipper, T. L., & Argo, R. (Eds.). (2003). *Involvement in campus activities and the retention of first-year college students.* Columbia, SC: National Resource Center for the First-Year Experience & Students in Transition and National Association of Campus Activities.

Contextual Statement Contributor
Jan Arminio, Shippensburg University, NACA

Campus Activities Programs
CAS Standards and Guidelines

Part 1. MISSION

The purpose of Campus Activities Programs (CAP) must be to enhance the overall educational experience of students through development of, exposure to, and participation in programs and activities that improve student cooperation and leadership while preparing students to be responsible advocates and citizens and complementing the institution's academic programs.

These activities could be intellectual, social, recreational, cultural, multicultural, and spiritual in nature. Programs could pertain to leadership, governance, community service, healthy lifestyles, and organizational development.

CAP must develop, disseminate, implement, and regularly review their missions. The mission must be consistent with the mission of the institution and with professional standards. The mission must be appropriate for the institution's student populations and community settings. Mission statements must reference student learning and development.

CAP must provide opportunities for students to
- participate in co-curricular activities
- participate in campus governance
- advocate for their organizations and interests
- develop leadership abilities
- develop healthy interpersonal relationships
- use leisure time purposefully
- develop ethical decision-making skills
- advocate for student organizations and interests

Part 2. PROGRAM

The formal education of students, consisting of the curriculum and the co-curriculum, must promote student learning and development outcomes that are purposeful, contribute to students' realization of their potential, and prepare students for satisfying and productive lives.

Campus Activities Programs (CAP) must collaborate with colleagues and departments across the institution to promote student learning and development, persistence, and success.

Consistent with the institutional mission, CAP must identify relevant and desirable student learning and development outcomes from among the six domains and related dimensions:

   Domain: knowledge acquisition, integration, construction, and application

- Dimensions: understanding knowledge from a range of disciplines; connecting knowledge to other knowledge, ideas, and experiences; constructing knowledge; and relating knowledge to daily life

Domain: cognitive complexity

- Dimensions: critical thinking, reflective thinking, effective reasoning, and creativity

Domain: intrapersonal development

- Dimensions: realistic self-appraisal, self-understanding, and self-respect; identity development; commitment to ethics and integrity; and spiritual awareness

Domain: interpersonal competence

- Dimensions: meaningful relationships, interdependence, collaboration, and effective leadership.

Domain: humanitarianism and civic engagement

- Dimensions: understanding and appreciation of cultural and human differences, social responsibility, global perspective, and sense of civic responsibility

Domain: practical competence

- Dimensions: pursuing goals, communicating effectively, technical competence, managing personal affairs, managing career development, demonstrating professionalism, maintaining health and wellness, and living a purposeful and satisfying life

[LD Outcomes: See The Council for the Advancement of Standards Learning and Developmental Outcomes statement for examples of outcomes related to these domains and dimensions.]

CAP must
- assess relevant and desirable student learning and development
- provide evidence of impact on outcomes
- articulate contributions to or support of student learning and development in the domains not specifically assessed
- articulate contributions to or support of student persistence and success
- use evidence gathered through this process to create strategies for improvement of programs and services

CAP must be
- **intentionally designed**
- **guided by theories and knowledge of learning and development**
- **integrated into the life of the institution**
- **reflective of developmental and demographic profiles of the student population**
- **responsive to needs of individuals, populations with distinct needs, and relevant constituencies**
- **delivered using multiple formats, strategies, and contexts**

Where institutions provide distance education, CAP must assist distance learners to achieve their educational goals by providing access to information about programs and services, to staff members who can address questions and concerns, and to counseling, advising, or other forms of assistance.

CAP must be comprehensive and reflect and promote the diversity of student interests and needs, allowing especially for the achievement of a sense of self-esteem and community pride.

A comprehensive CAP program should include offerings that vary in type, size, scheduling, and cost.

CAP must be of broad scope, inclusive of all educational domains for student learning and development.

Programs should include activities that
- complement classroom instruction and academic learning
- offer instruction and experience in leadership and working in groups
- promote physical and psychosocial wellbeing
- promote understanding of and interaction with people of one's own culture and other cultures
- foster meaningful interactions between students and members of the faculty, staff, and administration
- build specific group communities and identity with the campus community

CAP must offer and encourage student participation in student-led campus activities.

Additional encouragement can come from club advisors, faculty members, staff, parents, peers, administrators, and others.

CAP should create environments in which students can
- explore activities in individual and group settings for self-understanding and growth
- learn about diverse cultures and experiences
- explore ideas and issues through the arts
- design and implement programs to enhance social, cultural, multicultural, social justice, intellectual, recreational, service, and campus governance involvement
- comprehend institutional policies and procedures and their relationship to individual and group interests and activities
- learn of and use campus facilities and other resources
- plan, market, implement, and assess programs

CAP should enhance the retention and graduation of students and strengthen campus and community relations. Programs and events should be planned and implemented collaboratively by students, professional staff, and faculty members.

CAP must ensure that the institution has a policy for the registration and recognition of student organizations.

CAP must include these fundamental functions: implementing campus programs that add vibrancy to the campus, advising student organizations that implement programs or services, advising student governing organizations, ensuring the proper and efficient stewardship of funds including the student activity fee and institutional allocation, and implementing training, development, and educational opportunities.

Programs may evolve from CAP office or from student organizations and student governing bodies and should add richness to the institution and its integral functions. The CAP should strive to build student institutional loyalty and allegiance while promoting citizenship and civility.
Student and student organizations' awards programs should be based on fair and equitable criteria.

These functions may be achieved directly or in collaboration or consultation with other campus entities.

Programs sponsored by CAP must be produced and promoted according to professional and institutional practices and protocols.

Promotion methods CAP may use include the creation and dissemination, either in print or on-line, of activities calendars, organizational directories, student handbooks, and programming and financial management guides.

Entertainment programs should
- reflect the values stated in the institution and CAP mission statements
- maintain admission fees at levels that encourage widespread student attendance
- implement hospitality requirements that prohibit the provision of alcohol to entertainers where appropriate
- include a constituency-based advisory system for activities planning, implementation, and evaluation, to ensure coordination within the larger campus

academic calendar

Contracts must be signed by an appropriate authority identified by institutional policies and procedures.

CAP should provide guidance and training that enables students to recruit, negotiate with, and select performers.

Advising
CAP must provide effective administrative support for student organizations. Every student organization must have an advisor. The criteria for who may serve as an advisor and the role and responsibilities of advisors must be defined by the institution.

Responsibilities of advisors can include attending organization meetings, meeting with organization officers as a group or individually, overseeing budget and financial transactions, serving as an advocate for the organization, serving as a liaison between the institution and students, assisting the organization in problem-solving, and overseeing the election and/or appointment of new officers. Advising can take place through face-to-face meetings or via telephone, email, instant messaging, or other communication methods.

Advisors should be institutional faculty members, staff, or graduate student employees.

Advisors must be knowledgeable of legal issues and institutional policies, especially regarding risk management.

CAP must provide information and training opportunities for advisors.

CAP staff should be available to provide oversight and to consult and problem-solve with advisors. Advisors who volunteer their time should be recognized by the institution for their contributions.

Advisors should
- be knowledgeable of student development theory and philosophy to appropriately support students and also to encourage learning and development.
- have adaptive advising styles in order to be able to work with students with a variety of skill and knowledge levels
- have interest in the students involved in the organization
- have expertise in the topic for which the student group is engaged
- understand organizational development processes and team building

Student Governance
Student governance groups must have a written mission, purpose, and process for continuity of leadership that is regularly reviewed. Criteria for student involvement must be clear, widely publicized, easily accessible, and consistently followed. Budgeting and fiscal procedures must be clearly defined and must follow all applicable laws. Clearly defined grievance procedures must exist to settle disagreements regarding continuity of leadership, budgeting procedures, and ethics violations by student leaders.

Student governance groups could include undergraduate and graduate student government associations, residence hall associations, campus center governing boards, sports club councils, fraternity and sorority governance councils, media boards, and college councils.

Student governance groups must be encouraged to operate in accordance with institutional values, mission, and policies, and be informed of possible consequences for failure to do so.

Student governance groups may conduct a wide variety of activities and services, including executive, judicial, legislative, business or service functions, and educational or entertainment programming.

Institutions must have policies and procedures for providing an advisor to student governance organizations.

Training, Education, and Development
CAP must ensure that there are training, education, and development opportunities for students involved in student organizations.

Many CAP are responsible for the training, education, and development of students who are involved in student organizations. As outlined in the CAS Standards for Student Leadership Programs, training involves those activities designed to prepare students to assume leadership positions, improve performance of the individual in the role presently occupied, and enhance participants' knowledge and understanding of specific leadership theories, concepts, models, and institutional policies and procedures needed to work effectively. Successful developmental opportunities often occur in an environment that empowers students to mature and develop toward greater levels of leadership complexity.

CAP training, education, and development activities must be delivered by a diverse range of faculty members, students, and staff, using diverse pedagogies, and take place in a variety of ways.

Training, education, and development activities may take the form of retreats; one-on-one conversations; manuals, handbooks, and other publications; workshops and conferences; seminars; mentoring; and for-credit courses.

CAP training, education, and development opportunities must take into account differing student developmental levels.

Students should be trained in leadership concepts and skills, organizational development, ethical behavior, and other skills particular to distinctive programming requirements, such as contracting for entertainment.

Additional information on leadership programs for students can be found in the CAS Student Leadership Programs standards and guidelines.

Part 3. ORGANIZATION AND LEADERSHIP

To achieve student and program outcomes, Campus Activities Programs (CAP) must be structured purposefully and organized effectively. CAP must have

- clearly stated goals
- current and accessible policies and procedures
- written performance expectations for employees
- functional work flow graphics or organizational charts demonstrating clear channels of authority

Leaders with organizational authority for the programs and services must provide strategic planning, supervision, and management; advance the organization; and maintain integrity through the following functions:

Strategic Planning

- articulate a vision and mission that drive short- and long-term planning
- set goals and objectives based on the needs of the population served and desired student learning or development and program outcomes
- facilitate continuous development, implementation, and assessment of goal attainment congruent with institutional mission and strategic plans
- promote environments that provide meaningful opportunities for student learning, development, and engagement
- develop and continuously improve programs and services in response to the changing needs of students served and evolving institutional priorities
- intentionally include diverse perspectives to inform decision making

Supervising

- manage human resource processes including recruitment, selection, development, supervision, performance planning, evaluation, recognition, and reward
- influence others to contribute to the effectiveness and success of the unit
- empower professional, support, and student staff to accept leadership opportunities
- offer appropriate feedback to colleagues and

students on skills needed to become more effective leaders
- encourage and support professional development, collaboration with colleagues and departments across the institution, and scholarly contribution to the profession

Managing

- identify and address individual, organizational, and environmental conditions that foster or inhibit mission achievement
- plan, allocate, and monitor the use of fiscal, physical, human, intellectual, and technological resources
- use current and valid evidence to inform decisions
- incorporate sustainability practices in the management and design of programs, services, and facilities
- understand appropriate technologies and integrate them into programs and services
- be knowledgeable about codes and laws relevant to programs and services and ensure that staff members understand their responsibilities through appropriate training
- assess potential risks and take action to mitigate them

Advancing the Organization

- communicate effectively in writing, speaking, and electronic venues
- advocate for programs and services
- advocate for representation in strategic planning initiatives at appropriate divisional and institutional levels
- initiate collaborative interactions with internal and external stakeholders who have legitimate concerns about and interests in the functional area
- facilitate processes to reach consensus where wide support is needed
- inform other areas within the institution about issues affecting practice

Maintaining Integrity

- model ethical behavior and institutional citizenship
- share data used to inform key decisions in transparent and accessible ways
- monitor media used for distributing information about programs and services to ensure the content is current, accurate, appropriately referenced, and accessible

Opportunities for student learning and development could include activities boards; student governance bodies; academic, performance, cultural, arts, religious, recreational, and special interest organizations; program boards; theatrical productions; and media boards.

The CAP should be aware of the institutional strategic plan and be ready to respond to contemporary conditions and emergency preparedness. These conditions could include response to natural disasters, celebrations of notable achievements, and the changing nature of the student population.

CAP may be organized as an autonomous unit or may be organized in the same unit as the campus union or other programming units.

Part 4. HUMAN RESOURCES

Campus Activities Programs (CAP) must be staffed adequately by individuals qualified to accomplish mission and goals.

Within institutional guidelines, CAP must
- **establish procedures for staff recruitment and selection, training, performance planning, and evaluation**
- **set expectations for supervision and performance**
- **assess the performance of employees individually and as a team**
- **provide access to continuing and advanced education and appropriate professional development opportunities to improve the leadership ability, competence, and skills of all employees.**

Appropriate continuous training opportunities should be offered for all CAP staff members. This can include training in leadership, organizational planning, diversity, ethical decision making, and communication skills. Staff members should seek to enhance their resourcefulness, empathy, creativity, and openness to serving diverse student populations. Staff members should also seek to increase their knowledge of current issues. Training and development opportunities could be achieved through participation with professional organizations.

Depending upon the scope of campus activities programs, the staff may include an activities director, a program coordinator, organization and program advisors, orientation and leadership specialists, a technology specialist, and a bookkeeper/financial officer.

CAP must maintain position descriptions for all staff members.

To create a diverse staff, CAP must institute recruitment and hiring strategies that encourage individuals from under-represented populations to apply for positions.

CAP must develop promotion practices that are fair, inclusive, proactive, and non-discriminatory.

To further the recruitment and retention of staff, CAP must consider work life initiatives, such as compressed work schedules, flextime, job sharing, remote work, or telework.

CAP professional staff members must hold an earned graduate or professional degree in a field relevant to the position they hold or must possess an appropriate combination of educational credentials and related work experience.

Relevant fields may include college student affairs, higher education administration, organizational development, or other related programs. Graduate studies should include courses in the behavioral sciences, management, recreation, student affairs, student development, and research techniques. The CAP may require particular training and experience appropriate to serving distinct campus populations and specialized campus or community needs.

The primary functions of fulltime professional staff members may include the administration and coordination of campus activities programs; assessment of student interests and needs; planning, implementing, and evaluating programs with students; assisting student organizations in planning and implementing their programs; advising student groups; advising student governance organizations; and providing training, education, and development opportunities for students and advisors involved in student organizations.

Campus activities staff members should include the following additional qualifications:
- ability to collaborate with faculty members, administrators, staff colleagues, students, and all other constituencies
- capacity to interpret or advocate student concerns and interests to the campus community
- expertise in the development of students
- ability to create and deliver programs, activities, and services to students and to student groups
- experience in promoting student leadership
- capability of serving as a role model for ethical behavior
- commitment to professional and personal development
- knowledge of group dynamics and ability to work effectively with groups
- ability to supervise a variety of staff including students, support staff, and professional staff
- knowledge of contracting procedures and contract negotiations
- skills in working with agents and performers
- experience in effectively managing budgets
- appropriate expertise in the use of technology
- ability to supervise student staff members
- ability to balance the role of student advocate and the interest of the institution

At least one professional staff member should be assigned responsibility for campus activities programs.

CAP professional staff members must engage in continuing professional development activities to keep abreast of the research, theories, legislation, policies, and developments that affect their programs and services.

CAP must have technical and support staff members adequate to accomplish their mission. All members of the staff must be technologically proficient and qualified to perform their job functions, be knowledgeable about ethical and legal uses of technology, and have access to training and resources to support the performance of their assigned responsibilities.

Degree- or credential-seeking interns or graduate assistants must be qualified by enrollment in an appropriate field of study and by relevant experience. These individuals must be trained and supervised adequately by professional staff members holding educational credentials and related work experience appropriate for supervision. Supervisors must be cognizant of the roles of interns and graduate assistants as both student and employee and closely adhere to all parameters of their job descriptions, work hours, and schedules. Supervisors and the interns or graduate assistants must agree to compensatory time or other appropriate compensation if circumstances necessitate additional hours.

Student employees and volunteers must be carefully selected, trained, supervised, and evaluated. They must be educated on how and when to refer those in need of additional assistance to qualified staff members and must have access to a supervisor for assistance in making these judgments. Student employees and volunteers must be provided clear job descriptions, pre-service training based on assessed needs, and continuing development.

Thorough training should be provided for student employees and volunteers to enable them to carry out their duties and responsibilities and to enhance their personal experiences with campus activities programs.

All CAP staff members, including student employees and volunteers, must receive specific training on institutional policies pertaining to functions or activities they support and to privacy and confidentiality policies and laws regarding access to student records and other sensitive institutional information.

All CAP staff members must receive training on policies and procedures related to the use of technology to store or access student records and institutional data.

CAP must ensure that staff members are knowledgeable about and trained in emergency procedures, crisis response, and prevention efforts. Prevention efforts must address identification of threatening conduct or behavior of students, faculty and staff members, and others and must incorporate a system for responding and reporting.

CAP must ensure that staff members are knowledgeable of and trained in safety and emergency procedures for securing and vacating facilities.

Joint staff development efforts should be encouraged with colleagues in allied programs such as recreational sports, residence hall programming, and special programs for international students and students from traditionally underrepresented groups.

Identification of staff with authority to enter into binding contracts must be made by the institution and clearly disseminated and explained to students and advisors.

Part 5. ETHICS

Campus Activities Programs (CAP) must review relevant professional ethical standards and must adopt or develop and implement appropriate statements of ethical practice.

CAP must publish and adhere to statements of ethical practice and ensure their periodic review by relevant constituencies.

Applicable statements may include principles and standards pertaining to
- civil and ethical conduct
- accuracy of information (i.e., accurate presentation of institutional goals, services, and policies to the public and the college or university community, and fair and accurate representation in publicity and promotions)
- conflict of interest
- role conflicts
- fiscal accountability
- fair and equitable administration of institutional policies
- student involvement in relevant institutional decisions
- free and open exchange of ideas through campus activities programs
- fulfillment of contractual arrangements and agreements
- role modeling of ethical leadership practices

CAP must orient new staff members to relevant ethical standards and statements of ethical practice and related institutional policies.

Statements of ethical standards must specify that staff members respect privacy and maintain confidentiality in all communications and records to the extent that such communications and records are protected under relevant privacy laws.

Statements of ethical standards must specify limits on disclosure of information contained in students' educational records as well as requirements to disclose to appropriate authorities.

Statements of ethical standards must address personal and economic conflicts of interest, or appearance thereof, by staff members in the performance of their work.

Statements of ethical standards must reflect the responsibility of staff members to be fair, objective, and impartial in their interactions with others.

Statements of ethical standards must reference management of institutional funds.

Statements of ethical standards must reference appropriate behavior regarding research and assessment with human participants, confidentiality of research and assessment data, and students' rights and responsibilities.

Statements of ethical standards must include the expectation that CAP staff members confront and hold accountable other staff members who exhibit unethical behavior.

Statements of ethical standards must address issues surrounding scholarly integrity.

As appropriate, CAP staff members must inform users of programs and services of ethical obligations and limitations emanating from codes and laws or from licensure requirements.

CAP staff members must recognize and avoid conflicts of interest that could adversely influence their judgment or objectivity and, when unavoidable, recuse themselves from the situation.

CAP staff members must perform their duties within the limits of their position, training, expertise, and competence.

When these limits are exceeded, individuals in need of further assistance must be referred to persons possessing appropriate qualifications.

Promotional and descriptive information must be accurate and free of deception.

CAP must adhere to institutional policies regarding ethical and legal use of software and technology.

Part 6. LAW, POLICY, AND GOVERNANCE

Campus Activities Programs (CAP) must be in compliance with laws, regulations, and policies that relate to their respective responsibilities and that pose legal obligations, limitations, risks, and liabilities for the institution as a whole. Examples include constitutional, statutory, regulatory, and case law; relevant law and orders emanating from codes and laws; and the institution's policies.

CAP must inform staff members, appropriate officials, and users of programs and services about existing and changing legal obligations, risks and liabilities, and limitations.

CAP must have written policies on all relevant operations, transactions, or tasks that have legal implications.

CAP must regularly review policies. The revision and creation of policies must be informed by best practices, available evidence, and policy issues in higher education.

CAP staff members must use reasonable and informed practices to limit the liability exposure of the institution and its officers, employees, and agents. Staff members must be informed about institutional policies regarding risk management, personal liability, and related insurance coverage options and must be referred to external sources if the institution does not provide coverage.

The institution must provide access to legal advice for staff members as needed to carry out assigned responsibilities.

CAP must have procedures and guidelines consistent with institutional policy for responding to threats, emergencies, and crisis situations. Systems and procedures must be in place to disseminate timely and accurate information to students, other members of the institutional community, and appropriate external organizations during emergency situations.

CAP staff members must neither participate in nor condone any form of harassment or activity that demeans persons or creates an intimidating, hostile, or offensive environment.

CAP must obtain permission to use copyrighted materials and instruments. CAP must purchase the materials and instruments from legally compliant sources or seek alternative permission from the publisher or owner. References to copyrighted materials and instruments must include appropriate citations.

CAP staff members must be knowledgeable about

internal and external governance systems that affect programs and services.

CAP staff members should be well informed about current campus and student legal issues, including risk management, free speech, organization recognition and registration procedures, contractual issues, and student fees.

Part 7. DIVERSITY, EQUITY, AND ACCESS

Within the context of each institution's unique mission and in accordance with institutional polices and all applicable codes and laws, CAP must create and maintain educational and work environments that are

- welcoming, accessible, and inclusive to persons of diverse backgrounds
- equitable and non-discriminatory
- free from harassment

CAP must not discriminate on the basis of ability; age; cultural identity; ethnicity; family educational history (e.g., first generation to attend college); gender identity and expression; nationality; political affiliation; race; religious affiliation; sex; sexual orientation; economic, marital, social, or veteran status; or any other basis included in institutional policies and codes and laws.

CAP must

- advocate for greater sensitivity to multicultural and social justice concerns by the institution and its personnel
- modify or remove policies, practices, facilities, structures, systems, and technologies that limit access, discriminate, or produce inequities
- include diversity, equity, and access initiatives within their strategic plans
- foster communication that deepens understanding of identity, culture, self-expression, and heritage
- promote respect about commonalities and differences among people within their historical and cultural contexts
- address the characteristics and needs of a diverse population when establishing and implementing culturally relevant and inclusive programs, services, policies, procedures, and practices
- provide staff members with access to multicultural training and hold staff members accountable for integrating the training into their work
- respond to the needs of all students and other populations served when establishing hours of operation and developing methods of delivering programs, services, and resources
- ensure physical, program, and resource access for persons with disabilities
- recognize the needs of distance learning students by providing appropriate and accessible services and resources or by assisting them in gaining access to other appropriate services and resources in their geographic region

Outreach efforts could include electronic voting for student elections and student fee assessments and online communities.

CAP staff must design and implement strategies for involving and engaging diverse student populations.

CAP must provide educational programs that emphasize self assessment and personal responsibility for creating and improving relationships across differences.

CAP must support and participate in creating a welcoming and nurturing educational environment for all students.

Part 8. INSTITUTIONAL AND EXTERNAL RELATIONS

Campus Activities Programs (CAP) must reach out to relevant individuals, groups, communities, and organizations internal and external to the institution to

- establish, maintain, and promote understanding and effective relations with those that have a significant interest in or potential effect on the students or other constituents served by the programs and services
- garner support and resources for programs and services as defined by the mission statement
- disseminate information about the programs and services
- collaborate, where appropriate, to assist in offering or improving programs and services to meet the needs of students and other constituents and to achieve program and student outcomes
- engage diverse individuals, groups, communities, and organizations to enrich the educational environment and experiences of students and other constituents

CAP must have procedures and guidelines consistent with institutional policy for

- communicating with the media
- contracting with external organizations for delivery of programs and services
- cultivating, soliciting, and managing gifts
- applying to and managing funds from grants

CAP should encourage faculty and staff members throughout the campus community to be involved in campus activities. Faculty members should serve as valuable resources related to their academic disciplines, especially as lecturers, performers, artists, and workshop facilitators. Faculty and staff members who serve as advisors should work directly with organizations in program and leadership development and should be supported by CAP staff. Faculty and staff members, administrators, and students may serve together on advisory boards to provide leadership for important initiatives.

CAP is a highly visible operation both on and off campus and may be influential in forming public opinion about the institution and creating a positive environment for the entire community. In that regard, to build bridges and connections, CAP staff may volunteer for campus-wide or community-based committees, initiatives, and programs beyond the traditional student affairs areas.

Part 9. FINANCIAL RESOURCES

Campus Activities Programs (CAP) must have funding to accomplish the mission and goals. In establishing funding priorities and making significant changes, a comprehensive analysis must be conducted to determine the following elements: unmet needs of the unit, relevant expenditures, external and internal resources, and impact on students and the institution.

CAP must demonstrate efficient and effective use and responsible stewardship of fiscal resources consistent with institutional protocols.

Methods for establishing, collecting, and allocating student and user fees must be clear and equitable. The authority and processes for decisions relevant to campus activities fees must be clearly established and funds must be spent consistent with established priorities.

Authority for decisions relevant to campus activities fees should rest in large part with students and are typically initiated by a vote of the student body. The fees, once approved through institutional processes, may be managed and allocations distributed by representative student governing bodies or by other allocation boards or committees.

Finance committees of student organizations or student governments should work collaboratively with staff members to establish campus activities fees and priorities. Students and staff members should share responsibility for budget development and implementation according to mutually established program priorities.

Students who have fiscal responsibility must be provided with information and training regarding institutional regulations and policies that govern accounting and the appropriate handling of funds.

CAP should provide educational programs and training to students about the basics of financial management.

Due to the large amounts of money generated by campus activities and the transience of the student population, good business practice dictates that reasonable safeguards be established to ensure responsible management of and accounting for the funds involved. Student organizations may be required to maintain their funds with the institution's business office in which an account for each group is established and where bookkeeping and auditing services are provided. When possible, it is recommended that processes be established to permit individual student organizations to manage their own business transactions. Within this framework, CAP works collaboratively with student organizations on matters of bookkeeping, budgeting, and other matters of fiscal accountability, including contract negotiations, consistent with institutional practices.

Funds for CAP may be provided through state/provincial appropriations, institutional budgets, activities fees, user fees, membership and other specialized fees, revenues from programming or fundraising projects, grants, and foundation resources. Funds may be supplemented by income from ticket sales, sales of promotional items, and individual or group gifts consistent with institutional policies.

In conjunction with students, CAP must establish clear policies and procedures for funding and managing major campus events and entertainment programs necessitating large financial commitments, including concerts, athletic rivalries, homecoming, alumni days, campus traditions, and family weekend.

Part 10. TECHNOLOGY

Campus Activities Programs (CAP) must have adequate technology to support the achievement of their mission and goals. The technology and its use must comply with institutional policies and procedures and be evaluated for compliance with relevant codes and laws.

Technological capabilities should accommodate all common communication systems including email, on-line calendars, electronic portfolios, pod casts, instant messaging, web browsing, telephone and video conferencing, and other emerging technologies.

CAP must use current technology to provide updated information regarding mission, location, staffing, programs, services, and official contacts to students and designated clients.

CAP must explore the use of technology to enhance delivery of programs and services, especially for students at a distance or external constituencies.

When technology is used to facilitate student learning and development, CAP must select technology that

reflects intended outcomes.

CAP must

- maintain policies and procedures that address the security, confidentiality, and backup of data, as well as compliance with privacy laws
- have clearly articulated plans in place for protecting confidentiality and security of information when using Internet-based technologies
- develop plans for replacing and updating existing hardware and software as well as plans for integrating new technically-based or supported programs, including systems developed internally by the institution, systems available through professional associations, or private vendor-based systems

Technology, as well as workstations or computer labs maintained by programs and services for student use, must be accessible to all designated clients and must meet established technology standards for delivery to persons with disabilities.

When providing student access to technology, CAP must

- have policies on the use of technology that are clear, easy to understand, and available to all students
- provide assistance, information, or referral to appropriate support services to those needing help accessing or using technology
- provide instruction or training on how to use the technology
- inform students on the legal and ethical implications of misuse as it pertains to intellectual property, harassment, privacy, and social networks

Student violations of technology policies must follow established institutional student disciplinary procedures.

Students who experience negative emotional or psychological consequences from the use of technology must be referred to support services provided by the institution.

Part 11. FACILITIES AND EQUIPMENT

Campus Activities Programs (CAP) must have adequate, accessible, and suitably located facilities and equipment to support the mission and goals. If acquiring capital equipment as defined by the institution, CAP must take into account expenses related to regular maintenance and life cycle costs. Facilities and equipment must be evaluated on an established cycle, including consideration of

sustainability, and be in compliance with codes and laws to provide for access, health, safety, and security.

CAP staff members must have workspace that is well equipped, adequate in size, and designed to support their work and responsibilities. For conversations requiring privacy, staff members must have access to a private space.

CAP staff members who share workspace must be able to secure their own work.

The design of the facilities must guarantee the security and privacy of records and ensure the confidentiality of sensitive information.

The location and layout of the facilities must be sensitive to the needs of persons with disabilities as well as the needs of other constituencies.

Facilities should be located conveniently and designed with flexibility to serve the wide variety of functions associated with campus activities. Appropriate facilities, accessible to all members of the college community, should be provided, including student organization offices and adequately sized and equipped public performance spaces.

The CAP may be located in the college union. [See CAS Standards and Guidelines for College Unions.] In addition to their traditional programming, social, and service facilities, unions typically house campus activities programs, student organization offices, and related meeting, work, and storage rooms. Campus activities may also take place in residence halls, recreation centers, fraternity and sorority houses, sports facilities, worship centers, and other locations. CAP space should be designed to encourage maximum interaction among students and between staff members and students.

Part 12. ASSESSMENT AND EVALUATION

Campus Activities Programs (CAP) must have a clearly articulated assessment plan to document achievement of stated goals and learning outcomes, demonstrate accountability, provide evidence of improvement, and describe resulting changes in programs and services.

CAP must have adequate fiscal, human, professional development, and technological resources to develop and implement assessment plans.

Assessments must include direct and indirect evaluation and use qualitative and quantitative methodologies and existing evidence, as appropriate, to determine whether and to what degree the stated mission, goals, and intended outcomes are being met as effectively and efficiently as possible. The process must employ sufficient and sound measures to ensure comprehensiveness. Data collected must include

responses from students and other constituencies, and aggregated results must be shared with those groups. Results of assessments must be shared appropriately with multiple constituents.

Assessment instrumentation and methods should be scientifically designed and implemented, and when possible, staff should seek advice and guidance and work collaboratively with institutional research offices.

Results of assessments and evaluations must be used to identify needs and interests in revising and improving programs and services, recognizing staff performance, maximizing resource efficiency and effectiveness, improving student achievement of learning and development outcomes, and improving student persistence and success. Changes resulting from the use of assessments and evaluation must be shared with stakeholders.

The CAP should be evaluated regularly and the findings should be disseminated to appropriate campus agencies and constituencies including appropriate student organizations. Evaluation procedures should yield evidence relative to the achievement of program goals, student learning outcomes, quality and scope of program offerings, responsiveness to expressed interests, program attendance and effectiveness, cost effectiveness, quality and appearance of facilities, student success and retention, and equipment use and maintenance. Data sources should include students, staff, alumni, faculty members, administrators, community members, and relevant documents and records. Student self-assessment should be encouraged through the use of such techniques as electronic portfolios.

Records of program evaluations should be maintained in the office of the administrative leader of the CAP and should be accessible to planners of subsequent programs.

General Standards revised in 2011.
Campus Activities content developed/revised in 1986, 1997, & 2006

The Role of Campus Information and Visitor Services
CAS Standards Contextual Statement

The development of the campus information and visitor services field was a direct result of the increasing diversity, size, complexity, and specialization of institutions of higher learning during the 20th century. This pattern was particularly seen on campuses in the United States and necessitated the development of information centers to address the many informational needs of large and complex campus communities. Often these centers evolved into, or were combined with, visitor services to become comprehensive campus gateway operations providing entry points to institutions for all visitors, including prospective students, alumni, and others. The common objective of campus information and visitor services (CIVS) is to bring people, programs, and campus services and resources together through increased accessibility to information.

Some of the earliest examples of visitor services and centers include the establishment in 1951 of the Visitor Center at the U.S. Military Academy at West Point and the creation of the Visitor Information Center at the University of California at Berkeley in 1965. Historically, these programs originated as extensions of institutional recruitment activities and efforts. One of the earliest examples of specialized information and referral services can be traced to the 1970 establishment of the Campus Assistance Center at the University of Wisconsin-Madison. Specialized information and referral programs were often established as information and rumor control efforts responding to the rapid expansion of campuses and increasing lack of trust in traditional institutional communication methods. By providing inquirers with the information and services they needed, or referring them to the appropriate resources when necessary, these programs were quickly judged to be highly useful in providing improved communication opportunities and increasing the quality of campus life. These early campus information and visitor service programs quickly became permanent campus operations with philosophies focused on access and individualized service. Additionally, many of the programs established clear guidelines for assisting inquirers in a friendly, sensitive manner and assuring appropriate confidentiality. CIVS programs have had a profound impact on campus communities through commitment to the principle of providing inquirers with clear, concise, thorough, and nonjudgmental information and referrals in the most welcoming environment possible.

By the late 1980s, the increasing institutional pressure for better accountability, outreach, and service to the broader campus community resulted in an increase in the number of campus information and visitor services operations. Easy accessibility to appropriate and timely information is a critical component for institutions in reaching instructional, research, and outreach goals. For many constituents, especially during downtimes—evenings, weekends, and breaks—campus information and visitor services programs become the physical embodiment of an institution. Increasing emphasis on quality improvement and service within the higher education community has been another driving force in the growing number of campus information and visitor services programs. The importance of the Internet, mass communication (e.g., radio and cable television), and new media (e.g., streaming video, podcasts) in the provision of information, and the need for support services that can assure the accuracy and relevance of this information, have also served to increase the importance of campus information and visitor services programs. By having access to an easily available and credible information and visitor services program, inquirers are assisted in making well-informed choices, planning wise courses of action, and taking advantage of the available and/or unique resources of the institution and the surrounding community.

These standards and guidelines provide a framework for excellence in the provision of campus information and visitor services. CIVS is the process of linking people who have campus-related questions to the appropriate resources and services. Also, CIVS provides feedback to service providers and discovers gaps and duplication in campus programs and services that should be addressed. This feedback loop can lead to quality service improvements that make campus operations more efficient. Inquiries can comprise anything related to the campus community, such as directions to a campus building or event; how to contact a department or a faculty or staff member; or whom to contact or where to go for issues of a personal nature, to resolve a problem, or to apply for admission. Inquirers may be current students, faculty or staff members, alumni, prospective students and their families, other visitors, or anyone needing information about the institution. CIVS programs serve as a gateway to the institution, providing one-on-one information to inquirers. When a direct answer is not possible, then the goal is to make a referral, paying careful attention to the needs of the inquirer, assessment of appropriate resources and response modes, identification of programs and services capable of meeting those needs, provision of sufficient information about each program and service to help inquirers make informed choices, location of alternative resources when services are unavailable, and active linking of the inquirer to needed services when necessary. The standards and guidelines that follow are intended to assist in the development of CIVS programs that make such high quality service possible.

References, Readings, and Resources

Hefferlin, J.B. L. (1971). *Information services for academic administration.* San Francisco: Jossey-Bass

Alliance of Information and Referral Systems. (n.d.). *Out of the shadows: Information and referral bringing people and services together.* Seattle, Washington: Author.

Alliance of Information and Referral Systems. (n.d.). *The ABC's of I & R: A self-study guide for information and referral staff.* Seattle, Washington: Author.

Collegiate Information and Visitor Services Association (CIVSA), Rutgers - The State University of New Jersey Campus Information Services, 542 George Street New Brunswick, New Jersey. 08901. (732) 932-9342; (732) 932-9359 (fax); Publisher of *The Welcomer.* Web Site: www.civsa.org

Contextual Statement Contributor
Matthew J. Weismantel, Rutgers University, CIVS

Campus Information and Visitor Services
CAS Standards and Guidelines

Part 1. MISSION

The mission of Campus Information and Visitor Services (CIVS) is to facilitate welcome and access to the institution by providing timely and accurate information and appropriate referrals. CIVS offers a primary point of contact with and access to the institution by providing comprehensive contact information and general descriptions for many programs and services of the institution. CIVS must meet the introductory informational needs of the campus community: students, faculty members, staff, prospective students and their family members, alumni, and general visitors.

To accomplish this mission, CIVS must
- be readily accessible
- provide a welcoming environment
- emphasize personal communication and interaction
- provide accurate information and referrals

CIVS must have a strong commitment to student learning and development, contributing generally to institutional and other agency missions, and acknowledging that students play an integral part in mission delivery. This commitment must be reflected in its mission statement and demonstrated through quality supervision, staff development, and performance appraisals.

CIVS must develop, disseminate, implement, and regularly review their missions. The mission must be consistent with the mission of the institution and with professional standards. The mission must be appropriate for the institution's student populations and community settings. Mission statements must reference student learning and development.

Part 2. PROGRAM

Campus Information and Visitor Services (CIVS) must be responsive to the information and visitor needs and interests of all inquirers.

A broad array of programs and services must be available to ensure that accurate informational resources are provided in a timely manner that accommodates the needs of inquirers.

These services may include telephone or other electronic means of contact, or a walk-in facility, such as a visitor or information center, in which the inquirer has one-to-one, human contact and easy access to information resources such as catalogs, calendars, booklets, schedules, fliers, maps, books, and brochures. Additionally, this may include a variety of tour programs, presentation and conference facilities, and other information distribution methods across campus including video and Internet services.

Multiple media approaches must be used to provide information, services, and programs.

Such approaches may involve Internet-based resources including a website, virtual and downloadable applications, email, social networking, signage, maps, telephone information services, or emergency information devices.

The formal education of students, consisting of the curriculum and the co-curriculum, must promote student learning and development outcomes that are purposeful, contribute to students' realization of their potential, and prepare students for satisfying and productive lives.

CIVS must collaborate with colleagues and departments across the institution to promote student learning and development, persistence, and success.

Consistent with the institutional mission, CIVS must identify relevant and desirable student learning and development outcomes from among the six domains and related dimensions:

Domain: knowledge acquisition, integration, construction, and application

- Dimensions: understanding knowledge from a range of disciplines; connecting knowledge to other knowledge, ideas, and experiences; constructing knowledge; and relating knowledge to daily life

Domain: cognitive complexity

- Dimensions: critical thinking, reflective thinking, effective reasoning, and creativity

Domain: intrapersonal development

- Dimensions: realistic self-appraisal, self-understanding, and self-respect; identity development; commitment to ethics and integrity; and spiritual awareness

Domain: interpersonal competence

- Dimensions: meaningful relationships, interdependence, collaboration, and effective leadership.

Domain: humanitarianism and civic engagement

- **Dimensions: understanding and appreciation of cultural and human differences, social responsibility, global perspective, and sense of civic responsibility**

  Domain: practical competence

- **Dimensions: pursuing goals, communicating effectively, technical competence, managing personal affairs, managing career development, demonstrating professionalism, maintaining health and wellness, and living a purposeful and satisfying life**

[LD Outcomes: See *The Council for the Advancement of Standards Learning and Developmental Outcomes* statement for examples of outcomes related to these domains and dimensions.]

CIVS must

- **assess relevant and desirable student learning and development**
- **provide evidence of impact on outcomes**
- **articulate contributions to or support of student learning and development in the domains not specifically assessed**
- **articulate contributions to or support of student persistence and success**
- **use evidence gathered through this process to create strategies for improvement of programs and services**

CIVS must be

- **intentionally designed**
- **guided by theories and knowledge of learning and development**
- **integrated into the life of the institution**
- **reflective of developmental and demographic profiles of the student population**
- **responsive to needs of individuals, populations with distinct needs, and relevant constituencies**
- **delivered using multiple formats, strategies, and contexts**

Where institutions provide distance education, CIVS must assist distance learners to achieve their educational goals by providing access to information about programs and services, to staff members who can address questions and concerns, and to counseling, advising, or other forms of assistance.

CIVS must provide specific information and referral to existing campus programs and services or, when such programs do not exist, actively link inquirers to alternative community and other programs that can meet their specific needs.

CIVS programs must be easily accessible to assist a diverse populations of inquirers in making well-informed choices, planning appropriate courses of action, and taking advantage of available institutional resources.

CIVS must develop and maintain an accurate information retrieval and delivery system of available campus and community resources. This system must be updated regularly to ensure timeliness, accuracy, and comprehensiveness of information.

CIVS must be available at locations and times that meet the needs of the inquirers.

CIVS must provide feedback to appropriate campus officials regarding conditions that may negatively influence an inquirer's interaction with the institution and propose interventions to remedy such conditions.

Feedback topics may include statistics, data analysis, relevant documentation of service use (e.g., identifying unmet needs, gaps, and services duplication), service quality at other campus locations, and inquirer characteristics.

CIVS must strive to assist inquirers in a friendly, caring, sensitive, and non-judgmental manner and provide clear, concise information. CIVS must protect the privacy of individuals within the campus community from inappropriate inquiry.

CIVS must establish and maintain a planned program of activities to increase campus and community awareness of its services, mission, goals, and objectives.

Campus information and visitor services may include

- campus orientation and tour programs
- display and presentation space
- broadcast and electronic informational resources and support
- visitor reception space including appropriate support services and facilities adequate in size and scope to meet the volume of inquirers to be assisted

CIVS should be a principal provider of structure and content to the institution's on-line information systems.

A range of information should be provided to inquirers, including brief responses, such as names or phone numbers, as well as details about an organization's policies and procedures.

Program activities may include

- participation in training programs of other offices and departments
- provision of printed materials such as brochures, posters, directional information and exhibits
- public service announcements
- hosting informational tours and special events for diverse audiences
- information-based Web site
- role as a resource for other campus and community

support services

Part 3. ORGANIZATION AND LEADERSHIP

To achieve student and program outcomes, Campus Information and Visitor Services (CIVS) must be structured purposefully and organized effectively. CIVS must have

- clearly stated goals
- current and accessible policies and procedures
- written performance expectations for employees
- functional work flow graphics or organizational charts demonstrating clear channels of authority

Leaders with organizational authority for the programs and services must provide strategic planning, supervision, and management; advance the organization; and maintain integrity through the following functions:

Strategic Planning
- articulate a vision and mission that drive short- and long-term planning
- set goals and objectives based on the needs of the population served and desired student learning or development and program outcomes
- facilitate continuous development, implementation, and assessment of goal attainment congruent with institutional mission and strategic plans
- promote environments that provide meaningful opportunities for student learning, development, and engagement
- develop and continuously improve programs and services in response to the changing needs of students served and evolving institutional priorities
- intentionally include diverse perspectives to inform decision making

Supervising
- manage human resource processes including recruitment, selection, development, supervision, performance planning, evaluation, recognition, and reward
- influence others to contribute to the effectiveness and success of the unit
- empower professional, support, and student staff to accept leadership opportunities
- offer appropriate feedback to colleagues and students on skills needed to become more effective leaders
- encourage and support professional development, collaboration with colleagues and departments across the institution, and

scholarly contribution to the profession

Managing
- identify and address individual, organizational, and environmental conditions that foster or inhibit mission achievement
- plan, allocate, and monitor the use of fiscal, physical, human, intellectual, and technological resources
- use current and valid evidence to inform decisions
- incorporate sustainability practices in the management and design of programs, services, and facilities
- understand appropriate technologies and integrate them into programs and services
- be knowledgeable about codes and laws relevant to programs and services and ensure that staff members understand their responsibilities through appropriate training
- assess potential risks and take action to mitigate them

Advancing the Organization
- communicate effectively in writing, speaking, and electronic venues
- advocate for programs and services
- advocate for representation in strategic planning initiatives at appropriate divisional and institutional levels
- initiate collaborative interactions with internal and external stakeholders who have legitimate concerns about and interests in the functional area
- facilitate processes to reach consensus where wide support is needed
- inform other areas within the institution about issues affecting practice

Maintaining Integrity
- model ethical behavior and institutional citizenship
- share data used to inform key decisions in transparent and accessible ways
- monitor media used for distributing information about programs and services to ensure the content is current, accurate, appropriately referenced, and accessible

Campus Information and Visitor Services (CIVS) must be delivered in an atmosphere of staff teamwork, assessment, and continuous improvement.

The information retrieval and delivery system used by CIVS must be organized according to a standardized search system. The information system must have the capacity to accept changes in a very short time frame for information that may change in between

regularly scheduled updates.

CIVS must have well developed policies regarding the type, breadth, and currency of information contained in the information retrieval and delivery system.

CIVS must develop and maintain accurate, up-to-date information about available campus resources and procedures for verifying accuracy.

Informational resources should be profiled to include
- official name, common name, and acronym address (i.e., room, building name, street, city, zip code)
- e-mail address
- telephone number, fax number, hours and days of service
- Internet addresses
- type and description of service(s) provided
- population(s) served
- eligibility guidelines
- intake procedures
- required documents
- cost
- waiting period for service
- contact person
- auspices (i.e., city, state/province, private, social service, campus)
- date of last update

CIVS must establish and use a system of collecting and organizing inquirer data for appropriate referral and feedback to the campus community.

CIVS should pursue meaningful research to review and improve programs and services. Members of the campus community should be involved in the review of these findings, as well as in the design and governance of campus information and visitor services. Students, faculty members, staff, and appropriate external agencies should be involved through committees, councils, and boards.

Part 4. HUMAN RESOURCES

Campus Information and Visitor Services (CIVS) must be staffed adequately by individuals qualified to accomplish mission and goals.
Within institutional guidelines, CIVS must
- **establish procedures for staff recruitment and selection, training, performance planning, and evaluation**
- **set expectations for supervision and performance**
- **assess the performance of employees individually and as a team**
- **provide access to continuing and advanced education and appropriate professional development opportunities to improve the leadership ability, competence, and skills of all employees.**

Continuing staff development experiences should include in-service training programs, professional conferences, workshops, and on-site training to enhance employee familiarization with the institution's visitor destinations, programs, services, and employees.

CIVS staff positions must be filled based on a defined set of qualifications such as level of education, work experience, and personal characteristics (e.g., integrity, communication skills, leadership ability).

CIVS must maintain position descriptions for all staff members.

To create a diverse staff, CIVS must institute recruitment and hiring strategies that encourage individuals from under-represented populations to apply for positions.

CIVS must develop promotion practices that are fair, inclusive, proactive, and non-discriminatory.

To further the recruitment and retention of staff, CIVS must consider work life initiatives, such as compressed work schedules, flextime, job sharing, remote work, or telework.

CIVS professional staff members must hold an earned graduate or professional degree in a field relevant to the position they hold or must possess an appropriate combination of educational credentials and related work experience.

CIVS professional staff members must engage in continuing professional development activities to keep abreast of the research, theories, legislation, policies, and developments that affect their programs and services.

CIVS must have technical and support staff members adequate to accomplish their mission. All members of the staff must be technologically proficient and qualified to perform their job functions, be knowledgeable about ethical and legal uses of technology, and have access to training and resources to support the performance of their assigned responsibilities.

Degree- or credential-seeking interns or graduate assistants must be qualified by enrollment in an appropriate field of study and by relevant experience. These individuals must be trained and supervised adequately by professional staff members holding educational credentials and related work experience appropriate for supervision. Supervisors must be cognizant of the roles of interns and graduate assistants as both student and employee and closely adhere to all parameters of their job descriptions, work hours, and schedules. Supervisors and the interns or graduate assistants must agree to compensatory time

or other appropriate compensation if circumstances necessitate additional hours.

Student employees and volunteers must be carefully selected, trained, supervised, and evaluated. They must be educated on how and when to refer those in need of additional assistance to qualified staff members and must have access to a supervisor for assistance in making these judgments. Student employees and volunteers must be provided clear job descriptions, pre-service training based on assessed needs, and continuing development.

All CIVS staff members, including student employees and volunteers, must receive specific training on institutional policies pertaining to functions or activities they support and to privacy and confidentiality policies and laws regarding access to student records and other sensitive institutional information.

All CIVS staff members must receive training on policies and procedures related to the use of technology to store or access student records and institutional data.

A formal training program must be required for all staff, especially those who will be providing direct service.

Training programs should include experiences for initial employee orientations as well as on-the-job training, in-service group training, supervisory coaching, and individualized training based on employee needs.

Staff-training programs should include
- emergency /crisis management
- strategies for understanding campus and community resources
- information retrieval, delivery and data collection
- overview of mission, vision, strategic goals, role, purpose, function, structure, policies, and procedures of the unit
- student development theory and practice
- customer service and basic communication skills such as interviewing, listening, empathy, clarification and problem-solving
- strategies for supporting persons with disabilities and language differences

CIVS must ensure that staff members are knowledgeable about and trained in emergency procedures, crisis response, and prevention efforts. Prevention efforts must address identification of threatening conduct or behavior of students, faculty and staff members, and others and must incorporate a system for responding and reporting.

CIVS must ensure that staff members are knowledgeable of and trained in safety and emergency procedures for securing and vacating facilities.

Every CIVS staff member must show respect for all inquirers.

Periodic formal written evaluations of CIVS staff must be conducted and kept on record.

Part 5. ETHICS

Campus Information and Visitor Services (CIVS) must review relevant professional ethical standards and must adopt or develop and implement appropriate statements of ethical practice.

CIVS must publish and adhere to statements of ethical practice and ensure their periodic review by relevant constituencies.

CIVS must orient new staff members to relevant ethical standards and statements of ethical practice and related institutional policies.

Statements of ethical standards must specify that staff members respect privacy and maintain confidentiality in all communications and records to the extent that such communications and records are protected under relevant privacy laws.

Statements of ethical standards must specify limits on disclosure of information contained in students' educational records as well as requirements to disclose to appropriate authorities.

Statements of ethical standards must address personal and economic conflicts of interest, or appearance thereof, by staff members in the performance of their work.

Statements of ethical standards must reflect the responsibility of staff members to be fair, objective, and impartial in their interactions with others.

Statements of ethical standards must reference management of institutional funds.

Statements of ethical standards must reference appropriate behavior regarding research and assessment with human participants, confidentiality of research and assessment data, and students' rights and responsibilities.

Statements of ethical standards must include the expectation that CIVS staff members confront and hold accountable other staff members who exhibit unethical behavior.

Statements of ethical standards must address issues surrounding scholarly integrity.

As appropriate, CIVS staff members must inform users of programs and services of ethical obligations and limitations emanating from codes and laws or from licensure requirements.

CIVS staff members must recognize and avoid conflicts of interest that could adversely influence their judgment or objectivity and, when unavoidable, recuse themselves from the situation.

CIVS staff members must perform their duties within the limits of their position, training, expertise, and competence.

When these limits are exceeded, individuals in need of further assistance must be referred to persons possessing appropriate qualifications.

Promotional and descriptive information must be accurate and free of deception.

CIVS must adhere to institutional policies regarding ethical and legal use of software and technology.

Part 6. LAW, POLICY, AND GOVERNANCE

Campus Information and Visitor Services (CIVS) must be in compliance with laws, regulations, and policies that relate to their respective responsibilities and that pose legal obligations, limitations, risks, and liabilities for the institution as a whole. Examples include constitutional, statutory, regulatory, and case law; relevant law and orders emanating from codes and laws; and the institution's policies.

CIVS must inform staff members, appropriate officials, and users of programs and services about existing and changing legal obligations, risks and liabilities, and limitations.

CIVS must have written policies on all relevant operations, transactions, or tasks that have legal implications.

CIVS must regularly review policies. The revision and creation of policies must be informed by best practices, available evidence, and policy issues in higher education.

CIVS staff members must use reasonable and informed practices to limit the liability exposure of the institution and its officers, employees, and agents. CIVS staff members must be informed about institutional policies regarding risk management, personal liability, and related insurance coverage options and must be referred to external sources if the institution does not provide coverage.

The institution must provide access to legal advice for staff members as needed to carry out assigned responsibilities.

CIVS must have procedures and guidelines consistent with institutional policy for responding to threats, emergencies, and crisis situations. Systems and procedures must be in place to disseminate timely and accurate information to students, other members of the institutional community, and appropriate external organizations during emergency situations.

CIVS staff members must neither participate in nor condone any form of harassment or activity that demeans persons or creates an intimidating, hostile, or offensive environment.

CIVS must obtain permission to use copyrighted materials and instruments. CIVS must purchase the materials and instruments from legally compliant sources or seek alternative permission from the publisher or owner. References to copyrighted materials and instruments must include appropriate citations.

CIVS staff members must be knowledgeable about internal and external governance systems that affect programs and services.

Part 7. DIVERSITY, EQUITY, AND ACCESS

Within the context of each institution's unique mission and in accordance with institutional polices and all applicable codes and laws, Campus Information and Visitor Services (CIVS) must create and maintain educational and work environments that are
- welcoming, accessible, and inclusive to persons of diverse backgrounds
- equitable and non-discriminatory
- free from harassment

CIVS must not discriminate on the basis of ability; age; cultural identity; ethnicity; family educational history (e.g., first generation to attend college); gender identity and expression; nationality; political affiliation; race; religious affiliation; sex; sexual orientation; economic, marital, social, or veteran status; or any other basis included in institutional policies and codes and laws.

CIVS must
- advocate for greater sensitivity to multicultural and social justice concerns by the institution and its personnel
- modify or remove policies, practices, facilities, structures, systems, and technologies that limit access, discriminate, or produce inequities
- include diversity, equity, and access initiatives within their strategic plans
- foster communication that deepens understanding of identity, culture, self-expression, and heritage

- promote respect about commonalities and differences among people within their historical and cultural contexts
- address the characteristics and needs of a diverse population when establishing and implementing culturally relevant and inclusive programs, services, policies, procedures, and practices
- provide staff members with access to multicultural training and hold staff members accountable for integrating the training into their work
- respond to the needs of all students and other populations served when establishing hours of operation and developing methods of delivering programs, services, and resources
- ensure physical, program, and resource access for persons with disabilities
- recognize the needs of distance learning students by providing appropriate and accessible services and resources or by assisting them in gaining access to other appropriate services and resources in their geographic region

Part 8. INSTITUTIONAL AND EXTERNAL RELATIONS

Campus Information and Visitor Services (CIVS) must reach out to relevant individuals, groups, communities, and organizations internal and external to the institution to

- establish, maintain, and promote understanding and effective relations with those that have a significant interest in or potential effect on the students or other constituents served by the programs and services
- garner support and resources for programs and services as defined by the mission statement
- disseminate information about the programs and services
- collaborate, where appropriate, to assist in offering or improving programs and services to meet the needs of students and other constituents and to achieve program and student outcomes
- engage diverse individuals, groups, communities, and organizations to enrich the educational environment and experiences of students and other constituents

CIVS must have procedures and guidelines consistent with institutional policy for

- communicating with the media
- contracting with external organizations for delivery of programs and services

- cultivating, soliciting, and managing gifts
- applying to and managing funds from grants

CIVS should collaborate closely with other campus offices and external agencies to ensure accuracy, timeliness, and reliability of information being provided to inquirers.

When appropriate, inquirers should be referred to other resources, and staff may actively participate in this linking process. This referral process is often integrated with information dissemination, intervention, and advocacy. Inquirers should be encouraged to re-contact the CIVS if additional information or assistance is needed.

Within institutional guidelines, CIVS should intervene and advocate for inquirers when information is inaccurate or misleading and/or inquirer needs have not been addressed satisfactorily. Follow-up on more complex problem situations should occur to determine the extent to which inquirer needs have been met.

Part 9. FINANCIAL RESOURCES

Campus Information and Visitor Services (CIVS) must have funding to accomplish the mission and goals. In establishing funding priorities and making significant changes, a comprehensive analysis must be conducted to determine the following elements: unmet needs of the unit, relevant expenditures, external and internal resources, and impact on students and the institution.

CIVS must demonstrate efficient and effective use and responsible stewardship of fiscal resources consistent with institutional protocols.

Institutional funds for CIVS should be allocated on a permanent basis.

In addition to institutional commitment of general funds, other funding sources may be considered including state/provincial appropriations, federal resources, fees and generated revenue, local community funding, and donations.

Financial resources should be sufficient to provide inquirers with high quality personal interaction as well as print and electronic information.

Part 10. TECHNOLOGY

Campus Information and Visitor Services (CIVS) must have adequate technology to support the achievement of their mission and goals. The technology and its use must comply with institutional policies and procedures and be evaluated for compliance with relevant codes and laws.

CIVS must use current technology to provide updated information regarding mission, location, staffing, programs, services, and official contacts to students and designated clients.

CIVS must explore the use of technology to enhance delivery of programs and services, especially for students at a distance or external constituencies.

When technology is used to facilitate student learning and development, CIVS must select technology that reflects intended outcomes.

CIVS must

- maintain policies and procedures that address the security, confidentiality, and backup of data, as well as compliance with privacy laws
- have clearly articulated plans in place for protecting confidentiality and security of information when using Internet-based technologies
- develop plans for replacing and updating existing hardware and software as well as plans for integrating new technically-based or supported programs, including systems developed internally by the institution, systems available through professional associations, or private vendor-based systems

Technology, as well as workstations or computer labs maintained by programs and services for student use, must be accessible to all designated clients and must meet established technology standards for delivery to persons with disabilities.

When providing student access to technology, CIVS must

- have policies on the use of technology that are clear, easy to understand, and available to all students
- provide assistance, information, or referral to appropriate support services to those needing help accessing or using technology
- provide instruction or training on how to use the technology
- inform students on the legal and ethical implications of misuse as it pertains to intellectual property, harassment, privacy, and social networks

Student violations of technology policies must follow established institutional student disciplinary procedures.

Students who experience negative emotional or psychological consequences from the use of technology must be referred to support services provided by the institution.

Part 11. FACILITIES AND EQUIPMENT

Campus Information and Visitor Services (CIVS) must have adequate, accessible, and suitably located facilities and equipment to support the mission and goals. If acquiring capital equipment as defined by the institution, CIVS must take into account expenses related to regular maintenance and life cycle costs. Facilities and equipment must be evaluated on an established cycle, including consideration of sustainability, and be in compliance with codes and laws to provide for access, health, safety, and security.

CIVS staff members must have workspace that is well equipped, adequate in size, and designed to support their work and responsibilities. For conversations requiring privacy, staff members must have access to a private space.

CIVS staff members who share workspace must be able to secure their own work.

The design of the facilities must guarantee the security and privacy of records and ensure the confidentiality of sensitive information.

The location and layout of the facilities must be sensitive to the needs of persons with disabilities as well as the needs of other constituencies.

CIVS must play an active role in the design and decision-making process for campus signage.

The CIVS facility should include space for confidential interviewing, display of materials, visitor reception, and information and referral operations. State-of-the-art telephone and computer capability should be included.

The CIVS facility should be accessible to and by public transportation and be at a location that can best represent the "front door" of the institution.

Part 12. ASSESSMENT AND EVALUATION

Campus Information and Visitor Services (CIVS) must have a clearly articulated assessment plan to document achievement of stated goals and learning outcomes, demonstrate accountability, provide evidence of improvement, and describe resulting changes in programs and services.

CIVS must have adequate fiscal, human, professional development, and technological resources to develop and implement assessment plans.

Assessments must include direct and indirect evaluation and use qualitative and quantitative methodologies and existing evidence, as appropriate, to determine whether and to what degree the stated mission, goals, and intended outcomes are being met as effectively and efficiently as possible. The process must employ sufficient and sound measures to ensure comprehensiveness. Data collected must include responses from students and other constituencies, and aggregated results must be shared with those groups. **Results of assessments must be shared appropriately with multiple constituents.**

Results of assessments and evaluations must be used to identify needs and interests in revising and improving programs and services, recognizing staff performance, maximizing resource efficiency and effectiveness, improving student achievement of learning and development outcomes, and improving student persistence and success. Changes resulting from the use of assessments and evaluation must be shared with stakeholders.

CIVS must maintain an on-going process to collect inquirer use and inquirer satisfaction information.

General Standards revised in 2011;
CIVS content developed/revised in 2000 & 2010

The Role of Campus Police and Security Programs

CAS Standards Contextual Statement

The issue of crime on American college and university campuses has been around since at least the early 19th century when a series of student disruptions rocked the campuses of a number of colleges (Gregory, 2001). The image of campus crime in recent years is in stark relief to former impressions due to high-profile incidents on campus, the perception that institutions were hiding campus crime (Gregory, 2002), and suggestions that university officials needed to take more responsibility for the safety of their students (Bickel & Lake, 1999).

Campus Police and Security refers to that agency and those individuals who, either as employees of the institution or through some sort of contracted service, provide for a safer campus environment, protect members of the university community, and may enforce institutional policy and relevant laws and codes. There are a wide variety of arrangements on college and university campuses in the United States and Canada by which these services are provided. These may include "sworn" police agencies at public institutions that are operated as any municipal, state, or province police agency may be and in which officers are trained similarly. On some independent institution campuses, the agency may operate under state or provincial law as "company police" or "special deputies" who have law enforcement authority but whose authority is limited to the campus itself. Some institutions contract with local law enforcement agencies to provide services within the borders of the campus, hire private security companies to protect the university, or employ their own security officers who do not have arrest authority. Finally, some universities use a combination of these methods to provide services on and around campus.

In the United States, all campus police and security programs operating on university campuses that receive federal funds must adhere to the *Jeanne Clery Disclosure of Campus Security Policy and Campus Crime Statistics Act* (2000). This federal law, originally passed in 1990, requires the reporting of campus crime statistics in certain categories, includes reporting on campus fire safety, requires the provision of certain information about campus policies, and has a number of other requirements with which university officials must comply. In addition, all U.S. states and Canadian provinces have laws and regulations that control how and under what types of arrangements campus police and security may operate.

The United States Department of Education has responsibility for enforcement of the Clery Act (http://www2.ed.gov/admins/lead/safety/campus.html), may fine institutions for violation of the Act, and in extreme cases may remove the authority of institutions to receive federal funds. The U.S.

Department of Education also provides a great deal of information to assist university authorities to make their campuses safer and to comply with the Act.

The family of Jeanne Clery, for whom the Clery Act is named, set up a non-profit advocacy group called Security on Campus, Inc. (2012). This group monitors compliance of institutions with the act and provides information regarding campus law enforcement and safety issues. This group also advocates for strict enforcement of the law and lobbies Congress for additional law to improve safety on American university campuses.

The International Association of Campus Law Enforcement Administrators (IACLEA) advances public safety for educational institutions by providing educational resources, advocacy, and professional development services. IACLEA is the leading voice for the campus public safety community.

IACLEA was created by eleven college and university security directors who met in November of 1958 at Arizona State University to discuss job challenges and mutual problems and to create a clearinghouse for information and issues shared by campus public safety directors across the country. Today, IACLEA membership represents more than 1,200 colleges and universities in 20 countries. In addition to the colleges and universities that are institutional members, IACLEA has 2,000 individual memberships held by campus law enforcement staff, criminal justice faculty members, and municipal chiefs of police" (IACLEA, 2012).

According to Fisher and Sloan (2007), "[t]he past 20 or so years ha[ve] seen key development in the context of campus security: the *professionalization* of the individuals and departments charged with the sometimes daunting task of reducing opportunities for on-campus victimization, responding to calls for assistance, and providing services to crime victims. The professionalization has touched almost all aspects of campus security and has resulted in significant changes in, and upgrades to, security policies" (p. 14). The authors indicated that the movement from service as a "night watchman" to the current role on many campuses of high-tech police departments, which may also have "information security and infrastructure protection" (p. 14) responsibilities, has been a dramatic role change.

Sloan and Lanier (2007) described the evolution of community policing on college and university campuses and noted other current trends that related to campus police and security policies. Bromley (2007) explained the evolution of campus police and security services in some detail and laid out his view of the modern campus police and security agency. CAS standards should guide campus police and security programs to best practices in their new roles.

References, Readings, and Resources

Bickel, R. D., & Lake, P. F. (1999). *The rights and responsibilities of the modern university: Who assumes the risks of college life?* Chapel Hill, N.C.: Carolina Academic Press.

Bromley, M. L. (2007). The evolution of campus policing: Different models for different eras. In Fisher, B. S., & Sloan III, J. J. (Eds.). *Campus crime: Legal, social and policy issues* (2nd ed., pp. 280-304). Springfield, IL: Charles C. Thomas.

Fisher, B. S., & Sloan III, J. J. (Eds.). (2007). Campus crime policy: Legal, social and security contexts (pp 3-22) in *Campus crime: Legal, social and policy issues* (2nd ed., pp. 3-22). Springfield, IL: Charles C. Thomas.

Fisher, B. S., Hartman, J. L., Cullen, F. T., & Turner, M. G. (2002). Making campuses safer for students: The Clery Act as a symbolic legal reform. *Stetson Law Review, 32*(1), 61-89. Retrieved from http://www.law.stetson.edu/lawrev/abstracts/PDF/32-1Fisher.pdf

Gregory, D. E. (2001). Crime on campus: Compliance, liability and safety. *Campus Law Enforcement Journal, 31*(4), 27-32.

Gregory, D. E. (2002, November-December). Hiding crime on campus: Current reality or paranoia from the past? *Campus Safety and Student Development, 4*(2), 17, 30-32.

Gregory, D. E., & Janosik, S. M. (2002). The Clery Act: How effective is it? Perceptions from the field - The current state of the research and recommendations for improvement. *Stetson Law Review, 32*(1), 7-59. Retrieved from http://www.law.stetson.edu/lawrev/abstracts/PDF/32-1Gregory.pdf

International Association of Campus Law Enforcement Administrators (IACLEA). http://www.iaclea.org/visitors/about/

Janosik, S. M. (2004). Parents' views of the Clery Act and campus safety. *The Journal of College Student Development, 45*(1), 43-56.

Janosik, S. M., & Gehring, D. D. (2003). *The impact of the Jeanne Clery Act Disclosure of Campus Security Policy and the Campus Crime Statistics Act on student decision-making.* EPI Policy Paper No. 10. Blacksburg, VA: Virginia Tech.

Janosik, S. M., & Gregory, D. E. (2003). The Clery Act and its influence on campus law enforcement practices. *NASPA Journal, 44*(1), 182-199. Retrieved from http://publications.naspa.org/cgi/viewcontent.cgi?article=1311&context=naspajournal

Jeanne Clery Disclosure of Campus Security Policy and Campus Crime Statistics Act. (2000). 20 U.S.C. § 1092(f).

Nicoletti, J., Spencer-Thomas, S., & Bollinger, C. (Eds) (2010). *Violence goes to college: The authoritative guide to prevention and intervention (2nd Ed.).* Springfield, IL: Charles C. Thomas.

Security on Campus, Inc. (2012). Jeanne Clery and the SOC story. Retrieved from http://www.securityoncampus.org/

Seng, M. (1995). The Crime Awareness and Campus Security Act: Some observations, critical comments and suggestions. In B. Fisher & J. Sloan, III (Eds.), *Campus crime: Legal, social and policy perspectives.* (pp. 38-52). Springfield, IL: Charles C. Thomas.

Seng, M., & Koehler, N. (1993). The Crime Awareness and Campus Security Act: A critical analysis. *Journal of Crime and Justice, 16,* 97-110.

Sloan III, J. J., & Lanier, M. M. (2007). Community policing on university campuses: Tradition, practices, and outlook. In Fisher, B. S., & Sloan III, J. J.(Eds.). (2007). *Campus crime: Legal, social and policy issues* (2nd ed.). Springfield, IL: Charles C. Thomas.

Smith, M. C. (1988). *Coping with crime on campus.* New York, NY: American Council on Education: Macmillan

Smith, M. C. (1989). *Crime and campus police: A handbook for police officers and administrators.* Asheville, NC: College Administration Publications.

Smith, M. C., & Fossey, R. (1995). *Crime on campus: Legal issues and campus administration.* Westport, CT: Greenwood Press.

Contextual Statement Contributor

Dennis E. Gregory, Old Dominion University

Campus Police and Security Programs
CAS Standards and Guidelines

Part 1. MISSION

Campus Police and Security Programs (CPSP) serve to provide a safe and orderly campus by enforcing the law, enforcing institutional and community standards, and fostering students' learning and development through the provision of safety education.

CPSP must develop, disseminate, implement, and regularly review their missions. The mission must be consistent with the mission of the institution and with professional standards. The mission must be appropriate for the institution's student populations and community settings. Mission statements must reference student learning and development.

CPSP must develop goals that address the institution's needs to maintain a safe and orderly campus:
- communicate and enforce applicable laws and ordinances
- collaborate with appropriate institutional agencies and programs to develop, disseminate, interpret, and enforce campus policies and procedures
- protect rights of students, employees, pre-college program participants, and campus visitors in the administration of campus police and security programs and enforcement of the law
- respond to student behavioral problems and violations of the law in a fair and consistent manner
- facilitate and encourage respect for the law, campus safety, and institutional governance
- initiate and encourage educational activities that serve to reduce violations of the law and of campus regulations

CPSP should encourage appropriate individual and group behavior as well as serve the campus community by reducing disruption, harm, and violation of institutional policy and the law.

CPSP should be conducted in ways that will serve to foster the ethical development and personal integrity of students and promote an environment that is consistent with the overall educational goals of the institution.

Part 2. PROGRAM

The formal education of students, consisting of the curriculum and the co-curriculum, must promote student learning and development outcomes that are purposeful, contribute to students' realization of

their potential, and prepare students for satisfying and productive lives.

Campus Police and Security Programs (CPSP) must collaborate with colleagues and departments across the institution to promote student learning and development, persistence, and success.

Consistent with the institutional mission, CPSP must identify relevant and desirable student learning and development outcomes from among the six domains and related dimensions:

Domain: knowledge acquisition, integration, construction, and application
- Dimensions: understanding knowledge from a range of disciplines; connecting knowledge to other knowledge, ideas, and experiences; constructing knowledge; and relating knowledge to daily life

Domain: cognitive complexity
- Dimensions: critical thinking, reflective thinking, effective reasoning, and creativity

Domain: intrapersonal development
- Dimensions: realistic self-appraisal, self-understanding, and self-respect; identity development; commitment to ethics and integrity; and spiritual awareness

Domain: interpersonal competence
- Dimensions: meaningful relationships, interdependence, collaboration, and effective leadership.

Domain: humanitarianism and civic engagement
- Dimensions: understanding and appreciation of cultural and human differences, social responsibility, global perspective, and sense of civic responsibility

Domain: practical competence
- Dimensions: pursuing goals, communicating effectively, technical competence, managing personal affairs, managing career development, demonstrating professionalism, maintaining health and wellness, and living a purposeful and satisfying life

[LD Outcomes: See *The Council for the Advancement of Standards Learning and Developmental Outcomes* statement for examples of outcomes related to these domains and dimensions.]

CPSP must

- **assess relevant and desirable student learning and development**
- **provide evidence of impact on outcomes**
- **articulate contributions to or support of student learning and development in the domains not specifically assessed**
- **articulate contributions to or support of student persistence and success**
- **use evidence gathered through this process to create strategies for improvement of programs and services**

CPSP must be

- **intentionally designed**
- **guided by theories and knowledge of learning and development**
- **integrated into the life of the institution**
- **reflective of developmental and demographic profiles of the student population**
- **responsive to needs of individuals, populations with distinct needs, and relevant constituencies**
- **delivered using multiple formats, strategies, and contexts**

Where institutions provide distance education, CPSP must assist distance learners to achieve their educational goals by providing access to information about programs and services, to staff members who can address questions and concerns, and to counseling, advising, or other forms of assistance.

CPSP must establish authority and policies within the context of the mission and purpose. A written statement describing the authority, philosophy, jurisdiction, and procedures of the CPSP must be developed and disseminated to all members of the campus community.

This CPSP statement should address

- the jurisdiction
- the authority
- the distinction between security and policing responsibilities
- the relationship between campus police and security programs and external law enforcement agencies with a clear description, including guidelines regarding when external law enforcement authorities will be called in
- the relationship that campus police and security programs have with institutional student conduct programs
- the impact of the "Clery Act" in the USA and other laws governing CPSP operations
- the CPSP intention to respond to and protect the constitutional or contractual rights of members of the community and the community itself.

The institutional policy statement should

- describe whether the CPSP is a police agency, a campus security agency, or some combination thereof
- indicate whether the institution contracts with a security agency or a local law enforcement agency to provide services to the campus or whether the CPSP is a branch of the institution
- applicable laws, ordinances, or policies that govern the CPSP operations

If an institution chooses, or is required by law, to provide a CPSP that is maintained and operated by the institution as a separate internal agency, it must

- **clearly identify the authority of this agency**
- **determine the levels of authority within the agency (e.g., ranks of officers, supervisory structure, task assignments)**
- **determine whether the agency will include sworn police officers, non-sworn security personnel, or some combination of both.**

Roles and functions of CPSP personnel who operate within the institution as a separate agency, an external non-police agency, or a local law enforcement agency may include

- patrolling campus and surrounding property
- enforcing applicable laws
- enforcing institutional policy to include participation in the student conduct system
- investigating violations of law or institutional policy
- enforcing institutional traffic and parking regulations
- examining and ensuring the integrity and safety of institutional facilities
- advising students and others on their rights and responsibilities
- providing institutional safety and crime awareness programs for members of the community and external entities
- maintaining accurate records of all actions.

A CPSP officer may be assigned responsibility for training student conduct board members and other student conduct personnel regarding laws and policies related to the institution and for informing faculty, administration, and staff about legal and disciplinary matters.

If an institution chooses to contract with an external non-police agency such as a private security company, it must clearly identify the authority, responsibility, and limits of this agency and its personnel. The institution must make this information available to employees, students, and visitors and identify the institutional employee to whom this agency and its personnel report.

The institution must inform local law enforcement agencies of the authority, responsibility, and limits of any contracted agency and its personnel.

If an institution contracts with a local law enforcement agency to provide police and security services on campus, it must

- clearly identify any additional or extraordinary responsibilities of these personnel while working on behalf of the institution
- provide training to these personnel regarding their responsibility for enforcement of institutional policy
- identify an institutional employee to whom this agency and its personnel report while working on behalf of the institution.

Part 3. ORGANIZATION AND LEADERSHIP

To achieve student and program outcomes, Campus Police and Security Programs (CPSP) must be structured purposefully and organized effectively. CPSP must have

- clearly stated goals
- current and accessible policies and procedures
- written performance expectations for employees
- functional work flow graphics or organizational charts demonstrating clear channels of authority

Leaders with organizational authority for the programs and services must provide strategic planning, supervision, and management; advance the organization; and maintain integrity through the following functions:

Strategic Planning

- articulate a vision and mission that drive short- and long-term planning
- set goals and objectives based on the needs of the population served and desired student learning or development and program outcomes
- facilitate continuous development, implementation, and assessment of goal attainment congruent with institutional mission and strategic plans
- promote environments that provide meaningful opportunities for student learning, development, and engagement
- develop and continuously improve programs and services in response to the changing needs of students served and evolving institutional priorities
- intentionally include diverse perspectives to inform decision making

Supervising

- manage human resource processes including recruitment, selection, development, supervision, performance planning,

evaluation, recognition, and reward

- influence others to contribute to the effectiveness and success of the unit
- empower professional, support, and student staff to accept leadership opportunities
- offer appropriate feedback to colleagues and students on skills needed to become more effective leaders
- encourage and support professional development, collaboration with colleagues and departments across the institution, and scholarly contribution to the profession

Managing

- identify and address individual, organizational, and environmental conditions that foster or inhibit mission achievement
- plan, allocate, and monitor the use of fiscal, physical, human, intellectual, and technological resources
- use current and valid evidence to inform decisions
- incorporate sustainability practices in the management and design of programs, services, and facilities
- understand appropriate technologies and integrate them into programs and services
- be knowledgeable about codes and laws relevant to programs and services and ensure that staff members understand their responsibilities through appropriate training
- assess potential risks and take action to mitigate them

Advancing the Organization

- communicate effectively in writing, speaking, and electronic venues
- advocate for programs and services
- advocate for representation in strategic planning initiatives at appropriate divisional and institutional levels
- initiate collaborative interactions with internal and external stakeholders who have legitimate concerns about and interests in the functional area
- facilitate processes to reach consensus where wide support is needed
- inform other areas within the institution about issues affecting practice

Maintaining Integrity

- model ethical behavior and institutional citizenship
- share data used to inform key decisions in transparent and accessible ways
- monitor media used for distributing information about programs and services

to ensure the content is current, accurate, appropriately referenced, and accessible

A member of the campus community who possesses appropriate training and experience must be designated as the person to whom the CPSP reports.

This person should be at a senior administrative level, beyond the internal command structure of the CPSP.

The person responsible for the CPSP should have an educational background in the behavioral sciences (e.g., college student affairs, psychology, sociology, student development including moral and ethical development, higher education administration, counseling, law, criminology, or criminal justice).

The person responsible for the CPSP, the most senior person within the CPSP command structure, and all other professional staff members in CPSP should possess
- a clear understanding of the legal requirements for substantive and procedural due process
- legal knowledge sufficient to confer with attorneys involved in law enforcement as well as student disciplinary proceedings and other aspects of the student conduct services system
- a general interest in and commitment to the welfare and development of students who violate the law or institutional policies
- demonstrated skills in decision-making processes and conflict resolution
- teaching and consulting skills appropriate for educating, advising, and coordinating CPSP personnel
- the ability to communicate and interact with students and other members of the community regardless of race, sex, disability, sexual orientation, and other personal characteristics
- an understanding of the requirements relative to confidentiality and security of law enforcement and student conduct programs files
- the ability to create an atmosphere in which staff feel free to ask questions and obtain assistance.

Part 4. HUMAN RESOURCES

Campus Police and Security Programs (CPSP) must be staffed adequately by individuals qualified to accomplish mission and goals.

Within institutional guidelines, CPSP must
- establish procedures for staff recruitment and selection, training, performance planning, and evaluation
- set expectations for supervision and performance
- assess the performance of employees individually and as a team
- provide access to continuing and advanced education and appropriate professional development opportunities to improve the leadership ability, competence, and skills of all employees.

CPSP must maintain position descriptions for all staff members.

To create a diverse staff, CPSP must institute recruitment and hiring strategies that encourage individuals from under-represented populations to apply for positions.

CPSP must develop promotion practices that are fair, inclusive, proactive, and non-discriminatory.

To further the recruitment and retention of staff, CPSP must consider work life initiatives, such as compressed work schedules, flextime, job sharing, remote work, or telework.

CPSP professional staff members must hold an earned graduate or professional degree in a field relevant to the position they hold or must possess an appropriate combination of educational credentials and related work experience.

CPSP professional staff members must engage in continuing professional development activities to keep abreast of the research, theories, legislation, policies, and developments that affect their programs and services.

CPSP must have technical and support staff members adequate to accomplish their mission. All members of the staff must be technologically proficient and qualified to perform their job functions, be knowledgeable about ethical and legal uses of technology, and have access to training and resources to support the performance of their assigned responsibilities.

Degree- or credential-seeking interns or graduate assistants must be qualified by enrollment in an appropriate field of study and by relevant experience. These individuals must be trained and supervised adequately by professional staff members holding educational credentials and related work experience appropriate for supervision.   Supervisors must be cognizant of the roles of interns and graduate assistants as both student and employee and closely adhere to all parameters of their job descriptions, work hours, and schedules. Supervisors and the interns or graduate assistants must agree to compensatory time or other appropriate compensation if circumstances necessitate additional hours.

Student employees and volunteers must be carefully selected, trained, supervised, and evaluated. They must be educated on how and when to refer those in need of additional assistance to qualified staff members and must have access to a supervisor for assistance in making these judgments. Student employees and volunteers must be provided clear job descriptions, pre-service training based on assessed needs, and continuing development.

All CPSP staff members, including student employees and volunteers, must receive specific training on institutional policies pertaining to functions or activities they support and to privacy and confidentiality policies and laws regarding access to student records and other sensitive institutional information.

All CPSP staff members must receive training on policies and procedures related to the use of technology to store or access student records and institutional data.

CPSP must ensure that staff members are knowledgeable about and trained in emergency procedures, crisis response, and prevention efforts. Prevention efforts must address identification of threatening conduct or behavior of students, faculty and staff members, and others and must incorporate a system for responding and reporting.

CPSP must ensure that staff members are knowledgeable of and trained in safety and emergency procedures for securing and vacating facilities.

Initial and inservice training of all CPSP personnel must be provided.

In order for CPSP personnel to fulfill their roles and functions, initial training must include
- police-related training that is the same as or equal to the training provided to personnel of other police agencies
- a review of constitutional and other relevant individual and institutional legal rights and responsibilities
- a description of the organization of the CPSP
- information regarding the authority of the CPSP
- policies regarding the use and carry of weapons
- offensive and defensive weapons training if weapons are authorized to be carried
- information regarding informal and formal agreements with local law enforcement agencies off campus
- records documenting that the needs of the agency are addressed and that there is accountability for all training provided

Training for CPSP agencies that provide security

services and for CPSP personnel who do not provide policing duties (e.g., security and other non-sworn personnel) must be appropriate to their responsibilities. This training may differ from police training.

Because CPSP personnel may also be involved in the student conduct process, they must be provided with
- an overview of all student conduct policies and procedures of the institution
- an explanation of the operation of the student conduct process at all levels, including authority and jurisdiction
- an overview of the institution's philosophy on student conduct and the role of CPSP in this process
- roles and functions of all student conduct bodies and their members
- an explanation of sanctions
- an explanation of institutional policies and privacy laws regarding access to student records and other sensitive institutional information (e.g., in the U.S., the Family Educational Rights and Privacy Act, FERPA) and the differences between "education records" and "law enforcement records" that result from this law
- an explanation of pertinent ethics, including particularly the importance of privacy of student disciplinary records and addressing bias and conflict of interest in the student conduct process
- a description of available personal counseling programs and referral resources
- an outline of conditions and interactions that may involve external enforcement officials, attorneys, witnesses, parents of accused students, and the media
- training in the developmental and interpersonal issues likely to arise among college students

Evaluation of the CPSP should include
- performance evaluations of all staff members by their supervisors
- periodic performance evaluations of individual hearing boards
- ongoing evaluation of training programs and publications
- periodic review of applicable laws and current case law to ensure compliance

Inservice training should include participation in relevant and on-going workshops, seminars, and conferences. A library containing current resources about campus police and security issues should be maintained and be accessible to CPSP personnel.

Students in academic programs, particularly in areas such as police science, forensic science, criminalistics, law, or criminology, may assist the campus police and security programs through student employment, practicums, internships, and assistantships.

Students who participate in some services to the CPSPs (with proper supervision) may be awarded academic credit. Clear objectives and assignments should be outlined to ensure that a student's grade for this participation is in no way influenced by his or her decisions on a particular case.

Part 5. ETHICS

Campus Police and Security Programs (CPSP) must review relevant professional ethical standards and must adopt or develop and implement appropriate statements of ethical practice.

CPSP must publish and adhere to statements of ethical practice and ensure their periodic review by relevant constituencies.

CPSP must orient new staff members to relevant ethical standards and statements of ethical practice and related institutional policies.

Statements of ethical standards must specify that staff members respect privacy and maintain confidentiality in all communications and records to the extent that such communications and records are protected under relevant privacy laws.

Statements of ethical standards must specify limits on disclosure of information contained in students' educational records as well as requirements to disclose to appropriate authorities.

Statements of ethical standards must address personal and economic conflicts of interest, or appearance thereof, by staff members in the performance of their work.

Statements of ethical standards must reflect the responsibility of staff members to be fair, objective, and impartial in their interactions with others.

Statements of ethical standards must reference management of institutional funds.

Statements of ethical standards must reference appropriate behavior regarding research and assessment with human participants, confidentiality of research and assessment data, and students' rights and responsibilities.

Statements of ethical standards must include the expectation that CPSP staff members confront and hold accountable other staff members who exhibit unethical behavior.

Statements of ethical standards must address issues surrounding scholarly integrity.

As appropriate, CPSP staff members must inform users of programs and services of ethical obligations and limitations emanating from codes and laws or from licensure requirements.

CPSP staff members must recognize and avoid conflicts of interest that could adversely influence their judgment or objectivity and, when unavoidable, recuse themselves from the situation.

CPSP staff members must perform their duties within the limits of their position, training, expertise, and competence.

When these limits are exceeded, individuals in need of further assistance must be referred to persons possessing appropriate qualifications.

Promotional and descriptive information must be accurate and free of deception.

CPSP must adhere to institutional policies regarding ethical and legal use of software and technology.

Part 6. LAW, POLICY, AND GOVERNANCE

Campus Police and Security Programs (CPSP) must be in compliance with laws, regulations, and policies that relate to their respective responsibilities and that pose legal obligations, limitations, risks, and liabilities for the institution as a whole. Examples include constitutional, statutory, regulatory, and case law; relevant law and orders emanating from codes and laws; and the institution's policies.

CPSP must inform staff members, appropriate officials, and users of programs and services about existing and changing legal obligations, risks and liabilities, and limitations.

CPSP must have written policies on all relevant operations, transactions, or tasks that have legal implications.

CPSP must regularly review policies. The revision and creation of policies must be informed by best practices, available evidence, and policy issues in higher education.

CPSP staff members must use reasonable and informed practices to limit the liability exposure of the institution and its officers, employees, and agents. CPSP staff members must be informed about institutional policies regarding risk management, personal liability, and related insurance coverage options and must be referred to external sources if coverage is not provided by the institution.

The institution must provide access to legal advice for staff members as needed to carry out assigned responsibilities.

CPSP must have procedures and guidelines consistent with institutional policy for responding to threats, emergencies, and crisis situations. Systems and procedures must be in place to disseminate timely and accurate information to students, other members of the institutional community, and appropriate external organizations during emergency situations.

CPSP staff members must neither participate in nor condone any form of harassment or activity that demeans persons or creates an intimidating, hostile, or offensive environment.

CPSP must obtain permission to use copyrighted materials and instruments. The CPSP must purchase the materials and instruments from legally compliant sources or seek alternative permission from the publisher or owner. References to copyrighted materials and instruments must include appropriate citations.

CPSP staff members must be knowledgeable about internal and external governance systems that affect programs and services.

The institution's policies regarding the administration of applicable laws must be clearly described in writing. Elements to be addressed in this policy must include

- CPSP personnel arrest authority
- circumstances under which, and by whom, weapons will be carried by CPSP personnel
- the roles of various personnel within the CPSP
- a formal or informal agreement with local law enforcement personnel regarding jurisdiction
- policies regarding campus crime reports, crime logs, and other required documentation
- threat assessment procedures

Procedures and processes must be designed by the CPSP to ensure that all relevant legal requirements are met and, if within a private institution, how private status impacts the institution with regard to law enforcement.

CPSP should provide a statement of relevant state/provincial and local laws regarding status as "special police or deputies" or other designations that allow law enforcement responsibilities.

CPSP should assist all employees and students of the institution to understand the sources and lines of authority of the CPSP.

The institution must be clear about how it defines the jurisdiction of the CPSP to include whether officers have authority beyond the borders of the campus and policy addressing the pursuit of suspects who leave the campus, the areas of patrol for CPSP personnel, and the relationship of the CPSP with local law enforcement agencies beyond the surrounding community.

Agreements should be reached between law enforcement agencies in adjoining jurisdictions or within the agency's jurisdiction to provide assistance to each other in the event of disaster, mass disorder, terrorism, or other emergency situations.

CPSP must maintain records of patrol activities, actions taken by CPSP personnel, information for a campus crime log, evidence to be used by CPSP personnel in law enforcement activities, and student conduct proceedings on campus.

The institution must clearly state the legal issues and conduct regulations that apply to student organizations, the procedures that will be followed in the enforcement of cases related to student organizations, and the guidelines used to determine if actions of individual members or small groups within an organization constitute action by the organization.

The institution must clearly state the legal issues and conduct regulations that apply off campus and which are, as a result, the responsibility of CPSP personnel. These include dealing with individual students and dealing with off-campus enforcement at residential facilities owned and operated by student organizations.

Appropriate policies and practices to ensure compliance with regulations should include notification to all constituencies of their rights and responsibilities under applicable laws as well as the student conduct system; a written description; accurate record keeping of all aspects of the campus police and security operations; and regular reviews of the campus police and security policies and practices.

CPSP must work with the institution to develop clear policy about the protocols for the use of video surveillance.

Part 7. DIVERSITY, EQUITY, AND ACCESS

Within the context of each institution's unique mission and in accordance with institutional polices and all applicable codes and laws, Campus Police and Security Programs (CPSP) must create and maintain educational and work environments that are

- welcoming, accessible, and inclusive to persons of diverse backgrounds
- equitable and non-discriminatory
- free from harassment

CPSP must not discriminate on the basis of ability;

age; cultural identity; ethnicity; family educational history (e.g., first generation to attend college); gender identity and expression; nationality; political affiliation; race; religious affiliation; sex; sexual orientation; economic, marital, social, or veteran status; or any other basis included in institutional policies and codes and laws.

CPSP must

- advocate for greater sensitivity to multicultural and social justice concerns by the institution and its personnel
- modify or remove policies, practices, facilities, structures, systems, and technologies that limit access, discriminate, or produce inequities
- include diversity, equity, and access initiatives within their strategic plans
- foster communication that deepens understanding of identity, culture, self-expression, and heritage
- promote respect about commonalities and differences among people within their historical and cultural contexts
- address the characteristics and needs of a diverse population when establishing and implementing culturally relevant and inclusive programs, services, policies, procedures, and practices
- provide staff members with access to multicultural training and hold staff members accountable for integrating the training into their work
- respond to the needs of all students and other populations served when establishing hours of operation and developing methods of delivering programs, services, and resources
- ensure physical, program, and resource access for persons with disabilities
- recognize the needs of distance learning students by providing appropriate and accessible services and resources or by assisting them in gaining access to other appropriate services and resources in their geographic region
- be sensitive to the communities that it serves and prohibit profiling

Part 8. INSTITUTIONAL AND EXTERNAL RELATIONS

Campus Police and Security Programs (CPSP) must reach out to relevant individuals, groups, communities, and organizations internal and external to the institution to

- establish, maintain, and promote understanding and effective relations with those that have a significant interest in or potential effect on the students or other constituents served by the programs and services
- garner support and resources for programs and services as defined by the mission statement
- disseminate information about the programs and services
- collaborate, where appropriate, to assist in offering or improving programs and services to meet the needs of students and other constituents and to achieve program and student outcomes
- engage diverse individuals, groups, communities, and organizations to enrich the educational environment and experiences of students and other constituents

CPSP must have procedures and guidelines consistent with institutional policy for

- communicating with the media
- contracting with external organizations for delivery of programs and services
- cultivating, soliciting, and managing gifts
- applying to and managing funds from grants

Representatives of the CPSP should meet regularly with pertinent campus constituencies (e.g., student government, student development offices, staff, faculty members, academic administrators, legal counsel) to exchange information concerning their respective operations and to identify ways to work together to prevent behavioral problems and to correct existing problems. Such collaborative efforts may include educational programs and joint publications.

CPSP representatives should also meet periodically with relevant external agencies (e.g., local police, district attorneys, and service providers) to ensure their understanding about the campus police and security programs as well as to address student behavior problems in an effective manner.

CPSP must publish information about its specific programs for the campus community.

CPSP publications must contain

- the Clery Act (in the USA) campus crime statistics report
- campus policies, such as those concerning legal representation by campus legal services if available, the maintenance of law enforcement records, and the destruction of records
- campus procedures, such as filing a crime report or request for disciplinary action, gathering information, conducting an investigation
- a general explanation of how and when non-campus law enforcement officials are

engaged.

Publications must be distributed to all members of the campus community.

Dissemination methods may include electronic media; the institutional catalog; orientation programs; the student handbook; specific publications related to requirements of the Clery Act and the Drug Free Schools and Community Act (in the USA) and other legal requirements; and admissions, registration, and billing materials.

Part 9. FINANCIAL RESOURCES

Campus Police and Security Programs (CPSP) must have funding to accomplish the mission and goals. In establishing funding priorities and making significant changes, a comprehensive analysis must be conducted to determine the following elements: unmet needs of the unit, relevant expenditures, external and internal resources, and impact on students and the institution.

CPSP must demonstrate efficient and effective use and responsible stewardship of fiscal resources consistent with institutional protocols.

Part 10. TECHNOLOGY

Campus Police and Security Programs (CPSP) must have adequate technology to support the achievement of their mission and goals. The technology and its use must comply with institutional policies and procedures and be evaluated for compliance with relevant codes and laws.

CPSP must use current technology to provide updated information regarding mission, location, staffing, programs, services, and official contacts to students and designated clients.

CPSP must explore the use of technology to enhance delivery of programs and services, especially for students at a distance or external constituencies.

When technology is used to facilitate student learning and development, the CPSP must select technology that reflects intended outcomes.

CPSP must
- **maintain policies and procedures that address the security, confidentiality, and backup of data, as well as compliance with privacy laws**
- **have clearly articulated plans in place for protecting confidentiality and security of information when using Internet-based technologies**
- **develop plans for replacing and updating existing hardware and software as well as plans for integrating new technically-based or supported programs, including systems**

developed internally by the institution, systems available through professional associations, or private vendor-based systems

Technology, as well as workstations or computer labs maintained by programs and services for student use, must be accessible to all designated clients and must meet established technology standards for delivery to persons with disabilities.

When providing student access to technology, CPSP must
- **have policies on the use of technology that are clear, easy to understand, and available to all students**
- **provide assistance, information, or referral to appropriate support services to those needing help accessing or using technology**
- **provide instruction or training on how to use the technology**
- **inform students on the legal and ethical implications of misuse as it pertains to intellectual property, harassment, privacy, and social networks**

Student violations of technology policies must follow established institutional student disciplinary procedures.

Students who experience negative emotional or psychological consequences from the use of technology must be referred to support services provided by the institution.

Part 11. FACILITIES AND EQUIPMENT

Campus Police and Security Programs (CPSP) must have adequate, accessible, and suitably located facilities and equipment to support the mission and goals. If acquiring capital equipment as defined by the institution, CPSP must take into account expenses related to regular maintenance and life cycle costs. Facilities and equipment must be evaluated on an established cycle, including consideration of sustainability, and be in compliance with codes and laws to provide for access, health, safety, and security.

CPSP staff members must have workspace that is well-equipped, adequate in size, and designed to support their work and responsibilities. For conversations requiring privacy, staff members must have access to a private space.

CPSP staff members who share workspace must be able to secure their own work.

The design of the facilities must guarantee the security and privacy of records and ensure the

confidentiality of sensitive information.

The location and layout of the facilities must be sensitive to the needs of persons with disabilities as well as the needs of other constituencies.

CPSP facilities should include private rooms where individual consultations may be held, hearing room facilities, a meeting room for small groups, a library or resource area, and a secure location for records. The facilities should also be designed to promote the personal safety of the individuals involved in the CPSP (e.g., campus alert systems, multiple methods of egress, and panic buttons).

Part 12. ASSESSMENT AND EVALUATION

Campus Police and Security Programs (CPSP) must have a clearly articulated assessment plan to document achievement of stated goals and learning outcomes, demonstrate accountability, provide evidence of improvement, and describe resulting changes in programs and services.

CPSP must have adequate fiscal, human, professional development, and technological resources to develop and implement assessment plans.

Assessments must include direct and indirect evaluation and use qualitative and quantitative methodologies and existing evidence, as appropriate, to determine whether and to what degree the stated mission, goals, and intended outcomes are being met as effectively and efficiently as possible. The process must employ sufficient and sound measures to ensure comprehensiveness. Data collected must include responses from students and other constituencies, and aggregated results must be shared with those groups. Results of assessments must be shared appropriately with multiple constituents.

Results of assessments and evaluations must be used to identify needs and interests in revising and improving programs and services, recognizing staff performance, maximizing resource efficiency and effectiveness, improving student achievement of learning and development outcomes, and improving student persistence and success. Changes resulting from the use of assessments and evaluation must be shared with stakeholders.

Assessment and evaluation activities may include
- the degree to which CPSP personnel are appropriately following institutional procedures and guidelines to gather feedback from students, faculty, staff, and the community on the performance and effectiveness of the campus police and security system and the learning and development effects on students and other members of the institutional community

- annual trends in crime statistics, case load, rates of recidivism, and types of offenses
- the effects of programming designed to prevent crime, increase safety related behaviors, provide a safe environment, and prevent behavioral problems.

General Standards revised in 2011;
CPSP content developed in 2012

The Role of Campus Religious and Spiritual Programs
CAS Standards Contextual Statement

The pursuit of religious liberty drove the founding of colonial America. Many early colonists were religious dissenters. In order to reinforce and protect the ideal of free religious expression, they founded the early colleges to educate colonial leadership, weaving Protestant Christian values throughout the curriculum and college life. The continuing turmoil in England and Europe—wars, famine, population growth and urbanization, and religious intolerance—combined with expanding trade to increase the migration of settlers to the New World. With these immigrants came an increasing diversity of religious belief that challenged standing practices of religious liberty. New pragmatic pressures on the colonial colleges forced curricular changes to prepare the growing merchant and governing class. The central place initially afforded religion in the college began to see competition from the vocational needs of the growing colonies and, upon independence from England, of the new nation (Thelin, 2011; Waggoner, 2011).

The 19th century brought continued geographic and population expansion of the United States, and colleges grew and developed along with the needs of the country. Numerous Protestant and fewer Catholic colleges followed the westward expansion, and their missions continued to differentiate in response to the increasing complexity of the nation's activities. The achievements of Europe's new philosophical ideas and sciences began to traverse the Atlantic, fostering innovations in higher education; chief among these were German-style research and alternative critical study of Biblical texts that challenged traditional unmediated readings. Religion's primacy as the chief interpreter of experience was being challenged by the promise of science and technology (Reuben, 1996). The place of religion in education was debated in the United States, Canada, the United Kingdom, and Europe, and in the U.S. the implications of the First Amendment for a society of increasing religious plurality continued to be worked out in the courts.

As state-supported universities developed, particularly with federal land grants through the Morrill Acts of 1862 and 1890, the place of religion was mediated by the requirements of emergent constitutional doctrine. Direct university involvement with religion became more restrained, and new co-curricular outlets developed for facilitating religious expression on public campuses. These would later grow into organizations including the YMCA, InterVarsity Fellowship, Catholic Newman Clubs, Jewish Hillel Centers, the Muslim Student Association, and many more. In the meantime, religiously-affiliated institutions continued to flourish, providing a protected space for free religious expression along the lines of their particular beliefs. This differentiated

model of religion in higher education became the common practice through the 20th century (Thelin, 2011).

The 1960s brought a challenge to several cultural authorities, including religion. The Vatican Council of 1962 initiated what many saw as liberalizing reforms in the Roman Catholic Church. Several theologians announced the Death of God. Ruling in *Engel v. Vitale* in 1962, the U.S. Supreme Court decided that a prayer approved by the New York Board of Regents for use in opening exercises violated the Establishment Clause of the First Amendment and was therefore impermissible. One year later in *Abington School District v. Schempp*, the Court disallowed Bible reading for similar reasons. The reaction was immediate and intense. These decisions, however, opened the door to teaching about religion (as opposed to teaching religion), and religious studies departments began to appear in colleges and universities. The Immigration Act of 1965 initiated a stream of new citizens who brought with them Asian religious practices. The 60s counterculture helped popularize Eastern ideas, evolving them into a New Age Spirituality to challenge conventional U.S. religious practices. A period of experimentation ensued, much of which originated on college campuses. But this innovation was challenged in the larger society by new and vocal conservative religious leaders and their organizations (Waggoner, 2011).

The September 11, 2001, attacks on the U.S. represented a watershed event that brought Islam to the forefront of American consciousness and galvanized interest in religion throughout the world, especially on college campuses. Religious studies courses filled. Discussions and debates on religion and spirituality flourished across all campuses, in and out of classrooms. This is the milieu today—a heightened increase in the role of religion in public life with higher education as a major arena where these ideas are being explored. Faculty of all disciplines, student affairs staff, chaplains and campus ministers, and students themselves are all potential resources in this discussion. A rich literature addressing these topics has emerged, as have numerous promising practices.

Sharon Daloz Parks' seminal work, *Big Questions, Worthy Dreams* (2011), provided the theoretical base for conceptualizing faith and spiritual development in college by extending the work of James Fowler (1981) into young-adult, college-age development. Parker Palmer (1993; Palmer & Zajonc, 2010) made the case in a series of books over twenty years that spiritual development is inextricably bound up with the educational enterprise. Two important social science databases were developed by the Astin team (Astin, Astin, & Lindholm, 2010) at UCLA through the multiyear *Spirituality in Higher Education* national (U.S.) study and by Christian Smith and associates at the University of Notre Dame (Smith, 2009).

Professional associations began to focus on religion, spirituality, and higher education. Among them was the National Association of Student Personnel Administrators (NASPA), creating a Knowledge Community focusing on this area and sponsoring the online *Journal of College and Character*. The peer-reviewed *Journal of College Student Development* of the American College Personnel Association (ACPA) began to feature work in this area. Other journals published progress in this emerging area of interest; examples include *Religion & Education* for coverage across varying faith and spiritual perspectives and *Christian Higher Education* and *Catholic Education: A Journal of Inquiry and Practice* for tradition-specific concerns.

Campus religious and spiritual programs can and do vary widely in focus and intent. Spirituality, while it can be associated with religious traditions, is a perspective that deals with questions of meaning, purpose, and well-being apart from religion (Astin, Astin, & Lindholm, 2010). CAS standards and guidelines for campus religious and spiritual programs should be used as a guide to help assess the needs of students and to structure programs to meet the religious and spiritual needs of students. As students look toward more diverse options to fulfill their religious or spiritual development, and as professional practice in the field continues to evolve quickly, institutions must continue to equip their staff members with knowledge of relevant issues. Nash and Murray (2010) provide useful guidance for both faculty and student affairs administrators to help students with questions of purpose and meaning.

Campus religious and spiritual programs may be structured differently on individual campuses according to the needs and limitations of each institution. There is no preferred organizational or programming structure. Organizational structures may range from coordinating committees to individual staff members working directly with these organizations. Institutional type, size, goals, and mission are just a few of the factors that do and should guide both structure and function of religious and spiritual programs on a campus.

One major and important difference among institutions is between those affiliated with a religious tradition and those that are not. Religiously-affiliated institutions may have particular mission statements, creeds, training, or directives that can influence how programs are organized and implemented on their campuses. For institutions not so affiliated, organization and programming must be guided in the U.S. by Supreme Court decisions relative to First-Amendment guarantees prohibiting the establishment of religion yet allowing free religious expression. In general, the law provides that the state will be neutral in its relations with persons who profess belief or disbelief in any religion. Legal standards are continually evolving in the area of religion in public life. Consequently, those who administer Campus Religious and/or Spiritual Programs (CRSP) must maintain familiarity with relevant case law.

References, Readings, and Resources

Association of College and University Religious Affairs, www.acuraonline.org

Astin, A., Astin, H., & Lindholm, J. (2010). *Cultivating the spirit: How college can enhance students' inner lives.* San Francisco, CA: Jossey-Bass.

Catholic Education: A Journal of Inquiry and Practice, scholarship.bc.edu/ojs/index.php/catholic

Christian Higher Education, www.tofconline.com/uche

Fowler, J. W. (1981). *Stages of faith: The psychology of human development and the quest for meaning.* San Francisco, CA: Harper & Row.

Interfaith Youth Core, www.ifyc.org

Jewish Campus Life, www.hillel.org

Journal of College Student Development, www.jcsdonline.org/

Journal of College and Character, www.journals.naspa.org/jcc/

Muslim Student Association, www.msanational.org

National Association of College and University Chaplains, www.nacuc.net

National Association of Student Personnel Administrators (NASPA) Spirituality and Religion in Higher Education Knowledge Community, www.naspa.org/kc

National Campus Ministry Association, www.campusministry.net

Nash, R. J., & Murray, M. C. (2010). *Helping college students find purpose: The campus guide to meaning-making.* San Francisco, CA: Jossey-Bass.

Palmer, P. J. (1993). *To know as we are known: Education as a spiritual journey.* San Francisco, CA: Harper Collins.

Palmer, P. J., & Zajonc, A. (2010). *The heart of higher education: A call to renewal.* San Francisco, CA: Jossey-Bass.

Parks, S. D. (2011). *Big questions, worthy dreams: Mentoring emerging adults in their search for meaning, purpose, and faith* (2nd ed.). San Francisco, CA: Jossey-Bass.

Religion & Education, www.tofconline.com/urel

Reuben, J. A. (1996). *The making of the modern university: Intellectual transformation and the marginalization of morality.* Chicago, IL: University of Chicago Press.

Secular Student Alliance, www.secularstudents.org/

Smith, C. (2009). *Souls in transition: The religious and spiritual lives of emerging adults.* New York, NY: Oxford University Press.

Thelin, J. R. (2011). *A history of American higher education* (2nd ed.). Baltimore, MD: Johns Hopkins University Press.

Waggoner, M. D. (2011). *Sacred and secular tensions in higher education: Connecting parallel universities.* New York, NY: Routledge.

Contextual Statement Contributors
Current Edition:
Michael D. Waggoner, University of Northern Iowa

Previous Editions:
Diane L. Cooper, University of Georgia
Merrily S. Dunn, University of Georgia
S. Bryan Rush, University of Georgia/Erskine College
J.D. White, Universty of Georgia/Campus Labs

Campus Religious and Spiritual Programs
CAS Standards and Guidelines

Part 1. MISSION

The purpose of Campus Religious and Spiritual Programs (CRSP) is to provide access to programs that enable interested students to pursue full spiritual growth and development and to foster a campus atmosphere in which interested members of the college community may freely express their religion, spirituality, and faith.

A private or religiously affiliated institution may state its preference for a particular faith or spiritual tradition and may directly use its own resources for this purpose.

CRSP must develop, disseminate, implement, and regularly review their missions. The mission must be consistent with the mission of the institution and with professional standards. The mission must be appropriate for the institution's student populations and community settings. Mission statements must reference student learning and development.

Public institutions without formal religious and/or spiritual programs should make provisions for religious and spiritual programs indirectly, that is, through cooperation with off-campus agencies that provide religious services and programs.

The goals of CRSP should provide opportunities for interested students to
- receive the religious and/or spiritual support they seek
- articulate a personal philosophy
- acquire skills and knowledge to address issues of values, ethics, and morality
- examine the interaction of faith, intellectual inquiry, and social responsibility as bases for finding and affirming meaning and satisfaction in life
- participate in dialogue between and among representatives of the religious and/or spiritual and the secular
- participate with others in the expression of their faith(s)

Part 2. PROGRAM

The formal education of students, consisting of the curriculum and the co-curriculum, must promote student learning and development outcomes that are purposeful, contribute to students' realization of their potential, and prepare students for satisfying and productive lives.

Campus Religious and Spiritual Programs (CRSP) must collaborate with colleagues and departments across the institution to promote student learning and development, persistence, and success.

Consistent with the institutional mission, CRSP must identify relevant and desirable student learning and development outcomes from among the six domains and related dimensions:

> Domain: knowledge acquisition, integration, construction, and application

> - Dimensions: understanding knowledge from a range of disciplines; connecting knowledge to other knowledge, ideas, and experiences; constructing knowledge; and relating knowledge to daily life

> Domain: cognitive complexity

> - Dimensions: critical thinking, reflective thinking, effective reasoning, and creativity

> Domain: intrapersonal development

> - Dimensions: realistic self-appraisal, self-understanding, and self-respect; identity development; commitment to ethics and integrity; and spiritual awareness

> Domain: interpersonal competence

> - Dimensions: meaningful relationships, interdependence, collaboration, and effective leadership.

> Domain: humanitarianism and civic engagement

> - Dimensions: understanding and appreciation of cultural and human differences, social responsibility, global perspective, and sense of civic responsibility

> Domain: practical competence

> - Dimensions: pursuing goals, communicating effectively, technical competence, managing personal affairs, managing career development, demonstrating professionalism, maintaining health and wellness, and living a purposeful and satisfying life

[LD Outcomes: See *The Council for the Advancement of Standards Learning and Developmental Outcomes* statement for examples of outcomes related to these domains and dimensions.]

CRSP must
- assess relevant and desirable student learning and development

- provide evidence of impact on outcomes
- articulate contributions to or support of student learning and development in the domains not specifically assessed
- articulate contributions to or support of student persistence and success
- use evidence gathered through this process to create strategies for improvement of programs and services

CRSP must be
- intentionally designed
- guided by theories and knowledge of learning and development
- integrated into the life of the institution
- reflective of developmental and demographic profiles of the student population
- responsive to needs of individuals, populations with distinct needs, and relevant constituencies
- delivered using multiple formats, strategies, and contexts

Where institutions provide distance education, CRSP must assist distance learners to achieve their educational goals by providing access to information about programs and services, to staff members who can address questions and concerns, and to counseling, advising, or other forms of assistance.

CRSP will vary depending on the requirements and beliefs of specific denominations and faiths, as well as the needs and traditions of the particular institution.

To the extent either required or prohibited by constitutional, statutory, or regulatory provisions, institutions must provide reasonable opportunities for students to
- question, explore, understand, affiliate with or avoid, and express or reject various religious faiths and/or spiritual beliefs and practices
- seek individual counseling or group associations for the examination and application of religious and/or spiritual values and beliefs
- worship communally and individually
- pray and meditate

In public institutions, staff members may coordinate programs, while personnel associated with religious groups provide direct service to campus community.

In religiously affiliated and private secular colleges, religious programs and direct service may be provided by staff members of the institution.

The types of religious programs and activities offered may include

- co-curricular religious studies
- opportunities for religious and/or spiritual nurturance
- service opportunities
- where appropriate by law, regulation, or policy, opportunity to propagate religions or faiths
- where appropriate by law, regulation, or policy, opportunity to practice rituals of religion or faith
- advocacy for particular ethical or moral policies in public life
- opportunities to relate religious and spiritual beliefs to academic and professional programs
- programs that mark significant events or experiences in the life of the community, e.g., death, tragedy, memorials, or celebrations

In addition, institutions may provide guidance services to promote spiritual or religious growth. Co-curricular programs (e.g., lectures, discussions, service projects) that are designed to help students understand their faiths and the faiths of others may also be offered.

Part 3. ORGANIZATION AND LEADERSHIP

To achieve student and program outcomes, Campus Religious and Spiritual Programs (CRSP) must be structured purposefully and organized effectively. CRSP must have
- clearly stated goals
- current and accessible policies and procedures
- written performance expectations for employees
- functional work flow graphics or organizational charts demonstrating clear channels of authority

Leaders with organizational authority for the programs and services must provide strategic planning, supervision, and management; advance the organization; and maintain integrity through the following functions:

Strategic Planning
- articulate a vision and mission that drive short- and long-term planning
- set goals and objectives based on the needs of the population served and desired student learning or development and program outcomes
- facilitate continuous development, implementation, and assessment of goal attainment congruent with institutional mission and strategic plans
- promote environments that provide meaningful opportunities for student learning, development, and engagement
- develop and continuously improve programs and services in response to the changing

- needs of students served and evolving institutional priorities
- intentionally include diverse perspectives to inform decision making

Supervising

- manage human resource processes including recruitment, selection, development, supervision, performance planning, evaluation, recognition, and reward
- influence others to contribute to the effectiveness and success of the unit
- empower professional, support, and student staff to accept leadership opportunities
- offer appropriate feedback to colleagues and students on skills needed to become more effective leaders
- encourage and support professional development, collaboration with colleagues and departments across the institution, and scholarly contribution to the profession

Managing

- identify and address individual, organizational, and environmental conditions that foster or inhibit mission achievement
- plan, allocate, and monitor the use of fiscal, physical, human, intellectual, and technological resources
- use current and valid evidence to inform decisions
- incorporate sustainability practices in the management and design of programs, services, and facilities
- understand appropriate technologies and integrate them into programs and services
- be knowledgeable about codes and laws relevant to programs and services and ensure that staff members understand their responsibilities through appropriate training
- assess potential risks and take action to mitigate them

Advancing the Organization

- communicate effectively in writing, speaking, and electronic venues
- advocate for programs and services
- advocate for representation in strategic planning initiatives at appropriate divisional and institutional levels
- initiate collaborative interactions with internal and external stakeholders who have legitimate concerns about and interests in the functional area
- facilitate processes to reach consensus where wide support is needed
- inform other areas within the institution about issues affecting practice

Maintaining Integrity

- model ethical behavior and institutional citizenship
- share data used to inform key decisions in transparent and accessible ways
- monitor media used for distributing information about programs and services to ensure the content is current, accurate, appropriately referenced, and accessible

CRSP activities, policies, and procedures should be scrutinized regularly in light of the growing body of law in the area of religion and higher education.

Part 4. HUMAN RESOURCES

Campus Religious and Spiritual Programs (CRSP) must be staffed adequately by individuals qualified to accomplish mission and goals.

Within institutional guidelines, CRSP must
- establish procedures for staff recruitment and selection, training, performance planning, and evaluation
- set expectations for supervision and performance
- assess the performance of employees individually and as a team
- provide access to continuing and advanced education and appropriate professional development opportunities to improve the leadership ability, competence, and skills of all employees.

At public institutions, religious programs may be coordinated by a professional individual and/or a committee. Professional or volunteer persons named (and paid) by the religious and spiritual groups represented on the campus may carry out their respective activities. The title "director" or "coordinator" of religious programs is more appropriate because of the predominantly educational and liaison functions of the position.

At private institutions, campus religious programs are typically coordinated by a professional in an appropriate field or a committee. Additional staff members may be employed by the institution. Religious groups may also provide additional staff for the institution. Religiously related institutions should permit on-campus programs of religions or spiritual beliefs other than those espoused by the institution. Titles for the director or coordinator at private institutions include chaplain, director of religious life or spiritual development, or other title specific to a religious or spiritual tradition.

CRSP must maintain position descriptions for all staff members.

To create a diverse staff, CRSP must institute

recruitment and hiring strategies that encourage individuals from under-represented populations to apply for positions.

CRSP must develop promotion practices that are fair, inclusive, proactive, and non-discriminatory.

To further the recruitment and retention of staff, CRSP must consider work life initiatives, such as compressed work schedules, flextime, job sharing, remote work, or telework.

CRSP professional staff members must hold an earned graduate or professional degree in a field relevant to the position they hold or must possess an appropriate combination of educational credentials and related work experience.

When the coordinator of religious and/or spiritual programs represents a particular religious and/or spiritual body, that person should possess qualifications consistent with the particular body represented and appropriate for a higher education setting.

Any director or coordinator should have
- an understanding of and a commitment to spiritual and religious development as a part of a student's human growth
- the ability to treat fairly all varieties of campus religious experience and personal faith
- awareness and understanding of the beliefs of religious and spiritual groups affiliated with that campus

Depending upon the legal constraints of the institution, the responsibilities of the director or coordinator for religious and/or spiritual programs may include:
- the development and communication of policies relating to religious and spiritual programs that are educationally sound and legally acceptable
- the development of procedures whereby students may organize for religious, spiritual, or moral purposes and participate in programs and activities aimed at their spiritual and/or religious growth
- the provision of access to campus facilities for those responsible for religious or spiritual programs
- the provision of opportunities for guidance in relation to students' religious or spiritual needs
- coordination with other campus decision makers on matters related to religious and/or spiritual activities such as scheduling and examinations

CRSP professional staff members must engage in continuing professional development activities to keep abreast of the research, theories, legislation, policies, and developments that affect their programs and services.

CRSP must have technical and support staff members adequate to accomplish their mission. All members of the staff must be technologically proficient and qualified to perform their job functions, be knowledgeable about ethical and legal uses of technology, and have access to training and resources to support the performance of their assigned responsibilities.

Degree- or credential-seeking interns or graduate assistants must be qualified by enrollment in an appropriate field of study and by relevant experience. These individuals must be trained and supervised adequately by professional staff members holding educational credentials and related work experience appropriate for supervision. Supervisors must be cognizant of the roles of interns and graduate assistants as both student and employee and closely adhere to all parameters of their job descriptions, work hours, and schedules. Supervisors and the interns or graduate assistants must agree to compensatory time or other appropriate compensation if circumstances necessitate additional hours.

Officials should be fair and equitable in relationships with all agencies participating in the program.

Student employees and volunteers must be carefully selected, trained, supervised, and evaluated. They must be educated on how and when to refer those in need of additional assistance to qualified staff members and must have access to a supervisor for assistance in making these judgments. Student employees and volunteers must be provided clear job descriptions, pre-service training based on assessed needs, and continuing development.

All CRSP staff members, including student employees and volunteers, must receive specific training on institutional policies pertaining to functions or activities they support and to privacy and confidentiality policies and laws regarding access to student records and other sensitive institutional information.

All CRSP staff members must receive training on policies and procedures related to the use of technology to store or access student records and institutional data.

CRSP must ensure that staff members are knowledgeable about and trained in emergency procedures, crisis response, and prevention efforts. Prevention efforts must address identification of threatening conduct or behavior of students, faculty and staff members, and others and must incorporate a system for responding and reporting.

CRSP must ensure that staff members are knowledgeable of and trained in safety and emergency procedures for securing and vacating facilities.

Affiliation with appropriate professional organizations is encouraged.

When a staff member represents a particular religious and/or spiritual body, that person should possess qualifications consistent with the particular body they represent and appropriate for a higher education setting.

Part 5. ETHICS

Campus Religious and Spiritual Programs (CRSP) must review relevant professional ethical standards and must adopt or develop and implement appropriate statements of ethical practice.

CRSP must publish and adhere to statements of ethical practice and ensure their periodic review by relevant constituencies.

CRSP must orient new staff members to relevant ethical standards and statements of ethical practice and related institutional policies.

Statements of ethical standards must specify that staff members respect privacy and maintain confidentiality in all communications and records to the extent that such communications and records are protected under relevant privacy laws.

Statements of ethical standards must specify limits on disclosure of information contained in students' educational records as well as requirements to disclose to appropriate authorities.

Statements of ethical standards must address personal and economic conflicts of interest, or appearance thereof, by staff members in the performance of their work.

Statements of ethical standards must reflect the responsibility of staff members to be fair, objective, and impartial in their interactions with others.

Accommodation must be made so that students, faculty members, and staff from various religions and faiths may carry out the essential practices of their belief systems.

Statements of ethical standards must reference management of institutional funds.

Statements of ethical standards must reference appropriate behavior regarding research and assessment with human participants, confidentiality of research and assessment data, and students' rights and responsibilities.

Statements of ethical standards must include the expectation that CRSP staff members confront and hold accountable other staff members who exhibit unethical behavior.

Statements of ethical standards must address issues surrounding scholarly integrity.

As appropriate, CRSP staff members must inform users of programs and services of ethical obligations and limitations emanating from codes and laws or from licensure requirements.

CRSP staff members must recognize and avoid conflicts of interest that could adversely influence their judgment or objectivity and, when unavoidable, recuse themselves from the situation.

CRSP staff members must perform their duties within the limits of their position, training, expertise, and competence.

When these limits are exceeded, individuals in need of further assistance must be referred to persons possessing appropriate qualifications.

Promotional and descriptive information must be accurate and free of deception.

CRSP must adhere to institutional policies regarding ethical and legal use of software and technology.

CRSP staff members must avoid any actions that favor one particular faith over another.

As the institution carries out its academic program, fair and reasonable consideration should be given to the need of campus members to participate in the basic activities of their faiths. Institutional policies and practices should be reviewed regularly so as to avoid undue interference with the exercise of religious and/or spiritual traditions.

Private institutions that sponsor or require particular religious activities must clearly state so in their pre-admission literature, thus permitting a potential student to exercise choice in this regard before admission.

CRSP staff members must work to provide reasonable access for all groups and points of view to any public forums sponsored by the institution.

Membership requirements for on-campus religious organizations at public institutions must be consistent with the group's stated purposes. All religious and/or spiritual organizations must be accorded the same rights and privileges and be held accountable in the same manner as any other campus organization.

CRSP staff members must attempt to protect students, through policy and practice, from undue influence or harassment from persons advocating particular religious positions or activities.

Part 6. LAW, POLICY, AND GOVERNANCE

Campus Religious and Spiritual Programs (CRSP) must be in compliance with laws, regulations, and policies that relate to their respective responsibilities and that pose legal obligations, limitations, risks, and liabilities for the institution as a whole. Examples include constitutional, statutory, regulatory, and case law; relevant law and orders emanating from codes and laws; and the institution's policies.

CRSP must inform staff members, appropriate officials, and users of programs and services about existing and changing legal obligations, risks and liabilities, and limitations.

CRSP must have written policies on all relevant operations, transactions, or tasks that have legal implications.

CRSP must regularly review policies. The revision and creation of policies must be informed by best practices, available evidence, and policy issues in higher education.

CRSP staff members must use reasonable and informed practices to limit the liability exposure of the institution and its officers, employees, and agents. CRSP staff members must be informed about institutional policies regarding risk management, personal liability, and related insurance coverage options and must be referred to external sources if the institution does not provide coverage.

The institution must provide access to legal advice for staff members as needed to carry out assigned responsibilities.

CRSP must have procedures and guidelines consistent with institutional policy for responding to threats, emergencies, and crisis situations. Systems and procedures must be in place to disseminate timely and accurate information to students, other members of the institutional community, and appropriate external organizations during emergency situations.

CRSP staff members must neither participate in nor condone any form of harassment or activity that demeans persons or creates an intimidating, hostile, or offensive environment.

CRSP must obtain permission to use copyrighted materials and instruments. CRSP must purchase the materials and instruments from legally compliant sources or seek alternative permission from the publisher or owner. References to copyrighted materials and instruments must include appropriate citations.

CRSP staff members must be knowledgeable about internal and external governance systems that affect programs and services.

Part 7. DIVERSITY, EQUITY, AND ACCESS

Within the context of each institution's unique mission and in accordance with institutional polices and all applicable codes and laws, Campus Religious and Spiritual Programs (CRSP) must create and maintain educational and work environments that are

- welcoming, accessible, and inclusive to persons of diverse backgrounds
- equitable and non-discriminatory
- free from harassment

CRSP must not discriminate on the basis of ability; age; cultural identity; ethnicity; family educational history (e.g., first generation to attend college); gender identity and expression; nationality; political affiliation; race; religious affiliation; sex; sexual orientation; economic, marital, social, or veteran status; or any other basis included in institutional policies and codes and laws.

CRSP must

- advocate for greater sensitivity to multicultural and social justice concerns by the institution and its personnel
- modify or remove policies, practices, facilities, structures, systems, and technologies that limit access, discriminate, or produce inequities
- include diversity, equity, and access initiatives within their strategic plans
- foster communication that deepens understanding of identity, culture, self-expression, and heritage
- promote respect about commonalities and differences among people within their historical and cultural contexts
- address the characteristics and needs of a diverse population when establishing and implementing culturally relevant and inclusive programs, services, policies, procedures, and practices
- provide staff members with access to multicultural training and hold staff members accountable for integrating the training into their work
- respond to the needs of all students and other populations served when establishing hours of operation and developing methods of delivering programs, services, and resources
- ensure physical, program, and resource access for persons with disabilities
- recognize the needs of distance learning students by providing appropriate and

accessible services and resources or by assisting them in gaining access to other appropriate services and resources in their geographic region

Part 8. INSTITUTIONAL AND EXTERNAL RELATIONS

Campus Religious and Spiritual Programs (CRSP) must reach out to relevant individuals, groups, communities, and organizations internal and external to the institution to

- establish, maintain, and promote understanding and effective relations with those that have a significant interest in or potential effect on the students or other constituents served by the programs and services
- garner support and resources for programs and services as defined by the mission statement
- disseminate information about the programs and services
- collaborate, where appropriate, to assist in offering or improving programs and services to meet the needs of students and other constituents and to achieve program and student outcomes
- engage diverse individuals, groups, communities, and organizations to enrich the educational environment and experiences of students and other constituents

CRSP must have procedures and guidelines consistent with institutional policy for

- communicating with the media
- contracting with external organizations for delivery of programs and services
- cultivating, soliciting, and managing gifts
- applying to and managing funds from grants

Because religion and/or spirituality may be a concern of many academic disciplines and may have an important impact on student development, staff assigned to religious programs should consult with and coordinate their programs with interested colleagues.

The CRSP director or coordinator may interact with faculty and staff formally through advisory councils or through informal contacts.

Continuing attention should be given to developing and improving relationships with both on-campus and off-campus constituencies. Specific religious and/or spiritual programs and action projects may arise from many sources (e.g., academic departments, on-campus functional areas such as residence halls and campus centers, and off-campus organizations, whether local, regional, national, and/or international).

The coordinator, faculty, staff, and administrators of the institution should meet with personnel from religious and/or spiritual groups on a periodic basis.

Part 9. FINANCIAL RESOURCES

Campus Religious and Spiritual Programs (CRSP) must have funding to accomplish the mission and goals. In establishing funding priorities and making significant changes, a comprehensive analysis must be conducted to determine the following elements: unmet needs of the unit, relevant expenditures, external and internal resources, and impact on students and the institution.

All institutions must provide sufficient funding for any institutional staff member(s) and the operational costs related to religious and/or spiritual programs.

If this assignment accounts for only a part of an individual staff member's work load, the budget should clearly indicate the portion that is available for religious and spiritual programs.

CRSP must demonstrate efficient and effective use and responsible stewardship of fiscal resources consistent with institutional protocols.

Funding for personnel and programs of adjunct agencies (i.e., not directly provided by the institution) must be assumed by the sponsors of the adjunct agency.

Part 10. TECHNOLOGY

Campus Religious and Spiritual Programs (CRSP) must have adequate technology to support the achievement of their mission and goals. The technology and its use must comply with institutional policies and procedures and be evaluated for compliance with relevant codes and laws.

CRSP must use current technology to provide updated information regarding mission, location, staffing, programs, services, and official contacts to students and designated clients.

CRSP must explore the use of technology to enhance delivery of programs and services, especially for students at a distance or external constituencies.

When technology is used to facilitate student learning and development, CRSP must select technology that reflects intended outcomes.

CRSP must

- maintain policies and procedures that address the security, confidentiality, and backup of data, as well as compliance with privacy laws
- have clearly articulated plans in place for protecting confidentiality and security of

information when using Internet-based technologies

- develop plans for replacing and updating existing hardware and software as well as plans for integrating new technically-based or supported programs, including systems developed internally by the institution, systems available through professional associations, or private vendor-based systems

Technology, as well as workstations or computer labs maintained by programs and services for student use, must be accessible to all designated clients and must meet established technology standards for delivery to persons with disabilities.

When providing student access to technology, CRSP must

- have policies on the use of technology that are clear, easy to understand, and available to all students
- provide assistance, information, or referral to appropriate support services to those needing help accessing or using technology
- provide instruction or training on how to use the technology
- inform students on the legal and ethical implications of misuse as it pertains to intellectual property, harassment, privacy, and social networks

Student violations of technology policies must follow established institutional student disciplinary procedures.

Students who experience negative emotional or psychological consequences from the use of technology must be referred to support services provided by the institution.

Part 11. FACILITIES AND EQUIPMENT

Campus Religious and Spiritual Programs (CRSP) must have adequate, accessible, and suitably located facilities and equipment to support the mission and goals. If acquiring capital equipment as defined by the institution, CRSP must take into account expenses related to regular maintenance and life cycle costs. Facilities and equipment must be evaluated on an established cycle, including consideration of sustainability, and be in compliance with codes and laws to provide for access, health, safety, and security.

CRSP staff members must have workspace that is well equipped, adequate in size, and designed to support their work and responsibilities. For conversations requiring privacy, staff members must have access to a private space.

CRSP staff members who share workspace must be able to secure their own work.

The design of the facilities must guarantee the security and privacy of records and ensure the confidentiality of sensitive information.

The location and layout of the facilities must be sensitive to the needs of persons with disabilities as well as the needs of other constituencies.

Opportunity must be provided for all student religious and/or spiritual organizations to utilize campus facilities on the same basis as other student organizations.

In public institutions, whenever space is made permanently or exclusively available for specific staff of affiliated agencies, arrangements should be made whereby the institution is appropriately reimbursed for expenses.

Private institutions may provide facilities designed to suit the purpose(s) of a specific religious group(s).

Institutions should provide fair and equitable arrangements and facilities (including in campus centers, academic buildings, or residential units) for specific religious and/or spiritual groups' programming and practices.

Suitable areas should be provided for individual meditation and small group spiritual interaction.

The institution should provide for or coordinate student religious and/or spiritual dietary differences.

Part 12. ASSESSMENT AND EVALUATION

Campus Religious and Spiritual Programs (CRSP) must have a clearly articulated assessment plan to document achievement of stated goals and learning outcomes, demonstrate accountability, provide evidence of improvement, and describe resulting changes in programs and services.

Each institution should require evaluation of its religious program to determine the achievement of goals, the constituencies reached, and its overall effectiveness.

CRSP must have adequate fiscal, human, professional development, and technological resources to develop and implement assessment plans.

Assessments must include direct and indirect evaluation and use qualitative and quantitative methodologies and existing evidence, as appropriate, to determine whether and to what degree the stated mission, goals, and intended outcomes are being met as effectively and efficiently as possible. The process must employ sufficient and sound measures to ensure comprehensiveness. Data collected must include

responses from students and other constituencies, and aggregated results must be shared with those groups. Results of assessments must be shared appropriately with multiple constituents.

This evaluation may be made in concert with the periodic examination of the diverse needs and interests of students and other members of the campus community.

Data should be collected from officers and advisors of campus religious and spiritual organizations to determine the effectiveness of policies affecting religious activity.

Results of assessments and evaluations must be used to identify needs and interests in revising and improving programs and services, recognizing staff performance, maximizing resource efficiency and effectiveness, improving student achievement of learning and development outcomes, and improving student persistence and success. Changes resulting from the use of assessments and evaluation must be shared with stakeholders.

General Standards revised in 2011;
CRSP (formerly Religious Programs) content developed/revised in 1986, 1997, & 2006

The Role of Career Services
CAS Standards Contextual Statement

The first evidence of assistance in career services dates back to the 19th century, when commercial employment agencies began to place graduates of the nation's teacher training programs, also known as normal schools, into jobs. More than 200 such agencies existed by the late 1800s. By the turn of the century, an increasing number of institutions had begun to realize their responsibility to help graduates find jobs. When the first institutional appointment and placement services were established, faculty members typically took responsibility for them on a part-time basis. Soon many institutions established programs staffed by full-time "appointment secretaries." By 1920, approximately 75 percent of the nation's normal schools had established placement services; as a direct result of the increasing number of college-sponsored placement services, the number of external agencies decreased.

At the beginning of the twentieth century the concept and practice of choosing an occupation were becoming more prevalent, and much of the theory supporting occupational choice was based on the 1909 work of Frank Parsons in *Choosing Your Vocation*. Parsons developed a tripartite model—understanding one's self, understanding the requirements of available jobs, and making choices based on true logic. Often referred to as trait and factor theory, it was grounded in a logical, cognitive, and rational approach to selecting occupations. This model was the forerunner of modern theories of career development and was the foundation for career counseling and career development practice until the early 1950s.

Both of the first professional associations focusing on job placement for college graduates, the National Institutional Teacher Placement Association and the National Association of Appointment Secretaries, were established in 1924. In 1934, the National Institutional Teacher Placement Association evolved into the Association for School, College, and University Staffing (ASCUS), which later became the American Association for Employment in Education (AAEE).

From its inception, the mission of AAEE was to connect K-12 school recruiters with career services administrators and education faculty from higher education institutions that prepare educators. AAEE provides information, resources, and networking opportunities to assist schools, colleges, and universities in the employment of educators for staffing excellence in education.

The National Association of Appointment Secretaries became the American College Personnel Association (ACPA) in 1931. ACPA's membership and mission have broadened to include all student affairs professionals for the purpose of "support[ing] and foster[ing] college student learning

through the generation and dissemination of knowledge, which informs policies, practices, and programs for student affairs professionals and the higher education community." The ACPA Commission for Career Development offers members opportunities to "examine and address the changing and diverse role of career development in higher education within a student development framework."

In addition, others concerned with business and industrial placement established the Eastern College Personnel Officers in 1926, and by 1951 six other regional associations had been formed, due largely to Post World War II economic conditions. Those original seven organizations have since merged to form four independent regional associations, which together have memberships covering all fifty states.

Following World War II, the economy exploded and employers sought to hire the nation's college graduates to meet expanding needs. More than 65 percent of the current career services centers were established between 1947 and 1960. Over the years, the function of these offices shifted from solely providing placement activities to providing a broad range of career activities. Accordingly, this shift is reflected by office name changes from "placement office" to "career planning and placement office" to the most commonly used title, "career services."

Concurrent with the growth in institutional enrollments and creation of career services units, new theories began to emerge emphasizing a developmental approach exploring the stages of career development as a function of personal development, often exemplified in the blending of work identity and personal identity. As the complexity of individuals was further explored, the many factors that influence the career decision-making process became more evident and this coincided with the growth of student and career development theory. As career centers evolved so did career theories from vocational theory roots.

The choices of the individual are at the core of many of these more modern theories, but also required is an understanding of external factors that inevitably shape the multiple career decisions an individual will make over the course of their lifetime. Major career development theory categories and some seminal theorists for each include Trait and Factor Theory (Holland), Developmental Theory (Super, Gottfredson), Learning Theory (Krumboltz), Social Cognitive Theory (Bandura, Lent), Values-Based Theory (Brown), Career Information Processing Theory (Peterson, Sampson, and Reardon), Transition Theory (Schlossburg), Contextualist Theory (Young, Valach, and Collins), and Planned Happenstance Theory (Mitchell). These representative theories of career choice and development are indicative of the complexity of career decision-making and provide practitioners a broad-based framework to guide intervention with students and other clients. Modern career theory is also inclusive of race, gender, and class implications and the related impacts on career decision-making.

The National Association of Colleges and Employers (NACE) is a comprehensive national association for career services. A forerunner to NACE, the Association of School and College Placement, was formed in 1940. This group published the *School and College Placement* magazine, now known as the *NACE Journal*. In 1956, the national association was incorporated as the College Placement Publications Council and its name was shortened in 1957 to the College Placement Council. In 1995, the association became the National Association of Colleges and Employers. Today, the core purpose of NACE is to facilitate the employment of the college educated; it works to meet this mission in a variety of ways, especially by providing an important connection between college career services centers and HR/staffing offices focused on recruiting and hiring new college graduates.

Today, the majority of colleges and universities provide career services that often include career advising or career counseling; career resources; programming such as job-search workshops and networking events; career and job fairs; assistance with co-op, internship, and externship programs; on-campus recruiting; and job posting and resume referral services. Many of these services are available electronically through institutional web sites.

Programs and services offered by career services may vary based on the mission of the institution, its classification, and the constituents being served. For example, a community college career services office may place a greater emphasis on workforce preparation and gaining work-related experience; a 4-year liberal arts career services may offer more career counseling and preparation for graduate or professional school; and a for-profit institution career services may have an explicit expectation to "place" a high percentage of its students in jobs.

In the 21st century, career services is tasked to meet increasingly complex and sophisticated challenges that include responding to economic shifts, increasing diversity, changing demographics, globalization, and technology. Career services professionals need to be both culturally sensitive in working with students and knowledgeable about career options both in the United States and internationally. There is an increasing need to prepare students for multiple career transitions over a life span, and to engage in an entrepreneurial approach to personal and career development. Today's traditional-age students, characterized by their high comfort level with and expectation of technology, and "virtual" students, created through distance learning options, require that career services professionals have an increasingly high level of technical competence. Today's career services professionals must balance high-tech and high-touch service and delivery in serving students and employers. Career changers, including alumni, veterans, and others who are working on second, third, and fourth career transitions, are turning to career services to provide assistance through traditional and nontraditional means.

An increasing focus in higher education on assessment and accountability necessitates career services professionals to find meaningful measures by which to demonstrate their value to stakeholders that include students, faculty, administrators, parents, employers, and local communities. It has never been more important to develop productive and collaborative relationships not only with employers and community organizations but also with faculty and other campus constituencies such as services learning, leadership development, and international programs. Increased emphasis on the part of employers on internships/co-ops, electronic recruiting, and diversity recruiting require a corresponding emphasis on the part of career services professionals. Additionally, the growing emphasis on assessment of student learning, using measurable outcomes, and evidence based decision-making processes, requires careful planning, effective implementation, and transparent reporting to stakeholders.

Leadership for career services in the 21st century requires a broader range of skills and competencies beyond those once considered traditional for professionals involved in the career planning and development field. The complexity of work and life impacted by global economic pressures, the accelerating pace of knowledge creation, and ubiquitous technology use means career professionals must help students acquire the knowledge, skills, and ability to connect their educational experiences to work and life roles. Successful leadership in career services leading to employment of graduates will positively affect the admission and retention of students, collaboration with academic programs, and partnerships with community organizations. Leaders will need sales, management, technical, financial, marketing, public relations, assessment, and analytical skills in addition to a foundation in education, counseling, or student personnel services. NACE, AAEE, ACPA, the National Career Development Association, and other organizations play an increasingly important role in the development of this broader set of skills for career services professionals. They deliver value by conducting research on benchmarks and best practices, reporting on current and emerging issues and trends, providing timely and relevant resources and tools, offering training and professional development, and facilitating networking and affiliation among professional colleagues.

References, Readings, and Resources

American Association for Employment in Education (AAEE). 3040 Riverside Drive, Suite 125,Columbus,OH43221. Phone: 614/485-1111. FAX: 614/485-9609. Web site: www.aaee.org

American College Personnel Association (ACPA), Commission on Career Development. One DuPont Circle, Suite 300,Washington,DC 20036-1188. Phone: 202/835-2272. FAX: 202/296-3286. Web site: www.acpa.nche.edu.

Gysbers, N., Heppner, M., & Johnston, J. (1998). Career counseling: Process, issues & techniques. Boston: Allyn and Bacon

Hughey, K. E., Nelson, D. B., Damminger, J. K., McCalla-Wriggins, B., & Associates (2009). The handbook of career advising. San Francisco: Jossey-Bass

Isaacson, L. E., & Brown, D. (2000). Career information, career counseling, and career development (7th Ed.), Boston: Allyn and Bacon

Mitchell, K. Planned Happenstance. http://plannedhappenstance.com

NACE Attracting New Professionals Task Force. (2004). Career services in higher education (PowerPoint presentation). Bethlehem, PA: National Association of Colleges and Employers. http://www.naceweb.org/Knowledge/Career_Services/Career_Services_in_Higher_Education_(PPT).aspx

NACE Future Trends Committee. (2009). Looking ahead: highlights from the future trends survey. In NACE Journal (September 2009) Bethlehem, PA: National Association of Colleges and Employers. www.naceweb.org

National Association of Colleges and Employers (NACE). 62 Highland Avenue, Bethlehem, PA18017. Phone: 800/544-5272. FAX: 610/868-0208. Web site: www.naceweb.org

National Association of Colleges and Employers. NACE Organizational History. http://www.naceweb.org/About/NACE_Organizational_History.aspx

National Association of Colleges and Employers. The professional standards evaluation workbook (2010). www.naceweb.org

National Association of Colleges and Employers. The professional standards for college and university career services (2010). www.naceweb.org

National Career Development Association. 305 N. Booch Circle, Broken Arrow, OK 74012. Phone: 918-663-7060. Fax: 918-663-7058. Website: www.ncda.org

Ratcliffe, R. S. (2004). Use of the CAS standards by career services directors at four-year public colleges and universities (Doctoral Dissertation, Virginia Polytechnic Institute and State University, 2004). Available at http://scholar.lib.vt.edu/theses/available/etd-07262004-150008/

Reardon, R. C., Lenz, J. G., Sampson, J. P., & Peterson, G. W. (2009). Career development and planning: A comprehensive approach (3rd Ed.). Florence KY: Cengage Learning

Schnider, N. (Ed.). (2009). Educator supply and demand research report. Columbus, OH: American Association for Employment in Education.

Schnider, N. (Ed.). (2010). The job search handbook for educators. Columbus, OH: American Association for Employment in Education.

2011-12 Career Services Benchmark Survey (2012). Bethlehem, PA: National Association of Colleges and Employers. www.naceweb.org

Contextual Statement Contributors

Alison Angell, Lesley University, AAEE
Patricia Carretta, George Mason University, NACE
Mimi Collins, NACE
Mollie Starbuck Fout, Ball State University, NACE
R. Samuel Ratcliffe, Virginia Military Institute, NACE
Joseph A. Testani, University of Richmond, NACE

Career Services
CAS Standards and Guidelines

Part 1. MISSION

The primary mission of Career Services (CS) is to assist students and other designated clients in developing, evaluating, and implementing career, education, and employment plans.

Consistent with institutional mission, other designated clients may include alumni, faculty, staff, and community members.

In addition, CS must
- **be a resource to the institution on career and workplace issues and employment and workforce data**
- **develop productive relationships with faculty members, administrators, staff, employers, and other external constituencies**
- **support institutional outcomes assessment and relevant research endeavors**

CS must develop, disseminate, implement, and regularly review their missions. The mission must be consistent with the mission of the institution and with professional standards. The mission must be appropriate for the institution's student populations and community settings. Mission statements must reference student learning and development.

In assisting designated clients, CS must consider the needs of all their constituencies when designing the program and delivering services.

The stated mission should be to help students and designated clients to
- develop or clarify self-knowledge related to career choice and performance in the workplace
- develop understanding of the occupational information required to support career decision-making, including current and future trends and projections
- identify and select personally suitable academic programs and experiential opportunities that optimize future educational and employment options
- take responsibility for making informed career decisions and developing further education and employment plans
- understand how their professional interests and competencies relate to occupational and job requirements
- gain experience on or off campus for the purpose of exploring interests and developing their competencies
- develop effective job search and candidate presentation skills
- link with alumni, employers, professional organizations, and others who can provide opportunities to develop professional interests and competencies, integrate academic learning with work, and explore future career possibilities
- utilize technology throughout the career development and job search processes
- prepare to manage their careers after graduation

CS must promote awareness within the institution of the array of domestic and global occupations and the need for and nature of career development over the lifespan.

Because of expertise and knowledge on career-related subjects, CS should seek involvement in relevant administrative decisions related to student services, institutional development, curriculum planning, and external relations.

Because career-related subjects may also be addressed by other student services and academic programs within the institution, career services should consult with them, promote collaboration, and encourage linkages where appropriate.

Part 2. PROGRAM

Career Services (CS) must design programs and services to assist students and other designated clients to make career decisions and pursue the skill development necessary to compete in a rapidly changing, competency-based, global workplace.

CS must be informed by current career development and experiential learning theories and practices, employment and workforce trends, and appropriate assessments and evaluations.

The formal education of students, consisting of the curriculum and the co-curriculum, must promote student learning and development outcomes that are purposeful, contribute to students' realization of their potential, and prepare students for satisfying and productive lives.

CS must collaborate with colleagues and departments across the institution to promote student learning and development, persistence, and success.

Consistent with the institutional mission, CS must identify relevant and desirable student learning and development outcomes from among the six domains and related dimensions:

Domain: knowledge acquisition, integration,

construction, and application

- Dimensions: understanding knowledge from a range of disciplines; connecting knowledge to other knowledge, ideas, and experiences; constructing knowledge; and relating knowledge to daily life

Domain: cognitive complexity

- Dimensions: critical thinking, reflective thinking, effective reasoning, and creativity

Domain: intrapersonal development

- Dimensions: realistic self-appraisal, self-understanding, and self-respect; identity development; commitment to ethics and integrity; and spiritual awareness

Domain: interpersonal competence

- Dimensions: meaningful relationships, interdependence, collaboration, and effective leadership.

Domain: humanitarianism and civic engagement

- Dimensions: understanding and appreciation of cultural and human differences, social responsibility, global perspective, and sense of civic responsibility

Domain: practical competence

- Dimensions: pursuing goals, communicating effectively, technical competence, managing personal affairs, managing career development, demonstrating professionalism, maintaining health and wellness, and living a purposeful and satisfying life

[LD Outcomes: See *The Council for the Advancement of Standards Learning and Developmental Outcomes* statement for examples of outcomes related to these domains and dimensions.]

CS must

- assess relevant and desirable student learning and development
- provide evidence of impact on outcomes
- articulate contributions to or support of student learning and development in the domains not specifically assessed
- articulate contributions to or support of student persistence and success
- use evidence gathered through this process to create strategies for improvement of programs and services

CS must be

- intentionally designed
- guided by theories and knowledge of learning

and development

- integrated into the life of the institution
- reflective of developmental and demographic profiles of the student population
- responsive to needs of individuals, populations with distinct needs, and relevant constituencies
- delivered using multiple formats, strategies, and contexts

Where institutions provide distance education, CS must assist distance learners to achieve their educational goals by providing access to information about programs and services, to staff members who can address questions and concerns, and to counseling, advising, or other forms of assistance.

CS must be delivered in a variety of formats in recognition of institutional settings, different learning styles, cultural differences, distance learning, and special needs among clients.

Components of CS must be clearly defined, designed, and implemented in alignment with

- the career development needs and educational and occupational interests of students and other designated clients
- current research, theories, and knowledge of career development and learning
- contemporary career services standards and practices
- economic trends, opportunities, constraints, and/or the needs of external constituents
- institutional priorities
- technological advancements
- operational and personnel resources

Program goals must be reviewed and updated regularly, and communicated as appropriate, to stakeholders including students and other designated clients, administrators, faculty, staff, employers, and other constituencies.

CS should disseminate information on the availability, scope, and use of career services through institutional publications, campus media, presentations, outreach, and orientation programs.

CS must work collaboratively with academic divisions, departments, faculty members, student services, other relevant constituencies of the institution, and employers to enhance students' career development and participation in internships and other experiential education programs.

CS must develop and implement intentional marketing strategies and outreach programming to promote awareness and encourage use of the services.

For CS to effectively accomplish its stated purposes, it must include

- **career advising, counseling, and education**
- **information and resources on careers and further education**
- **opportunities for career exploration through experiential education**
- **job search services**
- **graduate and professional school or further education planning**
- **employer relations and recruitment services**
- **consultation services to faculty and administrators**

Career Advising, Counseling, and Education

Through CS or other units, the institution must offer career advising, counseling, and education that assist designated clients at any stage of their career development to

- **clarify interests, competencies, values, experiences, personal characteristics, and desired lifestyles using appropriate assessment tools**
- **explore occupational, educational, and employment possibilities**
- **make reasoned, informed educational and career decisions and plans based on accurate self-knowledge and occupational information**
- **establish short-term and long-term career goals**

The institution's career advising, counseling, and education services should

- encourage students to take advantage of career services as early as possible in their academic programs
- recognize that students' career decision-making is inextricably linked to additional psychosocial, personal, developmental, and cultural issues and beliefs
- assist students with career issues relevant to the individual (e.g., dual careers, sexual orientation, disabilities)
- provide scheduled appointments or drop-ins with individuals, group programs, career planning courses, outreach opportunities, special events, web- or computer-based programs, or any other available resources
- help students gain more self-awareness, apply knowledge and skills from their academic programs, and explore careers through part-time employment, internships, and other experiential programs
- assist students to assess their skills, values, and interests and understand how they relate to academic and co-curricular options and career opportunities
- help students develop and apply job search

competencies and decision-making skills

CS must refer students to appropriate counseling and resource agencies if assistance is needed beyond the scope of career advising, counseling, and education.

Career advising, counseling, and education should encourage designated clients to access employers and employment information as a part of their career exploration and decision-making process.

Information and Resources on Careers and Further Study

Career Services must make current and comprehensive career information accessible to designated clients and educate them on the effective use of information and resources in exploring and making educational and career decisions.

CS should provide information and resources

- to help clients assess and relate their interests, competencies, needs and expectations, education, experience, personal background, and desired lifestyle to the employment market
- for constituent groups on career and employment topics and the ethical obligations of students, employers, and others involved in the employment process
- on current employment opportunities and on employers to ensure that candidates have broad choices of employment
- to help students identify and pursue future educational objectives

Information and resources must be

- **current and reflective of economic, occupational, and workplace issues and trends**
- **organized with appropriate systems that are user-friendly, flexible, and adaptable to change**

The scope of information and resources available to clients should include

- individual self-assessment and career planning
- occupational and job market information
- options for further study (e.g., four-year colleges and universities; graduate and professional schools)
- job search information
- experiential learning, internship, and job listings
- employer information

Resources on careers and further study must be provided electronically where available for optimal student access.

Career information, resources, and means of delivery must be compatible with the size and nature of the student population, the career and geographic

interests of the students, and scope of academic programs.

Career information and resources should be conveniently available in a variety of media appropriate for different learning styles and special needs.

Career information facilities should be managed and staffed with persons who have the appropriate counseling, advising, and information technology competencies to assist students in accessing and using career information.

Opportunities for Career Exploration through Experiential Education

The institution must provide experiential education programs and services to enable students to integrate their academic studies with work experiences and career exploration.

Experiential education may include apprenticeships, cooperative education, internships, peer leadership experiences, service-learning, shadowing experiences, student teaching, undergraduate research, volunteer experiences, and work-study jobs and other campus employment.

CS should take a leadership role in working with their constituents to develop meaningful and intentional on-campus student employment opportunities.

CS may coordinate on-campus student employment.

Experiential education programs administered through CS must
- **provide students with opportunities to define both learning and career objectives and to reflect upon learning and other developmental aspects of their experience**
- **help students to identify employers for career development and potential employment**
- **teach students appropriate search and application techniques**
- **support institutional efforts to provide students with additional financial resources for attending college and/or opportunities for obtaining academic credit**
- **ensure adequate site supervision**
- **consider appropriate risk management strategies**

Experiential education programs administered through CS should promote mentor/mentee relationships. When experiential education opportunities are provided by other departments, CS should work closely with those departments.

Job Search Services

Job search services must assist students and other designated clients to
- **develop job-search competencies**
- **articulate their strengths, competencies, and**

achievements applicable to the positions they are seeking
- **present themselves effectively as candidates for employment**
- **identify and request appropriate references**
- **obtain information on employment opportunities, trends, and prospective employers**
- **connect with employers through campus recruitment programs, job listings, referrals, direct application, networking, publications, and information technology**
- **identify relevant career management issues (e.g., sex, gender, age, sexual orientation, dual career, disability, cultural, mental health)**
- **access and effectively use the Internet to access career and employer resources**
- **make informed choices among a variety of options**
- **identify and practice ethical job search behaviors**

CS must develop and implement strategies that cultivate employment opportunities for students.

Job search services may include offering site visits, campus recruiting, resumè referrals, information sessions, meetings with faculty members, access to alumni for networking, pre-recruiting activities, student access to employer information, posting job openings, and career and job fairs.

Job search services should help students and other designated clients develop skills to uncover less visible job markets related to their career interests.

If CS offers credential services for students and other clients, CS should
- establish a specific time period and procedures for maintaining information contained in student files and a systematic process for destruction of such records
- articulate clearly those record retention policies and procedures to students and other clients
- obtain signed written consent to disclose credential files prior to release of related information
- establish a process to verify legitimate release of information
- advise employers that CS does not verify accuracy of information contained in a credential file

CS should advise students and other clients about how to identify and approach individuals to provide a reference, what constitutes an effective reference, and legal and ethical considerations germane to students and other clients.

Job search services may assist clients in the development of portfolios.

Graduate and Professional School or Further Education Planning

Career services must offer programs and services that assist students and other designated clients to

- identify opportunities for further education that match their career goals
- obtain information on further education programs through a variety of sources
- connect with schools or programs offering further education
- present themselves effectively as candidates for further education
- identify and request appropriate references
- make appropriate decisions regarding further education

CS may provide information and resources on research and training opportunities; scholarships, grants and fellowships; and other information on financing further education.

Employer Relations and Recruitment Services

Because employers are both vital partners in the educational process and primary customers of career services, CS must offer a variety of services to employers that reflect the match between the students' and the employers' interests and needs.

Employer relations and recruitment services may include: site visits; campus recruiting; resumè referrals; pre-recruiting information sessions with students; student access to timely employer information; posting and publishing of job and internship openings; on-site or virtual career/job fairs; experiential learning options which may include shadowing experiences, internships, externships, student teaching, cooperative education assignments; remote electronic interviewing options; employer participation in career planning, work-force readiness courses, career conferences, resumè preparation, practice interviews, and job search readiness workshops.

To ensure quality employer relations and services, CS must

- develop strategic objectives for employer relations/services and job development that yield maximum opportunities for the institution's students, graduates, and designated clients
- inform and promote adherence to laws, policies, procedures, and instructions for using the services in accordance with federal, state/provincial, and institutional privacy and non-discrimination mandates
- develop, maintain and enhance relationships with employers who provide career development and employment opportunities
- enhance customer service and foster continuous improvement by using feedback from employers

- inform, educate, and consult with employers on the nature of services provided and candidates' availability
- actively involve employers in on-campus programs that meet students' and designated clients' career and employment needs
- facilitate employer involvement and communication with faculty, students, and administrators concerning career and employment issues
- consult with employers on opportunities and strategies for establishing long-term relationships with academic units
- promote adherence to professional and ethical standards that serve as conduct models for students and designated clients
- provide employer feedback to faculty, administrators, and students and designated clients on preparation for jobs, the curricula, and the hiring process

CS should

- provide timely, pertinent information to employers regarding the institution's operations, enrollment, academic calendar, academic programs and curricula, and student/class profile in accordance with institutional policy and guidelines and availability of data to the public
- provide information and services to assist employers to communicate their opportunities to targeted populations and enhance their visibility
- educate employers of student demographics, needs, issues, and perspectives
- encourage employers to provide timely information to career services staff on job offers, salaries, and hires
- provide guidance on working with student leaders and student clubs and organizations
- use employers' experiences and expertise in support of institutional activities
- invite employer membership in career advisory boards
- develop and implement marketing strategies as part of a comprehensive employer relations program
- maximize students' exposure to employers

CS must define the various types of employers it will serve and articulate policies that guide its working relationships with these employers.

CS must uniformly and consistently apply policies and procedures to all employers.

CS staff should understand the variety and diversity of needs and employment practices among businesses, corporations, government agencies, schools, and non-profit organizations.

CS must develop policies for working with third-party recruiting organizations. Policies must include recruiter disclosure of the identities of organizations they represent and agreement to abide by the ethical guidelines.

CS should encourage employers to share information related to their organization's policies and practices on such topics as sustainability, social justice, and family friendly work practices.

Consultation Services to Faculty and Administrators

To support the institution's mission and goals, CS must provide faculty and staff and administrative units with information, guidance, and support on career development, and employment issues and linkages with the broader community.

CS should support faculty and staff and administrative units by
- identifying and disseminating information on employment trends and top employing organizations and on co-op and internship sponsors
- providing employer feedback on the preparation of students for jobs, the curriculum, and the hiring process
- raising awareness of appropriate ethical and legal guidelines for student referrals
- providing guidance on effective strategies for engaging employers in programs offered by faculty and administrative units
- increasing awareness of career development issues and available resources
- providing and interpreting aggregate data on student learning, career-related and first-destination outcomes, and employer engagement for purposes such as accreditation, marketing, institutional development, and curriculum development

CS should develop and disseminate guidelines for serving as a reference and writing effective reference letters, including legal and ethical considerations and other key factors.

Part 3. ORGANIZATION AND LEADERSHIP

An institution must appoint, position, and empower a leader or leadership team to provide strategic direction, manage programs and services, and align Career Services (CS) with the mission of the institution and the needs of the constituencies served.

If components of career services are offered by several units, the institution must designate a leader or leadership team that will coordinate the institution's programs and services.

Such leadership is necessary to ensure adherence to institutional and unit missions and to enhance program effectiveness and efficiency.

To achieve student and program outcomes, CS must be structured purposefully and organized effectively.

CS must have
- clearly stated goals
- current and accessible policies and procedures
- written performance expectations for employees
- functional work flow graphics or organizational charts demonstrating clear channels of authority

Leaders with organizational authority for the programs and services must provide strategic planning, supervision, and management; advance the organization; and maintain integrity through the following functions:

Strategic Planning
- articulate a vision and mission that drive short- and long-term planning
- set goals and objectives based on the needs of the population served and desired student learning or development and program outcomes
- facilitate continuous development, implementation, and assessment of goal attainment congruent with institutional mission and strategic plans
- promote environments that provide meaningful opportunities for student learning, development, and engagement
- develop and continuously improve programs and services in response to the changing needs of students served and evolving institutional priorities
- intentionally include diverse perspectives to inform decision making

Supervising
- manage human resource processes including recruitment, selection, development, supervision, performance planning, evaluation, recognition, and reward
- influence others to contribute to the effectiveness and success of the unit
- empower professional, support, and student staff to accept leadership opportunities
- offer appropriate feedback to colleagues and students on skills needed to become more effective leaders
- encourage and support professional development, collaboration with colleagues and departments across the institution, and scholarly contribution to the profession

Managing
- identify and address individual,

organizational, and environmental conditions that foster or inhibit mission achievement
- plan, allocate, and monitor the use of fiscal, physical, human, intellectual, and technological resources
- use current and valid evidence to inform decisions
- incorporate sustainability practices in the management and design of programs, services, and facilities
- understand appropriate technologies and integrate them into programs and services
- be knowledgeable about codes and laws relevant to programs and services and ensure that staff members understand their responsibilities through appropriate training
- assess potential risks and take action to mitigate them

Advancing the Organization
- communicate effectively in writing, speaking, and electronic venues
- advocate for programs and services
- advocate for representation in strategic planning initiatives at appropriate divisional and institutional levels
- initiate collaborative interactions with internal and external stakeholders who have legitimate concerns about and interests in the functional area
- facilitate processes to reach consensus where wide support is needed
- inform other areas within the institution about issues affecting practice

Maintaining Integrity
- model ethical behavior and institutional citizenship
- share data used to inform key decisions in transparent and accessible ways
- monitor media used for distributing information about programs and services to ensure the content is current, accurate, appropriately referenced, and accessible

CS leaders must conduct regular program evaluations to improve operations and to adjust to changing client needs, evolving institutional priorities, and changes in the workforce and employment conditions.

CS leaders must annually review, update, and communicate goals and objectives to appropriate constituencies.

CS leaders should identify and find means to address individual, organizational, or environmental conditions that inhibit goal achievement.

CS leaders must participate in institutional decisions about career services objectives and policies. CS leaders must participate in institutional decisions related to the identification and designation of clients served.

Decisions about clients served should include type and scope of services offered and the fees, if any, that are charged.

The external and internal organization of CS, including its place within the institution, must support the CS mission and achievement of programmatic and student outcomes.

The unit to which CS reports should support efficient and effective delivery of career services within the institution.

Areas for consideration in determining structure and management of career services should include
- size, nature, and mission of the institution
- needs of students and designated clients
- number and scope of academic-related programs and services
- scope and intent of recruiting services
- philosophy and delivery system for services
- varied delivery methods (e.g., direct contact, technology)

CS should be coordinated with, and complementary to, employment-related services provided by other institutional units.

Part 4. HUMAN RESOURCES

Career Services (CS) must be staffed adequately by individuals qualified to accomplish mission and goals.

Within institutional guidelines, CS must
- establish procedures for staff recruitment and selection, training, performance planning, and evaluation
- set expectations for supervision and performance
- assess the performance of employees individually and as a team
- provide access to continuing and advanced education and appropriate professional development opportunities to improve the leadership ability, competence, and skills of all employees.

CS must embrace fair employment practices and must be proactive in attracting and retaining a diverse staff.

CS staff must be staffed by persons who, in combination, provide the core competencies to perform primary functions effectively.

The primary functions should include the following core competencies and knowledge domains.

Management and Administration
Core Competencies
Needs assessment and satisfaction measures; program design, implementation and evaluation; strategic & operational planning; program integration and integrity; staffing; staff development and supervision; budget planning and administration; political sensitivity and negotiation skills; synthesize, interpret and report information.
Knowledge Domains
Systems theory; organizational development; research design; statistics; accounting and budgeting procedures; revenue generation; principles; purchasing; staff selection; supervision; performance appraisals; management of information systems; customer service; marketing

Program and Event Administration
Core Competencies
Needs assessment; goal setting; program planning; implementation and evaluation; budget allocation; time management; problem solving; attention to detail.
Knowledge Domains
Systems, logistics, and procedures; project management; customer service.

Research and Student Learning/Development Outcomes
Core Competencies
Identification of relevant and desirable student learning and development outcomes; outcome-oriented programming; research-based evidence of program impact on student learning and development outcomes
Knowledge Domains
Student and adult development theory; research/assessment procedures; evidence-based decision-making; statistical procedures.

Career Advising/Counseling and Consultation
Core Competencies
Needs assessment and diagnosis; intervention design and implementation; test administration and interpretation; counseling; feedback; evaluation; advising; empathy and interpersonal sensitivity; work with individuals and groups; use of career, occupational, and employment information.
Knowledge Domains
Career development theories; adult development theory and unique issues for special populations; statistics; counseling processes; evaluation of person-job fit; job analysis; career decision making; behavior management; job search, interviews, and resumès.

Teaching/ Training/ Educating
Core Competencies
Needs assessment; program/workshop design; researching, evaluating, and integrating information; effective teaching strategies; career coaching; career mentoring; work with individuals and groups; work with diverse populations; use of technology for delivery of content.
Knowledge Domains
Setting learning objectives; designing curricula and learning resources for specific content areas; experiential learning; career development and job search process; learning styles.

Marketing/ Promoting/Outreach
Core Competencies
Needs assessment and goal setting; written and interpersonal communication; public speaking; domestic and international job and experiential learning opportunity development; relationship development and management; job development; effective use of print, web, personal presentation methods; sales and closing techniques; development/fundraising strategies; marketing principles/strategies.
Knowledge Domains
Customer service; knowledge of institution and its academic programs; career services; employer, alumni, and faculty needs and expectations; recruiting and staffing methods, trends.

Brokering/ Connecting/Linking
Core Competencies
Organize information, logistics, people, and processes toward a desired outcome; consulting; building and managing advisory boards; interpersonal skills.
Knowledge Domains
Systems and procedures; candidate/resumè referral; recruiting and experiential learning operations; human resource selection practices.

Information Management
Core Competencies
Organization and dissemination; storage and retrieval; computing systems and applications; data entry and analysis; acquisition of appropriate career resources; web design and management.
Knowledge Domains
Library/resources center organization; computer systems and applications; specific electronic management information systems.

CS must maintain position descriptions for all staff members.

To create a diverse staff, CS must institute recruitment and hiring strategies that encourage individuals from under-represented populations to apply for positions.

CS must develop promotion practices that are fair, inclusive, proactive, and non-discriminatory.

To further the recruitment and retention of staff, CS must consider work life initiatives, such as

compressed work schedules, flextime, job sharing, remote work, or telework.

CS professional staff members must hold an earned graduate or professional degree in a field relevant to the position they hold or must possess an appropriate combination of educational credentials and related work experience.

CS professional staff members must engage in continuing professional development activities to keep abreast of the research, theories, legislation, policies, and developments that affect their programs and services.

Training should include customer service, program procedures, and information and resource utilization.

CS must have technical and support staff members adequate to accomplish their mission. All members of the staff must be technologically proficient and qualified to perform their job functions, be knowledgeable about ethical and legal uses of technology, and have access to training and resources to support the performance of their assigned responsibilities.

A technical support person or support service should be available to maintain computer and information technology systems for career services.

Career information staff should have the appropriate competencies to assist designated clients to access and effectively use career information and resources.

Degree- or credential-seeking interns or graduate assistants must be qualified by enrollment in an appropriate field of study and by relevant experience. These individuals must be trained and supervised adequately by professional staff members holding educational credentials and related work experience appropriate for supervision. Supervisors must be cognizant of the roles of interns and graduate assistants as both student and employee and closely adhere to all parameters of their job descriptions, work hours, and schedules. Supervisors and the interns or graduate assistants must agree to compensatory time or other appropriate compensation if circumstances necessitate additional hours.

Student employees and volunteers must be carefully selected, trained, supervised, and evaluated. They must be educated on how and when to refer those in need of additional assistance to qualified staff members and must have access to a supervisor for assistance in making these judgments. Student employees and volunteers must be provided clear job descriptions, pre-service training based on assessed needs, and continuing development.

All CS staff members, including student employees and volunteers, must receive specific training on institutional policies pertaining to functions or activities they support and to privacy and confidentiality policies and laws regarding access to student records and other sensitive institutional information.

All CS staff members must receive training on policies and procedures related to the use of technology to store or access student records and institutional data.

CS must ensure that staff members are knowledgeable about and trained in emergency procedures, crisis response, and prevention efforts. Prevention efforts must address identification of threatening conduct or behavior of students, faculty and staff members, and others and must incorporate a system for responding and reporting.

CS must ensure that staff members are knowledgeable of and trained in safety and emergency procedures for securing and vacating facilities.

Staff training and development should be ongoing and promote knowledge and skill development across program components.

All staff must be trained in legal, confidential, and ethical issues related to career services.

Part 5. ETHICS

Career Services (CS) must review relevant professional ethical standards and must adopt or develop and implement appropriate statements of ethical practice.

CS must publish and adhere to statements of ethical practice and ensure their periodic review by relevant constituencies.

Ethical standards or other statements from relevant professional associations should be considered and if adopted for implementation, should be clearly communicated to relevant constituencies.

CS must orient new staff members to relevant ethical standards and statements of ethical practice and related institutional policies.

Statements of ethical standards must specify that staff members respect privacy and maintain confidentiality in all communications and records to the extent that such communications and records are protected under relevant privacy laws.

Statements of ethical standards must specify limits on disclosure of information contained in students' educational records as well as requirements to disclose to appropriate authorities.

Statements of ethical standards must address personal and economic conflicts of interest, or appearance thereof, by staff members in the performance of their work.

Statements of ethical standards must reflect the responsibility of staff members to be fair, objective, and impartial in their interactions with others.

Statements of ethical standards must reference management of institutional funds.

Statements of ethical standards must reference appropriate behavior regarding research and assessment with human participants, confidentiality of research and assessment data, and students' rights and responsibilities.

Statements of ethical standards must include the expectation that CS staff members confront and hold accountable other staff members who exhibit unethical behavior.

Statements of ethical standards must address issues surrounding scholarly integrity.

As appropriate, CS staff members must inform users of programs and services of ethical obligations and limitations emanating from codes and laws or from licensure requirements.

CS staff members must recognize and avoid conflicts of interest that could adversely influence their judgment or objectivity and, when unavoidable, recuse themselves from the situation.

CS staff members must perform their duties within the limits of their position, training, expertise, and competence.

When these limits are exceeded, individuals in need of further assistance must be referred to persons possessing appropriate qualifications.

Promotional and descriptive information must be accurate and free of deception.

CS must adhere to institutional policies regarding ethical and legal use of software and technology.

CS should provide guidance and education on these standards to all persons involved in providing career services, including, but not limited to, entry-level professionals, support staff, student staff, interns, graduate assistants, faculty and staff, employers, service providers, and other administrators. CS staff members should provide guidance regarding prevailing ethical expectations to students and other clients using career services.

Part 6. LAW, POLICY, AND GOVERNANCE

Career Services (CS) must be in compliance with laws, regulations, and policies that relate to their respective responsibilities and that pose legal obligations, limitations, risks, and liabilities for the institution as a whole. Examples include constitutional, statutory, regulatory, and case law; relevant law and orders emanating from codes and laws; and the institution's policies.

CS must inform staff members, appropriate officials, and users of programs and services about existing and changing legal obligations, risks and liabilities, and limitations.

CS must have written policies on all relevant operations, transactions, or tasks that have legal implications.

CS must regularly review policies. The revision and creation of policies must be informed by best practices, available evidence, and policy issues in higher education.

CS staff members must use reasonable and informed practices to limit the liability exposure of the institution and its officers, employees, and agents. CS staff members must be informed about institutional policies regarding risk management, personal liability, and related insurance coverage options and must be referred to external sources if the institution does not provide coverage.

The institution must provide access to legal advice for staff members as needed to carry out assigned responsibilities.

CS must have procedures and guidelines consistent with institutional policy for responding to threats, emergencies, and crisis situations. Systems and procedures must be in place to disseminate timely and accurate information to students, other members of the institutional community, and appropriate external organizations during emergency situations.

CS staff members must neither participate in nor condone any form of harassment or activity that demeans persons or creates an intimidating, hostile, or offensive environment.

CS must obtain permission to use copyrighted materials and instruments. CS must purchase the materials and instruments from legally compliant sources or seek alternative permission from the publisher or owner. References to copyrighted materials and instruments must include appropriate citations.

CS staff members must be knowledgeable about internal and external governance systems that affect programs and services.

CS staff members must be aware of and seek advice from the institution's legal counsel or other appropriate professional resources on

- privacy and disclosure of student information contained in education records
- defamation law regarding references and recommendations on the behalf of students and other designated clients
- laws regarding employment referral practices of the career services office and others employed by the institution that refer students for employment; affirmative action regulations and laws regarding programs for special populations
- liability issues pertaining to experiential learning programs
- laws regarding eligibility to work and contracts governing service provided by outside vendors
- privacy of data maintained in electronic format by entities engaged by career services
- laws regarding grant administration

Contracts with outside vendors must include adherence to ethics, confidentiality, security, and institutional policies, as well as reflect support of career services programs, goals, and standards.

CS must maintain appropriate records for future work with students and other designated clients.

Part 7. DIVERSITY, EQUITY, AND ACCESS

Within the context of each institution's unique mission and in accordance with institutional polices and all applicable codes and laws, Career Services (CS) must create and maintain educational and work environments that are

- welcoming, accessible, and inclusive to persons of diverse backgrounds
- equitable and non-discriminatory
- free from harassment

These groups may include traditionally under-represented, evening, part-time, commuter, LGBT, and international students, as well as students with disabilities, athletes, veterans, and distance learners.

To respond to the needs of students and other designated clients, career services should provide services in-person, online, and via telephone, e-mail, or other formats. CS should be responsive to the needs of all its constituencies through the establishment of office hours, customer service systems, and online operations.

CS must not discriminate on the basis of ability; age; cultural identity; ethnicity; family educational history (e.g., first generation to attend college); gender identity and expression; nationality; political affiliation; race; religious affiliation; sex; sexual orientation; economic, marital, social, or veteran status; or any other basis included in institutional policies and codes and laws.

CS must address non-adherence by employers to the word and spirit of equal employment opportunity and affirmative action.

CS staff should make every effort to inform or educate faculty members about issues relevant to discriminatory practices related to their referral of students directly to employers.

CS must

- advocate for greater sensitivity to multicultural and social justice concerns by the institution and its personnel
- modify or remove policies, practices, facilities, structures, systems, and technologies that limit access, discriminate, or produce inequities
- include diversity, equity, and access initiatives within their strategic plans
- foster communication that deepens understanding of identity, culture, self-expression, and heritage
- promote respect about commonalities and differences among people within their historical and cultural contexts
- address the characteristics and needs of a diverse population when establishing and implementing culturally relevant and inclusive programs, services, policies, procedures, and practices
- provide staff members with access to multicultural training and hold staff members accountable for integrating the training into their work
- respond to the needs of all students and other populations served when establishing hours of operation and developing methods of delivering programs, services, and resources
- ensure physical, program, and resource access for persons with disabilities
- recognize the needs of distance learning students by providing appropriate and accessible services and resources or by assisting them in gaining access to other appropriate services and resources in their geographic region

CS should collaborate with other departments and student organizations to provide educational programs that help clients from diverse backgrounds and individuals with disabilities to identify and address their needs related to career development and employment. CS should initiate partnerships and collaborative programming with other offices representing specific populations to ensure appropriate service delivery.

Part 8. INSTITUTIONAL AND EXTERNAL RELATIONS

Career Services (CS) must reach out to relevant individuals, groups, communities, and organizations internal and external to the institution to
- **establish, maintain, and promote understanding and effective relations with those that have a significant interest in or potential effect on the students or other constituents served by the programs and services**
- **garner support and resources for programs and services as defined by the mission statement**
- **disseminate information about the programs and services**
- **collaborate, where appropriate, to assist in offering or improving programs and services to meet the needs of students and other constituents and to achieve program and student outcomes**
- **engage diverse individuals, groups, communities, and organizations to enrich the educational environment and experiences of students and other constituents**

In order to achieve this, CS should
- develop institutional support for career development and employment services for students and other designated clients
- involve the academic administration and faculty in career planning and employment programs
- raise issues and concerns with the institution's legal counsel regarding compliance with employment laws as they pertain to recruitment and hiring of students, alumni, and other designated clients
- participate in campus activities such as faculty organizations, committees, student orientation programs, classroom presentations, academic courses in career planning, leadership training, and student organization programs
- exchange information with the academic administration and faculty concerning employment requirements, labor market trends, specific jobs, and employment that may be related to academic planning and curriculum development
- arrange appropriate programs that use alumni experience and expertise
- establish cooperative relationships with other offices and services in order to support mutual referrals, exchange of information, sharing of resources, and other program functions
- partner with other organizations and institutions to address the unique needs of special populations
- provide information and reports to the academic

administration, faculty and key offices of the institution regarding career services for students and other designated clients and for employers
- provide feedback to faculty, administrators, and students on the preparation of graduates for employment, graduate/professional school, or further education to aid curriculum development and individual career planning
- encourage dialogue among employers, faculty members, and administrators concerning career issues and trends for students, graduates, and other designated clients
- provide parents and family members with information and relevant data on career education programs and services and key results related to employment, graduate study, and further education outcomes as appropriate

In addition, CS should encourage staff participation in professional associations and community activities related to career and employment issues (e.g., chambers of commerce, workforce development functions, employer open houses, workshops, federally mandated one stop centers, school-to-work efforts).

CS must have procedures and guidelines consistent with institutional policy for
- **communicating with the media**
- **contracting with external organizations for delivery of programs and services**
- **cultivating, soliciting, and managing gifts**
- **applying to and managing funds from grants**

Part 9. FINANCIAL RESOURCES

Career Services (CS) must have funding to accomplish the mission and goals. In establishing funding priorities and making significant changes, a comprehensive analysis must be conducted to determine the following elements: unmet needs of the unit, relevant expenditures, external and internal resources, and impact on students and the institution.

CS must demonstrate efficient and effective use and responsible stewardship of fiscal resources consistent with institutional protocols.

Consistent with institutional policy, CS may
- develop a funding strategy that outlines projects, programs, and related activity that can be further enhanced with additional outside funding sources
- cultivate employer support of the institution, including scholarships and other forms of financial support

Outside revenue may be generated to supplement institutional funding.

Fees charged to employers, vendors, students, and other designated clients should be limited and reasonable to carry out stated CS objectives.

Part 10. TECHNOLOGY

Career Services (CS) must have adequate technology to support the achievement of their mission and goals. The technology and its use must comply with institutional policies and procedures and be evaluated for compliance with relevant codes and laws.

CS must use current technology to provide updated information regarding mission, location, staffing, programs, services, and official contacts to students and designated clients.

CS must explore the use of technology to enhance delivery of programs and services, especially for students at a distance or external constituencies.

When technology is used to facilitate student learning and development, CS must select technology that reflects intended outcomes.

CS must

- maintain policies and procedures that address the security, confidentiality, and backup of data, as well as compliance with privacy laws
- have clearly articulated plans in place for protecting confidentiality and security of information when using Internet-based technologies
- develop plans for replacing and updating existing hardware and software as well as plans for integrating new technically-based or -supported programs, including systems developed internally by the institution, systems available through professional associations, or private vendor-based systems

Technology selection must address distance learners and clients with unique needs and interests.

CS staff must be well informed about the array of career-based technological applications that are in current use.

In light of the rapidity of change associated with technology, CS must develop plans for the replacement/updating of existing hardware and software as well as plan for the integration of new technically-based or supported career programs, including systems developed internally by the institution, systems available through professional associations, or private vendor-based systems.

Technological applications specific to CS must include

- Internet-based resources that provide updated information regarding mission, location, staffing, programs, and services

available to students and designated clients, as well as contact information
- computer-based assessment and computer-assisted career guidance systems
- online recruiting and employment systems that include job listings and student résumés

Other applications may include student registration systems; student contact, record, and tracking systems; career portfolios; student surveys; employer satisfaction surveys; career fair management systems; resumè writing software; office intranet sites; e-mail-based career advising/counseling; video-based technology; mentoring; and social/professional networking sites.

Technology, as well as workstations or computer labs maintained by programs and services for student use, must be accessible to all designated clients and must meet established technology standards for delivery to persons with disabilities.

When providing student access to technology, CS must

- have policies on the use of technology that are clear, easy to understand, and available to all students
- provide assistance, information, or referral to appropriate support services to those needing help accessing or using technology
- provide instruction or training on how to use the technology
- inform students on the legal and ethical implications of misuse as it pertains to intellectual property, harassment, privacy, and social networks

Student violations of technology policies must follow established institutional student disciplinary procedures.

Students who experience negative emotional or psychological consequences from the use of technology must be referred to support services provided by the institution.

Part 11. FACILITIES AND EQUIPMENT

Career Services (CS) must have adequate, accessible, and suitably located facilities and equipment to support the mission and goals. If acquiring capital equipment as defined by the institution, CS must take into account expenses related to regular maintenance and life cycle costs. Facilities and equipment must be evaluated on an established cycle, including consideration of sustainability, and be in compliance with codes and laws to provide for access, health, safety, and security.

CS staff members must have workspace that is well

equipped, adequate in size, and designed to support their work and responsibilities. For conversations requiring privacy, staff members must have access to a private space.

CS should provide
- private offices for professional staff in order to perform advising, counseling, or other confidential work
- support staff work areas
- reception, student registration, and waiting area
- career resource center
- storage space sufficient to accommodate resources, supplies, and equipment
- access to computer labs and to conference and large group meeting rooms equipped with appropriate levels of technology
- private interview facilities for employers and a waiting area for students to accommodate the scope of the recruiting program
- private employer workspace

CS staff members who share workspace must be able to secure their own work.

The design of the facilities must guarantee the security and privacy of records and ensure the confidentiality of sensitive information.

The location and layout of the facilities must be sensitive to the needs of persons with disabilities as well as the needs of other constituencies.

CS should be in a convenient location for students and employers and project a welcoming, professional atmosphere for its users. Parking for visitors should be adequate and convenient.

Part 12. ASSESSMENT AND EVALUATION

Career Services (CS) must have a clearly articulated assessment plan to document achievement of stated goals and learning outcomes, demonstrate accountability, provide evidence of improvement, and describe resulting changes in programs and services.

CS must have adequate fiscal, human, professional development, and technological resources to develop and implement assessment plans.

Assessments must include direct and indirect evaluation and use qualitative and quantitative methodologies and existing evidence, as appropriate, to determine whether and to what degree the stated mission, goals, and intended outcomes are being met as effectively and efficiently as possible. The process must employ sufficient and sound measures to ensure comprehensiveness. Data collected must include responses from students and other constituencies,

and aggregated results must be shared with those groups. Results of assessments must be shared appropriately with multiple constituents.

For comparative studies, CS should identify and consult with peers and professional associations.

CS should collaborate with institutional research units, state agencies, accrediting bodies, and other relevant groups that produce assessment and evaluation data. CS should promote institutional efforts to conduct relevant research on career development, institutional issues such as academic success and retention, student learning outcomes, employment trends, and career interests.

Evaluations should include
- review of the strategic plan, mission, human resources needs, diversity efforts, and other areas covered in this document
- regular feedback from participants on events, programs, and services
- systematic needs assessment to guide program development
- first destination surveys at or following graduation
- employer and student feedback regarding experiential learning programs
- alumni follow-up surveys administered at specific times after graduation
- reports and satisfaction surveys from students and other constituencies interacting with career services such as employers, faculty, and other post-secondary institutions

Results of assessments and evaluations must be used to identify needs and interests in revising and improving programs and services, recognizing staff performance, maximizing resource efficiency and effectiveness, improving student achievement of learning and development outcomes, and improving student persistence and success. Changes resulting from the use of assessments and evaluation must be shared with stakeholders.

CS should prepare and disseminate annual and special reports, including career services philosophy, goals and objectives, current programs and services, service delivery information, first destination information, and graduate follow-up information.

General Standards revised in 2011;
CS content developed/revised in 1986, 1997, 2000, & 2010

The Role of Clinical Health Services
CAS Standards Contextual Statement

An institution of higher education (IHE), particularly one with a residential student body, has traditionally provided students with services not available in the surrounding community. Society has become increasingly aware of the need for universal access to basic healthcare services as well as the effects of policy and the built environment on an individual's physical, social, and emotional health. New partnerships are being forged so that clinical (individual) and systemic (population) concerns are addressed in the most effective way. The complexity and comprehensiveness of the Clinical Health Services (CHS) provided by an IHE varies extensively by student demographics, institutional mission, and the availability of community resources. The CHS can play a role in easing access to medical, nursing, and psychological care for college students and, on some campuses, employees and community members as well. The CHS also works with other campus and community departments and programs to address communicable diseases, emergency preparedness, and crisis management. Access to medical, psychological, nursing, and allied care as well as management of public health needs are important aspects of maintaining a productive living, learning, and working environment. In many cases, the services may be provided directly by the institution; in other cases, external resources may be used and coordinated with the institution.

The focus of the CHS, in most cases, is to attend to traditional student healthcare services, health centers, and campus clinics, thus maintaining an accredited ambulatory healthcare clinic, primarily serving only students, with additional emergency preparedness, crisis management, public health surveillance, and, occasionally, workers compensation responsibilities. The CHS places relatively little focus on wellness or primary prevention and the growing efforts to address the campus environment as a place that supports risk reduction, safety, and wellness.

Changes in the characteristics of healthcare and the availability of the CHS have led to an emphasis on financing through an insurance product and reasonable access. Access to clinical diagnosis, therapeutic procedures, pharmaceuticals, and psychological counseling, many of which are insurance reimbursable, are elements of comprehensive healthcare services made available to students on many campuses. The leadership on a campus must assess the student's level of insurance coverage, access to healthcare, and the quality of services on campus and in the surrounding community. Student populations vary widely; each campus has its own culture. As campuses respond to a broad range of student needs, they also have an opportunity to influence students who will become consumers of the healthcare system, leaders in public health, business leaders in the healthcare insurance industry, future decision and policy makers, and members of a constructive society.

As part of the educational mission of the institution, a health service must do all it can to engage the student in a consumer education process regarding access of clinical healthcare services. For many, college is the time when the individual student becomes responsible for many of life's daily experiences. This may include balancing a checkbook, grocery shopping, signing rental agreements, and initiating contact with a healthcare delivery system. Students need to know their rights and responsibilities. They need to have access to accurate information on cost, price, services, and providers. Orientation to the concepts and language of insurance could diminish significant financial risk. These students will be consumers of healthcare all their lives, so they must understand the prevailing system and alternatives. Regardless of the institution's specific policies requiring levels of healthcare insurance coverage beyond current law, students need to know how insurance is used as the financing vehicle for services in the United States and how to make an informed decision based on their particular situation. Immediate access to accurate information will allow students to take responsibility and affect change.

In 1860, Edward Hitchcock Jr., physician and professor of hygiene at Amherst College, was charged by the president of the college to develop methods to advance the health of students (Packwood, 1989). In response to this charge, Dr. Hitchcock used physical fitness and hygiene education. During the early part of the twentieth century in response to outbreaks and epidemics of communicable diseases and a lack of community resources, campus infirmaries were created to isolate students with infectious diseases. Given the lack, in the 1940s, of a single-payer system of universal healthcare access, infirmaries populated college campuses. In the 1950s as veterans returned and took advantage of the GI Bill, physicals and immunizations were added, as they were the standard of practice in the military. Societal and behavioral risk factors moved to the forefront in the 1970s, and in the 1990s the recognition of the impact of developmental and psychosocial concerns brought new institutional investments in mental health as an element of services.

Some of the historical reasons for providing the CHS on campus remain pertinent today. However, financing the delivery of healthcare is changing to universal access through private purchase third-party insurance, employment compensation packages, or taxpayer-provided insurance coverage. All three of these financing options often cover primary care and other medical services for students off campus or near their parent or spouse. Students who are underinsured may access care through community resources for the underinsured. Students who are underinsured may also have access to services that are financed by requiring all enrolled students to pay, on their tuition and fee bill, a student health fee or general fund. The CHS is rightly compared to other primary care ambulatory community health clinics or the public health department in the community. Traditionally, the CHS was just one of the programs and services financed by institutional appropriations or a "health fee." During these next few years, the integration of existing healthcare delivery and application of insurance (whether privately purchased, employer-purchased as part of a compensation package, or tax-payer purchased) will create changes in how and where students access healthcare.

Regardless of the financing and access to healthcare, the health issues that pose a threat to the student's academic success are currently more often psychosocial, behavioral, or environmental than risks from infection or other diseases. Data collected by the American College Health Association National College Health Assessment (ACHA-NCHA) show that colds, flu, sore throats, and sinus infections are still frequent in the student population and can pose a threat to academic success. The great majority of health-related causes for academic problems (intra- or interpersonal difficulties and stress resulting from a lack of routine exercise or balanced nutrition, excessive computer use, and sleep hygiene) cannot be addressed effectively by only accessing healthcare but rather by requiring environmental and community initiatives.

The CHS can be one of a variety of methods used to advance the health of students to the extent that such efforts enhance the learning environment. Clinical Healthcare Services must adapt and make it a priority to first address health risks and problems contextually appropriate to a student's capacity to learn. The most important aspect of any CHS will be its ability to create and maintain necessary, non-duplicate responsive services as well as collaborative relationships with the larger community, faculty, and staff. The maintenance of a comprehensive ambulatory healthcare facility may not be as important as other coordinated relevant and cost-effective initiatives. Campuses must maintain a focus on services that support priorities within this academic context.

Although institutions differ in size, scope, and setting, there are universal concepts that affect the level of healthcare services to college students. Current sociological trends, high-risk identification, public health issues, healthcare insurance finance reform, and changes in preventive medicine have broad institutional implications. The CHS has a unique opportunity to help meet those new challenges through a variety of services, programs, and approaches. The standards and guidelines are offered to serve this process.

References, Readings, and Resources

American College Health Association [ACHA]. ACHA National Office, P.O. Box 28937. Baltimore, MD 21240-8937. (410) 859-1500; Fax (410) 859-1510. http://www.acha.org

American College Health Association. (2004). American College Health Association - National College Health Assessment (ACHA-NCHA) Web Summary. Updated June 2004. Available at http://www.acha.org

American College Health Association. (2008). Guidelines and white Papers
Baltimore, MD: Author.

Centers for Disease Control and Prevention. (1997). Youth risk behavior surveillance: National college health risk behavior survey-United States. MMWR, 46(6), 1-56.

Jackson, M., & Weinstein, H. (1997). The importance of healthy communities of higher education. Journal of American College Health, 45, 237-241.

Keeling, R. P. (2000). Beyond the campus clinic: A holistic approach to student health. AAC&U Peer Review, 2(3), 13-18.

Neinstein, L. S. (2002). Adolescent health care: A practical guide. Philadelphia: Lippincott Williams & Wilkins.

Packwood, W. (1989). College student personnel services. Springfield, IL: Charles C. Thomas.

Patrick, K. (1988). Student health: Medical care within institutions of higher education. Journal of the American Medical Association, 260, 3301-3305.

Silverman, D., Underhile, R., & Keeling, R. (2008). Student health reconsidered: A radical proposal for thinking differently about health-related programs and services for students. Student Health Spectrum, June 2008, 4-11.

Swinford, P. (2002). Advancing the health of students: A viewpoint. Journal of American College Health, May 2002.

Contextual Statement Contributors

Paula Swinford, University of Southern California, ACHA
Kristen Buzzbee, CAS ACHA Alternate
Richard P. Keeling, MD, K&A, NYC, CAS Public Director
Mary Hoban and Victor Lieno, ACHA

Clinical Health Services
CAS Standards and Guidelines

Part 1. MISSION

The purpose of Clinical Health Services (CHS) is to provide, promote, support, and integrate individual healthcare, clinical preventive services, clinical treatment for illness, patient education, and public health responsibilities. Such services must take into consideration the health status of the student population and the learning environment. These services must be consistent with the educational mission of the institution and must comply with relevant legal requirements, state/provincial regulations, and professional standards. The mission must reflect the fundamental assumption that health and social justice are inextricably interconnected. CHS must serve as a method of advancing the health of the students, thereby enhancing the learning environment at the institution of higher education it serves.

The following characteristics exemplify CHS that are consistent with the environment of healthcare delivery and the environment of higher education:

- access to multiple data sources on the characteristics and health status of the population
- a spectrum of services that supports the learning mission of the campus community and health in its broadest sense
- easy and equal access to services by all students
- advocacy for a healthy campus community by providing leadership on policy issues regarding health risks of the population in the context of the learning environment
- evidence of measures of quality, such as accreditation of services, the use of recognized standards, and data on service delivery and effectiveness
- significant student involvement in advising the program's mission, goals, services, funding, and evaluation
- providing leadership during a health-related crises
- collaboration with other campus health-related programs and services

CHS must develop, disseminate, implement, and regularly review their missions. The mission must be consistent with the mission of the institution and with professional standards. The mission must be appropriate for the institution's student populations and community settings. Mission statements must reference student learning and development.

Part 2. PROGRAM

The formal education of students, consisting of the curriculum and the co-curriculum, must promote student learning and development outcomes that are purposeful, contribute to students' realization of their potential, and prepare students for satisfying and productive lives.

Clinical Health Services (CHS) must collaborate with colleagues and departments across the institution to promote student learning and development, persistence, and success.

Consistent with the institutional mission, CHS must identify relevant and desirable student learning and development outcomes from among the six domains and related dimensions:

Domain: knowledge acquisition, integration, construction, and application

- Dimensions: understanding knowledge from a range of disciplines; connecting knowledge to other knowledge, ideas, and experiences; constructing knowledge; and relating knowledge to daily life

Domain: cognitive complexity

- Dimensions: critical thinking, reflective thinking, effective reasoning, and creativity

Domain: intrapersonal development

- Dimensions: realistic self-appraisal, self-understanding, and self-respect; identity development; commitment to ethics and integrity; and spiritual awareness

Domain: interpersonal competence

- Dimensions: meaningful relationships, interdependence, collaboration, and effective leadership.

Domain: humanitarianism and civic engagement

- Dimensions: understanding and appreciation of cultural and human differences, social responsibility, global perspective, and sense of civic responsibility

Domain: practical competence

- Dimensions: pursuing goals, communicating effectively, technical competence, managing personal affairs, managing career development, demonstrating professionalism, maintaining health and wellness, and living a purposeful and satisfying life

[LD Outcomes: See *The Council for the Advancement of Standards Learning and Developmental Outcomes* statement for examples of outcomes related to these domains and dimensions.]

CHS must

- **assess relevant and desirable student learning and development**
- **provide evidence of impact on outcomes**
- **articulate contributions to or support of student learning and development in the domains not specifically assessed**
- **articulate contributions to or support of student persistence and success**
- **use evidence gathered through this process to create strategies for improvement of programs and services**

CHS must be

- **intentionally designed**
- **guided by theories and knowledge of learning and development**
- **integrated into the life of the institution**
- **reflective of developmental and demographic profiles of the student population**
- **responsive to needs of individuals, populations with distinct needs, and relevant constituencies**
- **delivered using multiple formats, strategies, and contexts**

Where institutions provide distance education, CHS must assist distance learners to achieve their educational goals by providing access to information about programs and services, to staff members who can address questions and concerns, and to counseling, advising, or other forms of assistance.

CHS must acknowledge that health and social justice are inextricably interconnected.

CHS must establish appropriate policies and procedures for responding to emergency situations, especially where CHS facilities, personnel, and resources are not equipped to handle emergencies and/or when services are closed.

CHS must provide an infrastructure to support its services. The program must also create and maintain a network of services throughout the campus and surrounding communities.

Regardless of the size or scope of the institution, CHS must conform to a general level of acceptable practice that is theory-based and data-driven, and compliant with pertinent statutes, regulations, and professional standards.

In determining the scope of services to be offered, the following guidelines should apply:

- data on the affordability and accessibility of local healthcare resources, the insurance coverage of individual students, and the health status of the population should be collected and used to set priorities and tailor the CHS to the specific campus context
- CHS should contribute to the general education of students in the areas of behaviors and environments that promote physical, psychological, spiritual, and social health
- the scope and objectives of the services should be planned and outlined according to standards of practice utilizing data, goals and objectives, focus populations, assessment strategies and evaluative methodologies
- the educational goals of CHS should be consistent with nationally and internationally developed healthcare objectives
- documented evidence of organized strategic planning and implementation should be available
- CHS should create opportunities to address documented health issues and medical services needs within the student community it serves
- appropriate interdisciplinary and interagency collaboration should occur regularly

In determining the quality of services provided, the following guidelines should apply:

- access for all students to essential medical, nursing, and counseling services
- provision of services in accordance with standards of professional practice and ethical conduct and concern for the costs versus benefits to the health status of the population
- maintenance of accreditation, staff certification, and licensure where appropriate
- cost-effective and relevant services designed to address unique campus configurations
- coordination of services to ensure coverage with no duplication
- identification of less expensive alternative resources for individual healthcare when appropriate
- provision of appropriate referrals for additional or alternative treatments or assessments

Part 3. ORGANIZATION AND LEADERSHIP

To achieve student and program outcomes, Clinical Health Services (CHS) must be structured purposefully and organized effectively. CHS must have

- **clearly stated goals**
- **current and accessible policies and procedures**
- **written performance expectations for employees**
- **functional work flow graphics or organizational charts demonstrating clear channels of authority**

Leaders with organizational authority for the programs and services must provide strategic planning, supervision, and management; advance the organization; and maintain integrity through the following functions:

Strategic Planning

- articulate a vision and mission that drive short- and long-term planning
- set goals and objectives based on the needs of the population served and desired student learning or development and program outcomes
- facilitate continuous development, implementation, and assessment of goal attainment congruent with institutional mission and strategic plans
- promote environments that provide meaningful opportunities for student learning, development, and engagement
- develop and continuously improve programs and services in response to the changing needs of students served and evolving institutional priorities
- intentionally include diverse perspectives to inform decision making

Supervising

- manage human resource processes including recruitment, selection, development, supervision, performance planning, evaluation, recognition, and reward
- influence others to contribute to the effectiveness and success of the unit
- empower professional, support, and student staff to accept leadership opportunities
- offer appropriate feedback to colleagues and students on skills needed to become more effective leaders
- encourage and support professional development, collaboration with colleagues and departments across the institution, and scholarly contribution to the profession

Managing

- identify and address individual, organizational, and environmental conditions that foster or inhibit mission achievement
- plan, allocate, and monitor the use of fiscal, physical, human, intellectual, and technological resources
- use current and valid evidence to inform decisions
- incorporate sustainability practices in the management and design of programs, services, and facilities
- understand appropriate technologies and

integrate them into programs and services

- be knowledgeable about codes and laws relevant to programs and services and ensure that staff members understand their responsibilities through appropriate training
- assess potential risks and take action to mitigate them

Advancing the Organization

- communicate effectively in writing, speaking, and electronic venues
- advocate for programs and services
- advocate for representation in strategic planning initiatives at appropriate divisional and institutional levels
- initiate collaborative interactions with internal and external stakeholders who have legitimate concerns about and interests in the functional area
- facilitate processes to reach consensus where wide support is needed
- inform other areas within the institution about issues affecting practice

Maintaining Integrity

- model ethical behavior and institutional citizenship
- share data used to inform key decisions in transparent and accessible ways
- monitor media used for distributing information about programs and services to ensure the content is current, accurate, appropriately referenced, and accessible

CHS leaders should continuously strive to eliminate duplicate coverage for care and contribute to a campus culture that supports health.

As the institution is legally constituted, the institution must have a defined governance structure that sets policy and is ultimately responsible for the CHS and its operations.

CHS should be defined by the size, nature, complexity, and mission of the institution and by the documented needs and capabilities of the population it serves, as well as the availability of local community resources.

CHS should establish and maintain an advisory board with broad constituent representation, with specific duties and responsibilities for policy, budget, services, facilities, and resources.

CHS should make initial staff appointments, reappointments, and assignment or curtailment of clinical privileges based upon a professional review of credentials and as directed by institutional policy and state/provincial regulations and statutes.

CHS should establish criteria and institute procedures for

assessment and evaluation of medical access insurance policies.

The CHS director or coordinator must be placed within the institution's organizational structure to be able to promote cooperative interactions with appropriate campus and community entities.

Part 4. HUMAN RESOURCES

Clinical Health Services (CHS) must be staffed adequately by individuals qualified to accomplish mission and goals.

Within institutional guidelines, CHS must
- **establish procedures for staff recruitment and selection, training, performance planning, and evaluation**
- **set expectations for supervision and performance**
- **assess the performance of employees individually and as a team**
- **provide access to continuing and advanced education and appropriate professional development opportunities to improve the leadership ability, competence, and skills of all employees.**

CHS should
- strive to improve the professional competence and skill, as well as the quality of performance of all personnel it employs
- provide personnel with convenient access to on-line library resources that include materials pertinent to operational, administrative, institutional, and research services
- encourage participation of personnel in seminars, workshops, and other educational activities pertinent to its mission, goals, objectives, and the professional role
- verify participation in relevant external professional development programs, when attendance at such activities is required of professional personnel
- monitor the use of resources available to its personnel to identify that activities are relevant to the mission, goals, and objectives, and to maintain the licensure and/or certification of professional personnel
- identify continuing education activities based on quality improvement findings and the education criteria established by recognized professional authorities

CHS must maintain position descriptions for all staff members.

To create a diverse staff, CHS must institute recruitment and hiring strategies that encourage individuals from under-represented populations to apply for positions.

CHS must develop promotion practices that are fair, inclusive, proactive, and non-discriminatory.

Staff members must take part in training sessions about gender, sexual orientation, racial, cultural, religious and/or spiritual, and ethnic sensitivity and should be aware of and involved in campus and community matters.

To further the recruitment and retention of staff, CHS must consider work life initiatives, such as compressed work schedules, flextime, job sharing, remote work, or telework.

CHS professional staff members must hold an earned graduate or professional degree in a field relevant to the position they hold or must possess an appropriate combination of educational credentials and related work experience.

CHS must establish criteria and implement a procedure to review and verify credentials of staff.

CHS professional staff members must engage in continuing professional development activities to keep abreast of the research, theories, legislation, policies, and developments that affect their programs and services.

CHS must have technical and support staff members adequate to accomplish their mission. All members of the staff must be technologically proficient and qualified to perform their job functions, be knowledgeable about ethical and legal uses of technology, and have access to training and resources to support the performance of their assigned responsibilities.

Degree- or credential-seeking interns or graduate assistants must be qualified by enrollment in an appropriate field of study and by relevant experience. These individuals must be trained and supervised adequately by professional staff members holding educational credentials and related work experience appropriate for supervision. Supervisors must be cognizant of the roles of interns and graduate assistants as both student and employee and closely adhere to all parameters of their job descriptions, work hours, and schedules. Supervisors and the interns or graduate assistants must agree to compensatory time or other appropriate compensation if circumstances necessitate additional hours.

Student employees and volunteers must be carefully selected, trained, supervised, and evaluated. They must be educated on how and when to refer those in need of additional assistance to qualified staff members and must have access to a supervisor for

assistance in making these judgments. **Student employees and volunteers must be provided clear job descriptions, pre-service training based on assessed needs, and continuing development.**

All CHS staff members, including student employees and volunteers, must receive specific training on institutional policies pertaining to functions or activities they support and to privacy and confidentiality policies and laws regarding access to student records and other sensitive institutional information.

All CHS staff members must receive training on policies and procedures related to the use of technology to store or access student records and institutional data.

Programs and services must ensure that staff members are knowledgeable about and trained in emergency procedures, crisis response, and prevention efforts. Prevention efforts must address identification of threatening conduct or behavior of students, faculty and staff members, and others and must incorporate a system for responding and reporting.

CHS must ensure that staff members are knowledgeable of and trained in safety and emergency procedures for securing and vacating facilities.

Specific aspects of the CHS for which staff should be assigned include business and financial management, community relations, and assessment.

Leaders should involve staff members in designing the organizational structure and in creating and reviewing policies and procedures that reinforce and foster health-engendering behaviors.

When CHS staff is involved in formal teaching or supervision, policies governing those activities must be consistent with the mission, goals, policies, and objectives of the institution.

When CHS staff is involved in research and publishing, policies governing those activities must be consistent with mission, goals, priorities, and objectives of the institution and capabilities of the program.

All CHS staff must be informed of the research policies of the institution and CHS.

Part 5. ETHICS

Clinical Health Services (CHS) must review relevant professional ethical standards and must adopt or develop and implement appropriate statements of ethical practice.

CHS must publish and adhere to statements of ethical practice and ensure their periodic review by relevant constituencies.

CHS must orient new staff members to relevant ethical standards and statements of ethical practice and related institutional policies.

Statements of ethical standards must specify that staff members respect privacy and maintain confidentiality in all communications and records to the extent that such communications and records are protected under relevant privacy laws.

Statements of ethical standards must specify limits on disclosure of information contained in students' educational records as well as requirements to disclose to appropriate authorities.

The task of media relations involving individual health status should be assigned to staff members who are knowledgeable about information that can be released.

Staff members should prevent visitors from entering the facility in any manner that would compromise confidentiality.

Statements of ethical standards must address personal and economic conflicts of interest, or appearance thereof, by staff members in the performance of their work.

Statements of ethical standards must reflect the responsibility of staff members to be fair, objective, and impartial in their interactions with others.

Statements of ethical standards must reference management of institutional funds.

Statements of ethical standards must reference appropriate behavior regarding research and assessment with human participants, confidentiality of research and assessment data, and students' rights and responsibilities.

Statements of ethical standards must include the expectation that CHS staff members confront and hold accountable other staff members who exhibit unethical behavior.

Statements of ethical standards must address issues surrounding scholarly integrity.

As appropriate, CHS staff members must inform users of programs and services of ethical obligations and limitations emanating from codes and laws or from licensure requirements.

CHS staff members must recognize and avoid conflicts of interest that could adversely influence their judgment or objectivity and, when unavoidable, recuse themselves from the situation.

Products and services should not be promoted for any other reason than the individual's or the community's benefit.

CHS staff members must perform their duties within the limits of their position, training, expertise, and competence.

When these limits are exceeded, individuals in need of further assistance must be referred to persons possessing appropriate qualifications.

Promotional and descriptive information must be accurate and free of deception.

CHS must adhere to institutional policies regarding ethical and legal use of software and technology.

All marketing and advertising concerning the clinical health services must communicate the scope and range of services provided without deception.

Clinical health services should inform individuals of their basic rights and responsibilities regarding service. Such rights and responsibilities should include

- service that is competent, considerate, and compassionate; recognizes basic human rights; safeguards personal dignity; and respects values and preferences
- provision of appropriate privacy, including protection from access to confidential information by faculty members, staff, student workers, and others
- ability to receive services from the staff member of choice
- accurate information regarding competencies and credentials of the clinical health services staff
- use of identified methods to express grievances and make suggestions
- information concerning individual health status and available services
- individual disclosure of complete and full information on health status that will be treated confidentially and for which the individual gives authority to approve or refuse release in compliance with applicable federal and state/provincial laws
- an explicit process to share necessary personal health information with mental health/counseling/psychotherapy services and other higher education faculty and staff on a need-to-know basis
- an explicit process for consent to share necessary personal health information with off-campus entities

Part 6. LAW, POLICY, AND GOVERNANCE

Clinical Health Services (CHS) must be in compliance with laws, regulations, and policies that relate to their respective responsibilities and that pose legal obligations, limitations, risks, and liabilities for the institution as a whole. Examples include constitutional, statutory, regulatory, and case law; relevant law and orders emanating from codes and laws; and the institution's policies.

CHS must inform staff members, appropriate officials, and users of programs and services about existing and changing legal obligations, risks and liabilities, and limitations.

CHS must inform the institutional community of its policies and procedures addressing

- **individual rights and responsibilities**
- **balancing protection of individual health and safety with individual rights to confidentiality and privacy**
- **risk management**
- **medical access insurance coverage**
- **informed consent**
- **access, release content, and maintenance of individual records in accordance with legal obligations and limitations**
- **research**
- **medical dismissal of students**

CHS must have written policies on all relevant operations, transactions, or tasks that have legal implications.

CHS must regularly review policies. The revision and creation of policies must be informed by best practices, available evidence, and policy issues in higher education.

CHS staff members must use reasonable and informed practices to limit the liability exposure of the institution and its officers, employees, and agents. CHS staff members must be informed about institutional policies regarding risk management, personal liability, and related insurance coverage options and must be referred to external sources if the institution does not provide coverage.

The institution must provide access to legal advice for staff members as needed to carry out assigned responsibilities.

CHS must have procedures and guidelines consistent with institutional policy for responding to threats, emergencies, and crisis situations. Systems and procedures must be in place to disseminate timely and accurate information to students, other members of the institutional community, and appropriate external organizations during emergency situations.

CHS staff members must neither participate in nor condone any form of harassment or activity that demeans persons or creates an intimidating, hostile, or offensive environment.

CHS must obtain permission to use copyrighted materials and instruments. CHS must purchase the

materials and instruments from legally compliant sources or seek alternative permission from the publisher or owner. References to copyrighted materials and instruments must include appropriate citations.

CHS staff members must be knowledgeable about internal and external governance systems that affect programs and services.

CHS must develop and maintain a systematic risk management program appropriate for the organization.

Risk management programs should focus on
- methods by which individuals may be dismissed from or refused services
- methods of collecting unpaid accounts
- review of litigation related to the institution's CHS
- review of all deaths, trauma, or adverse events where there is health risk
- communication with the liability insurance carrier
- methods of dealing with inquiries from government agencies, attorneys, consumer advocate groups, reporters, and the media
- methods of managing a situation with an impaired staff member
- methods for complying with governmental regulations and contractual agreements
- methods of transporting students with medical emergencies
- maintenance of confidential records

Part 7. DIVERSITY, EQUITY, AND ACCESS

Within the context of each institution's unique mission and in accordance with institutional polices and all applicable codes and laws, Clinical Health Services (CHS) must create and maintain educational and work environments that are
- welcoming, accessible, and inclusive to persons of diverse backgrounds
- equitable and non-discriminatory
- free from harassment

CHS must not discriminate on the basis of ability; age; cultural identity; ethnicity; family educational history (e.g., first generation to attend college); gender identity and expression; nationality; political affiliation; race; religious affiliation; sex; sexual orientation; economic, marital, social, or veteran status; or any other basis included in institutional policies and codes and laws.

CHS must
- advocate for greater sensitivity to multicultural and social justice concerns by the institution and its personnel
- modify or remove policies, practices, facilities,

structures, systems, and technologies that limit access, discriminate, or produce inequities
- include diversity, equity, and access initiatives within their strategic plans
- foster communication that deepens understanding of identity, culture, self-expression, and heritage
- promote respect about commonalities and differences among people within their historical and cultural contexts
- address the characteristics and needs of a diverse population when establishing and implementing culturally relevant and inclusive programs, services, policies, procedures, and practices
- provide staff members with access to multicultural training and hold staff members accountable for integrating the training into their work
- respond to the needs of all students and other populations served when establishing hours of operation and developing methods of delivering programs, services, and resources
- ensure physical, program, and resource access for persons with disabilities
- recognize the needs of distance learning students by providing appropriate and accessible services and resources or by assisting them in gaining access to other appropriate services and resources in their geographic region

CHS should accommodate the unique needs of individuals with disabilities and should encourage faculty, staff, and other students to develop awareness of and sensitivity to individuals with disabilities. Students with disabilities should be encouraged to self-identify individual needs as soon as possible following admission (pre-matriculation) so that accommodations can be made.

For students with physical disabilities, CHS staff should advocate that the institution meet special needs through clinical health services, housing, food services, and counseling services. Whenever possible, the institution should eliminate architectural barriers that create difficulties for students with physical disabilities.

Students with special health risks may be identified by information provided on health history or behavioral assessment forms, or through screening, surveillance, and education services.

Students with chronic health conditions may be identified and informed of support services.

CHS may provide services directly or identify appropriate resources in the community to meet the special needs of these students.

CHS must ensure that students are informed about the importance of medical and dental access insurance and how to make an informed decision based on their needs.

As a condition of enrollment, students may be required to provide evidence that they have adequate medical access through healthcare insurance coverage.

Medical access through insurance coverage should be available to all eligible students.

Every contact should be viewed as an opportunity to recognize and honor diversity to address specific concerns that might impact health and quality of life for the individual and community.

Students should be provided an environment of caring with an inclusive approach, which is essential for establishing levels of confidentiality, trust, and comfort.

CHS should establish procedures for students to discuss with staff their comfort or discomfort with various approaches in delivery of services.

Individuals should be accepted in a free and open manner and in an atmosphere of mutual respect to encourage candid discussion of sensitive personal issues. Staff members should demonstrate sensitivity and understanding to students from diverse backgrounds and cultures to provide satisfactory services.

Part 8. INSTITUTIONAL AND EXTERNAL RELATIONS

Clinical Health Services (CHS) must reach out to relevant individuals, groups, communities, and organizations internal and external to the institution to
- **establish, maintain, and promote understanding and effective relations with those that have a significant interest in or potential effect on the students or other constituents served by the programs and services**
- **garner support and resources for programs and services as defined by the mission statement**
- **disseminate information about the programs and services**
- **collaborate, where appropriate, to assist in offering or improving programs and services to meet the needs of students and other constituents and to achieve program and student outcomes**
- **engage diverse individuals, groups, communities, and organizations to enrich the educational environment and experiences of students and other constituents**

CHS must have procedures and guidelines consistent with institutional policy for
- **communicating with the media**
- **contracting with external organizations for delivery of programs and services**
- **cultivating, soliciting, and managing gifts**
- **applying to and managing funds from grants**

To ensure success, CHS must maintain good relations with students, faculty members, staff, alumni, the local community, contractors, and support agencies.

CHS must comply with these standards even when contracted for or outsourced by the Institution.

CHS staff should participate actively with their institution in designing policies and practices and developing further resources and services that have direct impact on the health status of the campus population.

CHS should review and assess health aspects of relevant institutional policies and practices. These issues may include but are not limited to drug use policies and treatment, blood-borne diseases, sexual harassment/assault, suicide and homicide threats, and discrimination of all types.

Policies on requirements for immunization prior to and during matriculation should be implemented and maintained to assure compliance, protect community health, and meet the needs of students at risk.

CHS should collaborate to minimize duplication of services with campus and community partners.

CHS should address the level and the priorities of campus services as determined by institution-specific population health status surveys, available community resources, user data and institutional context. CHS should review potential health hazards or problems related to academic activities.

CHS should identify and utilize community services, whenever appropriate, to build resource/service networks and create awareness within the community about special needs populations.

Part 9. FINANCIAL RESOURCES

Clinical Health Services (CHS) must have funding to accomplish the mission and goals. In establishing funding priorities and making significant changes, a comprehensive analysis must be conducted to determine the following elements: unmet needs of the unit, relevant expenditures, external and internal resources, and impact on students and the institution.

CHS must demonstrate efficient and effective use and responsible stewardship of fiscal resources consistent with institutional protocols.

Financial planning and projections should include budget data for both current and long-term expenditures that include capital expenditures and deferred maintenance costs.

Part 10. TECHNOLOGY

Clinical Health Services (CHS) must have adequate technology to support the achievement of their mission and goals. The technology and its use must comply with institutional policies and procedures and be evaluated for compliance with relevant codes and laws.

CHS must use current technology to provide updated information regarding mission, location, staffing, programs, services, and official contacts to students and designated clients.

CHS must explore the use of technology to enhance delivery of programs and services, especially for students at a distance or external constituencies.

When technology is used to facilitate student learning and development, CHS must select technology that reflects intended outcomes.

CHS must

- maintain policies and procedures that address the security, confidentiality, and backup of data, as well as compliance with privacy laws
- have clearly articulated plans in place for protecting confidentiality and security of information when using Internet-based technologies
- develop plans for replacing and updating existing hardware and software as well as plans for integrating new technically-based or supported programs, including systems developed internally by the institution, systems available through professional associations, or private vendor-based systems

Technology, as well as workstations or computer labs maintained by programs and services for student use, must be accessible to all designated clients and must meet established technology standards for delivery to persons with disabilities.

When providing student access to technology, CHS must

- have policies on the use of technology that are clear, easy to understand, and available to all students
- provide assistance, information, or referral to appropriate support services to those needing help accessing or using technology
- provide instruction or training on how to use the technology
- inform students on the legal and ethical implications of misuse as it pertains to

intellectual property, harassment, privacy, and social networks

Student violations of technology policies must follow established institutional student disciplinary procedures.

Students who experience negative emotional or psychological consequences from the use of technology must be referred to support services provided by the institution.

Part 11. FACILITIES AND EQUIPMENT

Clinical Health Services (CHS) must have adequate, accessible, and suitably located facilities and equipment to support the mission and goals. If acquiring capital equipment as defined by the institution, CHS must take into account expenses related to regular maintenance and life cycle costs. Facilities and equipment must be evaluated on an established cycle, including consideration of sustainability, and be in compliance with codes and laws to provide for access, health, safety, and security.

CHS staff members must have workspace that is well equipped, adequate in size, and designed to support their work and responsibilities. For conversations requiring privacy, staff members must have access to a private space.

CHS staff members who share workspace must be able to secure their own work.

The design of the facilities must guarantee the security and privacy of records and ensure the confidentiality of sensitive information.

The location and layout of the facilities must be sensitive to the needs of persons with disabilities as well as the needs of other constituencies.

CHS facilities should support a range of activities including clinical treatment, intervention and consultation, patient education, and policy development. A safe, functional, and efficient environment is crucial to providing appropriate services and achieving desired outcomes.

Depending upon services offered, environmental conditions should include

- necessary facilities, technology, and equipment to handle individual or campus emergencies
- regulations prohibiting smoking
- elimination of hazards that might lead to slipping, falling, electrical shock, burns, poisoning, or other trauma
- adequate reception areas, toilets, and telephones
- parking for guests, patients, and people with disabilities

- accommodations for persons with physical disabilities
- adequate lighting and ventilation
- clean and properly maintained facilities
- facilities that provide for confidentiality and privacy of services and records
- testing and proper maintenance of equipment
- a system for the proper identification, management, handling, transport, treatment, and disposition of hazardous materials and wastes whether solid, liquid, or gas
- appropriate alternative power sources in case of emergency
- technology to support services and facilities

Part 12. ASSESSMENT AND EVALUATION

Clinical Health Services (CHS) must have a clearly articulated assessment plan to document achievement of stated goals and learning outcomes, demonstrate accountability, provide evidence of improvement, and describe resulting changes in programs and services.

CHS must have adequate fiscal, human, professional development, and technological resources to develop and implement assessment plans.

Assessments must include direct and indirect evaluation and use qualitative and quantitative methodologies and existing evidence, as appropriate, to determine whether and to what degree the stated mission, goals, and intended outcomes are being met as effectively and efficiently as possible. The process must employ sufficient and sound measures to ensure comprehensiveness. Data collected must include responses from students and other constituencies, and aggregated results must be shared with those groups. Results of assessments must be shared appropriately with multiple constituents.

CHS should maintain an active, organized, peer-based, quality management and improvement program that links peer review, quality improvement activities, and risk management in an organized, systematic way.

Periodically, the organization should assess user and non-user satisfaction with services and facilities provided by the clinical health services and incorporate findings into quality improvement.

To develop criteria used to evaluate services, staff members should understand, support, and participate in programs of quality management and improvement. Data should be collected in an on-going manner to identify unacceptable or unexpected trends or occurrences.

The quality improvement program should address administrative and cost issues and service outcomes.

Results of assessments and evaluations must be used to identify needs and interests in revising and improving programs and services, recognizing staff performance, maximizing resource efficiency and effectiveness, improving student achievement of learning and development outcomes, and improving student persistence and success. Changes resulting from the use of assessments and evaluation must be shared with stakeholders.

General Standards revised in 2011;
CHS (formerly College Health Programs) developed/revised in 2001 & 2006

The Role of College Honor Societies
CAS Standards Contextual Statement

The purposes of honor societies in colleges and universities are threefold. First, they exist primarily to recognize the attainment of scholarship of a superior quality. Second, a few societies recognize the development of leadership qualities and commitment to service and excellence in research in addition to a strong scholarship record. Third, to the degree this recognition is coveted, they encourage the production of superior scholarship and leadership. To accomplish these objectives, it is clear that an honor society must define and maintain a truly high standard of eligibility for membership and achieve sufficient status by so doing that membership becomes something to be highly valued.

The honor society has followed the expansion and specialization of higher education in America. When Phi Beta Kappa was organized in 1776, there was no thought given to its field because all colleges then in existence were for the training of men for the service of the church and the state. With the expansion of education into new fields a choice had to be made, and Phi Beta Kappa elected to operate in the field of liberal arts and sciences. Although this was not finally decided until 1898, the trend was evident earlier; the 1880s saw the establishment of Tau Beta Pi in the field of engineering and Sigma Xi in scientific research.

Early in the 20th century, other honor societies came into being. Phi Kappa Phi was organized to accept membership from all academic fields in the university. A few others of this nature had origins in Black, Catholic, or Jesuit colleges and universities. These honor societies became known as general honor societies. Other variations have developed since that time. Leadership honor societies recognized meritorious attainments in all-around leadership and campus citizenship. Numerous societies drew membership from the various departments of study, recognizing good work in the student's special field of study. These societies are generally known as specialized honor societies. Another variation recognized scholastic achievement during the freshman or sophomore year. Yet other variations recognized achievement in associate degree programs and advanced study.

The national organization of each honor society sets standards for establishing collegiate chapters and requirements for administering them. Chapters are chartered to institutions and have a dual relationship: maintain national honor society standards and requirements and abide by institutional policies and procedures.

The Association of College Honor Societies was founded in 1925 to join forces for the establishment and maintenance of useful functions and desirable standards, including criteria for membership, for governance of each member society, and for chapter operation. In addition to defining honor societies, similar student organizations with more liberal membership requirements were named recognition societies. Baird's Manual*, for many years the definitive reference of college organizations, adopted the ACHS definitions for classification of honor societies and recognition societies.

The standards and functions originally named in the early history of ACHS still have relevance today as ACHS fulfills a certifying function in assuring candidates for membership as well as institutions that member societies have met the high standards. The standards also serve a role for judging credibility of non-member societies.

The challenge in the 21st century is the same as when ACHS was founded: to use academic and operational standards to allay the confusion prevailing on campuses and among the public regarding the credibility and legitimacy of newly emerging honor societies. A plethora of Internet societies, for-profit societies, and an increasingly narrow focus of specialized societies gives rise to the need for the CAS standards to guide colleges and universities in setting regulations for official recognition of campus honor societies. Students, parents, and the public can use the standards as criteria for judging quality.

References, Readings, and Resources

Association of College Honor Societies. (2012). *ACHS handbook*. 4990 Northwind Dr., Ste. 140, East Lansing, MI 48823-5031. Retrieved from http://www.achsnatl.org/member-directory.asp

Warren, J. W. (2000). *Prelude to the new millennium: Promoting honor for seventy-five years*. East Lansing, MI: Association of College Honor Societies. www.achsnatl.org/history.asp

* Note – *Baird's Manual of American College Fraternities*, last published in 1991 by Baird's Manual Foundation, was the authoritative reference work on college Greek-letter societies since first published in 1879.

Contextual Statement Contributor
Dorothy I. Mitstifer, ACHS

College Honor Societies
CAS Standards and Guidelines

Part 1. MISSION

The mission of College Honor Societies (CHS) is to confer distinction for high achievement in undergraduate, graduate, and professional studies; in student leadership; in service; and in research.

CHS must develop, disseminate, implement, and regularly review their missions. The mission must be consistent with the mission of the institution and with professional standards. The mission must be appropriate for the institution's student populations and community settings. Mission statements must reference student learning and development.

The following historical functions are properly served by CHS:
- foster a spirit of liberal education
- stimulate and encourage intellectual development
- stand for freedom of mind and spirit and for democracy of learning
- provide spiritual and intellectual leadership
- preserve valuable traditions and customs
- provide opportunities for members to associate in mutual understanding for the purpose of advancing society in the art of democratic living
- stimulate worthy attitudes for the improvement of the general welfare of the institution
- impose upon members high citizenship responsibilities and emphasize deeper study and discussion of the political-moral tradition—its characteristics, ideals, and possibilities

Part 2. PROGRAM

The formal education of students, consisting of the curriculum and the co-curriculum, must promote student learning and development outcomes that are purposeful, contribute to students' realization of their potential, and prepare students for satisfying and productive lives.

College Honor Societies (CHS) must collaborate with colleagues and departments across the institution to promote student learning and development, persistence, and success.

Consistent with the institutional mission, CHS must identify relevant and desirable student learning and development outcomes from among the six domains and related dimensions:

Domain: **knowledge acquisition, integration, construction, and application**
- Dimensions: **understanding knowledge from** a range of disciplines; connecting knowledge to other knowledge, ideas, and experiences; constructing knowledge; and relating knowledge to daily life

Domain: **cognitive complexity**
- Dimensions: **critical thinking, reflective thinking, effective reasoning, and creativity**

Domain: **intrapersonal development**
- Dimensions: **realistic self-appraisal, self-understanding, and self-respect; identity development; commitment to ethics and integrity; and spiritual awareness**

Domain: **interpersonal competence**
- Dimensions: **meaningful relationships, interdependence, collaboration, and effective leadership.**

Domain: **humanitarianism and civic engagement**
- Dimensions: **understanding and appreciation of cultural and human differences, social responsibility, global perspective, and sense of civic responsibility**

Domain: **practical competence**
- Dimensions: **pursuing goals, communicating effectively, technical competence, managing personal affairs, managing career development, demonstrating professionalism, maintaining health and wellness, and living a purposeful and satisfying life**

[LD Outcomes: See *The Council for the Advancement of Standards Learning and Developmental Outcomes* statement for examples of outcomes related to these domains and dimensions.]

CHS must
- **assess relevant and desirable student learning and development**
- **provide evidence of impact on outcomes**
- **articulate contributions to or support of student learning and development in the domains not specifically assessed**
- **articulate contributions to or support of student persistence and success**
- **use evidence gathered through this process to create strategies for improvement of programs and services**

CHS must be
- **intentionally designed**

- guided by theories and knowledge of learning and development
- integrated into the life of the institution
- reflective of developmental and demographic profiles of the student population
- responsive to needs of individuals, populations with distinct needs, and relevant constituencies
- delivered using multiple formats, strategies, and contexts

Programs of CHS must include the following elements:

- educational programming that complements the academic curriculum
- opportunities for recognition by the institution
- faculty, staff, and administrator involvement and interaction with students

The process for establishment of collegiate chapters of CHS must include:

- formal chartering of each chapter by institution and college/department petition
- approval by official action of the governing body of the national organization
- jointly defined relationship between the institution and the college honor society that must be formalized, documented, and disseminated
- candidate selection by the campus chapter
- membership invitation by the campus chapter

In order to maintain good standing with the national organization, CHS chapters must comply with the national organization's policies.

The national organization of a college honor society must be governed by its membership and must include:

- officers/board members elected by the national membership
- chapter representation in the governing body
- national membership participation in approving and revising by-laws
- independent financial review and full financial disclosure

Classifications of CHS include general scholarship, general leadership, specialized scholarship, and freshman and sophomore and two year honor societies. Minimum scholastic qualifications in each classification of CHS should include:

- general scholarship – top 20%, not earlier than 5th semester
- general leadership – top 35%, not earlier than 5th semester
- specialized scholarship – top 35%, not earlier than

4th semester
- freshman and sophomore and two-year (associate degree) honor societies – adherence to the same high standards with the exception of semesters completed

"Recognition Societies" are those organizations with lower scholastic criteria.

Where institutions provide distance education, CHS must assist distance learners to achieve their educational goals by providing access to information about programs and services, to staff members who can address questions and concerns, and to counseling, advising, or other forms of assistance.

Part 3. ORGANIZATION AND LEADERSHIP

Advisers (faculty or staff member) must represent the institution in advising chapters of College Honor Societies (CHS). The adviser must model leadership principles, establish a climate and structure that facilitates leadership development, determine expectations of accountability, and fairly assess student performance.

Chapter governance documents and the names of officers and advisers must be filed annually both with the institution and the national organization.

Institutions should maintain a centralized registry of CHS organizations.

To achieve student and program outcomes, CHS must be structured purposefully and organized effectively. CHS must have
- clearly stated goals
- current and accessible policies and procedures
- written performance expectations for employees
- functional work flow graphics or organizational charts demonstrating clear channels of authority

Leaders with organizational authority for the programs and services must provide strategic planning, supervision, and management; advance the organization; and maintain integrity through the following functions:

Strategic Planning
- articulate a vision and mission that drive short- and long-term planning
- set goals and objectives based on the needs of the population served and desired student learning or development and program outcomes
- facilitate continuous development, implementation, and assessment of goal attainment congruent with institutional

mission and strategic plans
- promote environments that provide meaningful opportunities for student learning, development, and engagement
- develop and continuously improve programs and services in response to the changing needs of students served and evolving institutional priorities
- intentionally include diverse perspectives to inform decision making

Supervising
- manage human resource processes including recruitment, selection, development, supervision, performance planning, evaluation, recognition, and reward
- influence others to contribute to the effectiveness and success of the unit
- empower professional, support, and student staff to accept leadership opportunities
- offer appropriate feedback to colleagues and students on skills needed to become more effective leaders
- encourage and support professional development, collaboration with colleagues and departments across the institution, and scholarly contribution to the profession

Managing
- identify and address individual, organizational, and environmental conditions that foster or inhibit mission achievement
- plan, allocate, and monitor the use of fiscal, physical, human, intellectual, and technological resources
- use current and valid evidence to inform decisions
- incorporate sustainability practices in the management and design of programs, services, and facilities
- understand appropriate technologies and integrate them into programs and services
- be knowledgeable about codes and laws relevant to programs and services and ensure that staff members understand their responsibilities through appropriate training
- assess potential risks and take action to mitigate them

Advancing the Organization
- communicate effectively in writing, speaking, and electronic venues
- advocate for programs and services
- advocate for representation in strategic planning initiatives at appropriate divisional and institutional levels
- initiate collaborative interactions with

internal and external stakeholders who have legitimate concerns about and interests in the functional area
- facilitate processes to reach consensus where wide support is needed
- inform other areas within the institution about issues affecting practice

Maintaining Integrity
- model ethical behavior and institutional citizenship
- share data used to inform key decisions in transparent and accessible ways
- monitor media used for distributing information about programs and services to ensure the content is current, accurate, appropriately referenced, and accessible

Leaders of CHS are elected by their peers to organize chapter activities.

Leaders of CHS should be students.

Part 4. HUMAN RESOURCES

College Honor Societies (CHS) must be staffed adequately by individuals qualified to accomplish mission and goals.

Within institutional guidelines, CHS must
- establish procedures for staff recruitment and selection, training, performance planning, and evaluation
- set expectations for supervision and performance
- assess the performance of employees individually and as a team
- provide access to continuing and advanced education and appropriate professional development opportunities to improve the leadership ability, competence, and skills of all employees.

CHS must maintain position descriptions for all staff members.

To create a diverse staff, CHS must institute recruitment and hiring strategies that encourage individuals from under-represented populations to apply for positions.

CHS must develop promotion practices that are fair, inclusive, proactive, and non-discriminatory.

To further the recruitment and retention of staff, CHS must consider work life initiatives, such as compressed work schedules, flextime, job sharing, remote work, or telework.

CHS professional staff members must hold an earned graduate or professional degree in a field relevant to the position they hold or must possess an appropriate combination of educational credentials and related work experience.

With very few exceptions, faculty and staff are not employed as CHS advisers; most are volunteers.

CHS professional staff members must engage in continuing professional development activities to keep abreast of the research, theories, legislation, policies, and developments that affect their programs and services.

CHS must have technical and support staff members adequate to accomplish their mission. All members of the staff must be technologically proficient and qualified to perform their job functions, be knowledgeable about ethical and legal uses of technology, and have access to training and resources to support the performance of their assigned responsibilities.

Degree- or credential-seeking interns or graduate assistants must be qualified by enrollment in an appropriate field of study and by relevant experience. These individuals must be trained and supervised adequately by professional staff members holding educational credentials and related work experience appropriate for supervision. Supervisors must be cognizant of the roles of interns and graduate assistants as both student and employee and closely adhere to all parameters of their job descriptions, work hours, and schedules. Supervisors and the interns or graduate assistants must agree to compensatory time or other appropriate compensation if circumstances necessitate additional hours.

Graduate student advisers of CHS must be qualified by enrollment in an appropriate field of study and by relevant experience. These individuals must be trained and supervised adequately by professional staff members holding educational credentials and related work experience appropriate for supervision.

Leaders and advisers must be carefully trained, supervised, and evaluated. They must be educated on how and when to refer those in need of additional assistance to qualified staff members and must have access to a supervisor for assistance in making these judgments. Student leaders must be provided clear and precise job descriptions, pre-service training based on assessed needs, and continuing leadership development.

Student employees and volunteers must be carefully selected, trained, supervised, and evaluated. They must be educated on how and when to refer those in need of additional assistance to qualified staff members and must have access to a supervisor for

assistance in making these judgments. Student employees and volunteers must be provided clear job descriptions, pre-service training based on assessed needs, and continuing development.

All CHS staff members, including student employees and volunteers, must receive specific training on institutional policies pertaining to functions or activities they support and to privacy and confidentiality policies and laws regarding access to student records and other sensitive institutional information.

All CHS staff members must receive training on policies and procedures related to the use of technology to store or access student records and institutional data.

CHS must ensure that staff members are knowledgeable about and trained in emergency procedures, crisis response, and prevention efforts. Prevention efforts must address identification of threatening conduct or behavior of students, faculty and staff members, and others and must incorporate a system for responding and reporting.

CHS must ensure that staff members are knowledgeable of and trained in safety and emergency procedures for securing and vacating facilities.

Part 5. ETHICS

College Honor Societies (CHS) must review relevant professional ethical standards and must adopt or develop and implement appropriate statements of ethical practice.

CHS must publish and adhere to statements of ethical practice and ensure their periodic review by relevant constituencies.

CHS must orient new staff members to relevant ethical standards and statements of ethical practice and related institutional policies.

Statements of ethical standards must specify that staff members respect privacy and maintain confidentiality in all communications and records to the extent that such communications and records are protected under relevant privacy laws.

Statements of ethical standards must specify limits on disclosure of information contained in students' educational records as well as requirements to disclose to appropriate authorities.

Statements of ethical standards must address personal and economic conflicts of interest, or appearance thereof, by staff members in the performance of their work.

Statements of ethical standards must reflect the responsibility of staff members to be fair, objective, and impartial in their interactions with others.

Statements of ethical standards must reference management of institutional funds.

Statements of ethical standards must reference appropriate behavior regarding research and assessment with human participants, confidentiality of research and assessment data, and students' rights and responsibilities.

Statements of ethical standards must include the expectation that CHS staff members confront and hold accountable other staff members who exhibit unethical behavior.

Statements of ethical standards must address issues surrounding scholarly integrity.

As appropriate, CHS staff members must inform users of programs and services of ethical obligations and limitations emanating from codes and laws or from licensure requirements.

CHS staff members must recognize and avoid conflicts of interest that could adversely influence their judgment or objectivity and, when unavoidable, recuse themselves from the situation.

CHS staff members must perform their duties within the limits of their position, training, expertise, and competence.

When these limits are exceeded, individuals in need of further assistance must be referred to persons possessing appropriate qualifications.

Promotional and descriptive information must be accurate and free of deception.

CHS must adhere to institutional policies regarding ethical and legal use of software and technology.

Part 6. LAW, POLICY, AND GOVERNANCE

College Honor Societies (CHS) must be in compliance with laws, regulations, and policies that relate to their respective responsibilities and that pose legal obligations, limitations, risks, and liabilities for the institution as a whole. Examples include constitutional, statutory, regulatory, and case law; relevant law and orders emanating from codes and laws; and the institution's policies.

CHS must inform staff members, appropriate officials, and users of programs and services about existing and changing legal obligations, risks and liabilities, and limitations.

CHS must have written policies on all relevant operations, transactions, or tasks that have legal implications.

CHS must regularly review policies. The revision and creation of policies must be informed by best practices, available evidence, and policy issues in higher education.

CHS staff members must use reasonable and informed practices to limit the liability exposure of the institution and its officers, employees, and agents. CHS staff members must be informed about institutional policies regarding risk management, personal liability, and related insurance coverage options and must be referred to external sources if the institution does not provide coverage.

The institution must provide access to legal advice for staff members as needed to carry out assigned responsibilities.

CHS must have procedures and guidelines consistent with institutional policy for responding to threats, emergencies, and crisis situations. Systems and procedures must be in place to disseminate timely and accurate information to students, other members of the institutional community, and appropriate external organizations during emergency situations.

CHS staff members must neither participate in nor condone any form of harassment or activity that demeans persons or creates an intimidating, hostile, or offensive environment.

CHS must obtain permission to use copyrighted materials and instruments. CHS must purchase the materials and instruments from legally compliant sources or seek alternative permission from the publisher or owner. References to copyrighted materials and instruments must include appropriate citations.

CHS staff members must be knowledgeable about internal and external governance systems that affect programs and services.

Part 7. DIVERSITY, EQUITY, AND ACCESS

Within the context of each institution's unique mission and in accordance with institutional polices and all applicable codes and laws, College Honor Societies (CHS) must create and maintain educational and work environments that are
- welcoming, accessible, and inclusive to persons of diverse backgrounds
- equitable and non-discriminatory
- free from harassment

CHS must not discriminate on the basis of ability; age; cultural identity; ethnicity; family educational history (e.g., first generation to attend college);

gender identity and expression; nationality; political affiliation; race; religious affiliation; sex; sexual orientation; economic, marital, social, or veteran status; or any other basis included in institutional policies and codes and laws.

CHS must

- advocate for greater sensitivity to multicultural and social justice concerns by the institution and its personnel
- modify or remove policies, practices, facilities, structures, systems, and technologies that limit access, discriminate, or produce inequities
- include diversity, equity, and access initiatives within their strategic plans
- foster communication that deepens understanding of identity, culture, self-expression, and heritage
- promote respect about commonalities and differences among people within their historical and cultural contexts
- address the characteristics and needs of a diverse population when establishing and implementing culturally relevant and inclusive programs, services, policies, procedures, and practices
- provide staff members with access to multicultural training and hold staff members accountable for integrating the training into their work
- respond to the needs of all students and other populations served when establishing hours of operation and developing methods of delivering programs, services, and resources
- ensure physical, program, and resource access for persons with disabilities
- recognize the needs of distance learning students by providing appropriate and accessible services and resources or by assisting them in gaining access to other appropriate services and resources in their geographic region

CHS must include outreach to underrepresented populations in membership recruitment activities.

Part 8. INSTITUTIONAL AND EXTERNAL RELATIONS

College Honor Societies (CHS) must reach out to relevant individuals, groups, communities, and organizations internal and external to the institution to

- establish, maintain, and promote understanding and effective relations with those that have a significant interest in or potential effect on the students or other constituents served by the programs and services
- garner support and resources for programs and services as defined by the mission statement
- disseminate information about the programs and services
- collaborate, where appropriate, to assist in offering or improving programs and services to meet the needs of students and other constituents and to achieve program and student outcomes
- engage diverse individuals, groups, communities, and organizations to enrich the educational environment and experiences of students and other constituents

CHS must have procedures and guidelines consistent with institutional policy for

- communicating with the media
- contracting with external organizations for delivery of programs and services
- cultivating, soliciting, and managing gifts
- applying to and managing funds from grants

Part 9. FINANCIAL RESOURCES

College Honor Societies (CHS) must have funding to accomplish the mission and goals. In establishing funding priorities and making significant changes, a comprehensive analysis must be conducted to determine the following elements: unmet needs of the unit, relevant expenditures, external and internal resources, and impact on students and the institution.

CHS must demonstrate efficient and effective use and responsible stewardship of fiscal resources consistent with institutional protocols.

Part 10. TECHNOLOGY

College Honor Societies (CHS) must have adequate technology to support the achievement of their mission and goals. The technology and its use must comply with institutional policies and procedures and be evaluated for compliance with relevant codes and laws.

CHS must use current technology to provide updated information regarding mission, location, staffing, programs, services, and official contacts to students and designated clients.

CHS must explore the use of technology to enhance delivery of programs and services, especially for students at a distance or external constituencies.

When technology is used to facilitate student learning and development, CHS must select technology that reflects intended outcomes.

CHS must

- maintain policies and procedures that address the security, confidentiality, and backup of data, as well as compliance with privacy laws
- have clearly articulated plans in place for protecting confidentiality and security of information when using Internet-based technologies
- develop plans for replacing and updating existing hardware and software as well as plans for integrating new technically-based or supported programs, including systems developed internally by the institution, systems available through professional associations, or private vendor-based systems

Technology, as well as workstations or computer labs maintained by programs and services for student use, must be accessible to all designated clients and must meet established technology standards for delivery to persons with disabilities.

When providing student access to technology, CHS must

- have policies on the use of technology that are clear, easy to understand, and available to all students
- provide assistance, information, or referral to appropriate support services to those needing help accessing or using technology
- provide instruction or training on how to use the technology
- inform students on the legal and ethical implications of misuse as it pertains to intellectual property, harassment, privacy, and social networks

Student violations of technology policies must follow established institutional student disciplinary procedures.

Students who experience negative emotional or psychological consequences from the use of technology must be referred to support services provided by the institution.

Part 11. FACILITIES AND EQUIPMENT

College Honor Societies (CHS) must have adequate, accessible, and suitably located facilities and equipment to support the mission and goals. If acquiring capital equipment as defined by the institution, CHS must take into account expenses related to regular maintenance and life cycle costs. Facilities and equipment must be evaluated on an established cycle, including consideration of sustainability, and be in compliance with codes and laws to provide for access, health, safety, and security.

Meeting space for chapter activities and storage space for chapter materials (memorabilia, documents, files) should be available. Chapter files should be stored electronically and securely. Storage space for other chapter property should be available.

CHS staff members must have workspace that is well equipped, adequate in size, and designed to support their work and responsibilities. For conversations requiring privacy, staff members must have access to a private space.

CHS staff members who share workspace must be able to secure their own work.

The design of the facilities must guarantee the security and privacy of records and ensure the confidentiality of sensitive information.

The location and layout of the facilities must be sensitive to the needs of persons with disabilities as well as the needs of other constituencies.

Part 12. ASSESSMENT AND EVALUATION

College Honor Societies (CHS) must have a clearly articulated assessment plan to document achievement of stated goals and learning outcomes, demonstrate accountability, provide evidence of improvement, and describe resulting changes in programs and services.

CHS must have adequate fiscal, human, professional development, and technological resources to develop and implement assessment plans.

Assessments must include direct and indirect evaluation and use qualitative and quantitative methodologies and existing evidence, as appropriate, to determine whether and to what degree the stated mission, goals, and intended outcomes are being met as effectively and efficiently as possible. The process must employ sufficient and sound measures to ensure comprehensiveness. Data collected must include responses from students and other constituencies, and aggregated results must be shared with those groups. Results of assessments must be shared appropriately with multiple constituents.

Results of assessments and evaluations must be used to identify needs and interests in revising and improving programs and services, recognizing staff performance, maximizing resource efficiency and effectiveness, improving student achievement of learning and development outcomes, and improving student persistence and success. Changes resulting from the use of assessments and evaluation must be shared with stakeholders.

General Standards revised in 2011;
CHS content developed in 2005

The Role of College Unions
CAS Standards Contextual Statement

Today's college union is a unifying force that brings together students, faculty, administrators, staff, alumni, and guests. It provides a forum for divergent viewpoints and creates an environment where all feel welcome. Optimally the union is a centrally located building where members of the campus community come together, formally and informally.

The word "union" implies a bringing together of the campus community, including its students, faculty, staff, and alumni. The word "university" derives from the Latin *universitas* meaning the whole; and the word "union" from *unio* meaning oneness—a whole made up of united parts. In the educational world the two concepts support and complement each other.

The college union, primarily referring to an organization or program, evolved from the debating tradition of British universities. The earliest college union, founded at Cambridge University in 1815, was literally a "union" of three debating societies. The first North American college union was organized at Harvard in 1832; like its British predecessors, it existed primarily for debating purposes. By the late 1800s, the Harvard Union had embraced the concept of being a general club. The first building erected explicitly for union purposes was Houston Hall at the University of Pennsylvania. Built in 1896, it housed lounges, dining rooms, reading and writing rooms, an auditorium, game rooms, and student offices; it was given to the university by the Houston family as a "place where all may meet on common ground."

In the 1930s, the success of civic recreational and cultural centers influenced college union leaders to view the union as the campus counterpart of the "community center" with an educational and recreational mission to perform. The first extensive period of union building construction took place following World War II, as enrollments surged and colleges and universities sought to better fulfill the needs of students and faculty. A second building boom occurred in the 1990s and 2000s as the original facilities were renovated or replaced. Numerous institutions built their first unions during this second boom as well.

Traditionally, the union was described as the "hearthstone" or "living room" of the campus. Today's union is the gathering place of the campus. In the 21st century, the college union movement has concentrated on building community, emphasizing its educational mission, and promoting student learning and leadership. During this time, the names of facilities that embody the union idea have expanded to include memorial union, student union, university commons, college or university center, student center, and campus center, among others. Funding and institutional preferences have led to the variety of names. Regardless of the facility's name, the fundamental principle of college unions remains to bring together and unify its campus community.

The contemporary college union meets many needs expressed by all members of the campus community. College union facilities often include banks, post offices, child care, dining facilities, study lounges, fitness centers, bookstores, and other services the campus community, especially students, relies on during the course of the day. In providing these services, the college union supports the community focus on academic and personal achievement. College unions vary by institutional size, scope, and purpose. No universal formula identifies the optimum size of a college union. However, the Association of College Unions International (ACUI) offers a benchmarking service that allows for institutional comparison in size and facilities.

In 2005, ACUI announced a set of 11 core competencies for the college union and student activities profession. Developed over six years, the core competencies are a composite set of knowledge and behaviors that provide the basis and foundation for professional practice in college union and student activities work. Subsequently, ACUI developed skill sets associated with each competency. The ACUI website (www.acui.org) has more information about these efforts, which may be used to complement the CAS standards.

The college union provides numerous educationally purposeful activities outside the classroom that are "key to enhancing learning and personal development," according to The Student Learning Imperative (ACPA, 1996). The union contributes to the education of the student body-at-large through its cultural, educational, social, and recreational programs; the union also educates students involved in its governance and program boards and those it employs. The Role of the College Union defines the union as "a student centered organization that values participatory decision making. Through volunteerism, its boards, committees, and student employment, the union offers firsthand experience in citizenship and educates students in leadership, social responsibility, and values" (ACUI, 2008). These models of college union governance foster student/staff partnerships that form the foundation for student development and leadership training.

The modern college union is a complex entity, offering a wide array of programs and services to the campus community. The standards and guidelines that follow outline the characteristics of a college union that offers high-quality experiences and uses informed practice to educate and serve a diverse range of constituents.

References, Readings, and Resources

American College Personnel Association. (1996). *The student learning imperative*. Washington, DC: Author.

Association of College Unions International (ACUI) Central Office, One City Centre, Suite 200, 120 W. Seventh St., Bloomington, IN 47404-3839. 812.245.2284, www.acui.org.

Association of College Unions International. (1998). *The role of the college union*. Bloomington, IN: Author.

Association of College Unions International. (2006). *51 facts about college unions*. Bloomington, IN: Author.

Butts, P. F. (1971). *The college union idea*. Bloomington, IN: Association of College Unions International.

Day, K., Payment, S., Grady, D., Pitts, K., Rodricks, D., Whittier, C., & Wahlquist, Z. (2009). *Task Force on Applying Core Competencies to the College Union and Student Activities Profession: Phase I final report*. Available from http://www.acui.org/about.

Delansky, B., Javinar, J., Morton, C., Perozzi, B., & Zarr, J. (2005). *Task Force on the Development of Core Competencies in the College Union and Student Activities Profession: Identification of core competencies report*. Available from http://www.acui.org/about.

Knell, P., & Latta, S. (2006). *College union dynamic: Flexible solutions for successful facilities*. Bloomington, IN: Association of College Unions International.

Maul, S. Y. (1994). *Building community on campus*. Bloomington, IN: Association of College Unions International.

McMillan, A., & Davis, N. T. (Eds.) (1989). *College unions: Seventy-five years*. Bloomington, IN: Association of College Unions International.

Mitchell, R. L. (1997). *Metaphors, semaphores and two-by-fours: Reflections on a personal profession*. Bloomington, IN: Association of College Unions International.

Perozzi, B.P. (Ed.). (2009). *Enhancing student learning through college employment*. Bloomington, IN: Association of College Unions International.

The Bulletin, ACUI publication, published bimonthly; available from the ACUI Central Office.

Contextual Statement Contributors

Current Edition:
Bob Rodda, College of Wooster, ACUI
Loren Rullman, University of Michigan, ACUI

Previous Editions:
Bob Rodda, College of Wooster, ACUI
Nancy Davis Metz, ACUI

College Unions
CAS Standards and Guidelines

Part 1. MISSION

The primary goals of College Unions (CU) must be to bring campus constituents together, build campus community, support and initiate programs, provide services, and maintain facilities that promote student learning and development.

CU must develop, disseminate, implement, and regularly review their missions. The mission must be consistent with the mission of the institution and with professional standards. The mission must be appropriate for the institution's student populations and community settings. Mission statements must reference student learning and development.

The CU should provide educational, social, cultural, and recreational programs, services, and facilities that enhance the quality of campus life.

Students must be the principal constituents of the CU.

The CU should provide opportunities for students to learn and practice leadership, program planning, organizational management, social and civic responsibility, and interpersonal skills.

The vitality, variety, and spontaneity of the CU's activities should stem primarily from student boards, committees, and student-directed initiatives.

The CU must be an inclusive environment where interaction and understanding among individuals from diverse backgrounds occurs.

Part 2. PROGRAM

The formal education of students, consisting of the curriculum and the co-curriculum, must promote student learning and development outcomes that are purposeful, contribute to students' realization of their potential, and prepare students for satisfying and productive lives.

College Unions (CU) must collaborate with colleagues and departments across the institution to promote student learning and development, persistence, and success.

Consistent with the institutional mission, CU must identify relevant and desirable student learning and development outcomes from among the six domains and related dimensions:

Domain: knowledge acquisition, integration, construction, and application

- Dimensions: understanding knowledge from a range of disciplines; connecting knowledge to other knowledge, ideas, and experiences; constructing knowledge; and relating knowledge to daily life

Domain: cognitive complexity

- Dimensions: critical thinking, reflective thinking, effective reasoning, and creativity

Domain: intrapersonal development

- Dimensions: realistic self-appraisal, self-understanding, and self-respect; identity development; commitment to ethics and integrity; and spiritual awareness

Domain: interpersonal competence

- Dimensions: meaningful relationships, interdependence, collaboration, and effective leadership.

Domain: humanitarianism and civic engagement

- Dimensions: understanding and appreciation of cultural and human differences, social responsibility, global perspective, and sense of civic responsibility

Domain: practical competence

- Dimensions: pursuing goals, communicating effectively, technical competence, managing personal affairs, managing career development, demonstrating professionalism, maintaining health and wellness, and living a purposeful and satisfying life

[LD Outcomes: See *The Council for the Advancement of Standards Learning and Developmental Outcomes* statement for examples of outcomes related to these domains and dimensions.]

CU must
- assess relevant and desirable student learning and development
- provide evidence of impact on outcomes
- articulate contributions to or support of student learning and development in the domains not specifically assessed
- articulate contributions to or support of student persistence and success
- use evidence gathered through this process to create strategies for improvement of programs and services

CU must be

- **intentionally designed**
- **guided by theories and knowledge of learning and development**
- **integrated into the life of the institution**
- **reflective of developmental and demographic profiles of the student population**
- **responsive to needs of individuals, populations with distinct needs, and relevant constituencies**
- **delivered using multiple formats, strategies, and contexts**

Where institutions provide distance education, CU must assist distance learners to achieve their educational goals by providing access to information about programs and services, to staff members who can address questions and concerns, and to counseling, advising, or other forms of assistance.

CU must include programs, activities and events, services, and facilities that address campus, community, and student needs.

CU programs, activities, and events could include
- student development programs
- social, cultural, intellectual, and diversity programs
- leisure activities and recreational opportunities
- student leadership development programs and opportunities
- service-learning and community service programs
- performances
- entertainment
- tournaments
- outdoor recreation and travel
- social events
- educational programs
- crafts and hobbies
- leisure activities
- continuing education opportunities

CU services could include
- food services
- retail stores and services
- communication technology
- mailing and duplication services
- information center
- campus and community information

CU facilities could include
- commuter accommodations
- rooms of various sizes and configurations for meetings, banquets, conferences, and programs
- office space for student organization including storage
- office space for relevant administrative functions
- recreational facilities
- rest rooms that meet all constituents needs
- technological capabilities including connectivity

to campus intranets, the Internet, and emerging technologies
- exhibit spaces
- art galleries
- quiet rooms, lounges, and study spaces
- conference facilities
- studios

CU must provide opportunities for student, staff, and faculty involvement in program planning, policy development, and facility operation.

CU should also provide appropriate opportunities for involvement, participation, and collaboration with alumni and other institutional stakeholders.

Spaces in CU should be comfortable, inviting, and attractive, and appropriate space should be consistently available for informal and spontaneous interactions.

CU should create and support programs that instill an enduring affinity for the institution, including the history, legacy, traditions, and culture of the institution.

Part 3. ORGANIZATION AND LEADERSHIP

To achieve student and program outcomes, College Unions (CU) must be structured purposefully and organized effectively. CU must have
- **clearly stated goals**
- **current and accessible policies and procedures**
- **written performance expectations for employees**
- **functional work flow graphics or organizational charts demonstrating clear channels of authority**

Leaders with organizational authority for the programs and services must provide strategic planning, supervision, and management; advance the organization; and maintain integrity through the following functions:

Strategic Planning
- **articulate a vision and mission that drive short- and long-term planning**
- **set goals and objectives based on the needs of the population served and desired student learning or development and program outcomes**
- **facilitate continuous development, implementation, and assessment of goal attainment congruent with institutional mission and strategic plans**
- **promote environments that provide meaningful opportunities for student learning, development, and engagement**
- **develop and continuously improve programs and services in response to the changing**

needs of students served and evolving institutional priorities

- intentionally include diverse perspectives to inform decision making

Supervising

- manage human resource processes including recruitment, selection, development, supervision, performance planning, evaluation, recognition, and reward
- influence others to contribute to the effectiveness and success of the unit
- empower professional, support, and student staff to accept leadership opportunities
- offer appropriate feedback to colleagues and students on skills needed to become more effective leaders
- encourage and support professional development, collaboration with colleagues and departments across the institution, and scholarly contribution to the profession

Managing

- identify and address individual, organizational, and environmental conditions that foster or inhibit mission achievement
- plan, allocate, and monitor the use of fiscal, physical, human, intellectual, and technological resources
- use current and valid evidence to inform decisions
- incorporate sustainability practices in the management and design of programs, services, and facilities
- understand appropriate technologies and integrate them into programs and services
- be knowledgeable about codes and laws relevant to programs and services and ensure that staff members understand their responsibilities through appropriate training
- assess potential risks and take action to mitigate them

Advancing the Organization

- communicate effectively in writing, speaking, and electronic venues
- advocate for programs and services
- advocate for representation in strategic planning initiatives at appropriate divisional and institutional levels
- initiate collaborative interactions with internal and external stakeholders who have legitimate concerns about and interests in the functional area
- facilitate processes to reach consensus where wide support is needed
- inform other areas within the institution about issues affecting practice

Maintaining Integrity

- model ethical behavior and institutional citizenship
- share data used to inform key decisions in transparent and accessible ways
- monitor media used for distributing information about programs and services to ensure the content is current, accurate, appropriately referenced, and accessible

In addition CU leaders must

- promote efforts to build community
- use principles of good organizational management
- facilitate good planning processes and philosophies
- use leadership skills to effectively manage facilities
- demonstrate intercultural competencies
- conduct outreach and marketing that describes and promotes the programs and services of the CU
- ensure excellent customer services
- utilize developmental and learning theories to design and implement learning initiatives and experiences for students
- engage in professional development activities to stay current with research and best practices

CU must be organized to provide effective social, cultural, intellectual, and recreational programming; offer appropriate business enterprises and services; and maintain its physical plant.

CU must involve members of the campus community in its governance and programming structure and in the formulation of CU policies.

Involvement of the campus community should include students, faculty and staff members, and alumni. Involvement could include parents and local community members. Typically such involvement is through advisory, governing, and program boards. These boards should address issues such as (a) facility operating policies related to the use and/or rental of CU facilities by campus and non-campus groups, (b) programming goals, (c) scheduling of events, (d) budget planning, fee structure, and allocation priorities, (e) employment policies, (f) space allocation priorities, and (g) hours of operation.

CU must assure that outsourced programs and services comply with the goals, policies, and procedures of the CU and the institution.

CU must have an emergency preparedness plan and a business continuity plan. The emergency preparedness plan must be compatible with the institution's emergency preparedness plan. The business continuity plan must be in place to respond after an emergency that compromises essential services and access to the facility.

Procedures must be in place to assess and manage events with large numbers of participants, potential volatile content, or dangerous materials and equipment.

Part 4. HUMAN RESOURCES

College Unions (CU) must be staffed adequately by individuals qualified to accomplish mission and goals.

Within institutional guidelines, CU must
- establish procedures for staff recruitment and selection, training, performance planning, and evaluation
- set expectations for supervision and performance
- assess the performance of employees individually and as a team
- provide access to continuing and advanced education and appropriate professional development opportunities to improve the leadership ability, competence, and skills of all employees.

CU must maintain position descriptions for all staff members.

To create a diverse staff, CU must institute recruitment and hiring strategies that encourage individuals from under-represented populations to apply for positions.

CU must develop promotion practices that are fair, inclusive, proactive, and non-discriminatory.

To further the recruitment and retention of staff, CU must consider work life initiatives, such as compressed work schedules, flextime, job sharing, remote work, or telework.

CU professional staff members must hold an earned graduate or professional degree in a field relevant to the position they hold or must possess an appropriate combination of educational credentials and related work experience.

Graduate degrees should be earned in fields relevant to the CU including, but not limited to, college student affairs; student development; public, business, or higher education administration; and recreation studies.

CU staff responsible for programs, services, and facilities must have appropriate combinations of education, experience, and credentials to adequately and safely provide a level of management and leadership consistent with relevant industry standards and institutional expectations.

Cross training should be made available to enable appropriate staff to assume critical operations and responsibilities during unforeseen situations.

Staff members should possess (a) knowledge of and ability to use management principles, including the effective management of volunteers; (b) understanding of and the ability to apply student development theory; (c) skills in assessment, planning, training, and evaluation; (d) interpersonal skills; (e) technical skills; (f) understanding of CU philosophy; (g) commitment to institutional mission; and (h) safety and emergency management skills.

CU professional staff members must engage in continuing professional development activities to keep abreast of the research, theories, legislation, policies, and developments that affect their programs and services.

CU must have technical and support staff members adequate to accomplish their mission. All members of the staff must be technologically proficient and qualified to perform their job functions, be knowledgeable about ethical and legal uses of technology, and have access to training and resources to support the performance of their assigned responsibilities.

Staff members may include food service personnel, audio visual technicians, stage hands, information technology staff, maintenance personnel, support staff, attendants, housekeepers, reservationists, sales clerks, and cashiers.

Degree- or credential-seeking interns or graduate assistants must be qualified by enrollment in an appropriate field of study and by relevant experience. These individuals must be trained and supervised adequately by professional staff members holding educational credentials and related work experience appropriate for supervision. Supervisors must be cognizant of the roles of interns and graduate assistants as both student and employee and closely adhere to all parameters of their job descriptions, work hours, and schedules. Supervisors and the interns or graduate assistants must agree to compensatory time or other appropriate compensation if circumstances necessitate additional hours

The CU should offer internships or practicums to graduate students pursuing advanced degrees in college student affairs; student development; public, business, or higher educational administration; and recreation studies. These students should be utilized in a manner consistent with the missions of the CU and graduate programs.

Student employees and volunteers must be carefully

selected, trained, supervised, and evaluated. They must be educated on how and when to refer those in need of additional assistance to qualified staff members and must have access to a supervisor for assistance in making these judgments. Student employees and volunteers must be provided clear job descriptions, pre-service training based on assessed needs, and continuing development.

Student employees and volunteers should be an integral part of the CU's operation. Their work experience should be an important part of their educational experience and contribute to increased engagement in the campus community. A thorough training program should be provided for part-time student employees and volunteers and, depending on their assigned duties, might include leadership training, group facilitation skills, communication skills, CU policies, and emergency procedures.

All CU staff members, including student employees and volunteers, must receive specific training on institutional policies pertaining to functions or activities they support and to privacy and confidentiality policies and laws regarding access to student records and other sensitive institutional information.

All CU staff members must receive training on policies and procedures related to the use of technology to store or access student records and institutional data.

CU must ensure that staff members are knowledgeable about and trained in emergency procedures, crisis response, and prevention efforts. Prevention efforts must address identification of threatening conduct or behavior of students, faculty and staff members, and others and must incorporate a system for responding and reporting.

CU must ensure that staff members are knowledgeable of and trained in safety and emergency procedures for securing and vacating facilities.

Part 5. ETHICS

College Unions (CU) must review relevant professional ethical standards and must adopt or develop and implement appropriate statements of ethical practice.

CU must publish and adhere to statements of ethical practice and ensure their periodic review by relevant constituencies.

CU must orient new staff members to relevant ethical standards and statements of ethical practice and related institutional policies.

Statements of ethical standards must specify

that staff members respect privacy and maintain confidentiality in all communications and records to the extent that such communications and records are protected under relevant privacy laws.

Statements of ethical standards must specify limits on disclosure of information contained in students' educational records as well as requirements to disclose to appropriate authorities.

Statements of ethical standards must address personal and economic conflicts of interest, or appearance thereof, by staff members in the performance of their work.

Statements of ethical standards must reflect the responsibility of staff members to be fair, objective, and impartial in their interactions with others.

Statements of ethical standards must reference management of institutional funds.

Statements of ethical standards must reference appropriate behavior regarding research and assessment with human participants, confidentiality of research and assessment data, and students' rights and responsibilities.

Statements of ethical standards must include the expectation that CU staff members confront and hold accountable other staff members who exhibit unethical behavior.

Statements of ethical standards must address issues surrounding scholarly integrity.

As appropriate, CU staff members must inform users of programs and services of ethical obligations and limitations emanating from codes and laws or from licensure requirements.

CU staff members must recognize and avoid conflicts of interest that could adversely influence their judgment or objectivity and, when unavoidable, recuse themselves from the situation.

CU staff members must perform their duties within the limits of their position, training, expertise, and competence.

When these limits are exceeded, individuals in need of further assistance must be referred to persons possessing appropriate qualifications.

Promotional and descriptive information must be accurate and free of deception.

CU must adhere to institutional policies regarding ethical and legal use of software and technology.

Marketing and advertising must be informative, respectful, socially responsible, and useful to students, faculty, staff, and visitors.

Part 6. LAW, POLICY, AND GOVERNANCE

College Unions (CU) must be in compliance with laws, regulations, and policies that relate to their respective responsibilities and that pose legal obligations, limitations, risks, and liabilities for the institution as a whole. Examples include constitutional, statutory, regulatory, and case law; relevant law and orders emanating from codes and laws; and the institution's policies.

CU must inform staff members, appropriate officials, and users of programs and services about existing and changing legal obligations, risks and liabilities, and limitations.

CU must have written policies on all relevant operations, transactions, or tasks that have legal implications.

CU must regularly review policies. The revision and creation of policies must be informed by best practices, available evidence, and policy issues in higher education.

CU staff members must use reasonable and informed practices to limit the liability exposure of the institution and its officers, employees, and agents. CU staff members must be informed about institutional policies regarding risk management, personal liability, and related insurance coverage options and must be referred to external sources if the institution does not provide coverage.

The institution must provide access to legal advice for staff members as needed to carry out assigned responsibilities.

CU must have procedures and guidelines consistent with institutional policy for responding to threats, emergencies, and crisis situations. Systems and procedures must be in place to disseminate timely and accurate information to students, other members of the institutional community, and appropriate external organizations during emergency situations.

CU staff members must neither participate in nor condone any form of harassment or activity that demeans persons or creates an intimidating, hostile, or offensive environment.

CU must obtain permission to use copyrighted materials and instruments. CU must purchase the materials and instruments from legally compliant sources or seek alternative permission from the publisher or owner. References to copyrighted materials and instruments must include appropriate citations.

CU staff members must be knowledgeable about internal and external governance systems that affect programs and services.

Part 7. DIVERSITY, EQUITY, AND ACCESS

Within the context of each institution's unique mission and in accordance with institutional polices and all applicable codes and laws, College Unions (CU) must create and maintain educational and work environments that are
- welcoming, accessible, and inclusive to persons of diverse backgrounds
- equitable and non-discriminatory
- free from harassment

CU must not discriminate on the basis of ability; age; cultural identity; ethnicity; family educational history (e.g., first generation to attend college); gender identity and expression; nationality; political affiliation; race; religious affiliation; sex; sexual orientation; economic, marital, social, or veteran status; or any other basis included in institutional policies and codes and laws.

CU must
- advocate for greater sensitivity to multicultural and social justice concerns by the institution and its personnel
- modify or remove policies, practices, facilities, structures, systems, and technologies that limit access, discriminate, or produce inequities
- include diversity, equity, and access initiatives within their strategic plans
- foster communication that deepens understanding of identity, culture, self-expression, and heritage
- promote respect about commonalities and differences among people within their historical and cultural contexts
- address the characteristics and needs of a diverse population when establishing and implementing culturally relevant and inclusive programs, services, policies, procedures, and practices
- provide staff members with access to multicultural training and hold staff members accountable for integrating the training into their work
- respond to the needs of all students and other populations served when establishing hours of operation and developing methods of delivering programs, services, and resources
- ensure physical, program, and resource access for persons with disabilities
- recognize the needs of distance learning students by providing appropriate and

accessible services and resources or by assisting them in gaining access to other appropriate services and resources in their geographic region

CU governing and programming boards should represent campus diversity and institutional goals for inclusion.

CU should conduct outreach to include and engage all populations in the life of the Union.

Outsourced programs and services are accountable to the institution. Therefore, CU should encourage providers of outsourced programs and services to offer a diverse workforce and inclusive environment.

Part 8. INSTITUTIONAL AND EXTERNAL RELATIONS

College Unions (CU) must reach out to relevant individuals, groups, communities, and organizations internal and external to the institution to

- establish, maintain, and promote understanding and effective relations with those that have a significant interest in or potential effect on the students or other constituents served by the programs and services
- garner support and resources for programs and services as defined by the mission statement
- disseminate information about the programs and services
- collaborate, where appropriate, to assist in offering or improving programs and services to meet the needs of students and other constituents and to achieve program and student outcomes
- engage diverse individuals, groups, communities, and organizations to enrich the educational environment and experiences of students and other constituents

Examples of relevant individuals, campus offices, and external agencies include students; student organizations, especially student government and program board(s); faculty members; administrative offices; alumni; local community members; contracted service providers, including lessees; and campus safety offices.

CU should use relevant and appropriate student and campus marketing and outreach resources to inform the campus community about CU programs and services. Staff and volunteers throughout CU should be considered for membership on various institutional committees and governing bodies.

CU must have procedures and guidelines consistent with institutional policy for
- communicating with the media

- contracting with external organizations for delivery of programs and services
- cultivating, soliciting, and managing gifts
- applying to and managing funds from grants

Part 9. FINANCIAL RESOURCES

College Unions (CU) must have funding to accomplish the mission and goals. In establishing funding priorities and making significant changes, a comprehensive analysis must be conducted to determine the following elements: unmet needs of the unit, relevant expenditures, external and internal resources, and impact on students and the institution.

CU must demonstrate efficient and effective use and responsible stewardship of fiscal resources consistent with institutional protocols.

CU should have financial resources to ensure reasonable pricing of services and adequate programming, staffing, maintenance, and professional development.

When handling student fee funds, CU must manage fees in accordance with approved accounting methods of the institution.

Student fee funds should be used to benefit students directly.

The institution should consider various methods and sources of financial support including, but not limited to (a) direct institutional support (e.g., salaries, utilities, housekeeping, maintenance, and membership fees); (b) student fees; (c) income from sales, services, rentals, and leases; and (d) fundraising initiatives.

Part 10. TECHNOLOGY

College Unions (CU) must have adequate technology to support the achievement of their mission and goals. The technology and its use must comply with institutional policies and procedures and be evaluated for compliance with relevant codes and laws.

CU must use current technology to provide updated information regarding mission, location, staffing, programs, services, and official contacts to students and designated clients.

CU must explore the use of technology to enhance delivery of programs and services, especially for students at a distance or external constituencies.

When technology is used to facilitate student learning and development, CU must select technology that reflects intended outcomes.

CU must
- maintain policies and procedures that address the security, confidentiality, and backup of data, as well as compliance with privacy laws

- **have clearly articulated plans in place for protecting confidentiality and security of information when using Internet-based technologies**
- **develop plans for replacing and updating existing hardware and software as well as plans for integrating new technically-based or supported programs, including systems developed internally by the institution, systems available through professional associations, or private vendor-based systems**

Technology, as well as workstations or computer labs maintained by programs and services for student use, must be accessible to all designated clients and must meet established technology standards for delivery to persons with disabilities.

When providing student access to technology, CU must
- **have policies on the use of technology that are clear, easy to understand, and available to all students**
- **provide assistance, information, or referral to appropriate support services to those needing help accessing or using technology**
- **provide instruction or training on how to use the technology**
- **inform students on the legal and ethical implications of misuse as it pertains to intellectual property, harassment, privacy, and social networks**

Student violations of technology policies must follow established institutional student disciplinary procedures.

Students who experience negative emotional or psychological consequences from the use of technology must be referred to support services provided by the institution.

The CU should use current and appropriate technology to facilitate, improve, assess, and extend access to its programs, products, services, and facilities.

Part 11. FACILITIES AND EQUIPMENT

College Unions (CU) must have adequate, accessible, and suitably located facilities and equipment to support the mission and goals. If acquiring capital equipment as defined by the institution, programs and services must take into account expenses related to regular maintenance and life cycle costs. Facilities and equipment must be evaluated on an established cycle, including consideration of sustainability, and be in compliance with codes and laws to provide for access, health, safety, and security.

Recycling, energy conservation, and other sustainability efforts must be addressed throughout the CU.

CU facilities should be proportional in size to the needs of the campus community and be centrally located.

CU should provide appropriate spaces that meet the unique needs of diverse groups, while simultaneously promoting interaction and community.

Facilities must be accessible, clean, reasonably priced, well maintained, and have adequate safety and security features.

New construction and renovation projects should be responsive to the current and future needs of the campus community. Decisions about new construction and renovation should be based upon clearly defined needs and consistent with the mission of the institution, which may include adherence to institutional standards for sustainability, accessibility, beautification, debt coverage, and historic preservation.

Members of the campus community and the CU staff should be involved in program development of new and renovated facilities. Such planning efforts should include representation by students, faculty, and staff.

Systematically planned replacement cycles should exist for furnishings, mechanical and electrical systems, maintenance equipment, floor/wall/window treatments, technology, and service equipment.

CU staff members must have workspace that is well equipped, adequate in size, and designed to support their work and responsibilities. For conversations requiring privacy, staff members must have access to a private space.

CU staff members who share workspace must be able to secure their own work.

The design of the facilities must guarantee the security and privacy of records and ensure the confidentiality of sensitive information.

The location and layout of the facilities must be sensitive to the needs of persons with disabilities as well as the needs of other constituencies.

Part 12. ASSESSMENT AND EVALUATION

College Unions (CU) must have a clearly articulated assessment plan to document achievement of stated goals and learning outcomes, demonstrate accountability, provide evidence of improvement, and describe resulting changes in programs and services.

CU must have adequate fiscal, human, professional development, and technological resources to develop

and implement assessment plans.

Assessments must include direct and indirect evaluation and use qualitative and quantitative methodologies and existing evidence, as appropriate, to determine whether and to what degree the stated mission, goals, and intended outcomes are being met as effectively and efficiently as possible. The process must employ sufficient and sound measures to ensure comprehensiveness. Data collected must include responses from students and other constituencies, and aggregated results must be shared with those groups. Results of assessments must be shared appropriately with multiple constituents.

Results of assessments and evaluations must be used to identify needs and interests in revising and improving programs and services, recognizing staff performance, maximizing resource efficiency and effectiveness, improving student achievement of learning and development outcomes, and improving student persistence and success. Changes resulting from the use of assessments and evaluation must be shared with stakeholders.

Evaluation should include goal-related progress on such considerations as student satisfaction, attendance at programs, cash flow, appearance of facilities, and vitality of volunteer groups such as programming and governing boards.

Results and summary data from assessment and evaluation should be broadly shared with all appropriate constituencies including students, faculty and staff members, cabinet members, and board members.

General Standards revised in 2011;
CU content developed/revised in 1986, 1997, 1998, & 2009

The Role of Commuter and Off-Campus Living Programs
CAS Standards Contextual Statement

Commuter and off-campus students are defined as those who do not live in institutional-owned housing on campus (Jacoby, 2000). Commuter and off-campus students attend virtually every institution of higher education and comprise over 85 percent of college enrollment (Horn & Nevill, 2006). Their numbers include students who live at home with their parents, in rental housing, or with their own families. They may attend college full time, part time, or alternate between the two. They may live near the campus or far away; they may commute by car, public transportation, walking, or bicycle. The majority of commuter and off-campus students work, mostly off-campus, and some are employed the equivalent of full-time and/or at more than one job.

Many professionals treat commuter students as a homogenous group and largely ignore the diversity within the group (Jacoby & Garland, 2004). Regardless of differences in backgrounds, living arrangements, and educational goals, commuter and off-campus students face common needs and concerns, such as finding safe and reliable transportation, managing multiple life roles, integrating their off-campus support systems into their higher education experience, and developing a sense of belonging in their campus community. Whether they attend a predominantly residential or commuter institution, the fact that they reside off-campus profoundly affects the nature of their educational experience.

Commuter and off-campus students are a rapidly growing segment of the postsecondary population. The long-standing residential tradition of American higher education has often impeded effective, comprehensive institutional responses to their wide range of lifestyles. Historically, the relationship of commuter and off-campus students to the institution has been neither well understood nor incorporated into the design of policies, programs, and practices. The CAS Standards and Guidelines take the approach that all students must have equitable access to institutional services, engagement opportunities, and the total educational process regardless of place of residence.

Institutions must critically and comprehensively examine their practices from the point of view of all types of commuter and off-campus students to correct any existing inequities. Because the population is so diverse and each institution's population is unique, it is important that each college and university regularly collect data about its commuter and off-campus students and the nature of their college experiences. These standards and guidelines provide a basis for institutional self-assessment and program development.

References, Readings, and Resources

American College Personnel Association, Commission for Commuter Students and Adult Learners. One Dupont Circle NW, Suite 300. Washington, DC 20036. (202) 835-2272. http://www.acpa.nche.edu

Chickering, A. W. (1974). *Commuting versus resident students.* San Francisco: Jossey-Bass.

Donaldson, J. F., & Townsend, B. K. (2007). Higher education journals' discourse about adult undergraduate students. *The Journal of Higher Education, 78*(1), 27-50.

Horn, L., and Nevill, S. (2006). P*rofile of Undergraduates in U.S. Postsecondary Education Institutions: 2003–04: With a Special Analysis of Community College Students* (NCES 2006-184). U.S. Department of Education. Washington, DC: National Center for Education Statistics.

Jacoby, B. (Ed.). (2000). *Involving commuter students in learning.* New Directions for Higher Education #109. San Francisco: Jossey-Bass

Jacoby, B. (2004). Engaging first-year commuter students in learning. *Metropolitan Universities, 15*(2).

Jacoby, B. & Garland, J. (2004). Strategies for enhancing commuter student success. *Journal of College Student Retention, 6*(1).

Jacoby, B. (1989). *The student as commuter: Developing a comprehensive institutional response.* ASHE-ERIC Higher Education Report No. 7. Washington, DC: School of Education and human Development, The George Washington University.

Jacoby, B., & Girrell, K. (1981). A model for improving service and programs for commuter students (The SPAR Model). *NASPA Journal, 18*(3).

Kodama, C. M. (2002). Marginality of transfer commuter students. *NASPA Journal, 39*(3), 233-250.

Mahan, M. (2010). NCCP has a new home. *Commuter Perspectives, 31*(3).

Mahan, M. (2011). *Learning about commuter students: Resources within reach (10th ed).* National Clearinghouse for Commuter Programs. http://nccp.nsuok.edu

National Clearinghouse for Commuter Programs, Northeastern State University, Broken Arrow, OK 74014. (918)449-6200. http://nccp.nsuok.edu

Schlossberg, N. K. Lynch, A. Q., & Chickering, A. W. (1989). *Improving higher education environments for adults.* San Francisco: Jossey-Bass.

Stewart, S. S. (Ed.). (1983). *Commuter students: Enhancing their educational experience.* New directions for Student Services #24. San Francisco: Jossey-Bass.

Contextual Statement Contributors
Current Edition:
Melissa Mahan, Northeastern State University, NCCP

Previous Editions:
Barbara Jacoby, University of Maryland

Commuter and Off-Campus Living Programs
CAS Standards and Guidelines

Part 1. MISSION

The primary mission of Commuter and Off-Campus Living Programs (COCLP) is to ensure that all students have equitable access to programs, services, and engagement opportunities regardless of place of residence.

In addition, COCLP must
- provide services and facilities to meet the basic needs of commuter and off-campus students as determined by institutional assessment
- ensure that all students benefit equitably from the institution's educational programs
- provide engagement opportunities to assist commuter and off-campus students and promote learning and development
- support the institution's vision for the student learning experience

COCLP must develop, disseminate, implement, and regularly review their missions. The mission must be consistent with the mission of the institution and with professional standards. The mission must be appropriate for the institution's student populations and community settings. Mission statements must reference student learning and development.

The COCLP mission should address not only programs and services but also education and advocacy on behalf of commuter and off-campus students.

Commuter and off-campus students may be defined differently at individual institutions; however, this document focuses on the equitable access of all students to institutional resources.

The number of commuter and off-campus students may range from a small minority to the entire student population. The commuter and off-campus students in any higher educational institution should have equitable benefits of the curricular and co-curricular programs and services offered, regardless of full-time or part-time credit load, family status, age, proximity to campus, day or evening enrollment, or dependent versus independent living status.

Part 2. PROGRAM

Commuter and Off-Campus Living Programs (COCLP) must provide direct delivery of essential programs and services meeting a wide variety of needs and interests, whether organized as a single office or distributed throughout the institution. In either case, these services and programs must be evaluated to ensure that all students have equitable access to programs, services, and engagement opportunities regardless of place of residence.

The formal education of students, consisting of the curriculum and the co-curriculum, must promote student learning and development outcomes that are purposeful, contribute to students' realization of their potential, and prepare students for satisfying and productive lives.

COCLP must collaborate with colleagues and departments across the institution to promote student learning and development, persistence, and success.

Consistent with the institutional mission, COCLP must identify relevant and desirable student learning and development outcomes from among the six domains and related dimensions:

Domain: knowledge acquisition, integration, construction, and application

- Dimensions: understanding knowledge from a range of disciplines; connecting knowledge to other knowledge, ideas, and experiences; constructing knowledge; and relating knowledge to daily life

Domain: cognitive complexity

- Dimensions: critical thinking, reflective thinking, effective reasoning, and creativity

Domain: intrapersonal development

- Dimensions: realistic self-appraisal, self-understanding, and self-respect; identity development; commitment to ethics and integrity; and spiritual awareness

Domain: interpersonal competence

- Dimensions: meaningful relationships, interdependence, collaboration, and effective leadership.

Domain: humanitarianism and civic engagement

- Dimensions: understanding and appreciation of cultural and human differences, social responsibility, global perspective, and sense of civic responsibility

Domain: practical competence

- Dimensions: pursuing goals, communicating

effectively, technical competence, managing personal affairs, managing career development, demonstrating professionalism, maintaining health and wellness, and living a purposeful and satisfying life

[LD Outcomes: See *The Council for the Advancement of Standards Learning and Developmental Outcomes* statement for examples of outcomes related to these domains and dimensions.]

COCLP must

- **assess relevant and desirable student learning and development**
- **provide evidence of impact on outcomes**
- **articulate contributions to or support of student learning and development in the domains not specifically assessed**
- **articulate contributions to or support of student persistence and success**
- **use evidence gathered through this process to create strategies for improvement of programs and services**

COCLP must be

- **intentionally designed**
- **guided by theories and knowledge of learning and development**
- **integrated into the life of the institution**
- **reflective of developmental and demographic profiles of the student population**
- **responsive to needs of individuals, populations with distinct needs, and relevant constituencies**
- **delivered using multiple formats, strategies, and contexts**

Where institutions provide distance education, COCLP must assist distance learners to achieve their educational goals by providing access to information about programs and services, to staff members who can address questions and concerns, and to counseling, advising, or other forms of assistance.

COCLP must assist students with access to institutional resources and in meeting basic needs such as housing, transportation, parking, security, information and referral, facilities, food, computer and internet access, and childcare.

COCLP should assist students in making informed choices about housing and should provide information about available housing, tenants' rights and responsibilities, utilities, and legal advice and assistance.

Provisions should be made for parking; carpools; emergency vehicle assistance; and walkway, bike path, and parking lot security. Information about transportation alternatives to campus should be provided.

Information about campus services, programs, and current events should be disseminated in a variety of media and formats. Access to services such as course registration should be available via the internet and telephone as well as in traditional modes.

Students should have adequate study and lounge spaces in convenient locations around the campus. These should include access to computers, printers, copiers, and lockers.

Food service should be available in convenient locations at hours when students are on campus, including evenings and weekends.

Institutions should address commuter and off-campus students' need for high-speed internet access for accomplishing course work, and should ensure equitable access to informational resources.

Institutions should provide adequate childcare services, either through the institution or through referrals to community childcare providers. On-campus facilities for infant feeding and changing should be available.

COCLP should work to ensure that all institutional services are available equitably to commuter and off-campus students, including scheduling of classes, events, campus employment, and office hours to accommodate students' varied schedules.

COCLP must provide programs that meet the specific needs of commuter and off-campus students and ensure that all students have equitable access to all educational, recreational, and social programming.

COCLP should provide educational programs that inform students of tenancy ordinances, tenants and landlord rights and responsibilities, legal advice and assistance, personal financial management, roommate and neighbor relations, and conflict-resolution skills. Additional educational programs can include defensive driving, personal security, proper nutrition, and time management.

COCLP should offer programs, or encourage the Institution to offer programs, that enable commuter and off-campus students to achieve learning and development outcomes. These include opportunities for interaction with faculty members and peers, activities scheduled at times convenient for commuter and off-campus students, peer mentoring, learning communities that do not require on-campus residence, experiential education, family-oriented activities, programs offered in off-campus locations with dense student populations, and programming using technology (e.g., virtual communities).

Institutions must include the commuter and off-campus student perspective at all appropriate levels of campus planning, policy making, budgeting, program delivery, and governance.

Commuter and off-campus student advocacy should focus on

- access to comprehensive academic advising, student support services, and information
- recognition of the diverse subgroups of the commuter and off-campus student population, including students who are older, married, fully employed, part-time, evening, veterans, or who live at home with parents or guardian.
- equitable fee structure for campus services
- fair representation of all types of commuter and off-campus students in areas of campus employment, internships, and financial aid awards
- faculty and institutional research programs that enhance understanding of the demographic characteristics and unique needs of commuter and off-campus students
- inclusion of the commuter and off-campus student perspective in community decision-making (e.g., transportation route planning, police coverage, and local ordinances)
- minimum standards for use as criteria for listing off-campus housing options

COCLP must collect data and encourage institutional research to understand the characteristics, needs, and experiences of commuter and off-campus students.

Research efforts may include demographic studies, needs assessments, retention studies, environmental assessments, involvement and satisfaction measures, longitudinal studies, and commuter-resident comparisons.

Part 3. ORGANIZATION AND LEADERSHIP

To achieve student and program outcomes, Commuter and Off-Campus Living Programs (COCLP) must be structured purposefully and organized effectively. COCLP must have
- **clearly stated goals**
- **current and accessible policies and procedures**
- **written performance expectations for employees**
- **functional work flow graphics or organizational charts demonstrating clear channels of authority**

Leaders with organizational authority for the programs and services must provide strategic planning, supervision, and management; advance the organization; and maintain integrity through the following functions:

Strategic Planning
- **articulate a vision and mission that drive short- and long-term planning**
- **set goals and objectives based on the needs of the population served and desired student learning or development and program outcomes**

- **facilitate continuous development, implementation, and assessment of goal attainment congruent with institutional mission and strategic plans**
- **promote environments that provide meaningful opportunities for student learning, development, and engagement**
- **develop and continuously improve programs and services in response to the changing needs of students served and evolving institutional priorities**
- **intentionally include diverse perspectives to inform decision making**

Supervising
- **manage human resource processes including recruitment, selection, development, supervision, performance planning, evaluation, recognition, and reward**
- **influence others to contribute to the effectiveness and success of the unit**
- **empower professional, support, and student staff to accept leadership opportunities**
- **offer appropriate feedback to colleagues and students on skills needed to become more effective leaders**
- **encourage and support professional development, collaboration with colleagues and departments across the institution, and scholarly contribution to the profession**

Managing
- **identify and address individual, organizational, and environmental conditions that foster or inhibit mission achievement**
- **plan, allocate, and monitor the use of fiscal, physical, human, intellectual, and technological resources**
- **use current and valid evidence to inform decisions**
- **incorporate sustainability practices in the management and design of programs, services, and facilities**
- **understand appropriate technologies and integrate them into programs and services**
- **be knowledgeable about codes and laws relevant to programs and services and ensure that staff members understand their responsibilities through appropriate training**
- **assess potential risks and take action to mitigate them**

Advancing the Organization
- **communicate effectively in writing, speaking, and electronic venues**
- **advocate for programs and services**
- **advocate for representation in strategic**

planning initiatives at appropriate divisional and institutional levels

- initiate collaborative interactions with internal and external stakeholders who have legitimate concerns about and interests in the functional area
- facilitate processes to reach consensus where wide support is needed
- inform other areas within the institution about issues affecting practice

Maintaining Integrity
- model ethical behavior and institutional citizenship
- share data used to inform key decisions in transparent and accessible ways
- monitor media used for distributing information about programs and services to ensure the content is current, accurate, appropriately referenced, and accessible

Part 4. HUMAN RESOURCES

Commuter and Off-Campus Living Programs (COCLP) must be staffed adequately by individuals qualified to accomplish mission and goals.

Within institutional guidelines, COCLP must
- establish procedures for staff recruitment and selection, training, performance planning, and evaluation
- set expectations for supervision and performance
- assess the performance of employees individually and as a team
- provide access to continuing and advanced education and appropriate professional development opportunities to improve the leadership ability, competence, and skills of all employees.

COCLP must maintain position descriptions for all staff members.

To create a diverse staff, COCLP must institute recruitment and hiring strategies that encourage individuals from under-represented populations to apply for positions.

COCLP must develop promotion practices that are fair, inclusive, proactive, and non-discriminatory.

To further the recruitment and retention of staff, COCLP must consider work life initiatives, such as compressed work schedules, flextime, job sharing, remote work, or telework.

COCLP professional staff members must hold an earned graduate or professional degree in a field relevant to the position they hold or must possess an appropriate combination of educational credentials and related work experience.

COCLP professional staff should possess the academic preparation, experience, abilities, professional interests, and competencies essential for the efficient operation of the office as charged, as well as the ability to identify and address needs of the commuter and off-campus student population. They should possess the following knowledge and skills:
- ability to work with diverse students
- knowledge of history and current trends in higher education
- knowledge of organizational development, group dynamics, strategies for changes and principles of community development
- ability to design and evaluate programs to meet desired outcomes
- effective written and oral communication skills
- knowledge of theories of college student learning and development
- knowledge of management and budgeting
- ability to work effectively with internal and external agencies
- ability to serve as an effective advocate

COCLP professional staff members must engage in continuing professional development activities to keep abreast of the research, theories, legislation, policies, and developments that affect their programs and services.

COCLP must have technical and support staff members adequate to accomplish their mission. All members of the staff must be technologically proficient and qualified to perform their job functions, be knowledgeable about ethical and legal uses of technology, and have access to training and resources to support the performance of their assigned responsibilities.

Degree- or credential-seeking interns or graduate assistants must be qualified by enrollment in an appropriate field of study and by relevant experience. These individuals must be trained and supervised adequately by professional staff members holding educational credentials and related work experience appropriate for supervision. Supervisors must be cognizant of the roles of interns and graduate assistants as both student and employee and closely adhere to all parameters of their job descriptions, work hours, and schedules. Supervisors and the interns or graduate assistants must agree to compensatory time or other appropriate compensation if circumstances necessitate additional hours.

Student employees and volunteers must be carefully selected, trained, supervised, and evaluated. They must be educated on how and when to refer those in need of additional assistance to qualified staff members and must have access to a supervisor for assistance in making these judgments. Student employees and volunteers must be provided clear job descriptions, pre-service training based on assessed needs, and continuing development.

All COCLP staff members, including student employees and volunteers, must receive specific training on institutional policies pertaining to functions or activities they support and to privacy and confidentiality policies and laws regarding access to student records and other sensitive institutional information.

All COCLP staff members must receive training on policies and procedures related to the use of technology to store or access student records and institutional data.

COCLP must ensure that staff members are knowledgeable about and trained in emergency procedures, crisis response, and prevention efforts. Prevention efforts must address identification of threatening conduct or behavior of students, faculty and staff members, and others and must incorporate a system for responding and reporting.

COCLP must ensure that staff members are knowledgeable of and trained in safety and emergency procedures for securing and vacating facilities.

Part 5. ETHICS

Commuter and Off-Campus Living Programs (COCLP) must review relevant professional ethical standards and must adopt or develop and implement appropriate statements of ethical practice.

COCLP must publish and adhere to statements of ethical practice and ensure their periodic review by relevant constituencies.

COCLP must orient new staff members to relevant ethical standards and statements of ethical practice and related institutional policies.

Statements of ethical standards must specify that staff members respect privacy and maintain confidentiality in all communications and records to the extent that such communications and records are protected under relevant privacy laws.

Statements of ethical standards must specify limits on disclosure of information contained in students' educational records as well as requirements to disclose to appropriate authorities.

Statements of ethical standards must address personal and economic conflicts of interest, or appearance thereof, by staff members in the performance of their work.

Statements of ethical standards must reflect the responsibility of staff members to be fair, objective, and impartial in their interactions with others.

Statements of ethical standards must reference management of institutional funds.

Statements of ethical standards must reference appropriate behavior regarding research and assessment with human participants, confidentiality of research and assessment data, and students' rights and responsibilities.

Statements of ethical standards must include the expectation that COCLP staff members confront and hold accountable other staff members who exhibit unethical behavior.

Statements of ethical standards must address issues surrounding scholarly integrity.

As appropriate, COCLP staff members must inform users of programs and services of ethical obligations and limitations emanating from codes and laws or from licensure requirements.

COCLP staff members must recognize and avoid conflicts of interest that could adversely influence their judgment or objectivity and, when unavoidable, recuse themselves from the situation.

COCLP staff members must perform their duties within the limits of their position, training, expertise, and competence.

When these limits are exceeded, individuals in need of further assistance must be referred to persons possessing appropriate qualifications.

Promotional and descriptive information must be accurate and free of deception.

COCLP must adhere to institutional policies regarding ethical and legal use of software and technology.

Part 6. LAW, POLICY, AND GOVERNANCE

Commuter and Off-Campus Living Programs (COCLP) must be in compliance with laws, regulations, and policies that relate to their respective responsibilities and that pose legal obligations, limitations, risks, and liabilities for the institution as a whole. Examples include constitutional, statutory, regulatory, and case law; relevant law and orders emanating from codes and laws; and the institution's policies.

COCLP must inform staff members, appropriate

officials, and users of programs and services about existing and changing legal obligations, risks and liabilities, and limitations.

COCLP must have written policies on all relevant operations, transactions, or tasks that have legal implications.

COCLP must regularly review policies. The revision and creation of policies must be informed by best practices, available evidence, and policy issues in higher education.

COCLP staff members must use reasonable and informed practices to limit the liability exposure of the institution and its officers, employees, and agents. COCLP staff members must be informed about institutional policies regarding risk management, personal liability, and related insurance coverage options and must be referred to external sources if the institution does not provide coverage.

The institution must provide access to legal advice for staff members as needed to carry out assigned responsibilities.

COCLP must have procedures and guidelines consistent with institutional policy for responding to threats, emergencies, and crisis situations. Systems and procedures must be in place to disseminate timely and accurate information to students, other members of the institutional community, and appropriate external organizations during emergency situations.

COCLP staff members must neither participate in nor condone any form of harassment or activity that demeans persons or creates an intimidating, hostile, or offensive environment.

COCLP must obtain permission to use copyrighted materials and instruments. COCLP must purchase the materials and instruments from legally compliant sources or seek alternative permission from the publisher or owner. References to copyrighted materials and instruments must include appropriate citations.

COCLP staff members must be knowledgeable about internal and external governance systems that affect programs and services.

Part 7. DIVERSITY, EQUITY, AND ACCESS

Within the context of each institution's unique mission and in accordance with institutional polices and all applicable codes and laws, Commuter and Off-Campus Living Programs (COCLP) must create and maintain educational and work environments that are

- welcoming, accessible, and inclusive to persons of diverse backgrounds
- equitable and non-discriminatory
- free from harassment

COCLP must not discriminate on the basis of ability; age; cultural identity; ethnicity; family educational history (e.g., first generation to attend college); gender identity and expression; nationality; political affiliation; race; religious affiliation; sex; sexual orientation; economic, marital, social, or veteran status; or any other basis included in institutional policies and codes and laws.

COCLP must

- advocate for greater sensitivity to multicultural and social justice concerns by the institution and its personnel
- modify or remove policies, practices, facilities, structures, systems, and technologies that limit access, discriminate, or produce inequities
- include diversity, equity, and access initiatives within their strategic plans
- foster communication that deepens understanding of identity, culture, self-expression, and heritage
- promote respect about commonalities and differences among people within their historical and cultural contexts
- address the characteristics and needs of a diverse population when establishing and implementing culturally relevant and inclusive programs, services, policies, procedures, and practices
- provide staff members with access to multicultural training and hold staff members accountable for integrating the training into their work
- respond to the needs of all students and other populations served when establishing hours of operation and developing methods of delivering programs, services, and resources
- ensure physical, program, and resource access for persons with disabilities
- recognize the needs of distance learning students by providing appropriate and accessible services and resources or by assisting them in gaining access to other appropriate services and resources in their geographic region

Part 8. INSTITUTIONAL AND EXTERNAL RELATIONS

Commuter and Off-Campus Living Programs (COCLP) must reach out to relevant individuals, groups, communities, and organizations internal and external to the institution to

- establish, maintain, and promote

understanding and effective relations with those that have a significant interest in or potential effect on the students or other constituents served by the programs and services

- garner support and resources for programs and services as defined by the mission statement
- disseminate information about the programs and services
- collaborate, where appropriate, to assist in offering or improving programs and services to meet the needs of students and other constituents and to achieve program and student outcomes
- engage diverse individuals, groups, communities, and organizations to enrich the educational environment and experiences of students and other constituents

COCLP must have procedures and guidelines consistent with institutional policy for

- communicating with the media
- contracting with external organizations for delivery of programs and services
- cultivating, soliciting, and managing gifts
- applying to and managing funds from grants

COCLP must maintain a high degree of visibility within the campus community through direct promotion and delivery of services, involvement with campus programs, and educational efforts to increase all campus community members' understanding of the needs of commuter and off-campus students.

COCLP should coordinate their activities with all offices and agencies whose efforts directly affect commuter and off-campus students. These include such areas as campus safety and security, transportation and parking, campus information and referral services, and other relevant offices and campus committees.

COCLP should maintain active relationship with various community agencies to ensure the inclusion of the commuter and off-campus student perspective in community decision-making.

Part 9. FINANCIAL RESOURCES

Commuter and Off-Campus Living Programs (COCLP) must have funding to accomplish the mission and goals. In establishing funding priorities and making significant changes, a comprehensive analysis must be conducted to determine the following elements: unmet needs of the unit, relevant expenditures, external and internal resources, and impact on students and the institution.

COCLP must demonstrate efficient and effective use and responsible stewardship of fiscal resources consistent with institutional protocols.

Fee-paying students should benefit equitably from fee-supported services. This is especially important regarding access to electronic services such as computer/internet and campus cable television systems.

Part 10. TECHNOLOGY

Commuter and Off-Campus Living Programs (COCLP) must have adequate technology to support the achievement of their mission and goals. The technology and its use must comply with institutional policies and procedures and be evaluated for compliance with relevant codes and laws.

COCLP must use current technology to provide updated information regarding mission, location, staffing, programs, services, and official contacts to students and designated clients.

COCLP must explore the use of technology to enhance delivery of programs and services, especially for students at a distance or external constituencies.

When technology is used to facilitate student learning and development, COCLP must select technology that reflects intended outcomes.

COCLP must

- maintain policies and procedures that address the security, confidentiality, and backup of data, as well as compliance with privacy laws
- have clearly articulated plans in place for protecting confidentiality and security of information when using Internet-based technologies
- develop plans for replacing and updating existing hardware and software as well as plans for integrating new technically-based or supported programs, including systems developed internally by the institution, systems available through professional associations, or private vendor-based systems

Technology, as well as workstations or computer labs maintained by programs and services for student use, must be accessible to all designated clients and must meet established technology standards for delivery to persons with disabilities.

Institutions that provide high speed internet access or campus based cable television programming to residential students should also consider options to increase accessibility to such services to commuter and off-campus students.

When providing student access to technology, COCLP must

- **have policies on the use of technology that are clear, easy to understand, and available to all students**
- **provide assistance, information, or referral to appropriate support services to those needing help accessing or using technology**
- **provide instruction or training on how to use the technology**
- **inform students on the legal and ethical implications of misuse as it pertains to intellectual property, harassment, privacy, and social networks**

Student violations of technology policies must follow established institutional student disciplinary procedures.

Students who experience negative emotional or psychological consequences from the use of technology must be referred to support services provided by the institution.

Part 11. FACILITIES AND EQUIPMENT

Commuter and Off-Campus Living Programs (COCLP) must have adequate, accessible, and suitably located facilities and equipment to support the mission and goals. If acquiring capital equipment as defined by the institution, COCLP must take into account expenses related to regular maintenance and life cycle costs. Facilities and equipment must be evaluated on an established cycle, including consideration of sustainability, and be in compliance with codes and laws to provide for access, health, safety, and security.

COCLP staff members must have workspace that is well equipped, adequate in size, and designed to support their work and responsibilities. For conversations requiring privacy, staff members must have access to a private space.

COCLP staff members who share workspace must be able to secure their own work.

The design of the facilities must guarantee the security and privacy of records and ensure the confidentiality of sensitive information.

The location and layout of the facilities must be sensitive to the needs of persons with disabilities as well as the needs of other constituencies.

The campus must provide adequate facilities for the use of commuter and off-campus students, including recreational, study, and lounge space; computer and internet access; and dining facilities.

Because commuter and off-campus students do not have a residence on campus in which to spend time before,

between, and after classes, a variety of comfortable spaces should be provided for their use. These spaces should be in classroom buildings, as well as in college union and student center buildings, and should include individual lockers, computer and copier access, food preparation facilities, and family support services (e.g., infant feeding and changing areas).

Part 12. ASSESSMENT AND EVALUATION

Commuter and Off-Campus Living Programs (COCL) must have a clearly articulated assessment plan to document achievement of stated goals and learning outcomes, demonstrate accountability, provide evidence of improvement, and describe resulting changes in programs and services.

COCLP must have adequate fiscal, human, professional development, and technological resources to develop and implement assessment plans.

Assessments must include direct and indirect evaluation and use qualitative and quantitative methodologies and existing evidence, as appropriate, to determine whether and to what degree the stated mission, goals, and intended outcomes are being met as effectively and efficiently as possible. The process must employ sufficient and sound measures to ensure comprehensiveness. Data collected must include responses from students and other constituencies, and aggregated results must be shared with those groups. Results of assessments must be shared appropriately with multiple constituents.

Results of assessments and evaluations must be used to identify needs and interests in revising and improving programs and services, recognizing staff performance, maximizing resource efficiency and effectiveness, improving student achievement of learning and development outcomes, and improving student persistence and success. Changes resulting from the use of assessments and evaluation must be shared with stakeholders.

General Standards revised 2011;
COCLP (formerly Commuter Student Programs) content developed/revised 1986, 1997, & 2005

The Role of Conference and Event Programs
CAS Standards Contextual Statement

A higher education campus is a community where people gather to learn, share, and discuss issues of interest in an open, non-threatening, and enlightened atmosphere. It is a place where topics important to society are addressed freely in a number of formats and settings. Campuses are centers for symposia, lectures, public events, demonstrations, conferences, and other teaching and learning programs attended by people from all walks of life, generations, occupations, and educational levels. These events help to identify the campus as a place where scholarly, cultural, social, artistic, athletic, and other activities can freely occur. As institutions become less constrained by physical borders, they have also become the source and home of conferences and events. A department responsible for developing, coordinating, and promoting on- and off-campus conferences and events is typically found at the core of this important educational responsibility.

Conference and event programs address a broad range of organizing, hosting, and logistical service needs. Services provided to a variety of constituents include program planning; managing conference centers; developing conferences in conjunction with faculty and staff members; providing services and support for summer youth camps; coordinating guest services and special celebrations; scheduling facilities; and organizing donor events, inaugurations, groundbreakings, commencements, homecomings, parents weekends, and other traditional gatherings.

Although the portfolios of program responsibilities will vary from campus to campus, one common element is that of helping institutions expand their activities, presence, and influence beyond the traditional roles of faculty, students, and staff. Conference and events programs make the campus a more effective and user-friendly place for all types of learners. They enhance diverse campus cultures, and conference subject matter adds depth and variety to campus dialogue. Conferences and events programs support institutional efforts to function as a center for celebrations and non-traditional educational activities. They provide a forum for free speech, venues for cultural events, opportunities for students and scholars to be exposed to research findings, and a chance for more people to observe what higher education is all about.

Conference and event programs provide activities during periods when fewer students are present to optimize efficient use of campus resources. They provide institutions with additional sources of revenue and contribute to the availability and continuity of employment for faculty and staff. Many of the support and coordination roles typically associated with student affairs are now tailored to these events through a single conference and event programs office.

The Association of Collegiate Conference and Event Directors–International (ACCED-I) estimates that more than 1,500 U.S. institutions of higher learning have offices providing conference and event planning. Their operations may include overseeing the summer operation of residence halls and classrooms; year-round management of full-service conference centers; coordination of large public events held in campus arenas and stadiums; and procurement of services and facilities at off-campus locations. Today, conference and event staff members provide everything from multi-department coordination of services to year-round academic support services and professional event planning consultation.

Several associations for campus conference and event professionals have come into being and flourished. As these associations matured, the need for professional standards became abundantly clear in dialogue among members. In the mid-1990s, a study of service practices by the Canadian University and College Conference Officers Association (CUCCOA) culminated in a summary report that called for establishing international standards for practitioners. In 1997 ACCED-I, CUCCOA, the Association of College and University Housing OfficersInternational (ACUHOI), and the British Universities Accommodation Consortium (BUAC), later merged into VENUEMASTERS, collectively agreed on the need for developing professional standards in collaboration with the CAS standards development initiative. The CAS standards and guidelines that follow provide a professional context for the campus conference and event industry and will serve as a useful tool for all who wish to provide conference and event programs in higher education settings.

References, Readings, and Resources

Association of College and University Housing OfficersInternational (ACUHOI) http://www.acuho-i.org
Association of Collegiate Conference and Event Directors–International (ACCED-I) http://www.acced-i.org/
Canadian University and College Conference Officers Association (CUCCOA) http://www.cuccoa.org/
United Kingdom: VENUEMASTERS http://www.venuemasters.co.uk/

Contextual Statement Contributors:
Thomas Flynn, University of Maryland, ACCED-I
Patrick Perfetto, University of Maryland, ACCED-I

Conference and Event Programs
CAS Standards and Guidelines

Part 1. MISSION

The primary mission of Conference and Event Programs (CEP) is to manage institutional resources for educational conferences, workshops, events, and activities that are relevant and complementary to the mission of the institution.

CEP must develop, disseminate, implement, and regularly review their missions. The mission must be consistent with the mission of the institution and with professional standards. The mission must be appropriate for the institution's student populations and community settings. Mission statements must reference student learning and development.

The program mission must recognize and accommodate the needs and relevant goals, of users of conference and event services as well as institutional agencies that are integral providers of service.

Part 2. PROGRAM

Conference and Event Programs (CEP) must provide leadership within and for the institution relative to conference and event planning and management.

CEP must communicate effectively among campus agencies concerning activities that may influence or conflict with planned or potential conferences and events and other campus activities.

CEP must provide clear and timely descriptions of conference and event activities on campus events calendars and related information sources.

CEP must be knowledgeable about institutional resources, including facilities, safety, and visitor services.

CEP should
- collaborate with clients and service providers to assure that programs have a positive and compatible presence in the campus community
- exercise state-of-the-art meeting and event planning concepts and procedures
- encourage understanding and appreciation of the values and mission of the institution

In addition, CEP may
- create opportunities for departments to fulfill their programmatic goals
- create opportunities for departments to extend employment for employees and interns beyond the regular academic calendar

- provide additional revenue derived from income-producing facilities and services
- provide employment and experiential opportunities for students and staff members
- enable educational opportunities for the community that would not otherwise exist

The formal education of students, consisting of the curriculum and the co-curriculum, must promote student learning and development outcomes that are purposeful, contribute to students' realization of their potential, and prepare students for satisfying and productive lives.

CEP must collaborate with colleagues and departments across the institution to promote student learning and development, persistence, and success.

Consistent with the institutional mission, CEP must identify relevant and desirable student learning and development outcomes from among the six domains and related dimensions:

Domain: knowledge acquisition, integration, construction, and application

- Dimensions: understanding knowledge from a range of disciplines; connecting knowledge to other knowledge, ideas, and experiences; constructing knowledge; and relating knowledge to daily life

Domain: cognitive complexity

- Dimensions: critical thinking, reflective thinking, effective reasoning, and creativity

Domain: intrapersonal development

- Dimensions: realistic self-appraisal, self-understanding, and self-respect; identity development; commitment to ethics and integrity; and spiritual awareness

Domain: interpersonal competence

- Dimensions: meaningful relationships, interdependence, collaboration, and effective leadership.

Domain: humanitarianism and civic engagement

- Dimensions: understanding and appreciation of cultural and human differences, social responsibility, global perspective, and sense of civic responsibility

Domain: practical competence

- Dimensions: pursuing goals, communicating effectively, technical competence, managing personal affairs, managing career development, demonstrating professionalism, maintaining health and wellness, and living a purposeful and satisfying life

[LD Outcomes: See *The Council for the Advancement of Standards Learning and Developmental Outcomes* statement for examples of outcomes related to these domains and dimensions.]

CEP must

- assess relevant and desirable student learning and development
- provide evidence of impact on outcomes
- articulate contributions to or support of student learning and development in the domains not specifically assessed
- articulate contributions to or support of student persistence and success
- use evidence gathered through this process to create strategies for improvement of programs and services

Avenues for learning and development may include

- students engaged in the development and implementation of the program
- program participants learning about the institution
- students benefitting from the program brought to the institution

CEP must be

- intentionally designed
- guided by theories and knowledge of learning and development
- integrated into the life of the institution
- reflective of developmental and demographic profiles of the student population
- responsive to needs of individuals, populations with distinct needs, and relevant constituencies
- delivered using multiple formats, strategies, and contexts

Where institutions provide distance education, CEP must assist distance learners to achieve their educational goals by providing access to information about programs and services, to staff members who can address questions and concerns, and to counseling, advising, or other forms of assistance.

Part 3. ORGANIZATION AND LEADERSHIP

To achieve student and program outcomes, Conference and Event Programs (CEP) must be structured purposefully and organized effectively. CEP must have

- clearly stated goals

- current and accessible policies and procedures
- written performance expectations for employees
- functional work flow graphics or organizational charts demonstrating clear channels of authority

Leaders with organizational authority for the programs and services must provide strategic planning, supervision, and management; advance the organization; and maintain integrity through the following functions:

Strategic Planning

- articulate a vision and mission that drive short- and long-term planning
- set goals and objectives based on the needs of the population served and desired student learning or development and program outcomes
- facilitate continuous development, implementation, and assessment of goal attainment congruent with institutional mission and strategic plans
- promote environments that provide meaningful opportunities for student learning, development, and engagement
- develop and continuously improve programs and services in response to the changing needs of students served and evolving institutional priorities
- intentionally include diverse perspectives to inform decision making

Supervising

- manage human resource processes including recruitment, selection, development, supervision, performance planning, evaluation, recognition, and reward
- influence others to contribute to the effectiveness and success of the unit
- empower professional, support, and student staff to accept leadership opportunities
- offer appropriate feedback to colleagues and students on skills needed to become more effective leaders
- encourage and support professional development, collaboration with colleagues and departments across the institution, and scholarly contribution to the profession

Managing

- identify and address individual, organizational, and environmental conditions that foster or inhibit mission achievement
- plan, allocate, and monitor the use of fiscal, physical, human, intellectual, and technological resources

- use current and valid evidence to inform decisions
- incorporate sustainability practices in the management and design of programs, services, and facilities
- understand appropriate technologies and integrate them into programs and services
- be knowledgeable about codes and laws relevant to programs and services and ensure that staff members understand their responsibilities through appropriate training
- assess potential risks and take action to mitigate them

Advancing the Organization
- communicate effectively in writing, speaking, and electronic venues
- advocate for programs and services
- advocate for representation in strategic planning initiatives at appropriate divisional and institutional levels
- initiate collaborative interactions with internal and external stakeholders who have legitimate concerns about and interests in the functional area
- facilitate processes to reach consensus where wide support is needed
- inform other areas within the institution about issues affecting practice

Maintaining Integrity
- model ethical behavior and institutional citizenship
- share data used to inform key decisions in transparent and accessible ways
- monitor media used for distributing information about programs and services to ensure the content is current, accurate, appropriately referenced, and accessible

Because of the likely involvement of multiple campus units in the delivery of conference and event services, CEP leaders may need special authorization to manage resources.

CEP leaders should
- ensure that programs are compatible with the mission and values of the institution
- be aware of the changing needs of clients to assure expectations are congruent with the capabilities of service providers
- encourage the highest possible service provider capabilities to meet changing client expectations
- ensure that effective and appropriate strategies exist for communicating with prospective and current program participants
- consider student as well as staff and faculty member needs, issues, and perspectives
- cultivate relationships with leaders of academic and administrative departments
- work cooperatively with campus organizations and units in developing effective programs
- ensure efficient and appropriate use of institutional resources
- promote equal access for program participants

CEP should be organized to reflect institutional characteristics, priorities, and organizational structures so that the needs of the intended primary customer may be effectively met. Accordingly, not all functions may exist within the same administrative unit. In such cases, coordination among the units is essential to ensure a cohesive system of services for program and event planners.

The institution may centralize most CEP functions in one administrative unit in order to provide one-stop access to, and coordination of, services to planners of conferences, events, and similar gatherings. To accomplish this, the CEP office should
- serve as a central point of contact for multiple campus services, particularly in a decentralized environment
- have reasonable access to campus resources and facilities
- provide effective coordination of multiple services
- exercise appropriate authority with regard to campus resources necessary to support conferences and events in collaboration with campus service providers, through, for example, service agreements and memoranda of understanding.

Before every conference and event, CEP must clearly communicate with clients and service providers about how the program is going to be managed and onsite issues resolved.

Other areas for consideration in determining structure and management of CEP may include
- availability and characteristics of facilities
- size, nature, and mission of the institution
- scope of related academic services
- philosophy and delivery system for services
- variety of delivery methods being employed or available to the institution
- degree of integration with other institutional units
- unique access or service needs of the relevant community

Part 4. HUMAN RESOURCES

Conference and Event Programs (CEP) must be staffed adequately by individuals qualified to accomplish mission and goals.

Within institutional guidelines, CEP must
- **establish procedures for staff recruitment and selection, training, performance planning, and evaluation**

- set expectations for supervision and performance
- assess the performance of employees individually and as a team
- provide access to continuing and advanced education and appropriate professional development opportunities to improve the leadership ability, competence, and skills of all employees.

CEP must maintain position descriptions for all staff members.

To create a diverse staff, CEP must institute recruitment and hiring strategies that encourage individuals from under-represented populations to apply for positions.

CEP must develop promotion practices that are fair, inclusive, proactive, and non-discriminatory.

To further the recruitment and retention of staff, CEP must consider work life initiatives, such as compressed work schedules, flextime, job sharing, remote work, or telework.

CEP professional staff members must hold an earned graduate or professional degree in a field relevant to the position they hold or must possess an appropriate combination of educational credentials and related work experience.

CEP staff members must be proficient in customer service techniques.

CEP staff members must be knowledgeable about services of institutional agencies and facilities such as housing, dining, recreation, parking, and technology services.

CEP staff members may consider obtaining relevant certifications through meeting planning and higher education associations, such as the Certified Meeting Professional (CMP) or Collegiate Conference and Event Professional (CCEP) designations.

CEP professional staff members must engage in continuing professional development activities to keep abreast of the research, theories, legislation, policies, and developments that affect their programs and services.

CEP must have technical and support staff members adequate to accomplish their mission. All members of the staff must be technologically proficient and qualified to perform their job functions, be knowledgeable about ethical and legal uses of technology, and have access to training and resources to support the performance of their assigned responsibilities.

Degree- or credential-seeking interns or graduate assistants must be qualified by enrollment in an appropriate field of study and by relevant experience. These individuals must be trained and supervised adequately by professional staff members holding educational credentials and related work experience appropriate for supervision. Supervisors must be cognizant of the roles of interns and graduate assistants as both student and employee and closely adhere to all parameters of their job descriptions, work hours, and schedules. Supervisors and the interns or graduate assistants must agree to compensatory time or other appropriate compensation if circumstances necessitate additional hours.

Student employees and volunteers must be carefully selected, trained, supervised, and evaluated. They must be educated on how and when to refer those in need of additional assistance to qualified staff members and must have access to a supervisor for assistance in making these judgments. Student employees and volunteers must be provided clear job descriptions, pre-service training based on assessed needs, and continuing development.

All CEP staff members, including student employees and volunteers, must receive specific training on institutional policies pertaining to functions or activities they support and to privacy and confidentiality policies and laws regarding access to student records and other sensitive institutional information.

All CEP staff members must receive training on policies and procedures related to the use of technology to store or access student records and institutional data.

CEP must ensure that staff members are knowledgeable about and trained in emergency procedures, crisis response, and prevention efforts. Prevention efforts must address identification of threatening conduct or behavior of students, faculty and staff members, and others and must incorporate a system for responding and reporting.

CEP must ensure that staff members are knowledgeable of and trained in safety and emergency procedures for securing and vacating facilities.

Part 5. ETHICS

Conference and Event Programs (CEP) must review relevant professional ethical standards and must adopt or develop and implement appropriate statements of ethical practice.

CEP must consider whether prospective clients, programs or events present ethical conflict for the institution. When potential conflict arises, CEP must consult with appropriate institutional authorities.

CEP must publish and adhere to statements of ethical practice and ensure their periodic review by relevant constituencies.

CEP must orient new staff members to relevant ethical standards and statements of ethical practice and related institutional policies.

Statements of ethical standards must specify that staff members respect privacy and maintain confidentiality in all communications and records to the extent that such communications and records are protected under relevant privacy laws.

Statements of ethical standards must specify limits on disclosure of information contained in students' educational records as well as requirements to disclose to appropriate authorities.

Advice and information disclosed by clients, students, and faculty and staff members in the course of conducting business should be considered confidential unless otherwise required by law or institutional policy to be disclosed.

Statements of ethical standards must address personal and economic conflicts of interest, or appearance thereof, by staff members in the performance of their work.

Statements of ethical standards must reflect the responsibility of staff members to be fair, objective, and impartial in their interactions with others.

Statements of ethical standards must reference management of institutional funds.

Statements of ethical standards must reference appropriate behavior regarding research and assessment with human participants, confidentiality of research and assessment data, and students' rights and responsibilities.

Statements of ethical standards must include the expectation that CEP staff members confront and hold accountable other staff members who exhibit unethical behavior.

Statements of ethical standards must address issues surrounding scholarly integrity.

As appropriate, CEP staff members must inform users of programs and services of ethical obligations and limitations emanating from codes and laws or from licensure requirements.

CEP staff members must recognize and avoid conflicts of interest that could adversely influence their judgment or objectivity and, when unavoidable, recuse themselves from the situation.

CEP staff members must perform their duties within the limits of their position, training, expertise, and competence.

When these limits are exceeded, individuals in need of further assistance must be referred to persons possessing appropriate qualifications.

Promotional and descriptive information must be accurate and free of deception.

CEP must adhere to institutional policies regarding ethical and legal use of software and technology.

Part 6. LAW, POLICY, AND GOVERNANCE

Conference and Event Programs (CEP) must be in compliance with laws, regulations, and policies that relate to their respective responsibilities and that pose legal obligations, limitations, risks, and liabilities for the institution as a whole. Examples include constitutional, statutory, regulatory, and case law; relevant law and orders emanating from codes and laws; and the institution's policies.

CEP must ensure crisis management policies and procedures are adapted for periods of time when the institution may be closed or operating at reduced capacity (such as break periods or summer months) or for periods during which operational responsibilities are temporarily transferred (such as for residence halls).

CEP must have the authority to initiate and fulfill contracts and written obligations. Agreements must be in place to fairly protect the interests of both the institution and its clients.

CEP must inform staff members, appropriate officials, and users of programs and services about existing and changing legal obligations, risks and liabilities, and limitations.

Relevant institutional policies must be clearly evident in agreements with clients.

CEP should be aware of client activities on campus and ensure compliance with institutional policies.

CEP must have written policies on all relevant operations, transactions, or tasks that have legal implications.

CEP must regularly review policies. The revision and creation of policies must be informed by best practices, available evidence, and policy issues in higher education.

CEP staff members must use reasonable and informed practices to limit the liability exposure of the institution and its officers, employees, and agents. CEP staff members must be informed about institutional policies regarding risk management, personal liability, and related insurance coverage options and must be referred to external sources if the institution does not provide coverage.

The institution must provide access to legal advice for staff members as needed to carry out assigned responsibilities.

CEP must have procedures and guidelines consistent with institutional policy for responding to threats, emergencies, and crisis situations. Systems and procedures must be in place to disseminate timely and accurate information to students, other members of the institutional community, and appropriate external organizations during emergency situations.

CEP staff members should be timely and forthright in informing conference and event staff, participants, and students of extraordinary or changing conditions.

CEP staff members must neither participate in nor condone any form of harassment or activity that demeans persons or creates an intimidating, hostile, or offensive environment.

CEP must obtain permission to use copyrighted materials and instruments. CEP must purchase the materials and instruments from legally compliant sources or seek alternative permission from the publisher or owner. References to copyrighted materials and instruments must include appropriate citations.

CEP staff members must be knowledgeable about internal and external governance systems that affect programs and services.

Part 7. DIVERSITY, EQUITY, AND ACCESS

Within the context of each institution's unique mission and in accordance with institutional polices and all applicable codes and laws, Conference and Event Programs (CEP) must create and maintain educational and work environments that are

- welcoming, accessible, and inclusive to persons of diverse backgrounds
- equitable and non-discriminatory
- free from harassment

CEP must not discriminate on the basis of ability; age; cultural identity; ethnicity; family educational history (e.g., first generation to attend college); gender identity and expression; nationality; political affiliation; race; religious affiliation; sex; sexual orientation; economic, marital, social, or veteran status; or any other basis included in institutional policies and codes and laws.

CEP should make reasonable efforts to inform and educate the community about conference and events that feature unique aspects of diversity.

CEP should provide access to services and information through a variety of formats.

Staff members should ensure that program services provided through non-institutional third parties are offered on a fair and equitable basis.

CEP must

- advocate for greater sensitivity to multicultural and social justice concerns by the institution and its personnel
- modify or remove policies, practices, facilities, structures, systems, and technologies that limit access, discriminate, or produce inequities
- include diversity, equity, and access initiatives within their strategic plans
- foster communication that deepens understanding of identity, culture, self-expression, and heritage
- promote respect about commonalities and differences among people within their historical and cultural contexts
- address the characteristics and needs of a diverse population when establishing and implementing culturally relevant and inclusive programs, services, policies, procedures, and practices
- provide staff members with access to multicultural training and hold staff members accountable for integrating the training into their work
- respond to the needs of all students and other populations served when establishing hours of operation and developing methods of delivering programs, services, and resources
- ensure physical, program, and resource access for persons with disabilities
- recognize the needs of distance learning students by providing appropriate and accessible services and resources or by assisting them in gaining access to other appropriate services and resources in their geographic region

Part 8. INSTITUTIONAL AND EXTERNAL RELATIONS

Conference and Event Programs (CEP) must reach out to relevant individuals, groups, communities, and organizations internal and external to the institution to

- establish, maintain, and promote understanding and effective relations with those that have a significant interest in or potential effect on the students or other

constituents served by the programs and services
- garner support and resources for programs and services as defined by the mission statement
- disseminate information about the programs and services
- collaborate, where appropriate, to assist in offering or improving programs and services to meet the needs of students and other constituents and to achieve program and student outcomes
- engage diverse individuals, groups, communities, and organizations to enrich the educational environment and experiences of students and other constituents

CEP must have procedures and guidelines consistent with institutional policy for
- communicating with the media
- contracting with external organizations for delivery of programs and services
- cultivating, soliciting, and managing gifts
- applying to and managing funds from grants

The program should ensure institutional support by
- establishing cooperative relationships with other offices (in addition to direct service providers) such as alumni, enrollment management, athletics, institutional advancement, communications, public relations, and campus information and visitor services
- sharing information, to stimulate program opportunities, and to enhance institutional visibility
- encouraging staff member participation in civic and community organizations (e.g., Convention and Visitors Bureau, Chamber of Commerce, service organizations) and active involvement in professional associations

CEP must adhere to institution-wide processes that systematically involve academic affairs, student affairs, and administrative units such as police and security, physical plant, and business offices.

CEP must collaborate and meet regularly with service providers to coordinate schedules and facility use and to review conferences and events under development.

CEP should serve as a resource to provide professional advice on conference and event-related issues and activities.

Part 9. FINANCIAL RESOURCES

Conference and Event Programs (CEP) must have funding to accomplish the mission and goals. In establishing funding priorities and making significant changes, a comprehensive analysis must be conducted to determine the following elements: unmet needs of the unit, relevant expenditures, external and internal resources, and impact on students and the institution.

CEP must demonstrate efficient and effective use and responsible stewardship of fiscal resources consistent with institutional protocols.

Funds to support the CEP, insofar as possible and desirable, should be self-generated from fees set at fair market rates.

Self-supported CEP should be authorized to establish reserve funds if higher-than-expected revenue results in a surplus, as a buffer against future shortfalls.

Part 10. TECHNOLOGY

Conference and Event Programs (CEP) must have adequate technology to support the achievement of their mission and goals. The technology and its use must comply with institutional policies and procedures and be evaluated for compliance with relevant codes and laws.

CEP must use current technology to provide updated information regarding mission, location, staffing, programs, services, and official contacts to students and designated clients.

CEP must explore the use of technology to enhance delivery of programs and services, especially for students at a distance or external constituencies.

When technology is used to facilitate student learning and development, CEP must select technology that reflects intended outcomes.

CEP must
- maintain policies and procedures that address the security, confidentiality, and backup of data, as well as compliance with privacy laws
- have clearly articulated plans in place for protecting confidentiality and security of information when using Internet based technologies
- develop plans for replacing and updating existing hardware and software as well as plans for integrating new technically-based or supported programs, including systems developed internally by the institution, systems available through professional associations, or private vendor-based systems

Technology, as well as workstations or computer labs maintained by programs and services for student use, must be accessible to all designated clients and must meet established technology standards for delivery to persons with disabilities.

When providing student access to technology, CEP must

- have policies on the use of technology that are clear, easy to understand, and available to all students
- provide assistance, information, or referral to appropriate support services to those needing help accessing or using technology
- provide instruction or training on how to use the technology
- inform students on the legal and ethical implications of misuse as it pertains to intellectual property, harassment, privacy, and social networks

Student violations of technology policies must follow established institutional student disciplinary procedures.

Students who experience negative emotional or psychological consequences from the use of technology must be referred to support services provided by the institution.

When CEP offers external constituents access to institutional computing resources, procedures should be in place to support users who encounter technical difficulties, and CEP policies should protect the integrity of institutional data, technological resources, and student access.

Part 11. FACILITIES AND EQUIPMENT

Conference and Event Programs (CEP) must have adequate, accessible, and suitably located facilities and equipment to support the mission and goals. If acquiring capital equipment as defined by the institution, CEP must take into account expenses related to regular maintenance and life cycle costs. Facilities and equipment must be evaluated on an established cycle, including consideration of sustainability, and be in compliance with codes and laws to provide for access, health, safety, and security.

CEP staff members must have workspace that is well equipped, adequate in size, and designed to support their work and responsibilities. For conversations requiring privacy, staff members must have access to a private space.

CEP staff members who share workspace must be able to secure their own work.

The design of the facilities must guarantee the security and privacy of records and ensure the confidentiality of sensitive information.

The location and layout of the facilities must be sensitive to the needs of persons with disabilities as well as the needs of other constituencies.

Agreements should exist with departments necessary to fulfill needs of the CEP.

Part 12. ASSESSMENT AND EVALUATION

Conference and Event Programs (CEP) must have a clearly articulated assessment plan to document achievement of stated goals and learning outcomes, demonstrate accountability, provide evidence of improvement, and describe resulting changes in programs and services.

CEP should collaborate with institutional research units to generate data to project CEP contributions to the local economy, increase student enrollment, or stimulate additional research.

A representative cross-section from appropriate campus communities should be involved in reviewing the CEP program on a regular basis.

CEP should produce and disseminate an annual report identifying overall goals, activities and programs served, financial contributions, representative participate feedback, and opportunities that contribute to the overall visibility and promotion of the institution.

Evaluation of CEP may include goal-related progress on such considerations as stakeholder satisfaction, attendance, cash flow, financial health, and appearance of facilities.

Results and summary data from assessment and evaluation should be broadly shared with all appropriate constituencies including students, faculty and staff members, senior administrators, and clients.

CEP must assess and evaluate regularly its effectiveness in providing students with quality learning and development opportunities.

CEP must have adequate fiscal, human, professional development, and technological resources to develop and implement assessment plans.

Assessments must include direct and indirect evaluation and use qualitative and quantitative methodologies and existing evidence, as appropriate, to determine whether and to what degree the stated mission, goals, and intended outcomes are being met as effectively and efficiently as possible. The process must employ sufficient and sound measures to ensure comprehensiveness. Data collected must include responses from students and other constituencies, and aggregated results must be shared with those groups. Results of assessments must be shared appropriately with multiple constituents.

Results of assessments and evaluations must be used to identify needs and interests in revising and improving programs and services, recognizing staff performance, maximizing resource efficiency and

effectiveness, improving student achievement of learning and development outcomes, and improving student persistence and success. Changes resulting from the use of assessments and evaluation must be shared with stakeholders.

General Standards revised in 2011;
CEP content developed/revised in 2002 & 2012

The Role of Counseling Services
CAS Standards Contextual Statement

The face of college counseling is changing to meet the needs of today's students. It continues to represent the integration of a helping profession activity with an educational environment (Dean & Meadows, 1995). The arrival of the current high-achieving generation of traditional college students, along with the influx of nontraditional, under-represented, and first-generation students, enhances the campus environment but also brings greater levels of anxiety, depression, and even suicidal ideation (Howard, Schiraldi, Pineda, & Campanella, 2006; Twenge, 2006).

The nature and type of the higher education environment and its effects on students are important tools for college counselors. Steenbarger (1990) noted that college counseling exemplifies the developmental framework that has produced a history of creative outreach and support work on campuses. The delivery of counseling services to students in higher education has been and is evolving to respond effectively to clientele in an ever-changing environment.

Historically, the role and function of college counseling has changed in response to both external and internal factors. Social needs, political environment, national economy, and changing demographics all exert shifting influences to which counseling services must respond. Change also occurs in response to internal factors unique to each campus environment (e.g., location of the counseling center within health services versus an office that combines the counseling services with career services or academic advising versus a stand-alone counseling center). As a result, the breadth and depth of counseling services reflect the intersection of these influences. Davis and Humphrey's (2000) comprehensive work provided a thorough review of the history of college counseling roles and service delivery models, the changing demographics of higher education, and implications for the future. With the rapid technological and cultural changes in our society, the counseling profession among other helping professions put forth standards of practice to meet the ever-changing needs of higher education clientele. College counselors have a responsibility to stay informed with a strong knowledge of current student needs (Upcraft, Gardner, & Barefoot, 2005).

The current challenges are created by external forces including changing ethnic, racial, national, and experiential backgrounds of students; increasing psychological, health, safety, and financial needs of students; increasing competition for resources in higher education; increased emphasis on accountability; new and changing regulations regarding client privacy; and the implications of health and mental health care reform (American College Health Association, 2007; Gallagher, 2007; Kadison & DiGeronimo,

2004; Magoon, 2002). Moreover, the aftermath of 9/11, Virginia Tech, and other global traumatic events highlight the necessity for college counseling programs to be responsive to unanticipated factors. The level of severity of college students' presenting concerns is much greater than the traditional presenting problems of adjustment issues and individuation that were typically identified in counseling center research from the 1950s through the early 1980s (Pledge, et al., 1998). Recent research indicates that the level of severity of presenting problems and the complexity of problems continue to increase (ACHA, 2007; Benton et al., 2003; Kadison, 2006). As the severity and complexity of clients' problems expand, it is increasingly important for college counseling professionals to be prepared to work with physicians, community mental health providers, other campus departments, and health care professionals. An increased focus on retention and outcomes assessment, generated in part by accreditation agencies, has challenged college counseling programs to be more intentional about demonstrating efficacy (Boyer, 2005; Dean & Meadows, 1995; Lifton, Seay, & Bushko, 2004; Tinto, 2006-07).

Based on these challenges, Stone and Archer (1990) stressed a need for counseling services to (a) clearly define boundaries on the types of problems and degree of severity of those clients for whom the counseling professionals will provide services and (b) develop and identify extensive referral and outreach services to transition effectively more severe clients to appropriate community resources. At the same time, college counselors strive to maintain the developmental, preventive, and consultative services that are integral to their work. As Stone and Archer (1990) noted, the concepts of working within limits and achieving balance between demands and resources are significant for college counseling services. Archer and Cooper (1998) further recognized the importance of demonstrating to institutions the positive outcomes of helping students maintain psychological health and develop personally in ways that support retention.

College counseling services work with other student support services to promote students' personal and educational success through activities that complement formal academic programs. College counselors offer remedial, preventive, crisis, outreach, and consultative services, depending on the nature of the campus and students served. A strong commitment to professional development, whether through conducting research, providing training and supervision, maintaining professional credentials, upholding ethical standards of practice, or actively participating in professional organizations or other scholarly activities, is the catalyst for competent responses to the changing social issues and complex developmental, psychosocial, and mental health concerns of students (Boyd, et al., 2003).

College attendance creates a unique set of circumstances and stresses that can stimulate significant student growth and development, especially when the many student support functions are well coordinated and working together. As students experience change, they often need to address personal issues, work through challenges, and deal with the implications of growth and change. The rapid changes that characterize today's society, compounded by the impact of global crisis, catastrophic natural events, and economic decline can exacerbate students' personal and psychological problems (Davis & Humphrey, 2000; Kadison & DiGeronimo, 2004). However, students' access to and success in higher education are maximized as counseling services embrace and use medical, technological, and psychological advances. Humphrey, Kitchens, and Patrick (2000) encouraged counseling services to expand and embrace the use of interactional and Internet-based technologies for additional service-delivery options; this is particularly important as more students enroll through distance education options. Counseling services must offer assistance and resources to students through innovative means in order to serve the needs of all students.

The CAS Counseling Services Standards and Guidelines that follow provide college counselors with criteria to develop, enhance, evaluate, and judge the quality of campus counseling services.

References, Readings, and Resources

American College Health Association. (2007). American College Health Association – National College Health Assessment: Reference Group Executive Summary Fall 2007. Baltimore, MD: American College Health Association.

Archer, J., Jr., & Cooper, S. (1998). *Counseling and mental health services on campus: A handbook of contemporary practices and challenges.* San Francisco: Jossey-Bass.

Benton, S., Robertson, J., Tseng, W., Newton, F., & Benton, S. (2003). Changes in counseling center client problems across 13 years, *Professional Psychology: Research and Practice, 34,* 66-72.

Boyd, V., Hattauer, E., Brandel, I. W., Buckles, N., Davidshofer, C., Deakin, S., et al. (2003). Accreditation standards for university and college counseling centers. *Journal of Counseling and Development, 81,* 168-177.

Boyer, P. G. (2005). College student persistence of first-time freshmen at a Midwest university: A longitudinal study. *Research for Educational Reform, 10 (1),* 16-27.

Dean, L. A., & Meadows, M. E. (1995). College counseling: Union and intersection. *Journal of Counseling and Development, 74,* 139-142.

Davis, D., & Humphrey, K. (2000). *College counseling: Issues and strategies for a new millennium.* Alexandria, VA: American Counseling Association.

Gallagher, R. P. (2006). *National survey of counseling center directors.* Alexandria, VA: International Association of Counseling Services.

Humphrey, K., Kitchens, H., & Patrick, J. (2000). Trends in college counseling in the 21st century. In D. Davis & K. Humphrey, (Eds.) *College counseling: Issues and strategies for a new millennium* (pp.289-305). Alexandria, VA: American Counseling Association.

Kadison, R. D. (2006). College psychiatry 2006: Challenges and opportunities. *Journal of American College Health, 54*(6), 338-340.

Kadison, R. D., & DiGeronimo, T. F. (2004). *College of the over-whelmed: The campus mental health crisis and what to do about it.* San Francisco: Jossey-Bass.

Lifton, D. E., Seay, S. & Bushko, A. (2004). Measuring undergraduate hardiness as an indicator of persistence to graduation within four years. In I. M. Duranczyk, J. L. Higbee, & D. B. Lundell (Eds.). *Best Practices for Access and Retention in Higher Education.* Minneapolis, MN: Center for Research on Developmental Education and Urban Literacy, General College, University of Minnesota.

Magoon, T. (2002). *College and university counseling center directors' 2001-2002 data bank.* College Park, MD: University of Maryland.

Pledge, D., Lapan, R., Heppner, P., Kivlighan, D., and Roehlke, H. (1998). Stability and severity of presenting problems at a university counseling center: A six year analysis. *Professional Psychology: Research and Practice, 29,* 386-389.

Seenbarger, B. N. (1990). Toward a developmental understanding of the counseling specialty. *Journal of Counseling and Development, 68,* 435-437.

Stone, G. L., & Archer, J., Jr. (1990). College and university counseling centers in the 1990s: Challenges and limits. *The Counseling Psychologist, 18,* 539-607.

Tinto, V. (2006-2007). Research and practice of retention: What next? *Journal of College Student Retention, 8 (1),* 1-19.

Twenge, J. M. (2004). *Generation me: Why today's young American's are more confident, assertive, entitled – and more miserable than ever before.* New York: Free Press.

Upcraft, M. L., Gardner, J. N., & Barefood, B. O. (2005). *Challenging and supporting the first-year student: A handbook for improving the first-year of college.* San Francisco: Jossey-Bass.

Additional Resources

American College Counseling Association (ACCA): http://www.collegecounseling.org

American College Health Association (ACHA): http://www.acha.org

American College Personnel Association (ACPA): http://myacpa.org;

Commission VII: Counseling & Psychological Services: http://myacpa.org

American Counseling Association (ACA): http://www.counseling.org

American Psychological Association (APA): http://www.apa.org/ and Division 17, Counseling Psychology http://www.apa.org/about/division/div17.html

Association for the Coordination of Counseling Center Clinical Services: http://accccs.appstate.edu/

Association of Counseling Center Training Agents (ACCTA): http://www.accta.net

Association of Counselor Education and Supervision (ACES): http://www.acesonline.net/

Association of Psychology Postdoctoral and Internship Centers (APPIC): http://www.appic.org/index.html

Association for University and College Counseling Center Directors (AUCCCD): http://www.aucccd.org

Clearinghouse for Structured/Thematic Groups & Innovative Programs, University of Texas at Austin: http://www. utexas.edu/student/cmhc/clearinghouse/index.html

Counseling Center Village: http://ub-counseling.buffalo.edu/ ccv.html

International Association of Counseling Services (IACS):   An Accreditation Association: http://www.iacsinc.org/

Contextual Statement Contributors

Current Edition:
Carolyn W. Kern, University of North Texas
Angela Shores, Meredith College

Previous Editions:
Laura A. Dean, University of Georgia, ACCA
Michelle (Stefanisko) Cooper, Western Carolina University

Counseling Services
CAS Standards and Guidelines

Part 1. MISSION

The primary mission of Counseling Services (CS) is to assist students in defining and accomplishing personal, academic, and career goals. To accomplish the mission, the scope of CS must include

- **individual and group counseling services to students who may be experiencing psychological, behavioral, or learning difficulties**
- **programming focused on the developmental needs of students to maximize their potential to benefit from the academic environment and experience**
- **consultative services to the institution to help foster an environment supportive of the intellectual, emotional, spiritual, and physical development of students**
- **advocacy for a healthy and diverse learning community**
- **assessment services to identify and address student needs through appropriate services and referrals**
- **crisis response, including threat assessment**

CS must develop, disseminate, implement, and regularly review their missions. The mission must be consistent with the mission of the institution and with professional standards. The mission must be appropriate for the institution's student populations and community settings. Mission statements must reference student learning and development.

A wide variety of counseling, consultative, evaluative, and training functions may be performed by CS as an expression of its institutional mission.

To effectively respond to the educational needs of the institution and of students, CS should have the following complementary functions:

Developmental. The developmental mission is to help students enhance their personal growth. Developmental interventions help students acclimate to and benefit from the academic environment. To facilitate this, counseling services should promote student growth in the areas of positive and realistic self-appraisal, intellectual development, appropriate personal and occupational choices, the ability to relate meaningfully and mutually with others, and the capacity to engage in a personally satisfying and effective lifestyle.

Clinical. The clinical mission recognizes that some students experience significant problems, ranging from serious adjustment issues to more severe psychological disorders that require immediate professional attention. Elements of the clinical mission include diagnosis, treatment, and crisis response, as well as consideration of the effect on the campus community. Clinical services often allow students to continue enrollment and achieve success.

Preventive. The preventive mission is to anticipate environmental conditions and developmental processes that may negatively influence students' wellbeing and initiate interventions that will promote personal adjustment and growth.

Although there are basic similarities in the overall goals of various types of institutions, differences in student populations and institutional priorities may affect emphases of functions within individual counseling services. For these reasons, counseling services at different institutions may emphasize combinations of personal counseling, academic counseling, career counseling, or student development services.

CS should be organized based on institutional characteristics, priorities, and organizational structures. Accordingly, not all functions may exist within the same administrative unit.

CS must be coordinated to ensure a cohesive system of support for students when counseling functions exist in separate administrative units.

Part 2. PROGRAM

The formal education of students, consisting of the curriculum and the co-curriculum, must promote student learning and development outcomes that are purposeful, contribute to students' realization of their potential, and prepare students for satisfying and productive lives.

Counseling Services (CS) must collaborate with colleagues and departments across the institution to promote student learning and development, persistence, and success.

Consistent with the institutional mission, CS must identify relevant and desirable student learning and development outcomes from among the six domains and related dimensions:

> **Domain: knowledge acquisition, integration, construction, and application**
>
> - **Dimensions: understanding knowledge from a range of disciplines; connecting knowledge to other knowledge, ideas, and experiences; constructing knowledge; and relating knowledge to daily life**

Domain: cognitive complexity

- Dimensions: critical thinking, reflective thinking, effective reasoning, and creativity

Domain: intrapersonal development

- Dimensions: realistic self-appraisal, self-understanding, and self-respect; identity development; commitment to ethics and integrity; and spiritual awareness

Domain: interpersonal competence

- Dimensions: meaningful relationships, interdependence, collaboration, and effective leadership.

Domain: humanitarianism and civic engagement

- Dimensions: understanding and appreciation of cultural and human differences, social responsibility, global perspective, and sense of civic responsibility

Domain: practical competence

- Dimensions: pursuing goals, communicating effectively, technical competence, managing personal affairs, managing career development, demonstrating professionalism, maintaining health and wellness, and living a purposeful and satisfying life

[LD Outcomes: See *The Council for the Advancement of Standards Learning and Developmental Outcomes* statement for examples of outcomes related to these domains and dimensions.]

CS must
- assess relevant and desirable student learning and development
- provide evidence of impact on outcomes
- articulate contributions to or support of student learning and development in the domains not specifically assessed
- articulate contributions to or support of student persistence and success
- use evidence gathered through this process to create strategies for improvement of programs and services

CS must be
- intentionally designed
- guided by theories and knowledge of learning and development
- integrated into the life of the institution
- reflective of developmental and demographic profiles of the student population
- responsive to needs of individuals, populations with distinct needs, and relevant constituencies

- delivered using multiple formats, strategies, and contexts

Where institutions provide distance education, CS must assist distance learners to achieve their educational goals by providing access to information about programs and services, to staff members who can address questions and concerns, and to counseling, advising, or other forms of assistance.

To fulfill its mission, CS must provide the following services directly, through referral, or in collaboration:
- individual counseling in areas of personal, educational, career development, interpersonal relationships, family, social, and psychological issues
- group interventions (e.g., counseling, psychotherapy, support) to help students establish satisfying personal relationships and to become more effective in areas such as interpersonal processes, communication skills, decision-making concerning personal relationships and educational or career matters, and the establishment of personal values
- psychological testing and other assessment techniques to foster client self-understanding and decision-making
- outreach efforts to address developmental needs and concerns of students
- outreach and counseling support for students from diverse backgrounds
- counseling support for students affected by addictions and substance abuse
- counseling support to help students assess and overcome specific deficiencies in educational preparation or skills
- psychiatric consultation, evaluation, and support services for students needing maintenance or monitoring of psychotropic medications
- crisis and violence assessment, intervention, and response
- disaster preparedness and response
- staff and faculty professional development programs

In those cases where other institutional agencies address similar issues, such as career counseling and educational counseling, CS must establish cooperative relationships and maintain appropriate mutual referrals.

In those cases where specialized and needed expertise is not available within counseling services, staff members must refer students to resources within the institution or the local community.

CS must play an active role in interpreting and, when appropriate, advocating for addressing the needs of students to administration, faculty members, and staff of the institution.

CS should provide to institutional leaders a perspective that reflects an appropriate balance between administrative requirements and the needs and interests of students. CS should interpret the institutional environment to students and intervene to either improve the quality of the environment or facilitate the development of better interactions between the student and environment.

CS should help identify and advocate for the removal of barriers to student retention. CS should be sensitive to the needs of traditionally underserved populations and students with distinct needs.

CS may engage in research that contributes to knowledge of student characteristics and needs and evaluation of student outcomes in its programs. CS may assist students, faculty, and staff members who conduct individual research on student characteristics or on the influence of specific student development activities.

CS should provide consultation and inservice professional development for faculty members, administrators, staff and student staff members, and paraprofessionals.

Training and supervision of paraprofessionals, practicum students, and interns is an appropriate and desirable responsibility of CS.

Wherever a fee-for-service model is employed, CS must understand students' health care insurance and work with students to utilize their coverage.

Part 3. ORGANIZATION AND LEADERSHIP

To achieve student and program outcomes, Counseling Services (CS) must be structured purposefully and organized effectively. CS must have
- clearly stated goals
- current and accessible policies and procedures
- written performance expectations for employees
- functional work flow graphics or organizational charts demonstrating clear channels of authority

Leaders with organizational authority for the programs and services must provide strategic planning, supervision, and management; advance the organization; and maintain integrity through the following functions:

Strategic Planning
- articulate a vision and mission that drive short- and long-term planning
- set goals and objectives based on the needs of the population served and desired student learning or development and program outcomes
- facilitate continuous development, implementation, and assessment of goal attainment congruent with institutional mission and strategic plans
- promote environments that provide meaningful opportunities for student learning, development, and engagement
- develop and continuously improve programs and services in response to the changing needs of students served and evolving institutional priorities
- intentionally include diverse perspectives to inform decision making

Supervising
- manage human resource processes including recruitment, selection, development, supervision, performance planning, evaluation, recognition, and reward
- influence others to contribute to the effectiveness and success of the unit
- empower professional, support, and student staff to accept leadership opportunities
- offer appropriate feedback to colleagues and students on skills needed to become more effective leaders
- encourage and support professional development, collaboration with colleagues and departments across the institution, and scholarly contribution to the profession

Managing
- identify and address individual, organizational, and environmental conditions that foster or inhibit mission achievement
- plan, allocate, and monitor the use of fiscal, physical, human, intellectual, and technological resources
- use current and valid evidence to inform decisions
- incorporate sustainability practices in the management and design of programs, services, and facilities
- understand appropriate technologies and integrate them into programs and services
- be knowledgeable about codes and laws relevant to programs and services and ensure that staff members understand their responsibilities through appropriate training
- assess potential risks and take action to mitigate them

Advancing the Organization
- communicate effectively in writing, speaking,

and electronic venues
- advocate for programs and services
- advocate for representation in strategic planning initiatives at appropriate divisional and institutional levels
- initiate collaborative interactions with internal and external stakeholders who have legitimate concerns about and interests in the functional area
- facilitate processes to reach consensus where wide support is needed
- inform other areas within the institution about issues affecting practice

Maintaining Integrity
- model ethical behavior and institutional citizenship
- share data used to inform key decisions in transparent and accessible ways
- monitor media used for distributing information about programs and services to ensure the content is current, accurate, appropriately referenced, and accessible

The director should have the ability to interact effectively with administrators, faculty and staff members, students, colleagues, and community members and should possess all the general qualifications of a counseling staff member.

The director role also should include the following responsibilities:
- provision of counseling information and services to students, faculty members, and staff and, in accordance with the mission of CS and the institution, to the community
- evaluation of services
- provision of consultation/leadership in campus-wide and internal policy formation and program development
- education of staff members regarding legal issues in mental health, medicine, and higher education, as well as those governing the delivery of counseling services

CS leaders should create a work environment inclusive of various professional credentials and preparation.

Because the functions of CS are essential to the overall mission of an institution, their value and impact should be clearly articulated to the institution, and their placement within the organizational structure should be such that it facilitates significant interaction with unit heads in academic and student affairs and other relevant areas.

CS should function independently of units directly responsible for making decisions concerning students' official matriculation status, such as student conduct, academic probation, and admissions or re-admissions actions.

Part 4. HUMAN RESOURCES

Counseling Services (CS) must be staffed adequately by individuals qualified to accomplish mission and goals.

Within institutional guidelines, CS must
- **establish procedures for staff recruitment and selection, training, performance planning, and evaluation**
- **set expectations for supervision and performance**
- **assess the performance of employees individually and as a team**
- **provide access to continuing and advanced education and appropriate professional development opportunities to improve the leadership ability, competence, and skills of all employees.**

Counseling functions must be performed by professionals from the disciplines of counseling and clinical psychology, counseling and counselor education, psychiatry, and clinical social work, as well as by others with appropriate training, credentials, and supervised experience.

CS must maintain position descriptions for all staff members.

To create a diverse staff, CS must institute recruitment and hiring strategies that encourage individuals from under-represented populations to apply for positions.

CS must develop promotion practices that are fair, inclusive, proactive, and non-discriminatory.

To further the recruitment and retention of staff, CS must consider work life initiatives, such as compressed work schedules, flextime, job sharing, remote work, or telework.

CS professional staff members must hold an earned graduate or professional degree in a field relevant to the position they hold or must possess an appropriate combination of educational credentials and related work experience.

The minimum qualification for counseling staff members must be a master's degree from a regionally accredited institution in a relevant discipline.

Staff members should have completed a supervised practicum/internship at the graduate level, preferably in the counseling of students within a higher education setting, or should be appropriately supervised until they can transfer their skills to this setting. Counseling staff members should hold, or be eligible for, state/provincial licensure or certification in their chosen discipline (e.g., counseling, psychology, social work) where such exists.

Counseling staff members should have appropriate course work and training in psychological assessment; theories of counseling, cognitive development, personality, abnormal psychology, or psychopathology; treatment planning; group counseling; crisis intervention and management; addictions and alcohol and other drug issues; career development; multicultural counseling; legal and ethical issues in counseling; and learning styles. Counseling staff members should keep abreast of current research, including outcome research. Counseling staff members should also demonstrate knowledge of technology, leadership, organizational development, consultation, and relevant federal, regional, and state/provincial statutes.

Counseling staff members, when responsible for supervision of colleagues or graduate interns, should have doctoral degrees, hold degrees commensurate with those being supervised, or meet professional and state/provincial standards for providing clinical supervision, including licensure or certification as a supervisor.

Counseling staff members should participate in appropriate professional organizations and should have the budgetary support to do so. Counseling staff members should be encouraged to participate in community activities related to their profession.

Practicum students and interns, as well as paraprofessional assistants, may perform, under supervision, such counseling functions as are appropriate to their preparation and experience.

CS professional staff members must engage in continuing professional development activities to keep abreast of the research, theories, legislation, policies, and developments that affect their programs and services.

CS must have technical and support staff members adequate to accomplish their mission. All members of the staff must be technologically proficient and qualified to perform their job functions, be knowledgeable about ethical and legal uses of technology, and have access to training and resources to support the performance of their assigned responsibilities.

Degree- or credential-seeking interns or graduate assistants must be qualified by enrollment in an appropriate field of study and by relevant experience. These individuals must be trained and supervised adequately by professional staff members holding educational credentials and related work experience appropriate for supervision. Supervisors must be cognizant of the roles of interns and graduate assistants as both student and employee and closely adhere to all parameters of their job descriptions, work

hours, and schedules. Supervisors and the interns or graduate assistants must agree to compensatory time or other appropriate compensation if circumstances necessitate additional hours.

Student employees and volunteers must be carefully selected, trained, supervised, and evaluated. They must be educated on how and when to refer those in need of additional assistance to qualified staff members and must have access to a supervisor for assistance in making these judgments. Student employees and volunteers must be provided clear job descriptions, pre-service training based on assessed needs, and continuing development.

All CS staff members, including student employees and volunteers, must receive specific training on institutional policies pertaining to functions or activities they support and to privacy and confidentiality policies and laws regarding access to student records and other sensitive institutional information.

All CS staff members must receive training on policies and procedures related to the use of technology to store or access student records and institutional data.

CS must ensure that staff members are knowledgeable about and trained in emergency procedures, crisis response, and prevention efforts. Prevention efforts must address identification of threatening conduct or behavior of students, faculty and staff members, and others and must incorporate a system for responding and reporting.

CS must ensure that staff members are knowledgeable of and trained in safety and emergency procedures for securing and vacating facilities.

CS should maintain an inservice and staff development program that includes supervision, case presentations, research reports, and discussion of relevant professional issues. Institutional budgetary support should be available to provide for inservice and professional development activities.

The director of counseling services must have an appropriate combination of graduate course work, formal training, and supervised experience.

The director of CS should have a doctoral degree in counseling psychology, clinical psychology, counselor education, medicine with completed specialty training in psychiatry, or other related discipline from an accredited institution, with a minimum of a master's degree in such areas. The director should hold or be eligible for state licensure or certification where such exists or should pursue such credentials. It is highly desirable that the director has a minimum of three years experience as a staff member or administrator in counseling services within higher education. The director should have received supervision (either pre- or post-doctorate) in counseling within higher education.

The level of CS staffing must be established and reviewed regularly with regard to service demands, enrollment, user surveys, diversity of services offered, institutional resources, and other mental health and student services that may be available on the campus and in the local community.

The level of staffing and workloads must be adequate and appropriate for program and service demands.

The student to counselor ratio should be determined locally in light of institutional size and type, student demographics, roles and responsibilities of professional staff members, scope of services provided, and unique features of CS.

In addition to providing direct services, staff time should be allowed for preparation of interviews and reports, updating institutional information, research, faculty and staff contacts, staff meetings, training and supervision, personal and professional development, consultation, and walk-in and emergency counseling interventions, in accordance with individual staff members' qualifications and task assignments. Similarly, teaching, administration, research, and other such responsibilities should be identified as relevant staff functions.

Support staff members who deal directly with students should be carefully selected, because they play an important role in the students' impressions of the counseling services, often must make some preliminary client-related decisions, and may have access to confidential information.

Part 5. ETHICS

Counseling Services (CS) must review relevant professional ethical standards and must adopt or develop and implement appropriate statements of ethical practice.

CS must publish and adhere to statements of ethical practice and ensure their periodic review by relevant constituencies.

CS must orient new staff members to relevant ethical standards and statements of ethical practice and related institutional policies.

Statements of ethical standards must specify that staff members respect privacy and maintain confidentiality in all communications and records to the extent that such communications and records are protected under relevant privacy laws.

Statements of ethical standards must specify limits on disclosure of information contained in students' educational records as well as requirements to disclose to appropriate authorities.

When the condition of a client is indicative of serious and foreseeable harm to the client or to others, counseling staff members must take reasonable personal action that may involve informing responsible authorities and, when possible, consulting with other professionals. In such cases, counseling staff members must be cognizant of pertinent ethical principles, state/provincial or federal statutes, and local mental health guidelines that stipulate the limits of confidentiality.

Information should be released only at the written request or concurrence of a client who has full knowledge of the nature of the information that is being released and of the parties to whom it is released.

Instances of limited confidentiality must be clearly articulated, reviewed with the client, and acknowledged by signature.

The decision to release information without consent may occur only after careful consideration and under the conditions described above.

Statements of ethical standards must address personal and economic conflicts of interest, or appearance thereof, by staff members in the performance of their work.

Statements of ethical standards must reflect the responsibility of staff members to be fair, objective, and impartial in their interactions with others.

Statements of ethical standards must reference management of institutional funds.

Statements of ethical standards must reference appropriate behavior regarding research and assessment with human participants, confidentiality of research and assessment data, and students' rights and responsibilities.

Statements of ethical standards must include the expectation that CS staff members confront and hold accountable other staff members who exhibit unethical behavior.

Statements of ethical standards must address issues surrounding scholarly integrity.

As appropriate, CS staff members must inform users of programs and services of ethical obligations and limitations emanating from codes and laws or from licensure requirements.

CS staff members must recognize and avoid conflicts of interest that could adversely influence their judgment or objectivity and, when unavoidable, recuse themselves from the situation.

CS staff members must perform their duties within

the limits of their position, training, expertise, and competence.

When these limits are exceeded, individuals in need of further assistance must be referred to persons possessing appropriate qualifications.

Promotional and descriptive information must be accurate and free of deception.

CS must adhere to institutional policies regarding ethical and legal use of software and technology.

Such uses include the use of online counseling.

CS staff members must conform to relevant federal, state/provincial, and local statutes that govern the delivery of counseling and psychological services.

Staff members must comply with applicable laws related to privacy and confidentiality.

CS staff members must be familiar with and adhere to relevant ethical standards in the field, including those professional procedures for intake, assessment, case notes, and termination summaries as well as the preparation, use, and distribution of psychological tests.

Client status and information disclosed in individual counseling sessions must remain confidential unless written permission to divulge the information is given by the client.

Clients must be made aware of issues such as the limits to confidentiality during intake or early in the counseling process so they can participate from a position of informed consent.

Consultation regarding individual students, as requested or needed with faculty and other institutional personnel is offered in the context of preserving the student's confidential relationship with the counseling services. Consultation with parents, partners, and public and private agencies that bear some responsibility for particular students may occur within the bounds of a confidential counseling relationship.

CS must maintain records in a confidential and secure manner while specifying procedures to monitor access, use, and maintenance of the records.

Part 6. LAW, POLICY, AND GOVERNANCE

Counseling Services (CS) must be in compliance with laws, regulations, and policies that relate to their respective responsibilities and that pose legal obligations, limitations, risks, and liabilities for the institution as a whole. Examples include constitutional, statutory, regulatory, and case law; relevant law and orders emanating from codes and laws; and the institution's policies.

CS must inform staff members, appropriate officials, and users of programs and services about existing and changing legal obligations, risks and liabilities, and limitations.

CS must have written policies on all relevant operations, transactions, or tasks that have legal implications.

CS must regularly review policies. The revision and creation of policies must be informed by best practices, available evidence, and policy issues in higher education.

CS staff members must use reasonable and informed practices to limit the liability exposure of the institution and its officers, employees, and agents. CS staff members must be informed about institutional policies regarding risk management, personal liability, and related insurance coverage options and must be referred to external sources if the institution does not provide coverage.

The institution must provide access to legal advice for staff members as needed to carry out assigned responsibilities.

CS must have procedures and guidelines consistent with institutional policy for responding to threats, emergencies, and crisis situations. Systems and procedures must be in place to disseminate timely and accurate information to students, other members of the institutional community, and appropriate external organizations during emergency situations.

CS staff members must neither participate in nor condone any form of harassment or activity that demeans persons or creates an intimidating, hostile, or offensive environment.

CS must obtain permission to use copyrighted materials and instruments. CS must purchase the materials and instruments from legally compliant sources or seek alternative permission from the publisher or owner. References to copyrighted materials and instruments must include appropriate citations.

CS staff members must be knowledgeable about internal and external governance systems that affect programs and services.

Part 7. DIVERSITY, EQUITY, AND ACCESS

Within the context of each institution's unique mission and in accordance with institutional polices and all applicable codes and laws, Counseling Services (CS) must create and maintain educational and work environments that are
- welcoming, accessible, and inclusive to

persons of diverse backgrounds
- equitable and non-discriminatory
- free from harassment

CS must not discriminate on the basis of ability; age; cultural identity; ethnicity; family educational history (e.g., first generation to attend college); gender identity and expression; nationality; political affiliation; race; religious affiliation; sex; sexual orientation; economic, marital, social, or veteran status; or any other basis included in institutional policies and codes and laws.

CS must
- advocate for greater sensitivity to multicultural and social justice concerns by the institution and its personnel
- modify or remove policies, practices, facilities, structures, systems, and technologies that limit access, discriminate, or produce inequities
- include diversity, equity, and access initiatives within their strategic plans
- foster communication that deepens understanding of identity, culture, self-expression, and heritage
- promote respect about commonalities and differences among people within their historical and cultural contexts
- address the characteristics and needs of a diverse population when establishing and implementing culturally relevant and inclusive programs, services, policies, procedures, and practices
- provide staff members with access to multicultural training and hold staff members accountable for integrating the training into their work
- respond to the needs of all students and other populations served when establishing hours of operation and developing methods of delivering programs, services, and resources
- ensure physical, program, and resource access for persons with disabilities
- recognize the needs of distance learning students by providing appropriate and accessible services and resources or by assisting them in gaining access to other appropriate services and resources in their geographic region

Part 8. INSTITUTIONAL AND EXTERNAL RELATIONS

Programs and services must reach out to relevant individuals, groups, communities, and organizations internal and external to the institution to
- establish, maintain, and promote understanding and effective relations with

those that have a significant interest in or potential effect on the students or other constituents served by the programs and services
- garner support and resources for programs and services as defined by the mission statement
- disseminate information about the programs and services
- collaborate, where appropriate, to assist in offering or improving programs and services to meet the needs of students and other constituents and to achieve program and student outcomes
- engage diverse individuals, groups, communities, and organizations to enrich the educational environment and experiences of students and other constituents

CS should develop close cooperation with institutional referral sources and with potential consumers of counseling services consultations. CS should also work closely with all other segments of the institution whose goal is the promotion of psychological, emotional, and career development.

CS should work closely with the senior student affairs and academic affairs administrators to ensure that institutional goals and objectives are met.

Within the institution, CS should establish close cooperation with career services, academic advising, specialized academic support units (e.g., reading and study skills programs, learning assistance programs), and student services (e.g., services for students with disabilities; international and multicultural students; lesbian, gay, bisexual and transgender students; TRIO programs; women; veterans; returning adult students).

CS should establish relationships with a wide range of student groups (e.g., student government; gay, lesbian, bisexual, transgender groups; fraternities and sororities; spiritual groups; organizations for students from underrepresented groups) to promote visibility and serve as a resource to them.

CS should establish and maintain a close working relationship with student health services as counseling staff members are often called upon to refer clients for medical concerns or hospitalization and to serve as consultants to, or to seek consultation from, health services professionals.

CS should foster relationships with academic units and with professionals in admissions, registrar's office, student activities, athletics, residence halls, and campus security where appropriate.

CS should establish effective relationships with the institutional legal counsel and the legal staff of relevant professional organizations in order to effectively respond to pertinent legal issues and precedents that underlie the delivery components of CS.

Where adequate mental health resources are not available on campus, CS must establish and maintain close working relationships with community mental health resources.

CS must have procedures for the referral of students who require counseling beyond the scope of institutional CS.

CS must have procedures and guidelines consistent with institutional policy for
- communicating with the media
- contracting with external organizations for delivery of programs and services
- cultivating, soliciting, and managing gifts
- applying to and managing funds from grants

CS must advocate for membership on critical institutional committees, especially those related to crisis response, students at risk, and threat assessment.

Part 9. FINANCIAL RESOURCES

Counseling Services (CS) must have funding to accomplish the mission and goals. In establishing funding priorities and making significant changes, a comprehensive analysis must be conducted to determine the following elements: unmet needs of the unit, relevant expenditures, external and internal resources, and impact on students and the institution.

CS must demonstrate efficient and effective use and responsible stewardship of fiscal resources consistent with institutional protocols.

Part 10. TECHNOLOGY

Counseling Services (CS) must have adequate technology to support the achievement of their mission and goals. The technology and its use must comply with institutional policies and procedures and be evaluated for compliance with relevant codes and laws.

CS must use current technology to provide updated information regarding mission, location, staffing, programs, services, and official contacts to students and designated clients.

CS must explore the use of technology to enhance delivery of programs and services, especially for students at a distance or external constituencies.

When technology is used to facilitate student learning and development, CS must select technology that reflects intended outcomes.

CS must
- maintain policies and procedures that address

the security, confidentiality, and backup of data, as well as compliance with privacy laws
- have clearly articulated plans in place for protecting confidentiality and security of information when using Internet-based technologies
- develop plans for replacing and updating existing hardware and software as well as plans for integrating new technically-based or supported programs, including systems developed internally by the institution, systems available through professional associations, or private vendor-based systems

Technology, as well as workstations or computer labs maintained by programs and services for student use, must be accessible to all designated clients and must meet established technology standards for delivery to persons with disabilities.

When providing student access to technology, CS must
- have policies on the use of technology that are clear, easy to understand, and available to all students
- provide assistance, information, or referral to appropriate support services to those needing help accessing or using technology
- provide instruction or training on how to use the technology
- inform students on the legal and ethical implications of misuse as it pertains to intellectual property, harassment, privacy, and social networks

Student violations of technology policies must follow established institutional student disciplinary procedures.

Students who experience negative emotional or psychological consequences from the use of technology must be referred to support services provided by the institution.

CS must maintain secure and ethical use in the application of technology for the provision of counseling services.

CS must select technology that reflects current best pedagogical practices when it is used to facilitate student learning and development.

Part 11. FACILITIES AND EQUIPMENT

Counseling Services (CS) must have adequate, accessible, and suitably located facilities and equipment to support the mission and goals. If acquiring capital equipment as defined by the institution, CS must take into account expenses related to regular maintenance and life cycle costs. Facilities and equipment must be evaluated on an established cycle, including consideration of sustainability, and be in compliance with codes and laws to provide for access, health, safety, and security.

CS staff members must have workspace that is well equipped, adequate in size, and designed to support their work and responsibilities. For conversations requiring privacy, staff members must have access to a private space.

CS staff members who share workspace must be able to secure their own work.

The design of the facilities must guarantee the security and privacy of records and ensure the confidentiality of sensitive information.

The location and layout of the facilities must be sensitive to the needs of persons with disabilities as well as the needs of other constituencies.

CS must maintain a physical and social environment that facilitates optimal functioning and ensures appropriate confidentiality.

CS, when feasible, should be physically separate from administrative offices, campus security, and student conduct units.

Individual offices for counseling staff members should be provided, appropriately equipped, and soundproofed. The offices should be designed to accommodate the functions performed by counseling staff members.

There should be a reception area that provides a comfortable and private waiting area for clients.

CS should maintain or have ready access to professional resource materials.

In those instances where counseling services include a career development unit, there should be a resource center that holds institutional catalogs and occupation and career information.

An area suitable for individual and group testing procedures should be available.

CS should maintain or have ready access to group meeting space that provides a confidential setting.

CS should maintain equipment that is capable of providing modern technical approaches, such as biofeedback and secure video conferencing accessibility, to treatment and record keeping and have access to equipment for research and media presentations.

CS with training components should have adequate facilities

for recording and, where possible, for direct observations.

Part 12. ASSESSMENT AND EVALUATION

Counseling Services (CS) must have a clearly articulated assessment plan to document achievement of stated goals and learning outcomes, demonstrate accountability, provide evidence of improvement, and describe resulting changes in programs and services.

CS must have adequate fiscal, human, professional development, and technological resources to develop and implement assessment plans.

Assessments must include direct and indirect evaluation and use qualitative and quantitative methodologies and existing evidence, as appropriate, to determine whether and to what degree the stated mission, goals, and intended outcomes are being met as effectively and efficiently as possible. The process must employ sufficient and sound measures to ensure comprehensiveness. Data collected must include responses from students and other constituencies, and aggregated results must be shared with those groups. Results of assessments must be shared appropriately with multiple constituents.

Results of assessments and evaluations must be used to identify needs and interests in revising and improving programs and services, recognizing staff performance, maximizing resource efficiency and effectiveness, improving student achievement of learning and development outcomes, and improving student persistence and success. Changes resulting from the use of assessments and evaluation must be shared with stakeholders.

General Standards revised in 2011;
CS content developed/revised in 1986, 1997, 1999, & 2011

The Role of Dining Services Programs
CAS Standards Contextual Statement

Institutions of higher education have provided a dining services program, initially as a component of student housing, since the first residential colleges were founded. Over the years the quality and variety of services provided varied greatly depending upon the specific institution. In 1958, with the creation of the National Association of College and University Food Services (NACUFS), the professionalism of those employed in dining services was enhanced, and the potential for the overall improvement of dining services was increased.

The basic principles that underlie any dining services program are to provide students, faculty, staff, and guests with high quality food service and products in a pleasant environment at a reasonable cost. Those principles are shared by professionals throughout the college and university arena, although the specific focus may vary from campus to campus. Although the original scope of the dining services program encompassed simply the providing of nourishment, currently that is only one of the basic elements of a quality program. Meals are important times and places for students, faculty, and staff to exchange ideas, discuss current issues, and share experiences; the design of facilities and menus needs to accommodate these functions. Although reasonable cost to the consumer is an expectation, providing a source of revenue to the institution is usually a desired outcome. Balancing those two imperatives is critical to the success of any program.

Additionally, modern dining services programs must address the dietary needs and wants of an increasingly diverse population. It is no longer sufficient to provide only good nutrition. Programs must address the rising sophistication of students in higher education and the dining experiences they bring with them to campus. Life-style choices must also be addressed in addition to dietary needs. Vegetarian/vegan and/or religious-based diets are but two of an ever growing list of eating choices made by today's student that must be accommodated successfully.

As dining services programs have dealt positively with the transition from supplying basic needs to providing for expanded expectations, they are now addressing an increasing list of current issues. Among these is the practice of outsourcing of the dining services program. It is incumbent upon the administration of each institution to make the decision to self-operate or privatize based upon what is in the best interest of that particular institution and its students, faculty, and staff. Sustainability is an issue that has recently emerged on many campuses. These institutions are providing products and services that support local businesses and industries in a manner that encourages the continued existence of those resources while balancing the budget.

Increasingly, students with food allergies are being served by dining services programs. One of the challenges in this area is to provide a specialized diet without students feeling as if they are being singled out as different. Finally, as mentioned above, students bring an increasingly sophisticated and diverse set of dining experiences to campus. Developing a "retail orientation" to better address these expectations is one of the more prevalent changes being implemented across campuses. There is a continuing need to provide a wide variety of services. At times, students may benefit from all-you-care-to-eat service; at other times, they prefer take-out services. Often, late-night service is a need. In other words, today's students want what they want, where they want it, and when they want it. It is the role of dining services to maintain high quality programs while seeking ways to meet these changing needs and expectations. The standards and guidelines that follow offer guidance for the development and assessment of high quality dining services programs.

References, Readings, and Resources

Administering Food Service Contracts: A Handbook for Contract Administrators in College and University Food Services. (n.d.). Okemos, MI: National Association of College and University Food Services (NACUFS).

Academy of Nutrition and Dietetic. http://www.eatright.org

Educational Foundation of the National Restaurant Association http://www.nraef.org

Foodservice Systems Management Education Council. http://www.fsmec.org

Journal of The National Association of College & University Food Services. (n.d.). Okemos, MI: National Association of College and University Food Services (NACUFS).

Professional Practices in College and University Food Services (5ᵗʰ ed.). Okemos, MI: National Association of College and University Food Services (NACUFS).

The National Association of College and University Food Services. http://www.nacufs.org

Contextual Statement Contributors

Russ Myer, University of Nevada, Reno; NACUFS
Joe Spina, NACUFS

Dining Services Programs
CAS Standards and Guidelines

Part 1. MISSION

The mission of Dining Services Programs (DSP) must address
- a dining environment that encourages both individual and community development
- engagement of students in learning about sound nutrition practices
- safe and secure facilities that are clean, attractive, well-maintained, and comfortable
- management services that ensure the orderly and effective administration and operation of all aspects of the program
- reasonably priced, quality, safe, diverse, and nutritious food offerings

DSP must develop, disseminate, implement, and regularly review their missions. The mission must be consistent with the mission of the institution and with professional standards. The mission must be appropriate for the institution's student populations and community settings. Mission statements must reference student learning and development.

DSP should clearly define and communicate its vision and mission to staff members and students, to provide the focus for departmental practices.

The institution, when outsourcing, should clearly define what role the contractor has in developing a mission statement or supporting the institution's mission statement.

In addition to dining services, the DSP mission must include, either directly or through collaboration, a provision for educational programs and services and management services.

Part 2. PROGRAM

The formal education of students, consisting of the curriculum and the co-curriculum, must promote student learning and development outcomes that are purposeful, contribute to students' realization of their potential, and prepare students for satisfying and productive lives.

Dining Services Programs (DSP) must collaborate with colleagues and departments across the institution to promote student learning and development, persistence, and success.

Consistent with the institutional mission, DSP must identify relevant and desirable student learning and development outcomes from among the six domains and related dimensions:

Domain: knowledge acquisition, integration, construction, and application
- Dimensions: understanding knowledge from a range of disciplines; connecting knowledge to other knowledge, ideas, and experiences; constructing knowledge; and relating knowledge to daily life

Domain: cognitive complexity
- Dimensions: critical thinking, reflective thinking, effective reasoning, and creativity

Domain: intrapersonal development
- Dimensions: realistic self-appraisal, self-understanding, and self-respect; identity development; commitment to ethics and integrity; and spiritual awareness

Domain: interpersonal competence
- Dimensions: meaningful relationships, interdependence, collaboration, and effective leadership.

Domain: humanitarianism and civic engagement
- Dimensions: understanding and appreciation of cultural and human differences, social responsibility, global perspective, and sense of civic responsibility

Domain: practical competence
- Dimensions: pursuing goals, communicating effectively, technical competence, managing personal affairs, managing career development, demonstrating professionalism, maintaining health and wellness, and living a purposeful and satisfying life

[LD Outcomes: See *The Council for the Advancement of Standards Learning and Developmental Outcomes* statement for examples of outcomes related to these domains and dimensions.]

DSP must
- assess relevant and desirable student learning and development
- provide evidence of impact on outcomes
- articulate contributions to or support of student learning and development in the domains not specifically assessed
- articulate contributions to or support of student persistence and success
- use evidence gathered through this process to create strategies for improvement of

programs and services

DSP must be
- intentionally designed
- guided by theories and knowledge of learning and development
- integrated into the life of the institution
- reflective of developmental and demographic profiles of the student population
- responsive to needs of individuals, populations with distinct needs, and relevant constituencies
- delivered using multiple formats, strategies, and contexts

Where institutions provide distance education, DSP must assist distance learners to achieve their educational goals by providing access to information about programs and services, to staff members who can address questions and concerns, and to counseling, advising, or other forms of assistance.

To fulfill its mission and goals effectively, DSP must provide students with access to experiences, services, and programs that facilitate
- interaction with faculty and staff members
- respect for self, others, and property
- appreciation of new ideas
- appreciation of cultural differences and other forms of diversity
- development of a balanced lifestyle embracing wellness
- orientation to community expectations, facilities, services, and staff
- understanding of institutional and dining policies, procedures, and expectations, including the potential consequences for violation
- involvement in programming and policy development
- responsibility for their community through confrontation of inappropriate or disruptive behavior

DSP should support and respond to student dietary and medical requirements, such as vegan diets and food allergies.

DSP should provide access to a registered dietician to assist students in meeting their dietary and medical needs.

DSP must establish appropriate policies and procedures for responding to emergency situations, especially where DSP facilities, personnel, and resources could assist the institution.

Dining Services should be involved in institution emergency planning.

DSP should provide an organizational avenue such as a food advisory board and should have a relationship with appropriate student governance organizations.

Part 3. ORGANIZATION AND LEADERSHIP

To achieve student and program outcomes, Dining Services Programs (DSP) must be structured purposefully and organized effectively. DSP must have
- clearly stated goals
- current and accessible policies and procedures
- written performance expectations for employees
- functional work flow graphics or organizational charts demonstrating clear channels of authority

Leaders with organizational authority for the programs and services must provide strategic planning, supervision, and management; advance the organization; and maintain integrity through the following functions:

Strategic Planning
- articulate a vision and mission that drive short- and long-term planning
- set goals and objectives based on the needs of the population served and desired student learning or development and program outcomes
- facilitate continuous development, implementation, and assessment of goal attainment congruent with institutional mission and strategic plans
- promote environments that provide meaningful opportunities for student learning, development, and engagement
- develop and continuously improve programs and services in response to the changing needs of students served and evolving institutional priorities
- intentionally include diverse perspectives to inform decision making

Supervising
- manage human resource processes including recruitment, selection, development, supervision, performance planning, evaluation, recognition, and reward
- influence others to contribute to the effectiveness and success of the unit
- empower professional, support, and student staff to accept leadership opportunities
- offer appropriate feedback to colleagues and students on skills needed to become more effective leaders
- encourage and support professional development, collaboration with colleagues and departments across the institution, and

scholarly contribution to the profession

Managing

- identify and address individual, organizational, and environmental conditions that foster or inhibit mission achievement
- plan, allocate, and monitor the use of fiscal, physical, human, intellectual, and technological resources
- use current and valid evidence to inform decisions
- incorporate sustainability practices in the management and design of programs, services, and facilities
- understand appropriate technologies and integrate them into programs and services
- be knowledgeable about codes and laws relevant to programs and services and ensure that staff members understand their responsibilities through appropriate training
- assess potential risks and take action to mitigate them

Advancing the Organization

- communicate effectively in writing, speaking, and electronic venues
- advocate for programs and services
- advocate for representation in strategic planning initiatives at appropriate divisional and institutional levels
- initiate collaborative interactions with internal and external stakeholders who have legitimate concerns about and interests in the functional area
- facilitate processes to reach consensus where wide support is needed
- inform other areas within the institution about issues affecting practice

Maintaining Integrity

- model ethical behavior and institutional citizenship
- share data used to inform key decisions in transparent and accessible ways
- monitor media used for distributing information about programs and services to ensure the content is current, accurate, appropriately referenced, and accessible

DSP must promote professionalism, integrity, and ethical behavior in dealing with colleagues, students, administration, faculty, vendors, and the public.

The institution must clearly articulate whether DSP is to be subsidized, self-sustaining, or revenue generating.

Institutions with significant commuter-based populations or other unique circumstances should recognize that subsidizing

the operation may be required, depending upon the level of service desired.

The institution, when outsourcing, must clearly state that the relationship is to be mutually beneficial.

It should recognize that when outsourced, the food service provider has a reasonable expectation of profit and should work with the institution to achieve mutual benefit.

DSP must comply with laws, regulations, and policies, with particular attention to health and safety requirements.

DSP should promote a positive relationship with all internal and external customers, especially students, and openly solicit comments from all customers.

DSP must have internal service control systems in place throughout the department to protect the customer and the department without sacrificing the underlying commitment to customer service.

DSP should have clear lines of authority and responsibility, assignment of span of control, and delineation of individual job responsibilities to achieve the mission of the department while maximizing efficient and effective use of human resources.

DSP must plan and conduct all activities around a fundamental commitment to providing quality service.

Resident dining and retail operations should provide a variety of features, offerings, and themes that deliver a quality food service experience, meet the expectations of customers, and contribute positively to the department and institution.

Nutrition education provided by the department should address the assessed needs of customers and staff and contribute to the overall health of the campus community.

Catering services should provide quality products and customer-centered services.

DSP must have written up-to-date internal policies and procedures covering each aspect of the operation.

Where the management of DSP is divided among different offices within the institution and/or contracted to an outside vendor, institutional leaders, stakeholders, and contractors must establish and maintain productive working relationships.

When DSP is contracted for or outsourced, the institution must identify the individual(s) responsible for administering the contract, supervising the service, and the conditions for the contract's continuance or renewal.

The institution and DSP, whether self-operated, contracted, or a combination of self-operated and

contracted, must collaborate in providing a balanced dining services program that meets the nutritional, educational, and social needs of students and the college or university community.

DSP should participate in campus emergency planning efforts to ensure that appropriate contingency plans are in place to feed students.

To fulfill its mission and goals effectively, DSP must maintain well-structured management functions, including planning, personnel, property management, purchasing, contract administration, financial control, and information systems.

DSP should use a planning process that increases the probability that the department will successfully accomplish its mission.

DSP should have a formal, written long-range strategic planning document that provides a vision of the future, reflects the department's long-range decision-making process, and supports its short-term operational planning.

DSP and each of its units should prepare operating or action plans for short-term periods that are consistent with the approved long-term plans.

DSP should develop capital improvement plans, guided by the department's long-term strategic plan, by working in cooperation with the institution to meet the projected needs for dining service facilities and programs that will support the future student enrollment of the institution.

DSP should conduct market research to provide an objective basis for planning how to market and manage the department to maximize customer satisfaction and achieve fiscal goals.

DSP should use a menu-planning process that results in a variety of appealing and wholesome food and beverage choices to meet the dining and nutritional needs of customers within the food cost budget goals.

DSP must use safe and effective procedures for preparing, presenting, and holding foods and maintaining the safety, appearance, and nutritional quality of the products.

DSP should have well-organized food production systems in place.

The organization of work flow within dining services should permit the efficient and safe movement of food and beverage products from receiving through storage, issue, preparation, production, holding, distribution, service, and storage of leftovers.

DSP should organize the purchasing functions to ensure the orderly and timely procurement of food products, supplies, services, and equipment at the defined quantity, cost, and quality levels to support the mission of the department.

DSP must fully comply with all applicable federal, state/provincial, and local food safety codes; compliance focuses on managing the food safety risk at critical control points in a manner consistent with a Hazard Analysis Critical Control Point (HACCP) or similar food safety system.

Part 4. HUMAN RESOURCES

Dining Services Programs (DSP) must be staffed adequately by individuals qualified to accomplish mission and goals.

Within institutional guidelines, DSP must
- establish procedures for staff recruitment and selection, training, performance planning, and evaluation
- set expectations for supervision and performance
- assess the performance of employees individually and as a team
- provide access to continuing and advanced education and appropriate professional development opportunities to improve the leadership ability, competence, and skills of all employees.

DSP must maintain position descriptions for all staff members.

To create a diverse staff, DSP must institute recruitment and hiring strategies that encourage individuals from under-represented populations to apply for positions.

DSP must develop promotion practices that are fair, inclusive, proactive, and non-discriminatory.

To further the recruitment and retention of staff, DSP must consider work life initiatives, such as compressed work schedules, flextime, job sharing, remote work, or telework.

DSP professional staff members must hold an earned graduate or professional degree in a field relevant to the position they hold or must possess an appropriate combination of educational credentials and related work experience.

DSP professional staff members must engage in continuing professional development activities to keep abreast of the research, theories, legislation, policies, and developments that affect their programs and services.

DSP must have technical and support staff members adequate to accomplish their mission. All members of the staff must be technologically proficient and qualified to perform their job functions, be knowledgeable about ethical and legal uses of technology, and have access to training and resources to support the performance of their assigned responsibilities.

Degree- or credential-seeking interns or graduate assistants must be qualified by enrollment in an appropriate field of study and by relevant experience. These individuals must be trained and supervised adequately by professional staff members holding educational credentials and related work experience appropriate for supervision. Supervisors must be cognizant of the roles of interns and graduate assistants as both student and employee and closely adhere to all parameters of their job descriptions, work hours, and schedules. Supervisors and the interns or graduate assistants must agree to compensatory time or other appropriate compensation if circumstances necessitate additional hours

Student employees and volunteers must be carefully selected, trained, supervised, and evaluated. They must be educated on how and when to refer those in need of additional assistance to qualified staff members and must have access to a supervisor for assistance in making these judgments. Student employees and volunteers must be provided clear job descriptions, pre-service training based on assessed needs, and continuing development.

Student employees should be considered as a part of the DSP staff.

Because student employment is an important component of student development, DSP should have an effective program for the recruitment, training, education, development, evaluation, and promotion of student employees.

All DSP staff members, including student employees and volunteers, must receive specific training on institutional policies pertaining to functions or activities they support and to privacy and confidentiality policies and laws regarding access to student records and other sensitive institutional information.

All DSP staff members must receive training on policies and procedures related to the use of technology to store or access student records and institutional data.

DSP must ensure that staff members are knowledgeable about and trained in emergency procedures, crisis response, and prevention efforts. Prevention efforts must address identification of threatening conduct or behavior of students, faculty and staff members, and others and must incorporate a system for responding and reporting.

DSP must ensure that staff members are knowledgeable of and trained in safety and emergency procedures for securing and vacating facilities.

DSP must maintain up-to-date, accurate, and complete personnel, payroll, and certification records for each staff member of the department.

DSP must provide emergency response training opportunities for staff to learn to respond to emergencies.

These opportunities could include CPR training, Heimlich maneuver, and basic first aid.

DSP should provide all new staff members, including students, a formal orientation, including policies, procedures, rules, and benefits that apply to them.

DSP should use a formal system for providing standardized and consistent job-specific training for staff members, including students.

Staff members include student staff where applicable.

DSP must follow an orderly system for salary and wage administration that complies with applicable laws and institutional policies and procedures.

DSP should provide personnel benefits beyond wage and salary that provide for the basic needs of all eligible staff members.

DSP should promote long-term career opportunities for all staff members.

DSP management should practice positive approaches to staff management designed to increase productivity, minimize turnover, and contribute to a high level of morale.

DSP should use a system for reviewing the job performance of all staff members, including student employees, on a scheduled basis as an integral part of a proactive human resource development process.

DSP should provide special recognition for staff members, including student employees, whose performance is superior as an incentive to all staff members to maximize their potential.

DSP must have a system for administering discipline on an objective and fair basis with a clear focus on human resource development.

DSP must provide procedures for filing, processing, and hearing employee grievances. All staff members, including students, must be aware of and support the goals, objectives, and philosophy of DSP.

Where collective bargaining agreements exist, DSP management must administer them in good faith and strive to maintain a positive working relationship between management and union staff members.

DSP must comply with applicable laws and regulations and institutional and department policies regarding posting of information for staff members, including students, about their rights and responsibilities.

DSP should have orderly separation procedures that follow institutional policies for processing resignations and involuntary termination of employment.

Part 5. ETHICS

Dining Services Programs (DSP) must review relevant professional ethical standards and must adopt or develop and implement appropriate statements of ethical practice.

DSP must publish and adhere to statements of ethical practice and ensure their periodic review by relevant constituencies.

DSP must orient new staff members to relevant ethical standards and statements of ethical practice and related institutional policies.

Statements of ethical standards must specify that staff members respect privacy and maintain confidentiality in all communications and records to the extent that such communications and records are protected under relevant privacy laws.

Statements of ethical standards must specify limits on disclosure of information contained in students' educational records as well as requirements to disclose to appropriate authorities.

Statements of ethical standards must address personal and economic conflicts of interest, or appearance thereof, by staff members in the performance of their work.

Statements of ethical standards must reflect the responsibility of staff members to be fair, objective, and impartial in their interactions with others.

Statements of ethical standards must reference management of institutional funds.

Statements of ethical standards must reference appropriate behavior regarding research and assessment with human participants, confidentiality of research and assessment data, and students' rights and responsibilities.

Statements of ethical standards must include the expectation that DSP staff members confront and hold accountable other staff members who exhibit unethical behavior.

Statements of ethical standards must address issues surrounding scholarly integrity.

As appropriate, DSP staff members must inform users of programs and services of ethical obligations and limitations emanating from codes and laws or from licensure requirements.

DSP staff members must recognize and avoid conflicts of interest that could adversely influence their judgment or objectivity and, when unavoidable, recuse themselves from the situation.

DSP staff members must perform their duties within the limits of their position, training, expertise, and competence.

When these limits are exceeded, individuals in need of further assistance must be referred to persons possessing appropriate qualifications.

Promotional and descriptive information must be accurate and free of deception.

DSP must adhere to institutional policies regarding ethical and legal use of software and technology.

Part 6. LAW, POLICY, AND GOVERNANCE

Dining Services Programs (DSP) must be in compliance with laws, regulations, and policies that relate to their respective responsibilities and that pose legal obligations, limitations, risks, and liabilities for the institution as a whole. Examples include constitutional, statutory, regulatory, and case law; relevant law and orders emanating from codes and laws; and the institution's policies.

DSP must inform staff members, appropriate officials, and users of programs and services about existing and changing legal obligations, risks and liabilities, and limitations.

DSP must have written policies on all relevant operations, transactions, or tasks that have legal implications.

DSP must regularly review policies. The revision and creation of policies must be informed by best practices, available evidence, and policy issues in higher education.

DSP staff members must use reasonable and informed practices to limit the liability exposure of the institution and its officers, employees, and agents. DSP staff members must be informed about institutional policies regarding risk management, personal liability, and related insurance coverage options and must be referred to external sources if the institution does not provide coverage.

The institution must provide access to legal advice for staff members as needed to carry out assigned responsibilities.

DSP must have procedures and guidelines consistent

with institutional policy for responding to threats, emergencies, and crisis situations. Systems and procedures must be in place to disseminate timely and accurate information to students, other members of the institutional community, and appropriate external organizations during emergency situations.

DSP staff members must neither participate in nor condone any form of harassment or activity that demeans persons or creates an intimidating, hostile, or offensive environment.

DSP must obtain permission to use copyrighted materials and instruments. DSP must purchase the materials and instruments from legally compliant sources or seek alternative permission from the publisher or owner. References to copyrighted materials and instruments must include appropriate citations.

DSP staff members must be knowledgeable about internal and external governance systems that affect programs and services.

Part 7. DIVERSITY, EQUITY, AND ACCESS

Within the context of each institution's unique mission and in accordance with institutional polices and all applicable codes and laws, Dining Services Programs (DSP) must create and maintain educational and work environments that are
- welcoming, accessible, and inclusive to persons of diverse backgrounds
- equitable and non-discriminatory
- free from harassment

DSP must not discriminate on the basis of ability; age; cultural identity; ethnicity; family educational history (e.g., first generation to attend college); gender identity and expression; nationality; political affiliation; race; religious affiliation; sex; sexual orientation; economic, marital, social, or veteran status; or any other basis included in institutional policies and codes and laws.

DSP structure should reflect an unbiased commitment to diversity and maximize the potential of all staff members, including students.

DSP must
- advocate for greater sensitivity to multicultural and social justice concerns by the institution and its personnel
- modify or remove policies, practices, facilities, structures, systems, and technologies that limit access, discriminate, or produce inequities
- include diversity, equity, and access initiatives within their strategic plans

- foster communication that deepens understanding of identity, culture, self-expression, and heritage
- promote respect about commonalities and differences among people within their historical and cultural contexts
- address the characteristics and needs of a diverse population when establishing and implementing culturally relevant and inclusive programs, services, policies, procedures, and practices
- provide staff members with access to multicultural training and hold staff members accountable for integrating the training into their work
- respond to the needs of all students and other populations served when establishing hours of operation and developing methods of delivering programs, services, and resources
- ensure physical, program, and resource access for persons with disabilities
- recognize the needs of distance learning students by providing appropriate and accessible services and resources or by assisting them in gaining access to other appropriate services and resources in their geographic region

DSP should acknowledge that it serves a multicultural community and provide products and services that recognize this ethnic and cultural diversity.

DSP should plan promotions that recognize religious or ethnic events, considering student body diversity, institutional support, and community diversity.

Part 8. INSTITUTIONAL AND EXTERNAL RELATIONS

Dining Services Programs (DSP) must reach out to relevant individuals, groups, communities, and organizations internal and external to the institution to
- establish, maintain, and promote understanding and effective relations with those that have a significant interest in or potential effect on the students or other constituents served by the programs and services
- garner support and resources for programs and services as defined by the mission statement
- disseminate information about the programs and services
- collaborate, where appropriate, to assist in offering or improving programs and services to meet the needs of students and other constituents and to achieve program and student outcomes

- **engage diverse individuals, groups, communities, and organizations to enrich the educational environment and experiences of students and other constituents**

DSP must have procedures and guidelines consistent with institutional policy for
- **communicating with the media**
- **contracting with external organizations for delivery of programs and services**
- **cultivating, soliciting, and managing gifts**
- **applying to and managing funds from grants**

DSP must comply with these standards even when contracted for or outsourced by the institution.

DSP should make a positive contribution to the educational, social, and economic development of the campus and local community.

The success of DSP is dependent on the maintenance of good relationships with students, faculty, administrators, alumni, the community at large, contractors, and support agencies. Staff members should encourage participation in campus programs by relevant groups.

When appropriate within the policies and procedures of the institution and department, DSP should sponsor campus and community nonprofit activities to promote goodwill and enhance the nonprofit mission of the community organization.

DSP departmental managers should encourage staff members, including students, to volunteer for community nonprofit and campus causes and activities in the name of the department to promote the community image of the department and enhance the quality of life of the volunteers.

Part 9. FINANCIAL RESOURCES

Dining Services Programs (DSP) must have funding to accomplish the mission and goals. In establishing funding priorities and making significant changes, a comprehensive analysis must be conducted to determine the following elements: unmet needs of the unit, relevant expenditures, external and internal resources, and impact on students and the institution.

DSP must demonstrate efficient and effective use and responsible stewardship of fiscal resources consistent with institutional protocols.

DSP must have in place an effective system of financial accountability controls to ensure responsible fiscal management.

The institution should recognize that when outsourced, the food service provider has a reasonable expectation of making profit.

DSP should prepare annual operating budgets to project

income and expenses for the year for each component of the operation and break down the budget to accurately forecast financial performance by accounting periods. DSP should strive to balance revenue and institutional expectations to provide necessary and desirable services.

DSP must use an accounting system that accurately accounts for all income and expenses, as approved by the institution, the department's controller, and auditors, as applicable.

Part 10. TECHNOLOGY

Dining Services Programs (DSP) must have adequate technology to support the achievement of their mission and goals. The technology and its use must comply with institutional policies and procedures and be evaluated for compliance with relevant codes and laws.

DSP must use current technology to provide updated information regarding mission, location, staffing, programs, services, and official contacts to students and designated clients.

DSP must explore the use of technology to enhance delivery of programs and services, especially for students at a distance or external constituencies.

When technology is used to facilitate student learning and development, DSP must select technology that reflects intended outcomes.

DSP must
- **maintain policies and procedures that address the security, confidentiality, and backup of data, as well as compliance with privacy laws**
- **have clearly articulated plans in place for protecting confidentiality and security of information when using Internet-based technologies**
- **develop plans for replacing and updating existing hardware and software as well as plans for integrating new technically-based or supported programs, including systems developed internally by the institution, systems available through professional associations, or private vendor-based systems**

Technology, as well as workstations or computer labs maintained by programs and services for student use, must be accessible to all designated clients and must meet established technology standards for delivery to persons with disabilities.

When providing student access to technology, DSP must
- **have policies on the use of technology that are clear, easy to understand, and available**

- to all students
- provide assistance, information, or referral to appropriate support services to those needing help accessing or using technology
- provide instruction or training on how to use the technology
- inform students on the legal and ethical implications of misuse as it pertains to intellectual property, harassment, privacy, and social networks

Student violations of technology policies must follow established institutional student disciplinary procedures.

Students who experience negative emotional or psychological consequences from the use of technology must be referred to support services provided by the institution.

DSP should use an objective process for evaluating technology needs and staying current with appropriate new information technologies. Areas for consideration include menu and inventory management, nutritional analysis, catering, event management, point-of-sale systems, concessions management, accounting systems, email, office production systems and services, and other specialty software such as that used for time and attendance.

DSP should make appropriate selections of technology systems, including hardware and software, to meet clearly-defined needs within budgetary limitations.

DSP should use a system for maintaining electronic and other computerized equipment and software.

Part 11. FACILITIES AND EQUIPMENT

Dining Services Programs (DSP) must have adequate, accessible, and suitably located facilities and equipment to support the mission and goals. If acquiring capital equipment as defined by the institution, DSP must take into account expenses related to regular maintenance and life cycle costs. Facilities and equipment must be evaluated on an established cycle, including consideration of sustainability, and be in compliance with codes and laws to provide for access, health, safety, and security.

DSP staff members must have workspace that is well equipped, adequate in size, and designed to support their work and responsibilities. For conversations requiring privacy, staff members must have access to a private space.

DSP staff members who share workspace must be able to secure their own work.

The design of the facilities must guarantee the security and privacy of records and ensure the confidentiality of sensitive information.

The location and layout of the facilities must be sensitive to the needs of persons with disabilities as well as the needs of other constituencies.

The facilities managed by DSP must be in full compliance with applicable federal, state/provincial, and local building codes, as well as institutional policies.

DSP should share dining facility spaces for campus programs and events, such as study halls and social events.

DSP should take extra precautions to provide a secure environment for customers and staff members.

DSP should have a capital improvement budget that supports the long-term strategic plan.

DSP must comply with all applicable federal, state/provincial, and local statutes, regulations, and codes when undertaking capital improvements, including new construction, renovations, and equipment installation.

DSP should use current sources of information in planning for capital equipment purchases, installation, and implementation to support the mission of the department within applicable federal, state/provincial, and local codes and regulations.

DSP facilities must be accessible, clean, attractive, properly designed, well-maintained, comfortable, conducive to a positive dining experience, and must have appropriate safety and security features.

DSP must maintain a high level of facilities sanitation through effective housekeeping.

DSP should have ongoing programs of planned and preventive maintenance to extend the life of facilities and equipment, ensure optimum working condition, and enhance safety and appearance.

Spaces must include adequate areas for seating as well as for service, preparation, storage, and receiving of food, and for disposal of waste.

DSP should design its facilities to support the mission of the department with optimum efficiency, while enhancing customer and staff satisfaction.

DSP must have a program for managing solid and liquid waste that complies with federal, state/provincial, and local regulations and coordinates the program with other solid and liquid waste efforts of the institution or community.

The focus of all capital improvement projects should be on designing for the future, based on the best available information and projections concerning future enrollment, shifts in student housing patterns, changes in the diversity of the student body, trends in college and university dining services, and market research of the off-campus dining service trends in the surrounding community.

Part 12. ASSESSMENT AND EVALUATION

Dining Services Programs (DSP) must have a clearly articulated assessment plan to document achievement of stated goals and learning outcomes, demonstrate accountability, provide evidence of improvement, and describe resulting changes in programs and services.

DSP should conduct market research such as comparing prices, offerings, menu, hours, and service levels.

DSP should promote a positive relationship with all internal and external customers, especially students, and openly solicit comments from all customers about how to improve the dining services program.

DSP must also evaluate customer satisfaction.

DSP must have adequate fiscal, human, professional development, and technological resources to develop and implement assessment plans.

Assessments must include direct and indirect evaluation and use qualitative and quantitative methodologies and existing evidence, as appropriate, to determine whether and to what degree the stated mission, goals, and intended outcomes are being met as effectively and efficiently as possible. The process must employ sufficient and sound measures to ensure comprehensiveness. Data collected must include responses from students and other constituencies, and aggregated results must be shared with those groups. Results of assessments must be shared appropriately with multiple constituents.

Results of assessments and evaluations must be used to identify needs and interests in revising and improving programs and services, recognizing staff performance, maximizing resource efficiency and effectiveness, improving student achievement of learning and development outcomes, and improving student persistence and success. Changes resulting from the use of assessments and evaluation must be shared with stakeholders.

General Standards revised in 2011;
DSP content developed in 2006

The Role of Disabilty Resources and Services
CAS Standards Contextual Statement

Professionals who serve students with disabilities have played a pivotal role in expanding access to college and university campus environments. Students with disabilities and their advocates have encouraged the adoption of the pedagogical principles and practices of Universal Design for Instruction (UDI) and have helped to transform sociopolitical consciousness of disability. Disability is now viewed as a part of the range of natural expression of difference in the human condition rather than a deficiency by definition.

In the United States prior to the mid-20th century, college students with disabilities were supported primarily by rehabilitation services. In the rehabilitation model, although college personnel and family members assisted students in many ways to overcome the challenges of postsecondary educational environments, buildings were not readily accessible, texts in accessible formats such as braille were very limited, and many aspects of campus life remained closed to students with disabilities.

U.S. veterans returning from World War II—many of them recently impaired—sought college educations and began a process of opening doors that coincided with the Disability Rights Movement (Church, 2009). Other voices for change included disability and independent living advocates like Ed Roberts, Judy Heumann, and Justin Dart, who knew that colleges needed to make their campuses and programs more accessible if disabled individuals were to have true equal opportunities for education. The Rehabilitation Act of 1973, which included Section 504 subpart E, stipulated that recipients of federal funds cannot deny access or admission based solely on disability and must provide auxiliary aids and services to accommodate for a person's disability. The Americans with Disabilities Act (ADA) of 1990, amended in 2008, expanded and further clarified the rights of persons with disabilities to equal access and accommodation in public and private spheres (ADA, 2008).

In the 1970s and 1980s, U.S. postsecondary institutions began to establish offices and departments to address the access needs of students with disabilities (Linton, 1998). These offices, whether aligned with Student Affairs or Academic Affairs, facilitated academic adjustments for disabled students. Services included administering tests when extra time or other accommodations were needed, arranging for sign language interpreters, securing accessible instructional materials, and advising on room assignments in residence halls. The medical or rehabilitation model of disability was the framework for much of this early disability services work on campuses. The work of the disability services professional on a brick-and-mortar or virtual college campus is now linked collaboratively with all sectors of the campus community, in a network of campus support that includes study abroad, residence life, food service, security, administration, financial aid, diversity, career services, library services, and advising.

The Association of Handicapped Student Service Personnel in Postsecondary Education (AHSSPPE) was established in 1977 as a professional association for those individuals working in disability resource and service offices around the U.S. In 1992 AHSSPPE became the Association on Higher Education And Disability (AHEAD), reflecting progress both in nomenclature and breadth of mission. With over 2,500 members, AHEAD is the principal professional resource for disability professionals in higher education. Driven by its vision, "education and societal environments that value disability and embody equality of opportunity," AHEAD provides professional development, professional engagement and networking, information, and technical assistance; has 34 state and multi-state affiliate groups around the country; and is active with allied international organizations sharing common missions. AHEAD produces a refereed publication, the *Journal on Postsecondary Education and Disability.*

Disability services professionals serving in colleges and universities have varied backgrounds, including counseling, social work, education, psychology, rehabilitation, and disability studies. The majority of directors and coordinators of disability resource and service departments have master's degrees, and many have doctorates across these areas of academic disciplines (Kasnitz, 2011).

In the 21st century, colleges and universities are being challenged to provide inclusive education to an expanding population of students with disabilities (United States Department of Education, 2008). The number of students with disabilities attending colleges and universities continues to grow (United States Government Accountability Office, 2009). Special education under the Individuals with Disabilities Education Act (IDEA) has resulted in more students with disabilities attending college than was true a couple of decades ago (Wagner, Newman, Cameto, Garza, & Levine, 2005). Learning Disability is the most prevalent type of disability, both in the PK-12 system and at the postsecondary level (Kasnitz, 2011).

In postsecondary settings, in order to qualify for accommodations, students must self-identify as having a disability, and they must do so through an office of disability resources and services. Disability resources and services offices vary in size. AHEAD's guideline is that each campus must have appropriate levels of full-time professional staff in these roles; rarely can this be accomplished by just one person. Over time, postsecondary disability offices are transitioning from a perspective of strict compliance to a resource-oriented model. This transition is in compliance with ADA regulations, as amended in 2008, and in alignment with emerging models of student development theory and disability philosophy.

Challenges for institutions of higher education and disability services professionals and departments are numerous. They include retrofitting and adapting poorly designed services, programs, and offerings where accessibility by all students was not a consideration at inception; adapting to a new and emerging population of students with disabilities; adapting to the rapidly evolving world of technology, in particular to technology designed for access by persons with disabilities; securing or facilitating use of accessible instructional materials; facilitating equal access in online course management systems; and educating campus personnel regarding the shared institutional responsibilities of creating just, equitable, and usable environments through the elimination of barriers in any and all areas of the academic experience.

References, Readings, and Resources

Americans With Disabilities Act of 1990, as Amended, 42 U.S.C. 12101 *et seq.* (2008). Retrieved from http://access-board. gov/about/laws/ADA.htm

Church, T. E. (2009). *Veterans with disabilities: Promoting success in higher education*. Available at http://www. ahead.org/publications#bo16

Kasnitz, D. (2011). *The 2010 biennial AHEAD survey of disability services and resource professionals in higher education*. Retrieved from http://www.ahead.org/ uploads/membersarea/Final%20AHEAD%202010%20 Biennial%20Initial%20Report.docx

Linton, S. (1998). *Claiming disability: Knowledge and identity*. New York, NY: New York University Press.

Rehabilitation Act of 1973, Section 504 as amended, 29 U.S.C 794 *et seq.* (1973). Subpart E retrieved from http:// ed.gov/policy/rights/reg/ocr/edlite-34cfr104.html#E

United States Department of Education. (2008). *The Higher Education Opportunity Act (Public Law 110-315)*. Retrieved from www.pacer.org/tatra/ TheHigherEducationOpportunityAct.doc

United States Government Accountability Office. (2009, October). *Higher education and disability: Education needs a coordinated approach to improve its assistance to schools in supporting students.* Washington, DC: Author. Retrieved from http://www.gao.gov/new.items/d1033.pdf

Wagner, M., Newman, L., Cameto, R., Garza, N., & Levine, P. (2005). *After high school: A first look at the postschool experiences of youth with disabilities.* A report from the National Longitudinal Transition Study-2 (NLTS2). Menlo Park, CA: SRI International. Available at www.nlts2.org/ reports/2005_04/nlts2_report_2005_04_complete.pdf

Contextual Statement Contributors

Jean Ashmore, President, AHEAD, and Disability Director Emerita, Rice University

Kate Broderick, Old Dominion University, AHEAD, assisted by David J. Thomas, Doctoral Graduate Assistant for the Office of Educational Accessibility

Beth Hunsinger, The Community College of Baltimore Maryland, AHEAD

Disability Resources and Services
CAS Standards and Guidelines

Part 1. MISSION

The primary mission of Disability Resources and Services (DRS) is to ensure equal access for students with disabilities to all curricular and co-curricular opportunities offered by the institution.

In addition, the mission of DRS must
- provide leadership to the campus community to enhance understanding and support of DRS
- provide guidance to the campus community to ensure compliance with legal requirements for access
  Relevant legal requirements may vary among governmental jurisdictions but would include minimally for U.S. institutions the requirements defined under Section 504 of the Rehabilitation Act of 1973, and the Americans with Disabilities Act of 1990.
- establish a clear set of policies and procedures that define the responsibilities of both the institution and the person eligible for accommodations

DRS must develop, disseminate, implement, and regularly review their missions. The mission must be consistent with the mission of the institution and with professional standards. The mission must be appropriate for the institution's student populations and community settings. Mission statements must reference student learning and development.

To accomplish its mission, DRS must
- ensure that qualified individuals with disabilities receive reasonable and appropriate accommodations so as to have equal access to all institutional programs and services regardless of the type and extent of the disability
- possess a clear set of policies and procedures
- inform the campus community about the location of disability services, the availability of equipment and technology helpful to those with disabilities, and identification of key individuals within the institution who can provide services to students with disabilities
- define and describe the procedures for obtaining services and   accommodations
- provide guidance and training for institutional staff and faculty members in the understanding of disability issues
  Institutional staff and faculty members should be educated about the stereotypes surrounding people with disabilities as well as appropriate protocols and language.
- advocate for equal access, accommodations, and respect for students with disabilities within the campus community

Part 2. PROGRAM

The formal education of students, consisting of the curriculum and the co-curriculum, must promote student learning and development outcomes that are purposeful, contribute to students' realization of their potential, and prepare students for satisfying and productive lives.

Disability Resources and Services (DRS) must collaborate with colleagues and departments across the institution to promote student learning and development, persistence, and success.

Consistent with the institutional mission, DRS must identify relevant and desirable student learning and development outcomes from among the six domains and related dimensions:

Domain: knowledge acquisition, integration, construction, and application

- Dimensions: understanding knowledge from a range of disciplines; connecting knowledge to other knowledge, ideas, and experiences; constructing knowledge; and relating knowledge to daily life

Domain: cognitive complexity

- Dimensions: critical thinking, reflective thinking, effective reasoning, and creativity

Domain: intrapersonal development

- Dimensions: realistic self-appraisal, self-understanding, and self-respect; identity development; commitment to ethics and integrity; and spiritual awareness

Domain: interpersonal competence

- Dimensions: meaningful relationships, interdependence, collaboration, and effective leadership.

Domain: humanitarianism and civic engagement

- Dimensions: understanding and appreciation of cultural and human differences, social responsibility, global perspective, and sense of civic responsibility

Domain: practical competence

- **Dimensions: pursuing goals, communicating effectively, technical competence, managing personal affairs, managing career development, demonstrating professionalism, maintaining health and wellness, and living a purposeful and satisfying life**

[LD Outcomes: See *The Council for the Advancement of Standards Learning and Developmental Outcomes* statement for examples of outcomes related to these domains and dimensions.]

DRS must

- **assess relevant and desirable student learning and development**
- **provide evidence of impact on outcomes**
- **articulate contributions to or support of student learning and development in the domains not specifically assessed**
- **articulate contributions to or support of student persistence and success**
- **use evidence gathered through this process to create strategies for improvement of programs and services**

DRS must be

- **intentionally designed**
- **guided by theories and knowledge of learning and development**
- **integrated into the life of the institution**
- **reflective of developmental and demographic profiles of the student population**
- **responsive to needs of individuals, populations with distinct needs, and relevant constituencies**
- **delivered using multiple formats, strategies, and contexts**

Where institutions provide distance education, DRS must assist distance learners to achieve their educational goals by providing access to information about programs and services, to staff members who can address questions and concerns, and to counseling, advising, or other forms of assistance.

If a formal DRS program does not exist, it must be the responsibility of the institution to ensure that the primary mission is accomplished, either through the direct delivery of essential programs and services by the person(s) designated by the institution as the point of contact for students or by assisting other offices in meeting those needs.

Institutions must make effective use of existing administrative structures and resources to avoid unnecessary duplication of services and to ensure that all campus offices and services have as a part of their mission the responsibility to meet the needs of persons with disabilities.

Depending on the institution, students with disabilities should be served within a decentralized system, with a central office providing those services not provided elsewhere on campus.

DRS must identify environmental conditions that negatively influence persons with disabilities and propose interventions that are designed to ameliorate such conditions.

The institution must regularly evaluate the campus for physical access. Maps and signage must reflect accessible routes, handicapped parking, building accessibility, entrances, and restroom facilities. Parking and transportation must comply with applicable accessibility regulations and laws.

The major components of DRS, each of which must be clearly identified to the campus and to the potential and current users of the services, include

- **a procedure for disclosure**
  Persons with disabilities should be given the opportunity to self-disclose to a disability services provider who is trained to evaluate the information and who understands and respects the confidentiality of the individual.

  Each person requesting services should be screened during an intake interview, should have documentation from a qualified professional, and should ensure that the service provider receives the documentation. The documentation should be current, state a diagnosis, and give evidence to support the impact of the disability and its effect on the academic or work environment. A referral list of qualified and competent professionals should be maintained for students who need more current or new documentation.

- **direct assistance to persons with disabilities**
  Services to qualified individuals should ensure equal access and also meet the requirements as required by current law and institutional policy. The actual services provided will vary among institutions based on the specific disability and on the location of services provided by other campus offices or the community. Staff members provide for accommodations that assist persons with disabilities in the accomplishment of educational, personal, social, and work goals.

  Examples of accommodation can include testing accommodations, readers, scribes, interpreters, note takers, brailed materials, screen magnification systems, text-to-speech, screen reading, voice dictation, and /or optical character recognition systems.

- **consultation to the campus community**
  DRS should act as a consultant and advocate to the campus community in ensuring physical and programmatic access to all institutional resources. This would include collaboration with faculty members about teaching and testing techniques for academic departments. DRS should work to ensure equal access to electronic communication and distance learning materials as well as access to print.

- **advising, counseling, and support for persons with disabilities**
  DRS should assist individuals in devising strategies to adjust to and succeed in higher education. When strategies include reasonable accommodations, the program should provide information about how to acquire them.

- **professional and community education**
  DRS should offer training and educational activities to faculty members, staff, and students and other community members that promote understanding, awareness, and advocacy.

- **dissemination of information**
  Information should include access issues, accommodations, and legal rights of persons with disabilities to the campus community. Information regarding the laws, the procedures for receiving services, documentation guidelines, and other related policies should be made readily available in both print and electronic formats. Additionally, general information about location, available hours, contact information, and procedures should be made widely available especially in institutional print and electronic publications including, but not limited to, course schedules, catalogs, bulletins, recruitment materials, student and faculty handbooks, and residence life publications. On-line information about DRS should be accessible with the use of assistive technology and must provide appropriate links to other useful services such as financial aid, admissions, residence life, security, parking, and campus information.

- **collaboration on institutional safety policies and procedures**
  The program should collaborate with appropriate campus offices and community agencies on the development and dissemination of safety, evacuation, and other emergency response plans.

Part 3. ORGANIZATION AND LEADERSHIP

To achieve student and program outcomes, Disability Resources and Services (DRS) must be structured purposefully and organized effectively. DRS must have

- clearly stated goals
- current and accessible policies and procedures
- written performance expectations for employees
- functional work flow graphics or organizational charts demonstrating clear channels of authority

Leaders with organizational authority for the programs and services must provide strategic planning, supervision, and management; advance the organization; and maintain integrity through the following functions:

Strategic Planning
- articulate a vision and mission that drive short- and long-term planning
- set goals and objectives based on the needs of the population served and desired student learning or development and program outcomes
- facilitate continuous development, implementation, and assessment of goal attainment congruent with institutional mission and strategic plans
- promote environments that provide meaningful opportunities for student learning, development, and engagement
- develop and continuously improve programs and services in response to the changing needs of students served and evolving institutional priorities
- intentionally include diverse perspectives to inform decision making

Supervising
- manage human resource processes including recruitment, selection, development, supervision, performance planning, evaluation, recognition, and reward
- influence others to contribute to the effectiveness and success of the unit
- empower professional, support, and student staff to accept leadership opportunities
- offer appropriate feedback to colleagues and students on skills needed to become more effective leaders
- encourage and support professional development, collaboration with colleagues and departments across the institution, and scholarly contribution to the profession

Managing
- identify and address individual, organizational, and environmental conditions that foster or inhibit mission achievement
- plan, allocate, and monitor the use of fiscal, physical, human, intellectual, and

technological resources

- **use current and valid evidence to inform decisions**
- **incorporate sustainability practices in the management and design of programs, services, and facilities**
- **understand appropriate technologies and integrate them into programs and services**
- **be knowledgeable about codes and laws relevant to programs and services and ensure that staff members understand their responsibilities through appropriate training**
- **assess potential risks and take action to mitigate them**

Advancing the Organization

- **communicate effectively in writing, speaking, and electronic venues**
- **advocate for programs and services**
- **advocate for representation in strategic planning initiatives at appropriate divisional and institutional levels**
- **initiate collaborative interactions with internal and external stakeholders who have legitimate concerns about and interests in the functional area**
- **facilitate processes to reach consensus where wide support is needed**
- **inform other areas within the institution about issues affecting practice**

Maintaining Integrity

- **model ethical behavior and institutional citizenship**
- **share data used to inform key decisions in transparent and accessible ways**
- **monitor media used for distributing information about programs and services to ensure the content is current, accurate, appropriately referenced, and accessible**

The leaders of a DRS must keep abreast of current litigation, interpretation of case law, changes in the field of medicine and diseases, changes in documenting disabilities, and trends in the field of secondary special education, and must use this information to advise their institutions and community how to best respond and react to these changes. Also, leaders must be informed of best practices within the field of disability services.

DRS must be situated within the administrative structure to develop and direct program activities effectively. Adequate staff, funding, and resources must be provided.

Such services normally function within divisions of student affairs or academic affairs. The services should involve advisory bodies which include students, faculty and staff members with disabilities.

Part 4. HUMAN RESOURCES

Disability Resources and Services (DRS) must be staffed adequately by individuals qualified to accomplish mission and goals.

Within institutional guidelines, DRS must
- **establish procedures for staff recruitment and selection, training, performance planning, and evaluation**
- **set expectations for supervision and performance**
- **assess the performance of employees individually and as a team**
- **provide access to continuing and advanced education and appropriate professional development opportunities to improve the leadership ability, competence, and skills of all employees.**

DRS must maintain position descriptions for all staff members.

To create a diverse staff, DRS must institute recruitment and hiring strategies that encourage individuals from under-represented populations to apply for positions.

DRS must develop promotion practices that are fair, inclusive, proactive, and non-discriminatory.

Staff assignments should take into account the benefits of employing persons with disabilities.

Sign language and oral interpreters must have appropriate qualifications, including appropriate coursework and certification.

To further the recruitment and retention of staff, DRS must consider work life initiatives, such as compressed work schedules, flextime, job sharing, remote work, or telework.

DRS professional staff members must hold an earned graduate or professional degree in a field relevant to the position they hold or must possess an appropriate combination of educational credentials and related work experience.

Designated staff members may serve as practicum instructors or intern supervisors.

Administrative and support staff must be provided with disability awareness training and possess knowledge and understanding of the needs of persons with disabilities.

DRS professional staff members must engage in continuing professional development activities to

keep abreast of the research, theories, legislation, policies, and developments that affect their programs and services.

DRS must have technical and support staff members adequate to accomplish their mission. All members of the staff must be technologically proficient and qualified to perform their job functions, be knowledgeable about ethical and legal uses of technology, and have access to training and resources to support the performance of their assigned responsibilities.

Degree- or credential-seeking interns or graduate assistants must be qualified by enrollment in an appropriate field of study and by relevant experience. These individuals must be trained and supervised adequately by professional staff members holding educational credentials and related work experience appropriate for supervision. Supervisors must be cognizant of the roles of interns and graduate assistants as both student and employee and closely adhere to all parameters of their job descriptions, work hours, and schedules. Supervisors and the interns or graduate assistants must agree to compensatory time or other appropriate compensation if circumstances necessitate additional hours.

Student employees and volunteers must be carefully selected, trained, supervised, and evaluated. They must be educated on how and when to refer those in need of additional assistance to qualified staff members and must have access to a supervisor for assistance in making these judgments. Student employees and volunteers must be provided clear job descriptions, pre-service training based on assessed needs, and continuing development.

All DRS staff members, including student employees and volunteers, must receive specific training on institutional policies pertaining to functions or activities they support and to privacy and confidentiality policies and laws regarding access to student records and other sensitive institutional information.

All DRS staff members must receive training on policies and procedures related to the use of technology to store or access student records and institutional data.

DRS must ensure that staff members are knowledgeable about and trained in emergency procedures, crisis response, and prevention efforts. Prevention efforts must address identification of threatening conduct or behavior of students, faculty and staff members, and others and must incorporate a system for responding and reporting.

DRS must ensure that staff members are knowledgeable of and trained in safety and emergency procedures for securing and vacating facilities.

Part 5. ETHICS

Disability Resources and Services (DRS) must review relevant professional ethical standards and must adopt or develop and implement appropriate statements of ethical practice.

DRS must publish and adhere to statements of ethical practice and ensure their periodic review by relevant constituencies.

Ethical standards or other statements from relevant professional associations should also be considered.

DRS must orient new staff members to relevant ethical standards and statements of ethical practice and related institutional policies.

Statements of ethical standards must specify that staff members respect privacy and maintain confidentiality in all communications and records to the extent that such communications and records are protected under relevant privacy laws.

Statements of ethical standards must specify limits on disclosure of information contained in students' educational records as well as requirements to disclose to appropriate authorities.

Statements of ethical standards must address personal and economic conflicts of interest, or appearance thereof, by staff members in the performance of their work.

Statements of ethical standards must reflect the responsibility of staff members to be fair, objective, and impartial in their interactions with others.

Statements of ethical standards must reference management of institutional funds.

Statements of ethical standards must reference appropriate behavior regarding research and assessment with human participants, confidentiality of research and assessment data, and students' rights and responsibilities.

Statements of ethical standards must include the expectation that DRS staff members confront and hold accountable other staff members who exhibit unethical behavior.

Statements of ethical standards must address issues surrounding scholarly integrity.

As appropriate, DRS staff members must inform users of programs and services of ethical obligations and limitations emanating from codes and laws or from licensure requirements.

DRS staff members must recognize and avoid conflicts of interest that could adversely influence their judgment or objectivity and, when unavoidable, recuse themselves from the situation.

DRS staff members must perform their duties within the limits of their position, training, expertise, and competence.

When these limits are exceeded, individuals in need of further assistance must be referred to persons possessing appropriate qualifications.

Promotional and descriptive information must be accurate and free of deception.

DRS must adhere to institutional policies regarding ethical and legal use of software and technology.

Part 6. LAW, POLICY, AND GOVERNANCE

Disability Resources and Services (DRS) must be in compliance with laws, regulations, and policies that relate to their respective responsibilities and that pose legal obligations, limitations, risks, and liabilities for the institution as a whole. Examples include constitutional, statutory, regulatory, and case law; relevant law and orders emanating from codes and laws; and the institution's policies.

DRS must inform staff members, appropriate officials, and users of programs and services about existing and changing legal obligations, risks and liabilities, and limitations.

DRS must have written policies on all relevant operations, transactions, or tasks that have legal implications.

DRS must regularly review policies. The revision and creation of policies must be informed by best practices, available evidence, and policy issues in higher education.

DRS staff members must use reasonable and informed practices to limit the liability exposure of the institution and its officers, employees, and agents. DRS staff members must be informed about institutional policies regarding risk management, personal liability, and related insurance coverage options and must be referred to external sources if the institution does not provide coverage.

The institution must provide access to legal advice for staff members as needed to carry out assigned responsibilities.

DRS must have procedures and guidelines consistent with institutional policy for responding to threats,

emergencies, and crisis situations. Systems and procedures must be in place to disseminate timely and accurate information to students, other members of the institutional community, and appropriate external organizations during emergency situations.

DRS staff members must neither participate in nor condone any form of harassment or activity that demeans persons or creates an intimidating, hostile, or offensive environment.

DRS must obtain permission to use copyrighted materials and instruments. DRS must purchase the materials and instruments from legally compliant sources or seek alternative permission from the publisher or owner. References to copyrighted materials and instruments must include appropriate citations.

DRS staff members must be knowledgeable about internal and external governance systems that affect programs and services.

DRS staff members must be aware of and seek advice from the institution's legal counsel on privacy and disclosure of student information contained in educational records, defamation law regarding references and recommendations on behalf of students, affirmative action laws, protective health information laws, and regulations regarding programs and liability issues pertaining to sponsored programs.

Higher education institutions must adhere to the law in appointing a disability compliance officer.

The DRS staff must, in conjunction with legal counsel, work to develop policies, procedures, and guidelines as required under relevant disability laws.

Interpretation of the laws and their application to the campus should be a coordinated effort with institutional legal counsel.

Part 7. DIVERSITY, EQUITY, AND ACCESS

Within the context of each institution's unique mission and in accordance with institutional polices and all applicable codes and laws, Disability Resources and Services (DRS) must create and maintain educational and work environments that are
- welcoming, accessible, and inclusive to persons of diverse backgrounds
- equitable and non-discriminatory
- free from harassment

DRS must not discriminate on the basis of ability; age; cultural identity; ethnicity; family educational history (e.g., first generation to attend college); gender identity and expression; nationality; political affiliation; race; religious affiliation; sex; sexual orientation; economic, marital, social, or veteran status; or any other basis included in institutional policies and codes and laws.

DRS must

- advocate for greater sensitivity to multicultural and social justice concerns by the institution and its personnel
- modify or remove policies, practices, facilities, structures, systems, and technologies that limit access, discriminate, or produce inequities
- include diversity, equity, and access initiatives within their strategic plans
- foster communication that deepens understanding of identity, culture, self-expression, and heritage
- promote respect about commonalities and differences among people within their historical and cultural contexts
- address the characteristics and needs of a diverse population when establishing and implementing culturally relevant and inclusive programs, services, policies, procedures, and practices
- provide staff members with access to multicultural training and hold staff members accountable for integrating the training into their work
- respond to the needs of all students and other populations served when establishing hours of operation and developing methods of delivering programs, services, and resources
- ensure physical, program, and resource access for persons with disabilities
- recognize the needs of distance learning students by providing appropriate and accessible services and resources or by assisting them in gaining access to other appropriate services and resources in their geographic region

DRS must educate the campus community about ensuring opportunities for individuals with disabilities in all facets of the institution.

Part 8. CAMPUS and EXTERNAL RELATIONS

Disability Resources and Services (DRS) must reach out to relevant individuals, groups, communities, and organizations internal and external to the institution to

- establish, maintain, and promote understanding and effective relations with those that have a significant interest in or potential effect on the students or other constituents served by the programs and services
- garner support and resources for programs and services as defined by the mission statement
- disseminate information about the programs and services
- collaborate, where appropriate, to assist in offering or improving programs and services to meet the needs of students and other constituents and to achieve program and student outcomes
- engage diverse individuals, groups, communities, and organizations to enrich the educational environment and experiences of students and other constituents

Such agencies would include vocational rehabilitation, the medical community, veterans administration, school districts, and social services agencies.

DRS must also work to maintain positive relations with students, faculty members, staff, the institutional legal counsel, the administration, all support offices, community agencies, the medical community, diagnosticians, and equal opportunity compliance officers.

DRS should take an active role in the coordination of the institution's response to the needs of persons with disabilities. This is essential to ensure the continuity of services, resource management, consistent institutional policies, and the integration of persons with disabilities into the total campus experience.

DRS should maintain a high degree of visibility with the academic units through the promotion and delivery of services, through involvement in determining what constitutes reasonable accommodations, and through promoting increased understanding of, and responsiveness to, the needs of persons with disabilities.

DRS should be informed about, and actively involved in, influencing and affecting the policies, practices, and planning of other units, which directly affect persons with disabilities.

DRS staff members must be available to participate in appropriate campus-wide committees.

Disability support service staff members may act as liaisons between student services, academic services, and community services on the behalf of persons with disabilities.

DRS must have procedures and guidelines consistent with institutional policy for

- communicating with the media
- contracting with external organizations for delivery of programs and services
- cultivating, soliciting, and managing gifts
- applying to and managing funds from grants

Part 9. FINANCIAL RESOURCES

Disability Resources and Services (DRS) must have funding to accomplish the mission and goals. In establishing funding priorities and making significant changes, a comprehensive analysis must be conducted to determine the following elements: unmet needs of the unit, relevant expenditures, external and internal resources, and impact on students and the institution.

DRS must demonstrate efficient and effective use and responsible stewardship of fiscal resources consistent with institutional protocols.

DRS should be funded as a separate institutional budget item.

The allocation of financial resources must be adequate to meet the obligations of the institution under applicable laws.

In addition to normal budget categories, the DRS program may have unusual budgetary requirements that can vary from term to term. These may include readers, interpreters, and special equipment such as a TTY/TDD (telephone communication devices for the deaf), screen readers, voice synthesizers, reading machines, device for enlarging print, Braille capabilities, additional technology to provide accommodated exams, and variable speed tape recorders. The institution is not obligated to provide personal equipment such as wheelchairs, hearing aids, or prosthetics. The number and nature of the devices can be determined based on the population of persons with disabilities requesting services.

The decision of whether to purchase mandated devices should not be weighed against competing departmental needs, such as additional computers or staff. Funding for disability accommodations should come from a centralized institutional source rather than from any one individual department.

Part 10. TECHNOLOGY

Disability Resources and Services (DRS) must have adequate technology to support the achievement of their mission and goals. The technology and its use must comply with institutional policies and procedures and be evaluated for compliance with relevant codes and laws.

DRS must use current technology to provide updated information regarding mission, location, staffing, programs, services, and official contacts to students and designated clients.

DRS must explore the use of technology to enhance delivery of programs and services, especially for students at a distance or external constituencies.

When technology is used to facilitate student learning and development, DRS must select technology that reflects intended outcomes.

DRS must

- maintain policies and procedures that address the security, confidentiality, and backup of data, as well as compliance with privacy laws
- have clearly articulated plans in place for protecting confidentiality and security of information when using Internet-based technologies
- develop plans for replacing and updating existing hardware and software as well as plans for integrating new technically-based or supported programs, including systems developed internally by the institution, systems available through professional associations, or private vendor-based systems

Technology, as well as workstations or computer labs maintained by programs and services for student use, must be accessible to all designated clients and must meet established technology standards for delivery to persons with disabilities.

When providing student access to technology, DRS must

- have policies on the use of technology that are clear, easy to understand, and available to all students
- provide assistance, information, or referral to appropriate support services to those needing help accessing or using technology
- provide instruction or training on how to use the technology
- inform students on the legal and ethical implications of misuse as it pertains to intellectual property, harassment, privacy, and social networks

Student violations of technology policies must follow established institutional student disciplinary procedures.

Students who experience negative emotional or psychological consequences from the use of technology must be referred to support services provided by the institution.

Part 11. FACILITIES AND EQUIPMENT

Disability Resources and Services (DRS) must have adequate, accessible, and suitably located facilities and equipment to support the mission and goals. If acquiring capital equipment as defined by the institution, DRS must take into account expenses related to regular maintenance and life cycle costs.

Facilities and equipment must be evaluated on an established cycle, including consideration of sustainability, and be in compliance with codes and laws to provide for access, health, safety, and security.

DRS staff members must have workspace that is well equipped, adequate in size, and designed to support their work and responsibilities. For conversations requiring privacy, staff members must have access to a private space.

DRS staff members who share workspace must be able to secure their own work.
The design of the facilities must guarantee the security and privacy of records and ensure the confidentiality of sensitive information.

The location and layout of the facilities must be sensitive to the needs of persons with disabilities as well as the needs of other constituencies.

Facilities available to DRS units should include
- offices and programmatic spaces within an accessible facility
- private offices for conducting intake interviews, counseling, or other meetings of a confidential nature
- private and quiet space for tape recording materials, and scribing or taking exams
- a receptionist area with accessible counter heights and TTY/TDD
- storage area to ensure the confidentiality of records
- conference room and training space adequate to accommodate persons in wheelchairs
- nearby availability of accessible rest rooms, water fountains, elevators, and corridors
- adequate handicapped parking convenient to the facility
- coat racks and bulletin boards
- warning devices such as strobe/buzzer fire alarms for emergencies.

DRS must ensure that staff members are knowledgeable of and trained in safety and emergency procedures for securing and vacating the facilities.

Part 12. ASSESSMENT AND EVALUATION

Disability Resources and Services (DRS) must have a clearly articulated assessment plan to document achievement of stated goals and learning outcomes, demonstrate accountability, provide evidence of improvement, and describe resulting changes in programs and services.

DRS must have adequate fiscal, human, professional development, and technological resources to develop and implement assessment plans.

Assessments must include direct and indirect evaluation and use qualitative and quantitative methodologies and existing evidence, as appropriate, to determine whether and to what degree the stated mission, goals, and intended outcomes are being met as effectively and efficiently as possible. The process must employ sufficient and sound measures to ensure comprehensiveness. Data collected must include responses from students and other constituencies, and aggregated results must be shared with those groups. Results of assessments must be shared appropriately with multiple constituents.

Results of assessments and evaluations must be used to identify needs and interests in revising and improving programs and services, recognizing staff performance, maximizing resource efficiency and effectiveness, improving student achievement of learning and development outcomes, and improving student persistence and success. Changes resulting from the use of assessments and evaluation must be shared with stakeholders.

Comprehensive, systematic, and periodic assessments should be conducted to address the academic, social, and physical needs of students as well as the psychological and physical environments of the campus. In turn, findings should be used to influence how present services should change for future development.

To determine the effectiveness of the organization and administration of the services, a data collection system should be developed and implemented. Program evaluations should be obtained from designated staff members, students, faculty members, and community.

Analyses of population characteristics and trends in the use of services should be performed regularly. Although not the sole measure of program's success, data may be compiled annually on attrition and graduation rates of students using the services.

General Standards revised in 2011;
DRS content developed/revised in 1986, 1997, & 2003

The Role of Education Abroad Programs and Services
CAS Standards Contextual Statement

U.S. students have been traveling abroad for higher education for centuries, but study abroad as we know it today officially began in the 1920's with Junior Year Abroad programs (Hoffa, 2007). More recently, there has been a sharp upward trend in U.S. students studying abroad. According to the Institute of International Education's *Open Doors* publication, during the 2009-2010 academic year a record 270,604 college students from colleges and universities in the United States participated in an education abroad program for academic credit. This figure marks a 4 percent rise from the preceding year and a 76 percent increase from 2000-2001 totals. There was a slight decline during the 2008-2009 academic year, the increases each year have slowed, but the general trend has been upward.

In addition to the increase in participation, there have been other recent trends. Students have been choosing destinations outside of Western Europe more frequently than before for their study abroad experiences, and they have been choosing short-term (one semester or shorter) study abroad programs much more frequently than yearlong programs. Besides the student numbers listed in *Open Doors*, U.S. students participated in experiential, volunteer, service-learning, and internship programs abroad. The visible trend toward greater interest and participation in education abroad among college students, both in the U.S. and in other countries, was concurrent with the proliferation of education abroad opportunities. Education abroad participants may now choose from a variety of programs that differ according to program location, type, duration, academic focus, method of instruction, and coordinating entity. Given the array of programs and the increasing interest in global education among students, their parents, educational institutions, state/provincial governments, and federal governments, as well as in other countries throughout the world, the need for Education Abroad Programs and Services (EAPS) to have and meet standards cannot be overstated.

For more than 40 years, guidelines and standards for providing EAPS have been developed by various groups, such as NAFSA, Association of International Educators, the Council on International Educational Exchange, the Institute for International Education, the Institute for the International Education of Students, The Forum on Education Abroad, and accreditation bodies such as the Middle States Association. The Forum is registered as the Standards Development Organization for education abroad with the Department of Justice and the Federal Trade Commission. CAS drew heavily on the publications of these groups in developing the CAS standards for EAPS. See the Resources section below for access to these organizations and some of their standards materials. They provide essential additional perspectives to any standards assessment of an education abroad office or organization.

On college and university campuses, EAPS responsibilities may be centralized in one office on campus or dispersed in multiple schools and departments across the institution. Education abroad directors and advisers must be familiar with a broad spectrum of campus services, processes, and systems, including but not limited to academic advising services, financial aid, registration, residence life, health services, counseling services, off-campus regulations and guidelines, disability services, risk management, judicial affairs, career services, alumni services, and development.

In times of global and economic uncertainty, education abroad directors and advisers must pay special attention to matters of safety, security, currency and market fluctuations, and access to financial assistance. These matters are of concern both to students and their families as well as to program development and management.

Assessment is a critical aspect of ensuring the integrity of EAPS. Among other areas, EAPS should systematically assess student learning and development outcomes. Research and practice in assessment and evaluation in study abroad programs have grown considerably, and there are many resources available to EAPS providers (see the lists below for suggestions).

Some education abroad opportunities are administered by the student's home campus, some by other institutions, and some by organizations. Whenever the programs are not administered by the home campus, the EAPS is responsible for investigating and approving the programs before allowing students to participate in and receive credit through them. The following standards and guidelines are aimed at home-country campus-based offices, although non-campus based EAPS organizations and overseas institutions will find many of the sections helpful. The provision of Education Abroad Programs and Services has become a global enterprise.

References, Readings, and Resources

Alliance for International Educational and Cultural Exchange: http://www.alliance-exchange.org/

American Council on Education. (n.d.). *Assessing international learning*. http://www.acenet.edu/Content/NavigationMenu/ProgramsServices/cii/res/assess/assess_resources.htm

American International Education Foundation: http://www.ief-usa.org/

Association for Studies in International Education: http://www.asie.org/index.htm

Bolen, M., Ed. (2007) *A guide to outcomesaAssessment in study abroad.* Carlisle, PA: Forum on Education Abroad.

Brockington, J. L., Hoffa W. W. and Martin, P.C. (2005). *NAFSA's guide to education abroad for advisers and administrators (3rd ed.).* Washington, D.C.: NAFSA: Association of International Educators.

Forum on education abroad: *Standards of good practice for education abroad,* 4th edition, 2011. Available at http://www.forumea.org/standards-standards.cfm

Frontiers, The Interdisciplinary Journal of Study Abroad: http://www.frontiersjournal.com/

Hoffa, W. W. (2007). A history of U.S. study abroad: Beginnings to 1965. A Special Publication of *Frontiers: The Interdisciplinary Journal of Study Abroad and The Forum on Education Abroa*d. Lancaster, PA.

IES MAP (Model Assessment Program): https://www.iesabroad.org/IES/Advisors_and_Faculty/iesMap.html

Institute of International Education, http://www.iienetwork.org/

Institute of International Education Annual Report *Open Doors,* http://opendoors.iienetwork.org/

Institute of International Education. (published annually). *Open doors 2011.* See http://www.iie.org/Research-and-Publications/Open-Doors

NAFSA: Association of International Educators: http://www.nafsa.org/

NAFSA's Statement of Ethical Principles: http://www.nafsa.org/_/File/_/ethical_principles_2009.pdf

Spencer, S. E., & Tuma, K. (Eds.). (2007). *The guide to successful short-term programs abroad (2nd ed.).* Washington, D.C.: NAFSA: Association of International Educators.

Strengthening study abroad: Recommendations for effective institutional management. (2008).   Washington, D.C.: NAFSA: Association of International Educators. Available at http://www.nafsa.org/imsa

The Center for Global Education: http://www.lmu.edu/globaled/index.html

The Forum on Education Abroad: http://www.forumea.org/

Contextual Statement Contributors
Current Edition:
Emily Gorlewski, Western Illinois University

Previous Editions:
Zaneeta Daver, University of Maryland, ACPA
Susan R. Komives, University of Maryland, ACPA

Education Abroad Programs and Services
CAS Standards and Guidelines

Part 1. MISSION

Education Abroad Programs and Services (EAPS) facilitate and oversee student participation in educational experiences that occur in countries outside the institution's home country.

EAPS must develop, disseminate, implement, and regularly review their missions. The mission must be consistent with the mission of the institution and with professional standards. The mission must be appropriate for the institution's student populations and community settings. Mission statements must reference student learning and development.

EAPS overall mission should address the following components:
- whom the program serves
- what the program values
- what the program seeks to accomplish (goals and objectives)
- a commitment to providing an appropriate variety of types of education abroad programs, in a variety of locations for academic credit
- a commitment to supporting students prior to, during, and after their education abroad experience
- a commitment to collaborating with internal and external stakeholders

Part 2. PROGRAM

The formal education of students, consisting of the curriculum and the co-curriculum, must promote student learning and development outcomes that are purposeful, contribute to students' realization of their potential, and prepare students for satisfying and productive lives.

Education Abroad Programs and Services (EAPS) must collaborate with colleagues and departments across the institution to promote student learning and development, persistence, and success.

Consistent with the institutional mission, EAPS must identify relevant and desirable student learning and development outcomes from among the six domains and related dimensions:

Domain: knowledge acquisition, integration, construction, and application
- Dimensions: understanding knowledge from a range of disciplines; connecting knowledge to other knowledge, ideas, and experiences; constructing knowledge; and relating knowledge to daily life

Domain: cognitive complexity
- Dimensions: critical thinking, reflective thinking, effective reasoning, and creativity

Domain: intrapersonal development
- Dimensions: realistic self-appraisal, self-understanding, and self-respect; identity development; commitment to ethics and integrity; and spiritual awareness

Domain: interpersonal competence
- Dimensions: meaningful relationships, interdependence, collaboration, and effective leadership.

Domain: humanitarianism and civic engagement
- Dimensions: understanding and appreciation of cultural and human differences, social responsibility, global perspective, and sense of civic responsibility

Domain: practical competence
- Dimensions: pursuing goals, communicating effectively, technical competence, managing personal affairs, managing career development, demonstrating professionalism, maintaining health and wellness, and living a purposeful and satisfying life

[LD Outcomes: See *The Council for the Advancement of Standards Learning and Developmental Outcomes* statement for examples of outcomes related to these domains and dimensions.]

EAPS must
- assess relevant and desirable student learning and development
- provide evidence of impact on outcomes
- articulate contributions to or support of student learning and development in the domains not specifically assessed
- articulate contributions to or support of student persistence and success
- use evidence gathered through this process to create strategies for improvement of programs and services

EAPS must be
- intentionally designed
- guided by theories and knowledge of learning and development
- integrated into the life of the institution
- reflective of developmental and demographic profiles of the student population

- **responsive to needs of individuals, populations with distinct needs, and relevant constituencies**
- **delivered using multiple formats, strategies, and contexts**

Where institutions provide distance education, EAPS must assist distance learners to achieve their educational goals by providing access to information about programs and services, to staff members who can address questions and concerns, and to counseling, advising, or other forms of assistance.

The EAPS should facilitate student participation in a variety of types of education abroad programs such as:

- programs where the student mobility is from the home institution (the school at which the student is seeking the degree) to a host institution (the school outside the institution's home country at which the student receives instruction and services while abroad)
- institutional exchanges where students from the home institution trade places with students from the host institution
- consortia programs that involve two or more institutions
- third-party programs where the program is administered outside the institution

To fulfill its mission and goals effectively, EAPS must include the following elements:

- **Clear and consisten academic policies and guidelines for home and host**

Admissions policies and procedures should be clearly articulated to students. Academic policies and procedures for awarding credit and understanding course grade equivalencies should also be clearly articulated to students before they depart for an education abroad program. Guidance with course selection should be offered regarding course transferability and equivalency. Coursework should be appropriately challenging; course requirements and methods of evaluating performance should be clearly stated; feedback should be provided to students periodically, in keeping with host country norms. Opportunities should be provided that allow the learning that occurs as a result of the EAPS experience to be integrated into subsequent educational experiences.

- **Curricular and co-curricular opportunities that are related to the mission and purpose of the specific education abroad program**

The curricular and co-curricular components of each education abroad opportunity should make effective use of the location and resources of the host country; students should be encouraged to engage with the host culture and to reflect on the differences and similarities between the intellectual, political, cultural, spiritual, and social institutions of the home and host countries. Students' curricular and co-curricular experiences should contribute to their appreciation and respect for cultural differences in general. Students should be encouraged to immerse themselves in the host culture, interact with host nationals, practice and improve their language and intercultural communication abilities, and reflect on their value systems in the context of living in another culture.

EAPS should provide opportunities for internships, service-learning, and other field study experiences that are related to the mission and purpose of the specific education abroad program. EAPS should incorporate opportunities to synthesize the learning that occurs as a result of these out-of-classroom experiences into future educational and life experiences.

Where field opportunities exist, they must be appropriately supervised and evaluated and must relate to the mission of the EAPS and institution. Awarding of credit for internships or field studies must be consistent with the policies of the home institution.

- **Pre-departure advising and orientation programs**

Pre-departure advising and orientation sessions must inform students about program requirements, academic credit and transfer policies, visa and passport requirements, and housing and travel arrangements, as well as financial, health, liability, insurance, safety, and security information. International students at the home institution must be advised to determine their re-entry status. Students must be asked directly and encouraged strongly to share information about any on-going health concerns before departing for their program locations. Home and host institution codes of conduct that apply to students while abroad must be clearly articulated; consequences of not following these codes of conduct must be clearly defined and communicated. Students must be provided with an introduction to intercultural communication and preparation for the cultural transition, including resources on culture shock and cultural adjustment. Orientation programs must identify resources for students so that they may educate themselves about the culture, customs, and laws of the host countries. EAPS must provide students with the contact the information of their home country's embassy or consulate at their host site.

Students should be advised to utilize the appropriate campus or community resources (e.g., travel medicine, financial aid, immigration status) before departure.

- **Information about student financial assistance**

- **On-going advising and support services for students while they are abroad**

  On-going advising and support services throughout the duration of the education abroad programs should be provided either through the home or host institution

- **Re-entry support and orientation programs for returning students**

  Upon return, re-entry programs and services must support re-acculturation to the home country, relationships, and the institution.

  Returning students should be encouraged to integrate their experience abroad into their continued learning, including sharing their stories and experiences with other students, faculty members, and staff members.

Part 3. ORGANIZATION AND LEADERSHIP

To achieve student and program outcomes, Education Abroad Programs and Services (EAPS) must be structured purposefully and organized effectively. EAPS must have
- clearly stated goals
- current and accessible policies and procedures
- written performance expectations for employees
- functional work flow graphics or organizational charts demonstrating clear channels of authority

Leaders with organizational authority for the programs and services must provide strategic planning, supervision, and management; advance the organization; and maintain integrity through the following functions:

Strategic Planning
- articulate a vision and mission that drive short- and long-term planning
- set goals and objectives based on the needs of the population served and desired student learning or development and program outcomes
- facilitate continuous development, implementation, and assessment of goal attainment congruent with institutional mission and strategic plans
- promote environments that provide meaningful opportunities for student learning, development, and engagement
- develop and continuously improve programs and services in response to the changing needs of students served and evolving institutional priorities
- intentionally include diverse perspectives to

inform decision making

Supervising
- manage human resource processes including recruitment, selection, development, supervision, performance planning, evaluation, recognition, and reward
- influence others to contribute to the effectiveness and success of the unit
- empower professional, support, and student staff to accept leadership opportunities
- offer appropriate feedback to colleagues and students on skills needed to become more effective leaders
- encourage and support professional development, collaboration with colleagues and departments across the institution, and scholarly contribution to the profession

Managing
- identify and address individual, organizational, and environmental conditions that foster or inhibit mission achievement
- plan, allocate, and monitor the use of fiscal, physical, human, intellectual, and technological resources
- use current and valid evidence to inform decisions
- incorporate sustainability practices in the management and design of programs, services, and facilities
- understand appropriate technologies and integrate them into programs and services
- be knowledgeable about codes and laws relevant to programs and services and ensure that staff members understand their responsibilities through appropriate training
- assess potential risks and take action to mitigate them

Advancing the Organization
- communicate effectively in writing, speaking, and electronic venues
- advocate for programs and services
- advocate for representation in strategic planning initiatives at appropriate divisional and institutional levels
- initiate collaborative interactions with internal and external stakeholders who have legitimate concerns about and interests in the functional area
- facilitate processes to reach consensus where wide support is needed
- inform other areas within the institution about issues affecting practice

Maintaining Integrity
- model ethical behavior and institutional

citizenship
- **share data used to inform key decisions in transparent and accessible ways**
- **monitor media used for distributing information about programs and services to ensure the content is current, accurate, appropriately referenced, and accessible**

EAPS leaders should establish working relationships with institutional agents, including provosts, academic deans, department chairs, risk managers, academic advisors, and student affairs professionals on the home campus to promote programs and engender support.

To fulfill its mission and goals effectively, EAPS must
- **provide leadership for integrating education abroad into the wider administrative and academic structure of the institution**
- **efficiently and effectively administer the programs they coordinate**
- **advise students appropriately, based on their interests, needs, financial ability, language proficiency, and academic background, as they choose an education abroad program**

EAPS should be housed within a centralized unit.

Information about education abroad opportunities and related institutional policies must be easily accessible.

Part 4. HUMAN RESOURCES

Education Abroad Programs and Services (EAPS) must be staffed adequately by individuals qualified to accomplish mission and goals.

Within institutional guidelines, EAPS must
- **establish procedures for staff recruitment and selection, training, performance planning, and evaluation**
- **set expectations for supervision and performance**
- **assess the performance of employees individually and as a team**
- **provide access to continuing and advanced education and appropriate professional development opportunities to improve the leadership ability, competence, and skills of all employees.**

EAPS must maintain position descriptions for all staff members.

To create a diverse staff, EAPS must institute recruitment and hiring strategies that encourage individuals from under-represented populations to apply for positions.

EAPS must develop promotion practices that are fair,

inclusive, proactive, and non-discriminatory.

To further the recruitment and retention of staff, EAPS must consider work life initiatives, such as compressed work schedules, flextime, job sharing, remote work, or telework.

EAPS professional staff members must hold an earned graduate or professional degree in a field relevant to the position they hold or must possess an appropriate combination of educational credentials and related work experience.

EAPS staff should have experience living or studying abroad. Entry into the profession by educators from a variety of academic backgrounds is encouraged.

EAPS professional staff members must be knowledgeable and competent in the following areas:
- **cultural sensitivity**
- **intercultural communication**
- **culture shock, reverse culture shock, and cultural adjustment**
- **student advising and counseling**
- **crisis management**
- **budgetary and financial management**
- **collaboration with faculty members and academic departments at home and host institutions**
- **organizational policies (e.g., admissions, credit transfer, financial aid, travel regulations, immigration policies, insurance)**
- **pre-departure and re-entry issues**
- **travel and living abroad**
- **technology**
- **country specific health, safety, and security concerns**

EAPS professional staff members should be knowledgeable and competent in such areas as:
- foreign language(s)
- countries, cultures, and regions where their students most frequently study (e.g. culture, customs, language, art, geography, political system, economic system, history, traditions, values, laws)
- other countries' educational systems
- human development
- marketing and promoting education abroad programs
- experiential education

EAPS professional staff members must engage in continuing professional development activities to keep abreast of the research, theories, legislation, policies, and developments that affect their programs and services.

EAPS must have technical and support staff members adequate to accomplish their mission. All

members of the staff must be technologically proficient and qualified to perform their job functions, be knowledgeable about ethical and legal uses of technology, and have access to training and resources to support the performance of their assigned responsibilities.

Degree- or credential-seeking interns or graduate assistants must be qualified by enrollment in an appropriate field of study and by relevant experience. These individuals must be trained and supervised adequately by professional staff members holding educational credentials and related work experience appropriate for supervision. Supervisors must be cognizant of the roles of interns and graduate assistants as both student and employee and closely adhere to all parameters of their job descriptions, work hours, and schedules. Supervisors and the interns or graduate assistants must agree to compensatory time or other appropriate compensation if circumstances necessitate additional hours.

Student employees and volunteers must be carefully selected, trained, supervised, and evaluated. They must be educated on how and when to refer those in need of additional assistance to qualified staff members and must have access to a supervisor for assistance in making these judgments. Student employees and volunteers must be provided clear job descriptions, pre-service training based on assessed needs, and continuing development.

All EAPS staff members, including student employees and volunteers, must receive specific training on institutional policies pertaining to functions or activities they support and to privacy and confidentiality policies and laws regarding access to student records and other sensitive institutional information.

All EAPS staff members must receive training on policies and procedures related to the use of technology to store or access student records and institutional data.

EAPS must ensure that staff members are knowledgeable about and trained in emergency procedures, crisis response, and prevention efforts. Prevention efforts must address identification of threatening conduct or behavior of students, faculty and staff members, and others and must incorporate a system for responding and reporting.

EAPS must ensure that staff members are knowledgeable of and trained in safety and emergency procedures for securing and vacating facilities.

Part 5. ETHICS

Education Abroad Programs and Services (EAPS) must review relevant professional ethical standards and must adopt or develop and implement appropriate statements of ethical practice.

EAPS must publish and adhere to statements of ethical practice and ensure their periodic review by relevant constituencies.

EAPS must orient new staff members to relevant ethical standards and statements of ethical practice and related institutional policies.

Statements of ethical standards must specify that staff members respect privacy and maintain confidentiality in all communications and records to the extent that such communications and records are protected under relevant privacy laws.

Statements of ethical standards must specify limits on disclosure of information contained in students' educational records as well as requirements to disclose to appropriate authorities.

Statements of ethical standards must address personal and economic conflicts of interest, or appearance thereof, by staff members in the performance of their work.

Statements of ethical standards must reflect the responsibility of staff members to be fair, objective, and impartial in their interactions with others.

Statements of ethical standards must reference management of institutional funds.

Statements of ethical standards must reference appropriate behavior regarding research and assessment with human participants, confidentiality of research and assessment data, and students' rights and responsibilities.

Statements of ethical standards must include the expectation that EAPS staff members confront and hold accountable other staff members who exhibit unethical behavior.

Statements of ethical standards must address issues surrounding scholarly integrity.

As appropriate, EAPS staff members must inform users of programs and services of ethical obligations and limitations emanating from codes and laws or from licensure requirements.

EAPS staff members must recognize and avoid conflicts of interest that could adversely influence their judgment or objectivity and, when unavoidable, recuse themselves from the situation.

EAPS staff members must perform their duties within the limits of their position, training, expertise, and competence.

When these limits are exceeded, individuals in need of further assistance must be referred to persons possessing appropriate qualifications.

Promotional and descriptive information must be accurate and free of deception.

EAPS must adhere to institutional policies regarding ethical and legal use of software and technology.

EAPS home and host staff members must have ethical and unbiased procedures in place for terminating participants.

Termination procedures should be made public and provided to participants prior to their participation in an education abroad program.

EAPS home and host staff members must have ethical guidelines in place for advising and interacting with students and their families.

In addition to standard records privacy and confidentiality policies, EAPS should develop procedures to assure the long-term protection of students' records.

Part 6. LAW, POLICY, AND GOVERNANCE

Education Abroad Programs and Services (EAPS) must be in compliance with laws, regulations, and policies that relate to their respective responsibilities and that pose legal obligations, limitations, risks, and liabilities for the institution as a whole. Examples include constitutional, statutory, regulatory, and case law; relevant law and orders emanating from codes and laws; and the institution's policies.

EAPS staff members must know where to refer program participants for information on host country laws and host institution policies and procedures. EAPS staff members must make participants aware of home institution consequences of breaking these laws, policies, and procedures.

EAPS must inform staff members, appropriate officials, and users of programs and services about existing and changing legal obligations, risks and liabilities, and limitations.

EAPS must have written policies on all relevant operations, transactions, or tasks that have legal implications.

EAPS must regularly review policies. The revision and creation of policies must be informed by best practices, available evidence, and policy issues in higher education.

EAPS staff members must use reasonable and informed practices to limit the liability exposure of the institution and its officers, employees, and agents. EAPS staff members must be informed about institutional policies regarding risk management, personal liability, and related insurance coverage options and must be referred to external sources if the institution does not provide coverage.

The institution must provide access to legal advice for staff members as needed to carry out assigned responsibilities.

EAPS must have procedures and guidelines consistent with institutional policy for responding to threats, emergencies, and crisis situations. Systems and procedures must be in place to disseminate timely and accurate information to students, other members of the institutional community, and appropriate external organizations during emergency situations.

EAPS staff members must neither participate in nor condone any form of harassment or activity that demeans persons or creates an intimidating, hostile, or offensive environment.

EAPS must obtain permission to use copyrighted materials and instruments. EAPS must purchase the materials and instruments from legally compliant sources or seek alternative permission from the publisher or owner. References to copyrighted materials and instruments must include appropriate citations.

EAPS staff members must be knowledgeable about internal and external governance systems that affect programs and services.

EAPS staff members must ensure that expectations for participant conduct—including but not limited to drug and alcohol abuse, sexual assault and harassment, academic integrity, and social conduct—are clearly articulated in program materials and in pre-departure and on-site orientations.

EAPS must have a clearly defined crisis management program.

The home institution should have a clearly defined crisis management program that integrates and supports the EAPS plan. The home institution should obtain the host institution crisis management plan.

EAPS staff members should develop collaborative relationships with relevant home and host institutional departments (e.g., general counsel, student conduct programs) in order to assess and minimize risk and develop appropriate resources for students.

Part 7. DIVERSITY, EQUITY, AND ACCESS

Within the context of each institution's unique mission and in accordance with institutional polices and all applicable codes and laws, **Education Abroad Programs and Services (EAPS) must create and maintain educational and work environments that are**

- welcoming, accessible, and inclusive to persons of diverse backgrounds
- equitable and non-discriminatory
- free from harassment

EAPS must not discriminate on the basis of ability; age; cultural identity; ethnicity; family educational history (e.g., first generation to attend college); gender identity and expression; nationality; political affiliation; race; religious affiliation; sex; sexual orientation; economic, marital, social, or veteran status; or any other basis included in institutional policies and codes and laws.

EAPS must

- advocate for greater sensitivity to multicultural and social justice concerns by the institution and its personnel
- modify or remove policies, practices, facilities, structures, systems, and technologies that limit access, discriminate, or produce inequities
- include diversity, equity, and access initiatives within their strategic plans
- foster communication that deepens understanding of identity, culture, self-expression, and heritage
- promote respect about commonalities and differences among people within their historical and cultural contexts
- address the characteristics and needs of a diverse population when establishing and implementing culturally relevant and inclusive programs, services, policies, procedures, and practices
- provide staff members with access to multicultural training and hold staff members accountable for integrating the training into their work
- respond to the needs of all students and other populations served when establishing hours of operation and developing methods of delivering programs, services, and resources
- ensure physical, program, and resource access for persons with disabilities
- recognize the needs of distance learning students by providing appropriate and accessible services and resources or by assisting them in gaining access to other appropriate services and resources in their geographic region

EAPS should encourage students from under-represented groups (e.g., gender, ethnicity, age, disability, marital status, socioeconomic status, academic major, religious affiliation, sexual orientation) to apply and participate in education abroad programs.

EAPS must intentionally foster students' understanding of cross-cultural differences and encourage participants to reflect on these differences at home and abroad.

EAPS must intentionally prepare participants for living and studying in the intended host country.

EAPS staff members must actively work with all interested participants to select an education abroad program suitable to their needs, skills, and eligibility.

EAPS should intentionally seek and promote diversity within education abroad program participants (including under-represented groups), faculty program leaders, and staff members.

Part 8. INSTITUTIONAL AND EXTERNAL RELATIONS

Education Abroad Programs and Services (EAPS) must reach out to relevant individuals, groups, communities, and organizations internal and external to the institution to

- establish, maintain, and promote understanding and effective relations with those that have a significant interest in or potential effect on the students or other constituents served by the programs and services
- garner support and resources for programs and services as defined by the mission statement
- disseminate information about the programs and services
- collaborate, where appropriate, to assist in offering or improving programs and services to meet the needs of students and other constituents and to achieve program and student outcomes
- engage diverse individuals, groups, communities, and organizations to enrich the educational environment and experiences of students and other constituents

EAPS must have procedures and guidelines consistent with institutional policy for

- communicating with the media
- contracting with external organizations for delivery of programs and services
- cultivating, soliciting, and managing gifts
- applying to and managing funds from grants

EAPS staff members should collaborate with

- departments on the home campus (i.e., academic

departments and programs, registrar, academic affairs, financial aid, financial services, student affairs, international student and scholar services, admissions, career advising, clinical health services, counseling services, institutional advancement, disability support services, multicultural centers, residential life)
- consulates of host countries
- home country embassies and consulates abroad
- faculty members at home and abroad who teach or do research in fields related to home institution education abroad opportunities
- administrative staff at the host institution responsible for students from abroad
- external program providers

EAPS staff members should collaborate with third-party program providers as appropriate to sustain existing programs and establish new opportunities to increase the diversity of options for students. Interested individuals (faculty members or other campus personnel) should be encouraged to become involved in education abroad by suggesting possible opportunities, proposing specific programs, or presenting and encouraging discussions about education abroad.

Agreements between EAPS and other institutions to promote education abroad, whether exchange agreements or co-sponsorship of programs, should be supportive of the institution's overall mission and collaborative with regard to academic objectives and standards.

EAPS should ensure that faculty members, administrators, staff members, and students are aware of education abroad opportunities. EAPS should work to ensure that programs are accurately described in advisory and promotional materials and that their purposes, financial implications, and educational objectives are clearly stated.

Part 9. FINANCIAL RESOURCES

Education Abroad Programs and Services (EAPS) must have funding to accomplish the mission and goals. In establishing funding priorities and making significant changes, a comprehensive analysis must be conducted to determine the following elements: unmet needs of the unit, relevant expenditures, external and internal resources, and impact on students and the institution.

EAPS must demonstrate efficient and effective use and responsible stewardship of fiscal resources consistent with institutional protocols.

EAPS should offer education abroad programs to students at affordable costs.

EAPS should consider grant writing and fundraising efforts to increase their financial resources, including funding for

need-based student scholarships.

EAPS should encourage their institution to create institutional education abroad scholarships and grants, both need and merit-based.

Part 10. TECHNOLOGY

Education Abroad Programs and Services (EAPS) must have adequate technology to support the achievement of their mission and goals. The technology and its use must comply with institutional policies and procedures and be evaluated for compliance with relevant codes and laws.

EAPS must use current technology to provide updated information regarding mission, location, staffing, programs, services, and official contacts to students and designated clients.

EAPS must explore the use of technology to enhance delivery of programs and services, especially for students at a distance or external constituencies.

When technology is used to facilitate student learning and development, EAPS must select technology that reflects intended outcomes.

EAPS must
- **maintain policies and procedures that address the security, confidentiality, and backup of data, as well as compliance with privacy laws**
- **have clearly articulated plans in place for protecting confidentiality and security of information when using Internet-based technologies**
- **develop plans for replacing and updating existing hardware and software as well as plans for integrating new technically-based or supported programs, including systems developed internally by the institution, systems available through professional associations, or private vendor-based systems**

Technology, as well as workstations or computer labs maintained by programs and services for student use, must be accessible to all designated clients and must meet established technology standards for delivery to persons with disabilities.

When providing student access to technology, EAPS must
- **have policies on the use of technology that are clear, easy to understand, and available to all students**
- **provide assistance, information, or referral to appropriate support services to those needing help accessing or using technology**
- **provide instruction or training on how to use**

the technology
- inform students on the legal and ethical implications of misuse as it pertains to intellectual property, harassment, privacy, and social networks

Student violations of technology policies must follow established institutional student disciplinary procedures.

Students who experience negative emotional or psychological consequences from the use of technology must be referred to support services provided by the institution.

Part 11. FACILITIES AND EQUIPMENT

Education Abroad Programs and Services (EAPS) must have adequate, accessible, and suitably located facilities and equipment to support the mission and goals. If acquiring capital equipment as defined by the institution, EAPS must take into account expenses related to regular maintenance and life cycle costs. Facilities and equipment must be evaluated on an established cycle, including consideration of sustainability, and be in compliance with codes and laws to provide for access, health, safety, and security.

EAPS staff members must have workspace that is well equipped, adequate in size, and designed to support their work and responsibilities. For conversations requiring privacy, staff members must have access to a private space.

EAPS staff members who share workspace must be able to secure their own work.

The design of the facilities must guarantee the security and privacy of records and ensure the confidentiality of sensitive information.

The location and layout of the facilities must be sensitive to the needs of persons with disabilities as well as the needs of other constituencies.

Office facilities at home and host institutions must be provided to accommodate EAPS goals. Home and host campus facilities must allow for privacy during student advising.

Residential and non-residential student facilities at host institutions must be provided to accommodate program goals, be safe and secure, and be maintained to meet student needs.

Residential and non-residential student facilities should be located conveniently at host institutions.

Host institutions should provide students with services equivalent to the services provided to host institution students (e.g., telephone, computer, Internet) at similar costs.

Part 12. ASSESSMENT AND EVALUATION

Education Abroad Programs and Services (EAPS) must have a clearly articulated assessment plan to document achievement of stated goals and learning outcomes, demonstrate accountability, provide evidence of improvement, and describe resulting changes in programs and services.

EAPS must have adequate fiscal, human, professional development, and technological resources to develop and implement assessment plans.

Assessments must include direct and indirect evaluation and use qualitative and quantitative methodologies and existing evidence, as appropriate, to determine whether and to what degree the stated mission, goals, and intended outcomes are being met as effectively and efficiently as possible. The process must employ sufficient and sound measures to ensure comprehensiveness. Data collected must include responses from students and other constituencies, and aggregated results must be shared with those groups. Results of assessments must be shared appropriately with multiple constituents.

Results of assessments and evaluations must be used to identify needs and interests in revising and improving programs and services, recognizing staff performance, maximizing resource efficiency and effectiveness, improving student achievement of learning and development outcomes, and improving student persistence and success. Changes resulting from the use of assessments and evaluation must be shared with stakeholders.

General Standards revised in 2011;
EAPS content developed in 2005

The Role of Fraternity and Sorority Advising Programs
CAS Standards Contextual Statement

Advising undergraduate fraternity and sorority organizations is a multifaceted function within student affairs. Professionals not only support individual student development but also work to advance organizational and community goals. Individuals selected to advise these organizations must have an understanding and appreciation for the history, culture (ethnic, gender, sexual orientation and religious), and organizational norms of the fraternities and sororities chartered on the campuses they serve (Johnson, Bradley, Bryant, Morton, & Sawyer, 2008). In some cases a much more hands-on approach must be employed by advisers in order to work effectively with these organizations (Kimbrough, 2002). Persons working with Fraternity and Sorority Advising Programs (FSAP) also work with a range of stakeholders outside of the college or university. Stakeholders include students, alumni, national and international fraternity/sorority staff, volunteer governing bodies of these organizations (e.g., the National Pan-Hellenic Council), parents, police and fire officials, and community members, among others (Mamarchev, Sina, & Heida, 2003). A question to be answered by fraternity/sorority professionals is to what extent these organizations augment the institution's educational mission.

Fraternities and sororities are distinctive in their historical and modern day function within higher education and have been a part of the fabric of student life on some campuses for more than two centuries, but the nature of this relationship is debated (Brown, Parks & Phillips, 2005; Gregory, 2003; Kimbrough, 2003; Rudolph, 1990; Whipple & Sullivan, 1998). The primary role for fraternity/sorority professionals is aiding stakeholders in positioning fraternities and sororities as a valued and relevant part of any campus (Bureau, 2007, Winter) and ensuring that these organizations act in accordance with the foundational principles on which they were founded. With this charge in mind, we present the context of supporting fraternity and sorority advising programs using the following model: identify the issues, generate ideas, and act with intention. This model can provide a basis for enacting the CAS Standards for Fraternity and Sorority Advising Programs to support the holistic development of students and positive and enduring principles of fraternities and sororities on college and university campuses.

Issues

Postsecondary organizational culture is certainly complex (Kuh & Whitt, 1988). Any collection of organized individuals can provide challenges for student affairs professionals; however, some argue the long-standing traditions in fraternities and sororities can make this culture particularly difficult to manage (Jelke & Kuh, 2003; Kimbrough, 2003; Whipple &

Sullivan, 1998). Culture is shaped in part by students but is also molded by stakeholders' influence. Therefore, issues are confounded by multiple agents, all of whom can make cultural change difficult. It may be too simplistic to divide the challenges and opportunities affecting the undergraduate fraternity and sorority movement into internal and external and into three different levels of individual, organization, and community, but this delineation may be the most effective way to understand the issues facing those working in FSAP.

Internal issues are those that immediate stakeholders must address to support student needs, organizational functions, and community-wide advancement. These include the challenges associated with alcohol misuse and abuse, hazing, recruitment and intake activities, and membership education practices. This is made more complex when there is a lack of collaboration amongst diverse fraternal organizations in the enactment of community policies and procedures. It can sometimes feel impossible to manage the different responsibilities that come with such dynamic organizations.

There are also opportunities to take an ordinary college experience and transform it into a powerful learning experience. Students learn through involvement in civic engagement, community service, philanthropic activities, leadership development, academic support, and friendships built upon common values. Additionally, some organizations contribute to an individual's personal identity development (Guardia & Evans, 2008). Ultimately these experiences offer students a unique challenge of managing individual and organizational expectations.

There are also issues within the international fraternal movement that impact fraternities and sororities on campuses: the management role of umbrella groups, ensuring that professionals have the skills necessary to support fraternities and sororities (such as those outlined in the *CAS Standards for Fraternity and Sorority Advising Programs* and the *AFA Core Competencies for Excellence in the Profession*) and a sometimes politically charged and potentially disjointed effort to assess the quality of the undergraduate experience.

External issues are those that influence fraternities and sororities and the FSAP in the larger scope of student affairs, higher education, and society. Challenges include institutional funding and staffing of student affairs functions, accountability and assessment in higher education, assessment of student learning outcomes, and the role of student affairs in supporting the mission of higher education (Sandeen & Barr, 2006). Student Affairs must align its activities with the mission of student learning (Schuh &

Upcraft, 2001); therefore, as a part of a larger student affairs division, FSAP must demonstrate the degree to which this important task is accomplished.

Within society, the perceptions of fraternities/sororities vary. Ardent supporters value the role these organizations can play in the development of students. The loudest critics question how fraternity and sorority life adds value to the student experience (Gregory, 2003; Parks, 2008; Kimbrough, 2003).

Ultimately, fraternities and sororities influence and are influenced by discourse on all of these issues. Efforts to solve the problems and accentuate the contributions of FSL require new and innovative ideas.

Ideas

If the consistently problematic issues could be easily solved, then the ills of fraternities and sororities would have been cured years ago. There are certainly individuals committed to improving these organizations and aligning them with the mission of higher education. However, students bring with them a world of ideas and expectations about fraternities and sororities. These perceptions and expectations will be difficult to alter. A list of action steps is beyond the scope of this statement; however, the accomplishment of any new idea must involve collaboration, embrace the never-ending process of change, and apply creativity and innovation.

As professionals support the advancement of their respective fraternity and sorority community, some comfort may be found in the idea that many are invested in the future of fraternities and sororities. Partnerships with fellow staff, faculty, alumni volunteers, national/international/fraternity/sorority professionals and volunteers, parents, and local service agencies and businesses can be forged to support the development of the students and the organizations. The FSAP standards certainly can be a launching point for such collaborations.

Applying new ideas can be tricky. However, innovation is required to make change stick (Koepsell, 2008). Tactics such as grounding policy discussions in a values-perspective, implementing activities that let students and stakeholders imagine reinventing the fraternity and sorority community, and transforming educational efforts to move from a *symptom approach* (for example, alcohol misuse and abuse) to a broader *disease approach* (people drink too much because they have low self-esteem) could be viewed as innovative. Even small tactics of innovation can make a difference in how fraternities and sororities contribute to the campus environment (Bureau, 2007, Summer).

Intentionality

With these issues and ideas in mind, we must be purposeful in our support of the positive development of students in fraternities and sororities. Student development theory is widely applied in student affairs to aid in the explanation of how students function (Hamrick, Evans, & Schuh, 2002; Johnson et al., 2008). Additionally, organizational theory can guide practice (Jelke & Kuh, 2003). When practitioners intentionally apply the theoretical foundations of student affairs, they can be most focused on student development.

In addition to theories, FSAP professionals can be effective in their roles if they understand the models and frameworks that guide good practice. There are many to consider (Gregory, 2003; Marmarchev, Sina, & Heida, 2003). One effective framework is that of assessment. Assessment is one way to be most intentional in how student affairs professionals conduct their work (Sandeen & Barr, 2006). Schuh and Upcraft (2001) provide guidance on how to support assessment in fraternity and sorority communities. If Fraternity and Sorority Advising Program (FSAP) leaders aspire to be more aligned with higher education priorities, it is particularly vital to assess the extent to which student learning occurs in fraternities and sororities (Bureau, 2011).

Conclusion

The *CAS* Standards for Fraternity and Sorority Advising Programs can be a powerful tool to enhance the fraternal experience. This document addresses the issues challenging the movement, offers a framework to apply new ideas, and provides an intentional approach to managing these complex organizations. Challenges exist but the application of the *CAS Standards for Fraternity and Sorority Advising Programs* can support efforts for student development in the context of fraternities and sororities and increase their relevance on college and university campuses.

References, Readings, and Resources

Association of Fraternity/Sorority Advisers (AFA) Website - http://afa1976.org/

Association of Fraternity Advisors (2007). *Core competencies for excellence in the profession*. Retrieved from http://www.fraternityadvisors.org/Business/CoreCompetencies.aspx

Brown, T. L., Parks, G. S., & Phillips, C. M. (2005). *African American fraternities and sororities: The legacy and the vision*. Lexington, KY: The University Press of Kentucky.

Bureau, D. (2007, Summer). Beyond the rhetoric and into the action of the values movement. *Perspectives,* 20-22

Bureau, D. (2007, Winter). Barriers to greatness: Using the concept of relevancy to create urgency for change. *Perspectives*, 8-11.

Bureau, D. (2011, Summer). Why reinvent the wheel? Using the CAS learning Domains and dimensions as a framework for fraternity and sorority advising program learning outcomes. *Perspectives*, 24-26.

Gregory, D. E. (2003). The dilemma facing fraternal organizations at the Millennium. In D. E. Gregory & Associates, *The administration of fraternal organizations on North American campuses*, 1-21. Asheville, N.C.: College Administration Publications.

Guardia, J.R., & Evans, N.J. (2008). The factors influencing the ethnic identity development of Latino fraternity members at a Hispanic Serving Institution. *Journal of College Student Development, 49,* 163-181.

Hamrick, F. A., Evans, N. J., & Schuh, J. H. (2002). *Foundations of student affairs practice.* San Francisco, CA: John Wiley & Sons.

Hayek, J. C., Carini, R. M., O'Day, P. T., & Kuh, G. D. (2002). Triumph or tragedy: Comparing student engagement levels of members of Greek-letter organizations and other students. *Journal of College Student Development, 43,* 643-663.

Jelke, T., & Kuh, G. (2003). High performing fraternities and sororities. In D. E. Gregory & Associates, *The administration of fraternal organizations on North American campuses,* 1-21. Asheville, N.C.: College Administration Publications.

Johnson, R., Bradley, D., Bryant, L., Morton, D., & Sawyer, D. (2008). Advising black Greek-letter organizations: A student development approach. In G.S. Parks (Ed.), *Black Greek-letter organizations in the 21st century: The fight has just begun,* pp. 437-458. Lexington, KY: The University Press of Kentucky.

Kimbrough, W. M. (2002, January 22). Guess who's coming to campus: The growth of Black, Latin and Asian fraternal organizations, NASPA's Net Results. Retrieved from http://www.nalfo.org/index.php/Resources/Resources.html

Kimbrough, W. M. (2003). Black Greek 101: The culture, customs, and challenges of Black fraternities and sororities. Madison, NJ: Fairleigh Dickinson University Press.

Koepsell, M. (2008, May). Utilizing community standards to align accountability, assessment and performance. *Essentials.* Retrieved from http://www.fraternityadvisors.org/Essentials/200805_Community_Standards.aspx

Kuh, G. D., & Whitt, E. J. (1988). The invisible tapestry: Culture in American colleges and universities. *ASHE-ERIC Higher Education Report Series,* No. 1. Washington, DC: Association for the Study of Higher Education.

Mamarchev, H. L., Sina, J. A., & Heida, D. E. (2003). Creating and managing a campus oversight plan: Do they work? What are the alternatives? In D. E. Gregory & Associates, *The administration of fraternal organizations on North American campuses,* 1-21. Asheville, N.C.: College Administration Publications.

Parks, G. S. (2008). *Black Greek-letter organizations in the 21st century: The fight has just begun.* Lexington, KY: The University Press of Kentucky.

Rudolph, F. (1990). *The American college and university* (2nd ed.). Athens, GA. The University of Georgia Press.

Sandeen, A., & Barr, M. J. (2006). *Critical issues for student affairs: Challenges and opportunities.* San Francisco, CA: Jossey-Bass.

Schuh, J. H., & Upcraft, M. L. (2001). *Assessment practice in student affairs: An applications manual.* San Francisco, CA: Jossey-Bass.

Whipple, E. G., & Sullivan, E. G. (1998). Greek-letter organizations: A community of learners? In E. G. Whipple (Ed.), *New challenges for Greek-letter organizations: Transforming fraternities and sororities into learning communities.* San Francisco, CA: Jossey-Bass.

Contextual Statement Contributors

Dan Bureau, Indiana University, AFA
(primary contributor)
Tanner Marcantel, Vanderbilt University
Monica Miranda Smalls, University of Rochester
Emily Perlow, Worcester Polytechnic Institute
Jeremiah Shinn, Indiana University
AFA Executive Board and Staff

Fraternity and Sorority Advising Programs
CAS Standards and Guidelines

Part 1. MISSION

The mission of the Fraternity and Sorority Advising Programs (FSAP) is to promote the learning and development of students who affiliate with fraternities and sororities. FSAP must support the fraternity and sorority community in efforts to be a relevant and contributing part of the institution.

To accomplish its mission, FSAP must
- promote the intellectual, physical, emotional, social, spiritual, ethical, civic, and career development of members
- provide education and experience in interpersonal relationships, leadership, group dynamics, and organization development
- promote member involvement in co-curricular activities
- promote sponsorship of and participation in community service, service-learning, and philanthropic projects
- promote an appreciation for differences and development of cross-cultural competencies
- recognize and encourage learning experiences that occur as a result of a diverse fraternity and sorority community
- advocate academic success of all members and for opportunities through which students can integrate in-class and out-of-class learning
- support members' efforts to align actions with espoused organizational mission and values
- collaborate with stakeholders who support the mission, including undergraduate and graduate/alumni members, faculty and other advisors, and organizational staff and/or volunteers,

FSAP must develop, disseminate, implement, and regularly review their missions. The mission must be consistent with the mission of the institution and with professional standards. The mission must be appropriate for the institution's student populations and community settings. Mission statements must reference student learning and development.

Part 2. PROGRAM

The formal education of students, consisting of the curriculum and the co-curriculum, must promote student learning and development outcomes that are purposeful, contribute to students' realization of their potential, and prepare students for satisfying and productive lives.

Fraternity and Sorority Advising Programs (FSAP) must collaborate with colleagues and departments across the institution to promote student learning and development, persistence, and success.

Consistent with the institutional mission, FSAP must identify relevant and desirable student learning and development outcomes from among the six domains and related dimensions:

Domain: knowledge acquisition, integration, construction, and application

- Dimensions: understanding knowledge from a range of disciplines; connecting knowledge to other knowledge, ideas, and experiences; constructing knowledge; and relating knowledge to daily life

Domain: cognitive complexity

- Dimensions: critical thinking, reflective thinking, effective reasoning, and creativity

Domain: intrapersonal development

- Dimensions: realistic self-appraisal, self-understanding, and self-respect; identity development; commitment to ethics and integrity; and spiritual awareness

Domain: interpersonal competence

- Dimensions: meaningful relationships, interdependence, collaboration, and effective leadership.

Domain: humanitarianism and civic engagement

- Dimensions: understanding and appreciation of cultural and human differences, social responsibility, global perspective, and sense of civic responsibility

Domain: practical competence

- Dimensions: pursuing goals, communicating effectively, technical competence, managing personal affairs, managing career development, demonstrating professionalism, maintaining health and wellness, and living a purposeful and satisfying life

[LD Outcomes: See *The Council for the Advancement of Standards Learning and Developmental Outcomes* statement for examples of outcomes related to these domains and dimensions.]

FSAP must

- assess relevant and desirable student learning and development
- provide evidence of impact on outcomes
- articulate contributions to or support of student learning and development in the domains not specifically assessed
- articulate contributions to or support of student persistence and success
- use evidence gathered through this process to create strategies for improvement of programs and services

FSAP must be

- intentionally designed
- guided by theories and knowledge of learning and development
- integrated into the life of the institution
- reflective of developmental and demographic profiles of the student population
- responsive to needs of individuals, populations with distinct needs, and relevant constituencies
- delivered using multiple formats, strategies, and contexts

Where institutions provide distance education, FSAP must assist distance learners to achieve their educational goals by providing access to information about programs and services, to staff members who can address questions and concerns, and to counseling, advising, or other forms of assistance.

To support a positive experience that emphasizes the learning and development of members, the FSAP must include educational programming, advising services, and social and recreational programming. FSAP focus on education must

- enhance new-member and member knowledge, understanding, and competencies essential for academic success, personal and moral development, organizational development, and the practice of leadership
- complement the academic mission of the institution
- complement the efforts of educational programs implemented by international, national, and/or regional organizations when applicable
- address aspects of the fraternity and sorority community that are currently or historically problematic, including applicable laws and institutional policies, housing safety, hazing, alcohol and other drug abuse, sexual harassment, sexual assault, racism, intolerance based on religion or sexual orientation, and other practices and attitudes

that diminish human dignity or physical and social security

FSAP should support the development of academic skills and the creation of environments that encourage academic success. FSAP should facilitate the application of knowledge and skills through experiential opportunities provided by the member's chapter and the overall fraternity and sorority community.

Leadership experiences should prepare members to effectively understand and support group processes, particularly the relevant aspects of self-governance, change management, problem solving, dynamics of power and influence, responsibility, accountability, and integrity. Leadership experiences also should enable members to gain knowledge about assessing leadership and management skills.

In their focus on individual chapters, FSAP must

- monitor academic performance of chapter members individually and collectively and recommending programs for scholastic improvement
- meet with chapter leaders to aid in the development of member and chapter goals
- assist members to understand their responsibilities to the group and to the overall community, including emphasis on demonstrating espoused organizational values
- attend new member and chapter meetings as appropriate
- evaluate chapter development and recommend programs for improvement
- provide assistance and advice in planning chapter programs (e.g., new member education, intake activities)
- encourage chapter members' attendance at their organization's leadership conferences and conventions
- support the development of standards and expectations for members
- complement efforts of educational programs offered by international, national, and/or regional organizations when applicable
- attend to the specific needs of chapters without international, national, or regional affiliation, oversight, and support

FSAP focus on the fraternity and sorority community and its immediate stakeholders (e.g., chapter advisors, house corporation members, chapter presidents, institutional administrators, faculty advisors) must include

- advising governing councils and organizations
- advising financial processes
- coordinating life safety, facility management,

and risk management programs in conjunction with local agencies

- facilitating or providing resources, including potential presenters of campus or national renown to conduct workshops, programs, retreats, and seminars on relevant topics (e.g., multicultural competence, leadership development, recruitment and intake, risk management)
- monitoring of membership statistics and academic retention by chapter and community (fraternity/sorority and non-fraternity/sorority) for purposes of improving academic support and recommending intervention strategies
- gathering and disseminating information via meetings, websites, newsletters, social media venues, and/or information bulletins to the various entities involved in fraternity and sorority life (e.g., campus involvement and service opportunities)
- providing assistance and advice in planning and assessing fraternity and sorority community programs (e.g., recruitment activities, stepshows, philanthropies, and alumni events)
- organizing and facilitating leadership programs/retreats/workshops
- connecting members to leadership opportunities across campus, in the local community, and within their national or international organizations
- publishing or sharing documents that focus on current events, leadership opportunities, trends, and other information regarding fraternity and sorority life
- providing for recording and archiving information about the fraternity and sorority community and encouraging chapter leaders to do the same for their organizations

FSAP focus on other stakeholders must include

- collaborating with national or international organizations when applicable and appropriate
- connecting faculty, staff, and administrators to fraternity and sorority members
- establishing and coordinating communication with local alumni volunteers
- providing resources for parents/guardians of members
- helping alumni and national and international volunteers support members' meeting of standards
- being available as an information resource for members, alumni, faculty, and administrators

In their focus on social and recreational programming, FSAP must enhance the members' knowledge, understanding, and skills necessary to promote social responsibility and develop a safe and healthy social culture within the fraternity and sorority community.

FSAP must develop appropriate processes for recognition of organizational status or registration by the institution.

Campus chapters should participate in the same student organization registration and recognition process as other campus student groups.

Because fraternities and sororities often have unique relationships with their institutions and operate under dual-authority structures, institutions may assign responsibility for fraternities and sororities to specific offices, departments, or personnel. In such cases, it may be important to articulate how fraternities and sororities are to contribute to the institution and vice versa. This may require a documented relationship statement. When applicable, the relationship statement should be formalized, signed, and disseminated.

The relationship between the institution and its chapters should be defined based upon the unique circumstances for the campus. Areas for consideration may include

- a description of each chapter's responsibility to recognize the shared expectations of and contributions to a productive fraternity/sorority community
- historical relationships
- educational role of fraternities and sororities
- conditions, privileges, and responsibilities of affiliation
- housing and other facilities
- support and program orientation
- governance and authority (e.g., national and international organization affiliation and expansion, self-governance)
- reference to comprehensive policy documents
- expectations of the institution and the fraternity and sorority community
- accountability to other student governing bodies
- support for organization growth

FSAP expectations of fraternities/sororities should not infringe upon the legal rights of student organizations.

FSAP at campuses where chapters exist without institutional recognition should mitigate any negative influence of these chapters on the campus community and inform stakeholders about the institution's position on these groups.

Part 3. ORGANIZATION AND LEADERSHIP

To achieve student and program outcomes, Fraternity and Sorority Advising Programs (FSAP) must be structured purposefully and organized effectively.

FSAP must have

- clearly stated goals
- current and accessible policies and procedures
- written performance expectations for employees
- functional work flow graphics or organizational charts demonstrating clear channels of authority

Leaders with organizational authority for the programs and services must provide strategic planning, supervision, and management; advance the organization; and maintain integrity through the following functions:

Strategic Planning

- articulate a vision and mission that drive short- and long-term planning
- set goals and objectives based on the needs of the population served and desired student learning or development and program outcomes
- facilitate continuous development, implementation, and assessment of goal attainment congruent with institutional mission and strategic plans
- promote environments that provide meaningful opportunities for student learning, development, and engagement
- develop and continuously improve programs and services in response to the changing needs of students served and evolving institutional priorities
- intentionally include diverse perspectives to inform decision making

Supervising

- manage human resource processes including recruitment, selection, development, supervision, performance planning, evaluation, recognition, and reward
- influence others to contribute to the effectiveness and success of the unit
- empower professional, support, and student staff to accept leadership opportunities
- offer appropriate feedback to colleagues and students on skills needed to become more effective leaders
- encourage and support professional development, collaboration with colleagues and departments across the institution, and scholarly contribution to the profession

Managing

- identify and address individual, organizational, and environmental conditions that foster or inhibit mission achievement
- plan, allocate, and monitor the use of fiscal, physical, human, intellectual, and technological resources
- use current and valid evidence to inform decisions
- incorporate sustainability practices in the management and design of programs, services, and facilities
- understand appropriate technologies and integrate them into programs and services
- be knowledgeable about codes and laws relevant to programs and services and ensure that staff members understand their responsibilities through appropriate training
- assess potential risks and take action to mitigate them

Advancing the Organization

- communicate effectively in writing, speaking, and electronic venues
- advocate for programs and services
- advocate for representation in strategic planning initiatives at appropriate divisional and institutional levels
- initiate collaborative interactions with internal and external stakeholders who have legitimate concerns about and interests in the functional area
- facilitate processes to reach consensus where wide support is needed
- inform other areas within the institution about issues affecting practice

Maintaining Integrity

- model ethical behavior and institutional citizenship
- share data used to inform key decisions in transparent and accessible ways
- monitor media used for distributing information about programs and services to ensure the content is current, accurate, appropriately referenced, and accessible

FSAP must assist members and chapters in understanding their rights and responsibilities as part of the institution.

This may include interpreting institutional policies, administering a conduct system that addresses inappropriate behavior in a manner that safeguards procedural fairness and is consistent with institutional conduct policies, and providing outreach programming to familiarize other departments and community agencies with fraternity and sorority life.

Staff members must avoid situations or actions that may pose conflicts of interest or create the appearance of preferential treatment.

Part 4. HUMAN RESOURCES

Fraternity and Sorority Advising Programs (FSAP) must be staffed adequately by individuals qualified to accomplish mission and goals.

Within institutional guidelines, FSAP must
- establish procedures for staff recruitment and selection, training, performance planning, and evaluation
- set expectations for supervision and performance
- assess the performance of employees individually and as a team
- provide access to continuing and advanced education and appropriate professional development opportunities to improve the leadership ability, competence, and skills of all employees.

FSAP must maintain position descriptions for all staff members.

To create a diverse staff, FSAP must institute recruitment and hiring strategies that encourage individuals from under-represented populations to apply for positions.

FSAP must develop promotion practices that are fair, inclusive, proactive, and non-discriminatory.

To further the recruitment and retention of staff, FSAP must consider work life initiatives, such as compressed work schedules, flextime, job sharing, remote work, or telework.

FSAP professional staff members must hold an earned graduate or professional degree in a field relevant to the position they hold or must possess an appropriate combination of educational credentials and related work experience.

Appropriate preparatory graduate level coursework may include organizational behavior and development, oral and written communication, research and evaluation, ethics, appraisal of educational practices, group dynamics, budgeting, counseling techniques, leadership development, learning and human development theories, higher education administration, performance appraisal and supervision, application of information technology, legal issues in higher education, and student affairs.

Effective supervision is critical to the success of the program, with knowledge often required in the areas of housing, dining, accounting, safety and risk management, student conduct, alumni relations, and programming. In addition, professional staff members should have experience in the development and implementation of educational programs for members. FSAP staff should be qualified to work with various internal and external agencies in formulating goals and directions for the chapters and community that are consistent with institutional policies.

FSAP professional staff members must engage in continuing professional development activities to keep abreast of the research, theories, legislation, policies, and developments that affect their programs and services.

FSAP must have technical and support staff members adequate to accomplish their mission. All members of the staff must be technologically proficient and qualified to perform their job functions, be knowledgeable about ethical and legal uses of technology, and have access to training and resources to support the performance of their assigned responsibilities.

Degree- or credential-seeking interns or graduate assistants must be qualified by enrollment in an appropriate field of study and by relevant experience. These individuals must be trained and supervised adequately by professional staff members holding educational credentials and related work experience appropriate for supervision. Supervisors must be cognizant of the roles of interns and graduate assistants as both student and employee and closely adhere to all parameters of their job descriptions, work hours, and schedules. Supervisors and the interns or graduate assistants must agree to compensatory time or other appropriate compensation if circumstances necessitate additional hours.

FSAP should utilize paraprofessionals such as graduate assistants and graduate student interns to expand staff capabilities and provide valuable experience for individuals who have an interest in the field of fraternity and sorority advising.

Student employees and volunteers must be carefully selected, trained, supervised, and evaluated. They must be educated on how and when to refer those in need of additional assistance to qualified staff members and must have access to a supervisor for assistance in making these judgments. Student employees and volunteers must be provided clear job descriptions, pre-service training based on assessed needs, and continuing development.

All FSAP staff members, including student employees and volunteers, must receive specific training on institutional policies pertaining to functions or activities they support and to privacy and confidentiality policies and laws regarding access to student records and other sensitive institutional information.

All FSAP staff members must receive training on policies and procedures related to the use of technology to store or access student records and institutional data.

FSAP must ensure that staff members are

knowledgeable about and trained in emergency procedures, crisis response, and prevention efforts. Prevention efforts must address identification of threatening conduct or behavior of students, faculty and staff members, and others and must incorporate a system for responding and reporting.

FSAP must ensure that staff members are knowledgeable of and trained in safety and emergency procedures for securing and vacating facilities.

The level of FSAP staffing services must be established and reviewed regularly with regard to demands, enrollment, diversity of services offered, institutional resources, and other services available on the campus and in the local community.

Part 5. ETHICS

Fraternity and Sorority Advising Programs (FSAP) must review relevant professional ethical standards and must adopt or develop and implement appropriate statements of ethical practice.

FSAP must adopt a statement of ethics intended to
- treat fairly prospective students who wish to affiliate with a fraternity/sorority
- eliminate illegal discrimination associated with the selection of members
- uphold applicable standards of conduct expressed by the institution and by the respective national or international organization

FSAP must publish and adhere to statements of ethical practice and ensure their periodic review by relevant constituencies.

FSAP must orient new staff members to relevant ethical standards and statements of ethical practice and related institutional policies.

Statements of ethical standards must specify that staff members respect privacy and maintain confidentiality in all communications and records to the extent that such communications and records are protected under relevant privacy laws.

Statements of ethical standards must specify limits on disclosure of information contained in students' educational records as well as requirements to disclose to appropriate authorities.

Statements of ethical standards must address personal and economic conflicts of interest, or appearance thereof, by staff members in the performance of their work.

Statements of ethical standards must reflect the responsibility of staff members to be fair, objective,

and impartial in their interactions with others.

Statements of ethical standards must reference management of institutional funds.

Statements of ethical standards must reference appropriate behavior regarding research and assessment with human participants, confidentiality of research and assessment data, and students' rights and responsibilities.

Statements of ethical standards must include the expectation that FSAP staff members confront and hold accountable other staff members who exhibit unethical behavior.

Statements of ethical standards must address issues surrounding scholarly integrity.

As appropriate, FSAP staff members must inform users of programs and services of ethical obligations and limitations emanating from codes and laws or from licensure requirements.

FSAP staff members must recognize and avoid conflicts of interest that could adversely influence their judgment or objectivity and, when unavoidable, recuse themselves from the situation.

FSAP staff members must perform their duties within the limits of their position, training, expertise, and competence.

When these limits are exceeded, individuals in need of further assistance must be referred to persons possessing appropriate qualifications.

Promotional and descriptive information must be accurate and free of deception.

FSAP must adhere to institutional policies regarding ethical and legal use of software and technology.

FSAP staff members should examine the distinct ethical challenges that come with serving the fraternity and sorority community, determine and implement appropriate approaches for addressing such challenges, and model relevant ethical standards in their everyday practice.

Part 6. LAW, POLICY, AND GOVERNANCE

Fraternity and Sorority Advising Programs (FSAP) must be in compliance with laws, regulations, and policies that relate to their respective responsibilities and that pose legal obligations, limitations, risks, and liabilities for the institution as a whole. Examples include constitutional, statutory, regulatory, and case law; relevant law and orders emanating from codes and laws; and the institution's policies.

FSAP must inform staff members, appropriate officials, and users of programs and services about existing and changing legal obligations, risks and liabilities, and limitations.

FSAP must have written policies on all relevant operations, transactions, or tasks that have legal implications.

FSAP should involve stakeholders in the administration of policies specific to the fraternity and sorority community.

FSAP may assist chapters and house corporations to identify appropriate levels of insurance.

Contracts with outside vendors must include adherence to ethical standards and institutional policies.

FSAP must regularly review policies. The revision and creation of policies must be informed by best practices, available evidence, and policy issues in higher education.

FSAP staff members must use reasonable and informed practices to limit the liability exposure of the institution and its officers, employees, and agents. FSAP staff members must be informed about institutional policies regarding risk management, personal liability, and related insurance coverage options and must be referred to external sources if the institution does not provide coverage.

The institution must provide access to legal advice for staff members as needed to carry out assigned responsibilities.

FSAP must have procedures and guidelines consistent with institutional policy for responding to threats, emergencies, and crisis situations. Systems and procedures must be in place to disseminate timely and accurate information to students, other members of the institutional community, and appropriate external organizations during emergency situations.

FSAP staff members must neither participate in nor condone any form of harassment or activity that demeans persons or creates an intimidating, hostile, or offensive environment.

FSAP must obtain permission to use copyrighted materials and instruments. FSAP must purchase the materials and instruments from legally compliant sources or seek alternative permission from the publisher or owner. References to copyrighted materials and instruments must include appropriate citations.

FSAP staff members must be knowledgeable about internal and external governance systems that affect programs and services.

FSAP must provide information on laws pertinent to the operation of chapters to fraternity and sorority

community stakeholders.

FSAP must ensure chapters without international, national, or regional affiliation understand applicable laws and policies.

FSAP must attend to the specific legal and policy issues of chapters without international, national, or regional affiliation, oversight, and support.

FSAP at campuses where chapters exist without institutional recognition should mitigate any negative influence of these chapters on the campus community and inform stakeholders about the institution's position on these groups.

Houses or common rooms that are owned, rented, or otherwise assigned to fraternities and sororities for their use must be managed in accordance with all applicable regulatory and statutory requirements of the host institution, international/national organization, and governmental authorities.

FSAP should establish a process for monitoring public discussions and informal communications, including social media and mobile networks.

Issues such as fire safety, noise control, parking, trash removal, security, facility and property maintenance, and life safety and health code compliance are of particular importance and should be monitored regularly.

FSAP staff members may be the principal representative of the administration to the fraternity and sorority community as well as the principal advocate for the fraternity and sorority community within the administration.

Processes used by the FSAP must emphasize positive working relationships with members and stakeholders.

These relationships may be fostered through the advising and administrative processes used by the FSAP.

The administrative organization of FSAP should reflect the mission and size of the institution. FSAP should be a fully integrated institutional component and organized, resourced, and administered in a manner that permits its stated mission to be fulfilled. The administrative leader of the program should be responsible to the senior student affairs officer or designee.

Part 7. DIVERSITY, EQUITY, AND ACCESS

Within the context of each institution's unique mission and in accordance with institutional polices and all applicable codes and laws, Fraternity and Sorority Advising Programs (FSAP) must create and maintain educational and work environments that are

- **welcoming, accessible, and inclusive to persons of diverse backgrounds**
- **equitable and non-discriminatory**

- **free from harassment**

FSAP must not discriminate on the basis of ability; age; cultural identity; ethnicity; family educational history (e.g., first generation to attend college); gender identity and expression; nationality; political affiliation; race; religious affiliation; sex; sexual orientation; economic, marital, social, or veteran status; or any other basis included in institutional policies and codes and laws.

FSAP must

- **advocate for greater sensitivity to multicultural and social justice concerns by the institution and its personnel**
- **modify or remove policies, practices, facilities, structures, systems, and technologies that limit access, discriminate, or produce inequities**
- **include diversity, equity, and access initiatives within their strategic plans**
- **foster communication that deepens understanding of identity, culture, self-expression, and heritage**
- **promote respect about commonalities and differences among people within their historical and cultural contexts**
- **address the characteristics and needs of a diverse population when establishing and implementing culturally relevant and inclusive programs, services, policies, procedures, and practices**
- **provide staff members with access to multicultural training and hold staff members accountable for integrating the training into their work**
- **respond to the needs of all students and other populations served when establishing hours of operation and developing methods of delivering programs, services, and resources**
- **ensure physical, program, and resource access for persons with disabilities**
- **recognize the needs of distance learning students by providing appropriate and accessible services and resources or by assisting them in gaining access to other appropriate services and resources in their geographic region**

FSAP should cultivate a range of opportunities for students to gain membership into fraternities and sororities that have diverse purposes, including those that are cultural, social, and professional in nature.

FSAP must address the characteristics and needs of a diverse campus population when establishing and implementing policies and procedures.

FSAP must enhance members' knowledge,

understanding, skills, and responsibilities associated with being a member of a pluralistic and global society. The program must provide educational efforts that develop appreciation of differences and cross-cultural competencies.

The FSAP should work with members to ensure recruitment and intake processes are accessible to all who choose to take part.

FSAP staff should maintain current knowledge of student demographics and characteristics on their campus and higher education in general.

FSAP should work with members to promote fraternity and sorority membership as a viable involvement option for all student populations. The FSAP should not interfere with the fraternity/sorority's right to select membership based on Title IX criteria and its status as a private organization.

Part 8. INSTITUTIONAL AND EXTERNAL RELATIONS

Fraternity and Sorority Advising Programs (FSAP) must reach out to relevant individuals, groups, communities, and organizations internal and external to the institution to

- **establish, maintain, and promote understanding and effective relations with those that have a significant interest in or potential effect on the students or other constituents served by the programs and services**
- **garner support and resources for programs and services as defined by the mission statement**
- **disseminate information about the programs and services**
- **collaborate, where appropriate, to assist in offering or improving programs and services to meet the needs of students and other constituents and to achieve program and student outcomes**
- **engage diverse individuals, groups, communities, and organizations to enrich the educational environment and experiences of students and other constituents**

FSAP must have procedures and guidelines consistent with institutional policy for

- **communicating with the media**
- **contracting with external organizations for delivery of programs and services**
- **cultivating, soliciting, and managing gifts**
- **applying to and managing funds from grants**

A team approach in working with members in the local chapters should be a common goal of the FSAP when it collaborates with advisors, alumni, house corporations, national or international representatives, and other community stakeholders.

Because alumni can serve as valuable resources, program staff members should encourage and enlist a productive level of alumni involvement and assist with information exchange and collaborative programming efforts.

FSAP should engage faculty and staff members to serve as chapter advisors and serve on committees that focus on institutional issues and policies affecting the fraternity and sorority community.

The FSAP should establish relationships with local nonprofit organizations that provide opportunities for service and philanthropic pursuits and involvement. Programs focused on philanthropic activities and community service/volunteer involvement, that have been traditional components of fraternity and sorority programs, should be developed, maintained, and encouraged. The FSAP should connect fraternity and sorority chapters to opportunities to serve their community.

Part 9. FINANCIAL RESOURCES

Fraternity and Sorority Advising Programs (FSAP) must have funding to accomplish the mission and goals. In establishing funding priorities and making significant changes, a comprehensive analysis must be conducted to determine the following elements: unmet needs of the unit, relevant expenditures, external and internal resources, and impact on students and the institution.

FSAP must demonstrate efficient and effective use and responsible stewardship of fiscal resources consistent with institutional protocols.

In some cases, FSAP may supplement institutional funding from sources such as development, fundraising, grants, and fees for services.

Part 10. TECHNOLOGY

Fraternity and Sorority Advising Programs (FSAP) must have adequate technology to support the achievement of their mission and goals. The technology and its use must comply with institutional policies and procedures and be evaluated for compliance with relevant codes and laws.

FSAP must use current technology to provide updated information regarding mission, location, staffing, programs, services, and official contacts to students and designated clients.

FSAP must explore the use of technology to enhance delivery of programs and services, especially for students at a distance or external constituencies.

When technology is used to facilitate student learning and development, FSAP must select technology that reflects intended outcomes.

FSAP must
- **maintain policies and procedures that address the security, confidentiality, and backup of data, as well as compliance with privacy laws**
- **have clearly articulated plans in place for protecting confidentiality and security of information when using Internet-based technologies**
- **develop plans for replacing and updating existing hardware and software as well as plans for integrating new technically-based or supported programs, including systems developed internally by the institution, systems available through professional associations, or private vendor-based systems**

Technology, as well as workstations or computer labs maintained by programs and services for student use, must be accessible to all designated clients and must meet established technology standards for delivery to persons with disabilities.

When providing student access to technology, FSAP must
- **have policies on the use of technology that are clear, easy to understand, and available to all students**
- **provide assistance, information, or referral to appropriate support services to those needing help accessing or using technology**
- **provide instruction or training on how to use the technology**
- **inform students on the legal and ethical implications of misuse as it pertains to intellectual property, harassment, privacy, and social networks**

Student violations of technology policies must follow established institutional student disciplinary procedures.

Students who experience negative emotional or psychological consequences from the use of technology must be referred to support services provided by the institution.

FSAP should centralize fraternity and sorority community resources with one website providing links to the websites of each recognized chapter and council along with other relevant sites.

FSAP should provide access to policies, procedures, standards, and relevant fraternity and sorority community documents. These documents provide insight into the operations and performance of the community and should be accessible to stakeholders.

Part 11. FACILITIES AND EQUIPMENT

Fraternity and Sorority Advising Programs (FSAP) must have adequate, accessible, and suitably located facilities and equipment to support the mission and goals. If acquiring capital equipment as defined by the institution, FSAP must take into account expenses related to regular maintenance and life cycle costs. Facilities and equipment must be evaluated on an established cycle, including consideration of sustainability, and be in compliance with codes and laws to provide for access, health, safety, and security.

Chapters that maintain facilities should have those living units assessed annually including life safety, sanitation, and quality of life inspections of all housing facilities, kitchens, building electrical systems, heating systems, and fire safety equipment.

FSAP staff members must have workspace that is well equipped, adequate in size, and designed to support their work and responsibilities. For conversations requiring privacy, staff members must have access to a private space.

FSAP staff members who share workspace must be able to secure their own work.

The design of the facilities must guarantee the security and privacy of records and ensure the confidentiality of sensitive information.

The location and layout of the facilities must be sensitive to the needs of persons with disabilities as well as the needs of other constituencies.

FSAP space should be integrated with other institutional student services.

Part 12. ASSESSMENT AND EVALUATION

Fraternity and Sorority Advising Programs (FSAP) must have a clearly articulated assessment plan to document achievement of stated goals and learning outcomes, demonstrate accountability, provide evidence of improvement, and describe resulting changes in programs and services.

Plans should complement assessment efforts initiated by organizations including the Association of Fraternity/Sorority Advisors (AFA) and umbrella groups.

FSAP must have adequate fiscal, human, professional development, and technological resources to develop and implement assessment plans.

Assessments must include direct and indirect evaluation and use qualitative and quantitative methodologies and existing evidence, as appropriate, to determine whether and to what degree the stated mission, goals, and intended outcomes are being met as effectively and efficiently as possible. The process must employ sufficient and sound measures to ensure comprehensiveness. Data collected must include responses from students and other constituencies, and aggregated results must be shared with those groups. Results of assessments must be shared appropriately with multiple constituents.

Results of assessments and evaluations must be used to identify needs and interests in revising and improving programs and services, recognizing staff performance, maximizing resource efficiency and effectiveness, improving student achievement of learning and development outcomes, and improving student persistence and success. Changes resulting from the use of assessments and evaluation must be shared with stakeholders.

Assessment should be conducted to determine the strength of leadership, the fulfillment of the community's purposes and priorities, academic performance (including chapter performance and contributions to retention), the effectiveness of self-governance procedures, individual chapter congruence with institutional and system purposes, the effectiveness of programs, and the availability and stability of resources.

Periodic assessment and evaluation of chapter and governing council needs, goals, and objectives should include chapter vitality and evaluation of each chapter's leadership, self-sufficiency, accountability to purpose, and productive activities.

An institutionally developed annual awards, recognition, or local accreditation program should be used to gauge chapter progress toward community goals.

When research is conducted, topics could include
- how student development is influenced by fraternity or sorority membership
- influence of participation on members' values, ethics, and actions
- skill development among members at various stages of membership
- the effect of participation in fraternities and sororities on members' matriculation, retention, and academic performance and progression
- involvement and influence of alumni advisors
- organizational and community development over time

Results of research and assessment initiatives should be shared with constituents and stakeholders (e.g., students, advisors, alumni, parents, national and international organizations, faculty, staff, and administrators).

General Standards revised in 2011;
FSAP content developed/revised in 1986, 1996, & 2012

The Role of Graduate and Professional Student Programs and Services
CAS Standards Contextual Statement

In light of the national conversation that global competitiveness of the United States and the capacity for innovation hinges on a strong system of graduate education (CGS & ETS, 2010), it is incumbent upon colleges and universities to increase graduate degree attainment – supporting, educating, and graduating more highly-skilled potential employees. Since the mid-1990s the higher education community recognized the unique needs, challenges and experiences of graduate and professional students – a growing and often underserved population. Today, institutions are conducting research and addressing the academic, personal, and professional needs and interests of graduate and professional students in a variety of ways: through a centralized graduate office; through offices reporting to academic departments, schools or colleges; or in collaboration with other institutional units. The variations in programs and services, organizational structures, and backgrounds of the professional administrators, coupled with the differences in the student populations served (e.g., degrees pursued, academic disciplines, distance programs, international and global enrollees), present unique challenges in development of standards and guidelines for graduate and professional student programs and services and underscores the need for these standards.

Since the 1990s, several notable initiatives occurred to address the challenges of graduate and professional students (Brandes, 2007). They include publications such as: the report, "Reshaping the Education of Scientists and Engineers" (Committee on Science, Engineering, and Public Policy, 1995), recommending a more student-centered model of education with attention on diversity and student professional development; and the first major monograph to address services for graduate and professional students, *Student Services for the Changing Graduate Student Population* (Logan & Isaac, 1995). A second monograph, *Supporting Graduate and Professional Students: The Role of Student Affairs* (Guentzel & Elkins Nesheim, 2006) was published in 2006. Universities such as Harvard, Cornell, and Yale took the lead in the latter half of the 1990s by establishing graduate student centers and appointing student affairs professionals (Brandes, 2007). These new professionals in graduate student affairs provided the vision and impetus for the formation in 1999 of a professional network within the National Association of Student Personnel Administrators (NASPA), which continues today as the Administrators in Graduate and Professional Student Services (AGAPSS). Several years later, the American College Personnel Association (ACPA) established its Commission for Graduate and Professional School Educators (Brandes, 2007), continuing today as the Commission for Graduate & Professional Student Affairs.

Among the emerging topics appearing in research studies and publications and at conferences and other gatherings of faculty and higher education administrators are the following:

- recruitment and retention of graduate and professional students, e.g., persistence to degree completion, especially among doctoral students; attrition rates; funding and support for STEM graduate studies
- academic job shortages and decline in students pursuing academic careers; students' socialization to a profession and how to best structure and deliver programs, services, and experience that involve and engage students and lead to their professional development
- attitudes that institutions only need to attend to the basic academic experience of graduate and professional students; that graduate students do not require the student services provided to undergraduates or places and opportunities for community building, involvement, and social integration
- increased recruitment, enrollment, and services for international students (CGS, 2011; Roberts, 2012)
- the increasingly heterogeneous graduate and professional student population, e.g., more diverse, nontraditional, commuting, part-time, full-time employed students; students with distinct needs pursuing different degrees, i.e., masters, doctoral, professional degrees; groups of students feeling marginalized, e.g., international students (Le, 2010), how to address the distinct needs of an increasingly more diverse, multicultural, and nontraditional graduate and professional student population enrolled in a growing number of masters, doctoral, professional, and certificate programs
- lack of research on developmental needs of graduate students and application of developmental theories and recommended practices to this population
- retention issues including lack of funding, advisor-advisee relationship, departmental issues, peer relationships
- the identification of needs and services provided for distance-education students,
- failure to address mental health, emotional, or stress-related problems that are common among graduate and professional students
- the focus of many divisions of student affairs on the undergraduate experience, resulting in lack of resources to address needs of graduate students
- the differences and variety of organizational and reporting structures, services offered, and locations of offices responsible for provision of services to graduate and professional students

- the varied knowledge, backgrounds, and experiences of professionals responsible for providing services and support to graduate and professional students
- how to build the professional communities and standards of practice for individuals with primary responsibility for student support services for graduate and professional students

The growing awareness of the unique needs of graduate and professional students led the authors of ACPA's and NASPA's seminal publication, *Learning Reconsidered: A Campus-Wide Focus on the Student Experience* (2004) to recommend that "Faculty members, student affairs professionals, academic administrators, and representative graduate students should work together to define strategies and resources that will support the comprehensive, holistic learning of graduate students" (p. 29). Other studies and findings, most notably Elkins Nesheim et al., 2007), also suggest that programs for graduate students are often most successful when delivered through partnerships between student affairs and academic affairs professionals.

In order to develop support at their institutions for a comprehensive and holistic approach to graduate student learning and development, members of NASPA's and ACPA's graduate and professional student services communities began discussions about the need for standards and practices to guide and support the development, assessment, and improvement of programs and services. Although CAS had developed separate standards for many of the programs and services that graduate and professional student services administer, e.g., admissions, advising, career services, orientation, etc., trying to apply these multiple standards to graduate and professional student services seemed daunting and difficult. The existing standards tended toward the undergraduate student services; did not take into account the wide-ranging roles and organizational structures of graduate and professional student services or the relationship to academic disciplines; and did not address the varied and specialized needs of graduate and professional students and their experiences.

In April 2007 CAS approved formation of a committee to develop standards for graduate and professional student programs and services. Members of NASPA's AGAPSS and ACPA's Commission for Graduate and Professional School Educators actively participated in the development of these standards and guidelines.

References, Readings, and Resources

American College Personnel Association & National Association of Student Personnel Administrators. (2004). *Learning reconsidered: A campus-wide focus on the student experience.* Washington, DC: American College Personnel Association and National Association of Student Personnel Administrators.

American College Student Personnel Association (ACPA) – Commission for Graduate and Professional School Educators, www.myacpa.org/comm/graduate

Brandes, L. C. O. (2007). Recent graduate and professional education issues: A timeline. Prepared for NASPA AGAPSS Pre-conference workshop at Harvard University, March 2007.

Cain, D. L., Marrara, C., Pitre, G. E., & Armour, S. (2003). Support services that matter: An exploration of the experiences and needs of graduate students in a distance learning environment. *Journal of Distance Education, 18*, 42-56.

Committee on Science, Engineering and Public Policy. (1995). *Reshaping the education of scientists and engineers.* Washington, DC: National Academy of Sciences.

Council of Graduate Schools and Educational Testing Service. (2010). *The path forward: The future of graduate education in the United States.* Retrieved from http://www.fgereport.org/rsc/pdf/CFGE_report.pdf

Council of Graduate Schools. (2011). *Findings from the 2011 CGS international graduate admissions survey.* Retrieved from http://www.cgsnet.org/ckfinder/userfiles/files/R_IntlAdm11_II.pdf

Elkins Nesheim, B., Guentzel, M. J., Kellogg, A. H., McDonald, W. M., Wells, C. A., & Whitt, E. J. (2007). Outcomes for student affairs-academic affairs partnership programs. *Journal of College Student Development, 48*(4), 435-454.

Gardner, S. K., & Barnes, B. J. (2007). Graduate student involvement: Socialization for the professional role. *Journal of College Student Development, 48*(4), 369-387.

Guentzel, M. J., & Elkins Nesheim, B. (2006). *Supporting graduate and professional students: The role of student affairs. New Directions in Student Services (No.115).* San Francisco, CA: Jossey Bass.

Hesli, V. L., Fink, E. C., & Duffy, D. M. (2003). The role of faculty in creating a positive graduate experience: survey results from the Midwest region, part II. *Political Science and Politics,* 3694), 801-804.

Hyun, J. K., Quinn, B. C., Madon, T., & Lustig, S. (2006). Graduate student mental health: Needs assessment and utilization of counseling services. *Journal of College Student Development, 47*(3), 247-266.

Kruger, K. (2005). *Technology in student affairs: Supporting student learning and services. New Directions in Student Services (No.112).* San Francisco, CA: Jossey Bass.

Le, T. (2010). Understanding the doctoral experience of Asian international students in the science, technology, engineering, and mathematics (STEM) fields: An exploration of one institutional context. *Journal of College Student Development, 51*, 252-264.

Logan, A. P., & Isaac, P. D. (1995). *Student services for the changing graduate student population. New Directions in Student Services (No.42).* San Francisco, CA: Jossey Bass.

National Association of Student Personnel Administrators (NASPA) – Administrators in Graduate and Professional Student Services (AGAPSS), www.naspa.org/kc/agapss/default.cfm

Polson, C. J. (2003, Summer). Adult graduate students challenge institutions to change. *New Directions for Student Services, 102,* 59-68.

Poock, M. C. (2004, Spring). Graduate student orientation

practices: Results from a national survey. *NASPA Journal 41*(3), 470-486.

Roberts, D. L. (2012). International graduate student mobility in the US: What more can we be doing. *Journal of College & Character, 13,* 1-7.

Contextual Statement Contributors

Lisa Brandes, Yale University, NASPA-AGAPSS
Pat Carretta, George Mason University, NACE
Lori Cohen, George Mason University
Eva DeCourcey, George Mason University
Janice Sutera Wolfe, George Mason University

Graduate and Professional Student Programs and Services
CAS Standards and Guidelines

Part 1. MISSION

The mission of Graduate and Professional Student Programs and Services (GPSPS) is to promote academic, personal, and professional growth and development of students enrolled in graduate and professional schools. In support of successful degree completion and achievement of other academic goals, GPSPS must ensure student access to programs and services that address students' needs, provide opportunities for involvement and engagement with students, staff, and faculty members, and facilitate community building and social integration across disciplines. Central to this mission is the necessity to connect students with appropriate resources through collaboration with campus partners and experts when services are not centrally provided by a GPSPS office.

GPSPS must develop, disseminate, implement, and regularly review their missions. The mission must be consistent with the mission of the institution and with professional standards. The mission must be appropriate for the institution's student populations and community settings. Mission statements must reference student learning and development.

Part 2. PROGRAM

Graduate and Professional Student Programs and Services (GPSPS) must provide programs and services to meet the academic, personal, and professional needs and interests of graduate and professional students, whether organized as a central office; located within an academic department, school, or college; or offered in collaboration with other student and academic affairs offices. GPSPS must use data about their graduate and professional students and their experiences to tailor programs and services for those students.

GPSPS should offer programs that reflect the diversity of their students. Demographics to consider include heterogeneity of students who are seeking degrees, disciplines studied, and the different types of institutions they have previously attended.

The formal education of students, consisting of the curriculum and the co-curriculum, must promote student learning and development outcomes that are purposeful, contribute to students' realization of their potential, and prepare students for satisfying and productive lives.

GPSPS must collaborate with colleagues and departments across the institution to promote student learning and development, persistence, and success.

Consistent with the institutional mission, GPSPS must identify relevant and desirable student learning and development outcomes from among the six domains and related dimensions:

Domain: knowledge acquisition, integration, construction, and application

- Dimensions: understanding knowledge from a range of disciplines; connecting knowledge to other knowledge, ideas, and experiences; constructing knowledge; and relating knowledge to daily life

Domain: cognitive complexity

- Dimensions: critical thinking, reflective thinking, effective reasoning, and creativity

Domain: intrapersonal development

- Dimensions: realistic self-appraisal, self-understanding, and self-respect; identity development; commitment to ethics and integrity; and spiritual awareness

Domain: interpersonal competence

- Dimensions: meaningful relationships, interdependence, collaboration, and effective leadership.

Domain: humanitarianism and civic engagement

- Dimensions: understanding and appreciation of cultural and human differences, social responsibility, global perspective, and sense of civic responsibility

Domain: practical competence

- Dimensions: pursuing goals, communicating effectively, technical competence, managing personal affairs, managing career development, demonstrating professionalism, maintaining health and wellness, and living a purposeful and satisfying life

[LD Outcomes: See The Council for the Advancement of Standards Learning and Developmental Outcomes statement for examples of outcomes related to these domains and dimensions.]

GPSPS must
- assess relevant and desirable student

learning and development
- provide evidence of impact on outcomes
- articulate contributions to or support of student learning and development in the domains not specifically assessed
- articulate contributions to or support of student persistence and success
- use evidence gathered through this process to create strategies for improvement of programs and services

GPSPS must be
- intentionally designed
- guided by theories and knowledge of learning and development
- integrated into the life of the institution
- reflective of developmental and demographic profiles of the student population
- responsive to needs of individuals, populations with distinct needs, and relevant constituencies
- delivered using multiple formats, strategies, and contexts

Where institutions provide distance education, GPSPS must assist distance learners to achieve their educational goals by providing access to information about programs and services, to staff members who can address questions and concerns, and to counseling, advising, or other forms of assistance.

Because of the potential impact on graduate student success, GPSPS must offer programs and services that promote students' continued cognitive, emotional, ethical, and social development.

GPSPS must provide opportunities for students to develop knowledge, skills, professional ethics, and values necessary for entry into and progress through the profession or career for which the graduate or professional degree programs offer preparation.

GPSPS must ensure that students have access to programs and services to assist in navigating the issues and coping with stress often associated with the transition into and progress through graduate or professional education. GPSPS must develop support systems for fostering retention and persistence.

Programs should address changes in lifestyle, relationships, work, and finances, as well as isolation and lack of support networks.

GPSPS should provide resources, services, and support to students who are or who become parents during their graduate program and should ensure that policies do not place an unfair burden on students who are parents.

GPSPS must offer programs and services that promote individual and community responsibility, academic integrity, and ethical practices.

GPSPS must advocate that students involved in research, teaching, or clinical work receive supervision and information, guidelines, and training on appropriate practices and policies.

GPSPS should be especially responsive to the needs of international, multicultural, women, and LGBT students and students with disabilities.

GPSPS must include an admissions function or work closely with admissions staff to
- ensure timely dissemination of information and materials
- provide equal access for all prospective students interested in and capable of pursuing graduate or professional education at the institution
- work with stakeholders to develop enrollment goals, related strategies, and resources that are needed to reach those goals
- coordinate programs for prospective students that present the realities of graduate education and promote deliberate educational planning

GPSPS must orient students to the academic unit, school/college, institution, and community or work closely with appropriate staff and resources to offer information in formats compatible with multiple constituencies, including residential, commuter, and distance learning students.

GPSPS should coordinate a series of orientation activities and transition services for new students that address the realities, norms, and expectations of graduate education; policies and regulations; resources within the academic department or school/college; and other campus and community resources beyond the department or school/college that offer programs and services essential or of interest to their students. GPSPS should provide information about student organizations and other formal or informal support groups and opportunities for involvement for all graduate students and especially for underrepresented students. GPSPS should employ the assistance of advanced graduate and professional students in planning and implementing the orientation program.

GPSPS must offer financial aid services or provide access to appropriate staff and resources to
- provide comprehensive and accurate information for students to make informed decisions on financing their education, managing loans and debt, research and training grants, and other financial matters while in graduate or professional school
- ensure clear and transparent procedures and policies for awarding financial aid
- ensure timeliness of delivery of financial aid

offered by the academic department, school/ college, or institution

GPSPS must assist students in adjusting to the academic demands of graduate or professional education or provide access to appropriate staff and resources.

GPSPS may

- provide information about grading and other policies; academic writing and citation style; the pace for learning; and other realities about academic demands and performance in their program of study
- provide professional development programs, resources, or referral to services on studying, test-taking, intellectual property, research methodologies, and research protocol
- arrange or facilitate study or tutor groups
- refer students with disabilities to staff or others who can conduct assessments and arrange accommodations
- discuss and clarify educational, career, and life goals and advise on the selection of appropriate courses and other educational experiences
- provide opportunities to assess appropriateness of academic program choice
- evaluate and monitor student academic progress and the impact on achievement of goals and degree completion
- support or refer students with supervisory, assistantship, or advising issues
- direct students with personal concerns to resources and programs on the campus or in the community
- provide information and referral to programs to improve oral communication and conversation skills
- encourage departments and students to develop strong mentorship programs

GPSPS must offer or provide access to resources that enhance the career and professional development of its students. Program components must be designed for and be reflective of the needs and interests of students.

GPSPS program components should include

- career counseling or coaching
- information and resources on careers, specializations within fields and professions, further education and training opportunities, and fellowships
- opportunities to explore career options available to those with graduate or professional degrees
- opportunities to gain experience related to the field or profession through internships, practicums, summer or part-time jobs, job shadowing, or volunteer work
- job search services
- access to advice and guidance from faculty, peer mentors, alumni, and other professionals

- information and support for travel grants and professional presentations

GPSPS may also encompass

- academic advising
- academic integrity and student conduct
- counseling and psychological services
- assistance with housing on and off campus
- disability services
- professional development programs in teaching, presentation of research, academic and research integrity, thesis and dissertation preparation, grant writing, ethical conduct, preparing future faculty, diversity training, and related topics
- information and advice on applying for scholarships and fellowships
- disciplinary or interdisciplinary scholarly events
- student organizations, governance support, and leadership development
- social and networking activities and programs
- international student programs and services
- multicultural activities and events
- access to sports events, recreation, and fitness and wellness activities
- community service opportunities
- services and accommodations for students with families including children
- graduation activities
- graduate alumni activities
- post-doctoral training and support services

GPSPS must disseminate relevant information about campus services, programs, and current events in a variety of media and formats.

Access to GPSPS services should be available via the Internet and telephone as well as through other channels of communication appropriate to the institution and community.

GPSPS must facilitate opportunities for community building and multicultural interaction within and across academic units.

GPSPS should offer students opportunities for interaction with faculty and staff members and peers within and outside their fields of study. GPSPS should encourage and support formation of student organizations and activities, multicultural communities, special-interest student organizations, honoraries, mentoring, and leadership programs.

Graduate and professional students should have adequate study, meeting, and lounge spaces that serve as gathering and community building spaces for students from different departments and academic programs. These spaces should encourage and support informal meetings, study groups, quiet study space, student organization activities, and co-curricular programs.

GPSPS should partner with graduate faculty members to offer

discipline specific co-curricular programs or collaborate with other departments, faculty members, and staff from related disciplines to offer such programs to a larger population of graduate students.

GPSPS must promote representation of graduate and professional students on all appropriate levels of campus planning, policy-making, budgeting, program delivery, and governance.

GPSPS must advocate for students and empower students to advocate for themselves.

Graduate and professional student advocacy should focus on
- access to comprehensive academic and student support services and information
- recognition of diverse subgroups within the graduate student population
- availability and equitable distribution of funds in support of student organizations, governance, conference travel, and research
- institutional research and assessment that enhance understanding of the demographic characteristics and special needs of graduate and professional students
- provision of on-campus housing designed for graduate and professional students, including housing for married students, students with domestic partners, older single students, and students with children
- assistance in locating accessible, affordable, and safe off-campus housing
- provision of child care services
- expanded access to libraries, laboratories, and studios as needed days, nights, and weekends throughout the year
- coordination of campus and community transit, parking, and security to access classes, libraries, laboratories, and studios

Part 3. ORGANIZATION AND LEADERSHIP

To achieve student and program outcomes, Graduate and Professional Student Programs and Services (GPSPS) must be structured purposefully and organized effectively. GPSPS must have
- clearly stated goals
- current and accessible policies and procedures
- written performance expectations for employees
- functional work flow graphics or organizational charts demonstrating clear channels of authority

Leaders with organizational authority for the programs and services must provide strategic planning, supervision, and management; advance the organization; and maintain integrity through the following functions:

Strategic Planning
- **articulate a vision and mission that drive short- and long-term planning**
- **set goals and objectives based on the needs of the population served and desired student learning or development and program outcomes**
- **facilitate continuous development, implementation, and assessment of goal attainment congruent with institutional mission and strategic plans**
- **promote environments that provide meaningful opportunities for student learning, development, and engagement**
- **develop and continuously improve programs and services in response to the changing needs of students served and evolving institutional priorities**
- **intentionally include diverse perspectives to inform decision making**

Supervising
- **manage human resource processes including recruitment, selection, development, supervision, performance planning, evaluation, recognition, and reward**
- **influence others to contribute to the effectiveness and success of the unit**
- **empower professional, support, and student staff to accept leadership opportunities**
- **offer appropriate feedback to colleagues and students on skills needed to become more effective leaders**
- **encourage and support professional development, collaboration with colleagues and departments across the institution, and scholarly contribution to the profession**

Managing
- **identify and address individual, organizational, and environmental conditions that foster or inhibit mission achievement**
- **plan, allocate, and monitor the use of fiscal, physical, human, intellectual, and technological resources**
- **use current and valid evidence to inform decisions**
- **incorporate sustainability practices in the management and design of programs, services, and facilities**
- **understand appropriate technologies and integrate them into programs and services**
- **be knowledgeable about codes and laws relevant to programs and services and ensure that staff members understand their responsibilities through appropriate training**
- **assess potential risks and take action to**

mitigate them

Advancing the Organization

- communicate effectively in writing, speaking, and electronic venues
- advocate for programs and services
- advocate for representation in strategic planning initiatives at appropriate divisional and institutional levels
- initiate collaborative interactions with internal and external stakeholders who have legitimate concerns about and interests in the functional area
- facilitate processes to reach consensus where wide support is needed
- inform other areas within the institution about issues affecting practice

Maintaining Integrity

- model ethical behavior and institutional citizenship
- share data used to inform key decisions in transparent and accessible ways
- monitor media used for distributing information about programs and services to ensure the content is current, accurate, appropriately referenced, and accessible

GPSPS leaders must collaborate with institutional leaders; academic departments within their college, school, or division; colleagues in other graduate programs at their institution; and with graduate offices, enrollment services, student affairs, academic support services, and alumni affairs for the purpose of developing strategies for connecting students to the larger community and positively affecting graduate student learning and development in and outside the classroom.

Staffing and reporting structures of GPSPS may vary. Whatever the structure, GPSPS should develop collaborative mechanisms, working groups, or relationships to coordinate their work to benefit all graduate and professional students.

Part 4. HUMAN RESOURCES

Graduate and Professional Student Programs and Services (GPSPS) must be staffed adequately by individuals qualified to accomplish mission and goals.

Within institutional guidelines, GPSPS must

- establish procedures for staff recruitment and selection, training, performance planning, and evaluation
- set expectations for supervision and performance
- assess the performance of employees individually and as a team
- provide access to continuing and advanced

education and appropriate professional development opportunities to improve the leadership ability, competence, and skills of all employees.

GPSPS must maintain position descriptions for all staff members.

To create a diverse staff, GPSPS must institute recruitment and hiring strategies that encourage individuals from under-represented populations to apply for positions.

GPSPS must develop promotion practices that are fair, inclusive, proactive, and non-discriminatory.

To further the recruitment and retention of staff, GPSPS must consider work life initiatives, such as compressed work schedules, flextime, job sharing, remote work, or telework.

GPSPS professional staff members must hold an earned graduate or professional degree in a field relevant to the position they hold or must possess an appropriate combination of educational credentials and related work experience.

GPSPS professional staff should be educated in student/ academic services in order to design and implement intentional support and services for graduate and professional students.

GPSPS professional staff members must engage in continuing professional development activities to keep abreast of the research, theories, legislation, policies, and developments that affect their programs and services.

GPSPS must have technical and support staff members adequate to accomplish their mission. All members of the staff must be technologically proficient and qualified to perform their job functions, be knowledgeable about ethical and legal uses of technology, and have access to training and resources to support the performance of their assigned responsibilities.

Degree- or credential-seeking interns or graduate assistants must be qualified by enrollment in an appropriate field of study and by relevant experience. These individuals must be trained and supervised adequately by professional staff members holding educational credentials and related work experience appropriate for supervision. Supervisors must be cognizant of the roles of interns and graduate assistants as both student and employee and closely adhere to all parameters of their job descriptions, work hours, and schedules. Supervisors and the interns or graduate assistants must agree to compensatory time or other appropriate compensation if circumstances necessitate additional hours.

Student employees and volunteers must be carefully selected, trained, supervised, and evaluated. They must be educated on how and when to refer those in need of additional assistance to qualified staff members and must have access to a supervisor for assistance in making these judgments. Student employees and volunteers must be provided clear job descriptions, pre-service training based on assessed needs, and continuing development.

All GPSPS staff members, including student employees and volunteers, must receive specific training on institutional policies pertaining to functions or activities they support and to privacy and confidentiality policies and laws regarding access to student records and other sensitive institutional information.

All GPSPS staff members must receive training on policies and procedures related to the use of technology to store or access student records and institutional data.

GPSPS must ensure that staff members are knowledgeable about and trained in emergency procedures, crisis response, and prevention efforts. Prevention efforts must address identification of threatening conduct or behavior of students, faculty and staff members, and others and must incorporate a system for responding and reporting.

GPSPS must ensure that staff members are knowledgeable of and trained in safety and emergency procedures for securing and vacating facilities.

Part 5. ETHICS

Graduate and Professional Student Programs and Services (GPSPS) must review relevant professional ethical standards and must adopt or develop and implement appropriate statements of ethical practice.

GPSPS must publish and adhere to statements of ethical practice and ensure their periodic review by relevant constituencies.

GPSPS must orient new staff members to relevant ethical standards and statements of ethical practice and related institutional policies.

Statements of ethical standards must specify that staff members respect privacy and maintain confidentiality in all communications and records to the extent that such communications and records are protected under relevant privacy laws.

Statements of ethical standards must specify limits on disclosure of information contained in students' educational records as well as requirements to disclose to appropriate authorities.

Statements of ethical standards must address personal and economic conflicts of interest, or appearance thereof, by staff members in the performance of their work.

Statements of ethical standards must reflect the responsibility of staff members to be fair, objective, and impartial in their interactions with others.

Statements of ethical standards must reference management of institutional funds.

Statements of ethical standards must reference appropriate behavior regarding research and assessment with human participants, confidentiality of research and assessment data, and students' rights and responsibilities.

Statements of ethical standards must include the expectation that GPSPS staff members confront and hold accountable other staff members who exhibit unethical behavior.

Statements of ethical standards must address issues surrounding scholarly integrity.

As appropriate, GPSPS staff members must inform users of programs and services of ethical obligations and limitations emanating from codes and laws or from licensure requirements.

GPSPS staff members must recognize and avoid conflicts of interest that could adversely influence their judgment or objectivity and, when unavoidable, recuse themselves from the situation.

GPSPS staff members must perform their duties within the limits of their position, training, expertise, and competence.

When these limits are exceeded, individuals in need of further assistance must be referred to persons possessing appropriate qualifications.

Promotional and descriptive information must be accurate and free of deception.

GPSPS must adhere to institutional policies regarding ethical and legal use of software and technology.

Part 6. LAW, POLICY, AND GOVERNANCE

Graduate and Professional Student Programs and Services (GPSPS) must be in compliance with laws, regulations, and policies that relate to their respective responsibilities and that pose legal obligations, limitations, risks, and liabilities for the institution as a whole. Examples include constitutional, statutory, regulatory, and case law; relevant law and orders emanating from codes and laws; and the institution's policies.

GPSPS must inform staff members, appropriate officials, and users of programs and services about existing and changing legal obligations, risks and liabilities, and limitations.

GPSPS must have written policies on all relevant operations, transactions, or tasks that have legal implications.

GPSPS must regularly review policies. The revision and creation of policies must be informed by best practices, available evidence, and policy issues in higher education.

GPSPS staff members must use reasonable and informed practices to limit the liability exposure of the institution and its officers, employees, and agents. GPSPS staff members must be informed about institutional policies regarding risk management, personal liability, and related insurance coverage options and must be referred to external sources if the institution does not provide coverage.

The institution must provide access to legal advice for staff members as needed to carry out assigned responsibilities.

GPSPS must have procedures and guidelines consistent with institutional policy for responding to threats, emergencies, and crisis situations. Systems and procedures must be in place to disseminate timely and accurate information to students, other members of the institutional community, and appropriate external organizations during emergency situations.

GPSPS staff members must neither participate in nor condone any form of harassment or activity that demeans persons or creates an intimidating, hostile, or offensive environment.

GPSPS must obtain permission to use copyrighted materials and instruments. GPSPS must purchase the materials and instruments from legally compliant sources or seek alternative permission from the publisher or owner. References to copyrighted materials and instruments must include appropriate citations.

GPSPS staff members must be knowledgeable about internal and external governance systems that affect programs and services.

Part 7. DIVERSITY, EQUITY, AND ACCESS

Within the context of each institution's unique mission and in accordance with institutional polices and all applicable codes and laws, Graduate and Professional Student Programs and Services (GPSPS) must create and maintain educational and work environments that are

- welcoming, accessible, and inclusive to persons of diverse backgrounds
- equitable and non-discriminatory
- free from harassment

GPSPS must not discriminate on the basis of ability; age; cultural identity; ethnicity; family educational history (e.g., first generation to attend college); gender identity and expression; nationality; political affiliation; race; religious affiliation; sex; sexual orientation; economic, marital, social, or veteran status; or any other basis included in institutional policies and codes and laws.

GPSPS must

- advocate for greater sensitivity to multicultural and social justice concerns by the institution and its personnel
- modify or remove policies, practices, facilities, structures, systems, and technologies that limit access, discriminate, or produce inequities
- include diversity, equity, and access initiatives within their strategic plans
- foster communication that deepens understanding of identity, culture, self-expression, and heritage
- promote respect about commonalities and differences among people within their historical and cultural contexts
- address the characteristics and needs of a diverse population when establishing and implementing culturally relevant and inclusive programs, services, policies, procedures, and practices
- provide staff members with access to multicultural training and hold staff members accountable for integrating the training into their work
- respond to the needs of all students and other populations served when establishing hours of operation and developing methods of delivering programs, services, and resources
- ensure physical, program, and resource access for persons with disabilities
- recognize the needs of distance learning students by providing appropriate and accessible services and resources or by assisting them in gaining access to other appropriate services and resources in their geographic region

Part 8. INSTITUTIONAL AND EXTERNAL RELATIONS

Graduate and Professional Student Programs

and Services (GPSPS) must reach out to relevant individuals, groups, communities, and organizations internal and external to the institution to

- establish, maintain, and promote understanding and effective relations with those that have a significant interest in or potential effect on the students or other constituents served by the programs and services
- garner support and resources for programs and services as defined by the mission statement
- disseminate information about the programs and services
- collaborate, where appropriate, to assist in offering or improving programs and services to meet the needs of students and other constituents and to achieve program and student outcomes
- engage diverse individuals, groups, communities, and organizations to enrich the educational environment and experiences of students and other constituents

The staff of GPSPS must work collaboratively with colleagues in other graduate programs at their institution and with departments including but not limited to graduate offices, enrollment services, international student services, student affairs, academic support services, research and grants offices, development, and alumni affairs.

GPSPS must have procedures and guidelines consistent with institutional policy for

- communicating with the media
- contracting with external organizations for delivery of programs and services
- cultivating, soliciting, and managing gifts
- applying to and managing funds from grants

Part 9. FINANCIAL RESOURCES

Graduate and Professional Student Programs and Services (GPSPS) must have funding to accomplish the mission and goals. In establishing funding priorities and making significant changes, a comprehensive analysis must be conducted to determine the following elements: unmet needs of the unit, relevant expenditures, external and internal resources, and impact on students and the institution.

GPSPS must demonstrate efficient and effective use and responsible stewardship of fiscal resources consistent with institutional protocols.

Part 10. TECHNOLOGY

Graduate and Professional Student Programs and Services (GPSPS) must have adequate technology to support the achievement of their mission and goals. The technology and its use must comply with institutional policies and procedures and be evaluated for compliance with relevant codes and laws.

GPSPS must use current technology to provide updated information regarding mission, location, staffing, programs, services, and official contacts to students and designated clients.

GPSPS must explore the use of technology to enhance delivery of programs and services, especially for students at a distance or external constituencies.

When technology is used to facilitate student learning and development, GPSPS must select technology that reflects intended outcomes.

GPSPS must

- maintain policies and procedures that address the security, confidentiality, and backup of data, as well as compliance with privacy laws
- have clearly articulated plans in place for protecting confidentiality and security of information when using Internet-based technologies
- develop plans for replacing and updating existing hardware and software as well as plans for integrating new technically-based or supported programs, including systems developed internally by the institution, systems available through professional associations, or private vendor-based systems

Technology, as well as workstations or computer labs maintained by programs and services for student use, must be accessible to all designated clients and must meet established technology standards for delivery to persons with disabilities.

When providing student access to technology, GPSPS must

- have policies on the use of technology that are clear, easy to understand, and available to all students
- provide assistance, information, or referral to appropriate support services to those needing help accessing or using technology
- provide instruction or training on how to use the technology
- inform students on the legal and ethical implications of misuse as it pertains to intellectual property, harassment, privacy, and social networks

Student violations of technology policies must follow established institutional student disciplinary procedures.

Students who experience negative emotional or psychological consequences from the use of technology must be referred to support services provided by the institution.

Part 11. FACILITIES AND EQUIPMENT

Graduate and Professional Student Programs and Services (GPSPS) must have adequate, accessible, and suitably located facilities and equipment to support the mission and goals. If acquiring capital equipment as defined by the institution, GPSPS must take into account expenses related to regular maintenance and life cycle costs. Facilities and equipment must be evaluated on an established cycle, including consideration of sustainability, and be in compliance with codes and laws to provide for access, health, safety, and security.

GPSPS staff members must have workspace that is well equipped, adequate in size, and designed to support their work and responsibilities. For conversations requiring privacy, staff members must have access to a private space.

GPSPS staff members who share workspace must be able to secure their own work.

GPSPS should advocate for adequate office and work space for research and teaching assistants located where meaningful interactions with students, faculty members, and staff members may take place.

GPSPS should ensure that graduate and professional students have adequate spaces for study groups; for socializing and networking with peers, faculty and staff members; and for holding co-curricular programs and events. These spaces should be for the specific use by graduate and professional students.

GPSPS should provide space for graduate student organizations and governance councils.

The design of the facilities must guarantee the security and privacy of records and ensure the confidentiality of sensitive information.

The location and layout of the facilities must be sensitive to the needs of persons with disabilities as well as the needs of other constituencies.

Part 12. ASSESSMENT AND EVALUATION

Graduate and Professional Student Programs and Services (GPSPS) must have a clearly articulated assessment plan to document achievement of stated goals and learning outcomes, demonstrate accountability, provide evidence of improvement, and describe resulting changes in programs and services.

These should include assessment of

- demographics and characteristics of the students
- student needs, experiences, and learning outcomes
- overall use of and satisfaction with programs and services
- attrition and persistence rates, such as time to degree completion and reasons for leaving prior to completion
- post-graduation career plans and outcomes
- adherence to national standards
- certification and licensing examination passing rates
- overall satisfaction with services and environment

GPSPS must have adequate fiscal, human, professional development, and technological resources to develop and implement assessment plans.

Assessments must include direct and indirect evaluation and use qualitative and quantitative methodologies and existing evidence, as appropriate, to determine whether and to what degree the stated mission, goals, and intended outcomes are being met as effectively and efficiently as possible. The process must employ sufficient and sound measures to ensure comprehensiveness. Data collected must include responses from students and other constituencies, and aggregated results must be shared with those groups. Results of assessments must be shared appropriately with multiple constituents.

Results of assessments and evaluations must be used to identify needs and interests in revising and improving programs and services, recognizing staff performance, maximizing resource efficiency and effectiveness, improving student achievement of learning and development outcomes, and improving student persistence and success. Changes resulting from the use of assessments and evaluation must be shared with stakeholders.

General Standards revised in 2011;
GPSPS content developed in 2008

The Role of Health Promotion Services
CAS Standards Contextual Statement

Health Promotion Services (HPS) engage students, faculty, and staff in developing personal skills, establishing strong communities, and building an academic environment where well-being advances the capacity to learn, work, and contribute. This includes employee wellness programs that help to establish an environment that values health and wellness as a resource for productivity, learning, and everyday life. Many variables (physical facilities, campus master plans, policies, traditions, enrollment demographics, the geography of the surrounding communities, and the employees as faculty or staff) contribute to the environment of an institution of higher education and are essential to the functional area of health promotion.

In 1986, the World Health Organization (WHO) defined health promotion in the "Ottawa Charter for Health Promotion":

> Health promotion is the process of enabling people to increase control over, and to improve, their health. To reach a state of complete physical, mental and social well-being, an individual or group must be able to identify and to realize aspirations, to satisfy needs, and to change or cope with the environment. Health is, therefore, seen as a resource for everyday life, not the objective of living. Health is a positive concept emphasizing social and personal resources, as well as physical capacities. Therefore, health promotion is not just the responsibility of the health sector, but goes beyond healthy life-styles to well-being. (p. 2)

Health and wellness are synonymous in their aspirations and desired results. Wellness usually has a more detailed list of descriptors for "well-being," often detailing six or more areas (physical, emotional, social, intellectual, spiritual, and occupational) rather than the three areas found in the WHO definition of health (physical, mental, social). Wellness, like health, can be used to mean a balance of the mind, body, and spirit that results in an overall feeling of well-being.

In 2007, WHO defined wellness, in the document "Health Promotion Glossary, New Terms":

> **Wellness** is the optimal state of health of individuals and groups. There are two focal concerns: the realization of the fullest potential of an individual physically, psychologically, socially, spiritually and economically, and the fulfillment of one's role expectations in the family, community, place of worship, workplace and other settings. (Smith, Tang, & Nutbeam, 2006)

If wellness is the optimal state of health and health is the complete state of well-being, can a "complete state" not be an "optimal state"? Perhaps, if health is reduced to just functional capacity and wellness becomes an unobtainable ideal. This reductive approach does not represent the spirit or the intent of common usage. Possibly wellness is a subjective valuation while health has a more objective nature. Wellness and health used as synonymous terms creates unity rather than division and focuses the work on shared outcomes.

On any given campus, regardless of whether health and wellness are used as synonyms, there are four essential goals: (a) the realization of the fullest potential of an individual physically, psychologically, socially, spiritually, and economically; (b) the fulfillment of an individual's role expectations in the family, community, place of worship, workplace, and other settings; (c) the achievement of more desirable outcomes for a group or population; and (d) the support and creation of environments that are enhancing of well-being for whole populations regardless of individual variables. Health and wellness described by these four key points is a positive concept emphasizing social and personal resources as well as the capacities of individuals, groups, populations, and environments.

Primary prevention and the socio-ecological model ground the integration of these four essential goals and lead the process that is state-of-the-art HPS. **Primary prevention** is essential to moving forward with health and wellness in a population. Primary prevention deters the development of health problems before they occur and therefore reduces risk factors and enhances protective factors. There are three subsets of primary prevention: universal, selective, and indicated. Universal prevention is wellness enhancing or risk reducing for broad populations without consideration of individual differences in risk. Selected prevention targets sub-populations of individuals identified on the basis of their membership in a group that has elevated risk. Indicated prevention is for individuals who are members of a group that exhibit high risk behaviors (Springer & Phillips, 2006). **The Socio-ecological Model** described in NASPA's _Leadership for a Healthy Campus: The Ecological Approach for Student Success_ receives strong national support as a model for addressing complex health issues. Health status and health behaviors are determined by influences at multiple levels, including personal (e.g., biological, psychological, etc.), organizational/institutional, environmental (both social and physical), and policy levels. Interventions are more effective when they address determinants at all levels due to the presence of significant and dynamic inter-relationships (McLeroy, 1988). Historically, health fields have focused on individual-level health determinants and interventions. This Socio-ecological Model reinforces the **Health Promotion Actions** listed in the Ottawa Charter for Health Promotion:
- build healthy public policy

- create supportive environments
- strengthen community actions
- develop personal skills
- reorient healthcare services (i.e., "reorient beyond its responsibility for providing clinical and curative services towards prevention of illness and promotion of health").

All of these actions are critical to health promotion. Unfortunately, too often the focus of HPS efforts is limited to only developing personal skills and even then only focused on involving some form of communication designed to improve health knowledge; health education that is focused only at the "remembering" level of Bloom's *Taxonomy of Educational Objectives* is never evaluated for actual skill development. Limited resources go to informing individuals rather than developing personal skills or any of the other five Health Promotion Actions. The Socio-ecological Model emphasizes the necessity for action at the contextual levels surrounding the individual. In fact, environmental management using policy and the built environment can reduce risk and enhance health without requiring each individual to develop a skill. Each of the five Health Promotion Actions are reinforced with the Socio-ecological Prevention Planning Model (McLeroy, 1988) and the IOM Prevention Planning Model (Springer & Phillips, 2006) in that they set individual-level skills and risk factors within complex layers of environment that can add population-level protection and enhancement.

Before the development of health promotion in the 1980s when health education was the focus, many professionals were relegated to executing health-awareness activities, giving presentations, distributing kitschy promotional items, and creating bulletin boards, brochures, and other non-evidence-based activities. In 2006, the *Journal of American College Health* published *Standards of Practice for Health Promotion in Higher Education* to guide daily efforts, facilitate assessment, assist in decisions to improve practice through professional development, and delineate a set of indicators to evaluate health promotion (Allen et al., 2006). Today, a mature office of wellness and health promotion has much more to offer the campus, placing a great emphasis on universal prevention leadership; theory-based and evidence-informed practice; understanding the correlations between health and learning; collaboration with faculty, staff, students, and community members to drive health enhancing change; achieving both health and learning outcomes; and creating the environments in which wellness and learning happen.

State-of-the-art strategies and initiatives not only include those actions that develop personal skills but also those that support built environments, enforce public policy, and empower communities. These actions all involve creating a culture that supports the health behaviors we want to see in our students and a culture that will change health behaviors on a population-level rather than "fixing" one individual at a time. Health promotion actions also include re-orienting the care delivered by medical, nursing, psychological, other allied healthcare professionals in the examination rooms, counseling offices, and other settings towards providing preventative, not just curative, health care. Re-orienting health services must be the responsibility of the professionals responsible for healthcare. The other health promotion actions listed--personal skills, built environments, policy, and community support--require moving beyond the health sector to coalition building, networking, leadership, policy change, community organizing, and the long-term efforts of wellness and health promotion professionals, administrators, students, alumni, parents, and the community members from surrounding the campus. It will be important to provide opportunities to articulate these definitions in mission and purpose statements, strategic plans, physical location, and resource allocations. It will also be important to describe the wellness and health promotion discipline to Student Life colleagues and to support campus-wide initiatives for continued development of a mature health promotion practice.

References, Readings, and Resources

Allen, N., Fabiano, P., Hong, L., Kennedy, S., Kenzig, M., Kodama, C., Swinford, P. L., & Zimmer, C. (2007). Introduction to the American College Health Association's "Standards of practice for health promotion in higher education." *Journal of American College Health, 55*(6), 374-379.

American College Personnel Association and National Association of Student Personnel Administrators. (2006). *Learning reconsidered 2: A practical guide to implementing a campus-wide focus on the student experience.* Washington, DC: ACPA and NASPA.

American College Health Association – National College Health Assessment (ACHA-NCHA) Spring 2007 Reference Group Data Report (Abridged). *Journal of American College Health*, 56(5), 469-480.

American College Health Association [ACHA]. ACHA National Office, P.O. Box 28937. Baltimore, MD 21240-8937. (410) 859-1500; Fax (410) 859-1510. www.acha.org

Bloom, B. S., Engelhart, M. D., Furst, E. J., Hill, W. H., & Krathwohl, D. R. (1956). *Taxonomy of educational objectives: the classification of educational goals; Handbook I: Cognitive Domain* New York, Longmans, Green, 1956.

Centers for Disease Control and Prevention. (2007). The social-ecological model: a framework for prevention. Retrieved from http://www.cdc.gov/ncipc/dvp/social-ecological-model_dvp.htm

Fertman, C. I., & Allensworth, D. D. (eds.). (2010). *Health promotion programs.* San Francisco, CA: Jossey-Bass.

Glantz, K., Lewis, F. M., & Rimer, B. K. (Eds.). (1997). *Health behavior and health education: Theory, research, and practice* (2nd ed.). San Francisco: Jossey-Bass.

Gordon, R. S. (1983). An operational classification of disease prevention. *Public Health Reports, 98*(2), 107- 109.

Green, L. W., & Kreuter, M. W. (1999). *Health promotion planning: An educational and ecological approach* (3rd ed). Boston: Mayfield Publishing Company.

Gullotta, T. P., & Bloom, M. (eds.). (2003). *The encyclopedia of primary prevention and health promotion*. New York, NY: Kluwer/Plenum.

Haddon, W. (1980). Advances in the epidemiology of injures as a basis for public policy. *Public Health Reports, 95*(5), 411-421.

Keeling, R. P. (1995). *The search for sexual health*. Article based on his keynote address at American Social Health Association, Canadian HELP Group Conference in June 1995. Available online at http://www.herpes.com/sexualHealth.html

McLeroy, K. R., Bibeau, D., Steckler, A., & Glanz, K. (1988). An ecological perspective on health promotion programs. *Health Education Quarterly, 15*(4), 351-377.

McLeroy, K. R., Steckler, A., & Bibeau, D. (Eds.) (1988). The social ecology of health promotion interventions. *Health Education Quarterly, 15*(4):351-495.

National Association of Student Personnel Administrators [NASPA]. NASPA National Office, 1875 Connecticut Ave., N.W., Suite 418. Washington, DC 20009. (202) 265-7500. www.naspa.org

National Association of Student Personnel Administrators – NASPA. (2010). Leadership for a healthy campus: An ecological approach for student success. Retrieved from http://www.naspa.org/membership/mem/pubs/ebooks/HealthyCampus.pdf.

Nutbeam, D. (1998). Health promotion glossary. *Health Promotion International, 13*(4), 349-364.

O'Donnell, M. P. (1989). Definition of health promotion: Part III: Expanding the definition. *American Journal of Health Promotion, 3*(3), 5.

O'Donnell, M. P. (2011). Editor's notes: Reflections on the 25th anniversary of publishing the American Journal of Health Promotion: People, scientific progress, and missteps. *American Journal of Health Promotion, 25*(4), iv-xi.

Silverman, D., Underhile, R., & Keeling, R. (2008). Student health reconsidered: A radical proposal for thinking differently about health-related programs and services for students. *Student Health Spectrum,* June 2008, 4-11.

Smith, B. J., Tang, K. C., & Nutbeam, D. (2006). WHO health promotion glossary: New terms. *Health Promotion International, 21*(4), 340-345.

Springer, F., & Phillips, J. L. (2006). The IOM Model: A Tool for Prevention Planning and Implementation. *Prevention Tactics.* 1-7.

Student Health Spectrum. (November 2005). *Health education and health promotion: Primary prevention and student health*, S. C. Caulfield (Ed.). Cambridge, MA: The Chickering Group.

Swinford, P. (2002). Advancing the health of students: A rationale for college health programs, *Journal of American College Health, 50*(6), 309-312.

US Department of Health and Human Services –DHHS (2008). Executive summary - phase I report: Recommendations for the framework and format of healthy people 2020. Retrieved from http://www.healthypeople.gov/hp2020/advisory/PhaseI/summary.htm#_Toc211942897.

World Health Organization. (1998). *Health promotion glossary.* Retrieved from http://www.who.int/hpr/NPH/docs/hp_glossary_en.pdf

World Health Organization. (1986). The Ottawa Charter for Health Promotion. (pp. 2). Retrieved from http://www.who.int/healthpromotion/conferences/previous/ottawa/en/index1.html

Zimmer, C. G., Hill, M. H., & Sonnad, S. R. (2003). A scope-of-practice survey leading to the development of standards of practice for health promotion in higher education. *Journal of American College Health, 51*(6), 247-54.

Zimmer, C. G. (2002). Health promotion in higher education. In S Turner & J. Hurley (Eds.), *The history and practice of college health*. Lexington, KY: The University Press of Kentucky, 311-327.

Contextual Statement Contributors

Patricia Fabiano, Western Washington University
Susan Kennedy, Pennsylvania State University
Nancy Allen, Michigan State University
Daisye Orr, Washington State Public Health Department
Paula Swinford, University of Southern California, ACHA
Dixie Bennett, Loyola University Chicago, NIRSA
Cathy Kodoma, University of California at Berkeley
Luoluo Hong, Arizona State University
Gina Baral Abrams, Princeton University

Health Promotion Services
CAS Standards and Guidelines

Part 1. MISSION

The mission and scope of practice of health promotion, sometimes referred to as wellness, must be reflective of the following fundamental assumptions about the role of health in higher education:

- there is a reciprocal relationship between learning and health, as well as a direct connection between the academic mission of higher education and the well-being of students
- in the broadest sense, health encompasses the capacity of individuals and communities to reach their potential
- health transcends individual factors and includes cultural, institutional, socioeconomic, and political influences
- health is not solely a biomedical quality measured through clinical indicators
- health and social justice are inextricably connected
- both individual and environmental approaches to health are critical

HPS must develop, disseminate, implement, and regularly review their missions. The mission must be consistent with the mission of the institution and with professional standards. The mission must be appropriate for the institution's student populations and community settings. Mission statements must reference student learning and development.

Part 2. PROGRAM

The formal education of students, consisting of the curriculum and the co-curriculum, must promote student learning and development outcomes that are purposeful, contribute to students' realization of their potential, and prepare students for satisfying and productive lives.

Health Promotion Services (HPS) must collaborate with colleagues and departments across the institution to promote student learning and development, persistence, and success.

Consistent with the institutional mission, HPS must identify relevant and desirable student learning and development outcomes from among the six domains and related dimensions:

Domain: knowledge acquisition, integration, construction, and application

- Dimensions: understanding knowledge from a range of disciplines; connecting knowledge to other knowledge, ideas, and experiences; constructing knowledge; and relating knowledge to daily life

Domain: cognitive complexity

- Dimensions: critical thinking, reflective thinking, effective reasoning, and creativity

Domain: intrapersonal development

- Dimensions: realistic self-appraisal, self-understanding, and self-respect; identity development; commitment to ethics and integrity; and spiritual awareness

Domain: interpersonal competence

- Dimensions: meaningful relationships, interdependence, collaboration, and effective leadership.

Domain: humanitarianism and civic engagement

- Dimensions: understanding and appreciation of cultural and human differences, social responsibility, global perspective, and sense of civic responsibility

Domain: practical competence

- Dimensions: pursuing goals, communicating effectively, technical competence, managing personal affairs, managing career development, demonstrating professionalism, maintaining health and wellness, and living a purposeful and satisfying life

[LD Outcomes: See *The Council for the Advancement of Standards Learning and Developmental Outcomes* statement for examples of outcomes related to these domains and dimensions.]

HPS must

- assess relevant and desirable student learning and development
- provide evidence of impact on outcomes
- articulate contributions to or support of student learning and development in the domains not specifically assessed
- articulate contributions to or support of student persistence and success
- use evidence gathered through this process to create strategies for improvement of programs and services

HSP must be
- intentionally designed

- guided by theories and knowledge of learning and development
- integrated into the life of the institution
- reflective of developmental and demographic profiles of the student population
- responsive to needs of individuals, populations with distinct needs, and relevant constituencies
- delivered using multiple formats, strategies, and contexts

Where institutions provide distance education, HPS must assist distance learners to achieve their educational goals by providing access to information about programs and services, to staff members who can address questions and concerns, and to counseling, advising, or other forms of assistance.

HPS must advance the health of students and contribute to the creation of an institutional and community climate of health and social justice.

HPS must review health promotion research and theories from interdisciplinary sources as a guide for the development of initiatives.

HPS must articulate the theoretical frameworks used in setting priorities and decision-making to the campus community.

HPS must apply professionally recognized constructs, tested theories, and evidence based strategies to the development of initiatives designed to improve the health of individuals and the campus environment.

HPS must involve students, faculty members, staff members, and community constituents to advance the health of students and to create campus and community environments that support students' health.

HPS professionals should strive to reduce risk, incidence, and severity for individual mental and physical distress, illness and injury; enhance health as a strategy to support student learning; and advocate for safety, social justice, economic opportunity, and human dignity.

HPS must acknowledge that health and social justice are inextricably connected.

HPS professionals should strive to identify and address the complex social, cultural, economic, and political factors that may contribute to or compromise the health of individuals or communities; advocate for inclusive and equal access to resources and services; and eliminate health disparities and increase the quality and years of healthy life for all.

HPS must include both individual and environmental prevention strategies.

HPS professionals should strive to reduce the risk of individual illness and injury, as well as build individual capacity and address larger institutional issues, priority health issues, community factors, and public policies that affect the health of students.

HPS professionals must advance the connection between the academic mission of higher education and the well-being of students.

HPS professionals should support the academic mission of student learning by assisting students in leading healthier lives and engaging individuals who will become political, social, and economic decision makers, thereby advancing the collective health of the community.

Part 3. ORGANIZATION AND LEADERSHIP

To achieve student and program outcomes, Health Promotion Services (HPS) must be structured purposefully and organized effectively. HPS must have

- clearly stated goals
- current and accessible policies and procedures
- written performance expectations for employees
- functional work flow graphics or organizational charts demonstrating clear channels of authority

Leaders with organizational authority for the programs and services must provide strategic planning, supervision, and management; advance the organization; and maintain integrity through the following functions:

Strategic Planning

- articulate a vision and mission that drive short- and long-term planning
- set goals and objectives based on the needs of the population served and desired student learning or development and program outcomes
- facilitate continuous development, implementation, and assessment of goal attainment congruent with institutional mission and strategic plans
- promote environments that provide meaningful opportunities for student learning, development, and engagement
- develop and continuously improve programs and services in response to the changing needs of students served and evolving institutional priorities
- intentionally include diverse perspectives to inform decision making

Supervising

- manage human resource processes including recruitment, selection, development, supervision, performance planning,

evaluation, recognition, and reward
- influence others to contribute to the effectiveness and success of the unit
- empower professional, support, and student staff to accept leadership opportunities
- offer appropriate feedback to colleagues and students on skills needed to become more effective leaders
- encourage and support professional development, collaboration with colleagues and departments across the institution, and scholarly contribution to the profession

Managing
- identify and address individual, organizational, and environmental conditions that foster or inhibit mission achievement
- plan, allocate, and monitor the use of fiscal, physical, human, intellectual, and technological resources
- use current and valid evidence to inform decisions
- incorporate sustainability practices in the management and design of programs, services, and facilities
- understand appropriate technologies and integrate them into programs and services
- be knowledgeable about codes and laws relevant to programs and services and ensure that staff members understand their responsibilities through appropriate training
- assess potential risks and take action to mitigate them

Advancing the Organization
- communicate effectively in writing, speaking, and electronic venues
- advocate for programs and services
- advocate for representation in strategic planning initiatives at appropriate divisional and institutional levels
- initiate collaborative interactions with internal and external stakeholders who have legitimate concerns about and interests in the functional area
- facilitate processes to reach consensus where wide support is needed
- inform other areas within the institution about issues affecting practice

Maintaining Integrity
- model ethical behavior and institutional citizenship
- share data used to inform key decisions in transparent and accessible ways
- monitor media used for distributing information about programs and services

to ensure the content is current, accurate, appropriately referenced, and accessible

Leaders of HPS must also
- develop health-related programs and policies that support student learning
- gather relevant data and review current literature
- develop strategic, operational, and resource utilization plans and policies

Leaders of HPS should advocate for campus-wide understanding of the connections between learning, culture, identity, social justice, and health.

Leaders of HPS should support others in strengthening their health promotion skills.

The HPS director must be placed within the institution's organizational structures so as to be able to promote cooperative interaction with appropriate campus and community entities and to develop the support of high-level administrators for the creation of safe and healthy campus environments. The placement of HPS within the organizational structure must clearly articulate the value of enhancing well-being and health promotion as essential to the overall mission of an institution.

HPS organizational placement should facilitate significant interaction with unit heads in academic and student affairs.

HPS must be located in an organizational structure to best provide for effective programs and services to achieve its mission.

HPS must play a principal role in creating and implementing institutional policies and programs in response to assessed student needs and capabilities.

HPS should function independent of clinical health services to ensure adequate attention is paid to prevention.

Part 4. HUMAN RESOURCES

Health Promotion Services (HPS) must be staffed adequately by individuals qualified to accomplish mission and goals.

Within institutional guidelines, HPS must
- establish procedures for staff recruitment and selection, training, performance planning, and evaluation
- set expectations for supervision and performance
- assess the performance of employees individually and as a team
- provide access to continuing and advanced education and appropriate professional development opportunities to improve the leadership ability, competence, and skills of

all employees.

HPS should encourage professional staff members to participate in regular self-reflection, assessment, and professional development planning to improve health promotion practice.

HPS should provide personnel with convenient access to on-line and other reference services that include materials pertinent to the operational, administrative, institutional, and research services offered by the institution.

HPS must maintain position descriptions for all staff members.

To create a diverse staff, HPS must institute recruitment and hiring strategies that encourage individuals from under-represented populations to apply for positions.

HPS must develop promotion practices that are fair, inclusive, proactive, and non-discriminatory.

To further the recruitment and retention of staff, HPS must consider work life initiatives, such as compressed work schedules, flextime, job sharing, remote work, or telework.

HPS professional staff members must hold an earned graduate or professional degree in a field relevant to the position they hold or must possess an appropriate combination of educational credentials and related work experience.

Professional staff members should have appropriate professional preparation and competencies in both theory and evidence-based practice for promoting health, advancing student learning, and contributing to student development.

The director of HPS should have an advanced degree in health education, public health, higher education administration, or other related discipline from an accredited institution.

The preferred qualification for HPS staff members should be an advanced degree from an accredited institution in a relevant discipline such as health education, public health, higher education administration, counseling, or community development with experience in higher education.

HPS staffing requirements must be established and reviewed regularly with regard to size of campus, institutional resources, student needs, and interdisciplinary health promotion collaborations on campus.

HPS professional staff members must engage in continuing professional development activities to keep abreast of the research, theories, legislation, policies, and developments that affect their programs and services.

HPS must have technical and support staff members adequate to accomplish their mission. All members of the staff must be technologically proficient and qualified to perform their job functions, be knowledgeable about ethical and legal uses of technology, and have access to training and resources to support the performance of their assigned responsibilities.**

Degree- or credential-seeking interns or graduate assistants must be qualified by enrollment in an appropriate field of study and by relevant experience. These individuals must be trained and supervised adequately by professional staff members holding educational credentials and related work experience appropriate for supervision. Supervisors must be cognizant of the roles of interns and graduate assistants as both student and employee and closely adhere to all parameters of their job descriptions, work hours, and schedules. Supervisors and the interns or graduate assistants must agree to compensatory time or other appropriate compensation if circumstances necessitate additional hours.

Student employees and volunteers must be carefully selected, trained, supervised, and evaluated. They must be educated on how and when to refer those in need of additional assistance to qualified staff members and must have access to a supervisor for assistance in making these judgments. Student employees and volunteers must be provided clear job descriptions, pre-service training based on assessed needs, and continuing development.

All HPS staff members, including student employees and volunteers, must receive specific training on institutional policies pertaining to functions or activities they support and to privacy and confidentiality policies and laws regarding access to student records and other sensitive institutional information.

All HPS staff members must receive training on policies and procedures related to the use of technology to store or access student records and institutional data.

HPS staff members must participate in training sessions and professional development that address gender, sexual orientation, racial, cultural, religious and/or spiritual, and ethnic sensitivity.

HPS staff members should be encouraged to demonstrate their commitment to these issues that affect individuals, the campus, and the community by participating in relevant events.

HPS staff members must demonstrate trustworthiness when dealing with sensitive information and a strict regard for confidentiality.

HPSmustensurethatstaffmembersareknowledgeable about and trained in emergency procedures, crisis response, and prevention efforts. Prevention efforts must address identification of threatening conduct or behavior of students, faculty and staff members, and others and must incorporate a system for responding and reporting.

HPS must ensure that staff members are knowledgeable of and trained in safety and emergency procedures for securing and vacating facilities.

Specific aspects of professional development should include theories of health promotion, student learning, and student development; assessment and evaluation; service delivery; coalition building; collaboration; and business and financial management.

HPS should maintain and financially support an in-service and staff development program, and budgetary support should be available to provide for in-service and professional development activities.

Part 5. ETHICS

Health Promotion Services (HPS) must review relevant professional ethical standards and must adopt or develop and implement appropriate statements of ethical practice.

HPS must publish and adhere to statements of ethical practice and ensure their periodic review by relevant constituencies.

HPS must orient new staff members to relevant ethical standards and statements of ethical practice and related institutional policies.

Statements of ethical standards must specify that staff members respect privacy and maintain confidentiality in all communications and records to the extent that such communications and records are protected under relevant privacy laws.

Statements of ethical standards must specify limits on disclosure of information contained in students' educational records as well as requirements to disclose to appropriate authorities.

Statements of ethical standards must address personal and economic conflicts of interest, or appearance thereof, by staff members in the performance of their work.

Statements of ethical standards must reflect the responsibility of staff members to be fair, objective, and impartial in their interactions with others.

Statements of ethical standards must reference management of institutional funds.

Statements of ethical standards must reference appropriate behavior regarding research and assessment with human participants, confidentiality of research and assessment data, and students' rights and responsibilities.

Statements of ethical standards must include the expectation that HPS staff members confront and hold accountable other staff members who exhibit unethical behavior.

Statements of ethical standards must address issues surrounding scholarly integrity.

As appropriate, HPS staff members must inform users of programs and services of ethical obligations and limitations emanating from codes and laws or from licensure requirements.

HPS staff members must recognize and avoid conflicts of interest that could adversely influence their judgment or objectivity and, when unavoidable, recuse themselves from the situation.

HPS staff members must perform their duties within the limits of their position, training, expertise, and competence.

When these limits are exceeded, individuals in need of further assistance must be referred to persons possessing appropriate qualifications.

Promotional and descriptive information must be accurate and free of deception.

HPS must adhere to institutional policies regarding ethical and legal use of software and technology.

Part 6. LAW, POLICY, AND GOVERNANCE

Health Promotion Services (HPS) must be in compliance with laws, regulations, and policies that relate to their respective responsibilities and that pose legal obligations, limitations, risks, and liabilities for the institution as a whole. Examples include constitutional, statutory, regulatory, and case law; relevant law and orders emanating from codes and laws; and the institution's policies.

HPS must inform staff members, appropriate officials, and users of programs and services about existing and changing legal obligations, risks and liabilities, and limitations.

HPS must have written policies on all relevant operations, transactions, or tasks that have legal implications.

HPS must regularly review policies. The revision and creation of policies must be informed by best practices, available evidence, and policy issues in higher education.

HPS staff members must use reasonable and informed practices to limit the liability exposure of the institution and its officers, employees, and agents. HPS staff members must be informed about institutional policies regarding risk management, personal liability, and related insurance coverage options and must be referred to external sources if the institution does not provide coverage.

The institution must provide access to legal advice for staff members as needed to carry out assigned responsibilities.

HPS must have procedures and guidelines consistent with institutional policy for responding to threats, emergencies, and crisis situations. Systems and procedures must be in place to disseminate timely and accurate information to students, other members of the institutional community, and appropriate external organizations during emergency situations.

HPS staff members must neither participate in nor condone any form of harassment or activity that demeans persons or creates an intimidating, hostile, or offensive environment.

HPS must obtain permission to use copyrighted materials and instruments. HPS must purchase the materials and instruments from legally compliant sources or seek alternative permission from the publisher or owner. References to copyrighted materials and instruments must include appropriate citations.

HPS staff members must be knowledgeable about internal and external governance systems that affect programs and services.

Part 7. DIVERSITY, EQUITY, AND ACCESS

Within the context of each institution's unique mission and in accordance with institutional polices and all applicable codes and laws, Health Promotion Services (HPS) must create and maintain educational and work environments that are
- welcoming, accessible, and inclusive to persons of diverse backgrounds
- equitable and non-discriminatory
- free from harassment

HPS must not discriminate on the basis of ability; age; cultural identity; ethnicity; family educational history (e.g., first generation to attend college); gender identity and expression; nationality; political affiliation; race; religious affiliation; sex; sexual orientation; economic, marital, social, or veteran status; or any other basis included in institutional policies and codes and laws.

HPS must

- advocate for greater sensitivity to multicultural and social justice concerns by the institution and its personnel
- modify or remove policies, practices, facilities, structures, systems, and technologies that limit access, discriminate, or produce inequities
- include diversity, equity, and access initiatives within their strategic plans
- foster communication that deepens understanding of identity, culture, self-expression, and heritage
- promote respect about commonalities and differences among people within their historical and cultural contexts
- address the characteristics and needs of a diverse population when establishing and implementing culturally relevant and inclusive programs, services, policies, procedures, and practices
- provide staff members with access to multicultural training and hold staff members accountable for integrating the training into their work
- respond to the needs of all students and other populations served when establishing hours of operation and developing methods of delivering programs, services, and resources
- ensure physical, program, and resource access for persons with disabilities
- recognize the needs of distance learning students by providing appropriate and accessible services and resources or by assisting them in gaining access to other appropriate services and resources in their geographic region

HPS should identify any social, cultural, political, and economic disparities that influence the health of students so that any disparities may be adequately addressed to improve equity and access to health-related services.

HPS staff members must demonstrate cultural competency and inclusiveness in advancing the health of individuals and communities.

HPS should design health promotion initiatives that reflect the social, cultural, and economic diversity of students.

HPS should create health promotion mission statements, program policies, staff member recruitment and retention practices, and professional development goals that reflect the social, cultural, and economic diversity of the campus.

HPS should provide leadership for campus-wide understanding of the connection between culture, identity, social justice, and health status.

Part 8. INSTITUTIONAL AND EXTERNAL RELATIONS

Health Promotion Services (HPS) must reach out to relevant individuals, groups, communities, and organizations internal and external to the institution to
- **establish, maintain, and promote understanding and effective relations with those that have a significant interest in or potential effect on the students or other constituents served by the programs and services**
- **garner support and resources for programs and services as defined by the mission statement**
- **disseminate information about the programs and services**
- **collaborate, where appropriate, to assist in offering or improving programs and services to meet the needs of students and other constituents and to achieve program and student outcomes**
- **engage diverse individuals, groups, communities, and organizations to enrich the educational environment and experiences of students and other constituents**

Sustaining partnerships should
- advocate for a shared vision that health promotion is the responsibility of all campus and community members
- develop and participate in campus and community partnerships that advance health promotion initiatives
- use campus and community resources to maximize the effectiveness of health promotion initiatives
- advocate for campus, local, state/provincial, national, and international policies that address campus and community health issues
- institutionalize health promotion initiatives through inclusion in campus strategic planning and resource allocation processes

HPS must have procedures and guidelines consistent with institutional policy for
- **communicating with the media**
- **contracting with external organizations for delivery of programs and services**
- **cultivating, soliciting, and managing gifts**
- **applying to and managing funds from grants**

To ensure success, HPS must maintain productive relations with students, faculty members, staff members, alumni, the community at large, contractors, and support agencies.

HPS staff members should participate actively with their institutions in designing policies and practices and developing further resources and services that have direct effects on the health of the campus population.

HPS should work closely with the senior administrators to ensure the meeting of institutional goals and objectives.

HPS should establish relationships with a wide range of constituencies, such as student affairs professionals, faculty members, and student groups, to promote collaboration and serve as a resource.

HPS should foster relationships with academic units and campus professionals in residence halls, recreational facilities, student activities, and athletics, where appropriate.

HPS should foster reciprocal relationships with clinical health services and counseling services to refer students for medical concerns and to serve as colleagues and consultants.

Part 9. FINANCIAL RESOURCES

Health Promotion Services (HPS) must have funding to accomplish the mission and goals. In establishing funding priorities and making significant changes, a comprehensive analysis must be conducted to determine the following elements: unmet needs of the unit, relevant expenditures, external and internal resources, and impact on students and the institution.

HPS must demonstrate efficient and effective use and responsible stewardship of fiscal resources consistent with institutional protocols.

Funding for HPS should be provided and sustained by the institution's budget or through a designated health fee applied to all enrolled students.

Part 10. TECHNOLOGY

Health Promotion Services (HPS) must have adequate technology to support the achievement of their mission and goals. The technology and its use must comply with institutional policies and procedures and be evaluated for compliance with relevant codes and laws.

HPS must use current technology to provide updated information regarding mission, location, staffing, programs, services, and official contacts to students and designated clients.

HPS must explore the use of technology to enhance delivery of programs and services, especially for students at a distance or external constituencies.

When technology is used to facilitate student learning and development, HPS must select technology that reflects intended outcomes.

HPS must
- **maintain policies and procedures that address the security, confidentiality, and backup of**

data, as well as compliance with privacy laws
- **have clearly articulated plans in place for protecting confidentiality and security of information when using Internet-based technologies**
- **develop plans for replacing and updating existing hardware and software as well as plans for integrating new technically-based or supported programs, including systems developed internally by the institution, systems available through professional associations, or private vendor-based systems**

Technology, as well as workstations or computer labs maintained by programs and services for student use, must be accessible to all designated clients and must meet established technology standards for delivery to persons with disabilities.

When providing student access to technology, HPS must
- **have policies on the use of technology that are clear, easy to understand, and available to all students**
- **provide assistance, information, or referral to appropriate support services to those needing help accessing or using technology**
- **provide instruction or training on how to use the technology**
- **inform students on the legal and ethical implications of misuse as it pertains to intellectual property, harassment, privacy, and social networks**

Student violations of technology policies must follow established institutional student disciplinary procedures.

Students who experience negative emotional or psychological consequences from the use of technology must be referred to support services provided by the institution.

Part 11. FACILITIES AND EQUIPMENT

Health Promotion Services (HPS) must have adequate, accessible, and suitably located facilities and equipment to support the mission and goals. If acquiring capital equipment as defined by the institution, HPS must take into account expenses related to regular maintenance and life cycle costs. Facilities and equipment must be evaluated on an established cycle, including consideration of sustainability, and be in compliance with codes and laws to provide for access, health, safety, and security.

To promote holistic health, the facilities of HPS should include

- a safe, functional, effective, and conveniently located positive environment for students, faculty and staff members, and community partners
- office space that is functionally autonomous rather than housed as a component of other units on campus
- office space that is physically separate from clinical health services
- quality space to ensure maximum effectiveness in providing health promotion resources for the campus community
- adequate meeting space for training student volunteers and supporting their work
- adequate physical facilities, equipment, and technology to monitor and report population health status data

HPS staff members must have workspace that is well equipped, adequate in size, and designed to support their work and responsibilities. For conversations requiring privacy, staff members must have access to a private space.

HPS staff members who share workspace must be able to secure their own work.

The design of the facilities must guarantee the security and privacy of records and ensure the confidentiality of sensitive information.

The location and layout of the facilities must be sensitive to the needs of persons with disabilities as well as the needs of other constituencies.

Part 12. ASSESSMENT AND EVALUATION

Health Promotion Services (HPS) must have a clearly articulated assessment plan to document achievement of stated goals and learning outcomes, demonstrate accountability, provide evidence of improvement, and describe resulting changes in programs and services.

HPS must have adequate fiscal, human, professional development, and technological resources to develop and implement assessment plans.

Assessments must include direct and indirect evaluation and use qualitative and quantitative methodologies and existing evidence, as appropriate, to determine whether and to what degree the stated mission, goals, and intended outcomes are being met as effectively and efficiently as possible. The process must employ sufficient and sound measures to ensure comprehensiveness. Data collected must include responses from students and other constituencies, and aggregated results must be shared with those groups. Results of assessments must be shared appropriately with multiple constituents.

Assessment and evaluation should include
- data gathered from published research on international, national, state/provincial, local, and campus health priorities
- population-based assessment of health status, needs, and assets of students
- environmental assessment of campus-community health needs and resources
- measurable goals and objectives for health promotion initiatives

Results of assessments and evaluations must be used to identify needs and interests in revising and improving programs and services, recognizing staff performance, maximizing resource efficiency and effectiveness, improving student achievement of learning and development outcomes, and improving student persistence and success. Changes resulting from the use of assessments and evaluation must be shared with stakeholders.

HPS should report evaluation data and research results to students, faculty members, staff members, and the campus community.

General Standards revised in 2011;
HPS content developed in 2006

The Role of Housing and Residential Life Programs
CAS Standards Contextual Statement

Although American institutions of higher learning have provided student housing in one form or another since the first colleges were founded (Frederiksen, 1993), the professionalization of those employed in housing was greatly enhanced when the Association of College and University Housing Officers-International (ACUHO-I) held its first annual conference in 1949. This meeting marked a significant step forward in the development of college and university student housing programs as a profession.

Until the middle of the last century, college and university "dormitories" were administered by "housemothers," often under the supervision of deans of men or women. These staff members assumed parental responsibility (in loco parentis) for the students housed in the residence halls. During the 1960s, dramatic changes in laws and education produced changes in the operation of residence halls. Housemothers were replaced by full-time staff with professional training in counseling and administration. These student affairs professionals focused on using the residence hall environment as a tool to complement formal classroom education. Since the 1960s, student housing has become increasingly more specialized and complex. The influence of the residential experience on the lives of students has been widely researched over the years.

> Group living influences maturation by exposing students to a variety of experiences and community-building activities. What distinguishes group living in campus residence from most other forms of housing is the involvement of both professional and paraprofessional staff members in providing intentional, as opposed to random, educational experiences for students. Students living in residence halls participate in more extracurricular, social, and cultural events; are more likely to graduate; and exhibit greater positive gains in psychosocial development, intellectual orientation, and self-concept than students living at home or commuting. In addition, they demonstrate significantly greater increases in aesthetic, cultural, and intellectual values; social and political liberalism; and secularism. (Schroeder & Mable, 1993)

More recently, the quality of residence halls has been acknowledged as not only essential to the quality of campus life but as an increasingly important factor in attracting students to a given institution. There has been a renaissance in college and university housing with many campuses significantly renovating halls and constructing new facilities to respond to today's students and to better meet expectations. One challenge for housing professionals

has indeed been the increasing demand for amenities in residence halls, which is often necessary to not only respond to the needs of today's students but to remain competitive with housing in the local market or with other institutions that are considered peers for enrollment management purposes. Some of the more obvious amenity enhancements include air conditioning, wireless connectivity, and conversion of traditional double loaded corridor rooms to suite style or single room accommodations, including bathrooms.

Another facility enhancement that cannot be overlooked is additions to the safety features provided in housing and residence life programs. In addition to electronic card access found on exterior doors, more programs are adding this feature to the individual room doors to eliminate the need for keys and to facilitate a very timely response minimizing any threat to building security. Throughout these facility enhancements, housing professionals are continually faced with balancing students' desire for convenience with the university's needs related to security and public safety. Many colleges and universities have added video surveillance capability to exterior doors, stairwells, elevator lobbies, halls, high tech learning facilities, or specialized classrooms while being sensitive to privacy issues on individual floors and rooms. Housing and Residence Life professionals are often members of the campus emergency management and/or threat-assessment teams and play a key role in emergency planning and response.

One of the most impactful concepts in higher education today is that of learning communities; many universities have developed living learning communities (LLCs) within residential communities as a means to be more intentional about student learning. LLCs provide valuable opportunities to integrate the more formal academic and student life experience, provide increased interaction between students and faculty, and provide critical avenues to enhance campus community building activities and traditions. Living learning communities can be developed around themes, majors, or concepts. In addition to providing a seamless learning experience and increased student engagement, LLCs are seen as critical to increasing retention, especially from the first to the second year.

College and university student housing operations employ staff members with wide varieties of skills and functions. Areas administered by institutional housing and residence life programs include such functions as
- Apartment, graduate and family housing
- Fraternities and sororities
- Student conduct and/or contract violations
- Housing for students with disabilities and other

- special needs
- Conference and guest housing
- Residence Education, including academic initiatives, LLCs, programming, and diversity education
- Facilities management (custodial and maintenance) and capital projects
- Financial planning and administration (assignments, contracting, billing, collections)
- Dining services (including catering and retail venues)
- Administration of in-hall information technology capabilities, media, and facilities (cable TV, various software systems, network and wireless access, computer learning centers, and classrooms)
- Off-campus housing services
- Research and assessment
- Safety and security measures (fire safety, electronic access systems, video surveillance, hall security)
- Identification and "one card" programs

Assessment efforts, particularly incorporating assessment of services, programs, staffing, and student learning can provide valuable information to housing administrators as they shape their housing and residential life programs. Administrators can work to develop clear student learning outcomes and design assessment to analyze these outcomes. Assessment lenses (e.g., interviews, focus groups, surveys, tracking) can help administrators document student learning and make efforts to improve the residential experience. Association of College and University Housing Officers–International (ACUHO-I) Educational Benchmarking Inc., the National Survey of Student Engagement (NSSE), and National Study of Living-Learning Programs (NSLLP) are examples of national surveys that are often administered to collect assessment data.

Many institutional student-housing operations are self-supported auxiliaries that do not receive financial support from the institution or other public sources; in effect, student housing in that context is an education "business." Privatization of residence halls/collegiate housing is part of the landscape of 21st century housing on college campuses. Some schools have opted to privatize aspects of their residence halls (development, construction, and management), utilizing housing management companies to address residence hall capacity shortages, aging facilities, a desire to house more students on campus, and changing student expectations (Fickes, 2007). Regardless of the status of the operation, planning is usually initiated institution-wide due to the wide scope and function of student housing. Likewise, although housing encompasses many functions, most administrations agree that students are best served when all housing and residential life functions fall under the responsibility of a single administrator, usually the director of housing and/or residential life. When public-private partnerships are undertaken, and "privatized" housing

developments have a formal relationship with the college or university and are located on campus, it is expected that these entities follow the same CAS Standards as the institution's program. As higher education prepares students with the knowledge and skills required for the challenges of the 21st century and as learning becomes more a lifetime responsibility, residence halls will continue to be a critical component of the undergraduate experience. The standards and guidelines that follow provide guidance to those who work in this field and accountability to the public they serve.

References, Readings, and Resources

American Association of Higher Education, American College Personnel Association, National Association of Student Personnel Administrators. (1998). *Powerful partnerships: A shared responsibility for learning.* Washington, DC: Authors.

American College Personnel Association. Commission on Housing and Residence Life. http://www.acpa.nche.edu/comms/comm03/index.html

American College Personnel Association and National Association of Student Personnel Administrators. (2004). *Learning reconsidered: A campus-wide focus on the student experience.* Washington DC: Authors.

Association of College and University Housing Officers-International (ACUHO-I). (1999). *Educational programming and student learning in college and university residence halls.* Columbus, OH: Author.

Association of College and University Housing Officers-International (ACUHO-I). (1992). *Ethical principles and standards for college and university housing professionals.* Columbus, OH: Author.

Association of College and University Housing Officers - International. (2008b). *Recruitment and retention of entry-level staff in housing and residence life: A report on activities supported by the ACUHO-I commissioned research program.* Columbus, OH: Author.

Blimling, G. S. (1993). New challenges and goals for residential life programs. In R. B. Winston, Jr., S. Anchors, & Associates (Eds.), *Student housing and residential life* (pp. 1-20). San Francisco, CA: Jossey-Bass.

Blimling, G. (1998). *The resident assistant: Applications and strategies for working with college students in residence halls* (5th ed.). Dubuque, IA: Kendall/Hunt.

Dunkel, N. W., & Schreiber, P. J. (1992). Competency development of housing professionals. *Journal of College and University Student Housing, 22*(2), 19-23.

Fickes, M. (2007, November 15). Privatized housing moves on-campus. *College Planning & Management.* ww.peterli.com/archive/cpm/122.shtm.

Frederiksen, C. F. (1993). A brief history of collegiate housing. In R. B. Winston, Jr., & S. Anchors (Eds.), *Student housing and residential life: A handbook for student affairs professionals committed to student development goals* (pp. 167-183). San Francisco: Jossey-Bass.

Keeling, R. P. (Ed.). (2006). *Learning reconsidered 2: A practical guide to implementing a campus-wide focus on the student experience.* Washington, D.C.: American

College Personnel Association, Association of College and University Housing Officers International, Association of College Unions International, National Academic Advising Association, National Association of Campus Activities, National Association of Student Personnel Administrators, & National Intramural-Recreational Sports Association.

Kuh, G. D., Sheed, J. D., Whitt, E. J., & Associates. (1991). *Involving colleges: Successful approaches to fostering student learning and development outside the classroom.* San Francisco: Jossey-Bass.

Laufgraben, J. L., Shipiro, N. S., & Associates. (2004). *Sustaining and improving learning communities.* San Francisco: Jossey-Bass.

National Leadership Council for Liberal Education and America's Promise. (2007). *College learning for the new global century.* Washington, DC: Author.

Schroeder, C. C., Mable, P., & Associates. (1993). *Realizing the educational potential of residence halls.* San Francisco: Jossey-Bass.

Shuh, J. (Ed.). (1999). *Educational programming and student learning in college and university residence halls.* Columbus, OH: Association of College and University Housing Officers-International.

The Journal of College and University Student Housing. Published by the Association of College and University Housing Officers-International (ACUHO-I), 941 Chatham Lane, Suite 318 Columbus, OH 43221-2416 Phone: 614.292.0099 Fax: 614.292.3205

Winston, R. B, Jr., Anchors, S., & Associates. (1993). *Student housing and residential life: A handbook for student affairs professionals committed to student development goals.* San Francisco: Jossey-Bass.

Contextual Statement Contributors

Current Edition:
Carole Henry, Old Dominion University, ACUHO-I

Previous Editions:
Mike Eyster, University of Oregon

Housing and Residential Life Programs
CAS Standards and Guidelines

Part 1. MISSION

The mission of Housing and Residential Life Programs (HRLP) is accomplished through the coordination of several interdependent specialized areas: residence education/programming, business operations, and housing/facilities management.

The standards in this document also apply to additional specialized areas that may include food services, apartment/family housing, special interest housing, conference housing, faculty/staff housing, and off-campus housing services.

The mission of HRLP must address
- **the living environment, including programs and services, that promotes learning and development in the broadest sense, with an emphasis on academic success**
- **reasonably priced living facilities that are clean, attractive, well-maintained, comfortable, and which include contemporary safety features maintained by systematic operations**
- **orderly and effective management of HRLP that consists of meeting the needs of students and other constituents in a courteous, efficient, and effective manner**
- **the provision of a variety of nutritious and pleasing meals, in pleasant surroundings, at a reasonable cost, and related services that effectively meet institutional goals (catering, retail/cash operations, convenience stores), in programs that include food services**

HRLP must develop, disseminate, implement, and regularly review their missions. The mission must be consistent with the mission of the institution and with professional standards. The mission must be appropriate for the institution's student populations and community settings. Mission statements must reference student learning and development.

Part 2. PROGRAM

The formal education of students, consisting of the curriculum and the co-curriculum, must promote student learning and development outcomes that are purposeful, contribute to students' realization of their potential, and prepare students for satisfying and productive lives.

Housing and Residential Life Programs (HRLP) must collaborate with colleagues and departments across the institution to promote student learning and development, persistence, and success.

Consistent with the institutional mission, HRLP must identify relevant and desirable student learning and development outcomes from among the six domains and related dimensions:

Domain: knowledge acquisition, integration, construction, and application
- **Dimensions: understanding knowledge from a range of disciplines; connecting knowledge to other knowledge, ideas, and experiences; constructing knowledge; and relating knowledge to daily life**

Domain: cognitive complexity
- **Dimensions: critical thinking, reflective thinking, effective reasoning, and creativity**

Domain: intrapersonal development
- **Dimensions: realistic self-appraisal, self-understanding, and self-respect; identity development; commitment to ethics and integrity; and spiritual awareness**

Domain: interpersonal competence
- **Dimensions: meaningful relationships, interdependence, collaboration, and effective leadership.**

Domain: humanitarianism and civic engagement
- **Dimensions: understanding and appreciation of cultural and human differences, social responsibility, global perspective, and sense of civic responsibility**

Domain: practical competence
- **Dimensions: pursuing goals, communicating effectively, technical competence, managing personal affairs, managing career development, demonstrating professionalism, maintaining health and wellness, and living a purposeful and satisfying life**

[LD Outcomes: See *The Council for the Advancement of Standards Learning and Developmental Outcomes* statement for examples of outcomes related to these domains and dimensions.]

HRLP must
- **assess relevant and desirable student learning and development**
- **provide evidence of impact on outcomes**
- **articulate contributions to or support of student learning and development in the**

domains not specifically assessed
- articulate contributions to or support of student persistence and success
- use evidence gathered through this process to create strategies for improvement of programs and services

HRLP must be
- intentionally designed
- guided by theories and knowledge of learning and development
- integrated into the life of the institution
- reflective of developmental and demographic profiles of the student population
- responsive to needs of individuals, populations with distinct needs, and relevant constituencies
- delivered using multiple formats, strategies, and contexts

Where institutions provide distance education, HRLP must assist distance learners to achieve their educational goals by providing access to information about programs and services, to staff members who can address questions and concerns, and to counseling, advising, or other forms of assistance.

HRLP must provide educational opportunities for students and other members of the campus community that support the strategic initiatives of the institution.

Partnerships with faculty members, academic administrators, and other campus constituents should be developed to utilize student residences as an integral part of the educational experience. These activities may include offering any of the following: partnerships with enrollment management to attract and retain students; faculty-staff interaction with students through workshop and lecture presentations; scholars in residence programs, residential colleges, classrooms (traditional and electronic) and computer labs in the residence halls; opportunities for faculty to hold office hours and meet with students; partnerships with departments and colleges to offer living-learning communities by academic program, theme, or special interest; residentially-based tutoring programs, study skills, and related workshops; and activities that contribute to achieving the academic mission.

Staff members must provide a variety of educational opportunities that promote academic success and the achievement of learning and student development outcomes.

HRLP should provide an environment that assists residents to remain in good academic standing, earn higher GPAs, and be retained. This may occur through early alert intervention programs; educating staff and students about available campus academic resources; offering living-learning communities which can be linked with course blocking;

transition or bridging programs; partnerships with first-year experience programs; or establishment of first-year interest groups, year-two programs, informal study groups, senior year experience programs, or other academic initiatives.

HRLP must provide access to experiences and services that facilitate
- a seamless learning environment
- opportunities to interact with faculty and staff members
- encouragement and assistance in forming study groups
- access to academic resources through technology
- opportunities to develop a mature style of relating to others and living cooperatively with others
- opportunities for analyzing, forming, and confirming values
- activities and educational opportunities that promote independence and self-sufficiency
- educational opportunities that assist residents in developing and confirming a sense of identity
- experiences that lead to the respect for self, others, and property
- experiences that promote a sense of justice and fair play
- opportunities to appreciate new ideas
- opportunities to appreciate cultural differences and other forms of diversity
- opportunities to apply knowledge, skills, and values
- opportunities for leadership development and decision-making
- opportunities to make career choices through planned activities
- opportunities to develop a balanced life style embracing wellness
- opportunities to learn life skills, e.g., personal finance and time management

Educational and community development programming, advising and counseling, and administrative activities of the HRLP staff will vary according to assessed student needs and institutional priorities.

In education and community development programs, staff members must
- introduce and orient residents to community expectations, facilities, services, and staff
- document institutional and residential living policies, procedures, and expectations including the potential consequences for violation
- involve students in programming, policy

development, and self-governance
- provide educational programs that focus on awareness of cultural differences and self-assessment of possible prejudices
- offer social, recreational, educational, cultural, and community service programs
- promote and provide education about the effects and risks of drug and alcohol use
- encourage residents to exercise responsibility for their community through confrontation of inappropriate or disruptive behavior
- encourage residents to participate in mediating conflict within the community
- encourage residents to learn about their rights as students, tenants, residents, and consumers

   Off-campus housing services should include referrals to available housing opportunities, listings, information about leases, landlord/tenant law, information about local ordinances, community resources, and other related information.

- promote appropriate student use of technological resources

In advising, counseling, and crises intervention, staff members must
- provide individual advising or counseling support within the scope of their training and expertise, and make appropriate referrals
- create relationships with students that demonstrate genuine interest in students' educational and personal development

In administrative activities, staff members must
- provide a clear and complete written agreement between the resident and the institution that conveys mutual commitments and responsibilities

   The agreement should include contract eligibility and duration; room assignments and changes; rates and payment policies; dining options; procedures for canceling, subleasing, or being released from the housing and/or dining agreement; room entry and inspection procedures; and pertinent rules and regulations.

- encourage residents to participate in evaluating HRLP
- provide information on safety, security, and emergency procedures
- create and maintain an environment and atmosphere which is conducive to educational pursuits
- provide emergency response and crisis intervention management in coordination with relevant campus and community resources
- ensure that the safety and security of the

residents and their property are taken into consideration as policies are developed
- assess needs of the housing population annually, specifically addressing the needs for special interest programming and for upgrading or modifying facilities

When food services is included within HRLP, it must include
- high quality food products
- orderly, secure, and sanitary food storage
- compliance with all pertinent environmental, health, and safety codes as well as sanitation procedures
- timely delivery of services
- high quality customer services
- pleasant environment in dining areas
- materials that educate students about nutrition and its relationship to good health
- suggestions and input from users regarding menu selection, satisfaction, and
- on-going evaluation

When a residential dining program is included within HRLP, it must include the above standards and
- menu planning to provide optimum nutrition and variety
- recipes and preparation processes that ensure appetizing food
- attention to students' cultural differences and special dietary needs
- hours of dining service operations sufficient to reasonably accommodate student needs
- dining meal plan options that are clear, affordable, and responsive to student needs
- involvement in educational programming that contributes to student learning and resident satisfaction

The standards and procedures developed and published by professional associations should be used for operating institutional food service operations.

Part 3. ORGANIZATION AND LEADERSHIP

To achieve student and program outcomes, Housing and Residential Life Programs (HRLP) must be structured purposefully and organized effectively. HRLP must have
- clearly stated goals
- current and accessible policies and procedures
- written performance expectations for employees
- functional work flow graphics or organizational charts demonstrating clear channels of authority

Leaders with organizational authority for the programs and services must provide strategic planning, supervision, and management; advance the organization; and maintain integrity through the following functions:

Strategic Planning

- articulate a vision and mission that drive short- and long-term planning
- set goals and objectives based on the needs of the population served and desired student learning or development and program outcomes
- facilitate continuous development, implementation, and assessment of goal attainment congruent with institutional mission and strategic plans
- promote environments that provide meaningful opportunities for student learning, development, and engagement
- develop and continuously improve programs and services in response to the changing needs of students served and evolving institutional priorities
- intentionally include diverse perspectives to inform decision making

Supervising

- manage human resource processes including recruitment, selection, development, supervision, performance planning, evaluation, recognition, and reward
- influence others to contribute to the effectiveness and success of the unit
- empower professional, support, and student staff to accept leadership opportunities
- offer appropriate feedback to colleagues and students on skills needed to become more effective leaders
- encourage and support professional development, collaboration with colleagues and departments across the institution, and scholarly contribution to the profession

Managing

- identify and address individual, organizational, and environmental conditions that foster or inhibit mission achievement
- plan, allocate, and monitor the use of fiscal, physical, human, intellectual, and technological resources
- use current and valid evidence to inform decisions
- incorporate sustainability practices in the management and design of programs, services, and facilities
- understand appropriate technologies and integrate them into programs and services
- be knowledgeable about codes and laws

relevant to programs and services and ensure that staff members understand their responsibilities through appropriate training

- assess potential risks and take action to mitigate them

Advancing the Organization

- communicate effectively in writing, speaking, and electronic venues
- advocate for programs and services
- advocate for representation in strategic planning initiatives at appropriate divisional and institutional levels
- initiate collaborative interactions with internal and external stakeholders who have legitimate concerns about and interests in the functional area
- facilitate processes to reach consensus where wide support is needed
- inform other areas within the institution about issues affecting practice

Maintaining Integrity

- model ethical behavior and institutional citizenship
- share data used to inform key decisions in transparent and accessible ways
- monitor media used for distributing information about programs and services to ensure the content is current, accurate, appropriately referenced, and accessible

An organizational chart should define both the responsibilities and relationships of staff members with the understanding that HRLP leadership should emphasize fluidity, adaptability, and cross-functional collaboration.

Where the management of the HRLP is divided among different agencies within the institution, it is the responsibility of insitutional leaders to establish and maintain productive working relationships.

A unified organizational structure, including all housing and residential life functions, should be used so as to effectively deliver the services to users and to avoid multiple hierarchical lines of communication and authority.

HRLP must maintain well-structured management functions, including planning, personnel, property management, purchasing, contract administration, financial control, and information systems.

Evaluation of the organization is based on progress toward the achievement of short- and long-range organizational goals. Planning must be adequate to project and accommodate both immediate and future needs.

Part 4. HUMAN RESOURCES

Housing and Residential Life Programs (HRLP) must be staffed adequately by individuals qualified to accomplish mission and goals.

Within institutional guidelines, HRLP must
- establish procedures for staff recruitment and selection, training, performance planning, and evaluation
- set expectations for supervision and performance
- assess the performance of employees individually and as a team
- provide access to continuing and advanced education and appropriate professional development opportunities to improve the leadership ability, competence, and skills of all employees.

HRLP must maintain position descriptions for all staff members.

HRLP position descriptions should include adequate time for planning as well as for program implementation.

To create a diverse staff, HRLP must institute recruitment and hiring strategies that encourage individuals from under-represented populations to apply for positions.

HRLP must develop promotion practices that are fair, inclusive, proactive, and non-discriminatory.

To further the recruitment and retention of staff, HRLP must consider work life initiatives, such as compressed work schedules, flextime, job sharing, remote work, or telework.

HRLP professional staff members must hold an earned graduate or professional degree in a field relevant to the position they hold or must possess an appropriate combination of educational credentials and related work experience.

There must be at least one professional staff member responsible for the administration and coordination of the department.   This individual must be knowledgeable about the goals and mission of the program.

Individual residence halls and apartment areas should be supervised by professional staff that have earned a master's degree from accredited institutions in a field of study such as college student personnel, college counseling, or higher education administration, or other fields as appropriate.

HRLP professional staff members must engage in continuing professional development activities to keep abreast of the research, theories, legislation, policies, and developments that affect their programs and services.

HRLP must have technical and support staff members adequate to accomplish their mission. All members of the staff must be technologically proficient and qualified to perform their job functions, be knowledgeable about ethical and legal uses of technology, and have access to training and resources to support the performance of their assigned responsibilities.

Degree- or credential-seeking interns or graduate assistants must be qualified by enrollment in an appropriate field of study and by relevant experience. These individuals must be trained and supervised adequately by professional staff members holding educational credentials and related work experience appropriate for supervision. Supervisors must be cognizant of the roles of interns and graduate assistants as both student and employee and closely adhere to all parameters of their job descriptions, work hours, and schedules. Supervisors and the interns or graduate assistants must agree to compensatory time or other appropriate compensation if circumstances necessitate additional hours.

Demonstrated skills of leadership and communication, maturity, a well-developed sense of responsibility, sensitivity to individual differences, a positive self-concept, an understanding of how to promote student learning and academic success, and an obvious interest and enthusiasm for working with students are desirable characteristics for professional, pre-professional, and paraprofessional staff members.

Student employees and volunteers must be carefully selected, trained, supervised, and evaluated. They must be educated on how and when to refer those in need of additional assistance to qualified staff members and must have access to a supervisor for assistance in making these judgments. Student employees and volunteers must be provided clear job descriptions, pre-service training based on assessed needs, and continuing development.

All HRLP staff members, including student employees and volunteers, must receive specific training on institutional policies pertaining to functions or activities they support and to privacy and confidentiality policies and laws regarding access to student records and other sensitive institutional information.

All HRLP staff members must receive training on policies and procedures related to the use of technology to store or access student records and institutional data.

Resident/community   assistants   and   other

paraprofessionals are expected to contribute to the accomplishment of the following functions: (a) educational programming, (b) administration, (c) group and activity advising, (d) leadership development, (e) discipline, (f) role modeling, (g) individual assistance and referral, and (h) providing information.

HRLP must ensure that staff members are knowledgeable about and trained in emergency procedures, crisis response, and prevention efforts. Prevention efforts must address identification of threatening conduct or behavior of students, faculty and staff members, and others and must incorporate a system for responding and reporting.

HRLP must ensure that staff members are knowledgeable of and trained in safety and emergency procedures for securing and vacating facilities.

HRLP staff members should have a written personal development plan that reflects the goals and objectives of the organization and areas for professional growth.

HRLP staff members must have a working knowledge of all relevant policies and procedures, the rationale for policies and procedures, and the relationship of policies and procedures to the organization's mission statement, goals, and objectives.

HRLP policies and procedures are reviewed annually and updated as appropriate.

HRLP staff members must be knowledgeable about and remain current with respect to the obligations and limitations placed upon the institution by constitutional, statutory, and common law, by external governmental agencies, and by institutional policies.

Part 5. ETHICS

Housing and Residential Life Programs (HRLP) must review relevant professional ethical standards and must adopt or develop and implement appropriate statements of ethical practice.

HRLP must publish and adhere to statements of ethical practice and ensure their periodic review by relevant constituencies.

HRLP must orient new staff members to relevant ethical standards and statements of ethical practice and related institutional policies.

Statements of ethical standards must specify that staff members respect privacy and maintain confidentiality in all communications and records to the extent that such communications and records are protected under relevant privacy laws.

Statements of ethical standards must specify limits on disclosure of information contained in students' educational records as well as requirements to disclose to appropriate authorities.

Statements of ethical standards must address personal and economic conflicts of interest, or appearance thereof, by staff members in the performance of their work.

Statements of ethical standards must reflect the responsibility of staff members to be fair, objective, and impartial in their interactions with others.

Statements of ethical standards must reference management of institutional funds.

Statements of ethical standards must reference appropriate behavior regarding research and assessment with human participants, confidentiality of research and assessment data, and students' rights and responsibilities.

Statements of ethical standards must include the expectation that HRLP staff members confront and hold accountable other staff members who exhibit unethical behavior.

Statements of ethical standards must address issues surrounding scholarly integrity.

As appropriate, HRLP staff members must inform users of programs and services of ethical obligations and limitations emanating from codes and laws or from licensure requirements.

HRLP staff members must recognize and avoid conflicts of interest that could adversely influence their judgment or objectivity and, when unavoidable, recuse themselves from the situation.

HRLP staff members must perform their duties within the limits of their position, training, expertise, and competence.

When these limits are exceeded, individuals in need of further assistance must be referred to persons possessing appropriate qualifications.

Promotional and descriptive information must be accurate and free of deception.

HRLP must adhere to institutional policies regarding ethical and legal use of software and technology.

HRLP staff members should remain abreast of ethical codes and practices through involvement in professional associations.

Part 6. LAW, POLICY, AND GOVERNANCE

Housing and Residential Life Programs (HRLP) must be in compliance with laws, regulations, and policies that relate to their respective responsibilities and that pose legal obligations, limitations, risks, and liabilities for the institution as a whole. Examples include constitutional, statutory, regulatory, and case law; relevant law and orders emanating from codes and laws; and the institution's policies.

HRLP must inform staff members, appropriate officials, and users of programs and services about existing and changing legal obligations, risks and liabilities, and limitations.

HRLP must have written policies on all relevant operations, transactions, or tasks that have legal implications.

HRLP must regularly review policies. The revision and creation of policies must be informed by best practices, available evidence, and policy issues in higher education.

HRLP staff members must use reasonable and informed practices to limit the liability exposure of the institution and its officers, employees, and agents. HRLP staff members must be informed about institutional policies regarding risk management, personal liability, and related insurance coverage options and must be referred to external sources if the institution does not provide coverage.

The institution must provide access to legal advice for staff members as needed to carry out assigned responsibilities.

HRLP must have procedures and guidelines consistent with institutional policy for responding to threats, emergencies, and crisis situations. Systems and procedures must be in place to disseminate timely and accurate information to students, other members of the institutional community, and appropriate external organizations during emergency situations.

HRLP staff members must neither participate in nor condone any form of harassment or activity that demeans persons or creates an intimidating, hostile, or offensive environment.

HRLP must obtain permission to use copyrighted materials and instruments. HRLP must purchase the materials and instruments from legally compliant sources or seek alternative permission from the publisher or owner. References to copyrighted materials and instruments must include appropriate citations.

HRLP staff members must be knowledgeable about internal and external governance systems that affect programs and services.

Part 7. DIVERSITY, EQUITY, AND ACCESS

Within the context of each institution's unique mission and in accordance with institutional polices and all applicable codes and laws, Housing and Residential Life Programs (HRLP) must create and maintain educational and work environments that are

- welcoming, accessible, and inclusive to persons of diverse backgrounds
- equitable and non-discriminatory
- free from harassment

HRLP must not discriminate on the basis of ability; age; cultural identity; ethnicity; family educational history (e.g., first generation to attend college); gender identity and expression; nationality; political affiliation; race; religious affiliation; sex; sexual orientation; economic, marital, social, or veteran status; or any other basis included in institutional policies and codes and laws.

HRLP must

- advocate for greater sensitivity to multicultural and social justice concerns by the institution and its personnel
- modify or remove policies, practices, facilities, structures, systems, and technologies that limit access, discriminate, or produce inequities
- include diversity, equity, and access initiatives within their strategic plans
- foster communication that deepens understanding of identity, culture, self-expression, and heritage
- promote respect about commonalities and differences among people within their historical and cultural contexts
- address the characteristics and needs of a diverse population when establishing and implementing culturally relevant and inclusive programs, services, policies, procedures, and practices
- provide staff members with access to multicultural training and hold staff members accountable for integrating the training into their work
- respond to the needs of all students and other populations served when establishing hours of operation and developing methods of delivering programs, services, and resources
- ensure physical, program, and resource access for persons with disabilities
- recognize the needs of distance learning students by providing appropriate and accessible services and resources or by assisting them in gaining access to other appropriate services and resources in their geographic region

Policies must be in place to encourage the hiring and promotion of a diverse and multicultural staff.

Part 8. INSTITUTIONAL AND EXTERNAL RELATIONS

Housing and Residential Life Programs (HRLP) must reach out to relevant individuals, groups, communities, and organizations internal and external to the institution to

- establish, maintain, and promote understanding and effective relations with those that have a significant interest in or potential effect on the students or other constituents served by the programs and services
- garner support and resources for programs and services as defined by the mission statement
- disseminate information about the programs and services
- collaborate, where appropriate, to assist in offering or improving programs and services to meet the needs of students and other constituents and to achieve program and student outcomes
- engage diverse individuals, groups, communities, and organizations to enrich the educational environment and experiences of students and other constituents

Particular efforts should be made by the staff to develop positive relationships with campus and off-campus agencies responsible for judicial affairs, counseling services, learning assistance, disability services, student health services, student activities, security and safety, academic advising, admissions, campus mail and telephone services, physical plant services, institutional budgeting and planning, computer centers, vendors and suppliers of products used in residence and dining halls, and private housing operators.

Special attention must be paid to the relationships with those units who use housing facilities to carry out their programs, such as conference services.

HRLP staff should be aware of the importance of housing and residential life as a critical institutional asset, its opportunity to contribute to academic programs and the delivery of services, and its effect on attracting and retaining students.

HRLP staff must develop and maintain staff relationships in a climate of mutual respect, support, trust, and interdependence, recognizing the strengths and limitations of each colleague.

HRLP must have procedures and guidelines consistent with institutional policy for
- communicating with the media
- contracting with external organizations for delivery of programs and services

- cultivating, soliciting, and managing gifts
- applying to and managing funds from grants

Part 9. FINANCIAL RESOURCES

Housing and Residential Life Programs (HRLP) must have funding to accomplish the mission and goals. In establishing funding priorities and making significant changes, a comprehensive analysis must be conducted to determine the following elements: unmet needs of the unit, relevant expenditures, external and internal resources, and impact on students and the institution.

HRLP must demonstrate efficient and effective use and responsible stewardship of fiscal resources consistent with institutional protocols.

Administration of funds must be handled in accordance with established, responsible accounting procedures.

Procedures should be present to ensure reconciliation between goods paid for and goods ordered and received.

Adequate and appropriate internal controls must exist to ensure full accountability of financial processes.

Financial reports must provide and reflect an accurate financial overview of the organization.

Financial reports should provide clear, understandable, timely data on which staff can plan and make informed decisions.

Purchasing procedures must be consistent with institutional policies and be cost effective.

The budget must be used as a planning and goal-setting document that reflects commitment to the mission and goals of the HRLP and of the institution.

Budgets should be flexible and capable of being adjusted during the year.

A portion of fees collected must be dedicated to the immediate support and long-term improvement of housing and residential life programs and facilities. Funding must be available to provide for the continuous upkeep of facilities, equipment and furnishings, on-going repairs, educational programming, and services to residents. Reserves must be available for major maintenance and renovation of facilities, replacement of equipment, and other capital improvements.

Student governance units (e.g., hall or campus-wide residential councils) should have access to accounting offices and services to carry out their functions effectively. Dues collected from students for programs and services should be managed within the institution.

Representatives of residence hall and apartment housing communities should be given opportunity to comment on proposed rate increases and the operating budget. Rate increases should be announced at least 90 days in advance of their implementation and discussed well in advance of their effective date.

Part 10. TECHNOLOGY

Housing and Residential Life Programs (HRLP) must have adequate technology to support the achievement of their mission and goals. The technology and its use must comply with institutional policies and procedures and be evaluated for compliance with relevant codes and laws.

HRLP must use current technology to provide updated information regarding mission, location, staffing, programs, services, and official contacts to students and designated clients.

HRLP must explore the use of technology to enhance delivery of programs and services, especially for students at a distance or external constituencies.

When technology is used to facilitate student learning and development, HRLP must select technology that reflects intended outcomes.

HRLP must

- maintain policies and procedures that address the security, confidentiality, and backup of data, as well as compliance with privacy laws
- have clearly articulated plans in place for protecting confidentiality and security of information when using Internet-based technologies
- develop plans for replacing and updating existing hardware and software as well as plans for integrating new technically-based or supported programs, including systems developed internally by the institution, systems available through professional associations, or private vendor-based systems

Technology, as well as workstations or computer labs maintained by programs and services for student use, must be accessible to all designated clients and must meet established technology standards for delivery to persons with disabilities.

When providing student access to technology, HRLP must

- have policies on the use of technology that are clear, easy to understand, and available to all students
- provide assistance, information, or referral to appropriate support services to those needing help accessing or using technology
- provide instruction or training on how to use the technology
- inform students on the legal and ethical implications of misuse as it pertains to intellectual property, harassment, privacy, and social networks

Student violations of technology policies must follow established institutional student disciplinary procedures.

Students who experience negative emotional or psychological consequences from the use of technology must be referred to support services provided by the institution.

Part 11. FACILITIES AND EQUIPMENT

Housing and Residential Life Programs (HRLP) must have adequate, accessible, and suitably located facilities and equipment to support the mission and goals. If acquiring capital equipment as defined by the institution, HRLP must take into account expenses related to regular maintenance and life cycle costs. Facilities and equipment must be evaluated on an established cycle, including consideration of sustainability, and be in compliance with codes and laws to provide for access, health, safety, and security.

HRLP staff members must have workspace that is well equipped, adequate in size, and designed to support their work and responsibilities. For conversations requiring privacy, staff members must have access to a private space.

HRLP staff members who share workspace must be able to secure their own work.

The design of the facilities must guarantee the security and privacy of records and ensure the confidentiality of sensitive information.

The location and layout of the facilities must be sensitive to the needs of persons with disabilities as well as the needs of other constituencies.

HRLP must ensure the physical environment is attractive, conducive to academic success and other learning opportunities, functional, in compliance with codes, and adequately provided with safety features.

Individual rooms and apartments must be furnished and equipped to accommodate the designated number of occupants.

Adequate space must be provided for student study, recreation, socializing, and group meetings.

Facilities should include private offices for counseling, advising, interviewing, or other meetings of a confidential nature, and office, reception, and storage space sufficient to accommodate assigned staff, supplies, equipment, library resources, conference rooms, classrooms, and meeting spaces.

Public, common, study, recreational areas and computer labs must be adequately furnished to accommodate the number of users.

Housekeeping programs must be required to provide a clean and orderly environment in all housing facilities. All community bathrooms, as well as public areas, must be cleaned and sanitized at least daily on weekdays.

A weekend housekeeping program should be in place.

Sufficient space for custodial work and storage must be available in close proximity to the assigned custodial area.

Maintenance and renovation programs must be implemented in all housing operations and include four major areas: (a) a preventive maintenance program designed to realize or exceed the projected life expectancy of the equipment and facilities, (b) a program designed to repair or upgrade equipment, facilities, and building systems as they become inoperable or obsolete, (c) a renovation program that modifies physical facilities and building systems to make them more accessible, effective, attractive, efficient, and safe, and (d) a program designed to provide emergency response 24 hours a day.

Periodic inspections must be made to (a) ensure compliance with fire and safety codes; (b) identify and address potential safety and security hazards including fire extinguishers, exit doors, automatic door closers, outside building lighting; and (c) identify other potentially dangerous spaces. Data from inspections must be used for repair and replacement schedules.

A system of access control must be in place to provide for building security, monitoring of exterior doors, and stringent controls on the use of master keys/access cards.

Systematically planned equipment replacement programs must exist for furnishings; mechanical, fire safety, and electrical systems; maintenance equipment; carpeting; window coverings; and dining equipment where applicable.

Painting must be done on the basis of current need and a pre-planned cyclical schedule.

Waste disposal, recycling, and handling and storage of chemicals and hazardous materials must be in compliance with federal, state/provincial, and local health, safety, and environmental protection requirements. HRLP staff must identify work place hazards and strive to minimize the risk to employees through education, training, and provision of personal protective equipment.

Grounds, including streets, walks, recreational areas, and parking lots, must be attractively maintained, with attention given to safety features.

Appropriate parking policies should exist for resident students, be developed collaboratively, and define responsibility and options.

Student housing construction project planning must be responsive to the current and future needs of residents. HRLP staff must be involved in the design and development of new housing construction.

Students should be consulted on the design and development of new housing construction.

A master plan for maintaining and renovating all facilities must exist and include timelines for addressing specific needs.

Laundry facilities should be provided within or in close proximity to living areas, be well maintained, and be reasonably priced.

Suggestions from residents should be regularly and consistently sought and considered regarding physical plant improvements and renovations to college/university housing and dining facilities.

A systematic energy conservation program should be implemented through assessment, programming, education, renovation, and replacement.

An up-to-date inventory of housing property and furnishings should be maintained.

Physical plant renovations should be scheduled to minimize disruption to residents and diners.

Acceptable accommodations and amenities should be provided for professional live-in staff members with appropriate consideration provided for the following needs: adequate living space for the staff member and any family, furnishings and equipment, telecommunications package, appropriate access, and parking.

Part 12. ASSESSMENT AND EVALUATION

Housing and Residential Life Programs (HRLP) must have a clearly articulated assessment plan to document achievement of stated goals and learning outcomes, demonstrate accountability, provide evidence of improvement, and describe resulting changes in programs and services.

HRLP must have adequate fiscal, human, professional development, and technological resources to develop and implement assessment plans.

Assessments must include direct and indirect evaluation and use qualitative and quantitative methodologies and existing evidence, as appropriate, to determine whether and to what degree the stated mission, goals, and intended outcomes are being met as effectively and efficiently as possible. The process must employ sufficient and sound measures to ensure comprehensiveness. Data collected must include responses from students and other constituencies, and aggregated results must be shared with those groups. Results of assessments must be shared appropriately with multiple constituents.

Results of assessments and evaluations must be used to identify needs and interests in revising and improving programs and services, recognizing staff performance, maximizing resource efficiency and effectiveness, improving student achievement of learning and development outcomes, and improving student persistence and success. Changes resulting from the use of assessments and evaluation must be shared with stakeholders.

General Standards revised in 2011;
HRLP content developed/revised in 1986, 1992, 1997, & 2004

The Role of International Student Programs and Services
CAS Standards Contextual Statement

In 2010-11, the number of international students at colleges and universities in the United States increased by five percent to 723,277, a 32 percent increase since 2000/01 (IIE, 2011). International students studying in the United States pursue undergraduate and graduate degrees as well as English-language training; they are drawn to this country because of the high quality programs and the wide range of academic options offered in the United States. International students bring with them rich experiences and unique cross-cultural perspectives that help to internationalize the campus and give American students first-hand opportunities to learn about the world. International students face unique challenges as they attempt to adjust to a different campus life and culture, master written and spoken languages, comply with immigration regulations, meet the requirements of their academic programs, and prepare to begin their careers.

The events of September 11, 2001, drew widespread attention and scrutiny of International Student Programs and Services (ISPS), which resulted in dramatic changes to the roles and responsibilities. A key change since then is the additional record keeping and reporting that is now required for an institution to remain in compliance with immigration regulations.

The ISPS functions and roles on campuses vary greatly. Some ISPS offices may serve only a handful of students, while others serve thousands as well as the academic departments that enroll and depend on these students. Some offices only serve international students; other offices serve international students, visiting scholars, and US students studying abroad. As more institutions open campuses in other countries, ISPS may be responsible for helping prepare institutional officials from both countries for the cross-cultural, procedural, and governmental issues that could arise. International student and scholar advising has progressed over the years from being an "add-on" activity for a faculty member or administrator to being a robust profession with a body of knowledge and any number of necessary key skill sets, including those listed below.

It is important for international student and scholar advisers to be current on immigration regulations and policies. They need to effectively communicate these regulations to students, scholars, and key campus community members; establish and maintain working relationships with individuals on and off-campus to address and advocate for students' and scholars' needs; be competent in crisis intervention in case of illness or serious legal, financial, or personal problems; have strong cross-cultural competencies to allow them to interact effectively with students and scholars from diverse cultures; understand how to develop effective and creative social and cultural programming; and be good at setting priorities and managing time and resources.

Advisers frequently serve as the liaison between international students and scholars and all those with whom these students and scholars come into contact, including faculty members, students, and staff; local citizens; officials of host country and foreign government agencies; and the student's sponsor or family at home to represent the students' best interests and advise them accordingly. They should be knowledgeable and articulate about host country culture and how it differs from the cultures of other countries and should understand the social and psychological processes of cross-cultural adjustment. They should be familiar with the educational systems and political, economic, historical, and social issues and trends framing the contexts of the countries from which their students come.

As more campuses continue to emphasize internationalization efforts, International Student Programs and Services should be prepared to step forward and initiate partnerships that will advance these goals. Collaboration with education abroad, admissions, international studies and international education, and student affairs organizations will sustain these efforts. Although this statement and the accompanying standards and guidelines are mostly focused on international students studying in the U.S., many of the challenges and other aspects described may also apply to any students who are studying outside their home country.

References, Readings, and Resources

Institute of International Education (published annually). *Open doors* report 2011: Report on international educational exchange. See http://www.iie.org/en/Research-and-Publications/Open-Doors

Institute of International Education: 809 United Nations Plaza, New York, NY 10017-3580 (212) 883-8200, http://www.iie.org

NAFSA: Association of International Educators: 1307 New York Avenue, NW, 8th Floor, Washington, DC 20005-4701; (202) 737-3699, http://www.nafsa.org

NAFSA's Knowledge Community for International Student and Scholar Services:
http://www.nafsa.org/istanetwork
http://www.nafsa.org/iscanetwork
http://www.nafsa.org/ccpnetwork

NAFSA Adviser's Manual On-line: http://www.nafsa.org/am

NAFSA's Statement of Ethical Principles:
http://www.nafsa.org/_/File/_/ethical_principles_2009.pdf

U. S. Citizenship and Immigration Services: http://www.uscis.gov

U.S. Immigration and Customs Enforcement: http://www.ice.gov

U.S. Department of Homeland Security: http://www.dhs.gov
U.S. Department of State: http://travel.state.gov

Additional Resources

From Intercultural Press (http://www.interculturalpress.com)
Bennett, M. (Ed.). (1998). *Basic Concepts of Intercultural Communication: Selected Readings.*
Cold Water. (1987). (video) This movie is about cross-cultural adaptation and culture shock and includes a comprehensive instructional guide. Twelve Boston University international students (plus one U.S. American student and three cross-cultural specialists) are interviewed about the experience of living and studying in a new culture.
Lanier, A. (2004). *Living in the U.S.A.* (6th ed.). Revised by Jef C. Davis.
Storti, C. (1998). *Figuring Foreigners Out: A Practical Guide.*
The Aliens: Being a Foreign Student. (2001). (video) In this film, six international students are interviewed about their experiences coming to the United States and attending a U.S. American college.

From NAFSA: Association of International Educators (http://www.nafsa.org)
Althen, G. (Ed.). (1994). *Learning Across Cultures*
Assaf, M., & Gentile, L. (Eds.). (2004). *Basic F-1 Procedures for Beginners*
Burak, P. A., & Hoffa, W. W. (Eds.). (2001). *Crisis Management in a Cross-Cultural Setting*
Gooding, M., & Wood, M. (Eds.). (2006). *Finding Your Way: Navigational Tools For International Student and Scholar Advisers*
O'Connell, B. (Ed.). (1994). *Foreign Student Education at Two-Year Colleges*

Contextual Statement Contributors
Current Edition:
Louis Gecenok, San Jose State University
Monica Sharp, University of Oklahoma

Previous Editions:
Katherine Hammett, Carroll University
Janice Bogen, Thomas Jefferson University

International Student Programs and Services
CAS Standards and Guidelines

Part 1. MISSION

The mission of International Student Programs and Services (ISPS) is to provide support and assistance necessary for international students to achieve their educational goals and to ensure institutional compliance with governmental immigration regulations. The ISPS must provide the documents for students to enter the country and maintain their legal status.

ISPS must develop, disseminate, implement, and regularly review their missions. The mission must be consistent with the mission of the institution and with professional standards. The mission must be appropriate for the institution's student populations and community settings. Mission statements must reference student learning and development.

Part 2. PROGRAM

The formal education of students, consisting of the curriculum and the co-curriculum, must promote student learning and development outcomes that are purposeful, contribute to students' realization of their potential, and prepare students for satisfying and productive lives.

International Student Programs and Services (ISPS) must collaborate with colleagues and departments across the institution to promote student learning and development, persistence, and success.

Consistent with the institutional mission, ISPS must identify relevant and desirable student learning and development outcomes from among the six domains and related dimensions:

Domain: knowledge acquisition, integration, construction, and application

- Dimensions: understanding knowledge from a range of disciplines; connecting knowledge to other knowledge, ideas, and experiences; constructing knowledge; and relating knowledge to daily life

Domain: cognitive complexity

- Dimensions: critical thinking, reflective thinking, effective reasoning, and creativity

Domain: intrapersonal development

- Dimensions: realistic self-appraisal, self-understanding, and self-respect; identity development; commitment to ethics and integrity; and spiritual awareness

Domain: interpersonal competence

- Dimensions: meaningful relationships, interdependence, collaboration, and effective leadership.

Domain: humanitarianism and civic engagement

- Dimensions: understanding and appreciation of cultural and human differences, social responsibility, global perspective, and sense of civic responsibility

Domain: practical competence

- Dimensions: pursuing goals, communicating effectively, technical competence, managing personal affairs, managing career development, demonstrating professionalism, maintaining health and wellness, and living a purposeful and satisfying life

[LD Outcomes: See The Council for the Advancement of Standards Learning and Developmental Outcomes statement for examples of outcomes related to these domains and dimensions.]

ISPS must
- assess relevant and desirable student learning and development
- provide evidence of impact on outcomes
- articulate contributions to or support of student learning and development in the domains not specifically assessed
- articulate contributions to or support of student persistence and success
- use evidence gathered through this process to create strategies for improvement of programs and services

ISPS must be
- intentionally designed
- guided by theories and knowledge of learning and development
- integrated into the life of the institution
- reflective of developmental and demographic profiles of the student population
- responsive to needs of individuals, populations with distinct needs, and relevant constituencies
- delivered using multiple formats, strategies, and contexts

Where institutions provide distance education, ISPS must assist distance learners to achieve their

educational goals by providing access to information about programs and services, to staff members who can address questions and concerns, and to counseling, advising, or other forms of assistance.

ISPS should provide the campus and larger community with multiple and varied opportunities for discussion to maximize learning, to minimize cultural conflict, or to deal with conflict.

ISPS must
- assess the needs of the international student population and set priorities among those needs
- offer or provide access to professional services for students in the areas of immigration and other government regulations, financial matters, employment, obtaining health care insurance, navigating the health care system, host-country language needs, and personal and cultural concerns
- assure institutional compliance with government regulations and procedures, including record-keeping and reporting responsibilities
- interpret immigration policies to the campus and local communities
- develop and offer educational programs to the campus community to enhance positive interaction between domestic and international students, to develop sensitivity regarding cultural differences and international student needs, and to assist in the understanding of adjustment to a host country's educational system and culture
- orient international students to the expectations, policies, and culture of the institution and to the educational system and culture of the host country
- facilitate the enrollment and retention of international students
- prepare students for re-entry and cultural re-adjustment related to the students' return home
- provide appropriate referrals for students whose individual needs may be in conflict with the home culture
- provide appropriate and timely referral services to other relevant agencies
- determine the educational goals; developmental levels; and social, emotional, and cultural needs of individual international students and specific populations
- collaborate effectively with other services areas, student organizations, and academic departments to meet international students' needs
- facilitate international students' participation

in campus life
- advocate to all areas of the institution for the needs of international students
- facilitate sensitivity within the institution and the community at large to the cultural needs of international students

Part 3. ORGANIZATION AND LEADERSHIP

To achieve student and program outcomes, International Student Programs and Services (ISPS) must be structured purposefully and organized effectively. ISPS must have
- clearly stated goals
- current and accessible policies and procedures
- written performance expectations for employees
- functional work flow graphics or organizational charts demonstrating clear channels of authority

Leaders with organizational authority for the programs and services must provide strategic planning, supervision, and management; advance the organization; and maintain integrity through the following functions:

Strategic Planning
- articulate a vision and mission that drive short- and long-term planning
- set goals and objectives based on the needs of the population served and desired student learning or development and program outcomes
- facilitate continuous development, implementation, and assessment of goal attainment congruent with institutional mission and strategic plans
- promote environments that provide meaningful opportunities for student learning, development, and engagement
- develop and continuously improve programs and services in response to the changing needs of students served and evolving institutional priorities
- intentionally include diverse perspectives to inform decision making

Supervising
- manage human resource processes including recruitment, selection, development, supervision, performance planning, evaluation, recognition, and reward
- influence others to contribute to the effectiveness and success of the unit
- empower professional, support, and student staff to accept leadership opportunities
- offer appropriate feedback to colleagues and

students on skills needed to become more effective leaders

- encourage and support professional development, collaboration with colleagues and departments across the institution, and scholarly contribution to the profession

Managing

- identify and address individual, organizational, and environmental conditions that foster or inhibit mission achievement
- plan, allocate, and monitor the use of fiscal, physical, human, intellectual, and technological resources
- use current and valid evidence to inform decisions
- incorporate sustainability practices in the management and design of programs, services, and facilities
- understand appropriate technologies and integrate them into programs and services
- be knowledgeable about codes and laws relevant to programs and services and ensure that staff members understand their responsibilities through appropriate training
- assess potential risks and take action to mitigate them

Advancing the Organization

- communicate effectively in writing, speaking, and electronic venues
- advocate for programs and services
- advocate for representation in strategic planning initiatives at appropriate divisional and institutional levels
- initiate collaborative interactions with internal and external stakeholders who have legitimate concerns about and interests in the functional area
- facilitate processes to reach consensus where wide support is needed
- inform other areas within the institution about issues affecting practice

Maintaining Integrity

- model ethical behavior and institutional citizenship
- share data used to inform key decisions in transparent and accessible ways
- monitor media used for distributing information about programs and services to ensure the content is current, accurate, appropriately referenced, and accessible

Institutional compliance issues must be considered in creating and maintaining effective office organization structure and management.

The institution should be aware of and ready to respond to government requirements for enrolling international students. For instance, the institution may be required to designate specific employees who will ensure institutional compliance with government immigration regulations.

Part 4. HUMAN RESOURCES

International Student Programs and Services (ISPS) must be staffed adequately by individuals qualified to accomplish mission and goals.

Within institutional guidelines, ISPS must

- **establish procedures for staff recruitment and selection, training, performance planning, and evaluation**
- **set expectations for supervision and performance**
- **assess the performance of employees individually and as a team**
- **provide access to continuing and advanced education and appropriate professional development opportunities to improve the leadership ability, competence, and skills of all employees.**

ISPS must maintain position descriptions for all staff members.

To create a diverse staff, ISPS must institute recruitment and hiring strategies that encourage individuals from under-represented populations to apply for positions.

ISPS must develop promotion practices that are fair, inclusive, proactive, and non-discriminatory.

To further the recruitment and retention of staff, ISPS must consider work life initiatives, such as compressed work schedules, flextime, job sharing, remote work, or telework.

ISPS professional staff members must hold an earned graduate or professional degree in a field relevant to the position they hold or must possess an appropriate combination of educational credentials and related work experience.

ISPS professional staff members must be knowledgeable about research and practice in areas related to international student programs and services and stay abreast of developments in policies, laws, and regulations affecting international students.

ISPS professional staff members must have an understanding of and demonstrate appreciation for various cultures served in the student population.

ISPS professional staff members must possess the required interpersonal skills and be competent in the

areas of effective communication, group facilitation, leadership training and development, and crisis intervention.

ISPS professional staff members should be familiar with multicultural theory, organizational development, counseling theory and practice, group dynamics, leadership development, human development, and research and evaluation. ISPS professional staff members should have proficiency in a second language and extended travel and/ or living experiences abroad.

ISPS professional staff members must engage in continuing professional development activities to keep abreast of the research, theories, legislation, policies, and developments that affect their programs and services.

ISPS must have technical and support staff members adequate to accomplish their mission. All members of the staff must be technologically proficient and qualified to perform their job functions, be knowledgeable about ethical and legal uses of technology, and have access to training and resources to support the performance of their assigned responsibilities.

Degree- or credential-seeking interns or graduate assistants must be qualified by enrollment in an appropriate field of study and by relevant experience. These individuals must be trained and supervised adequately by professional staff members holding educational credentials and related work experience appropriate for supervision. Supervisors must be cognizant of the roles of interns and graduate assistants as both student and employee and closely adhere to all parameters of their job descriptions, work hours, and schedules. Supervisors and the interns or graduate assistants must agree to compensatory time or other appropriate compensation if circumstances necessitate additional hours.

Student employees and volunteers must be carefully selected, trained, supervised, and evaluated. They must be educated on how and when to refer those in need of additional assistance to qualified staff members and must have access to a supervisor for assistance in making these judgments. Student employees and volunteers must be provided clear job descriptions, pre-service training based on assessed needs, and continuing development.

ISPS should hire graduate assistants and interns with an interest in international student programs and services. These individuals expand staff abilities, provide peer role models, and gain valuable pre-professional experience. Particular attention should be given to preparing assistants and interns to be sensitive to cultural differences and the special needs of international students.

All ISPS staff members, including student employees and volunteers, must receive specific training on institutional policies pertaining to functions or activities they support and to privacy and confidentiality policies and laws regarding access to student records and other sensitive institutional information.

All ISPS staff members must receive training on policies and procedures related to the use of technology to store or access student records and institutional data.

ISPS must ensure that staff members are knowledgeable about and trained in emergency procedures, crisis response, and prevention efforts. Prevention efforts must address identification of threatening conduct or behavior of students, faculty and staff members, and others and must incorporate a system for responding and reporting.

ISPS must ensure that staff members are knowledgeable of and trained in safety and emergency procedures for securing and vacating facilities.

Part 5. ETHICS

International Student Programs and Services (ISPS) must review relevant professional ethical standards and must adopt or develop and implement appropriate statements of ethical practice.

ISPS must publish and adhere to statements of ethical practice and ensure their periodic review by relevant constituencies.

ISPS must orient new staff members to relevant ethical standards and statements of ethical practice and related institutional policies.

Statements of ethical standards must specify that staff members respect privacy and maintain confidentiality in all communications and records to the extent that such communications and records are protected under relevant privacy laws.

Statements of ethical standards must specify limits on disclosure of information contained in students' educational records as well as requirements to disclose to appropriate authorities.

ISPS must also make exceptions to privacy and confidentiality of information contained in students' education records when mandated by governmental regulations and legislation.

In the United States, this includes the U.S. Department of Homeland Security or the U.S. Department of State.

Statements of ethical standards must address

personal and economic conflicts of interest, or appearance thereof, by staff members in the performance of their work.

Statements of ethical standards must reflect the responsibility of staff members to be fair, objective, and impartial in their interactions with others.

Statements of ethical standards must reference management of institutional funds.

Statements of ethical standards must reference appropriate behavior regarding research and assessment with human participants, confidentiality of research and assessment data, and students' rights and responsibilities.

Statements of ethical standards must include the expectation that ISPS staff members confront and hold accountable other staff members who exhibit unethical behavior.

Statements of ethical standards must address issues surrounding scholarly integrity.

As appropriate, ISPS staff members must inform users of programs and services of ethical obligations and limitations emanating from codes and laws or from licensure requirements.

ISPS staff members must recognize and avoid conflicts of interest that could adversely influence their judgment or objectivity and, when unavoidable, recuse themselves from the situation.

ISPS staff members must perform their duties within the limits of their position, training, expertise, and competence.

When these limits are exceeded, individuals in need of further assistance must be referred to persons possessing appropriate qualifications.

Promotional and descriptive information must be accurate and free of deception.

ISPS must adhere to institutional policies regarding ethical and legal use of software and technology.

Part 6. LAW, POLICY, AND GOVERNANCE

International Student Programs and Services (ISPS) must be in compliance with laws, regulations, and policies that relate to their respective responsibilities and that pose legal obligations, limitations, risks, and liabilities for the institution as a whole. Examples include constitutional, statutory, regulatory, and case law; relevant law and orders emanating from codes and laws; and the institution's policies.

ISPS staff must be well versed in and remain current on immigration laws and regulations that impact students. ISPS staff must understand and be able to communicate short-term issues related to and long-term impacts of immigration tracking systems, such as SEVIS, the Student and Exchange Visitor Information System.

ISPS staff must also be familiar with constitutional issues of due process, with rights and responsibilities afforded international students, and with privacy laws, and staff must be able to communicate such to students.

ISPS must inform staff members, appropriate officials, and users of programs and services about existing and changing legal obligations, risks and liabilities, and limitations.

ISPS must have written policies on all relevant operations, transactions, or tasks that have legal implications.

ISPS must regularly review policies. The revision and creation of policies must be informed by best practices, available evidence, and policy issues in higher education.

ISPS staff members must use reasonable and informed practices to limit the liability exposure of the institution and its officers, employees, and agents. ISPS staff members must be informed about institutional policies regarding risk management, personal liability, and related insurance coverage options and must be referred to external sources if the institution does not provide coverage.

The institution must provide access to legal advice for staff members as needed to carry out assigned responsibilities.

Staff members should establish and maintain positive working relationships with the institution's legal counsel.

ISPS must have procedures and guidelines consistent with institutional policy for responding to threats, emergencies, and crisis situations. Systems and procedures must be in place to disseminate timely and accurate information to students, other members of the institutional community, and appropriate external organizations during emergency situations.

ISPS staff members must neither participate in nor condone any form of harassment or activity that demeans persons or creates an intimidating, hostile, or offensive environment.

ISPS must obtain permission to use copyrighted materials and instruments. ISPS must purchase the materials and instruments from legally compliant sources or seek alternative permission from the publisher or owner. **References to copyrighted materials and instruments must include appropriate citations.**

ISPS staff members must be knowledgeable about internal and external governance systems that affect programs and services.

Part 7. DIVERSITY, EQUITY, AND ACCESS

Within the context of each institution's unique mission and in accordance with institutional polices and all applicable codes and laws, International Student Programs and Services (ISPS) must create and maintain educational and work environments that are

- **welcoming, accessible, and inclusive to persons of diverse backgrounds**
- **equitable and non-discriminatory**
- **free from harassment**

ISPS must not discriminate on the basis of ability; age; cultural identity; ethnicity; family educational history (e.g., first generation to attend college); gender identity and expression; nationality; political affiliation; race; religious affiliation; sex; sexual orientation; economic, marital, social, or veteran status; or any other basis included in institutional policies and codes and laws.

ISPS must
- **advocate for greater sensitivity to multicultural and social justice concerns by the institution and its personnel**
- **modify or remove policies, practices, facilities, structures, systems, and technologies that limit access, discriminate, or produce inequities**
- **include diversity, equity, and access initiatives within their strategic plans**
- **foster communication that deepens understanding of identity, culture, self-expression, and heritage**
- **promote respect about commonalities and differences among people within their historical and cultural contexts**
- **address the characteristics and needs of a diverse population when establishing and implementing culturally relevant and inclusive programs, services, policies, procedures, and practices**
- **provide staff members with access to multicultural training and hold staff members accountable for integrating the training into their work**
- **respond to the needs of all students and other populations served when establishing hours of operation and developing methods of**

delivering programs, services, and resources
- **ensure physical, program, and resource access for persons with disabilities**
- **recognize the needs of distance learning students by providing appropriate and accessible services and resources or by assisting them in gaining access to other appropriate services and resources in their geographic region**

ISPS must orient international students to the culture of the host country and promote and deepen international students' understanding of cross-cultural differences while building cross-cultural competencies.

ISPS should encourage coordinated efforts to promote multicultural sensitivity and the elimination of prejudicial behaviors in all functional areas.

Considering the long-term wellbeing of both individual international students and the institution's international educational exchange programs, ISPS staff members must anticipate and balance the wants, needs, and requirements of students with institutional policies, laws, and sponsors.

ISPS staff members should develop procedures to respond to anticipated conflicts between the needs of individual international students and institutional policies, governmental laws and regulations, or sponsor policies.

ISPS staff members should develop systems to address unanticipated conflicts between the needs of individual international students and institutional policies, governmental laws and regulations, or sponsor policies.

ISPS staff members must demonstrate a high degree of cross-cultural competency and sensitivity, while treating differences between value systems and cultures non-judgmentally and avoiding use of pejorative stereotypical statements.

Part 8. INSTITUTIONAL AND EXTERNAL RELATIONS

International Student Programs and Services (ISPS) must reach out to relevant individuals, groups, communities, and organizations internal and external to the institution to
- **establish, maintain, and promote understanding and effective relations with those that have a significant interest in or potential effect on the students or other constituents served by the programs and services**
- **garner support and resources for programs and services as defined by the mission statement**
- **disseminate information about the programs**

and services
- collaborate, where appropriate, to assist in offering or improving programs and services to meet the needs of students and other constituents and to achieve program and student outcomes
- engage diverse individuals, groups, communities, and organizations to enrich the educational environment and experiences of students and other constituents

ISPS must have procedures and guidelines consistent with institutional policy for
- communicating with the media
- contracting with external organizations for delivery of programs and services
- cultivating, soliciting, and managing gifts
- applying to and managing funds from grants

ISPS professional staff must be aware of and respond to changes in government activity affecting international students.

ISPS professional staff members should establish and maintain a positive working relationship with the institutional government liaison. Staff members should participate in advocacy as appropriate and necessary.

Part 9. FINANCIAL RESOURCES

International Student Programs and Services (ISPS) must have funding to accomplish the mission and goals. In establishing funding priorities and making significant changes, a comprehensive analysis must be conducted to determine the following elements: unmet needs of the unit, relevant expenditures, external and internal resources, and impact on students and the institution.

ISPS must demonstrate efficient and effective use and responsible stewardship of fiscal resources consistent with institutional protocols.

When considering a special student fee as a means of supporting international student programs and services, ISPS should carefully review the related ethical issues of such a fee and bring them to the attention of appropriate institutional leaders.

Part 10. TECHNOLOGY

International Student Programs and Services (ISPS) must have adequate technology to support the achievement of their mission and goals. The technology and its use must comply with institutional policies and procedures and be evaluated for compliance with relevant codes and laws.

ISPS must use current technology to provide updated information regarding mission, location, staffing,

programs, services, and official contacts to students and designated clients.

ISPS must explore the use of technology to enhance delivery of programs and services, especially for students at a distance or external constituencies.

When technology is used to facilitate student learning and development, ISPS must select technology that reflects intended outcomes.

ISPS must
- maintain policies and procedures that address the security, confidentiality, and backup of data, as well as compliance with privacy laws
- have clearly articulated plans in place for protecting confidentiality and security of information when using Internet-based technologies
- develop plans for replacing and updating existing hardware and software as well as plans for integrating new technically-based or supported programs, including systems developed internally by the institution, systems available through professional associations, or private vendor-based systems

Technology, as well as workstations or computer labs maintained by programs and services for student use, must be accessible to all designated clients and must meet established technology standards for delivery to persons with disabilities.

When providing student access to technology, ISPS must
- have policies on the use of technology that are clear, easy to understand, and available to all students
- provide assistance, information, or referral to appropriate support services to those needing help accessing or using technology
- provide instruction or training on how to use the technology
- inform students on the legal and ethical implications of misuse as it pertains to intellectual property, harassment, privacy, and social networks

Student violations of technology policies must follow established institutional student disciplinary procedures.

Students who experience negative emotional or psychological consequences from the use of technology must be referred to support services provided by the institution.

Part 11. FACILITIES AND EQUIPMENT

International Student Programs and Services (ISPS) must have adequate, accessible, and suitably located facilities and equipment to support the mission and goals. If acquiring capital equipment as defined by the institution, programs and services must take into account expenses related to regular maintenance and life cycle costs. Facilities and equipment must be evaluated on an established cycle, including consideration of sustainability, and be in compliance with codes and laws to provide for access, health, safety, and security.

ISPS staff members must have workspace that is well equipped, adequate in size, and designed to support their work and responsibilities. For conversations requiring privacy, staff members must have access to a private space.

ISPS staff members who share workspace must be able to secure their own work.

The design of the facilities must guarantee the security and privacy of records and ensure the confidentiality of sensitive information.

The location and layout of the facilities must be sensitive to the needs of persons with disabilities as well as the needs of other constituencies.

Part 12. ASSESSMENT AND EVALUATION

International Student Programs and Services (ISPS) must have a clearly articulated assessment plan to document achievement of stated goals and learning outcomes, demonstrate accountability, provide evidence of improvement, and describe resulting changes in programs and services.

ISPS must have adequate fiscal, human, professional development, and technological resources to develop and implement assessment plans.

Assessments must include direct and indirect evaluation and use qualitative and quantitative methodologies and existing evidence, as appropriate, to determine whether and to what degree the stated mission, goals, and intended outcomes are being met as effectively and efficiently as possible. The process must employ sufficient and sound measures to ensure comprehensiveness. Data collected must include responses from students and other constituencies, and aggregated results must be shared with those groups. Results of assessments must be shared appropriately with multiple constituents.

Results of assessments and evaluations must be used to identify needs and interests in revising and improving programs and services, recognizing staff performance, maximizing resource efficiency and effectiveness, improving student achievement of learning and development outcomes, and improving student persistence and success. Changes resulting from the use of assessments and evaluation must be shared with stakeholders.

General Standards revised in 2011;
ISPS content developed/revised in 1996 & 2008

The Role of Internship Programs
CAS Standards Contextual Statement

In the 1960s, with its social upheaval, a movement gained considerable momentum to make the college curriculum more relevant and to apply the knowledge of theoretical disciplines to solve societal problems. As higher education institutions revamped their curricula, they began to recognize that supervised learning experiences outside the classroom were relevant to the educational process and that ways could be found to evaluate these experiences, possibly for academic credit.

In the early 1970s, two professional associations, the Society for Field Experience and National Center for Public Service Internship Programs, were formed among those involved in college-based field experiences and in policy issues and government-based projects, such as the Urban Corps. These organizations merged in 1978 to form the organization known today as the National Society for Experiential Education (NSEE). Other experiential education organizations include the Cooperative Education and Internship Association (CEIA), the Association for Experiential Education (AEE), NAFSA: The Association of International Educators, the National Association of Colleges and Employers (NACE), and the Association for Experiential Education (AEE), among others. Increasingly, discipline-based academic associations formed sections for developing good practice for internships within their fields. NSEE, for example, now has a series of training modules, the Experiential Education Academy, which awards a certificate from NSEE. A goal of these organizations has been to advocate experiential and related forms of active or engaged learning, both within and outside the classroom or campus setting, and to establish appropriate standards and ethics.

As a result of the efforts of these organizations, as well as the demand by students and parents for a more career-oriented curriculum, internships became an integral part of a college education. What distinguishes internships from other forms of active learning is that there is a degree of supervision and self-study that allows students to "learn by doing" and to reflect upon that learning in a way that achieves certain learning goals and objectives. Feedback for improvement and the development or refinement of learning goals is also essential. What distinguishes an intern from a volunteer is the deliberative form of learning that takes place. There must be a balance between learning and contributing, and the student, the student's institution, and the internship placement site must share in the responsibility to ensure that the balance is appropriate and that the learning is of sufficiently high quality to warrant the effort, which might include academic credit.

Major questions and concerns arise regarding how colleges and universities can provide an appropriate internship experience, given the various goals of the institution, the academic and student affairs divisions, and the student. For example, some institutions encourage internships but refuse to grant academic credit for them. Some have policies that restrict academic credit to internships only outside the major. Also, accreditation standards within a professional field may conflict with institutional policy, restricting the opportunities for internships in professional fields. Some may prohibit students from receiving academic credit for internships that provide compensation, although this attitude is declining as quality placements increase. Then there are the variable standards as to what constitutes a credit-worthy internship (i.e., how many hours equal how many credits) and concern for the liability of students and their institution should mistakes be made.

In the past few years, a spotlight has been placed on the U.S. Department of Labor's Wage and Hours Divisions' interpretation of the Federal Fair Labor Standards Act and its application to internships and internship programs. If an employment relationship is deemed to exist, the intern is required to be paid at least the required minimum wage and with overtime compensation. Although interns who sue corporations and other for-profits for back wages are making headlines, educational institutions using the CAS and other standards of good practice are helping avoid these problems by educating the staff members, students, and internship sites regarding expectations, rules, and the law.

The kind of internship experience sanctioned by an institution may vary. Some emphasize a form of cooperative education in which compensation for professional work is a high expectation, although credit for the experience is not necessarily expected. Some may involve a heavily supervised semester or summer-long experience either for or not for academic credit, while others might utilize a form of externship, which is similar to short-term, field-based learning with minimal or limited interaction with an organization.

Setting standards for internship programs will establish for administrators, faculty, and staff members a set of benchmarks that identify what a quality internship program on a college campus should be. But it is important that we distinguish between an academic internship within academic affairs and the co-curricular internship found in the student affairs division. The CAS Internship Program standards take into account the importance of establishing standards within each of these areas to meet student academic, career, and personal goals. It also assumes that there is sufficient communication between the two areas so that the appropriate expertise can be utilized across divisions and throughout the campus.

Of considerable significance is the intent of CAS to include the notion that an internship program is not the sole purview of a career center or off-campus programs office. Academic departments that grant credit for internships have faculty (or a committee of faculty) designated to oversee internships, or have faculty members who accompany students on a short-term or long-term basis to locations off-campus, such as the popular destinations of Washington or London, should be considered as having internship programs that are expected to meet these CAS standards.

Although professionalism in experiential education has made significant leaps in the past decade, the establishment of these standards is an important milestone within the field. For the first time, a major statement is made that defines an internship within the context of an academic institution of higher education. It emphasizes that careful thought, planning, administration, implementation, and feedback are important in the entire learning process and that sufficient resources should be available to accomplish the established goals of the learning experience. Also, this professionalism must exist within both the academic and the co-curricular areas of the institution.

With the proliferation of internships at the local, state/provincial, national and international levels, administrators and faculty have a special obligation not only to ensure the high quality of the learning environment for their students, but also to assess the risk management and safety of students in these settings. Both faculty and staff members need to be sufficiently trained to appropriately oversee an internship, to recognize the warning signs, and to take appropriate action. Increasingly, institutions work with third party organizations to place, supervise, and evaluate students and assess outcomes because these organizations have dedicated personnel who are expert in these areas. Yet, similar diligence must b e paid to the evaluation of these organizations' performance as well.

Internships and other forms of experiential education have become much more accepted as part of the college experience. Many new faculty members are often former interns who understand the value of an internship and understand the appropriate ways of measuring student performance. More agencies understand how to utilize interns and to give them substantive work and responsibilities. More financial assistance is available either through the institution or the placement site to help cover the student's costs. Technology is providing career centers, internship offices, or off-campus programs with the ability to match the interests of the student with an appropriate placement more efficiently and effectively. Also, the movement toward online portfolio systems allows more participation in the development and evaluation of the student by all those involved in the internship experience. Such advances will very likely lead to greater advances in assessment of student outcomes in internships and other forms of experiential learning.

References, Readings, and Resources

Chickering, A. W. (1977). *Experience and learning: An introduction to experiential learning.* Rochelle, NY: Change Magazine Press.

Cooperative Education and Internship Association, P.O. Box 42506, Cincinnati, Ohio 45242. Retrieved from http://www.ceiainc.org.

Inkster, R. P., & Ross, R. G. (1998) *The Internship as partnership: A handbook for businesses, nonprofits, and government agencies.* Raleigh, NC: National Society for Experiential Education.

Inkster, R. P., & Ross, R. G. (1995). *The Internship as partnership: A handbook for campus based coordinators and advisors.* Raleigh, NC: National Society for Experiential Education.

Kendall, J. C., Duley, J. S., Little, T. C., Permaul, J. S., & Rubin, S. (1986). *Strengthening experiential education within your institution.* Raleigh, NC: National Society for Internships and Experiential Education.

Kiser, P. M. (2000). *Getting the most out of your internship: Learning from experience.* Belmont, CA: Wadsworth/Thomson Learning.

Kolb, D. A. (1984). *Experiential learning: Experience as the source of learning and development.* Upper Saddle River, N.J.: Prentice-Hall.

Stanton, T., & Ali, K. (1994). *The experienced hand: A student manual for making the most of an internship (2nd ed.).* New York: Carroll Press.

Sweitzer, H. F., & King, Mary A. (2008). *The successful internship: Transformation and empowerment in experiential learning.* Belmont, CA: Brooks Cole.

National Society for Experiential Education, 19 Mantua Road, Mt. Royal, NJ 08061. Retrieved from http://www.nsee.org

U.S. Department of Labor, Wage and Hour Division, Fact Sheet #71, April 2010. Retrieved from http://www.dol.gov/whd/regs/compliance/whdfs71.htm

Contextual Statement Contributor

Eugene J. Alpert, The Washington Center for Internships and Academic Seminars, NSEE

Internship Programs
CAS Standards and Guidelines

Part 1. MISSION

The primary mission of Internship Programs (IP) is to engage students in planned, educationally-related work and learning experiences that integrate knowledge and theory with practical application and skill development in a professional setting.

IP must develop, disseminate, implement, and regularly review their missions. The mission must be consistent with the mission of the institution and with professional standards. The mission must be appropriate for the institution's student populations and community settings. Mission statements must reference student learning and development.

Part 2. PROGRAM

The formal education of students, consisting of the curriculum and the co-curriculum, must promote student learning and development outcomes that are purposeful, contribute to students' realization of their potential, and prepare students for satisfying and productive lives.

Internship Programs (IP) must collaborate with colleagues and departments across the institution to promote student learning and development, persistence, and success.

Consistent with the institutional mission, IP must identify relevant and desirable student learning and development outcomes from among the six domains and related dimensions:

Domain: knowledge acquisition, integration, construction, and application

- Dimensions: understanding knowledge from a range of disciplines; connecting knowledge to other knowledge, ideas, and experiences; constructing knowledge; and relating knowledge to daily life

Domain: cognitive complexity

- Dimensions: critical thinking, reflective thinking, effective reasoning, and creativity

Domain: intrapersonal development

- Dimensions: realistic self-appraisal, self-understanding, and self-respect; identity development; commitment to ethics and integrity; and spiritual awareness

Domain: interpersonal competence

- Dimensions: meaningful relationships, interdependence, collaboration, and effective leadership.

Domain: humanitarianism and civic engagement

- Dimensions: understanding and appreciation of cultural and human differences, social responsibility, global perspective, and sense of civic responsibility

Domain: practical competence

- Dimensions: pursuing goals, communicating effectively, technical competence, managing personal affairs, managing career development, demonstrating professionalism, maintaining health and wellness, and living a purposeful and satisfying life

[LD Outcomes: See *The Council for the Advancement of Standards Learning and Developmental Outcomes* statement for examples of outcomes related to these domains and dimensions.]

IP must
- assess relevant and desirable student learning and development
- provide evidence of impact on outcomes
- articulate contributions to or support of student learning and development in the domains not specifically assessed
- articulate contributions to or support of student persistence and success
- use evidence gathered through this process to create strategies for improvement of programs and services

IP must be
- intentionally designed
- guided by theories and knowledge of learning and development
- integrated into the life of the institution
- reflective of developmental and demographic profiles of the student population
- responsive to needs of individuals, populations with distinct needs, and relevant constituencies
- delivered using multiple formats, strategies, and contexts

Where institutions provide distance education, IP must assist distance learners to achieve their educational goals by providing access to information about programs and services, to staff members who can address questions and concerns, and to counseling, advising, or other forms of assistance.

Learning goals of IP must

- **be clear about the educational purpose and expected student learning outcomes of the internship experience**
- **encourage the learner to test assumptions and hypotheses about the outcomes of decisions and actions taken, then weigh the outcomes against past learning and future implications**
- **develop and document intentional goals and objectives for the internship experience and measure learning outcomes against these goals and objectives**
- **maintain intellectual rigor in the field experience**

IP must

- **ensure that the participants enter the experience with sufficient foundation to support a successful experience**
- **engage students in appropriate and relevant internships that facilitate practical application of theory and knowledge**
- **provide the learner, the facilitator, and any organizational partners with important background information about each other and about the context and environment in which the experience will operate**
- **articulate the relationship of the internship experience to the expected learning outcomes**
- **determine criteria for internship sites and train appropriate internship personnel to ensure productive and appropriate learning opportunities for students**
- **ensure that all parties engaged in the experience are included in the recognition of progress and accomplishment**

When course credit is offered for an internship, the credit must primarily be for learning, not just for the practical work completed at the internship. Whether the internship is for credit or not, the focus must be on learning and educational objectives, not just on hours accrued at the site.

IP must offer a wide range of internship experiences appropriate for students at various developmental levels, abilities, and with various life circumstances.

Examples may include older students, commuter students, parents, part-time students, fully employed students, and students with disabilities.

IP must initiate collaborative relations among faculty and staff members within the institution for the design and implementation of internship experiences. They must also develop partnerships with external organizations to meet student learning and development outcomes and the organizations' needs.

Whether integrated into a course, completed as an independent study, or designed for co-curricular learning or personal development, internships should encourage practical application of knowledge and theory, development of skills and interests, and exploration of career options in a professional setting. Internships may be for pay or non-pay, for credit or non-credit, and for a variety of lengths or terms. IP experiences could include the following:

Discipline-specific course-based internships: These can be designed to achieve a variety of student learning outcomes relevant to the course and discipline within which the internship is based, including introducing students to career opportunities as a critical aspect of their college education and their chosen field of study, enabling students to learn what types of work within their chosen field of study best suit their interests, and helping students to understand the different career opportunities available to them both inside and outside their curriculum. These experiences should be part of the academic curriculum for credit.

Student-initiated internships: These internships can be designed to enable students to explore internship opportunities within or outside their course of study and their discipline, to apply knowledge learned in their academic program to practice in different situations and venues, and to gain exposure to a broader array of internship experiences than a course- or discipline-based internship might allow. These experiences, if approved in advance, should be considered for academic credit. These experiences could also add to co-curricular learning and personal development.

Short-term internships: These internship programs offer students the opportunity to explore career opportunities through internships without the long-term commitment required by a quarter-term program, academic semester, or year. Typically these occur during week-long breaks or during the short sessions between fall and spring semesters and summer (i.e., January or May term). These experiences can be integrated into the academic curriculum or serve as a co-curricular experience, for credit or not-for-credit, in the student's discipline, or in a broader learning context.

Paid internships: Whether integrated into a course, completed as independent-study, or planned during the summer or semester breaks, these internships are designed to provide students with exposure to career opportunities within a paid employment environment. Structured within a real-world context, students are encouraged to apply theory and knowledge in the career setting while receiving financial compensation for their work and time.

Internship experiences must be described in a syllabus or plan.

The internship course syllabus or plan for academic or co-curricular experiences should describe
- purpose of the internship
- desired learning and development outcomes of the internship for all participants
- assignments that link the internship to academic, career, or personal goals
- opportunities to reflect on one's personal reactions to internship experiences
- logistics (e.g., time required, transportation, materials required, access to services and resources, credit/non-credit, paid/unpaid, financial costs, and benefits)
- roles and responsibilities of students and site personnel
- risk management procedures
- supervision and accommodation requirements by institution personnel and internship site
- evaluation of the internship experience and assessment of the extent to which desired outcomes were achieved
- course requirements (if for credit), including criteria for grading

Part 3. ORGANIZATION AND LEADERSHIP

To achieve student and program outcomes, Internship Programs (IP) must be structured purposefully and organized effectively. IP must have
- clearly stated goals
- current and accessible policies and procedures
- written performance expectations for employees
- functional work flow graphics or organizational charts demonstrating clear channels of authority

Leaders with organizational authority for the programs and services must provide strategic planning, supervision, and management; advance the organization; and maintain integrity through the following functions:

Strategic Planning
- articulate a vision and mission that drive short- and long-term planning
- set goals and objectives based on the needs of the population served and desired student learning or development and program outcomes
- facilitate continuous development, implementation, and assessment of goal attainment congruent with institutional mission and strategic plans
- promote environments that provide meaningful opportunities for student learning, development, and engagement
- develop and continuously improve programs

and services in response to the changing needs of students served and evolving institutional priorities
- intentionally include diverse perspectives to inform decision making

Supervising
- manage human resource processes including recruitment, selection, development, supervision, performance planning, evaluation, recognition, and reward
- influence others to contribute to the effectiveness and success of the unit
- empower professional, support, and student staff to accept leadership opportunities
- offer appropriate feedback to colleagues and students on skills needed to become more effective leaders
- encourage and support professional development, collaboration with colleagues and departments across the institution, and scholarly contribution to the profession

Managing
- identify and address individual, organizational, and environmental conditions that foster or inhibit mission achievement
- plan, allocate, and monitor the use of fiscal, physical, human, intellectual, and technological resources
- use current and valid evidence to inform decisions
- incorporate sustainability practices in the management and design of programs, services, and facilities
- understand appropriate technologies and integrate them into programs and services
- be knowledgeable about codes and laws relevant to programs and services and ensure that staff members understand their responsibilities through appropriate training
- assess potential risks and take action to mitigate them

Advancing the Organization
- communicate effectively in writing, speaking, and electronic venues
- advocate for programs and services
- advocate for representation in strategic planning initiatives at appropriate divisional and institutional levels
- initiate collaborative interactions with internal and external stakeholders who have legitimate concerns about and interests in the functional area
- facilitate processes to reach consensus where wide support is needed

- inform other areas within the institution about issues affecting practice

Maintaining Integrity
- model ethical behavior and institutional citizenship
- share data used to inform key decisions in transparent and accessible ways
- monitor media used for distributing information about programs and services to ensure the content is current, accurate, appropriately referenced, and accessible

Part 4. HUMAN RESOURCES

Internship Programs (IP) must be staffed adequately by individuals qualified to accomplish mission and goals.

Within institutional guidelines, IP must
- **establish procedures for staff recruitment and selection, training, performance planning, and evaluation**
- **set expectations for supervision and performance**
- **assess the performance of employees individually and as a team**
- **provide access to continuing and advanced education and appropriate professional development opportunities to improve the leadership ability, competence, and skills of all employees.**

IP must maintain position descriptions for all staff members.

To create a diverse staff, IP must institute recruitment and hiring strategies that encourage individuals from under-represented populations to apply for positions.

IP must develop promotion practices that are fair, inclusive, proactive, and non-discriminatory.

To further the recruitment and retention of staff, IP must consider work life initiatives, such as compressed work schedules, flextime, job sharing, remote work, or telework.

IP professional staff members must hold an earned graduate or professional degree in a field relevant to the position they hold or must possess an appropriate combination of educational credentials and related work experience.

To facilitate the process of identifying internship sites, professional development of staff and faculty members engaged in IP should include enhancing their ability to
- identify the compatibility between site needs and student interests
- build relationship with business, organizations,

institutions, and other career and professional settings
- establish and maintain collaborative relationships with academic and other units on campus
- understand career and workforce trends

To ensure goal achievement of the IP experience, the professional development of staff and faculty members engaged in IP should include

A. Development of assessment skills:
- access previous evaluations of internship sites and make appropriate recommendations as to the learning value of the internship
- develop, implement, and evaluate internship and learning goals
- ensure the time commitment for the internship is appropriate
- ensure that the time spent at internships produces an appropriate balance between the objectives of the site and the learning objectives of the student
- match the unique needs of students and internship sites

B. Proper communication with students:
- prepare, mentor, and monitor students to fulfill internship requirements according to legal and risk management policies
- clarify the responsibilities of students, the institution, and internship sites

C. Enhancement of student learning:
- engage students in internship experiences to enhance student learning and exposure to career opportunities
- use active learning strategies that are effective in achieving identified learning outcomes
- engage students in structured opportunities for self-reflection and reflection on the internship experience
- sustain genuine and active commitment of students, the institution, and internship sites
- educate, train, and support students to apply learning from internship experiences to future endeavors

D. Management skills:
- foster participation by and with diverse populations
- develop fiscal and other resources for program support

IP professional staff members must engage in continuing professional development activities to keep abreast of the research, theories, legislation, policies, and developments that affect their programs and services.

Internship Programs (IP) must have technical and support staff members adequate to accomplish

their mission. All members of the staff must be technologically proficient and qualified to perform their job functions, be knowledgeable about ethical and legal uses of technology, and have access to training and resources to support the performance of their assigned responsibilities.

Degree- or credential-seeking interns or graduate assistants must be qualified by enrollment in an appropriate field of study and by relevant experience. These individuals must be trained and supervised adequately by professional staff members holding educational credentials and related work experience appropriate for supervision. Supervisors must be cognizant of the roles of interns and graduate assistants as both student and employee and closely adhere to all parameters of their job descriptions, work hours, and schedules. Supervisors and the interns or graduate assistants must agree to compensatory time or other appropriate compensation if circumstances necessitate additional hours.

Student employees and volunteers must be carefully selected, trained, supervised, and evaluated. They must be educated on how and when to refer those in need of additional assistance to qualified staff members and must have access to a supervisor for assistance in making these judgments. Student employees and volunteers must be provided clear job descriptions, pre-service training based on assessed needs, and continuing development.

All IP staff members, including student employees and volunteers, must receive specific training on institutional policies pertaining to functions or activities they support and to privacy and confidentiality policies and laws regarding access to student records and other sensitive institutional information.

All IP staff members must receive training on policies and procedures related to the use of technology to store or access student records and institutional data.

IP must ensure that staff members are knowledgeable about and trained in emergency procedures, crisis response, and prevention efforts. Prevention efforts must address identification of threatening conduct or behavior of students, faculty and staff members, and others and must incorporate a system for responding and reporting.

IP must ensure that staff members are knowledgeable of and trained in safety and emergency procedures for securing and vacating facilities.

Part 5. ETHICS

Internship Programs (IP) must review relevant professional ethical standards and must adopt or develop and implement appropriate statements of ethical practice.

IP must publish and adhere to statements of ethical practice and ensure their periodic review by relevant constituencies.

IP must orient new staff members to relevant ethical standards and statements of ethical practice and related institutional policies.

Statements of ethical standards must specify that staff members respect privacy and maintain confidentiality in all communications and records to the extent that such communications and records are protected under relevant privacy laws.

Statements of ethical standards must specify limits on disclosure of information contained in students' educational records as well as requirements to disclose to appropriate authorities.

Statements of ethical standards must address personal and economic conflicts of interest, or appearance thereof, by staff members in the performance of their work.

Statements of ethical standards must reflect the responsibility of staff members to be fair, objective, and impartial in their interactions with others.

Statements of ethical standards must reference management of institutional funds.

Statements of ethical standards must reference appropriate behavior regarding research and assessment with human participants, confidentiality of research and assessment data, and students' rights and responsibilities.

Statements of ethical standards must include the expectation that IP staff members confront and hold accountable other staff members who exhibit unethical behavior.

Statements of ethical standards must address issues surrounding scholarly integrity.

As appropriate, IP staff members must inform users of programs and services of ethical obligations and limitations emanating from codes and laws or from licensure requirements.

IP staff members must recognize and avoid conflicts of interest that could adversely influence their judgment or objectivity and, when unavoidable, recuse themselves from the situation.

IP staff members must perform their duties within the limits of their position, training, expertise, and competence.

When these limits are exceeded, individuals in need of further assistance must be referred to persons possessing appropriate qualifications.

All IP faculty and staff members responsible for supervising internship activities must monitor student performance and alter placements as needed.

Promotional and descriptive information must be accurate and free of deception.

IP must adhere to institutional policies regarding ethical and legal use of software and technology.

Part 6. LAW, POLICY, AND GOVERNANCE

Internship Programs (IP) must be in compliance with laws, regulations, and policies that relate to their respective responsibilities and that pose legal obligations, limitations, risks, and liabilities for the institution as a whole. Examples include constitutional, statutory, regulatory, and case law; relevant law and orders emanating from codes and laws; and the institution's policies.

IP staff and faculty members and internship site personnel engaged in internships must be knowledgeable about and responsive to laws and regulations that relate to their respective responsibilities.

IP must inform staff members, appropriate officials, and users of programs and services about existing and changing legal obligations, risks and liabilities, and limitations.

IP must have written policies on all relevant operations, transactions, or tasks that have legal implications.

IP must regularly review policies. The revision and creation of policies must be informed by best practices, available evidence, and policy issues in higher education.

IP staff members must use reasonable and informed practices to limit the liability exposure of the institution and its officers, employees, and agents. IP staff members must be informed about institutional policies regarding risk management, personal liability, and related insurance coverage options and must be referred to external sources if the institution does not provide coverage.

IP staff members must establish, review, and disseminate company safety and emergency procedures and policies for the work site and accompanying residential facility.

The institution must provide access to legal advice for staff members as needed to carry out assigned responsibilities.

IP must have procedures and guidelines consistent with institutional policy for responding to threats, emergencies, and crisis situations. Systems and procedures must be in place to disseminate timely and accurate information to students, other members of the institutional community, and appropriate external organizations during emergency situations.

IP staff members must neither participate in nor condone any form of harassment or activity that demeans persons or creates an intimidating, hostile, or offensive environment.

IP must obtain permission to use copyrighted materials and instruments. IP must purchase the materials and instruments from legally compliant sources or seek alternative permission from the publisher or owner. References to copyrighted materials and instruments must include appropriate citations.

IP staff members must be knowledgeable about internal and external governance systems that affect programs and services.

Part 7. DIVERSITY, EQUITY, AND ACCESS

Within the context of each institution's unique mission and in accordance with institutional polices and all applicable codes and laws, Internship Programs (IP) must create and maintain educational and work environments that are
- welcoming, accessible, and inclusive to persons of diverse backgrounds
- equitable and non-discriminatory
- free from harassment

IP must not discriminate on the basis of ability; age; cultural identity; ethnicity; family educational history (e.g., first generation to attend college); gender identity and expression; nationality; political affiliation; race; religious affiliation; sex; sexual orientation; economic, marital, social, or veteran status; or any other basis included in institutional policies and codes and laws.

IP must
- advocate for greater sensitivity to multicultural and social justice concerns by the institution and its personnel
- modify or remove policies, practices, facilities, structures, systems, and technologies that limit access, discriminate, or produce inequities
- include diversity, equity, and access initiatives within their strategic plans
- foster communication that deepens understanding of identity, culture, self-expression, and heritage

- **promote respect about commonalities and differences among people within their historical and cultural contexts**
- **address the characteristics and needs of a diverse population when establishing and implementing culturally relevant and inclusive programs, services, policies, procedures, and practices**
- **provide staff members with access to multicultural training and hold staff members accountable for integrating the training into their work**
- **respond to the needs of all students and other populations served when establishing hours of operation and developing methods of delivering programs, services, and resources**
- **ensure physical, program, and resource access for persons with disabilities**
- **recognize the needs of distance learning students by providing appropriate and accessible services and resources or by assisting them in gaining access to other appropriate services and resources in their geographic region**

IP staff members must select sites that adhere to this nondiscrimination standard.

Part 8. INSTITUTIONAL AND EXTERNAL RELATIONS

Internship Programs (IP) must reach out to relevant individuals, groups, communities, and organizations internal and external to the institution to
- **establish, maintain, and promote understanding and effective relations with those that have a significant interest in or potential effect on the students or other constituents served by the programs and services**
- **garner support and resources for programs and services as defined by the mission statement**
- **disseminate information about the programs and services**
- **collaborate, where appropriate, to assist in offering or improving programs and services to meet the needs of students and other constituents and to achieve program and student outcomes**
- **engage diverse individuals, groups, communities, and organizations to enrich the educational environment and experiences of students and other constituents**

These agencies include government, private business, and nonprofit organizations at the local, national, or international level.

If there is more than one campus unit that facilitates internship experiences, those offices should share information and collaborate as appropriate.

IP should develop productive working relationships with a wide range of campus agencies.

IP must have procedures and guidelines consistent with institutional policy for
- **communicating with the media**
- **contracting with external organizations for delivery of programs and services**
- **cultivating, soliciting, and managing gifts**
- **applying to and managing funds from grants**

IP must be concerned about issues of risk management and consult with appropriate campus offices and officials to insure proper procedures.

IP flourishes best when the institution as a whole is engaged as part of its surrounding community.

IP should advocate for the institution to share its resources with its community and to develop a wide range of mutually beneficial campus-community partnerships. The "community" may include individuals and organizations beyond the immediate physical location of the campus and include state/provincial, national, and international relationships.

Part 9. FINANCIAL RESOURCES

Internship Programs (IP) must have funding to accomplish the mission and goals. In establishing funding priorities and making significant changes, a comprehensive analysis must be conducted to determine the following elements: unmet needs of the unit, relevant expenditures, external and internal resources, and impact on students and the institution.

IP must demonstrate efficient and effective use and responsible stewardship of fiscal resources consistent with institutional protocols.

Part 10. TECHNOLOGY

Internship Programs (IP) must have adequate technology to support the achievement of their mission and goals. The technology and its use must comply with institutional policies and procedures and be evaluated for compliance with relevant codes and laws.

IP must use current technology to provide updated information regarding mission, location, staffing, programs, services, and official contacts to students and designated clients.

IP must explore the use of technology to enhance delivery of programs and services, especially for students at a distance or external constituencies. When technology is used to facilitate student learning and development, IP must select technology that

reflects intended outcomes.

IP must

- maintain policies and procedures that address the security, confidentiality, and backup of data, as well as compliance with privacy laws
- have clearly articulated plans in place for protecting confidentiality and security of information when using Internet-based technologies
- develop plans for replacing and updating existing hardware and software as well as plans for integrating new technically-based or supported programs, including systems developed internally by the institution, systems available through professional associations, or private vendor-based systems

Technology, as well as workstations or computer labs maintained by programs and services for student use, must be accessible to all designated clients and must meet established technology standards for delivery to persons with disabilities.

When providing student access to technology, IP must

- have policies on the use of technology that are clear, easy to understand, and available to all students
- provide assistance, information, or referral to appropriate support services to those needing help accessing or using technology
- provide instruction or training on how to use the technology
- inform students on the legal and ethical implications of misuse as it pertains to intellectual property, harassment, privacy, and social networks

Student violations of technology policies must follow established institutional student disciplinary procedures.

Students who experience negative emotional or psychological consequences from the use of technology must be referred to support services provided by the institution.

Part 11. FACILITIES AND EQUIPMENT

Internship Programs (IP) must have adequate, accessible, and suitably located facilities and equipment to support the mission and goals. If acquiring capital equipment as defined by the institution, IP must take into account expenses related to regular maintenance and life cycle costs. Facilities and equipment must be evaluated on an established cycle, including consideration of sustainability, and be in compliance with codes and laws to provide for access, health, safety, and security.

IP staff members must have workspace that is well equipped, adequate in size, and designed to support their work and responsibilities. For conversations requiring privacy, staff members must have access to a private space.

IP staff members who share workspace must be able to secure their own work.

The design of the facilities must guarantee the security and privacy of records and ensure the confidentiality of sensitive information.

The location and layout of the facilities must be sensitive to the needs of persons with disabilities as well as the needs of other constituencies.

Part 12. ASSESSMENT AND EVALUATION

Internship Programs (IP) must have a clearly articulated assessment plan to document achievement of stated goals and learning outcomes, demonstrate accountability, provide evidence of improvement, and describe resulting changes in programs and services.

IP must have adequate fiscal, human, professional development, and technological resources to develop and implement assessment plans.

Assessments must include direct and indirect evaluation and use qualitative and quantitative methodologies and existing evidence, as appropriate, to determine whether and to what degree the stated mission, goals, and intended outcomes are being met as effectively and efficiently as possible. The process must employ sufficient and sound measures to ensure comprehensiveness. Data collected must include responses from students and other constituencies, and aggregated results must be shared with those groups. Results of assessments must be shared appropriately with multiple constituents.

Results of assessments and evaluations must be used to identify needs and interests in revising and improving programs and services, recognizing staff performance, maximizing resource efficiency and effectiveness, improving student achievement of learning and development outcomes, and improving student persistence and success. Changes resulting from the use of assessments and evaluation must be shared with stakeholders.

IP must regularly evaluate, assess, and respond appropriately regarding the extent to which internship sites add to student learning.

General Standards revised in 2011;
IP standards developed in 2006

The Role of Learning Assistance Programs
CAS Standards Contextual Statement

Learning assistance programs (LAP) help students to succeed academically (Ryan & Glenn, 2004; Stone & Jacobs, 2008) and to facilitate student development and academic success by developing appropriate strategies and behaviors to increase learning efficiency (Dansereau, 1985). Participation in learning assistance programs and services can also improve student retention (Beal, 1980; Ryan and Glenn, 2004) and academic engagement, providing the kinds of rewarding interactions that foster student intellectual and social growth (Tinto, 1987, 2004). The LAP may serve all students at the institution or targeted populations from first-year through graduate and professional students, as well as faculty, staff, administrators, and other students in the community (Kerstiens, 1995).

Ideally, the LAP operates "at the crossroads of academic affairs, student affairs, and enrollment management" (Arendale, 2010, p. 3). The LAP uniquely complements classroom and online instruction by helping students make the most of their intellectual opportunities, making learning accessible to students, and encouraging communities of learning on campus.

The LAP usually provides individualized instruction (tutoring, mentoring, academic coaching, and counseling) that accommodates students' learning styles, learning goals, and current development. Learning centers may also provide Supplemental Instruction (SI), Structured Learning Assistance (SLA), and a variety of other programs and services that help students master content and learn how to learn. Sometimes the LAP provides credit and non-credit courses, including developmental education, tutor training classes or workshops, first-year seminars, linked courses, and learning strategies instruction. These programs are intentionally diverse because they are designed and implemented to be consistent with institutional missions as well as educational best practices.

High-quality learning assistance programs are characterized by a focus on processes and strategies of learning, intellectual development, and effective assessment of academic performance. These programs respect students' cultures while acquainting them with the conventions, discourses, and expectations of higher education. The LAP also engages faculty, staff, and administrators in broader conversations about academic success.

Learning assistance programs generally share certain theoretical perspectives and assumptions.
- Academic assistance programs should be ethically and professionally managed, guided by student learning outcomes and assessment, and consistent with current knowledge of student learning.
- Students should have access to the academic tools that will help them succeed.
- Learning assistance should be designed to meet the demands of the institutional setting and student populations.

Assisting students to achieve their academic goals, meet the expectations of their instructors and requirements of their degree programs, and succeed on standardized exams requires professional knowledge, experience, and expertise. To augment professional expertise, LAP professionals often train student staff to provide services (e.g., peer tutoring and mentoring, study groups, SI, SLA); the learning and development of student staff as well as of student clients thus become important parts of the mission.

Formal and informal learning assistance has been essential to student success and retention since the opening of the first U.S. colleges (Maxwell, 1997). The reading clinics, intensive writing, and study methods laboratories of the 1930s and 1940s and self-help programs, learning modules, and programmed instruction of the 1950s and 1960s formed part of the historical foundation for learning assistance programs (Arendale, 2004; Carino, 1995; Enright, 1975; Lissner, 1990; Sullivan, 1980). In the U.S., more holistic learning assistance grew out of demographic shifts in student populations in the 1970s, spearheaded in colleges and universities on the West Coast (Christ, 1980; Walker, 1980) and in the Midwest, coupled with a growing national sense of college as a necessary part of a complete education. The open university movement, which broadened admissions to students who had not traditionally sought or been admitted to academically-oriented postsecondary institutions, led to development of learning assistance centers to keep the open door to college from becoming a revolving door at institutions that otherwise did not intend to adapt to the new student body.

The growth of academic success programs across the U.S. and Canada into and through the 1980s was consistent with traditional American ideals of democratic education and equal opportunity. With the passage of the Americans with Disabilities Act in 1990, the last decade of the 20th century saw comprehensive academic support become a standard part of the postsecondary landscape.

CAS Standards provided the impetus for certification and professional development programs in learning assistance. In 1989, the College Reading and Learning Association (CRLA) initiated International Tutor Training Program Certification to ensure minimum standards for tutor training. Nine years later CRLA developed International Mentor Training Program Certification. The *CRLA Tutor Training Handbook* (Deese-

Roberts, 2003) and *CRLA Handbook for Training Peer Tutors and Mentors* (Agee & Hodges, 2012) provide examples of best practices that meet certification standards. The National Association for Developmental Education (NADE) developed the *NADE Self-Evaluation Guides* (Clark-Thayer, 2009) in the 1990s. All three certification programs are endorsed by the Council of Learning Assistance and Developmental Education Associations (CLADEA), through which five organizations continue to examine and approve certifications in the field.

Despite productive research in the field, challenges and issues remain to be addressed more fully in the future.

- How can the LAP best gather data to measure student learning and improve programs? What services and programs demonstrate best practices for student learning and academic success at different institutions and different LAP models? Academic assistance programs must do more than provide services; they must also demonstrate effectiveness (Trammell, 2005).
- How should the LAP respond to challenges of shifting student demographics, the changing culture of K-12 schooling, and diversity of needs? In short, how can the LAP improve access to higher education (Arendale, 2010)?
- How will brain research impact learning theory and inform LAP practices?
- How should the LAP move beyond the content, modes, and discourses of the Western model of education to embrace internationalization and globalization?
- How can the LAP help students deal with their high (and often unmet) grade expectations and see learning as a process?
- How can professional organizations and institutions facilitate the recruitment and professional development of LAP directors and staff members?
- How should the LAP resolve information technology concerns and use technology to deliver services?
- How can learning assistance and developmental education programs work together to best meet the needs of students and institutions?
- How can the LAP best assist students in becoming lifelong, independent learners?

References, Readings, and Resources

Agee, K., & Hodges, R. (Eds.).(2012). *Handbook for training peer tutors and mentors.* Mason, OH: Cengage Learning.

Arendale, D. R. (2004). Mainstreamed academic assistance and enrichment for all students: The historical origins of learning assistance centers. *Research for Educational Reform, 9*(4), 3-20.

Arendale, D. R. (2010). *Access at the crossroads: Learning assistance in higher education. ASHE Higher Education Report, 35*(6). San Francisco, CA: Jossey-Bass.

Association for the Tutoring Profession, www.myatp.org: *Synergy*

Association of Colleges for Tutoring and Learning Assistance, www.actla.info

Beal, P. E. (1980). Learning centers and retention. In O. T. Lenning & D. L. Wayman (Eds.), *New roles for learning assistance* (pp. 59-73). San Francisco, CA: Jossey-Bass.

Carino, P. (1995). Early writing centers: Toward a history. *The Writing Center Journal, 15*(2), 103-115.

Christ, F. L. (1980). Learning assistance at a state university: A cybernetic model. In K. V. Lauridsen (Ed.), *New directions for college learning assistance: Examining the scope of learning centers* (pp. 45-56). San Francisco, CA: Jossey-Bass.

Christ, F., Sheets, R., & Smith, K. (Eds.). (2000). *Starting a learning assistance center: Conversations with CRLA members who have been there and done that.* Clearwater, FL: H&H.

Clark-Thayer, S. (Ed.). (2009). *NADE self-evaluation guides (2nd ed.).* Clearwater, FL: H&H.

College Reading and Learning Association, www.crla.net: *Journal of College Reading and Learning*

Council of Learning Assistance and Developmental Education Associations, www.cladea.net

Dansereau, D. F. (1985). Learning strategy research. In J. W. Segal, S. F. Chipman, & R. Glaser (Eds.), *Thinking and learning skills: Relating learning to basic research* (pp. 209-240). Hillsdale, NJ: Erlbaum.

Deese-Roberts, S. (Ed.). (2003). *CRLA tutor training handbook* (rev. ed.). Hastings, NE: College Reading & Learning Association.

Enright, G. (1975). College learning skills: Frontierland origins of the learning assistance center. In R. Sugimoto (Ed.), *College learning skills today and tomorrowland: Proceedings of the Eighth Annual Conference of the Western College Reading Association* (pp. 81-92).

ETL Project, Enhancing Teaching-Learning Environments in Undergraduate Courses http://www.etl.tla.ed.ac.uk/project.html

Journal of Academic Language and Learning, http://journal.aall.org.au/

Journal of Learning Development in Higher Education, http://www.aldinhe.ac.uk/ojs/index.php?journal=jldhe

Journal of Adolescent and Adult Literacy, http://www.reading.org/General/Publications/Journals/jaal.aspx?mode=redirect

Kerstiens, G. (1995). A taxonomy of learning support services. In S. Mioduski and G. Enright (Eds.), *Proceedings of the 15th and 16th Annual Institutes for Learning Assistance Professionals* (pp. 48-51).

Lissner, L. S. (1990). The learning center from 1829 to the year 2000 and beyond. In R. M. Hashway (Ed.), *Handbook of Developmental Education* (pp. 128-154). New York, NY: Praeger.

LRNASST listserv archives, www.lists.ufl.edu/archives/lrnasst-l.html

LSCHE, Learning Support Centers in Higher Education web portal, www. lsche.net

Maxwell, M., Ed. (1994). *From access to success: A book of readings on college developmental education and learning* assistance programs. Clearwater, FL: H&H.

Maxwell, M. (1997). *Improving student learning skills: A new edition*. Clearwater, FL: H&H.

National Association for Developmental Education, www.nade. net: *NADE Digest* and *NADE Monograph Series*

National Center for Developmental Education, Appalachian State University, www.ncde.appstate.edu: *Journal of Developmental Education* and *Research in Developmental Education*

National College Learning Center Association, www.nclca.org: *The Learning Assistance Review*

Oxford Learning Institute, Oxford University, http://www. learning.ox.ac.uk/

Ryan, M. P., & Glenn, P. A. (2004). What do first-year students need most: Learning strategies instruction or academic socialization? *Journal of College Reading & Learning, 34*(2), 4-28.

Stone, M. E., & Jacobs, G. (Eds.). (2008). *Supplemental Instruction: Improving first-year student success in high-risk courses* (Monograph No. 7, 3rd ed.). Columbia, SC: University of South Carolina, National Resource Center for The First-Year Experience and Students in Transition.

Sullivan, L. L. (1980). Growth and influence in the learning center movement. In K. V. Lauridsen (Ed.), *Examining the scope of learning centers* (pp. 1-8). San Francisco, CA: Jossey-Bass.

Tinto, V. (1987). *Leaving college: Rethinking the causes and cures of student attrition*. Chicago, IL: University of Chicago Press.

Tinto, V. (2004). *Student retention and graduation: Facing the truth, living with the consequences*. Retrieved from http:// www.pellinstitute.org/downloads/publications-Student_ Retention_and_Graduation_July_2004.pdf

Trammell, J. (2005). Learning about the learning center: Program evaluation for learning assistance programs. *The Learning Assistance Review, 10*(2), 31-40.

Walker, C. (1980). The learning assistance center in a selective institution. In K. V. Lauridsen (Ed.), *New directions for college learning assistance: Examining the scope of learning centers* (pp. 57-68). San Francisco, CA: Jossey-Bass.

Contextual Statement Contributors

Karen S. Agee, University of Northern Iowa
Mickey Hay, Southwestern Michigan College
Becky Johnen, Educational Consulting Services, Inc.
Janet Norton, University of Iowa
Karen Patty-Graham, Southern Illinois University, Edwardsville
Melissa Thomas, The University of Texas at San Antonio
Linda Thompson, Harding University
John K. Trammell, Randolph-Macon College
Nic Voge, Princeton University
Nancy Wilson, Texas State University, San Marcos

Learning Assistance Programs
CAS Standards and Guidelines

Part 1. MISSION

The primary mission of Learning Assistance Programs (LAP) must be to provide students with resources and opportunities to improve their ability to learn and to achieve academic success.

LAP must develop, disseminate, implement, and regularly review their missions. The mission must be consistent with the mission of the institution and with professional standards. The mission must be appropriate for the institution's student populations and community settings. Mission statements must reference student learning and development.

LAP must collaborate with faculty members, staff, and administrators in addressing the learning needs, academic performance, and retention of students.

Models of LAP vary, but must have the following goals:
- ensure that students are the central focus of the program
- assist students in achieving their personal potential for learning
- introduce students to the academic expectations of the institution, the faculty members, and the culture of higher education
- help students develop positive attitudes toward learning and confidence in their ability to learn
- foster students' personal responsibility and accountability for their own learning
- provide a variety of instructional approaches appropriate to the skill levels and learning styles of students
- assist students in applying newly learned skills and strategies to their academic work
- support the academic standards and requirements of the institution

Models of LAP should also share the following common goals:
- provide instruction and services that address the cognitive, affective, and sociocultural dimensions of learning
- provide to faculty members, staff, and administrators, both services and resources that enhance and support student learning, instruction, and professional development

Part 2. PROGRAM

The formal education of students, consisting of the curriculum and the co-curriculum, must promote student learning and development outcomes that are purposeful, contribute to students' realization of their potential, and prepare students for satisfying and productive lives.

Learning Assistance Programs (LAP) must collaborate with colleagues and departments across the institution to promote student learning and development, persistence, and success.

Consistent with the institutional mission, LAP must identify relevant and desirable student learning and development outcomes from among the six domains and related dimensions:

Domain: knowledge acquisition, integration, construction, and application
- Dimensions: understanding knowledge from a range of disciplines; connecting knowledge to other knowledge, ideas, and experiences; constructing knowledge; and relating knowledge to daily life

Domain: cognitive complexity
- Dimensions: critical thinking, reflective thinking, effective reasoning, and creativity

Domain: intrapersonal development
- Dimensions: realistic self-appraisal, self-understanding, and self-respect; identity development; commitment to ethics and integrity; and spiritual awareness

Domain: interpersonal competence
- Dimensions: meaningful relationships, interdependence, collaboration, and effective leadership.

Domain: humanitarianism and civic engagement
- Dimensions: understanding and appreciation of cultural and human differences, social responsibility, global perspective, and sense of civic responsibility

Domain: practical competence
- Dimensions: pursuing goals, communicating effectively, technical competence, managing personal affairs, managing career development, demonstrating professionalism, maintaining health and wellness, and living a purposeful and satisfying life

[LD Outcomes: See *The Council for the Advancement of Standards*

Learning and Developmental Outcomes statement for examples of outcomes related to these domains and dimensions.]

LAP must

- **assess relevant and desirable student learning and development**
- **provide evidence of impact on outcomes**
- **articulate contributions to or support of student learning and development in the domains not specifically assessed**
- **articulate contributions to or support of student persistence and success**
- **use evidence gathered through this process to create strategies for improvement of programs and services**

LAP must be

- **intentionally designed**
- **guided by theories and knowledge of learning and development**
- **integrated into the life of the institution**
- **reflective of developmental and demographic profiles of the student population**
- **responsive to needs of individuals, populations with distinct needs, and relevant constituencies**
- **delivered using multiple formats, strategies, and contexts**

Where institutions provide distance education, LAP must assist distance learners to achieve their educational goals by providing access to information about programs and services, to staff members who can address questions and concerns, and to counseling, advising, or other forms of assistance.

The scope of programs and services must be determined by the needs of the student populations whom LAP are charged to serve.

LAP should serve all students at the institution. Individual LAP may serve specific populations such as culturally and ethnically diverse students, international and Englishasa-second-language students, student athletes, returning students, students with disabilities, and those provisionally admitted or on academic probation.

LAP should provide instruction and services for the development of reading, mathematics and quantitative reasoning, writing, critical thinking, problem-solving, technological literacy, scientific literacy, and learning strategies. Other programs may include subject-matter tutoring, course-based instructional programs such as Supplemental Instruction, time management programs, college success courses, first-year student seminars, and preparation for graduate and professional school admissions tests and for professional certification requirements.

In recognition of the fact that all students do not learn in the same manner, modes of delivering learning assistance programs should be diverse, including individual and group instruction and/or tutoring, cooperative learning, peer assisted learning, and accelerated learning. A variety of instructional media such as print, electronic, and skills laboratories should be incorporated. Instruction and programs may be delivered traditionally or via technology, either on or off site.

Formal and informal screening or diagnostic procedures must be conducted to identify the knowledge, skills, and motivation that students need to develop to achieve the level of proficiency prescribed or required by the institution, program, or instructor.

Assessment results must be shared with the student to formulate recommendations and a plan of instruction.

LAP should provide systematic feedback to students concerning their progress in reaching cognitive and affective goals; teach methods of self-regulation; and give students practice in applying and transferring skills and strategies learned through the LAP.

LAP professional staff must have access to institutional databases with student information relevant to its work.

LAP must promote, either directly or by referral, the cognitive and affective skills that influence learning, such as stress management, test anxiety reduction, assertiveness, time management, concentration, and motivation.

LAP must refer students to appropriate campus and community resources for assistance with personal problems, learning disabilities, financial difficulties, and other areas of need that may be outside the purview or beyond the expertise of the learning assistance program.

LAP must promote an understanding among campus community members of the learning needs of the student population.

Actions to promote this understanding may include

- establishing advisory boards consisting of members from key segments of the campus community
- holding periodic informational meetings and consulting with staff, faculty members, and administrators
- participating in staff and faculty development and inservice programs on curriculum and instructional approaches that address the development of learning skills, attitudes and behaviors, and the assessment of student learning outcomes
- encouraging the use of learning assistance program

resources, materials, instruction, and services as integral or supplemental classroom activities
- conducting inclass workshops that demonstrate the application of learning strategies to course content
- disseminating information that describes programs and services, hours of operation, and procedures for registering or scheduling appointments
- training and supervising paraprofessionals and pre-professionals to work in such capacities as tutors, peer mentors, and other group leaders, such as Supplemental Instruction (SI) leaders
- providing jobs, practicums, courses, internships, mentoring, and assistantships for students interested in learning assistance and related careers
- collaborating with other community groups and educational institutions to provide college preparation assistance

Part 3. ORGANIZATION AND LEADERSHIP

To achieve student and program outcomes, Learning Assistance Programs (LAP) must be structured purposefully and organized effectively. LAP must have
- clearly stated goals
- current and accessible policies and procedures
- written performance expectations for employees
- functional work flow graphics or organizational charts demonstrating clear channels of authority

Leaders with organizational authority for the programs and services must provide strategic planning, supervision, and management; advance the organization; and maintain integrity through the following functions:

Strategic Planning
- articulate a vision and mission that drive short- and long-term planning
- set goals and objectives based on the needs of the population served and desired student learning or development and program outcomes
- facilitate continuous development, implementation, and assessment of goal attainment congruent with institutional mission and strategic plans
- promote environments that provide meaningful opportunities for student learning, development, and engagement
- develop and continuously improve programs and services in response to the changing needs of students served and evolving institutional priorities
- intentionally include diverse perspectives to inform decision making

Supervising
- manage human resource processes including recruitment, selection, development, supervision, performance planning, evaluation, recognition, and reward
- influence others to contribute to the effectiveness and success of the unit
- empower professional, support, and student staff to accept leadership opportunities
- offer appropriate feedback to colleagues and students on skills needed to become more effective leaders
- encourage and support professional development, collaboration with colleagues and departments across the institution, and scholarly contribution to the profession

Managing
- identify and address individual, organizational, and environmental conditions that foster or inhibit mission achievement
- plan, allocate, and monitor the use of fiscal, physical, human, intellectual, and technological resources
- use current and valid evidence to inform decisions
- incorporate sustainability practices in the management and design of programs, services, and facilities
- understand appropriate technologies and integrate them into programs and services
- be knowledgeable about codes and laws relevant to programs and services and ensure that staff members understand their responsibilities through appropriate training
- assess potential risks and take action to mitigate them

Advancing the Organization
- communicate effectively in writing, speaking, and electronic venues
- advocate for programs and services
- advocate for representation in strategic planning initiatives at appropriate divisional and institutional levels
- initiate collaborative interactions with internal and external stakeholders who have legitimate concerns about and interests in the functional area
- facilitate processes to reach consensus where wide support is needed
- inform other areas within the institution about issues affecting practice

Maintaining Integrity
- model ethical behavior and institutional citizenship

- share data used to inform key decisions in transparent and accessible ways
- monitor media used for distributing information about programs and services to ensure the content is current, accurate, appropriately referenced, and accessible

LAP leaders must be knowledgeable about issues, trends, theories, research, and methodologies related to student learning and retention.

LAP leaders should
- participate in institutional planning, policy, procedural, and fiscal decisions that affect learning assistance for students
- seek opportunities for additional funding, resources, and facilities, as needed
- represent the learning assistance program on institutional committees
- collaborate with leaders of academic departments and support services in addressing the learning needs and retention of students
- be involved in research, publication, presentations, consultation, and activities of professional organizations
- communicate with professional colleagues in the learning assistance field and related professions
- promote and advertise their programs and services

The mission and goals of LAP, the needs and demographics of their clients, and their institutional role should determine where the unit is located in the organizational structure of the institution. Learning assistance programs are frequently organized as units in the academic affairs or the student affairs division.

Regardless of where LAP is positioned within the organization structure, it must communicate and collaborate with a network of key units across the institution to ensure coordination of related functions, programs, services, policies, and procedures, and to expedite student referrals.

LAP should have a broadly constituted advisory board to share information and make suggestions to strengthen the program.

LAP must provide written goals, objectives, and anticipated outcomes for each program and service.

Written procedures should exist for collecting, processing, and reporting student assessment and program data.

LAP must hold regularly scheduled meetings to share information; coordinate the planning, scheduling, and delivery of programs and services; identify and discuss potential and actual problems and concerns; and collaborate on making decisions and solving problems.

Part 4. HUMAN RESOURCES

Learning Assistance Programs (LAP) must be staffed adequately by individuals qualified to accomplish mission and goals.

Within institutional guidelines, LAP must
- **establish procedures for staff recruitment and selection, training, performance planning, and evaluation**
- **set expectations for supervision and performance**
- **assess the performance of employees individually and as a team**
- **provide access to continuing and advanced education and appropriate professional development opportunities to improve the leadership ability, competence, and skills of all employees.**

Staff and faculty who hold a joint appointment with LAP must be committed to the mission, philosophy, goals, and priorities of the program and must possess the necessary expertise for assigned responsibilities.

LAP must maintain position descriptions for all staff members.

To create a diverse staff, programs and services must institute recruitment and hiring strategies that encourage individuals from under-represented populations to apply for positions.

LAP must develop promotion practices that are fair, inclusive, proactive, and non-discriminatory.

To further the recruitment and retention of staff, LAP must consider work life initiatives, such as compressed work schedules, flextime, job sharing, remote work, or telework.

LAP professional staff members must hold an earned graduate or professional degree in a field relevant to the position they hold or must possess an appropriate combination of educational credentials and related work experience.

Relevant disciplines include English, reading, mathematics, student affairs professional preparation, student development, higher education, counseling, psychology, or education.

LAP professionals should be competent and experienced in
- the content areas in which they teach, conduct labs, or provide assistance
- learning theory, instruction and assessment, and the theory and professional standards of practice for their areas of specialization and responsibility
- understanding the unique characteristics and needs of the populations they assist and teach

- demonstrating the ability to adjust pedagogical approaches according to the learning needs and styles of their students, the nature of the learning task, and the content of academic disciplines across the curriculum
- working with college students with different learning styles and abilities, including those with disabilities
- writing and communicating at a professional level
- working in culturally and academically diverse environments
- consulting, collaborating, and negotiating with staff, faculty members, and administrators of academic and student affairs units
- designing, implementing, and utilizing instructional strategies, materials, and technologies
- training, supervising, and mentoring paraprofessionals and pre-professionals
- identifying and establishing lines of communication for student referral to other institutional and student support units

LAP professional staff members must engage in continuing professional development activities to keep abreast of the research, theories, legislation, policies, and developments that affect their programs and services.

LAP must have technical and support staff members adequate to accomplish their mission. All members of the staff must be technologically proficient and qualified to perform their job functions, be knowledgeable about ethical and legal uses of technology, and have access to training and resources to support the performance of their assigned responsibilities.

Degree- or credential-seeking interns or graduate assistants must be qualified by enrollment in an appropriate field of study and by relevant experience. These individuals must be trained and supervised adequately by professional staff members holding educational credentials and related work experience appropriate for supervision. Supervisors must be cognizant of the roles of interns and graduate assistants as both student and employee and closely adhere to all parameters of their job descriptions, work hours, and schedules. Supervisors and the interns or graduate assistants must agree to compensatory time or other appropriate compensation if circumstances necessitate additional hours.

Student employees and volunteers must be carefully selected, trained, supervised, and evaluated. They must be educated on how and when to refer those in need of additional assistance to qualified staff members and must have access to a supervisor for assistance in making these judgments. Student employees and volunteers must be provided clear job descriptions, pre-service training based on assessed needs, and continuing development.

LAP professionals must be knowledgeable of the policies and procedures to be followed for internships and practicums as required by students' academic departments.

Roles and responsibilities of LAP and those of the academic department should be clearly defined.

All LAP staff members, including student employees and volunteers, must receive specific training on institutional policies pertaining to functions or activities they support and to privacy and confidentiality policies and laws regarding access to student records and other sensitive institutional information.

All LAP staff members must receive training on policies and procedures related to the use of technology to store or access student records and institutional data.

LAP must ensure that staff members are knowledgeable about and trained in emergency procedures, crisis response, and prevention efforts. Prevention efforts must address identification of threatening conduct or behavior of students, faculty and staff members, and others and must incorporate a system for responding and reporting.

LAP must ensure that staff members are knowledgeable of and trained in safety and emergency procedures for securing and vacating facilities.

Administrative and technical staff should be knowledgeable about changes in programs, services, policies, and procedures in order to expedite smooth and efficient assistance to students. Appropriate staff development opportunities should be available.

Faculty members assigned to LAP must be informed about the implications for tenure and promotion.

Part 5. ETHICS

Learning Assistance Programs (LAP) must review relevant professional ethical standards and must adopt or develop and implement appropriate statements of ethical practice.

LAP must publish and adhere to statements of ethical practice and ensure their periodic review by relevant constituencies.

LAP must orient new staff members to relevant ethical standards and statements of ethical practice and related institutional policies.

Specific attention must be given to properly

orienting and advising student staff about matters of confidentiality. Clear statements must be distributed and reviewed with student staff regarding what information is not appropriate for them to access or communicate.

Statements of ethical standards must specify that staff members respect privacy and maintain confidentiality in all communications and records to the extent that such communications and records are protected under relevant privacy laws.

Statements of ethical standards must specify limits on disclosure of information contained in students' educational records as well as requirements to disclose to appropriate authorities.

Statements of ethical standards must address personal and economic conflicts of interest, or appearance thereof, by staff members in the performance of their work.

Statements of ethical standards must reflect the responsibility of staff members to be fair, objective, and impartial in their interactions with others.

Statements of ethical standards must reference management of institutional funds.

Statements of ethical standards must reference appropriate behavior regarding research and assessment with human participants, confidentiality of research and assessment data, and students' rights and responsibilities.

Statements of ethical standards must include the expectation that LAP staff members confront and hold accountable other staff members who exhibit unethical behavior.

Statements of ethical standards must address issues surrounding scholarly integrity.

As appropriate, LAP staff members must inform users of programs and services of ethical obligations and limitations emanating from codes and laws or from licensure requirements.

LAP staff members must recognize and avoid conflicts of interest that could adversely influence their judgment or objectivity and, when unavoidable, recuse themselves from the situation.

LAP staff members must perform their duties within the limits of their position, training, expertise, and competence.

When these limits are exceeded, individuals in need of further assistance must be referred to persons possessing appropriate qualifications.

Promotional and descriptive information must be accurate and free of deception.

LAP must adhere to institutional policies regarding ethical and legal use of software and technology.

Because LAP staff work with students' academic coursework, they must be knowledgeable of policies related to academic integrity, plagiarism, student code of conduct, students' rights and responsibilities and other similar policies. All staff members must be cognizant of the implications of these policies.

Statements or claims made about outcomes that can be achieved from participating in learning assistance programs and services must be truthful and realistic.

LAP funds acquired through grants and other noninstitutional resources must be managed according to the regulations and guidelines of the funding source and the institution.

Part 6. LAW, POLICY, AND GOVERNANCE

Learning Assistance Programs (LAP) must be in compliance with laws, regulations, and policies that relate to their respective responsibilities and that pose legal obligations, limitations, risks, and liabilities for the institution as a whole. Examples include constitutional, statutory, regulatory, and case law; relevant law and orders emanating from codes and laws; and the institution's policies.

LAP must inform staff members, appropriate officials, and users of programs and services about existing and changing legal obligations, risks and liabilities, and limitations.

LAP must have written policies on all relevant operations, transactions, or tasks that have legal implications.

LAP must regularly review policies. The revision and creation of policies must be informed by best practices, available evidence, and policy issues in higher education.

LAP staff members must use reasonable and informed practices to limit the liability exposure of the institution and its officers, employees, and agents. Staff members must be informed about institutional policies regarding risk management, personal liability, and related insurance coverage options and must be referred to external sources if the institution does not provide coverage.

The institution must provide access to legal advice for staff members as needed to carry out assigned responsibilities.

LAP must have procedures and guidelines consistent with institutional policy for responding to threats, emergencies, and crisis situations. Systems and procedures must be in place to disseminate timely and accurate information to students, other members of the institutional community, and appropriate external organizations during emergency situations.

LAP staff members must neither participate in nor condone any form of harassment or activity that demeans persons or creates an intimidating, hostile, or offensive environment.

LAP must obtain permission to use copyrighted materials and instruments. LAP must purchase the materials and instruments from legally compliant sources or seek alternative permission from the publisher or owner. References to copyrighted materials and instruments must include appropriate citations.

LAP staff members must be knowledgeable about internal and external governance systems that affect programs and services.

Staff development programs should be available to educate LAP staff of changing legal obligations.

Part 7. DIVERSITY, EQUITY, AND ACCESS

Within the context of each institution's unique mission and in accordance with institutional polices and all applicable codes and laws, Learning Assistance Programs (LAP) must create and maintain educational and work environments that are
- welcoming, accessible, and inclusive to persons of diverse backgrounds
- equitable and non-discriminatory
- free from harassment

LAP must not discriminate on the basis of ability; age; cultural identity; ethnicity; family educational history (e.g., first generation to attend college); gender identity and expression; nationality; political affiliation; race; religious affiliation; sex; sexual orientation; economic, marital, social, or veteran status; or any other basis included in institutional policies and codes and laws.

LAP must
- advocate for greater sensitivity to multicultural and social justice concerns by the institution and its personnel
- modify or remove policies, practices, facilities, structures, systems, and technologies that limit access, discriminate, or produce inequities
- include diversity, equity, and access initiatives within their strategic plans
- foster communication that deepens understanding of identity, culture, self-expression, and heritage
- promote respect about commonalities and differences among people within their historical and cultural contexts
- address the characteristics and needs of a diverse population when establishing and implementing culturally relevant and inclusive programs, services, policies, procedures, and practices
- provide staff members with access to multicultural training and hold staff members accountable for integrating the training into their work
- respond to the needs of all students and other populations served when establishing hours of operation and developing methods of delivering programs, services, and resources
- ensure physical, program, and resource access for persons with disabilities
- recognize the needs of distance learning students by providing appropriate and accessible services and resources or by assisting them in gaining access to other appropriate services and resources in their geographic region

The program should facilitate student adjustment to the academic culture of the institution by orienting students to the practices, resources, responsibilities, and behaviors that contribute to academic success.

The instructional content, materials, and activities of learning assistance programs should provide opportunities to increase awareness and appreciation of the individual and cultural differences of students, staff, and faculty members.

Part 8. INSTITUTIONAL AND EXTERNAL RELATIONS

Learning Assistance Programs (LAP) must reach out to relevant individuals, groups, communities, and organizations internal and external to the institution to
- establish, maintain, and promote understanding and effective relations with those that have a significant interest in or potential effect on the students or other constituents served by the programs and services
- garner support and resources for programs and services as defined by the mission statement
- disseminate information about the programs and services
- collaborate, where appropriate, to assist in offering or improving programs and services to meet the needs of students and other constituents and to achieve program and student outcomes

- engage diverse individuals, groups, communities, and organizations to enrich the educational environment and experiences of students and other constituents

LAP must have procedures and guidelines consistent with institutional policy for
- **communicating with the media**
- **contracting with external organizations for delivery of programs and services**
- **cultivating, soliciting, and managing gifts**
- **applying to and managing funds from grants**

LAP should
- be integrated into the academic program of the institution
- establish communication with academic units and student services
- collaborate with appropriate academic departments and faculty members when providing course-based learning assistance
- encourage the exchange of ideas, knowledge, and expertise
- provide mutual consultation, as needed, on student cases
- expedite student referrals to and from the LAP
- collaborate on programs and services that efficiently and effectively address student needs
- have representation on institutional committees relevant to the mission and goals of the program such as committees on retention, orientation, basic skills, learning communities, first-year student seminars, probation review (e.g., academic, financial aid), academic standards and requirements, curriculum design, assessment and placement, and professional development
- solicit and use trained volunteers from the local community to contribute their skills and talents to the services of the learning assistance program, consistent with the LAP mission and goals and the institution's risk management policies
- provide training and consultation to community based organizations, e.g., literacy associations, corporate training, and school-to-college transitions, initiatives, and programs

Part 9. FINANCIAL RESOURCES

Learning Assistance Programs (LAP) must have funding to accomplish the mission and goals. In establishing funding priorities and making significant changes, a comprehensive analysis must be conducted to determine the following elements: unmet needs of the unit, relevant expenditures, external and internal resources, and impact on students and the institution.

Adequate funds should be provided for the following

budget categories: staff and student salaries, general office functions, student assessment and instructional activities, data management and program evaluation processes, staff training and professional development activities, instructional materials and media, and instructional and office technology.

LAP must demonstrate efficient and effective use and responsible stewardship of fiscal resources consistent with institutional protocols.

A financial analysis of costs and available resources must be completed before implementing new programs or changing existing ones. This analysis must include an assessment of the impact on students served prior to making significant changes

Opportunities for additional funding should be pursued; however, these sources should not be expected to supplant institutional funding.

Part 10. TECHNOLOGY

Learning Assistance Programs (LAP) must have adequate technology to support the achievement of their mission and goals. The technology and its use must comply with institutional policies and procedures and be evaluated for compliance with relevant codes and laws.

Electronic systems for scheduling and record keeping must be secure.

Such systems should be integrated with institutional systems.

LAP must use current technology to provide updated information regarding mission, location, staffing, programs, services, and official contacts to students and designated clients.

LAP must explore the use of technology to enhance delivery of programs and services, especially for students at a distance or external constituencies.

When technology is used to facilitate student learning and development, LAP must select technology that reflects intended outcomes.

LAP must
- **maintain policies and procedures that address the security, confidentiality, and backup of data, as well as compliance with privacy laws**
- **have clearly articulated plans in place for protecting confidentiality and security of information when using Internet-based technologies**
- **develop plans for replacing and updating existing hardware and software as well as plans for integrating new technically-based or supported programs, including systems developed internally by the institution, systems available through professional**

associations, or private vendor-based systems

Technology, as well as workstations or computer labs maintained by programs and services for student use, must be accessible to all designated clients and must meet established technology standards for delivery to persons with disabilities.

When providing student access to technology, LAP must

- have policies on the use of technology that are clear, easy to understand, and available to all students
- provide assistance, information, or referral to appropriate support services to those needing help accessing or using technology
- provide instruction or training on how to use the technology
- inform students on the legal and ethical implications of misuse as it pertains to intellectual property, harassment, privacy, and social networks

Student violations of technology policies must follow established institutional student disciplinary procedures.

Students who experience negative emotional or psychological consequences from the use of technology must be referred to support services provided by the institution.

Part 11. FACILITIES AND EQUIPMENT

Learning Assistance Programs (LAP) must have adequate, accessible, and suitably located facilities and equipment to support the mission and goals. If acquiring capital equipment as defined by the institution, LAP must take into account expenses related to regular maintenance and life cycle costs. Facilities and equipment must be evaluated on an established cycle, including consideration of sustainability, and be in compliance with codes and laws to provide for access, health, safety, and security.

LAP staff members must have workspace that is well equipped, adequate in size, and designed to support their work and responsibilities. For conversations requiring privacy, staff members must have access to a private space.

Facilities and equipment should support the instructional, service, and office functions of the learning assistance program. Facilities should include flexible space to accommodate different delivery modes and student needs. Consideration should be given to universal instructional design in creating classrooms, labs, resource rooms, media

and computer centers, and group and one-to-one tutorial space to support instruction. Adequate space should be provided for quiet areas to support testing and other activities that require concentration.

There must be adequate and secure storage for equipment, supplies, instructional and testing materials, and confidential records.

Environmental conditions such as appropriate acoustics, lighting, ventilation, heating, and air-conditioning should enhance the teaching/learning process.

LAP staff members who share workspace must be able to secure their own work.

The design of the facilities must guarantee the security and privacy of records and ensure the confidentiality of sensitive information.

The location and layout of the facilities must be sensitive to the needs of persons with disabilities as well as the needs of other constituencies.

Part 12. ASSESSMENT AND EVALUATION

Learning Assistance Programs (LAP) must have a clearly articulated assessment plan to document achievement of stated goals and learning outcomes, demonstrate accountability, provide evidence of improvement, and describe resulting changes in programs and services.

LAP must have adequate fiscal, human, professional development, and technological resources to develop and implement assessment plans.

Assessments must include direct and indirect evaluation and use qualitative and quantitative methodologies and existing evidence, as appropriate, to determine whether and to what degree the stated mission, goals, and intended outcomes are being met as effectively and efficiently as possible. The process must employ sufficient and sound measures to ensure comprehensiveness. Data collected must include responses from students and other constituencies, and aggregated results must be shared with those groups. Results of assessments must be shared appropriately with multiple constituents.

Qualitative methods may include standard evaluation forms, questionnaires, interviews, focus groups, observations, or case studies, with input solicited from faculty members, staff, and students.

Quantitative measurements range from data on an individual student's performance to data on campus retention rates and success for various cohorts. Quantitative methods may include follow-up studies on students' grades in targeted courses, gain scores, grade point averages, graduation, reenrollment, and retention figures. Program effectiveness may also be measured by comparing data of learning assistance program participants and nonparticipants. Quantitative program measures may include data on the size of the user population, numbers utilizing particular services and number of contact hours, sources of student referrals to the program, or numbers of students who may be on a waiting list or who have requested services not provided by the learning assistance program. Quantitative data should be collected within specific time periods as well as longitudinally to reveal trends.

Results of assessments and evaluations must be used to identify needs and interests in revising and improving programs and services, recognizing staff performance, maximizing resource efficiency and effectiveness, improving student achievement of learning and development outcomes, and improving student persistence and success. Changes resulting from the use of assessments and evaluation must be shared with stakeholders.

LAP should have the ability to collect and analyze data through its own resources as well as through access to appropriate data generated by the institution.

Periodic evaluations of LAP or services may be performed by on-campus experts and outside consultants. Evaluations should be disseminated to appropriate administrators and constituencies.

LAP should conduct periodic selfassessments, utilizing selfstudy processes endorsed by professional organizations. The assessments should examine the quality of services provided as well as the potential impact on student learning over time. Additionally, learning outcomes associated with LAP instructional courses should reflect what students learn or do better as a result of being exposed to course materials and instructional strategies.

Various means of individual assessment should be conducted for the purpose of identifying the learning needs of the students and guiding them to appropriate programs and services. Assessment results should be communicated to students confidentially, honestly, and sensitively. Students should be advised and directed to appropriate, alternative educational opportunities when there is reasonable cause to believe that students may not be able to meet requirements for academic success.

LAP should periodically review and revise its goals and services based on evaluation outcomes and based on changes in institutional goals, priorities, and plans. Data that reveal trends or changes in student demographics, characteristics, needs, and outcomes should be utilized for learning assistance program short and longterm planning.

General Standards revised in 2011;
LAP content developed/revised in 1986, 1996, & 2007

The Role of Lesbian, Gay, Bisexual, Transgender Programs
CAS Standards Contextual Statement

In referencing lesbian, gay, bisexual, and transgender people, the acronym *LGBT* has become standard on most campuses. It should be understood, however, to be broadly inclusive of many related identities with nomenclature going far beyond these four terms. These may include queer, questioning, intersex, bi-affectionate, pansexual, fluid, asexual, genderqueer, men who have sex with men (MSM), and women who partner with women, in addition to terms rooted primarily in communities of color, such as same gender loving (SGL) in African American communities, *khush* in South Asian populations, and *two spirit* among American Indian peoples. Gender identity, gender expression, and sexual orientation are the identities being addressed.

From the late 1960s when the first Student Homophile Association formed at Columbia University, LGBT students made themselves visible on college campuses in ever increasing numbers. Positive institutional responses have usually begun with adding sexual orientation to non-discrimination policies and, typically much later, gender identity and gender expression. Over time, institutions have added services and programs that address the specific needs of LGBT students.

Dedicated resources delivered through a unit created specifically for that purpose began in 1971 when the University of Michigan created a Human Sexuality Office with a one-room office, two quarter-time positions, and a small budget (Burris, n.d.). Growth in the number of campuses with such units was slow initially and accelerated exponentially in the late 1990s and early years of the twenty-first century. Higher education professionals began to organize to provide support and information, share best practices, and otherwise develop this specialty first within existing professional organizations such as the Standing Committee for Lesbian, Gay, Bisexual, and Transgender/Awareness within ACPA and the Gay, Lesbian, Bisexual, and Transgender Knowledge Community within NASPA. However, the professional organization that has best met the needs of these educators—the Consortium of Higher Education LGBT Resource Professionals (lgbtcampus.org)—was officially founded in 1997 within the context of an advocacy organization, The National Gay and Lesbian Task Force. An activist element continues to be part of the work of these professionals, and the Consortium continues to be the most vital organization supporting them.

Services and programs addressing the specific needs of LGBT students may be delivered by a LGBT Resource Center through a unit with a broader mission such as a Multicultural Center, a Gender and Sexuality Center, or other organizational structures. Regardless of how the needs of LGBT students are addressed, two basic principles are observed: (a) all units must be responsible for meeting the needs of LGBT students within their functional areas and (b) some identifiable unit must be responsible for addressing the needs of LGBT students globally, including those needs that require a specific, articulated mission to address their unique needs. Also, regardless of organizational structure (LGBT Resource Center, Multicultural Center), these standards and guidelines apply.

The successful LGBT program targets individual students and creates and maintains a healthy LGBT campus community. Although recruitment and retention are central issues, lack of uniformity in terminology underscores the difficulty of producing statistical data similar to those that are used in developing and assessing programs for recruitment and retention of other populations. Of greater relevance than terminology, questions about gender identity, gender expression, and sexual orientation are not routinely asked, unlike questions of race and sex. Best practices for collecting these data have begun to emerge for sexual orientation, although many different approaches exist for gender identity and gender expression (SMART, 2009). Now that there is developing a degree of consensus regarding how to gather these data, it remains to be seen if higher education will find appropriate means for routinely collecting the data.

In the absence of institution-specific data, we must rely on individual studies generally produced by researchers who examine these issues nationally within the United States. For example, the ongoing collection of data about LGBT students in K-12 environments show continuing problems of hostile school climate, absenteeism, lowered educational aspirations and academic achievement, and poorer psychological well-being (Kosciw, Greytak, Diaz, & Bartkiewicz, 2010). The existing data indicate these problems continue and are compounded after LGBT students step onto college campuses (Rankin, Weber, Blumenfeld, & Frazer, 2010). In particular, LGBT students report significantly higher rates of harassment and discrimination than their non-LGBT peers. This is particularly true for students with multiple minority identities (e.g., racial identity and sexual identity; racial identity and gender identity). These data demonstrate that LGBT students are among the most likely to experience conduct that interferes with their ability to live and learn on campus.

None of the data regarding harassment, discrimination, and hostile climate for LGBT college students comes as a surprise to the professionals working in this area. It is from the collective wisdom of these professionals that CAS standards emerge.

References, Readings, and Resources

Burris, N. (n.d.).   History of the Spectrum Center. Retrieved from http://spectrumcenter.umich.edu/about/history

Kosciw, J., Greytak, E., Diaz, E., & Bartkiewicz, M. (2010). The 2009 national school climate survey. New York, NY: Gay, Lesbian and Straight Education Network.

Rankin, S., Weber, G., Blumenfeld, W., & Frazer, S. (2010). 2010 state of higher education for lesbian, gay, bisexual & transgender people. Charlotte, NC: Campus Pride.

Sexual Minority Assessment Research Team (SMART). (2009). Best practices for asking questions about sexual orientation on surveys. Los Angeles, CA: The Williams Institute.

Contextual Statement Contributor

Luke Jensen, University of Maryland, College Park

Lesbian, Gay, Bisexual, Transgender Programs and Services
CAS Standards and Guidelines

Part 1. MISSION

The mission of the Lesbian, Gay, Bisexual, Transgender Programs and Services (LGBT Programs and Services) must be to
- promote academic and personal growth of all LGBT and questioning students
- build and maintain campus LGBT communities
- advance access and equity in higher education
- establish and maintain coalitions with other campus constituencies and allies to create a more socially just institution and community
- offer programs to educate the campus about sexual orientation and gender identity and expression

Programming should address how sexual orientation and gender identity and expression differ in concept while remaining intertwined in daily life.

The term *LGBT* includes a broad spectrum of identities in addition to the four terms comprising the acronym.

LGBT Programs and Services must develop, disseminate, implement, and regularly review their missions. The mission must be consistent with the mission of the institution and with professional standards. The mission must be appropriate for the institution's student populations and community settings. Mission statements must reference student learning and development.

The mission of LGBT Programs and Services and the goals of its initiatives must be based on assessment of the needs of and campus climate for LGBT students. LGBT Programs and Services must select priorities among those needs and respond accordingly.

LGBT Programs and Services must not be the only institutional unit meeting the needs of LGBT students.

All institutional units should share responsibility for identifying and meeting the needs of LGBT students and eliminating prejudicial behaviors.

Part 2. PROGRAM

The formal education of students, consisting of the curriculum and the co-curriculum, must promote student learning and development outcomes that are purposeful, contribute to students' realization of their potential, and prepare students for satisfying and productive lives.

Lesbian, Gay, Bisexual, Transgender Programs and Services (LGBT Programs and Services) must collaborate with colleagues and departments across the institution to promote student learning and development, persistence, and success.

Consistent with the institutional mission, LGBT Programs and Services must identify relevant and desirable student learning and development outcomes from among the six domains and related dimensions:

Domain: knowledge acquisition, integration, construction, and application

- **Dimensions: understanding knowledge from a range of disciplines; connecting knowledge to other knowledge, ideas, and experiences; constructing knowledge; and relating knowledge to daily life**

Domain: cognitive complexity

- **Dimensions: critical thinking, reflective thinking, effective reasoning, and creativity**

Domain: intrapersonal development

- **Dimensions: realistic self-appraisal, self-understanding, and self-respect; identity development; commitment to ethics and integrity; and spiritual awareness**

Domain: interpersonal competence

- **Dimensions: meaningful relationships, interdependence, collaboration, and effective leadership.**

Domain: humanitarianism and civic engagement

- **Dimensions: understanding and appreciation of cultural and human differences, social responsibility, global perspective, and sense of civic responsibility**

Domain: practical competence

- **Dimensions: pursuing goals, communicating effectively, technical competence, managing personal affairs, managing career development, demonstrating professionalism, maintaining health and wellness, and living a purposeful and satisfying life**

[LD Outcomes: See *The Council for the Advancement of Standards Learning and Developmental Outcomes* statement for examples of outcomes related to these domains and dimensions.]

LGBT Programs and Services must

- assess relevant and desirable student learning and development
- provide evidence of impact on outcomes
- articulate contributions to or support of student learning and development in the domains not specifically assessed
- articulate contributions to or support of student persistence and success
- use evidence gathered through this process to create strategies for improvement of programs and services

LGBT Programs and Services must be
- intentionally designed
- guided by theories and knowledge of learning and development
- integrated into the life of the institution
- reflective of developmental and demographic profiles of the student population
- responsive to needs of individuals, populations with distinct needs, and relevant constituencies
- delivered using multiple formats, strategies, and contexts

Where institutions provide distance education, LGBT Programs and Services must assist distance learners to achieve their educational goals by providing access to information about programs and services, to staff members who can address questions and concerns, and to counseling, advising, or other forms of assistance.

LGBT Programs and Services must promote student learning and development outcomes of particular concern to LGBT students:
- realistic self-appraisal, self-understanding, and self-respect
- identity development
- effective leadership

LGBT Programs and Services must promote and advocate for services addressing the unique needs of LGBT students that are generally offered by other functional areas:
- individual and group psychological counseling
  - coming-out support with particular attention to multiple identities, especially race, ethnicity, disability, religion, family-of-origin issues, and to internalized homophobia and biphobia
  - support for individuals facing difficulties regarding gender identity and expression and for those experiencing internalized transphobia
  - services for victims, survivors, and perpetrators of homophobia, biphobia, and transphobia
  - services to address family issues
  - services to address dating issues for those who date only people of the same sex, who may date individuals of either sex, and who are transgender or may date someone who is transgender
  - services to address domestic and relationship violence
  - services to address body image concerns
  - support for LGBT victims of hate crimes
  - support for the education and recovery of perpetrators of hate crimes
  - support for understanding racial, ethnic, national, cultural, and religious issues and differences

- health services
  - health forms with inclusive language
  - LGBT health issues brochures
  - safer sex information for LGBT people
  - safer sex supplies
  - HIV/STD testing services with intake and follow-up protocols appropriate for LGBT people
  - sex-specific services for those whose sex and gender may not align (e.g., pap smears for female-bodied individuals who identify as male)
  - access to or referral for hormone therapy
  - inclusion of transgender specific health care coverage by any insurance offered by the institution

- career services
  - job search preparation
  - information on LGBT-friendly employers
  - employer mentoring programs for LGBT students
  - information on LGBT issues in the workplace, including coming out and transitioning on the job

- academic advising, including support of students' educational choices

- public safety
  - training for police officers and other public safety officials to respond appropriately when an LGBT person is involved in any incident
  - avoidance of re-victimization of LGBT students who have experienced bias
  - management of incidents related to bias against LGBT individuals

- admissions and registration, including maintenance of records and documentation that facilitates a change in name and sex and supports individuals who are in the process of transitioning with the use of a preferred name

- housing and residential Life
  - housing assignments that respect students' gender when it conflicts with their legal sex
  - the availability of married student housing options for same sex couples
- library services, including library and research guides for students interested in LGBT issues, especially when they cross traditional lines of academic disciplines
- facilities, including restroom and locker room policies and facilities that accommodate and support individuals who are transitioning or whose appearance may not fit a traditional male/female division
- recreational sports and intercollegiate athletics, including intramural, club, and varsity sports and other recreational opportunities that include and support individuals who do not fit into traditional sex segregated categories
- student life, activities, and organizations
  - access to opportunities for membership in student activities, including fraternities and sororities
  - supportive culture for LGBT students
  - support for LGBT students engaged in these activities

LGBT Programs and Services must promote resources that may not be the logical responsibility of other functional areas:
- identification of and networking with role models and mentors
- identification of courses with LGBT specific content especially at institutions with no LGBT studies or similar programs
- support of LGBT students in achieving academic success
- identification of supports for families of LGBT students
- identification of appropriate religious and faith communities
- support of international LGBT students
- identification of global LGBT laws and practices that may affect students studying abroad

LGBT Programs and Services must promote issues regarding the overall climate and general support for LGBT students on the campus as a whole:
- advocacy for the creation and maintenance of a campus climate that is free from harassment and violence
- training for students, staff, and faculty members in providing a supportive environment
- training and support for allies
- identification of environmental conditions that negatively influence student welfare and advocacy for their solutions
- creation within the institution of policies and procedures that promote and maintain a hospitable climate

Additionally, LGBT Programs and Services must work to assure equitable access to and involvement in all educational programs.

Particular attention should be given to financial aid, athletic scholarships, fraternity and sorority life, employment opportunities, and campus engagement and co-curricular activities on campus.

LGBT Programs and Services must promote learning opportunities for LGBT students and for all students on issues regarding sexual orientation and gender identity and expression.

LGBT Programs and Services must include examination of the intersection of sexual orientation, gender identity, and gender expression with race, class, gender, disability, ethnicity, religion, and age.

LGBT Programs and Services must promote the knowledge base of all students on issues regarding sexual orientation and gender identity and expression.

LGBT Programs and Services must assist other functional areas to meet the needs of LGBT students, because all institutional units share responsibility for meeting the needs of LGBT students.

LGBT Programs and Services must support campus efforts to eliminate prejudicial behavior based on sexual orientation and/or gender identity and expression.

LGBT Programs and Services should work closely with campus compliance officers or other campus officials charged with enforcing nondiscrimination policies and charged with promoting broad diversity efforts.

LGBT Programs and Services must educate the campus community when decisions or policies may affect LGBT students; publicize services, events, and issues of concern to LGBT students; and sponsor events that meet educational, personal, physical, and safety needs of LGBT students and their allies.

LGBT Programs and Services should take the following actions:

- encourage awareness of off campus networks and other support systems for LGBT students, including affiliation with local, state or provincial, regional, and national organizations
- increase campus awareness of the complex identity issues inherent in the lives of LGBT students
- publicize and celebrate the accomplishments of LGBT students, faculty, staff, and alumni
- represent LGBT concerns and issues on campus-wide committees
- promote scholarship, research, and assessment on LGBT issues
- encourage campus-wide inclusion of LGBT students and avoidance of negative stereotyping in campus media.

LGBT Programs and Services must address the needs of all LGBT students inclusive of their race, class, socio-economic status, gender, disability, ethnicity, religion, age, and degree or enrollment status. In addition, LGBT Programs and Services must plan for and recognize the diversity among the LGBT student population.

LGBT Programs and Services should partner with other institutional efforts to recognize and celebrate other areas of diversity such as race, ethnicity, gender, and disability.

LGBT Programs and Services must advocate for the human rights of LGBT persons to promote a more socially just institution and community.

LGBT Programs and Services should work with campus administration in outreach to local, state/provincial, and federal or national leaders to effect positive change for LGBT people in education, employment, and other issues with a direct relevance for campus life.

Part 3. ORGANIZATION AND LEADERSHIP

To achieve student and program outcomes, Lesbian, Gay, Bisexual, Transgender Programs and Services (LGBT Programs and Services) must be structured purposefully and organized effectively. LGBT Programs and Services must have

- **clearly stated goals**
- **current and accessible policies and procedures**
- **written performance expectations for employees**
- **functional work flow graphics or organizational charts demonstrating clear channels of authority**

Leaders with organizational authority for the programs and services must provide strategic planning, supervision, and management; advance the organization; and maintain integrity through the following functions:

Strategic Planning

- **articulate a vision and mission that drive short- and long-term planning**
- **set goals and objectives based on the needs of the population served and desired student learning or development and program outcomes**
- **facilitate continuous development, implementation, and assessment of goal attainment congruent with institutional mission and strategic plans**
- **promote environments that provide meaningful opportunities for student learning, development, and engagement**
- **develop and continuously improve programs and services in response to the changing needs of students served and evolving institutional priorities**
- **intentionally include diverse perspectives to inform decision making**

Supervising

- **manage human resource processes including recruitment, selection, development, supervision, performance planning, evaluation, recognition, and reward**
- **influence others to contribute to the effectiveness and success of the unit**
- **empower professional, support, and student staff to accept leadership opportunities**
- **offer appropriate feedback to colleagues and students on skills needed to become more effective leaders**
- **encourage and support professional development, collaboration with colleagues and departments across the institution, and scholarly contribution to the profession**

Managing

- **identify and address individual, organizational, and environmental conditions that foster or inhibit mission achievement**
- **plan, allocate, and monitor the use of fiscal, physical, human, intellectual, and technological resources**
- **use current and valid evidence to inform decisions**
- **incorporate sustainability practices in the management and design of programs, services, and facilities**
- **understand appropriate technologies and integrate them into programs and services**
- **be knowledgeable about codes and laws relevant to programs and services and ensure that staff members understand their**

responsibilities through appropriate training
- assess potential risks and take action to mitigate them

Advancing the Organization
- communicate effectively in writing, speaking, and electronic venues
- advocate for programs and services
- advocate for representation in strategic planning initiatives at appropriate divisional and institutional levels
- initiate collaborative interactions with internal and external stakeholders who have legitimate concerns about and interests in the functional area
- facilitate processes to reach consensus where wide support is needed
- inform other areas within the institution about issues affecting practice

Maintaining Integrity
- model ethical behavior and institutional citizenship
- share data used to inform key decisions in transparent and accessible ways
- monitor media used for distributing information about programs and services to ensure the content is current, accurate, appropriately referenced, and accessible

Program leaders must possess the academic preparation, experience, abilities, professional interests, competencies essential for the efficient operation of the office as charged, as well as the ability to identify additional areas of concern about LGBT students.

LGBT Programs and Services leaders should have coursework in organizational development, counseling, group dynamics, leadership development, student and human development, LGBT studies, multicultural education, women's studies, higher education, and research and assessment.

LGBT Programs and Services leaders should
- participate in institutional planning, policy, procedural, and fiscal decisions that affect LGBT students
- seek opportunities for additional funding, resources, and facilities, as needed
- represent the interests of LGBT students on relevant institutional committees
- collaborate with leaders of academic departments and support services in addressing the learning needs and retention of students
- be involved in research, publication, presentations, consultation, and activities of professional organizations
- interact with professional colleagues from LGBT

Programs and Services units at other institutions
- participate with relevant LGBT community organizations
- promote and advertise their programs and services

Whether as a separate unit or as part of a unit with a broader scope, LGBT Programs and Services must be structured to promote academic and personal growth of LGBT students.

LGBT Programs and Services must play a major role in implementing institutional programs developed in response to the assessed needs of LGBT students.

Access to the policymakers of the institution should be readily available.

LGBT Programs and Services must be afforded the opportunity to organize in a manner that is efficient and best promotes equity concerns.

Emphasis should be placed on achieving an organization in which services are not limited to a specific group of LGBT students (e.g., solely undergraduate students) but inclusive of many groups that make up a campus community (e.g., undergraduate, graduate, and prospective students, alumni, faculty, staff, and families).

Regardless of where LGBT Programs and Services are positioned within the organizational structure, they must be empowered to work with all functional areas of the institution to meet the needs of LGBT students and eliminate prejudicial behaviors. All institutional units share responsibility for meeting the needs of LGBT students in their area of service.

Part 4. HUMAN RESOURCES

Lesbian, Gay, Bisexual, Transgender Programs and Services (LGBT Programs and Services) must be staffed adequately by individuals qualified to accomplish mission and goals.

Within institutional guidelines, LGBT Programs and Services must
- establish procedures for staff recruitment and selection, training, performance planning, and evaluation
- set expectations for supervision and performance
- assess the performance of employees individually and as a team
- provide access to continuing and advanced education and appropriate professional development opportunities to improve the leadership ability, competence, and skills of all employees.

Where LGBT Programs and Services is part of a unit with a broader scope, such as a multicultural center or college union, it must be adequately staffed to promote academic and personal growth of LGBT students.

Staff members should have adequate time for student advising, reporting and updating institutional information, contact with faculty members and staff, staff meetings, training, supervision, personal and professional development, and consultation with other experts. Similarly, teaching, administration, research, and other responsibilities should be identified as relevant staff functions.

LGBT Programs and Services must maintain position descriptions for all staff members.

To create a diverse staff, LGBT Programs and Services must institute recruitment and hiring strategies that encourage individuals from under-represented populations to apply for positions.

LGBT Programs and Services must develop promotion practices that are fair, inclusive, proactive, and non-discriminatory.

To further the recruitment and retention of staff, LGBT Programs and Services must consider work life initiatives, such as compressed work schedules, flextime, job sharing, remote work, or telework.

LGBT Programs and Services professional staff members must hold an earned graduate or professional degree in a field relevant to the position they hold or must possess an appropriate combination of educational credentials and related work experience.

Program staff members should have a combination of graduate course work, formal training (including LGBT issues), and supervising experience.

LGBT Programs and Services professional staff members must engage in continuing professional development activities to keep abreast of the research, theories, legislation, policies, and developments that affect their programs and services.

LGBT Programs and Services must have technical and support staff members adequate to accomplish their mission. All members of the staff must be technologically proficient and qualified to perform their job functions, be knowledgeable about ethical and legal uses of technology, and have access to training and resources to support the performance of their assigned responsibilities.

Support staff should have a thorough knowledge of the institution and be able to perform office and administrative functions, including receiving visitors and identifying issues. Special emphasis should be placed on development of skills in the areas of public relations, information delivery,

identification problems, and referral protocols.

All LGBT Programs and Services staff members must be responsive to and knowledgeable about LGBT issues with special attention to rapidly changing trends in working with transgender individuals and to the intersection of sexual orientation and gender identity and expression with other elements of identity.

Degree- or credential-seeking interns or graduate assistants must be qualified by enrollment in an appropriate field of study and by relevant experience. These individuals must be trained and supervised adequately by professional staff members holding educational credentials and related work experience appropriate for supervision. Supervisors must be cognizant of the roles of interns and graduate assistants as both student and employee and closely adhere to all parameters of their job descriptions, work hours, and schedules. Supervisors and the interns or graduate assistants must agree to compensatory time or other appropriate compensation if circumstances necessitate additional hours.

Student employees and volunteers must be carefully selected, trained, supervised, and evaluated. They must be educated on how and when to refer those in need of additional assistance to qualified staff members and must have access to a supervisor for assistance in making these judgments. Student employees and volunteers must be provided clear job descriptions, pre-service training based on assessed needs, and continuing development.

All LGBT Programs and Services staff members, including student employees and volunteers, must receive specific training on institutional policies pertaining to functions or activities they support and to privacy and confidentiality policies and laws regarding access to student records and other sensitive institutional information.

All LGBT Programs and Services staff members must receive training on policies and procedures related to the use of technology to store or access student records and institutional data.

LGBT Programs and Services must ensure that staff members are knowledgeable about and trained in emergency procedures, crisis response, and prevention efforts. Prevention efforts must address identification of threatening conduct or behavior of students, faculty and staff members, and others and must incorporate a system for responding and reporting.

LGBT Programs and Services must ensure that staff members are knowledgeable of and trained in safety and emergency procedures for securing and vacating facilities.

LGBT Programs and Services must provide opportunities for professional development including but not limited to additional credit courses, seminars, and access to current research.

Additionally, staff members should participate in appropriate professional organizations and should have the budgetary support to do so. Staff members should be encouraged to participate in community activities related to the student population being served.

LGBT Programs and Services staff members must ensure that the privacy of students' sexual orientation and gender identity and expression are protected.

The staffing, level, and diversity of services must be established and reviewed regularly with regard to service demands, enrollment, user surveys, institutional resources and climate, and other student services available on the campus and in the local community.

LGBT Programs and Services staff must be open to and interested in working with LGBT students.

Part 5. ETHICS

Lesbian, Gay, Bisexual, Transgender Programs and Services (LGBT Programs and Services) must review relevant professional ethical standards and must adopt or develop and implement appropriate statements of ethical practice.

LGBT Programs and Services must publish and adhere to statements of ethical practice and ensure their periodic review by relevant constituencies.

LGBT Programs and Services must orient new staff members to relevant ethical standards and statements of ethical practice and related institutional policies.

Statements of ethical standards must specify that staff members respect privacy and maintain confidentiality in all communications and records to the extent that such communications and records are protected under relevant privacy laws.

LGBT Programs and Services staff members must ensure that the privacy of individuals' sexual orientation and gender identity and expression is protected.

Information should be released only at the written request of a student who has full knowledge of the nature of the information that is being released and of the parties to whom it is being released. Instances of limited confidentiality should be clearly articulated. The decision to release information without consent should occur only after careful consideration

and under the conditions described above.

Statements of ethical standards must specify limits on disclosure of information contained in students' educational records as well as requirements to disclose to appropriate authorities.

Statements of ethical standards must address personal and economic conflicts of interest, or appearance thereof, by staff members in the performance of their work.

Statements of ethical standards must reflect the responsibility of staff members to be fair, objective, and impartial in their interactions with others.

Statements of ethical standards must reference management of institutional funds.

Statements of ethical standards must reference appropriate behavior regarding research and assessment with human participants, confidentiality of research and assessment data, and students' rights and responsibilities.

Statements of ethical standards must include the expectation that LGBT Programs and Services staff members confront and hold accountable other staff members who exhibit unethical behavior.

Statements of ethical standards must address issues surrounding scholarly integrity.

As appropriate, LGBT Programs and Services staff members must inform users of programs and services of ethical obligations and limitations emanating from codes and laws or from licensure requirements.

LGBT Programs and Services staff members must recognize and avoid conflicts of interest that could adversely influence their judgment or objectivity and, when unavoidable, recuse themselves from the situation.

LGBT Programs and Services staff members must perform their duties within the limits of their position, training, expertise, and competence.

When these limits are exceeded, individuals in need of further assistance must be referred to persons possessing appropriate qualifications.

Promotional and descriptive information must be accurate and free of deception.

LGBT Programs and Services must adhere to institutional policies regarding ethical and legal use of software and technology.

Part 6. LAW, POLICY, AND GOVERNANCE

Lesbian, Gay, Bisexual, Transgender Programs and Services (LGBT Programs and Services) must be in compliance with laws, regulations, and policies that relate to their respective responsibilities and that pose legal obligations, limitations, risks, and liabilities for the institution as a whole. Examples include constitutional, statutory, regulatory, and case law; relevant law and orders emanating from codes and laws; and the institution's policies.

LGBT Programs and Services must inform staff members, appropriate officials, and users of programs and services about existing and changing legal obligations, risks and liabilities, and limitations.

LGBT Programs and Services must have written policies on all relevant operations, transactions, or tasks that have legal implications.

LGBT Programs and Services must regularly review policies. The revision and creation of policies must be informed by best practices, available evidence, and policy issues in higher education.

LGBT Programs and Services staff members must use reasonable and informed practices to limit the liability exposure of the institution and its officers, employees, and agents. LGBT Programs and Services staff members must be informed about institutional policies regarding risk management, personal liability, and related insurance coverage options and must be referred to external sources if the institution does not provide coverage.

The institution must provide access to legal advice for staff members as needed to carry out assigned responsibilities.

LGBT Programs and Services must have procedures and guidelines consistent with institutional policy for responding to threats, emergencies, and crisis situations. Systems and procedures must be in place to disseminate timely and accurate information to students, other members of the institutional community, and appropriate external organizations during emergency situations.

LGBT Programs and Services staff members must neither participate in nor condone any form of harassment or activity that demeans persons or creates an intimidating, hostile, or offensive environment.

LGBT Programs and Services must obtain permission to use copyrighted materials and instruments. LGBT Programs and Services must purchase the materials and instruments from legally compliant sources or seek alternative permission from the publisher or owner. References to copyrighted materials and instruments must include appropriate citations.

LGBT Programs and Services staff members must

be knowledgeable about internal and external governance systems that affect programs and services.

Resources should be available to educate LGBT Programs and Services staff on changing legal obligations.

Part 7. DIVERSITY, EQUITY, AND ACCESS

Within the context of each institution's unique mission and in accordance with institutional polices and all applicable codes and laws, Lesbian, Gay, Bisexual, Transgender Programs and Services (LGBT Programs and Services) must create and maintain educational and work environments that are

- welcoming, accessible, and inclusive to persons of diverse backgrounds
- equitable and non-discriminatory
- free from harassment

LGBT Programs and Services must not discriminate on the basis of ability; age; cultural identity; ethnicity; family educational history (e.g., first generation to attend college); gender identity and expression; nationality; political affiliation; race; religious affiliation; sex; sexual orientation; economic, marital, social, or veteran status; or any other basis included in institutional policies and codes and laws.

LGBT Programs and Services must

- advocate for greater sensitivity to multicultural and social justice concerns by the institution and its personnel
- modify or remove policies, practices, facilities, structures, systems, and technologies that limit access, discriminate, or produce inequities
- include diversity, equity, and access initiatives within their strategic plans
- foster communication that deepens understanding of identity, culture, self-expression, and heritage
- promote respect about commonalities and differences among people within their historical and cultural contexts
- address the characteristics and needs of a diverse population when establishing and implementing culturally relevant and inclusive programs, services, policies, procedures, and practices
- provide staff members with access to multicultural training and hold staff members accountable for integrating the training into their work
- respond to the needs of all students and other populations served when establishing hours of operation and developing methods of delivering programs, services, and resources

- ensure physical, program, and resource access for persons with disabilities
- recognize the needs of distance learning students by providing appropriate and accessible services and resources or by assisting them in gaining access to other appropriate services and resources in their geographic region

LGBT Programs and Services staff should display a statement of commitment or non-discrimination within physical office space as well as in LGBT Programs and Services electronic and print communications.

Part 8. INSTITUTIONAL AND EXTERNAL RELATIONS

Lesbian, Gay, Bisexual, Transgender Programs and Services (LGBT Programs and Services) must reach out to relevant individuals, groups, communities, and organizations internal and external to the institution to

- establish, maintain, and promote understanding and effective relations with those that have a significant interest in or potential effect on the students or other constituents served by the programs and services
- garner support and resources for programs and services as defined by the mission statement
- disseminate information about the programs and services
- collaborate, where appropriate, to assist in offering or improving programs and services to meet the needs of students and other constituents and to achieve program and student outcomes
- engage diverse individuals, groups, communities, and organizations to enrich the educational environment and experiences of students and other constituents

LGBT Programs and Services should pay particular attention to relationships with alumni, the community at large, contractors, vendors, and support agencies.

LGBT Programs and Services must collaborate with campus referral agencies for LGBT students, staff, faculty, and administration (e.g., multicultural, student affairs, visitor services, women's centers, special academic support units, campus security, health centers, counseling centers, religious programs, and career services).

LGBT Programs and Services must establish relationships with a wide range of student groups (e.g., LGBT student association, student government association, fraternities and sororities, and athletics) to promote visibility and to serve as a resource to the entire campus community.

LGBT Programs and Services must foster relationships with academic units (especially in LGBT studies, ethnic studies, women's studies, higher education, counseling and human services, and student affairs) and with campus professionals (e.g., student activities, athletics, commuter affairs, and residential life).

LGBT Programs and Services staff should be actively involved in appropriate campus networks to effectively participate in the establishment of institution-wide policies and practices and to collaborate with other staff and faculty to provide services.

LGBT Programs and Services must have adequate access to institutional legal counsel and legal staff of relevant professional organizations.

Where adequate LGBT resources are not available on campus, LGBT Programs and Services must establish and maintain close working relationships with off-campus community LGBT agencies that provide such services as counseling, community involvement, and health care.

An advisory board made up of students, faculty, staff, alumni, and community members may be established to advise, support, and guide the LGBT Programs and Services.

LGBT Programs and Services must have procedures and guidelines consistent with institutional policy for

- communicating with the media
- contracting with external organizations for delivery of programs and services
- cultivating, soliciting, and managing gifts
- applying to and managing funds from grants

Part 9. FINANCIAL RESOURCES

Lesbian, Gay, Bisexual, Transgender Programs and Services (LGBT Programs and Services) must have funding to accomplish the mission and goals. In establishing funding priorities and making significant changes, a comprehensive analysis must be conducted to determine the following elements: unmet needs of the unit, relevant expenditures, external and internal resources, and impact on students and the institution.

Funding for LGBT Programs and Services must be equitable in relationship to other comparable Programs and Services.

LGBT Programs and Services must demonstrate efficient and effective use and responsible stewardship of fiscal resources consistent with institutional protocols.

Funding for LGBT Programs and Services may come from

a variety of sources, including grant money, student government funds or fees, foundation donations, alumni development initiatives, and government contracts; however non-institutional funding should not be expected to supplant institutional funding.

Part 10. TECHNOLOGY

Lesbian, Gay, Bisexual, Transgender Programs and Services (LGBT Programs and Services) must have adequate technology to support the achievement of their mission and goals. The technology and its use must comply with institutional policies and procedures and be evaluated for compliance with relevant codes and laws.

LGBT Programs and Services must use current technology to provide updated information regarding mission, location, staffing, programs, services, and official contacts to students and designated clients.

LGBT Programs and Services must explore the use of technology to enhance delivery of programs and services, especially for students at a distance or external constituencies.

When technology is used to facilitate student learning and development, LGBT Programs and Services must select technology that reflects intended outcomes.

LGBT Programs and Services must

- maintain policies and procedures that address the security, confidentiality, and backup of data, as well as compliance with privacy laws
- have clearly articulated plans in place for protecting confidentiality and security of information when using Internet-based technologies
- develop plans for replacing and updating existing hardware and software as well as plans for integrating new technically-based or supported programs, including systems developed internally by the institution, systems available through professional associations, or private vendor-based systems

Technology, as well as workstations or computer labs maintained by programs and services for student use, must be accessible to all designated clients and must meet established technology standards for delivery to persons with disabilities.

When providing student access to technology, LGBT Programs and Services must

- have policies on the use of technology that are clear, easy to understand, and available to all students
- provide assistance, information, or referral to appropriate support services to those needing help accessing or using technology
- provide instruction or training on how to use the technology
- inform students on the legal and ethical implications of misuse as it pertains to intellectual property, harassment, privacy, and social networks

Student violations of technology policies must follow established institutional student disciplinary procedures.

Students who experience negative emotional or psychological consequences from the use of technology must be referred to support services provided by the institution.

Information about LGBT programs, services, and resources must be available in electronic formats.

LGBT Programs and Services should also provide multiple contact points using instant messaging services and social networking sites to provide access to potential visitors who prefer to be anonymous when seeking information, services, guidance, and advice.

Part 11. FACILITIES AND EQUIPMENT

Lesbian, Gay, Bisexual, Transgender Programs and Services (LGBT Programs and Services) must have adequate, accessible, and suitably located facilities and equipment to support the mission and goals. If acquiring capital equipment as defined by the institution, LGBT Programs and Services must take into account expenses related to regular maintenance and life cycle costs. Facilities and equipment must be evaluated on an established cycle, including consideration of sustainability, and be in compliance with codes and laws to provide for access, health, safety, and security.

LGBT Programs and Services should maintain a physical and social environment that facilitates appropriate attention to safety factors. In addition, private, individual, and group meeting space should be provided.

LGBT Programs and Services should have access to resources for research, including access to private computer space.

LGBT Programs and Services staff members must have workspace that is well equipped, adequate in size, and designed to support their work and responsibilities. For conversations requiring privacy, staff members must have access to a private space.

LGBT Programs and Services staff members who share workspace must be able to secure their own work.

The design of the facilities must guarantee the

security and privacy of records and ensure the confidentiality of sensitive information.

The location and layout of the facilities must be sensitive to the needs of persons with disabilities as well as the needs of other constituencies.

Part 12. ASSESSMENT AND EVALUATION

Lesbian, Gay, Bisexual, Transgender Programs and Services (LGBT Programs and Services) must have a clearly articulated assessment plan to document achievement of stated goals and learning outcomes, demonstrate accountability, provide evidence of improvement, and describe resulting changes in programs and services.

LGBT Programs and Services must have adequate fiscal, human, professional development, and technological resources to develop and implement assessment plans.

Assessments must include direct and indirect evaluation and use qualitative and quantitative methodologies and existing evidence, as appropriate, to determine whether and to what degree the stated mission, goals, and intended outcomes are being met as effectively and efficiently as possible. The process must employ sufficient and sound measures to ensure comprehensiveness. Data collected must include responses from students and other constituencies, and aggregated results must be shared with those groups. Results of assessments must be shared appropriately with multiple constituents.

Results of assessments and evaluations must be used to identify needs and interests in revising and improving programs and services, recognizing staff performance, maximizing resource efficiency and effectiveness, improving student achievement of learning and development outcomes, and improving student persistence and success. Changes resulting from the use of assessments and evaluation must be shared with stakeholders.

Both internal and external on-going evaluations are encouraged as part of a thoughtful plan of continuous evaluation of the LGBT Programs and Services mission and goals. Periodic reports, statistically valid research, outside reviews, and studies exploring student needs and opinions should be utilized.

General Standards revised in 2011;
LGBT Programs and Services content developed/revised in 2000 & 2010

The Role of Masters-Level Student Affairs Preparation Programs
CAS Standards Contextual Statement

Master's-level professional preparation programs provide individuals entering the field of student affairs the requisite knowledge, perspectives, and skills to serve students and foster their learning and development. Aside from acquiring skills and knowledge, students that complete a master's program in student affairs are socialized into the field. They learn about the culture of the profession and the values that guide it. These preparation programs may have different foci, including administration, counseling, or student development; all, however, should prepare students to work in a wide variety of functional areas. Although this diversity of preparation programs is valuable to the field, a set of shared standards is essential to serve as a foundation for all programs. The primary value of the CAS student affairs professional preparation standard is to assist in ensuring that an academic program is offering what the profession, through representative consensus, has deemed necessary to graduate prepared student affairs and student services professionals.

Standards for the professional education of student affairs practitioners have largely been established during the past five decades. In 1964 the Council of Student Personnel Associations in Higher Education (COSPA) drafted *A Proposal for Professional Preparation in College Student Personnel Work*, which subsequently evolved into *Guidelines for Graduate Programs in the Preparation of Student Personnel Workers in Higher Education*, dated March 5, 1967. The change in title from "proposal for" in the 1964 version to "guidelines for" in the fourth revision exemplifies the movement from a rather tentative statement of what professional preparation should entail to one asserting specific guidelines that should be followed in graduate education programs. A final statement, popularly recognized as the COSPA Report, was actually published some time after the dissolution of the Council (1975).

During this period, others concerned with the graduate education of counselors and other helping professionals established counselor education standards and explored the possibilities for accrediting graduate academic programs. A moving force in this effort was the Association of Counselor Educators and Supervisors (ACES), a division of the American Personnel and Guidance Association (APGA), now called the American Counseling Association (ACA). In 1978, ACES published a set of professional standards to accredit counseling and personnel services education programs. APGA recognized ACES as its official counselor education accrediting body and moved to establish an inter-association committee to guide counselor education program accreditation activity and the review and revision of the ACES/APGA preparation standards. In response to

this initiative, the American College Personnel Association (ACPA) established an *ad hoc* Preparation Standards Drafting Committee to create a set of standards designed to focus on the special concerns of student affairs graduate education. At its March 1979 meetings, the ACPA Executive Council adopted the Committee's statement entitled "Standards for the Preparation of Counselors and College Student Affairs Specialists at the Master's Degree Level."

ACPA then initiated a two-pronged effort in the area of professional standards. One was a collaborative effort with the National Association of Student Personnel Administrators (NASPA) to establish a profession-wide program of standards creation, and the other was a concerted effort to work under the then-APGA organizational umbrella to establish an agency for the accreditation of counseling and student affairs preparation programs. The former initiative resulted in the creation of the Council for the Advancement of Standards in Higher Education (CAS) and the latter in the establishment of the Council for the Accreditation of Counseling and Other Related Educational Programs (CACREP), an academic program-accrediting agency. Both the CAS and CACREP professional preparation standards reflected the influence of the ACPA standards for student affairs preparation.

The foregoing process was a prelude to the *CAS Masters-Level Student Affairs Professional Preparation Program Standards and Guidelines*, which follow. A major value of graduate standards is that they provide criteria by which an academic program of professional preparation can judge its educational efforts. Whether used for accreditation or program development purposes, standards provide faculty, staff, administrators, and students alike a tool to measure a program's characteristics against a set of well-conceived criteria designed to ensure educational quality.

The CAS standards for student affairs graduate programs were revised in 2002 and offer standards and guidelines based on profession-wide inter-association collaboration; a standards review is underway in 2012. Topics addressed in the standards include the program's mission; recruitment and admission policies and procedures; curriculum policies; pedagogy; the curriculum; equity and access; academic and student support; professional ethics and legal responsibilities; and program evaluation. The standards recognize that each program must also be responsive to the host department and institution. The standards support the need for life-long learning and professional development for all professionals. The ACPA and NASPA document of *Professional Competency Areas for Student Affairs* (2011) is a useful guide for professional preparation and professional development.

Curriculum standards are organized around Foundation Studies, Professional Studies, and Supervised Practice. Foundation Studies pertains to the historical and philosophical foundations of higher education and student affairs. This includes historical documents of the profession such as *Learning Reconsidered I and II (2004, 2006)*, *Student Personnel Point of View* (ACE, 1937), *Return to the Academy* (Brown, 1972), the *Student Learning Imperative* (ACPA, 1996), *Principles of Good Practice* (Blimling & Whitt, 1999), *Powerful Partnerships* (Joint Task Force, 1998), and *Reasonable Expectations* (Kuh et al, 1994) among others. Professional Studies pertains to student development theory, student characteristics, the effects of college on students, individual and group interventions, the organization and administration of student affairs, and assessment, evaluation, and research. Supervised Practice includes practica, internships, and externships under professionally supervised work conditions.

There are a number of emerging trends influencing today's professional preparation programs. Students entering these programs are more diverse than they have been in the past. More adult students have entered preparation programs as advanced degrees become more important for promotion and advancement. Changes in higher education, such as the increased emphasis on accountability, including assessment of graduate learning outcomes, are influencing curriculum. Graduates of professional preparation programs need to be ready to document the impact of programs and services they provide. The tools of the profession are changing; technology from hardware to software to social media is having a significant impact on how we connect with students and do our work. Finally, there is an emerging discussion of professionalism in the field, including consideration of the ACPA/NASPA Professional Competencies. Standards for preparation programs provide anchors guiding students with a strong foundation while adapting to emerging issues affecting the field.

Two groups that exist to support and promote the preparation of professionals are the Commission for Professional Preparation of ACPA and NASPA's Faculty Fellows. The Association for the Study of Higher Education (ASHE) has a commission on graduate preparation that has drafted standards for the study of higher education as a discipline. Through the use of the CAS Professional Preparation standards, programs can ensure that what the field has deemed appropriate education will produce succession student affairs and services professionals.

References, Readings, and Resources

ACPA: College Student Educators International. Commission for Professional Preparation. ACPA National Office, One Dupont Circle, N.W., Suite 300. Washington, DC 20036-1110. (202) 835-2272; Fax (202) 296-3286. http://www.myacpa.org/comm/profprep/

ACPA/NASPA (2011). *Professional competency areas for student affairs*. Washington, DC: Author. http://www2.myacpa.org/img/Professional_Competencies.pdf

American College Personnel Association (1996). The student learning imperative: Implications for student affairs. *Journal of College Student Development, 37,* 118-122.

American Council on Education (ACE) (1937). *The student personnel point of view* (Ser. 1, Vol. 1, No. 3,). Washington, DC: Author. [revised in 1949 and 1989].

Association of Counselor Educators and Supervisors (ACES). (1978). *Standards for the preparation of counselors and other personnel services specialists at the master's degree level.* Washington, DC: Author.

Blimling, G. S. & Whitt, E. J. (1999). *Good practice in student affairs.* San Francisco, CA: Jossey-Bass.

Brown, R. D. (1972). Student development in tomorrow's higher education - A return to the academy. *Student Personnel Series, 16.* Washington, DC: American College Personnel Association.

Bryant, W. A., Winston, R. B. Jr., & Miller, T. K. (Eds.) (1991). Using professional standards in student affairs, No. 53. *New Directions for Student Affairs.* San Francisco, CA: Jossey-Bass.

Cooper, D. L., Saunders, S. A., Winston, R. B., Jr., Hirt, J. B., Creamer, D. G., Janosik, S, M. (2002). *Learning through supervised practice in student affairs.* New York, NY: Taylor Francis.

Council of Student Personnel Associations (COSPA). (1964). *A proposal for professional preparation in college student personnel work.* Unpublished manuscript, Indianapolis: Author.

Council of Student Personnel Associations (COSPA). (March, 1967). *Guidelines for graduate programs in the preparation of student personnel workers in higher education.* Unpublished manuscript, Washington, DC: Author.

Council of Student Personnel Associations (COSPA). (1975). Student development services in post-secondary education. *Journal of College Student Personnel, 16,* 524-528.

Evans, N., & Phelps Tobin, C. (1996). *State of the art of preparation and practice in student affairs: Another look.* Lanham, MD: University Press of America.

Joint Task Force of Student Learning. (1998). *Powerful partnerships: A shared responsibility for learning.* Washington, DC: American Association for Higher Education.

Kuh, G. D. (1994). *Reasonable expectations: Renewing the educational compact between institutions and students.* Washington, DC: National Association of Student Personnel Administrators.

Magolda, P & Carnaghi, J. (Eds.). (2004). *Job one: Experiences of new professionals in student affairs.* New York, NY: University Press of America.

National Association of Student Personnel Administrators (NASPA). (1987). *A perspective on student affairs: A statement issued on the 50th anniversary of the student personnel point of view.* Washington, DC: Author.

National Student Affairs Archives, Bowling Green State

University, http://www.bgsu.edu/colleges/library/cac/bib/page39347.html

Schuh, J., Jones, S. R., & Harper, S. (Eds.) (2010). *Student services: A handbook for the profession (5th ed).* San Francisco, CA: Jossey-Bass.

Stringer, J. & McClelland, G. (Eds.) (2009). *The handbook of student affairs administration (3rd ed.).* San Francisco, CA: Jossey-Bass.

Whitt, E. J., Carnaghi, J. E., Matkin, J., Scalese-Love, P., & Nestor, D. (1990). Believing is seeing: Alternative perspectives on a statement of professional philosophy for student affairs. *NASPA Journal, 27*, 178-184.

Winston, R. B. Jr., Creamer, D. G., Miller, T. K., & Associates (2001). *The professional student affairs administrator: Educator, leader, and manager.* Philadelphia, PA: Taylor and Francis.

Contextual Statement Contributors

Current Edition:
Gavin Henning, Dartmouth College, ACPA
Susan R. Komives, University of Maryland, ACPA

Previous Editions:
Jan Arminio, Shippensburg University, NACA

Masters-Level Student Affairs Professional Preparation Programs
CAS Standards and Guidelines

Part 1. MISSION AND OBJECTIVES

The mission of professional preparation programs shall be to prepare persons through graduate education for professional positions in student affairs in schools, colleges, and universities. Each program mission must be consistent with the mission of the institution offering the program.

Program missions should reflect a particular emphasis, such as administration, counseling, student learning and development, student cultures, or other appropriate emphases as long as the standards herein are met.

The program's mission may include providing in-service education, professional development, research, and consultation for student affairs professional staff members at the institution.

Each professional preparation program must publish a clear statement of mission and objectives prepared by the program faculty in consultation with collaborating student affairs professionals and relevant advisory committees. The statement must be readily available to current and prospective students and to appropriate faculty and staff members and agencies. It must be written to allow accurate assessment of student learning and program effectiveness. The statement must be reviewed periodically.

This review may be conducted with the assistance of current students and faculty, graduates of the program, student affairs professionals, and personnel in cooperating agencies.

The program faculty should consider recommendations of local, state/provincial, regional, and national legislative bodies and professional groups concerned with student affairs when developing, revising, and publishing the program's mission and objectives. The mission and objectives should reflect consideration of the current issues and needs of society, of higher education, and of the student populations served. Personnel in cooperating agencies and faculty members with primary assignments in other disciplines should be aware of and encouraged to support and work toward the achievement of the program's mission and stated objectives.

The mission and objectives should specify both mandatory and optional areas of study and should include a plan for assessing student progress throughout the program of study. The mission and objectives may address recruitment, selection, retention, employment recommendations, curriculum, instructional methods, research activities, administrative policies, governance, and program evaluation.

Part 2. RECRUITMENT AND ADMISSION

Accurate descriptions of the graduate program, including the qualifications of its faculty and records of its students' persistence, degree completion, and subsequent study and employment, must be made readily available for review by both current and prospective students.

Students selected for admission to the program must meet the institution's criteria for admission to graduate study. Program faculty members must make admission decisions using written criteria that are disseminated to all faculty members and to prospective students.

Admissions materials must be clear about preferences for particular student status, such as full-time students, currently employed students, or students seeking learning opportunities by distance, and the manner in which such preferences may affect admissions decisions.

Students admitted to the program should have ample intellectual capacities, strong interpersonal skills, serious interest in the program, commitment to pursuing a career in student affairs, the potential to serve a wide range of students of varying developmental levels and backgrounds, and the capacity to be open to self-assessment and growth. Criteria known to predict success in the program for students of various backgrounds and characteristics should be used in their selection. Students from diverse backgrounds should be encouraged to apply.

Students from diverse backgrounds must be given equal opportunity for entry into the program.

Part 3. CURRICULUM POLICIES

The preparation program must specify in writing and distribute to prospective students its curriculum and graduation requirements. The program must conform to institutional policy and must be fully approved by the institution's administrative unit responsible for graduate programs. The institution must employ only faculty members with credentials that clearly reflect professional knowledge, ability, and skill to teach, advise, or supervise in the program.

Any revisions to the publicized program of studies must be published and distributed to students in a timely fashion. Course syllabi must be available that reflect purposes, teaching/learning methods, and outcome objectives.

All prerequisite studies and experiences should be identified clearly in course descriptions and syllabi.

The equivalent of two years full-time academic study must be required for the masters degree.

Ordinarily, to accomplish the goals of the curriculum as outlined later in this document, a program should include a total of 42-48 semester credit hours.

Programs must demonstrate that the full curriculum, as outlined in Part 5 of these standards and guidelines, is covered and that graduates reflect relevant proficiency.

Because of the benefits of immersion-like educational experiences characterized by full-time study, full-time enrollment should be encouraged. However, to serve those students for whom full-time study is not possible, programs may provide opportunities for part-time study. Part-time enrollment will result in a program of more than two academic years of study.

Appropriate consideration and provisions for admission and curriculum decisions should be made for students with extensive student affairs experience.

Distance learning options may be used in the program.

There must be a sequence of basic to advanced studies. Any required associated learning experiences must be included in the required program of studies.

Associated learning experiences may include comprehensive examinations, degree candidacy, and research requirements.

Opportunity for students to develop understandings and skills beyond minimum program requirements must be provided through elective course options, supervised individual study, and/or enrichment opportunities.

Programs should encourage students to take advantage of special enrichment opportunities and education that encourages learning beyond the formal curriculum, such as experiences in student affairs organizations, professional associations and conferences, and outreach projects.

An essential feature of the preparation program must be to foster an appreciation of spirit of inquiry, in faculty members and students, as evidenced by active involvement in producing and using research, evaluation, and assessment information in student affairs.

Research, program evaluation, and assessment findings should be used frequently in instructional and supervised practicum offerings. The study of methods of inquiry should be provided in context of elected program emphasis, such as administration, counseling, student learning and development, student cultures, or other program options.

Part 4. PEDAGOGY

Each program must indicate its pedagogical philosophy in the program literature. In addition, the individual faculty member must identify his or her pedagogical strategies. Faculty members must accommodate multiple student learning styles. Teaching approaches must be employed that lead to the accomplishment of course objectives, achievement of student learning outcomes, and are subject to evaluation by academic peers for the purpose of program improvement.

Such teaching approaches include active collaboration, service-learning, problem-based learning, experiential learning, and constructivist learning. Faculty members should elect to use multiple teaching strategies. Recognition of the student's role in learning should play a significant role in choice of teaching approach.

Part 5. THE CURRICULUM

All programs of study must include (a) foundational studies, (b) professional studies, and c) supervised practice. Foundational studies must include the study of the historical and philosophical foundations of higher education and student affairs. Professional studies must include (a) student development theory, (b) student characteristics and the effects of college on students, (c) individual and group interventions, (d) organization and administration of student affairs, and (e) assessment, evaluation, and research. Supervised practice must include practicums and/or internships consisting of supervised work involving at least two distinct experiences.

Demonstration of minimum knowledge and skill in each area is required of all program graduates.

The curriculum described above represents areas of study and should not be interpreted as specific course titles. The precise nature of courses should be determined by a variety of factors, including institutional mission, policies and practices, faculty judgment, current issues, and student needs. It is important that appropriate courses be available within the institution or from another institution, but it is not necessary that all be provided directly within the department or college in which the program is located administratively. Although all areas of study must be incorporated into the academic program, the precise nature of study may vary by institution, program emphasis, and student preference. The requirements for demonstration of competence and minimum knowledge in each area should be established by the faculty and regularly reviewed to assure that students are learning the essentials that underlie successful student affairs practice. A formal comprehensive examination or other culminating assessment project designed to provide students the opportunity to exhibit their knowledge and competence toward the end of their programs of study is encouraged.

Programs of study may be designed to emphasize one or more distinctive perspectives on student affairs such as educational program design, implementation, and evaluation; individual and group counseling and advising; student learning and human development; and/or administration of student affairs in higher education. Such program designs should include the most essential forms of knowledge and groupings of skills and competencies needed by practicing professionals and should be fashioned consistent with basic curriculum requirements. The wide range of expertise and interest of program faculty members and other involved and qualified contributors to curriculum content should be taken into account when designing distinctive perspectives in programs of study.

Each program must specify the structure of its degree options including which courses are considered core, which are considered thematic, which are required, and which are elective.

A "core" course is one that is principal to the student affairs preparation program. Theme courses are those that center on a common content area (such as introduction to student development theory, the application of student development theory, and using student development theory for environmental assessment).

Programs may structure their curriculum according to their distinctive perspectives and the nature of their students insuring adequacy of knowledge in foundation, professional, and supervised experience studies.

Part 5a: Foundation Studies
This component of the curriculum must include study in the historical, philosophical, ethical, cultural, and research foundations of higher education that inform student affairs practice. The study of the history and philosophy of student affairs are essential components of this standard.

Graduates must be able to reference historical and current documents that state the philosophical foundations of the profession and to communicate their relevance to current student affairs practice.

Graduates must also be able to articulate the inherent values of the profession that are stipulated in these documents in a manner that indicates how these values guide practice.

These values may include educating the whole student, treating each student as a unique individual, offering seamless learning opportunities, and ensuring the basic rights of all students.

This standard encompasses studies in other disciplines that inform student affairs practice, such as cultural contexts of higher education; governance, public policy, and finance of higher education; the impact of environments on behavior, especially learning; and international education and global understanding. Studies in this area should emphasize the diverse character of higher education environments. The foundational studies curriculum component should be designed to enhance students' understanding of higher education systems and exhibit how student affairs programs are infused into the larger educational picture.

Graduates must be knowledgeable about and be able to apply a code of ethics or ethical principles sanctioned by a recognized professional organization that provides ethical guidance for their work.

Part 5b: Professional Studies
This component of the curriculum must include studies of basic knowledge for practice and all programs must encompass at least five related areas of study including (a) student development theory; (b) student characteristics and effects of college on students; (c) individual and group interventions; (d) organization and administration of student affairs; and (e) assessment, evaluation, and research.

Other areas of study, especially when used as enrichment or cognate experiences, are encouraged. Studies in disciplines such as sociology, psychology, political science, and ethnic studies, for example, may be helpful to students depending upon the particular program emphasis. Communication skills and using technology as a learning tool should be emphasized in all the professional studies areas listed above.

Part 5b.1: Student Development Theory

This component of the curriculum must include studies of student development theories and research relevant to student learning and personal development. There must be extensive examination of theoretical perspectives that describe students' growth in the areas of intellectual, moral, ego, psychosocial, career, and spiritual development; racial, cultural, ethnic, gender, and sexual identity; the intersection of multiple identities; and learning styles throughout the late adolescent and adult lifespan. Study of collegiate environments and how person-environment interactions affect student development is also required.

Graduates must be able to demonstrate the ability to use appropriate development theory to understand, support, and advocate for student learning and development by assessing learning and developmental needs and creating learning and developmental opportunities.

This component should include studies of and research about human development from late adolescence through the adult life span and models and processes for translating theory and research into practice. Studies should stress differential strengths and applications of student development theories relative to student age, gender, ethnicity, race, culture, sexual identity, disability, spirituality, national origin, socioeconomic status, and resident/commuter status. Studies should also include specialized theories of development particular to certain populations or groups.

Subpart 5b.2: Student Characteristics and Effects of College on Students

This component of the curriculum must include studies of student characteristics, how such attributes influence student educational and developmental needs, and effects of the college experience on student learning and development.

Graduates must be able to demonstrate knowledge of how student learning and learning opportunities are influenced by student characteristics and by collegiate environments so that graduates can design and evaluate learning experiences for students.

This area should include studies of the effects of college on students, satisfaction with the college experience, student involvement in college, and factors that correlate with student persistence and attrition. This curriculum component should include, but is not limited to, student characteristics such as age, gender, ethnicity, race, religion, sexual identity, academic ability and preparation, learning styles, socioeconomic status, national origin, immigrant status, disability, developmental status, cultural background and orientation, transfer status, and family situation. Also included should be the study of specific student populations such as resident, commuter, and distance learners, part-time and full-time students, student athletes, members of fraternities and sororities, adult learners, first generation students and international students.

Subpart 5b.3: Individual and Group Interventions

This component of the curriculum must include studies of techniques and methods of interviewing; helping skills; and assessing, designing, and implementing developmentally appropriate interventions with individuals and organizations.

Graduates must be able to demonstrate knowledge and skills necessary to design and evaluate effective educational interventions for individuals and groups. Graduates must be able to identify and appropriately refer persons who need additional resources.

This curriculum component should include opportunities for study, skill building, and strategies for the implementation of advising, counseling, disciplining, instructing, mediating, and facilitating to assist individuals and groups. The program of study should include substantial instruction in counseling and group dynamics. Students should be exposed to a variety of theoretical perspectives, provided opportunities to practice individual and group interventions, and receive extensive supervision and feedback. Intervention skills are complex and require periods of time to practice under supervised conditions.

In addition to exposure to intervention theory, programs of study should include instruction in individual and group techniques and practices for addressing personal crises as well as problem solving, self-examination, and growth needs. Further, studies should include problem analyses, intervention design, and subsequent evaluation. Studies should emphasize theory plus individual and group interventions that are appropriate for and applicable to diverse populations.

Subpart 5b.4: Organization and Administration of Student Affairs

This component of the curriculum must include studies of organizational, management, and leadership theory and practice; student affairs functions; legal issues in higher education; and professional issues, ethics, and standards of practice.

Graduates must be able to identify and apply leadership, organizational, and management practices that assist institutions in accomplishing their mission.

This curriculum component should include opportunities for the study of student affairs programs and services including but not limited those for which CAS has developed standards and guidelines such as admissions, financial aid, orientation, counseling, academic advising, residence life, judicial services, campus activities, commuter student programs, recreational sports, career services, fraternity and sorority advising, religious programs, service-learning, disability services, academic support services, education opportunity programs, multicultural student affairs, international student affairs, and health services, among others. Studies of organizational culture, budgeting and finance, planning, technology as applied to organizations, and the selection, supervision, development, and evaluation of personnel should be included as well.

Subpart 5b.5: Assessment, Evaluation, and Research

This component of the curriculum must include the study of assessment, evaluation, and research. Studies must include both qualitative and quantitative research methodologies, measuring learning processes and outcomes, assessing

environments and organizations, measuring program and environment effectiveness, and critiques of published studies.

Graduates must be able to critique a sound study or evaluation and be able to design, conduct, and report on a sound research study, assessment study, or program evaluation, grounded in the appropriate literature.

Graduates must be aware of research ethics and legal implications of research, including the necessity of adhering to a human subjects review.

This curriculum component should include studies of the assessment of student needs and developmental attributes, the assessment of educational environments that influence student learning, and the assessment of student outcomes of the educational experience particular to student affairs work. This curriculum component also should include studies of program evaluation models and processes suitable for use in making judgments about the value of a wide range of programs and services. Students should be introduced to methodologies and techniques of quantitative and qualitative research, plus the philosophical foundations, assumptions, methodologies, methods, and criteria of worthiness of both. Students should be familiar with prominent research in student affairs that has greatly influenced the profession.

Part 5c: Supervised Practice

A minimum of 300 hours of supervised practice, consisting of at least two distinct experiences, must be required. Students must gain exposure to both the breadth and depth of student affairs work. Students must gain experience in developmental work with individual students and groups of students in: program planning, implementation, or evaluation; staff training, advising, or supervision; and administration functions or processes.

Supervision must be provided on-site by competent professionals working in cooperation with qualified program faculty members. On-site supervisors must provide direct regular supervision and evaluation of students' experiences and comply with all ethical principles and standards of the ACPA—College Student Educators International, NASPA—Student Affairs Administrators in Higher Education, and other recognized professional associations.

Qualified student affairs professionals possessing appropriate student affairs education and experience should be invited to sponsor and supervise students for practicum and internship experiences. Typical qualifications include at least a master's degree in student affairs or a related area of professional study, several years of successful professional

experience, and experience at that institution. Student affairs professionals serving as on-site supervisors and evaluators of students in training should be approved by the responsible faculty member as competent to accomplish this task.

Site supervisors must be approved in advance by program faculty. Program faculty must offer clear expectations of learning goals and supervision practices to site supervisors.

Supervised practice includes practicums and internships consisting of supervised work completed for academic credit in student programs and services in higher education. The exposure of students to diverse settings and work with diverse clientele or populations should be encouraged.

Because individual supervision of students in practicums and internships is labor intensive for faculty with this instructional responsibility, supervision must be limited to a small group to enable close regular supervision. Students must be supervised closely by faculty individually, in groups, or both.

When determining practicum and internship course loads, faculty members who provide direct practicum or internship supervision during any academic term should receive instructional credit for the equivalent of one academic course for each small group. Likewise, students enrolled in such internships should receive academic credit.

A graduate assistantship in programs and services in higher education, which provides both substantive experience and professional supervision, may be used in lieu of a practicum or internship. For this to be effective, faculty members responsible for assuring quality learning outcomes should work closely with graduate assistantship supervisors in students' assignment and evaluation processes. Appropriate consideration and provisions should be made for students with extensive experience in student affairs.

Preparation of students for practicums and internships is required. Practicums and internship experiences must be reserved for students who have successfully completed a sequence of courses pertaining to basic foundational knowledge of professional practice. This must include basic knowledge and skills in interpersonal communication, consultation, and referral skills. Students must comply with all ethical principles and standards of appropriate professional associations.

Preparation of students for supervised practice may be accomplished through special pre-practicums seminars, laboratory experiences, and faculty tutorials as well as coursework.

Student membership in professional associations should be expected. Attendance at professional conferences, meetings, or other professional development opportunities should also be encouraged.

Part 6. EQUITY AND ACCESS

A graduate program must adhere to the spirit and intent of equal opportunity in all activities. The program must encourage establishment of an ethical community in which diversity is viewed as an ethical obligation. The program must ensure that its services and facilities are programmatically and physically accessible. Programs that indicate in their admissions materials convenience and encouragement for working students must provide services, classes, and resources that respond to the needs of evening, part-time, and commuter students.

Discrimination must be avoided on the basis of ability; age; cultural identity; ethnicity; family educational history (e.g., first generation to attend college); gender identity and expression; nationality; political affiliation; race; religious affiliation; sex; sexual orientation; economic, marital, social, or veteran status; or any other basis included in institutional policies and codes and laws.

Graduate programs must be provided on a fair, equitable, and non-discriminatory basis in accordance with institutional policies and with all applicable state/provincial and federal statutes and regulations. Graduate programs must maintain an educational and work environment free from discrimination in accordance with law and institutional policy.

Consistent with the mission and goals, programs must take action to remedy significant imbalances in student participation and staffing patterns.

The program should recognize the important educational opportunities that diversity among its students and faculty brings to student affairs preparation. Therefore, programs should encourage the recognition of and adherence to the spirit of multiculturalism by all who are allied with the program's educational enterprise.

Part 7. ACADEMIC AND STUDENT SUPPORT

Institutions must provide sufficient faculty and staff members, resource materials, advising, career services, student financial support, facilities, and funding resources for the program.

Outcome indicators to determine whether a program has adequate resources could include student retention.

Part 7a: Faculty and Staff Members
The institution must provide adequate faculty and support staff members for the various aspects of the student affairs graduate program.

The institution must provide an academic program coordinator who is qualified by preparation and experience to manage the program.

The program coordinator or administrative director should have responsibility for managing the program's day to day operations, convening the program faculty as required, developing curriculum, and generally administering the preparation program within the context of the academic unit to which it is assigned. This individual should be the person responsible for guiding faculty teaching assignments, establishing and maintaining connections with student affairs staff members who serve as practicum/internship site supervisors, guiding general program activities, and representing the program to external constituencies.

Faculty assignments must demonstrate a serious commitment to the preparation of student affairs professionals. Sufficient full-time core faculty members must be devoted to teaching and administering the program to graduate not only employable students but also students capable of designing, creating, and implementing learning opportunities. At least one faculty member must be designated full-time to the program.

Faculty members should be available according to a reasonable faculty-student ratio that permits quality teaching, advising, supervision, research, and professional service. A core faculty member is one who identifies principally with the preparation program. Primary teaching responsibility in the program is recognized when core faculty member's instructional responsibilities are dedicated half-time or greater to teaching the program's curriculum. Devoted full-time to the program is defined as a faculty member whose institutional responsibilities are fully dedicated to the program. Teaching loads should be established on the basis of institutional policy and faculty assignments for service, research, and supervision. A system within the program and the institution should exist for involving professional practitioners who are qualified to assist with faculty responsibilities. Collaboration between full-time faculty members and student affairs practitioners is recommended for the instruction, advisement, and practicum and internship supervision of students in the preparation program. Student affairs practitioners should be consulted in the design, implementation, and evaluation of the preparation program, particularly regarding practicum and internship requirements.

Faculty members must be skilled as teachers and knowledgeable about student affairs in general, plus current theory, research, and practice in areas appropriate to their teaching or supervision assignments. Faculty members must also have current knowledge and skills appropriate for designing, conducting, and evaluating learning experiences using multiple pedagogies.

Faculty must maintain regular office hours that are clearly listed on course syllabi and in other prominent locations.

Faculty must act in accordance with ethical principals and standards of good practice disseminated by recognized professional organizations.

The institution must provide opportunity and resources for the continuing professional development of program faculty members. To ensure that faculty members can devote adequate time to professional duties, the academic program must have sufficient clerical and technical support staff.

Technical support must be of sufficient quality and quantity to accomplish word processing, data management, scheduling, electronic instructional material development, and distance learning. Equipment sufficient for electronic communications and Internet use is essential.

Technical support should include regular training in software upgrades and new hardware developments, hardware and software repairs, virus protection, access to the web, on-line journals, courseware, and presentation software.

Classroom facilities should have the capacity to offer classes using electronic technologies.

Adjunct and part-time faculty must be fully qualified and adequately trained to serve as teachers, advisors, and internship supervisors.

Adjuncts and part-time faculty should be provided with information about institutional policies and procedures, access to program resources and faculty, and feedback about their performance.

Part 7b: Resource Materials
Adequate resource materials must be provided to support the curriculum.

Resources may include career information; standardized tests and technical manuals; and materials for simulations, structured group experiences, human relations training, and data-based interventions for human and organization development. In addition, resources may include instruments and assessment tools that measure development and leadership from various theoretical points of view and materials that facilitate leadership, organizational design, management style, conflict management, and time management development. Resources should include software that allows for the analysis of qualitative and quantitative data.

Library resources must be provided for the program including current and historical books, periodicals, on-line journals, search mechanisms, and other media for the teaching and research aspects of the program. Library resources must be accessible to students and must be selected carefully, reviewed,

and updated periodically by the program faculty.

The library resources should be available days, evenings, and weekends and should include adequate interlibrary loan services, ERIC and similar data sources, computerized search capabilities, and photocopy services.

Research support must be adequate for both program faculty and students.

Computing services, data collection and storage services, research design consultation services, and adequate equipment should be available in support of research activities of both students and faculty members. The program should provide students with individualized research project development and implementation.

Part 7c: Advising
Faculty members must provide high quality academic and professional advising.

Academic advising should be viewed as a continuous process of clarification and evaluation. High quality academic advising should include, but is not limited to, development of suitable educational plans; selection of appropriate courses and other educational experiences; clarification of professional and career goals; knowledge of and interpretation of institutional and program policies, procedures, and requirements; knowledge of course contents, sequences, and support resources; evaluation of student progress; referrals to and use of institutional and community support services; support for and evaluation of scholarly endeavors including research and assessment; and knowledge and interpretation of professional ethics and standards. Advisors should be readily available to students and should possess abilities to facilitate a student's career exploration, self-assessment, decision-making, and responsible behavior in interactions with others. Advisors should be able to interpret the scores of assessment tools used in the advising process. These might include the Graduate Record Examination, Myers-Briggs Type Indicator, and Learning Styles Inventory. The number of faculty advisees should be monitored and adjusted as necessary to ensure that faculty can give adequate attention to all advisees.

Part 7d: Career Services
The institution must provide professional career assistance, either by institutional career services or by the program faculty.

Students should be assisted in clarifying objectives and establishing goals; exploring the full range of career possibilities; preparing for the job search including presenting oneself effectively as a candidate for employment; and making the transition from graduate student to professional practitioner. Faculty members should collaborate with campus career service providers to develop an active program of assistance including acquiring job listings; the preparation of credentials such as recommending applications, correspondence, and resumes; development of employment interview skills; identification of appropriate job search networks including professional associations; selection of suitable positions; and communication of ethical obligations of those involved in the employment process. Ideally, these services should be available to graduates throughout their professional careers.

Part 7e: Student Financial Support

Information must be provided to students about the availability of graduate assistantships, fellowships, work-study, research funding, travel support, and other financial aid opportunities.

Graduate assistantships should be made available to students to provide both financial assistance and opportunities for supervised work experience.

Part 7f: Facilities and Funding Resources

The institution must provide facilities accessible to all students and a budget that ensures continuous operation of all aspects of the program.

A program office should be located in reasonable proximity to faculty offices, classrooms, and laboratory facilities. Adequate and appropriate space, equipment, and supplies should be provided for faculty members, staff members, and graduate assistants. There should be facilities for advising, counseling, and student development activities that are private, adequate in size, and properly equipped. Special facilities and equipment may include audio and video recording devices, one-way observation rooms, small group rooms, and computer labs. Adequate classroom, seminar, and laboratory facilities to meet program needs also should be available. Adequate office and technical equipment should be provided including access to e-mail and other relevant technological resources.

Part 8. PROFESSIONAL ETHICS AND LEGAL RESPONSIBILITIES

Faculty members must comply with institutional policies and ethical principles and standards of ACPA— College Student Educators International, NASPA— Student Affairs Administrators in Higher Education, American Association of University Professors, and the CAS functional area ethical standards. Faculty members must demonstrate the highest standards of ethical behavior and academic integrity in all forms of teaching, research, publication, and professional service and must instruct students in ethical practice and in the principles and standards of conduct of the profession.

Ethical expectations of graduate students must be disseminated in writing on a regular basis to all students.

Ethical principles and standards of all relevant professional organizations should be consulted and used as appropriate. An ethical climate should prevail throughout the preparation program wherein faculty members model appropriate ethical behavior at all times for students to experience, observe, and emulate. Faculty members should present various theoretical positions and encourage students to make comparisons and to develop personally meaningful theoretical positions. Faculty members are expected to ensure that educational experiences focusing on self-understanding and personal growth are voluntary or, if such experiences are program requirements, that reasonable effort is made to inform prospective students of them prior to admission to the program. Students should be held accountable for appropriate ethical behavior at all times with special attention paid to the ethics components of the various CAS functional area standards when students participate in related practicum and internship assignments.

Faculty members must strive to ensure the fair and impartial treatment of students and others.

Faculty members must maintain ethical relationships with students exemplifying respect and the ideals of pedagogy.

Faculty members must not teach, supervise, or advise any student with whom they have an intimate relationship. When a student enters an academic program having a pre-existing intimate relationship with a faculty member, both must notify a third party, such as a department chair, to monitor the pedagogical relationship and assign appropriate teaching, supervisory, and advising responsibilities.

Graduate program faculty members must evaluate annually all students' progress and suitability for entry into the student affairs profession. Evaluation of students' ethical behaviors must be included. Faculty members must keep students informed about their progress toward successful program completion.

Through continual evaluation and appraisal of students, faculty members are expected to be aware of ethically problematic student behaviors, inadequate academic progress, and other behaviors or characteristics that may make a student unsuitable for the profession. Appropriate responses leading to remediation of the behaviors related to students' academic progress or professional suitability should be identified, monitored, evaluated, and shared with individual students as needed. Faculty members are expected in cases of significant problematic behaviors to communicate to the student the problems identified and the remediation required to avoid being terminated from the preparation program. After appropriate remediation has been proposed and evaluated, students who continue to be evaluated as being unsuitable for the profession, making poor academic progress, or having ethically problematic behaviors should be dismissed from the preparation program following appropriate due process procedures. If termination is enforced, faculty members are expected to explain to the student the grounds for the decision.

Faculty members must ensure that privacy is maintained with respect to all communication and records considered to be educational records unless written permission is given by the student or when the disclosure is allowable under the law and institution policy.

Faculty members must respond to requests for employment-related recommendations by students. When endorsement cannot be provided for a particular position, the student must be informed of the reason for non-endorsement.

Faculty members should base endorsements on knowledge of the student's competencies, skills, and personal characteristics.

Each candidate should be informed of procedures for endorsement, certification, registry, and licensure, if applicable.

Faculty members must inform all students of the institutional and program policies regarding graduate student liability.

Program policy should be established to ensure that all students are periodically informed of their liabilities and options for protection. Programs may wish to establish policies requiring students to hold membership in particular professional associations and to purchase liability insurance prior to entering into practicums or internships.

Part 9. PROGRAM EVALUATION

Planned procedures for continuing evaluation of the program must be established and implemented, and the evaluation information must be used for appropriate program enhancements.

Criteria for program evaluation should include knowledge and competencies learned by students, employment rates of graduates, professional contributions to the field made by graduates, and quality of faculty teaching, advising, and research. Evaluation of program effectiveness should reflect evidence obtained from former students; course evaluations; supervisors from institutions and agencies employing graduates of the program; personnel in state/provincial, regional, and national accrediting agencies during formal reviews; and clientele served by graduates.

Review of policies and procedures relating to recruitment, selection, retention, and career services should be included in program evaluations. The timing and regularity of evaluations should be determined in accordance with institutional policy. Generally, the length of time between comprehensive program evaluations by the program faculty

should not exceed five years.

General Standards revised in 2011
Preparation Program content developed/revised in 1979, 1986, 1997 & 2002

The Role of Multicultural Student Programs and Services
CAS Standards Contextual Statement

The expansion of the civil rights movement begun in the 1960s provided increased access to students whose attendance in higher education had been highly under-represented, especially at predominately White institutions. Although some under-represented student enrollments have increased since the 1960s through the Economic Opportunity Act of 1964 and the Higher Education Act of 1965 that launched the TRIO programs and Pell grants respectfully, enrollment that is representative of the national population, as well as the retention and degree completion of students of color, continues to be of considerable concern. For example, *The Chronicle of Higher Education* sited the report "A Matter of Degree" that "while 64 percent of fulltime students at four-year colleges graduate within six years, less than half of black students and less than half of Hispanic students do so in that period of time. The rates from low-income families are only slightly better" (Burd, 2004, p. A19). The report went on to state that the difference in graduation rates between Latino/a and White students is (at the average college) seven percentage points and 15 percent at a quarter of all four-year institutions. More recent data, resulting from a 2009 study conducted by the College Board Advocacy & Policy Center, found that only 19.2 percent of Latinos between the ages of 25 and 34 had earned a two or four year degree, compared with 41 percent nationally. Additionally, there are more data on the growing education gap between the rich and the poor. An article in the February 10, 2012 issue of the *New York Times* highlighted several recent studies suggesting that education gaps between the rich and the poor are growing—from elementary school through college. At the same time, race-based gaps are narrowing. "We have moved from a society in the 1950s and 1960s, in which race was more consequential than family income, to one today in which family income appears to be more determinative of educational success than race," said Sean F. Reardon, a Stanford University sociologist. Even so, the intersection of race and socio-economic status cannot be forgotten as we continue to close any and all gaps in educational attainment for all groups.

A contributing factor in the disparity of retention rates has been the initial lack of readiness by institutions to serve expanded student populations. The establishment of Multicultural Student Programs and Services (MSPS) was initially created to respond to this lack of readiness, but more recently has developed to offer proactively programs and services that serve to create environments where all students can thrive. Although the MSPS may vary in structure and purpose from institution to institution, most advocate for the academic success of students. This often includes advocating for changing policies, practices, and attitudes of the campus and its students and employees that inhibit student confidence and success; offering mentoring and other community building opportunities including cultural support systems where students can feel comfortable rather than feeling that they have to assimilate into the dominant culture; implementing programs to educate the campus community about various cultures and to promote awareness of multicultural and social justice issues; facilitating cooperation among campus affinity groups and integrating campus activities and majority organizations; ensuring access to academic support services including tutoring, special study skills training, supplemental instruction, referral to other learning assistance resources, distinctive orientation programs, affinity group advisement, academic advising, personal counseling, financial assistance counseling, career development, and graduate school advising; and offering an academic curricula where multicultural perspectives are embedded. The MSPS staff should be equipped to help educate college/university staff on cultural competency, multicultural issues, and appropriate inclusionary practices. On campuses where academic departments for ethnic, women, or queer studies exist, the MSPS sometimes coordinates services with these academic departments. Some MSPS organize services to address specific populations, while others seek to serve all under-represented and oppressed students collectively. Some have autonomous facilities that include programming, advising, classroom, and counseling space, whereas other MSPS are located in spaces under the management of other campus entities such as the campus union or housing and residence life.

Although underserved populations (Black/Latino) continue to be a special group to nurture and provide support services for retention and graduation rate improvement, the rapidly changing racial demographics of Asian American, multiracial, and international students have great impact on previously predominant White institutions and create a need for intercultural dialogue programs and services to foster an inclusive campus. Given the changing demographics, limiting the MSPS to historically underrepresented and oppressed groups risks the prospect of marginalization and isolation of those very groups. Involving all students (including White students) in diversity education programs is vital to community building and creating a welcoming, integrated climate. As a consequence, more multicultural offices have changed their names to signal the evolving changes to the title of Intercultural Offices.

Strong MSPS are essential to the academic and social integration and, thus, retention and graduation rates of students as well as the multicultural education of the campus. Clearly, institutions exhibit their commitment to providing quality education for all their students through the level of support they provide to the MSPS. Many multicultural offices and centers have been established to serve under-represented students including students of color, women students, and LGBT students separately. These standards will focus on general programs and services for under-represented and oppressed students. For standards related to programs and services for other under-represented students see the CAS Standards for Lesbian, Gay, Bisexual, and Transgender Programs; Women Student Programs; and Disability Services.

References, Readings, and Resources

Burd, S. (June 4, 2004). Colleges permit too many needy students to drop out, says report on graduation rates. *The Chronicle of Higher Education*, A19.

California Council of Cultural Centers in Higher Education: www.caccche.org

Cox, T., Jr. (2001). *Creating the multicultural organization*. San Francisco: Jossey Bass, 2001.

Helms, J. E. (1992). *A race is a nice thing to have*. Topeka: Content Communications. [available through www.emicrotraining.com]

"How colleges organize themselves to increase student persistence: four-year institutions." (April 2009). College Board Advocacy and Policy Center.

Komives, S. R., & Woodard, Jr., D. B. (Eds.). (2003). *Student Services: A handbook for the profession (4th ed.)*. San Francisco: Jossey-Bass.

McEwen, M. K., Kodoma, C. M., Alvarez, A., Lee, S., & Liang, C. T. H. (2002). *Working with Asian college students*. San Francisco: Jossey Bass: New Directions for Student Services Series.

Milem, J. F., Chang, M. J., & Antonio, A. L. (2005). *Making diversity work on campus: A research-based perspective*. Association of American Colleges and Universities.

Pope, R. L., & Reynolds, A. L. (1997). Student affairs core competencies: Integrating multicultural awareness, knowledge, and skills. *Journal of College Student Development, 38,* 266-277.

Pope, R. L., Reynolds, A. L., & Mueller, J. A. (2004). *Multicultural competence in student affairs*. San Francisco: Jossey-Bass.

Sidanius, J., Levin, S., & Van Laar, C. (2008). The diversity challenge: social identity and intergroup relations on the college campus. Sears, D. O. (Ed). New Yprk: Russell Sage Foundation

Talbot, D. (2003). Multiculturalism. In S. R. Komives & D. B. Woodard, Jr., (Eds.), *Student Services: A handbook for the profession (4th ed.)* (pp. 423-446). San Francisco: Jossey-Bass.

Tatum, B. D. (1999). *Why are all the Black kids sitting together in the cafeteria?: And other questions about race*. New York: Basic Books.

Contextual Statement Contributors

Current Edition:
Donna Wong, Emory University
Creston Lynch, Southern Methodist University
Ernest Jeffries, Davidson College
Alonzo Jones, Arizona State University

Previous Editions:
Jan Arminio, Shippensburg University

Multicultural Student Programs and Services
CAS Standards and Guidelines

Part 1. MISSION

Multicultural Student Programs and Services (MSPS) must promote academic and personal growth of traditionally underserved students, work with the entire campus to create an institutional and community climate of justice, promote access and equity in higher education, and offer programs that educate the campus about diversity.

MSPS must develop, disseminate, implement, and regularly review their missions. The mission must be consistent with the mission of the institution and with professional standards. The mission must be appropriate for the institution's student populations and community settings. Mission statements must reference student learning and development.

MSPS must assist the institution in developing shared goals and creating a sense of common community that serves all its constituents fairly and equitably and is marked by
- access to academic, social, cultural, recreational, and other groups and activities
- opportunities for intentional interaction and engagement
- integration

MSPS must encourage the institution to hold units responsible for meeting the needs of traditionally underserved students in their area of responsibility; this includes under-represented or oppressed students, such as students of color; lesbian, gay, bisexual and transgender students; and students with disabilities.

Institutions may have more than one MSPS organization. Each of these MSPS organizations' missions may address the needs of a particular student group or groups. These missions should be complementary. If only one MSPS organization exists, the mission should address the needs of students of the many cultural and oppressed groups.

In addition, MSPS should encourage all units to include explicitly in their mission serving a wide range of underserved students fairly and equitably.

Part 2. PROGRAM

The formal education of students, consisting of the curriculum and the co-curriculum, must promote student learning and development outcomes that are purposeful, contribute to students' realization of their potential, and prepare students for satisfying and productive lives.

Multicultural Student Programs and Services (MSPS) must collaborate with colleagues and departments across the institution to promote student learning and development, persistence, and success.

Consistent with the institutional mission, MSPS must identify relevant and desirable student learning and development outcomes from among the six domains and related dimensions:

Domain: knowledge acquisition, integration, construction, and application

- **Dimensions: understanding knowledge from a range of disciplines; connecting knowledge to other knowledge, ideas, and experiences; constructing knowledge; and relating knowledge to daily life**

Domain: cognitive complexity

- **Dimensions: critical thinking, reflective thinking, effective reasoning, and creativity**

Domain: intrapersonal development

- **Dimensions: realistic self-appraisal, self-understanding, and self-respect; identity development; commitment to ethics and integrity; and spiritual awareness**

Domain: interpersonal competence

- **Dimensions: meaningful relationships, interdependence, collaboration, and effective leadership.**

Domain: humanitarianism and civic engagement

- **Dimensions: understanding and appreciation of cultural and human differences, social responsibility, global perspective, and sense of civic responsibility**

Domain: practical competence

- **Dimensions: pursuing goals, communicating effectively, technical competence, managing personal affairs, managing career development, demonstrating professionalism, maintaining health and wellness, and living a purposeful and satisfying life**

[LD Outcomes: See *The Council for the Advancement of Standards Learning and Developmental Outcomes* statement for examples of outcomes related to these domains and dimensions.]

MSPS must
- **assess relevant and desirable student**

learning and development
- provide evidence of impact on outcomes
- articulate contributions to or support of student learning and development in the domains not specifically assessed
- articulate contributions to or support of student persistence and success
- use evidence gathered through this process to create strategies for improvement of programs and services

MSPS must be
- intentionally designed
- guided by theories and knowledge of learning and development
- integrated into the life of the institution
- reflective of developmental and demographic profiles of the student population
- responsive to needs of individuals, populations with distinct needs, and relevant constituencies
- delivered using multiple formats, strategies, and contexts

Where institutions provide distance education, MSPS must assist distance learners to achieve their educational goals by providing access to information about programs and services, to staff members who can address questions and concerns, and to counseling, advising, or other forms of assistance.

MSPS must be based on models, approaches, or theories that address students across developmental levels.

MSPS must provide educational programs and services for all students that focus on awareness of cultural differences, cultural commonalties, privilege, and identity; self-assessment of cultural awareness and possible prejudices; and changing prejudicial, oppressive, and stereotypical attitudes or behavior.

MSPS may support other institutional functional areas such as recruitment, career services, academic advising, counseling, health services, and alumni relations.

MSPS must promote academic success of students by
- offering distinctive programs that introduce students to a community network and teach students how to negotiate processes within the institution (e. g., registration, academic advising, financial aid, housing, campus employment)
- assisting them to determine and assess their educational goals and academic skills
- providing support services that assist in achieving educational goals and attaining or refining academic skills
- informing students of educational

opportunities, such as internships, special scholarship opportunities, study abroad programs, research, seminars, and conferences
- promoting intellectual, career, social, ethical, and social justice development
- networking with staff and faculty members
- connecting them to campus networks and groups and organizations.

MSPS should act as a liaison for referrals and interventions with staff and faculty members and administrators on behalf of students when appropriate.

MSPS must promote personal growth of students by
- enhancing students' understanding of their own culture, heritage, and identities
- enhancing students' understanding of cultures, heritages, and identities other than their own
- providing opportunities for students to establish satisfying interpersonal relationships
- providing opportunities for interactions, exchange of ideas, and reflection

MSPS must work to create an engaging climate for students by advocating for and encouraging students to take advantage of the following opportunities:
- campus and community service including leadership opportunities
- practice in leadership including training, education, and development
- access to appropriate mentors and role models
- shared inter- and intra-social experiences

MSPS must work to create a just campus climate by
- challenging tacit and overt prejudices or discrimination against students
- coordinating efforts to promote multicultural sensitivity and the elimination of prejudicial behaviors
- facilitating desired changes with the cooperation of other campus entities
- identifying and addressing impediments to the growth and development of full participation of students

If institutional practices or policies have prejudicial effects, staff members must bring these facts to the attention of the proper authorities in the institution and work to change them.

MSPS must offer to the campus community programs that increase multicultural awareness, knowledge, and skills by
- promoting and enhancing the understanding of a variety of cultures and historical

experiences
- **promoting and enhancing the understanding of privilege, power, and prejudicial and stereotypical assumptions**
- **promoting and enhancing identity development**
- **teaching skills on how to combat racism, homophobia, sexism, and other forms of discrimination**
- **complementing the academic curricula**

MSPS must serve as a resource for multicultural training, education, and development.

Educational programs may be provided in collaboration with efforts by academic and student affairs units and other program support services. Staff members in MSPS should coordinate their efforts with academic and student affairs units and other support services. Various dimensions of students' cultures, such as history, philosophy, worldview, literature, and various forms of communication and artistic expression, should be explored. Human relations programs should be designed to assist faculty members, staff members, and students in developing more tolerance, understanding, and ability to relate to others around issues of privilege; age; color; creed; cultural heritage; disability; ethnicity; gender identity; nationality; political affiliation; religious affiliation; sex; sexual orientation; or social, economic, marital, or veteran status.

Activities that attempt to promote students' development should be based upon assessments and should reflect unique dimensions of the multicultural student experience.

MSPS must assist students across the range of their experiences at the institution.

These areas may include
- monitoring scholastic progress of groups and individual students and recommending strategies for improvement
- providing workshops, programs, retreats, and seminars on relevant topics and encouraging attendance at activities and services sponsored by other campus offices
- encouraging student attendance at conferences, meetings, and programs
- advising student organizations that advance the equality and interests of specific groups (e. g., Black/African American students, Asian/Pacific Islander students, Latino/a students, Native students, LGBT students, and allies), editorial staffs of multicultural publications, fraternal groups, pre-professional clubs, and program councils
- providing assistance and advice in planning multicultural student celebrations (e.g., Black/African American History Month, Kwanzaa, Stonewall Anniversary, Day of Silence, Take Back the Night, Transgender Day of Remembrance)
- assisting multicultural student groups or individuals in identifying and gaining access, where appropriate, to institutional services such as printing, bulk mailing, and computer services
- providing a directory of multicultural faculty and staff members
- providing a directory of faculty and staff members who have agreed to provide mentoring and assistance
- publishing a newsletter, website, or other means of focusing on current events, leadership opportunities, and other relevant information

Part 3. ORGANIZATION AND LEADERSHIP

To achieve student and program outcomes, Multicultural Student Programs and Services (MSPS) must be structured purposefully and organized effectively. MSPS must have
- **clearly stated goals**
- **current and accessible policies and procedures**
- **written performance expectations for employees**
- **functional work flow graphics or organizational charts demonstrating clear channels of authority**

Leaders with organizational authority for the programs and services must provide strategic planning, supervision, and management; advance the organization; and maintain integrity through the following functions:

Strategic Planning
- **articulate a vision and mission that drive short- and long-term planning**
- **set goals and objectives based on the needs of the population served and desired student learning or development and program outcomes**
- **facilitate continuous development, implementation, and assessment of goal attainment congruent with institutional mission and strategic plans**
- **promote environments that provide meaningful opportunities for student learning, development, and engagement**
- **develop and continuously improve programs and services in response to the changing needs of students served and evolving institutional priorities**
- **intentionally include diverse perspectives to inform decision making**

Supervising
- **manage human resource processes including recruitment, selection, development,**

supervision, performance planning, evaluation, recognition, and reward
- influence others to contribute to the effectiveness and success of the unit
- empower professional, support, and student staff to accept leadership opportunities
- offer appropriate feedback to colleagues and students on skills needed to become more effective leaders
- encourage and support professional development, collaboration with colleagues and departments across the institution, and scholarly contribution to the profession

Managing
- identify and address individual, organizational, and environmental conditions that foster or inhibit mission achievement
- plan, allocate, and monitor the use of fiscal, physical, human, intellectual, and technological resources
- use current and valid evidence to inform decisions
- incorporate sustainability practices in the management and design of programs, services, and facilities
- understand appropriate technologies and integrate them into programs and services
- be knowledgeable about codes and laws relevant to programs and services and ensure that staff members understand their responsibilities through appropriate training
- assess potential risks and take action to mitigate them

Advancing the Organization
- communicate effectively in writing, speaking, and electronic venues
- advocate for programs and services
- advocate for representation in strategic planning initiatives at appropriate divisional and institutional levels
- initiate collaborative interactions with internal and external stakeholders who have legitimate concerns about and interests in the functional area
- facilitate processes to reach consensus where wide support is needed
- inform other areas within the institution about issues affecting practice

Maintaining Integrity
- model ethical behavior and institutional citizenship
- share data used to inform key decisions in transparent and accessible ways
- monitor media used for distributing

information about programs and services to ensure the content is current, accurate, appropriately referenced, and accessible

MSPS leaders must base their work on models and approaches that are theory-based and data driven.

MSPS must be located in an organizational structure that can best provide for effective programs and services for achievement of its mission.

Wherever located MSPS should collaborate and form close alliances with student affairs.

In response to assessed student needs, MSPS must play a principal role in creating and implementing institutional policies and programs.

Part 4. HUMAN RESOURCES

Multicultural Student Programs and Services (MSPSP) must be staffed adequately by individuals qualified to accomplish mission and goals.

Within institutional guidelines, MSPS must
- establish procedures for staff recruitment and selection, training, performance planning, and evaluation
- set expectations for supervision and performance
- assess the performance of employees individually and as a team
- provide access to continuing and advanced education and appropriate professional development opportunities to improve the leadership ability, competence, and skills of all employees.

MSPS must maintain position descriptions for all staff members.

To create a diverse staff, MSPS must institute recruitment and hiring strategies that encourage individuals from under-represented populations to apply for positions.

MSPS must develop promotion practices that are fair, inclusive, proactive, and non-discriminatory.

To further the recruitment and retention of staff, MSPS must consider work life initiatives, such as compressed work schedules, flextime, job sharing, remote work, or telework.

MSPS professional staff members must hold an earned graduate or professional degree in a field relevant to the position they hold or must possess an appropriate combination of educational credentials and related work experience.

MSPS professional staff members must possess the requisite multicultural knowledge, awareness, and

skills.

MSPS professional staff should possess the awareness that cultural differences are valuable.

MSPS professional staff should value the significance of their own cultural heritage and understand that of different cultures. They should have insight into the interpersonal process of how one's own behavior impacts others. They should be aware of when change is necessary for the realization of a positive and just campus.

MSPS professional staff must have knowledge about identity development and the intersections of various aspects of diversity (i.e., race and class, race and gender, race and sexual orientation) on identity development and the acculturation process.

MSPS professional staff must know how various groups experience the campus and what institutional and societal barriers limit their access and their success.

MSPS professional staff must know how culture affects verbal and non-verbal communication.

Professional staff must be knowledgeable about research and practice in areas appropriate to their programming with students.

MSPS professional staff must be skilled in identifying cultural issues and assessing their impact.

MSPS professional staff must be able to develop empathetic and trusting relationships with students.

MSPS professional staff must recognize individual, cultural, and universal similarities.

MSPS professional staff must be able to make culturally appropriate interventions to seek to optimize learning experiences for students.

MSPS professional staff must demonstrate respect for cultural values.

The professional staff of MSPS should reflect the various student cultures involved in MSPS.

In addition to professional staff being knowledgeable in their areas of responsibility, they should be knowledgeable about career planning and development, health promotion, group facilitation, leadership training and development, workshop design, social-interpersonal development, individual and group counseling, and campus resources.

MSPS professional staff should complete specific coursework in organizational development, counseling theory and practice, identity development theory, group dynamics, leadership development, human development, and research and assessment.

MSPS professional staff must have a personal commitment to justice and social change.

MSPS professional staff members must engage in continuing professional development activities to keep abreast of the research, theories, legislation, policies, and developments that affect their programs and services.

MSPS must have technical and support staff members adequate to accomplish their mission. All members of the staff must be technologically proficient and qualified to perform their job functions, be knowledgeable about ethical and legal uses of technology, and have access to training and resources to support the performance of their assigned responsibilities.

Degree- or credential-seeking interns or graduate assistants must be qualified by enrollment in an appropriate field of study and by relevant experience. These individuals must be trained and supervised adequately by professional staff members holding educational credentials and related work experience appropriate for supervision. Supervisors must be cognizant of the roles of interns and graduate assistants as both student and employee and closely adhere to all parameters of their job descriptions, work hours, and schedules. Supervisors and the interns or graduate assistants must agree to compensatory time or other appropriate compensation if circumstances necessitate additional hours.

The use of graduate assistants and interns should be encouraged to expand staff abilities, provide peer role models, and give valuable pre-professional experience. Particular attention should be given to preparing all pre-professional assistants to be especially sensitive to cultural differences of focus populations.

Student employees and volunteers must be carefully selected, trained, supervised, and evaluated. They must be educated on how and when to refer those in need of additional assistance to qualified staff members and must have access to a supervisor for assistance in making these judgments. Student employees and volunteers must be provided clear job descriptions, pre-service training based on assessed needs, and continuing development.

Student employees and volunteers from multicultural groups should be utilized.

Student employees must be assigned responsibilities that are within their scope of competence.

Training and activities for student employees could include retreats, leadership classes, and workshops.

All MSPS staff members, including student employees and volunteers, must receive specific training

on institutional policies pertaining to functions or activities they support and to privacy and confidentiality policies and laws regarding access to student records and other sensitive institutional information.

All MSPS staff members must receive training on policies and procedures related to the use of technology to store or access student records and institutional data.

MSPS must ensure that staff members are knowledgeable about and trained in emergency procedures, crisis response, and prevention efforts. Prevention efforts must address identification of threatening conduct or behavior of students, faculty and staff members, and others and must incorporate a system for responding and reporting.

MSPS must ensure that staff members are knowledgeable of and trained in safety and emergency procedures for securing and vacating facilities.

Part 5. ETHICS

Multicultural Student Programs and Services (MSPS) must review relevant professional ethical standards and must adopt or develop and implement appropriate statements of ethical practice.

MSPS must publish and adhere to statements of ethical practice and ensure their periodic review by relevant constituencies.

MSPS must orient new staff members to relevant ethical standards and statements of ethical practice and related institutional policies.

Statements of ethical standards must specify that staff members respect privacy and maintain confidentiality in all communications and records to the extent that such communications and records are protected under relevant privacy laws.

Statements of ethical standards must specify limits on disclosure of information contained in students' educational records as well as requirements to disclose to appropriate authorities.

Statements of ethical standards must address personal and economic conflicts of interest, or appearance thereof, by staff members in the performance of their work.

Statements of ethical standards must reflect the responsibility of staff members to be fair, objective, and impartial in their interactions with others.

Statements of ethical standards must reference management of institutional funds.

Statements of ethical standards must reference appropriate behavior regarding research and assessment with human participants, confidentiality of research and assessment data, and students' rights and responsibilities.

Statements of ethical standards must include the expectation that MSPS staff members confront and hold accountable other staff members who exhibit unethical behavior.

Statements of ethical standards must address issues surrounding scholarly integrity.

As appropriate, MSPS staff members must inform users of programs and services of ethical obligations and limitations emanating from codes and laws or from licensure requirements.

MSPS staff members must recognize and avoid conflicts of interest that could adversely influence their judgment or objectivity and, when unavoidable, recuse themselves from the situation.

MSPS staff members must perform their duties within the limits of their position, training, expertise, and competence.

When these limits are exceeded, individuals in need of further assistance must be referred to persons possessing appropriate qualifications.

Promotional and descriptive information must be accurate and free of deception.

MSPS must adhere to institutional policies regarding ethical and legal use of software and technology.

Part 6. LAW, POLICY, AND GOVERNANCE

Multicultural Student Programs and Services (MSPS) must be in compliance with laws, regulations, and policies that relate to their respective responsibilities and that pose legal obligations, limitations, risks, and liabilities for the institution as a whole. Examples include constitutional, statutory, regulatory, and case law; relevant law and orders emanating from codes and laws; and the institution's policies.

MSPS must inform staff members, appropriate officials, and users of programs and services about existing and changing legal obligations, risks and liabilities, and limitations.

MSPS must have written policies on all relevant operations, transactions, or tasks that have legal implications.

MSPS must regularly review policies. The revision and creation of policies must be informed by best practices, available evidence, and policy issues in higher education.

MSPS staff members must use reasonable and informed practices to limit the liability exposure of the institution and its officers, employees, and agents. MSPS staff members must be informed about institutional policies regarding risk management, personal liability, and related insurance coverage options and must be referred to external sources if the institution does not provide coverage.

The institution must provide access to legal advice for staff members as needed to carry out assigned responsibilities.

MSPS must have procedures and guidelines consistent with institutional policy for responding to threats, emergencies, and crisis situations. Systems and procedures must be in place to disseminate timely and accurate information to students, other members of the institutional community, and appropriate external organizations during emergency situations.

MSPS staff members must neither participate in nor condone any form of harassment or activity that demeans persons or creates an intimidating, hostile, or offensive environment.

MSPS must obtain permission to use copyrighted materials and instruments. MSPS must purchase the materials and instruments from legally compliant sources or seek alternative permission from the publisher or owner. References to copyrighted materials and instruments must include appropriate citations.

MSPS staff members must be knowledgeable about internal and external governance systems that affect programs and services.

Part 7. DIVERSITY, EQUITY, AND ACCESS

Within the context of each institution's unique mission and in accordance with institutional polices and all applicable codes and laws, Multicultural Student Programs and Services (MSPS) must create and maintain educational and work environments that are
- welcoming, accessible, and inclusive to persons of diverse backgrounds
- equitable and non-discriminatory
- free from harassment

MSPS must not discriminate on the basis of ability; age; cultural identity; ethnicity; family educational history (e.g., first generation to attend college); gender identity and expression; nationality; political affiliation; race; religious affiliation; sex; sexual orientation; economic, marital, social, or veteran status; or any other basis included in institutional policies and codes and laws.

MSPS must
- advocate for greater sensitivity to multicultural and social justice concerns by the institution and its personnel
- modify or remove policies, practices, facilities, structures, systems, and technologies that limit access, discriminate, or produce inequities
- include diversity, equity, and access initiatives within their strategic plans
- foster communication that deepens understanding of identity, culture, self-expression, and heritage
- promote respect about commonalities and differences among people within their historical and cultural contexts
- address the characteristics and needs of a diverse population when establishing and implementing culturally relevant and inclusive programs, services, policies, procedures, and practices
- provide staff members with access to multicultural training and hold staff members accountable for integrating the training into their work
- respond to the needs of all students and other populations served when establishing hours of operation and developing methods of delivering programs, services, and resources
- ensure physical, program, and resource access for persons with disabilities
- recognize the needs of distance learning students by providing appropriate and accessible services and resources or by assisting them in gaining access to other appropriate services and resources in their geographic region

Part 8. INSTITUTIONAL AND EXTERNAL RELATIONS

Multicultural Student Programs and Services (MSPS) must reach out to relevant individuals, groups, communities, and organizations internal and external to the institution to
- establish, maintain, and promote understanding and effective relations with those that have a significant interest in or potential effect on the students or other constituents served by the programs and services
- garner support and resources for programs and services as defined by the mission statement
- disseminate information about the programs and services

- collaborate, where appropriate, to assist in offering or improving programs and services to meet the needs of students and other constituents and to achieve program and student outcomes
- engage diverse individuals, groups, communities, and organizations to enrich the educational environment and experiences of students and other constituents

MSPS professional staff members must coordinate, or where appropriate, collaborate with staff and faculty members and other staff in providing services and programs to meet the needs of multicultural students.

MSPS must identify and address retention issues of underserved populations and advocate for the creation of welcoming surrounding community.

This could include MSPS involvement in community collaborations and coalitions that confront racism, sexism, and homophobia. Community services necessities should be available for all students.

MSPS must have procedures and guidelines consistent with institutional policy for
- communicating with the media
- contracting with external organizations for delivery of programs and services
- cultivating, soliciting, and managing gifts
- applying to and managing funds from grants

Part 9. FINANCIAL RESOURCES

Multicultural Student Programs and Services (MSPS) must have funding to accomplish the mission and goals. In establishing funding priorities and making significant changes, a comprehensive analysis must be conducted to determine the following elements: unmet needs of the unit, relevant expenditures, external and internal resources, and impact on students and the institution.

MSPS must demonstrate efficient and effective use and responsible stewardship of fiscal resources consistent with institutional protocols.

As programs grow and student diversity increases, institutions should increase financial support.

Part 10. TECHNOLOGY

Multicultural Student Programs and Services (MSPS) must have adequate technology to support the achievement of their mission and goals. The technology and its use must comply with institutional policies and procedures and be evaluated for compliance with relevant codes and laws.

MSPS must use current technology to provide updated information regarding mission, location, staffing, programs, services, and official contacts to students and designated clients.

MSPS must explore the use of technology to enhance delivery of programs and services, especially for students at a distance or external constituencies.

When technology is used to facilitate student learning and development, MSPS must select technology that reflects intended outcomes.

MSPS must
- maintain policies and procedures that address the security, confidentiality, and backup of data, as well as compliance with privacy laws
- have clearly articulated plans in place for protecting confidentiality and security of information when using Internet-based technologies
- develop plans for replacing and updating existing hardware and software as well as plans for integrating new technically-based or supported programs, including systems developed internally by the institution, systems available through professional associations, or private vendor-based systems

Technology, as well as workstations or computer labs maintained by programs and services for student use, must be accessible to all designated clients and must meet established technology standards for delivery to persons with disabilities.

When providing student access to technology, MSPS must
- have policies on the use of technology that are clear, easy to understand, and available to all students
- provide assistance, information, or referral to appropriate support services to those needing help accessing or using technology
- provide instruction or training on how to use the technology
- inform students on the legal and ethical implications of misuse as it pertains to intellectual property, harassment, privacy, and social networks

Student violations of technology policies must follow established institutional student disciplinary procedures.

Students who experience negative emotional or psychological consequences from the use of technology must be referred to support services provided by the institution.

Part 11. FACILITIES AND EQUIPMENT

Multicultural Student Programs and Services (MSPS) must have adequate, accessible, and suitably located facilities and equipment to support the mission and goals. If acquiring capital equipment as defined by the institution, MSPS must take into account expenses related to regular maintenance and life cycle costs. Facilities and equipment must be evaluated on an established cycle, including consideration of sustainability, and be in compliance with codes and laws to provide for access, health, safety, and security.

Adequate space should be provided for a resource library, private individual consultations, group workshops, and work areas for support staff. Many of the activities offered by MSPS require the same level of privacy as individual and group counseling.

Wherever it is located, MSPS should provide a safe haven for students. In addition, MSPS should provide a place for all students to learn to become more multi-culturally competent.

MSPS staff members must have workspace that is well equipped, adequate in size, and designed to support their work and responsibilities. For conversations requiring privacy, staff members must have access to a private space.

MSPS staff members who share workspace must be able to secure their own work.

The design of the facilities must guarantee the security and privacy of records and ensure the confidentiality of sensitive information.

The location and layout of the facilities must be sensitive to the needs of persons with disabilities as well as the needs of other constituencies.

Part 12. ASSESSMENT AND EVALUATION

Multicultural Student Programs and Services (MSPS) must have a clearly articulated assessment plan to document achievement of stated goals and learning outcomes, demonstrate accountability, provide evidence of improvement, and describe resulting changes in programs and services.

MSPS must have adequate fiscal, human, professional development, and technological resources to develop and implement assessment plans.

Assessments must include direct and indirect evaluation and use qualitative and quantitative methodologies and existing evidence, as appropriate, to determine whether and to what degree the stated mission, goals, and intended outcomes are being met as effectively and efficiently as possible. The process must employ sufficient and sound measures to ensure comprehensiveness. Data collected must include responses from students and other constituencies, and aggregated results must be shared with those groups. Results of assessments must be shared appropriately with multiple constituents.

Assessments may involve many methods. Survey instruments, interviews, behavioral observations, or some combination of these methods may be appropriate in a given institution.

General evaluation of the multicultural student programs and services must be conducted on a regularly scheduled basis. MSPS must solicit evaluative data from current multicultural students.

MSPS should solicit evaluative and developmental data from alumni.

Assessments must be conducted in a manner to assure an effective response.

MSPS should consult with the population to be assessed on the nature of the assessment.

Results of assessments and evaluations must be used to identify needs and interests in revising and improving programs and services, recognizing staff performance, maximizing resource efficiency and effectiveness, improving student achievement of learning and development outcomes, and improving student persistence and success. Changes resulting from the use of assessments and evaluation must be shared with stakeholders.

MSPS should assess the degree of congruence between students' educational goals and offerings of the institution and communicate the results of the assessment to appropriate decision makers.

General Standards revised in 2011;
MSPS (formerly Minority Student Programs) content developed/ revised in 1986, 1997, & 2006

The Role of Orientation Programs
CAS Standards Contextual Statement

To understand current trends in orientation programs, it is helpful to view today's practice within a historical context. The history of orientation programs in the United States is virtually as old as the history of the country's higher education. Harvard College was the first to formalize a system by which experienced students assisted new students in their transition to the institution. In addition to a personalized support system, students also experienced certain rites of passage that, from today's perspective, would likely be considered hazing. Although the system was somewhat flawed, it was the beginning of the formalization of orientation as a process that included support of students and their families as the transition to higher education began.

Later in the 19th century, Harvard institutionalized faculty-student contact by assigning faculty members educational and administrative responsibilities outside the classroom. One of these responsibilities was the orientation of new students. Soon other colleges also took an interest in the concerns specific to freshman students.

The National Orientation Directors Association (NODA) was chartered in 1976 and continues the tradition of orientation, retention, and transition professionals who have met annually for over 45 years. A Board of Directors consisting of regional representatives and officers governs the Association. Editors for the various NODA publications, regional coordinators, and other appointed positions work closely with the Board to plan and implement activities and services. National and regional networks address special interests such as nontraditional students, two-year and small colleges, Canadian colleges, multicultural affairs, and LGBT issues as well as transfer and parent and family services.

Today's orientation programs have responded to changing demographics by modifying institutional agendas. Programs have evolved from simply providing individualized faculty attention to focusing on important issues and responding to the needs of an increasingly diverse student and family population. Many programs rely extensively on highly trained and motivated peer groups (orientation leaders) in the achievement of the orientation mission.

Today, most orientation programs provide a clear and cogent introduction to an institution's academic community. Orientation is viewed as an important tool for student recruitment and retention. Most institutions include academic advising and registration for classes in their orientation programs as an impetus for active participation. Many institutions are implementing continuing orientation programs via a first-year experience course. Because of such changes, colleges and universities are taking steps to encourage student and parent and family attendance by marketing orientation programs from a decidedly academic perspective to address many issues of wider interest and concern related to matriculation, student support services, and campus life. A growing trend has been the high level of attendance at orientation programs by parents and families who often are very involved in the transition process. Many institutions deliver parent and family orientation programs separate from the student.

One of the most important changes is that orientation is now viewed as a comprehensive process rather than as a minimal program. Examples include programs lasting from one day to a week in length, welcome weeks, and tradition camps. National and international colleges and universities are developing wide-ranging orientation programs that truly address the transitional needs of diverse students and families.

What trends will guide future approaches to orientation programs? It is certain that recruitment and retention will continue to be major forces in the development of orientation programs. Likewise, attempts to foster an environment responsive to the individual needs of students and families will have a significant effect on orientation programming. Orientation professionals will need to evaluate ways to deliver orientation content as new technologies emerge. Funding for orientation programs will continue as a matter of concern. Demographic changes in institutions of higher education and in society at large will require institutional and programmatic responses. Maintaining current orientation and transitional programs by simply reacting to change does little to address the interests of all constituents. New and creative programs and methodologies must be assessed if the personal and educational needs of new and transfer students and their families are to be met.

Research, assessment, and evaluation are vital for orientations programs and must include evidence of program impact on the achievement of student learning and development outcomes. The CAS Orientation Programs Standards and Guidelines that follow have utility for national and international institutions and provide criteria by which to evaluate the quality and appropriateness of orientation programs.

References, Readings, and Resources

Designing Successful Transitions: A Guide for Orienting Students to College. Columbia, SC: University of South Carolina
Empowering Parents of First-Year College Students: A Guide for Success. Columbia, SC: University of South Carolina
National Orientation Directors Association: www.nodaweb.org
National Orientation Directors Data Bank. College Park, MD:

University of Maryland at College Park.

National Orientation Directors Association Member Handbook. Minneapolis: University of Minnesota.

National Orientation Directors Association: *The Orientation Review.* Minneapolis: University of Minnesota

National Orientation Directors Association: *Orientation Planning Manual.* Minneapolis: University of Minnesota

The Journal of College Orientation and Transition: DeKalb, IL: Northern Illinois University

Contextual Statement Contributor:

Current Edition:

J. Ann Hower, University of Michigan, Ann Arbor, NODA

Previous Editions:

Ralph Busby, Stephen F. Austin State University, NODA

Gerry Strumpf, University of Maryland, NODA

Orientation Programs
CAS Standards and Guidelines

Part 1. MISSION

The mission of Orientation Programs (OP) must facilitate the transition of new students into the institution; prepare students for the institution's educational opportunities and student responsibilities; initiate the integration of new students into the intellectual, cultural, and social climate of the institution; and support the parents, partners, guardians, and children of the new student.

OP must develop, disseminate, implement, and regularly review their missions. The mission must be consistent with the mission of the institution and with professional standards. The mission must be appropriate for the institution's student populations and community settings. Mission statements must reference student learning and development.

Part 2. PROGRAM

The formal education of students, consisting of the curriculum and the co-curriculum, must promote student learning and development outcomes that are purposeful, contribute to students' realization of their potential, and prepare students for satisfying and productive lives.

Orientation Programs (OP) must collaborate with colleagues and departments across the institution to promote student learning and development, persistence, and success.

Consistent with the institutional mission, OP must identify relevant and desirable student learning and development outcomes from among the six domains and related dimensions:

Domain: knowledge acquisition, integration, construction, and application

- Dimensions: understanding knowledge from a range of disciplines; connecting knowledge to other knowledge, ideas, and experiences; constructing knowledge; and relating knowledge to daily life

Domain: cognitive complexity

- Dimensions: critical thinking, reflective thinking, effective reasoning, and creativity

Domain: intrapersonal development

- Dimensions: realistic self-appraisal, self-understanding, and self-respect; identity development; commitment to ethics and integrity; and spiritual awareness

Domain: interpersonal competence

- Dimensions: meaningful relationships, interdependence, collaboration, and effective leadership.

Domain: humanitarianism and civic engagement

- Dimensions: understanding and appreciation of cultural and human differences, social responsibility, global perspective, and sense of civic responsibility

Domain: practical competence

- Dimensions: pursuing goals, communicating effectively, technical competence, managing personal affairs, managing career development, demonstrating professionalism, maintaining health and wellness, and living a purposeful and satisfying life

[LD Outcomes: See *The Council for the Advancement of Standards Learning and Developmental Outcomes* statement for examples of outcomes related to these domains and dimensions.]

OP must
- assess relevant and desirable student learning and development
- provide evidence of impact on outcomes
- articulate contributions to or support of student learning and development in the domains not specifically assessed
- articulate contributions to or support of student persistence and success
- use evidence gathered through this process to create strategies for improvement of programs and services

OP must be
- intentionally designed
- guided by theories and knowledge of learning and development
- integrated into the life of the institution
- reflective of developmental and demographic profiles of the student population
- responsive to needs of individuals, populations with distinct needs, and relevant constituencies
- delivered using multiple formats, strategies, and contexts

Where institutions provide distance education, OP must assist distance learners to achieve their

educational goals by providing access to information about programs and services, to staff members who can address questions and concerns, and to counseling, advising, or other forms of assistance.

OP must aid students and their families (i.e., parents, guardians, partners, and children) in understanding the nature and purpose of the institution, their membership in the academic community, and their relationship to the intellectual, cultural, and social climate of the institution.

OP should introduce students to the learning and development that will occur throughout the collegiate experience.

OP must continue as a process to address, as appropriate, transitional events, issues, and needs. The orientation process must include pre-enrollment, entry, and post-matriculation services and programs.

Components of OP may include credit and non-credit courses, seminars, adventure programs, service-learning, summer readings, learning communities, Freshmen Interest Groups (FIGs), web-based educational opportunities, comprehensive mailings, electronic communications, and campus visitations and may be administered through multiple institutional offices.

OP must
- be based on stated goals and objectives
- be coordinated with the relevant programs and activities of other institutional units
- be available to all students new to the institution, as well as to families
  First-year, transfer, and entering graduate students, as well as their families, should be served as distinct populations with specific attention given to the needs of sub-groups such as students with disabilities, athletes, adult learners, under-prepared students, under-represented students, honor students, and international students.
- assist new students as well as their families in understanding the purposes of higher education and the mission of the institution
  New students should have a clear understanding of the overall purpose of higher education and how this general purpose translates to the institution they are attending. The roles, responsibilities, and expectations of students, faculty and staff members, and families should be included.
- articulate the institution's expectations of students (e.g., scholarship, integrity, conduct, financial obligations, ethical use of technology) and provide information that clearly identifies relevant administrative policies and procedures and programs to enable students to make well-reasoned and well-informed choices

- provide new students with information and opportunities for academic and personal self-assessment
  OP should assist students in the selection of appropriate courses and course levels, making use of relevant placement examinations, entrance examinations, and academic records.
- use qualified faculty members, staff, or peer advisors to explain class scheduling, registration processes, and campus life
- provide new students, as well as their families, with information about laws and policies regarding educational records and other protected information
  OP should emphasize the independence of students in accomplishing their goals while acknowledging their interdependence with their peers and families.
- inform new students, as well as their families, about the availability of services and programs
- assist new students, as well as their families, in becoming familiar with the campus and local environment
  OP for students and families should provide information about the physical layout of the campus, including the location and purposes of campus facilities, support services, co-curricular venues, and administrative offices. Information about personal health, safety, and security should also be included.
- assist new students, as well as their families, in becoming familiar with the wide range of electronic and information resources available and expectations for their use
  OP should provide information about technological resources used to conduct institutional business and scholarly work including information about student information systems, electronic databases, email, and online course software. Information about how to manage responsible and ethical use of institutional technological resources should also be presented.
- provide time for students to become acquainted with their new environment
- provide intentional opportunities for new students to interact with fellow new students as well as continuing students and faculty and staff members
  OP should design and facilitate opportunities for new students to discuss their expectations and perceptions of the campus and to clarify their personal and educational goals.
  OP should design and facilitate opportunities for new students to meet their peers and begin forming new relationships.

OP must inform students about the history, traditions,

and campus cultures to facilitate an identification with and integration into the institution.

Part 3. ORGANIZATION AND LEADERSHIP

To achieve student and program outcomes, Orientation Programs (OP) must be structured purposefully and organized effectively. OP must have

- clearly stated goals
- current and accessible policies and procedures
- written performance expectations for employees
- functional work flow graphics or organizational charts demonstrating clear channels of authority

Leaders with organizational authority for the programs and services must provide strategic planning, supervision, and management; advance the organization; and maintain integrity through the following functions:

Strategic Planning

- articulate a vision and mission that drive short- and long-term planning
- set goals and objectives based on the needs of the population served and desired student learning or development and program outcomes
- facilitate continuous development, implementation, and assessment of goal attainment congruent with institutional mission and strategic plans
- promote environments that provide meaningful opportunities for student learning, development, and engagement
- develop and continuously improve programs and services in response to the changing needs of students served and evolving institutional priorities
- intentionally include diverse perspectives to inform decision making

Supervising

- manage human resource processes including recruitment, selection, development, supervision, performance planning, evaluation, recognition, and reward
- influence others to contribute to the effectiveness and success of the unit
- empower professional, support, and student staff to accept leadership opportunities
- offer appropriate feedback to colleagues and students on skills needed to become more effective leaders
- encourage and support professional development, collaboration with colleagues and departments across the institution, and

scholarly contribution to the profession

Managing

- identify and address individual, organizational, and environmental conditions that foster or inhibit mission achievement
- plan, allocate, and monitor the use of fiscal, physical, human, intellectual, and technological resources
- use current and valid evidence to inform decisions
- incorporate sustainability practices in the management and design of programs, services, and facilities
- understand appropriate technologies and integrate them into programs and services
- be knowledgeable about codes and laws relevant to programs and services and ensure that staff members understand their responsibilities through appropriate training
- assess potential risks and take action to mitigate them

Advancing the Organization

- communicate effectively in writing, speaking, and electronic venues
- advocate for programs and services
- advocate for representation in strategic planning initiatives at appropriate divisional and institutional levels
- initiate collaborative interactions with internal and external stakeholders who have legitimate concerns about and interests in the functional area
- facilitate processes to reach consensus where wide support is needed
- inform other areas within the institution about issues affecting practice

Maintaining Integrity

- model ethical behavior and institutional citizenship
- share data used to inform key decisions in transparent and accessible ways
- monitor media used for distributing information about programs and services to ensure the content is current, accurate, appropriately referenced, and accessible

All institutional offices involved in program delivery should be involved in the review of administrative policies and procedures.

Coordination of OP must occur even though a number of offices may be involved in the delivery of structured activities.

The size, nature, and complexity of the institution should guide the administrative scope and structure of OP.

Part 4. HUMAN RESOURCES

Orientation Programs (OP) must be staffed adequately by individuals qualified to accomplish mission and goals.

Within institutional guidelines, OP must
- establish procedures for staff recruitment and selection, training, performance planning, and evaluation
- set expectations for supervision and performance
- assess the performance of employees individually and as a team
- provide access to continuing and advanced education and appropriate professional development opportunities to improve the leadership ability, competence, and skills of all employees.

Faculty involvement in the development and delivery of OP is essential to its success. Faculty members should be included as part of the overall staffing.

OP must maintain position descriptions for all staff members.

To create a diverse staff, OP must institute recruitment and hiring strategies that encourage individuals from under-represented populations to apply for positions.

OP must develop promotion practices that are fair, inclusive, proactive, and non-discriminatory.

To further the recruitment and retention of staff, OP must consider work life initiatives, such as compressed work schedules, flextime, job sharing, remote work, or telework.

OP professional staff members must hold an earned graduate or professional degree in a field relevant to the position they hold or must possess an appropriate combination of educational credentials and related work experience.

OP professional staff members must engage in continuing professional development activities to keep abreast of the research, theories, legislation, policies, and developments that affect their programs and services.

OP must have technical and support staff members adequate to accomplish their mission. All members of the staff must be technologically proficient and qualified to perform their job functions, be knowledgeable about ethical and legal uses of technology, and have access to training and resources to support the performance of their assigned responsibilities.

Degree- or credential-seeking interns or graduate assistants must be qualified by enrollment in an appropriate field of study and by relevant experience. These individuals must be trained and supervised adequately by professional staff members holding educational credentials and related work experience appropriate for supervision. Supervisors must be cognizant of the roles of interns and graduate assistants as both student and employee and closely adhere to all parameters of their job descriptions, work hours, and schedules. Supervisors and the interns or graduate assistants must agree to compensatory time or other appropriate compensation if circumstances necessitate additional hours.

Student employees and volunteers must be carefully selected, trained, supervised, and evaluated. They must be educated on how and when to refer those in need of additional assistance to qualified staff members and must have access to a supervisor for assistance in making these judgments. Student employees and volunteers must be provided clear job descriptions, pre-service training based on assessed needs, and continuing development.

Student staff must be informed as to the limits of their authority, the expectation for appropriate role modeling, and their potential influence on new students.

All OP staff members, including student employees and volunteers, must receive specific training on institutional policies pertaining to functions or activities they support and to privacy and confidentiality policies and laws regarding access to student records and other sensitive institutional information.

All OP staff members must receive training on policies and procedures related to the use of technology to store or access student records and institutional data.

OP must ensure that staff members are knowledgeable about and trained in emergency procedures, crisis response, and prevention efforts. Prevention efforts must address identification of threatening conduct or behavior of students, faculty and staff members, and others and must incorporate a system for responding and reporting.

OP must ensure that staff members are knowledgeable of and trained in safety and emergency procedures for securing and vacating facilities.

Part 5. ETHICS

Orientation Programs (OP) must review relevant professional ethical standards and must adopt or develop and implement appropriate statements of ethical practice.

OP must publish and adhere to statements of ethical practice and ensure their periodic review by relevant constituencies.

OP must orient new staff members to relevant ethical standards and statements of ethical practice and related institutional policies.

Statements of ethical standards must specify that staff members respect privacy and maintain confidentiality in all communications and records to the extent that such communications and records are protected under relevant privacy laws.

Statements of ethical standards must specify limits on disclosure of information contained in students' educational records as well as requirements to disclose to appropriate authorities.

Statements of ethical standards must address personal and economic conflicts of interest, or appearance thereof, by staff members in the performance of their work.

Statements of ethical standards must reflect the responsibility of staff members to be fair, objective, and impartial in their interactions with others.

Statements of ethical standards must reference management of institutional funds.

Statements of ethical standards must reference appropriate behavior regarding research and assessment with human participants, confidentiality of research and assessment data, and students' rights and responsibilities.

Statements of ethical standards must include the expectation that OP staff members confront and hold accountable other staff members who exhibit unethical behavior.

Statements of ethical standards must address issues surrounding scholarly integrity.

As appropriate, OP staff members must inform users of programs and services of ethical obligations and limitations emanating from codes and laws or from licensure requirements.

OP staff members must recognize and avoid conflicts of interest that could adversely influence their judgment or objectivity and, when unavoidable, recuse themselves from the situation.

OP staff members must perform their duties within the limits of their position, training, expertise, and competence.

When these limits are exceeded, individuals in need of further assistance must be referred to persons possessing appropriate qualifications.

Promotional and descriptive information must be accurate and free of deception.

OP must adhere to institutional policies regarding ethical and legal use of software and technology.

Part 6. LAW, POLICY, AND GOVERNANCE

Orientation Programs (OP) must be in compliance with laws, regulations, and policies that relate to their respective responsibilities and that pose legal obligations, limitations, risks, and liabilities for the institution as a whole. Examples include constitutional, statutory, regulatory, and case law; relevant law and orders emanating from codes and laws; and the institution's policies.

OP must inform staff members, appropriate officials, and users of programs and services about existing and changing legal obligations, risks and liabilities, and limitations.

OP must have written policies on all relevant operations, transactions, or tasks that have legal implications.

OP must regularly review policies. The revision and creation of policies must be informed by best practices, available evidence, and policy issues in higher education.

OP staff members must use reasonable and informed practices to limit the liability exposure of the institution and its officers, employees, and agents. OP staff members must be informed about institutional policies regarding risk management, personal liability, and related insurance coverage options and must be referred to external sources if the institution does not provide coverage.

The institution must provide access to legal advice for staff members as needed to carry out assigned responsibilities.

OP must have procedures and guidelines consistent with institutional policy for responding to threats, emergencies, and crisis situations. Systems and procedures must be in place to disseminate timely and accurate information to students, other members of the institutional community, and appropriate external organizations during emergency situations.

OP staff members must neither participate in nor condone any form of harassment or activity that demeans persons or creates an intimidating, hostile, or offensive environment.

OP must obtain permission to use copyrighted materials and instruments. OP must purchase the materials and instruments from legally compliant sources or seek alternative permission from the publisher or owner. References to copyrighted materials and instruments must include appropriate citations.

OP staff members must be knowledgeable about internal and external governance systems that affect programs and services.

Part 7. DIVERSITY, EQUITY, AND ACCESS

Within the context of each institution's unique mission and in accordance with institutional polices and all applicable codes and laws, Orientation Programs (OP) must create and maintain educational and work environments that are

- welcoming, accessible, and inclusive to persons of diverse backgrounds
- equitable and non-discriminatory
- free from harassment

OP must not discriminate on the basis of ability; age; cultural identity; ethnicity; family educational history (e.g., first generation to attend college); gender identity and expression; nationality; political affiliation; race; religious affiliation; sex; sexual orientation; economic, marital, social, or veteran status; or any other basis included in institutional policies and codes and laws.

OP must

- advocate for greater sensitivity to multicultural and social justice concerns by the institution and its personnel
- modify or remove policies, practices, facilities, structures, systems, and technologies that limit access, discriminate, or produce inequities
- include diversity, equity, and access initiatives within their strategic plans
- foster communication that deepens understanding of identity, culture, self-expression, and heritage
- promote respect about commonalities and differences among people within their historical and cultural contexts
- address the characteristics and needs of a diverse population when establishing and implementing culturally relevant and inclusive programs, services, policies, procedures, and practices
- provide staff members with access to multicultural training and hold staff members accountable for integrating the training into their work

- respond to the needs of all students and other populations served when establishing hours of operation and developing methods of delivering programs, services, and resources
- ensure physical, program, and resource access for persons with disabilities
- recognize the needs of distance learning students by providing appropriate and accessible services and resources or by assisting them in gaining access to other appropriate services and resources in their geographic region

Part 8. INSTITUTIONAL AND EXTERNAL RELATIONS

Orientation Programs (OP) must reach out to relevant individuals, groups, communities, and organizations internal and external to the institution to

- establish, maintain, and promote understanding and effective relations with those that have a significant interest in or potential effect on the students or other constituents served by the programs and services
- garner support and resources for programs and services as defined by the mission statement
- disseminate information about the programs and services
- collaborate, where appropriate, to assist in offering or improving programs and services to meet the needs of students and other constituents and to achieve program and student outcomes
- engage diverse individuals, groups, communities, and organizations to enrich the educational environment and experiences of students and other constituents

OP should be an institution-wide process that systematically involves student affairs, academic affairs, and other administrative units, such as public safety, physical plant, and the business office.

OP should establish policies and practices that address how the institution should interact with parents and families.

OP must have procedures and guidelines consistent with institutional policy for

- communicating with the media
- contracting with external organizations for delivery of programs and services
- cultivating, soliciting, and managing gifts
- applying to and managing funds from grants

Part 9. FINANCIAL RESOURCES

Orientation Programs (OP) must have funding to accomplish the mission and goals. In establishing funding priorities and making significant changes, a comprehensive analysis must be conducted to determine the following elements: unmet needs of the unit, relevant expenditures, external and internal resources, and impact on students and the institution.

OP must demonstrate efficient and effective use and responsible stewardship of fiscal resources consistent with institutional protocols.

OP should be funded through institutional resources. In addition to institutional funding, other sources may be considered, including state appropriations, student fees, user fees, donations, contributions, concession and store sales, rentals, and dues.

Overnight programs may require students and their families to stay on campus. Recovering room and board costs directly from participants is an acceptable practice.

Resources, such as grants or loans, should be available to those students unable to afford the cost associated with orientation.

Part 10. TECHNOLOGY

Orientation Programs (OP) must have adequate technology to support the achievement of their mission and goals. The technology and its use must comply with institutional policies and procedures and be evaluated for compliance with relevant codes and laws.

OP must use current technology to provide updated information regarding mission, location, staffing, programs, services, and official contacts to students and designated clients.

OP must explore the use of technology to enhance delivery of programs and services, especially for students at a distance or external constituencies.

When technology is used to facilitate student learning and development, OP must select technology that reflects intended outcomes.

OP must
- maintain policies and procedures that address the security, confidentiality, and backup of data, as well as compliance with privacy laws
- have clearly articulated plans in place for protecting confidentiality and security of information when using Internet-based technologies
- develop plans for replacing and updating existing hardware and software as well as plans for integrating new technically-based or supported programs, including systems developed internally by the institution, systems available through professional associations, or private vendor-based systems

Technology, as well as workstations or computer labs maintained by programs and services for student use, must be accessible to all designated clients and must meet established technology standards for delivery to persons with disabilities.

When providing student access to technology, OP must
- have policies on the use of technology that are clear, easy to understand, and available to all students
- provide assistance, information, or referral to appropriate support services to those needing help accessing or using technology
- provide instruction or training on how to use the technology
- inform students on the legal and ethical implications of misuse as it pertains to intellectual property, harassment, privacy, and social networks

Student violations of technology policies must follow established institutional student disciplinary procedures.

Students who experience negative emotional or psychological consequences from the use of technology must be referred to support services provided by the institution.

Part 11. FACILITIES AND EQUIPMENT

Orientation Programs (OP) must have adequate, accessible, and suitably located facilities and equipment to support the mission and goals. If acquiring capital equipment as defined by the institution, OP must take into account expenses related to regular maintenance and life cycle costs. Facilities and equipment must be evaluated on an established cycle, including consideration of sustainability, and be in compliance with codes and laws to provide for access, health, safety, and security.

OP staff members must have workspace that is well equipped, adequate in size, and designed to support their work and responsibilities. For conversations requiring privacy, staff members must have access to a private space.

OP staff members who share workspace must be able to secure their own work.

The design of the facilities must guarantee the security and privacy of records and ensure the confidentiality of sensitive information.

The location and layout of the facilities must be sensitive to the needs of persons with disabilities as well as the needs of other constituencies.

Cooperation from the campus community is necessary to provide appropriate facilities to implement orientation programs. Whenever possible, a single office location to house personnel and provide adequate workspace should be conveniently located and suitable for its high level of interaction with the public.

Part 12. ASSESSMENT AND EVALUATION

Orientation Programs (OP) must have a clearly articulated assessment plan to document achievement of stated goals and learning outcomes, demonstrate accountability, provide evidence of improvement, and describe resulting changes in programs and services.

OP must have adequate fiscal, human, professional development, and technological resources to develop and implement assessment plans.

Assessments must include direct and indirect evaluation and use qualitative and quantitative methodologies and existing evidence, as appropriate, to determine whether and to what degree the stated mission, goals, and intended outcomes are being met as effectively and efficiently as possible. The process must employ sufficient and sound measures to ensure comprehensiveness. Data collected must include responses from students and other constituencies, and aggregated results must be shared with those groups. Results of assessments must be shared appropriately with multiple constituents.

Results of assessments and evaluations must be used to identify needs and interests in revising and improving programs and services, recognizing staff performance, maximizing resource efficiency and effectiveness, improving student achievement of learning and development outcomes, and improving student persistence and success. Changes resulting from the use of assessments and evaluation must be shared with stakeholders.

Evaluation of student and institutional needs, goals, objectives, and the effectiveness of orientation programs should occur on a regular basis. A representative cross-section of appropriate people from the campus community should be involved in reviews of orientation programs.

General Standards revised in 2011;
OP content developed/revised in 1986, 1996, & 2005

The Role of Parent and Family Programs
CAS Standards Contextual Statement

Parent involvement at the college level is not a new concept. Parents and families of college students have been involved in campus life since the first child set off to engage in higher learning. How the parental and family involvement manifested itself within the life of the institution has changed throughout the history of higher education. Beginning with the basic tenet of *in loco parentis*, as expressed through the faculty as monitors of student behavior, to the uprising of student rights as expressed in the Family Education Rights and Privacy Act (FERPA) of the 1970s, to a campus environment of *in consortio cum parentibus* (Henning 2007), parents and families have made their influence known with faculty, staff, and administrators on campuses across the nation.

As early as 1920, Mothers' Clubs and Dads' Clubs were active at such universities as Texas A & M, Southern Methodist University, and Stanford University. These early organizations, which sought to bring the stability and security of the family home to the campus, became the foundations of and models for the parent and family organizations active today on these and many other American campuses. As they evolved, these early groups began to incorporate fundraising for campus improvements and scholarships into their clubs' agendas. The Stanford Mothers' Club, after two years of taking convalescing students into their own homes, decided to provide and fund a Men's and a Women's Rest Home that, after 35 years, became part of the permanent Stanford Student Health facilities. This is an example of how parents and family members working with faculty, staff, and administrators established an understanding of the mutual roles necessary to serve students well. Examples such as this have led to the development of today's Parent and Family Programs offices.

Research overwhelmingly demonstrates that parent involvement in children's learning is positively related to achievement. Further, the research shows that the more intensively parents are involved in their children's learning, the greater the achievement effects. At the elementary school level, "family involvement is linked broadly with school achievement across different socioeconomic and ethnic groups" (Harvard Family Research Project, Winter 2006-2007, page 3).

Students' perceptions of their parents' values about achievement are strongly related to motivation and competence (Harvard Family Research Project, Spring 2007, page 5). Family involvement during adolescence is a predictor of such positive outcomes as school success and positive social and emotional outcomes.

Adolescents with supportive parents have higher grade point averages, and they exhibit higher rates of self-reliance, identity formation, school performance, and positive career-planning aspirations, They are more likely to discuss information with their parents that will keep them out of trouble, and they have higher rates of college enrollment (Harvard Family Research Project, Spring 2007).

During the college years, family support continues to be critical. Traditional student development theories support separation from the family for the purpose of individuation and developing as an independent adult. In contrast, other theories suggest that family involvement continues to have a positive effect during the college years, even supporting the goals of individuation. Attachment theory, for example, suggests that for students leaving home, having parents as a secure base may actually support rather than threaten the development of competence and autonomy (Kenny & Donaldson, 1992).

Research proves that parent/family involvement is an important resource that improves a student's productivity (Astone *et al*, 1999; Bourdieu & Passeron, 1977; Coleman, 1988; Lareau, 2001; Lin, 2001; Perna & Titus, 2005). Students bring a bank of social capital to their college experience that is earned through their involvement with family, school and community friends, and high school teachers. Some of the positive influences of this social capital include engagement with students' schools and communities, supportive families, and greater trust in the institution (Goddard, 2003). Successful college admittance at selective institutions rarely occurs without a structural network that includes a high level of commitment and involvement from a student's parents and family (Perna & Titus, 2005). Therefore, creating an environment for overall student success should include a mutually beneficial and appropriate parent and family program. The Parent Program Director at one of the country's largest public institutions says, "When we treat parents as valued partners and give them information about student development, they can be our best allies in student success, retention, and graduation" (Savage, 2007, personal communication).

Parents and families of undergraduate students are important stakeholders in institutions of higher education. Most importantly, evidence demonstrates that students benefit from the involvement of their parents in their education more now than ever before (National Survey of Student Engagement, Annual Report 2007). Additionally, parents have a significant emotional and financial investment in their student's success. Finally, parents discuss the effectiveness and quality of the institution in their communities with friends, prospective students, donors, voters, and taxpayers. When an institution commits to involving parents in appropriate and effective ways, it produces an outcome of parental support for student success and a group of life-long advocates eager to promote and support its vision and mission.

The mission of Parent and Family Programs should be the success and development of the college undergraduate student through education, communication, and the collaboration of the wisdom of parents and families with the expertise and wisdom of the university and its resources. The CAS standards and guidelines that follow provide a basis for institutional self-assessment and program development.

References, Readings, and Resources

Astone, N. A. , Nathanson, C. A., Schoen, R., & Kim, Y. J. (1999). Family demography, social theory, and investment in social capital. *Population and Development , 25,* 1–31.

Bourdieu, P., & Passeron, J. (1977). *Reproduction in education, society and culture.* (Nice, R., Trans.). Beverly Hills, CA: Sage.

Coleman, James S. 1988. Social capital in the creation of human capital. *The American Journal of Sociology, 94,* S95-120.

Goddard, R. D. (2003). Relational networks, social trust, and norms: A social capital perspective on students' chances of academic success. *Educational Evaluation and Policy Analysis, 25*(1), 59–74.

Harvard Family Research Project, Winter 2006-2007. *Family involvement in elementary school children's education.* No. 2 in a series. Retrieved from http://www.hfrp.org/publications-resources/publications-series/family-involvement-makes-a-difference/family-involvement-in-elementary-school-children-s-education

Harvard Family Research Project, Spring 2007. *Family Involvement in middle and high school students' education.* No. 3 in a series. Retrieved from http://www.hfrp.org/publications-resources/publications-series/family-involvement-makes-a-difference/family-involvement-in-middle-and-high-school-students-education

Henning, G. (2007). Is in corsortio cum parentibus the new in loco parentis? *NASPA Journal, 44*(3), 538–560.

Horvat, E. M. & Lareau, A. (1999). Moments of social inclusion and exclusion. Race, class, and cultural capital in family-school relationships. *Sociology of Education, 72,* 37–53.

Kenny, M. and Donaldson, G.A. (1992). The relationship of parental attachment and psychological separation to the adjustment of first-year college women. *Journal of College Student Development, 33* (5), 431-438.

Lareau, Annette. 2001. Linking Bourdieu's concept of capital to the broader field: The case of family-school relationships. In B. J. Biddle, (Ed.), *Social Class, Poverty, and Education: Policy and Practice* (pp. 77-100). New York: Routledge Falmer.

Lin, N. (2001). Building a network theory of social capital. In N. Lin, K. Cook, & R. S. Burt, (Eds.), *Social capital: Theory and research* (pp. 3–30). New York: Aldine de Gruyter.

National Survey of Student Engagement Annual Report. (2007). Retrieved from http://nsse.iub.edu/NSSE_2007_Annual_Report/docs/withhold/NSSE_2007_Annual_Report.pdf

Perna, L. W., & Titus, M. A. (2005). The relationship between parental involvement as social capital and college enrollment: An examination of racial and ethnic group differences. *Journal of Higher Education, 76*(5), 485–518.

Contextual Statement Contributors

Marjorie Savage, University of Minnesota
Kristine E. Stewart, Miami University

Parent and Family Programs
CAS Standards and Guidelines

Part 1. MISSION

The mission of Parent and Family Programs (PFP) is to build collaboration between parents and families and the institution for the common goals of student learning, development, and success.

PFP must develop, disseminate, implement, and regularly review their missions. The mission must be consistent with the mission of the institution and with professional standards. The mission must be appropriate for the institution's student populations and community settings. Mission statements must reference student learning and development.

Inherent in the mission statement should be a vision for students and their families to develop lifelong affinity for the institution and its initiatives.

Part 2. PROGRAM

The formal education of students, consisting of the curriculum and the co-curriculum, must promote student learning and development outcomes that are purposeful, contribute to students' realization of their potential, and prepare students for satisfying and productive lives.

Parent and Family Programs (PFP) must collaborate with colleagues and departments across the institution to promote student learning and development, persistence, and success.

Consistent with the institutional mission, PFP must identify relevant and desirable student learning and development outcomes from among the six domains and related dimensions:

Domain: knowledge acquisition, integration, construction, and application

- Dimensions: understanding knowledge from a range of disciplines; connecting knowledge to other knowledge, ideas, and experiences; constructing knowledge; and relating knowledge to daily life

Domain: cognitive complexity

- Dimensions: critical thinking, reflective thinking, effective reasoning, and creativity

Domain: intrapersonal development

- Dimensions: realistic self-appraisal, self-understanding, and self-respect; identity development; commitment to ethics and

integrity; and spiritual awareness

Domain: interpersonal competence

- Dimensions: meaningful relationships, interdependence, collaboration, and effective leadership.

Domain: humanitarianism and civic engagement

- Dimensions: understanding and appreciation of cultural and human differences, social responsibility, global perspective, and sense of civic responsibility

Domain: practical competence

- Dimensions: pursuing goals, communicating effectively, technical competence, managing personal affairs, managing career development, demonstrating professionalism, maintaining health and wellness, and living a purposeful and satisfying life

[LD Outcomes: See *The Council for the Advancement of Standards Learning and Developmental Outcomes* statement for examples of outcomes related to these domains and dimensions.]

PFP must
- assess relevant and desirable student learning and development
- provide evidence of impact on outcomes
- articulate contributions to or support of student learning and development in the domains not specifically assessed
- articulate contributions to or support of student persistence and success
- use evidence gathered through this process to create strategies for improvement of programs and services

PFP must be
- intentionally designed
- guided by theories and knowledge of learning and development
- integrated into the life of the institution
- reflective of developmental and demographic profiles of the student population
- responsive to needs of individuals, populations with distinct needs, and relevant constituencies
- delivered using multiple formats, strategies, and contexts

Where institutions provide distance education, PFP must assist distance learners to achieve their

educational goals by providing access to information about programs and services, to staff members who can address questions and concerns, and to counseling, advising, or other forms of assistance.

PFP must help families maintain a connection to the institution.

PFP should provide programming and services in person and online, information about issues related to student learning and development, and opportunities to interact with other families and students.

Programming and services may include parent and family orientation programs, parent and family weekends, move-in and send-off events, educational workshops and seminars, newsletters, and fundraising. Other programs should be specifically reflective of the institutional history, traditions, and culture.

PFP must
- **distribute information on a timely basis to take advantage of the impact of naturally occurring developmental stages experienced by students and families**
- **encourage parents and families to work with their student so that the student will learn to access institutional resources independently**
- **assist parents and families to investigate and navigate institutional resources, services, and programs**
- **collaborate with essential campus partners**
- **consider diverse perspectives in developing parent and family programs**
- **provide information for faculty members and staff to help them interact effectively with parents and families and understand their expectations**
- **advocate for the appropriate distribution of emergency information to parents and families in accordance with institutional policy**

Programming should address topics such as
- educational planning (academic advising, selection of major)
- standards of academic progress and other academic policies
- career planning
- student budgeting and money management
- educational costs, financial aid, and financial planning
- health and wellness
- resources to support students with disabilities
- resources through visitor services
- institutional support services (study skills, tutoring, and other learning assistance programs)
- diversity, multicultural, and international programs

and services
- membership in a diverse community and interactions across differences
- involvement in co-curricular activities
- campus safety
- global citizenship
- on-campus, off-campus, commuter, or distance learner student issues
- information related to the transition to college and the potential change in family dynamics
- organization and roles of the institution's administration
- realistic parent and family expectations of their student
- appropriate levels of involvement with their student and the institution
- campus policies on rights and responsibilities, conduct, and access to educational records

Part 3. ORGANIZATION AND LEADERSHIP

To achieve student and program outcomes, Parent and Family Programs (PFP) must be structured purposefully and organized effectively. PFP must have
- **clearly stated goals**
- **current and accessible policies and procedures**
- **written performance expectations for employees**
- **functional work flow graphics or organizational charts demonstrating clear channels of authority**

Leaders with organizational authority for the programs and services must provide strategic planning, supervision, and management; advance the organization; and maintain integrity through the following functions:

Strategic Planning
- **articulate a vision and mission that drive short- and long-term planning**
- **set goals and objectives based on the needs of the population served and desired student learning or development and program outcomes**
- **facilitate continuous development, implementation, and assessment of goal attainment congruent with institutional mission and strategic plans**
- **promote environments that provide meaningful opportunities for student learning, development, and engagement**
- **develop and continuously improve programs and services in response to the changing needs of students served and evolving institutional priorities**
- **intentionally include diverse perspectives to**

inform decision making

Supervising

- manage human resource processes including recruitment, selection, development, supervision, performance planning, evaluation, recognition, and reward
- influence others to contribute to the effectiveness and success of the unit
- empower professional, support, and student staff to accept leadership opportunities
- offer appropriate feedback to colleagues and students on skills needed to become more effective leaders
- encourage and support professional development, collaboration with colleagues and departments across the institution, and scholarly contribution to the profession

Managing

- identify and address individual, organizational, and environmental conditions that foster or inhibit mission achievement
- plan, allocate, and monitor the use of fiscal, physical, human, intellectual, and technological resources
- use current and valid evidence to inform decisions
- incorporate sustainability practices in the management and design of programs, services, and facilities
- understand appropriate technologies and integrate them into programs and services
- be knowledgeable about codes and laws relevant to programs and services and ensure that staff members understand their responsibilities through appropriate training
- assess potential risks and take action to mitigate them

Advancing the Organization

- communicate effectively in writing, speaking, and electronic venues
- advocate for programs and services
- advocate for representation in strategic planning initiatives at appropriate divisional and institutional levels
- initiate collaborative interactions with internal and external stakeholders who have legitimate concerns about and interests in the functional area
- facilitate processes to reach consensus where wide support is needed
- inform other areas within the institution about issues affecting practice

Maintaining Integrity

- model ethical behavior and institutional

citizenship
- share data used to inform key decisions in transparent and accessible ways
- monitor media used for distributing information about programs and services to ensure the content is current, accurate, appropriately referenced, and accessible

PFP should maintain a website that can be accessed from the institution's home page to address the information needs of parents and families.

PFP must be located in an organizational structure that can best provide for effective programs and services for achievement of its mission.

Such locations may include student affairs, enrollment management, or advancement.

Part 4. HUMAN RESOURCES

Parent and Family Programs (PFP) must be staffed adequately by individuals qualified to accomplish mission and goals.

PFP staff should include full-time professionals.

Within institutional guidelines, PFP must

- establish procedures for staff recruitment and selection, training, performance planning, and evaluation
- set expectations for supervision and performance
- assess the performance of employees individually and as a team
- provide access to continuing and advanced education and appropriate professional development opportunities to improve the leadership ability, competence, and skills of all employees.

PFP must maintain position descriptions for all staff members.

To create a diverse staff, PFP must institute recruitment and hiring strategies that encourage individuals from under-represented populations to apply for positions.

PFP must develop promotion practices that are fair, inclusive, proactive, and non-discriminatory.

To further the recruitment and retention of staff, PFP must consider work life initiatives, such as compressed work schedules, flextime, job sharing, remote work, or telework.

PFP professional staff members must hold an earned graduate or professional degree in a field relevant to the position they hold or must possess an appropriate combination of educational credentials and related

work experience.

PFP professional staff members must engage in continuing professional development activities to keep abreast of the research, theories, legislation, policies, and developments that affect their programs and services.

PFP must have technical and support staff members adequate to accomplish their mission. All members of the staff must be technologically proficient and qualified to perform their job functions, be knowledgeable about ethical and legal uses of technology, and have access to training and resources to support the performance of their assigned responsibilities.

PFP should have sufficient and specifically trained staff to support technology including the maintenance of program websites, social networks, communication systems, and developing emerging technology.

Degree- or credential-seeking interns or graduate assistants must be qualified by enrollment in an appropriate field of study and by relevant experience. These individuals must be trained and supervised adequately by professional staff members holding educational credentials and related work experience appropriate for supervision. Supervisors must be cognizant of the roles of interns and graduate assistants as both student and employee and closely adhere to all parameters of their job descriptions, work hours, and schedules. Supervisors and the interns or graduate assistants must agree to compensatory time or other appropriate compensation if circumstances necessitate additional hours.

Student employees and volunteers must be carefully selected, trained, supervised, and evaluated. They must be educated on how and when to refer those in need of additional assistance to qualified staff members and must have access to a supervisor for assistance in making these judgments. Student employees and volunteers must be provided clear job descriptions, pre-service training based on assessed needs, and continuing development.

All PFP staff members, including student employees and volunteers, must receive specific training on institutional policies pertaining to functions or activities they support and to privacy and confidentiality policies and laws regarding access to student records and other sensitive institutional information.

PFP must also receive specific training on the Health Insurance Portability & Accountability Act (HIPAA) if appropriate for institutional policies.

All PFP staff members must receive training on policies and procedures related to the use of technology to store or access student records and institutional data.

PFP must ensure that staff members are knowledgeable about and trained in emergency procedures, crisis response, and prevention efforts. Prevention efforts must address identification of threatening conduct or behavior of students, faculty and staff members, and others and must incorporate a system for responding and reporting.

PFP must ensure that staff members are knowledgeable of and trained in safety and emergency procedures for securing and vacating facilities.

PFP staff should pursue opportunities for support, professional development, and networking.

Part 5. ETHICS

Parent and Family Programs (PFP) must review relevant professional ethical standards and must adopt or develop and implement appropriate statements of ethical practice.

PFP must publish and adhere to statements of ethical practice and ensure their periodic review by relevant constituencies.

PFP must orient new staff members to relevant ethical standards and statements of ethical practice and related institutional policies.

Statements of ethical standards must specify that staff members respect privacy and maintain confidentiality in all communications and records to the extent that such communications and records are protected under relevant privacy laws.

Statements of ethical standards must specify limits on disclosure of information contained in students' educational records as well as requirements to disclose to appropriate authorities.

Statements of ethical standards must address personal and economic conflicts of interest, or appearance thereof, by staff members in the performance of their work.

Statements of ethical standards must reflect the responsibility of staff members to be fair, objective, and impartial in their interactions with others.

Statements of ethical standards must reference management of institutional funds.

Statements of ethical standards must reference appropriate behavior regarding research and assessment with human participants, confidentiality of research and assessment data, and students' rights and responsibilities.

Statements of ethical standards must include the expectation that PFP staff members confront and hold accountable other staff members who exhibit unethical behavior.

Statements of ethical standards must address issues surrounding scholarly integrity.

As appropriate, PFP staff members must inform users of programs and services of ethical obligations and limitations emanating from codes and laws or from licensure requirements.

PFP staff members must recognize and avoid conflicts of interest that could adversely influence their judgment or objectivity and, when unavoidable, recuse themselves from the situation.

PFP staff members must perform their duties within the limits of their position, training, expertise, and competence.

When these limits are exceeded, individuals in need of further assistance must be referred to persons possessing appropriate qualifications.

Promotional and descriptive information must be accurate and free of deception.

PFP must adhere to institutional policies regarding ethical and legal use of software and technology.

Part 6. LAW, POLICY, AND GOVERNANCE

Parent and Family Programs (PFP) must be in compliance with laws, regulations, and policies that relate to their respective responsibilities and that pose legal obligations, limitations, risks, and liabilities for the institution as a whole. Examples include constitutional, statutory, regulatory, and case law; relevant law and orders emanating from codes and laws; and the institution's policies.

PFP must inform staff members, appropriate officials, and users of programs and services about existing and changing legal obligations, risks and liabilities, and limitations.

PFP that use volunteers must provide appropriate training and support to ensure that guidelines and legal standards are followed.

PFP must have written policies on all relevant operations, transactions, or tasks that have legal implications.

PFP must regularly review policies. The revision and creation of policies must be informed by best practices, available evidence, and policy issues in higher education.

PFP staff members must use reasonable and informed practices to limit the liability exposure of the institution and its officers, employees, and agents. PFP staff members must be informed about institutional policies regarding risk management, personal liability, and related insurance coverage options and must be referred to external sources if the institution does not provide coverage.

The institution must provide access to legal advice for staff members as needed to carry out assigned responsibilities.

PFP must have procedures and guidelines consistent with institutional policy for responding to threats, emergencies, and crisis situations. Systems and procedures must be in place to disseminate timely and accurate information to students, other members of the institutional community, and appropriate external organizations during emergency situations.

PFP staff members must neither participate in nor condone any form of harassment or activity that demeans persons or creates an intimidating, hostile, or offensive environment.

PFP must obtain permission to use copyrighted materials and instruments. PFP must purchase the materials and instruments from legally compliant sources or seek alternative permission from the publisher or owner. References to copyrighted materials and instruments must include appropriate citations.

PFP staff members must be knowledgeable about internal and external governance systems that affect programs and services.

Part 7. DIVERSITY, EQUITY, AND ACCESS

Within the context of each institution's unique mission and in accordance with institutional polices and all applicable codes and laws, Parent and Family Programs (PFP) must create and maintain educational and work environments that are
- welcoming, accessible, and inclusive to persons of diverse backgrounds
- equitable and non-discriminatory
- free from harassment

PFP must not discriminate on the basis of ability; age; cultural identity; ethnicity; family educational history (e.g., first generation to attend college); gender identity and expression; nationality; political affiliation; race; religious affiliation; sex; sexual orientation; economic, marital, social, or veteran status; or any other basis included in institutional policies and codes and laws.

PFP must

- **advocate for greater sensitivity to multicultural and social justice concerns by the institution and its personnel**
- **modify or remove policies, practices, facilities, structures, systems, and technologies that limit access, discriminate, or produce inequities**
- **include diversity, equity, and access initiatives within their strategic plans**
- **foster communication that deepens understanding of identity, culture, self-expression, and heritage**
- **promote respect about commonalities and differences among people within their historical and cultural contexts**
- **address the characteristics and needs of a diverse population when establishing and implementing culturally relevant and inclusive programs, services, policies, procedures, and practices**
- **provide staff members with access to multicultural training and hold staff members accountable for integrating the training into their work**
- **respond to the needs of all students and other populations served when establishing hours of operation and developing methods of delivering programs, services, and resources**
- **ensure physical, program, and resource access for persons with disabilities**
- **recognize the needs of distance learning students by providing appropriate and accessible services and resources or by assisting them in gaining access to other appropriate services and resources in their geographic region**

PFP should include statements related to disability and equal opportunity laws in all print and electronic materials in accordance with institutional policy.

PFP should respect the diversity of the families of students, acknowledging the many different cultures and backgrounds represented by the families, including non-traditional family structures such as single parent households and foster families.

PFP should educate parents and families in general about all aspects of diversity in the college community and within society and be prepared to identify resources for support both on campus and locally as needed.

PFP staff must be knowledgeable of current trends and changing demographics of their institution as well as how they relate at the national level.

PFP should include programming for the unique family needs of student populations such as commuter, transfer, foster,

homeless, international, LGBT, and first generation students.

PFP should provide access to the institution's policies and procedures and resources in multiple language formats including printed forms for families who do not have technology.

Part 8. INSTITUTIONAL AND EXTERNAL RELATIONS

Parent and Family Programs (PFP) must reach out to relevant individuals, groups, communities, and organizations internal and external to the institution to

- **establish, maintain, and promote understanding and effective relations with those that have a significant interest in or potential effect on the students or other constituents served by the programs and services**
- **garner support and resources for programs and services as defined by the mission statement**
- **disseminate information about the programs and services**
- **collaborate, where appropriate, to assist in offering or improving programs and services to meet the needs of students and other constituents and to achieve program and student outcomes**
- **engage diverse individuals, groups, communities, and organizations to enrich the educational environment and experiences of students and other constituents**

PFP should create a role for parents and family members within the institution through a parent/families organization, association, or club. Such a group should develop family affinity for the institution, offer referral to programs and services, and provide opportunities for parents and families to have input on institutional matters affecting their students. A staff member of the institution should be charged with supporting and advising such an organization.

PFP should inform family members about issues that impact the health, well-being, and success of students through a variety of delivery methods communication methods, including newsletters, e-newsletters, websites, social networking, and educational programming. This material should display appropriate institutional branding.

PFP should provide a parents and family resource guide or handbook to address student-life topics of priority to the institution (e.g., drug and alcohol abuse, service-learning and study abroad opportunities, research opportunities, financial literacy, health and wellness), resources and benefits available to parents and families, institutional policies and procedures, the academic calendar, and support services for students and their families.

PFP must have procedures and guidelines consistent with institutional policy for

- **communicating with the media**
- **contracting with external organizations for delivery of programs and services**
- **cultivating, soliciting, and managing gifts**
- **applying to and managing funds from grants**

PFP should be represented on the institutional crisis response team. PFP should advocate for appropriate information to be sent to parents in the event of an emergency or campus crisis in accordance with institutional procedures.

Part 9. FINANCIAL RESOURCES

Parent and Family Programs (PFP) must have funding to accomplish the mission and goals. In establishing funding priorities and making significant changes, a comprehensive analysis must be conducted to determine the following elements: unmet needs of the unit, relevant expenditures, external and internal resources, and impact on students and the institution.

PFP may supplement institutional funding by developing revenue from sources such as fundraising, grants, and fees for services provided.

PFP must demonstrate efficient and effective use and responsible stewardship of fiscal resources consistent with institutional protocols.

Part 10. TECHNOLOGY

Parent and Family Programs (PFP) must have adequate technology to support the achievement of their mission and goals. The technology and its use must comply with institutional policies and procedures and be evaluated for compliance with relevant codes and laws.

PFP must use current technology to provide updated information regarding mission, location, staffing, programs, services, and official contacts to students and designated clients.

PFP must explore the use of technology to enhance delivery of programs and services, especially for students at a distance or external constituencies.

When technology is used to facilitate student learning and development, PFP must select technology that reflects intended outcomes.

PFP must

- **maintain policies and procedures that address the security, confidentiality, and backup of data, as well as compliance with privacy laws**
- **have clearly articulated plans in place for protecting confidentiality and security of information when using Internet-based technologies**

- **develop plans for replacing and updating existing hardware and software as well as plans for integrating new technically-based or supported programs, including systems developed internally by the institution, systems available through professional associations, or private vendor-based systems**

Technology, as well as workstations or computer labs maintained by programs and services for student use, must be accessible to all designated clients and must meet established technology standards for delivery to persons with disabilities.

When providing student access to technology, PFP must

- **have policies on the use of technology that are clear, easy to understand, and available to all students**
- **provide assistance, information, or referral to appropriate support services to those needing help accessing or using technology**
- **provide instruction or training on how to use the technology**
- **inform students on the legal and ethical implications of misuse as it pertains to intellectual property, harassment, privacy, and social networks**

Student violations of technology policies must follow established institutional student disciplinary procedures.

Students who experience negative emotional or psychological consequences from the use of technology must be referred to support services provided by the institution.

Part 11. FACILITIES AND EQUIPMENT

Parent and Family Programs (PFP) must have adequate, accessible, and suitably located facilities and equipment to support the mission and goals. If acquiring capital equipment as defined by the institution, PFP must take into account expenses related to regular maintenance and life cycle costs. Facilities and equipment must be evaluated on an established cycle, including consideration of sustainability, and be in compliance with codes and laws to provide for access, health, safety, and security.

PFP staff members must have workspace that is well equipped, adequate in size, and designed to support their work and responsibilities. For conversations requiring privacy, staff members must have access to a private space.

PFP staff members who share workspace must be able to secure their own work.

The design of the facilities must guarantee the security and privacy of records and ensure the confidentiality of sensitive information.

The location and layout of the facilities must be sensitive to the needs of persons with disabilities as well as the needs of other constituencies.

Part 12. ASSESSMENT AND EVALUATION

Parent and Family Programs (PFP) must have a clearly articulated assessment plan to document achievement of stated goals and learning outcomes, demonstrate accountability, provide evidence of improvement, and describe resulting changes in programs and services.

PFP must have adequate fiscal, human, professional development, and technological resources to develop and implement assessment plans.

Assessments must include direct and indirect evaluation and use qualitative and quantitative methodologies and existing evidence, as appropriate, to determine whether and to what degree the stated mission, goals, and intended outcomes are being met as effectively and efficiently as possible. The process must employ sufficient and sound measures to ensure comprehensiveness. Data collected must include responses from students and other constituencies, and aggregated results must be shared with those groups. Results of assessments must be shared appropriately with multiple constituents.

PFP should employ multiple methods to evaluate and assess the program's effectiveness in meeting the needs of families.

Results of assessments and evaluations must be used to identify needs and interests in revising and improving programs and services, recognizing staff performance, maximizing resource efficiency and effectiveness, improving student achievement of learning and development outcomes, and improving student persistence and success. Changes resulting from the use of assessments and evaluation must be shared with stakeholders.

General Standards revised in 2011;
PFP content developed in 2010

The Role of Recreational Sports Programs
CAS Standards Contextual Statement

The concept and practice of providing activities to enhance student growth during college is grounded in various student developmental theories and postulates. Among the most noted are theories related to identity development (Chickering, 1969; Marcia, 1966); cognitive process (Perry, 1968), moral development (Kohlberg & Hersh, 1977; Gilligan, 1982); spirituality and authenticity (Chickering, Dalton, & Stamm, 2006); interpersonal and intrapersonal changes (Knefelkamp, Widick, & Parker, 1978); and gender identity (McCewan, 1996). Student services practice also focuses on involvement and engagement in on and off-campus curricular and co-curricular activities as a method to enhance student retention and success (Astin, 1984; Pascarella & Terrenzini, 2005; Tinto, 1994). *Learning Reconsidered* provided and galvanized the recent focus on student service based learning by defining learning as "a comprehensive, holistic, transformative activity that integrates academic learning and student development, processes that have often been considered separate and even independent of each other" (American College Personnel Association & National Association of Student Personnel Administrators, 2004, p. 2). The context in which development, engagement, and learning occurs on a college campus is important and ranges from the curricular offerings connected with academic units to those associated with co-curricular units provided by a myriad of student services, including recreational sports.

Student involvement in sports activities has been part of the college experience since the earliest days of the colonial colleges. Organized by students, sports activities were considered a diversion from the rigors of academic life and limited to competitive activities between classmates within the institution. More formalized "intramurals," a term derived from the Latin words *intra*, meaning within, and *muralis*, meaning walls, began in U.S. colleges and universities during the 19th century and were, for the first part of that century, almost exclusively the only form of structured competition for students (Mueller, 1971). By the century's mid-point interest in competitive sport intensified and intercollegiate athletics was born, overshadowing intramural contests as the primary sport engagement focus on campus.

A resurgence of the intramural movement occurred in the late 19th and early 20th centuries and was formalized by the construction of the first dedicated intramural facilities in 1913, and the employment of professional staff members focused on providing increasingly popular sport related programs. The formation of a national professional organization for intramural sports directors first occurred in 1950 when the National Intramural Association (NIA) was formed (NIRSA, 2006e; Clark, 1978).

Over-time, intramural programs diversified to broader recreational pursuits and participation increased. The rise in popularity of aerobic exercise and a societal push toward greater gender equity, including implementation of Title IX of the Education Amendments of 1972, produced an influx of women into competitive athletics resulting in even higher levels of interest and participation for varied recreational pursuits. The NIA changed its name in 1975 to the National Intramural and Recreational Sports Association (NIRSA) to reflect the "sport-for-all" mindset held by the organization's membership. Separate standards and guidelines for specializations are governed by professional organizations associated with the specific functional area and/or published by NIRSA. As programs continued to grow and gain both student and institutional support, additional multi-faceted facilities were built, many exclusively, for recreational sports activities. By the late 1980s, the field of recreational sports witnessed a period of rapid growth in programs and the advent of new and better campus facilities for physical activities.

The beginning of the 21st Century found even greater expansion of collegiate recreational sports opportunities and facilities, reaching an estimated combined enrollment of 7.1 million students, with an estimated 5.3 million students considered heavy or regular users of established programs and facilities (NIRSA, 2005). New construction and refurbishing of existing facilities continues unabated and has helped to provide needed services to students to enhance their growth and maturation, particularly in the areas of health, fitness, and wellness. NIRSA reported that, between 2005–2010, at least $3.17 billion will be spent in new construction and renovations for indoor campus recreational sports facilities at 333 NIRSA member institutions at an average cost of $14.2 million. Total student enrollment for the reporting colleges and universities is 3.8 million (NIRSA, 2005).

During this period of tremendous growth, recreational sports programs experienced changed perceptions about institutional roles and standards of practice. Recreational sports programs are placed under the administrative auspices of a division of student affairs at 72 percent of NIRSA member institutions (Franklin, 2007), though some programs are found within a variety of other administrative structures including intercollegiate athletic departments, academic programs, and business units. NIRSA suggests that, while organizational designs vary among institutions, the full realization of recreational sports contributions to any campus depends upon institutional commitment to that endeavor.

NIRSA (2004) found that, at schools with established campus recreational sports departments, 75 percent of students participated in recreational sports programs and that participation in these programs was a key determinant of college satisfaction, success, recruitment, and retention. Student participation also encouraged the development of critical thinking skills and the creation of problem-solving strategies, honed decision-making skills, enhanced creativity, and promoted the synthesis and integration of information into all aspects of their lives. In this way, students both perform more effectively in an academic environment and flourish throughout all phases of the collegiate experience. Research also found that recreational sports programs contributed to the development of a student's positive self-image, awareness of strengths, increased tolerance and self-control, stronger social interaction skills, and maturity. These programs have been endorsed by institutions for their value in helping students maintain good physical and mental health by providing a respite from rigorous academic work and in teaching recreational skills with a carryover for leisure time exercise throughout life.

Viewed as an essential component of higher education, the field of recreational sports has grown into a dynamic organized profession contributing to the educational process through the enhancement of students' physical, mental, social, and emotional development. Recreational sports practitioners provide quality co-curricular opportunities to enhance the overall growth and development of students by remaining grounded to a commitment to student development and learning; a set of ethical codes and standards; and continuous professional improvement.

References, Readings, and Resources

Astin, A. W. (1984). Student involvement: A developmental theory for higher education. *Journal of College Student Personnel, 25,* 297-308.

Chickering, A. W. (1969). Education and identity. San Francisco: Jossey-Bass.

Chickering, A. W., Dalton, J. C., & Stamm, L. (2006). *Encouraging authenticity and spirituality in higher education*. San Francisco: Jossey-Bass.

Clarke, J. S. (1978). *Challenge and change: A history of the development of the National Intramural and Recreational Sports Association* 1950-1976. West Point, NY: Leisure Press, p.100.

Franklin, D. S. (2007). Student development and learning in campus recreation: Assessing recreational sports directors' awareness, perceived importance, application of and satisfaction with CAS standards. (Doctoral dissertation). Retrieved November 6, 2007, from ProQuest Digital Dissertations database. (Publication No. AAT 3269236).

Gilligan, C. (1982). In a different voice: Psychological theory and women's development. Cambridge, MA: Harvard University Press.

Hossler, D., Bean, J. P., & Associates. (1990). *The strategic management of college enrollments*. San Francisco: Jossey-Bass.

Keeling, R. (Ed.). (2004). *Learning reconsidered: A campus-wide focus on the student experience*. Washington, DC: American College Personnel Association & National Association of Student Personnel Administrators.

Keeling, R. (Ed.). (2006). *Learning reconsidered 2: A campus-wide focus on the student experience.* Washington, DC: American College Personnel Association & National Association of Student Personnel Administrators.

Knefelkamp, L. L., Widick, C., & Parker, C. A. (1978). Applying new developmental findings. *New Directions for Student Services, 4,* 69-78. San Francisco: Jossey-Bass.

Kohlberg, L., & Hersh, R. H. (1977). Moral development: A review of the theory. *Theory into Practice. 16,* 53-59

Marcia, J. E. (1966). Development and validation of ego-identity status. *Journal of Personality and Social Psychology, 3,* 551-558.

Mueller, P. (1971). *Intramurals: Programming and administration* (4th ed.). New York: Ronald Press Co.

Mull, R. F., Bayless, K. G., & Ross, C. M. (1987). *Recreational sports programming.* North Palm Beach, FL: The Athletic Institute.

National Center for Education Statistics. (October, 2003). *College/University Enrollment as Found in Projections of Education Statistics to 2013*. Washington, DC: Author.

National Intramural Recreational Sports Association, NIRSA National Center, 4185 SW Research Way, Corvallis, OR 97333-1067; Phone: 541-766-8211; Fax: 541-766-8284; e-mail: nirsa@nirsa.org; website: www.nirsa.org.

National Intramural-Recreational Sports Association. (1996). *General and specialty standards for collegiate recreational sports.* Champaign, IL: Human Kinetics.

National Intramural-Recreational Sports Association. (2004). *The value of recreational sports in higher education – Impact on student enrollment, success, and buying power.* Champaign, IL: Human Kinetics.

National Intramural-Recreational Sports Association. (2005). *Collegiate recreational sports facility construction report.* Champaign, IL: Human Kinetics.

Pascarella, E. T., & Terrenzini, P. T. (2005). *How college affects students: A third decade of research.* San Francisco: Jossey-Bass.

Perry, W. G. (1968). *Forms of intellectual and ethical development In the college years: A scheme.* New York: Holt, Rinehart & Winston.

Tinto, V. (1994). *Leaving college: Rethinking the causes and cures of student attrition (2nd ed.).* Chicago, IL: University Of Chicago Press.

Contextual Statement Contributors
Current Edition:
Doug Franklin, Ohio University

Previous Editions:
Dixie Bennett, Director of Campus Recreation & Student Union, Loyola University Chicago.

Recreational Sports Programs
CAS Standards and Guidelines

Part 1. MISSION

The mission of Recreational Sports Programs (RSP) must be to enhance the mind, body, and spirit of students and other eligible individuals by providing programs, services, and facilities that are responsive to the physical, social, recreational, and lifelong educational needs of the campus community as they relate to health, fitness, and learning.

To accomplish this mission, RSP should
- provide programs and services for participants that are conducive to the development of holistic health, particularly fitness and wellness
- provide comprehensive programs and services in a variety of program formats that reflect and promote the diversity of participant interests, needs, and ability levels
- provide participation, employment, and leadership opportunities designed to enhance learning, growth, and development
- provide participation, employment, and leadership opportunities designed to increase interaction and understanding among individuals from various backgrounds
- contribute to the public relations efforts of the institution, including the recruitment and retention of students, faculty members, and staff members
- facilitate service-learning opportunities for students
- work in collaboration with academic units to facilitate professional preparation opportunities for students
- provide programs, facilities, and equipment that are delivered in a safe, healthy, clean, accessible, and enjoyable environment
- ensure the effective administration, operation, and stewardship of all aspects of the RSP, working in collaboration with other services, programs, campus affiliates (e.g., faculty, staff, alumni, guests, families, general public), and academic units where appropriate

RSP must develop, disseminate, implement, and regularly review their missions. The mission must be consistent with the mission of the institution and with professional standards. The mission must be appropriate for the institution's student populations and community settings. Mission statements must reference student learning and development.

Part 2. PROGRAM

The formal education of students, consisting of the curriculum and the co-curriculum, must promote student learning and development outcomes that are purposeful, contribute to students' realization of their potential, and prepare students for satisfying and productive lives.

Recreational Sports Programs (RSP) must collaborate with colleagues and departments across the institution to promote student learning and development, persistence, and success.

Consistent with the institutional mission, RSP must identify relevant and desirable student learning and development outcomes from among the six domains and related dimensions:

Domain: knowledge acquisition, integration, construction, and application

- **Dimensions: understanding knowledge from a range of disciplines; connecting knowledge to other knowledge, ideas, and experiences; constructing knowledge; and relating knowledge to daily life**

Domain: cognitive complexity

- **Dimensions: critical thinking, reflective thinking, effective reasoning, and creativity**

Domain: intrapersonal development

- **Dimensions: realistic self-appraisal, self-understanding, and self-respect; identity development; commitment to ethics and integrity; and spiritual awareness**

Domain: interpersonal competence

- **Dimensions: meaningful relationships, interdependence, collaboration, and effective leadership.**

Domain: humanitarianism and civic engagement

- **Dimensions: understanding and appreciation of cultural and human differences, social responsibility, global perspective, and sense of civic responsibility**

Domain: practical competence

- **Dimensions: pursuing goals, communicating effectively, technical competence, managing personal affairs, managing career development, demonstrating professionalism, maintaining health and wellness, and living a purposeful and satisfying life**

[LD Outcomes: See *The Council for the Advancement of Standards Learning and Developmental Outcomes* statement for examples of outcomes related to these domains and dimensions.]

RSP must
- **assess relevant and desirable student learning and development**
- **provide evidence of impact on outcomes**
- **articulate contributions to or support of student learning and development in the domains not specifically assessed**
- **articulate contributions to or support of student persistence and success**
- **use evidence gathered through this process to create strategies for improvement of programs and services**

RSP must be
- **intentionally designed**
- **guided by theories and knowledge of learning and development**
- **integrated into the life of the institution**
- **reflective of developmental and demographic profiles of the student population**
- **responsive to needs of individuals, populations with distinct needs, and relevant constituencies**
- **delivered using multiple formats, strategies, and contexts**

Where institutions provide distance education, RSP must assist distance learners to achieve their educational goals by providing access to information about programs and services, to staff members who can address questions and concerns, and to counseling, advising, or other forms of assistance.

RSP must reflect the needs and interests of students and other eligible users.

Valid indicators include needs assessment surveys, research findings, and documented best practices.

RSP, in collaboration with other campus units and community providers when appropriate, should design programs and services through participation, employment, volunteerism, and leadership opportunities to encourage, enhance, and highlight the value of learning outcomes.

RSP should utilize various program delivery formats including
- informal - to provide for self-directed, individualized approach to participation. Specific times and facility locations should be reserved to provide a variety of self-directed individual or small group participation opportunities.
- intramural - to provide structured contests, challenges, meets, tournaments, and leagues for participants within the institution
- club - to provide opportunities for individuals to organize around a common interest. Opportunities should be available to students for a variety of interests within or beyond the institution.
- instructional - to provide individualized or group learning opportunities, knowledge, and skills through activity sessions, lessons, clinics, workshops, and various media
- extramural - to provide structured tournaments, contests, and meets between campus participants and other institutions

In addition to these program formats, the RSP may utilize specialized designations to describe programs or service delivery, including aquatics, fitness, wellness, outdoor, special events, special populations, and facilities.

Program planning and implementation process must be inclusive and include
- **equitable participation for men and women, with opportunities to participate at various levels of ability and disability**
- **interpretation of institutional policies and procedures**
- **a variety of opportunities that reflect and address cultural diversity**
- **participant involvement in shaping program content and procedures**
- **co-recreational activity with opportunities to participate at various levels of ability and disability**

Program operational planning and implementation process must include
- **participant safety through the use of rules, regulations, and facilities management**
- **effective risk management policies, procedures, and practices**
- **supervision of recreational sports activities and facilities**
- **facility coordination and scheduling**
- **consultation with groups and organizations for sport and fitness programming**
- **training of office and field staff**
- **conflict resolution management protocols**
- **procedures for the inventory, maintenance, and use and security of equipment**
- **recognition for participants, employees, and volunteers**
- **publicity, promotion, and media relations**
- **volunteerism in service delivery and leadership**
- **customer service practices**
- **promotion of socially responsible behaviors**

Part 3. ORGANIZATION AND LEADERSHIP

To achieve student and program outcomes, Recreational Sports Programs (RSP) must be

structured purposefully and organized effectively. RSP must have

- clearly stated goals
- current and accessible policies and procedures
- written performance expectations for employees
- functional work flow graphics or organizational charts demonstrating clear channels of authority

Leaders with organizational authority for the programs and services must provide strategic planning, supervision, and management; advance the organization; and maintain integrity through the following functions:

Strategic Planning

- articulate a vision and mission that drive short- and long-term planning
- set goals and objectives based on the needs of the population served and desired student learning or development and program outcomes
- facilitate continuous development, implementation, and assessment of goal attainment congruent with institutional mission and strategic plans
- promote environments that provide meaningful opportunities for student learning, development, and engagement
- develop and continuously improve programs and services in response to the changing needs of students served and evolving institutional priorities
- intentionally include diverse perspectives to inform decision making

Supervising

- manage human resource processes including recruitment, selection, development, supervision, performance planning, evaluation, recognition, and reward
- influence others to contribute to the effectiveness and success of the unit
- empower professional, support, and student staff to accept leadership opportunities
- offer appropriate feedback to colleagues and students on skills needed to become more effective leaders
- encourage and support professional development, collaboration with colleagues and departments across the institution, and scholarly contribution to the profession

Managing

- identify and address individual, organizational, and environmental conditions that foster or inhibit mission achievement
- plan, allocate, and monitor the use of fiscal, physical, human, intellectual, and technological resources
- use current and valid evidence to inform decisions
- incorporate sustainability practices in the management and design of programs, services, and facilities
- understand appropriate technologies and integrate them into programs and services
- be knowledgeable about codes and laws relevant to programs and services and ensure that staff members understand their responsibilities through appropriate training
- assess potential risks and take action to mitigate them

Advancing the Organization

- communicate effectively in writing, speaking, and electronic venues
- advocate for programs and services
- advocate for representation in strategic planning initiatives at appropriate divisional and institutional levels
- initiate collaborative interactions with internal and external stakeholders who have legitimate concerns about and interests in the functional area
- facilitate processes to reach consensus where wide support is needed
- inform other areas within the institution about issues affecting practice

Maintaining Integrity

- model ethical behavior and institutional citizenship
- share data used to inform key decisions in transparent and accessible ways
- monitor media used for distributing information about programs and services to ensure the content is current, accurate, appropriately referenced, and accessible

RSP leaders also must

- empower student staff and participants to build their own leadership skills
- value diversity through effective recruitment and retention of professional and student staff
- identify organization values and innovative opportunities
- establish risk management, technology, and marketing plans
- establish strategic, operational, and resource utilization plans
- manage facility resources
- advocate for financial and physical resources

RSP leaders must educate other institutional leaders about the significant differences in mission among intercollegiate athletics, physical education and recreation academic units, and the recreational sports programs.

Leaders should establish effective working relationships throughout their institution, with special emphasis on those units that impact, affect, or support the mission of the RSP. Leaders should actively seek opportunities for collaboration that may result in partnerships that benefit the institution as well as the RSP.

Members of the campus community should be involved in the selection, design, governance, and administration of programs and facilities. Students and other eligible users may be involved through participant, employee, and living unit committees, councils, and boards.

The organizational placement of recreational sports within the institution should ensure the accomplishment of the program's mission.

To fulfill its mission and goals effectively, RSP must maintain well-structured management functions, including planning, personnel, property and risk management, emergency response, purchasing, contract administration, marketing, financial control, and information systems.

A short and long range planning document that specifies goals, objectives, student learning outcomes, strategies, and timelines should be developed to provide direction for the program. This plan should be reviewed annually.

Purchasing and property management procedures should be designed to ensure value for money spent, security for equipment and supplies, and maintenance of property inventories.

Other areas for consideration in determining structure and management of the RSP should include
- size, nature, and mission of the institution
- scope of recreational sports programs
- philosophy and method of service delivery
- financial resources
- availability and characteristics of facilities

Part 4. HUMAN RESOURCES

Recreational Sports Programs (RSP) must be staffed adequately by individuals qualified to accomplish mission and goals.

Within institutional guidelines, RSP must
- establish procedures for staff recruitment and selection, training, performance planning, and evaluation
- set expectations for supervision and performance

- assess the performance of employees individually and as a team
- provide access to continuing and advanced education and appropriate professional development opportunities to improve the leadership ability, competence, and skills of all employees.

RSP must maintain position descriptions for all staff members.

To create a diverse staff, RSP must institute recruitment and hiring strategies that encourage individuals from under-represented populations to apply for positions.

RSP must develop promotion practices that are fair, inclusive, proactive, and non-discriminatory.

To further the recruitment and retention of staff, RSP must consider work life initiatives, such as compressed work schedules, flextime, job sharing, remote work, or telework.

RSP professional staff members must hold an earned graduate or professional degree in a field relevant to the position they hold or must possess an appropriate combination of educational credentials and related work experience.

RSP professional staff members must engage in continuing professional development activities to keep abreast of the research, theories, legislation, policies, and developments that affect their programs and services.

RSP must have technical and support staff members adequate to accomplish their mission. All members of the staff must be technologically proficient and qualified to perform their job functions, be knowledgeable about ethical and legal uses of technology, and have access to training and resources to support the performance of their assigned responsibilities.

Technical and support staff includes those positions with an expertise in such areas as customer service, facility/equipment maintenance and operations, marketing, information technology, fundraising, research, and business services.

Degree- or credential-seeking interns or graduate assistants must be qualified by enrollment in an appropriate field of study and by relevant experience. These individuals must be trained and supervised adequately by professional staff members holding educational credentials and related work experience appropriate for supervision. Supervisors must be cognizant of the roles of interns and graduate assistants as both student and employee and closely adhere to all parameters of their job descriptions, work hours, and schedules. Supervisors and the interns or graduate assistants must agree to compensatory time or other appropriate compensation if circumstances necessitate additional hours.

RSP should provide graduate assistant and/or internship opportunities to enhance professional preparation experiences. Desirable characteristics of interns and graduate assistants should include: knowledge of the principles and philosophy of recreational sports, demonstrated skills on leadership and communication, a well-developed sense of responsibility, sensitivity to individual differences, academic success, enthusiasm for working with students, and an understanding of current issues facing students.

Student employees and volunteers must be carefully selected, trained, supervised, and evaluated. They must be educated on how and when to refer those in need of additional assistance to qualified staff members and must have access to a supervisor for assistance in making these judgments. Student employees and volunteers must be provided clear job descriptions, pre-service training based on assessed needs, and continuing development.

RSP should develop mechanisms designed to recognize employees and volunteers. These efforts should recognize contributions, improvements, and involvement.

All RSP staff members, including student employees and volunteers, must receive specific training on institutional policies pertaining to functions or activities they support and to privacy and confidentiality policies and laws regarding access to student records and other sensitive institutional information.

All RSP staff members must receive training on policies and procedures related to the use of technology to store or access student records and institutional data.

RSP must ensure that staff members are knowledgeable about and trained in emergency procedures, crisis response, and prevention efforts. Prevention efforts must address identification of threatening conduct or behavior of students, faculty and staff members, and others and must incorporate a system for responding and reporting.

RSP must ensure that staff members are knowledgeable of and trained in safety and emergency procedures for securing and vacating facilities.

Part 5. ETHICS

Recreational Sports Programs (RSP) must review relevant professional ethical standards and must adopt or develop and implement appropriate statements of ethical practice.

RSP must publish and adhere to statements of ethical practice and ensure their periodic review by relevant constituencies.

RSP must orient new staff members to relevant ethical standards and statements of ethical practice and related institutional policies.

Ethical standard statements utilized by relevant professional associations should be reviewed in the formulation of RSP ethical standards.

Statements of ethical standards must specify that staff members respect privacy and maintain confidentiality in all communications and records to the extent that such communications and records are protected under relevant privacy laws.

Statements of ethical standards must specify limits on disclosure of information contained in students' educational records as well as requirements to disclose to appropriate authorities.

Statements of ethical standards must address personal and economic conflicts of interest, or appearance thereof, by staff members in the performance of their work.

Statements of ethical standards must reflect the responsibility of staff members to be fair, objective, and impartial in their interactions with others.

Statements of ethical standards must reference management of institutional funds.

Statements of ethical standards must reference appropriate behavior regarding research and assessment with human participants, confidentiality of research and assessment data, and students' rights and responsibilities.

Statements of ethical standards must include the expectation that RSP staff members confront and hold accountable other staff members who exhibit unethical behavior.

Statements of ethical standards must address issues surrounding scholarly integrity.

As appropriate, RSP staff members must inform users of programs and services of ethical obligations and limitations emanating from codes and laws or from licensure requirements.

RSP staff members must recognize and avoid conflicts of interest that could adversely influence their judgment or objectivity and, when unavoidable, recuse themselves from the situation.

RSP staff members must perform their duties within the limits of their position, training, expertise, and competence.

When these limits are exceeded, individuals in need of further assistance must be referred to persons possessing appropriate qualifications.

Promotional and descriptive information must be accurate and free of deception.

RSP must adhere to institutional policies regarding ethical and legal use of software and technology.

Part 6. LAW, POLICY, AND GOVERNANCE

Recreational Sports Programs (RSP) must be in compliance with laws, regulations, and policies that relate to their respective responsibilities and that pose legal obligations, limitations, risks, and liabilities for the institution as a whole. Examples include constitutional, statutory, regulatory, and case law; relevant law and orders emanating from codes and laws; and the institution's policies.

To address and minimize the risks inherent in RSP, a comprehensive risk management plan must be implemented.

Development and implementation of a risk management plan should include: identification of appropriate certifications, training and development of personnel, development and implementation of emergency action and critical incident plans, accident care and documentation, participant waivers and consents, participant conduct policies, and the inspection, supervision, and care of facilities and equipment.

RSP must inform staff members, appropriate officials, and users of programs and services about existing and changing legal obligations, risks and liabilities, and limitations.

RSP must have written policies on all relevant operations, transactions, or tasks that have legal implications.

RSP must regularly review policies. The revision and creation of policies must be informed by best practices, available evidence, and policy issues in higher education.

RSP staff members must use reasonable and informed practices to limit the liability exposure of the institution and its officers, employees, and agents. RSP staff members must be informed about institutional policies regarding risk management, personal liability, and related insurance coverage options and must be referred to external sources if the institution does not provide coverage.

The institution must provide access to legal advice for staff members as needed to carry out assigned responsibilities.

Recreational sports professionals should understand legal responsibilities related to individual rights and liability including but not limited to due process, employment procedures, equal opportunity, civil rights and liberties, and liability of wrongful or negligent acts.

RSP should conduct a periodic audit of its policies and practices with university counsel and risk management officials.

RSP must have procedures and guidelines consistent with institutional policy for responding to threats, emergencies, and crisis situations. Systems and procedures must be in place to disseminate timely and accurate information to students, other members of the institutional community, and appropriate external organizations during emergency situations.

RSP staff members must neither participate in nor condone any form of harassment or activity that demeans persons or creates an intimidating, hostile, or offensive environment.

RSP must obtain permission to use copyrighted materials and instruments. RSP must purchase the materials and instruments from legally compliant sources or seek alternative permission from the publisher or owner. References to copyrighted materials and instruments must include appropriate citations.

RSP staff members must be knowledgeable about internal and external governance systems that affect programs and services.

Part 7. DIVERSITY, EQUITY, AND ACCESS

Within the context of each institution's unique mission and in accordance with institutional polices and all applicable codes and laws, Recreational Sports Programs (RPS) must create and maintain educational and work environments that are
- welcoming, accessible, and inclusive to persons of diverse backgrounds
- equitable and non-discriminatory
- free from harassment

RSP must not discriminate on the basis of ability; age; cultural identity; ethnicity; family educational history (e.g., first generation to attend college); gender identity and expression; nationality; political affiliation; race; religious affiliation; sex; sexual orientation; economic, marital, social, or veteran status; or any other basis included in institutional policies and codes and laws.

RSP must
- advocate for greater sensitivity to

multicultural and social justice concerns by the institution and its personnel
- modify or remove policies, practices, facilities, structures, systems, and technologies that limit access, discriminate, or produce inequities
- include diversity, equity, and access initiatives within their strategic plans
- foster communication that deepens understanding of identity, culture, self-expression, and heritage
- promote respect about commonalities and differences among people within their historical and cultural contexts
- address the characteristics and needs of a diverse population when establishing and implementing culturally relevant and inclusive programs, services, policies, procedures, and practices
- provide staff members with access to multicultural training and hold staff members accountable for integrating the training into their work
- respond to the needs of all students and other populations served when establishing hours of operation and developing methods of delivering programs, services, and resources
- ensure physical, program, and resource access for persons with disabilities
- recognize the needs of distance learning students by providing appropriate and accessible services and resources or by assisting them in gaining access to other appropriate services and resources in their geographic region

RSP must adhere to applicable government standards and legal directives regarding access.

RSP must define the eligible user population, with consideration given to such groups as undergraduate and graduate students, faculty members, staff, retirees, alumni, and the general public.

RSP should
- consider the impact of fees and charges on access to programs and services
- participate in establishing institutional facility scheduling policies to support and encourage appropriate and equitable utilization of resources

In support of diversity, RSP must
- **publish, post, and circulate a statement to articulate a commitment to diversity in programs, services, and staffing**
- **recruit, hire, and seek to retain a diverse professional and student staff**
- **include diversity education for its employees**

and volunteers
- **reach out to diverse and under-represented populations through such means as surveys, assessments, focus groups, and campus organizations to identify needs and interests used in program design and delivery and in student employment practices**

Part 8. INSTITUTIONAL AND EXTERNAL RELATIONS

Recreational Sports Programs (RSP) must reach out to relevant individuals, groups, communities, and organizations internal and external to the institution to
- establish, maintain, and promote understanding and effective relations with those that have a significant interest in or potential effect on the students or other constituents served by the programs and services
- garner support and resources for programs and services as defined by the mission statement
- disseminate information about the programs and services
- collaborate, where appropriate, to assist in offering or improving programs and services to meet the needs of students and other constituents and to achieve program and student outcomes
- engage diverse individuals, groups, communities, and organizations to enrich the educational environment and experiences of students and other constituents

RSP must have procedures and guidelines consistent with institutional policy for
- communicating with the media
- contracting with external organizations for delivery of programs and services
- cultivating, soliciting, and managing gifts
- applying to and managing funds from grants

RSP should establish advisory councils to facilitate communication and collaboration with other campus and community units to improve programs and services. Representatives should be solicited from a variety of units and should represent diverse users. This may include representatives from student organizations, student union, clinical health services, health promotion services, counseling services, campus information visitor services, career services, student government, faculty and staff governance councils, conference services, residence halls/apartments, cultural centers, fraternity and sorority affairs, academics, campus police/public safety, athletics, alumni affairs, financial affairs, and physical plant. Community organizations may include hospitals and recreation and fitness centers.

Part 9. FINANCIAL RESOURCES

Recreational Sports Programs (RSP) must have funding to accomplish the mission and goals. In establishing funding priorities and making significant changes, a comprehensive analysis must be conducted to determine the following elements: unmet needs of the unit, relevant expenditures, external and internal resources, and impact on students and the institution.

RSP must demonstrate efficient and effective use and responsible stewardship of fiscal resources consistent with institutional protocols.

Institutional funds for RSP should be allocated to ensure long-term viability. Sources of income may include governmental appropriations, student fees (e.g., general, recreational, or health), user fees, donations, contributions, sponsorships, fines, entry fees, rentals, grants, contracts, dues, concessions, and retail sales.

If student funds from any source are dedicated to RSP, those funds should be designated for programs and services that directly benefit students, and the students should retain first priority for the use of facilities, programs, equipment, and services.

The budget process must include consideration of all expenses that are incurred in order to produce a quality RSP.

Expenses include but are not limited to programs and operations, human resource processes and labor costs, support area expenses (e.g., technology, facility support, member services, marketing, research and development), equipment replacement, capital improvement, administrative cost recovery, and reserve account allocations.

Expenditures should be based upon departmental and institutional goals and protocols, periodic needs assessments, and cost/benefit analysis.

All members of RSP staff should be accountable for financial and other resources.

Part 10. TECHNOLOGY

Recreational Sports Programs (RSP) must have adequate technology to support the achievement of their mission and goals. The technology and its use must comply with institutional policies and procedures and be evaluated for compliance with relevant codes and laws.

RSP must use current technology to provide updated information regarding mission, location, staffing, programs, services, and official contacts to students and designated clients.

RSP must explore the use of technology to enhance

delivery of programs and services, especially for students at a distance or external constituencies.

When technology is used to facilitate student learning and development, RSP must select technology that reflects intended outcomes.

RSP must
- maintain policies and procedures that address the security, confidentiality, and backup of data, as well as compliance with privacy laws
- have clearly articulated plans in place for protecting confidentiality and security of information when using Internet-based technologies
- develop plans for replacing and updating existing hardware and software as well as plans for integrating new technically-based or supported programs, including systems developed internally by the institution, systems available through professional associations, or private vendor-based systems

Technology, as well as workstations or computer labs maintained by programs and services for student use, must be accessible to all designated clients and must meet established technology standards for delivery to persons with disabilities.

When providing student access to technology, RSP must
- have policies on the use of technology that are clear, easy to understand, and available to all students
- provide assistance, information, or referral to appropriate support services to those needing help accessing or using technology
- provide instruction or training on how to use the technology
- inform students on the legal and ethical implications of misuse as it pertains to intellectual property, harassment, privacy, and social networks

Student violations of technology policies must follow established institutional student disciplinary procedures.

Students who experience negative emotional or psychological consequences from the use of technology must be referred to support services provided by the institution.

Part 11. FACILITIES AND EQUIPMENT

Recreational Sports Programs (RSP) must have adequate, accessible, and suitably located facilities and equipment to support the mission and goals.

If acquiring capital equipment as defined by the institution, RSP must take into account expenses related to regular maintenance and life cycle costs. Facilities and equipment must be evaluated on an established cycle, including consideration of sustainability, and be in compliance with codes and laws to provide for access, health, safety, and security.

RSP staff members must have workspace that is well equipped, adequate in size, and designed to support their work and responsibilities. For conversations requiring privacy, staff members must have access to a private space.

RSP staff members who share workspace must be able to secure their own work.

The design of the facilities must guarantee the security and privacy of records and ensure the confidentiality of sensitive information.

The location and layout of the facilities must be sensitive to the needs of persons with disabilities as well as the needs of other constituencies.

The institution must provide adequate indoor and outdoor facilities with a documented facility usage schedule that includes prioritized blocks of time for RSP to accommodate the needs and interests of the campus community. The use of the facilities must be coordinated to provide efficient and effective utilization.

The schedule should be disseminated to all user groups and reviewed periodically.

Institutions should use available research and assessment data when assessing facility needs. Consideration should be given to sustainability and to a balance of facilities that support the program delivery formats of RSP. Examples of such facilities include swimming pools, strength and cardiovascular training facilities, multi-purpose activity spaces, multi-use fields, nature trails, group exercise and dance rooms, challenge adventure facilities, martial arts mat/ studio rooms, personal training rooms, mind-body studios, health and wellness labs, skateboard and rollerblade venues, and racquet sport courts. Facilities should provide activity areas that are diverse as well as flexible and spaces for such support activities as offices, member services, repair rooms, locker/shower rooms, and storage.

Social space should be provided for users to encourage socialization and an inclusive environment. Examples of such facilities include lounges, lobbies, or food service areas.

Renovation, design, and development of facilities must adhere to applicable laws.

RSP may also refer to separate standards and guidelines for specializations governed by professional organizations for the use of facilities.

Technology resources including software and hardware as well as resources for training should be available to support RSP.

RSP must provide equipment adequate to meet the needs of participants.

Institutions should use available research and other assessment data when assessing technology and equipment needs.

RSP must require personal protective equipment and safety devices as appropriate.

Processes must be established for determining needs, inspecting, cleaning, maintaining, repairing, and replacing equipment.

RSP must establish appropriate policies and procedures for responding to emergency situations, especially where RSP facilities, personnel, and resources could assist the institution.

Part 12. ASSESSMENT AND EVALUATION

Recreational Sports Programs (RSP) must have a clearly articulated assessment plan to document achievement of stated goals and learning outcomes, demonstrate accountability, provide evidence of improvement, and describe resulting changes in programs and services.

RSP must have adequate fiscal, human, professional development, and technological resources to develop and implement assessment plans.

Assessments must include direct and indirect evaluation and use qualitative and quantitative methodologies and existing evidence, as appropriate, to determine whether and to what degree the stated mission, goals, and intended outcomes are being met as effectively and efficiently as possible. The process must employ sufficient and sound measures to ensure comprehensiveness. Data collected must include responses from students and other constituencies, and aggregated results must be shared with those groups. Results of assessments must be shared appropriately with multiple constituents.

Evaluation procedures should yield evidence relative to student/staff recruitment and retention, the achievement of program goals, scope of program offerings, responsiveness to expressed interests, program attendance and effectiveness, participant satisfaction, cost effectiveness, quality of facilities, equipment use and maintenance, staff performance, recruitment and retention, and data as a result of benchmarking against other programs.

Data sources should include student and other eligible users and nonusers. Data should include program evaluations and internal or external assessments and should be maintained in the office of the RSP administrator. They should be accessible to planners of subsequent programs.

RSP should pursue best practices and meaningful research to review and improve programs and services.

Results of assessments and evaluations must be used to identify needs and interests in revising and improving programs and services, recognizing staff performance, maximizing resource efficiency and effectiveness, improving student achievement of learning and development outcomes, and improving student persistence and success. Changes resulting from the use of assessments and evaluation must be shared with stakeholders.

General Standards revised in 2011;
RSP content developed/revised in 1986, 1996, & 2007

The Role of Registrar Programs and Services
CAS Standards Contextual Statement

Registrars, at least in function, were the first administrative positions created after institutional presidents. The position dates back to the end of the 12th century in Europe, and the title, "Registrar," first appeared at Oxford University in 1446.

Registrars were the original, all-purpose campus administrators. The role initially developed from the faculty, with a primary function to be an administrative officer that supported the academic functions of the institution. Everything from admissions, collecting tuition, keeping records of faculty meetings, and maintaining student records were included in the job responsibilities. The Registrar has always been somewhat of a generalist—and still is today, even if the role is not quite as diverse as it was a few hundred years ago.

Organizationally, the Registrar's Office is most often found in either Academic Affairs or Student Affairs. Because the position evolved out of the faculty, it was and still is integrated with academic issues. There has been an ebb and flow of the Registrar's Office between Academic Affairs and Student Affairs, depending upon where other academic support services, such as financial aid and admission, have been located.

The Office of the Registrar supports the academic mission of institutions through providing services (often in-person and virtually) such as (not an exhaustive list) course set up and subsequent registration opportunity; classroom assignment; establishment and enforcement of educational policy; academic record creation and maintenance; institutional compliance with state and federal regulations; records privacy education and regulation; grade processing; transfer credit evaluation; transcripts and certification of enrollment; degree progress monitoring; data management and reporting (i.e., graduation rates, degree progress data, course demand, predictive analytics); degree clearance and diploma preparation; and graduation ceremonies. The exact set of responsibilities within the Office of the Registrar varies widely by institutional type, size, and reporting structure.

As a service provider, Registrars' offices face similar trends and challenges that all of higher education is currently experiencing. Quickly and ever evolving technologies require the office to be mindful of new and improved ways of doing business; however, being nimble is a challenge because competing campus projects continually stretch information technology resources. Technology is not a panacea, and as budgets shrink technology can only replace so many functions that people used to do. State and federal calls for accountability and outcomes-based assessment land squarely in Registrars' offices as these offices regularly have responsibility for reporting. Students increasingly demand integrated services, so the office must work closely with areas that they may not have in the past; this is not a bad thing, just a new reality.

References, Readings, and Resources

American Association of Registrars and Admissions Officers (AACRAO): www.aacrao.org\

Lauren, B. (2006). *The registrar's guide: Evolving best practices in records and registration.* Washington, DC: American Association of Collegiate Registrars and Admissions Officers.

Pace, H. L. (2011). The evolving office of the registrar. *College and University, 86*(3), pp. 3-7.

Rooker, L. (ed.), Falkner, T. M., Hicks, D. J., Myers, B. A, & Shirley, S. *2010 FERPA Guide,* American Association of Collegiate Registrars and Admissions Officers.

Contextual Statement Contributors
Tina Falkner, University of Minnesota
Brad Myers, The Ohio State University

Registrar Programs and Services
CAS Standards and Guidelines

Part 1. MISSION

The mission of Registrar Programs and Services (RPS) is to maintain stewardship and integrity of student academic records and manage student and institutional academic policies. Therefore, RPS must
- maintain student academic records in perpetuity
- collaborate with complementary services regarding enrollment management functions
- coordinate academic calendars and academic registration
- support academic advising activities
- interpret, implement, and ensure compliance with policies and procedures related to academic record-keeping
- provide accurate individual and aggregate data to internal and external constituencies

Such constituencies needing data may include but are not limited to offices of institutional research, assessment, or enrollment management; faculty members and administrators; accreditation or certification agencies; athletic associations with whom the institution holds membership; entities providing services for veterans or students with special needs; and provincial/state/federal government agencies, such as Homeland Security in the US.

RPS must develop, disseminate, implement, and regularly review their missions. The mission must be consistent with the mission of the institution and with professional standards. The mission must be appropriate for the institution's student populations and community settings. Mission statements must reference student learning and development.

Part 2. PROGRAM

The formal education of students, consisting of the curriculum and the co-curriculum, must promote student learning and development outcomes that are purposeful, contribute to students' realization of their potential, and prepare students for satisfying and productive lives.

Registrar Programs and Services (RPS) must collaborate with colleagues and departments across the institution to promote student learning and development, persistence, and success.

Consistent with the institutional mission, RPS must identify relevant and desirable student learning and development outcomes from among the six domains and related dimensions:

Domain: knowledge acquisition, integration, construction, and application
- **Dimensions: understanding knowledge from a range of disciplines; connecting knowledge to other knowledge, ideas, and experiences; constructing knowledge; and relating knowledge to daily life**

Domain: cognitive complexity
- **Dimensions: critical thinking, reflective thinking, effective reasoning, and creativity**

Domain: intrapersonal development
- **Dimensions: realistic self-appraisal, self-understanding, and self-respect; identity development; commitment to ethics and integrity; and spiritual awareness**

Domain: interpersonal competence
- **Dimensions: meaningful relationships, interdependence, collaboration, and effective leadership.**

Domain: humanitarianism and civic engagement
- **Dimensions: understanding and appreciation of cultural and human differences, social responsibility, global perspective, and sense of civic responsibility**

Domain: practical competence
- **Dimensions: pursuing goals, communicating effectively, technical competence, managing personal affairs, managing career development, demonstrating professionalism, maintaining health and wellness, and living a purposeful and satisfying life**

[LD Outcomes: See *The Council for the Advancement of Standards Learning and Developmental Outcomes* statement for examples of outcomes related to these domains and dimensions.]

RPS must
- **assess relevant and desirable student learning and development**
- **provide evidence of impact on outcomes**
- **articulate contributions to or support of student learning and development in the domains not specifically assessed**
- **articulate contributions to or support of student persistence and success**
- **use evidence gathered through this process to create strategies for improvement of**

programs and services

RPS must be
- intentionally designed
- guided by theories and knowledge of learning and development
- integrated into the life of the institution
- reflective of developmental and demographic profiles of the student population
- responsive to needs of individuals, populations with distinct needs, and relevant constituencies
- delivered using multiple formats, strategies, and contexts

Where institutions provide distance education, RPS must assist distance learners to achieve their educational goals by providing access to information about programs and services, to staff members who can address questions and concerns, and to counseling, advising, or other forms of assistance.

RPS must
- treat students courteously with respect for them as individuals
- ensure that relevant policies and procedures, including record changes, are communicated effectively to students, faculty members, and other affected constituents
- provide accurate information to all constituents
- provide timely service to all constituents
- ensure the accuracy and reliability of the data collected and distributed
- provide for the maintenance, upkeep, security, integrity, and proper dissemination of academic information
- develop and implement effective and secure processes for exchange of transcripts between institutions
- provide leadership on the implementation of cooperative academic programs, articulation agreements, and other programs involving academic credit
- ensures that cooperative agreements articulate the responsibility for student support and services and the appropriate student conduct policies
- develop a workable disaster recovery plan that will allow RPS to function in the event of catastrophic circumstances
- educate the institutional community with regard to the security and release of student data

In support of the overall mission of the institution, and when responsibility is assigned, RPS must
- provide leadership for developing and maintaining the student record data base and archival files
- provide campus leadership for the application of information technology to academic processes, records, and information
- ensure that the security and confidentiality of student record data are maintained throughout the institution
- contribute to the enrollment management efforts of the institution
- provide a registration process for enrolling students in classes each term, which may include the calculation of tuition and fees
- verify student academic eligibility for graduation, honors, academic probation, or dismissal
- coordinate course schedules to provide information on courses and sections being offered in any given term with their day, time, location, and delivery formats
- coordinate the scheduling of appropriate space and resources for classes, including non-classroom-based courses
- manage the transfer of matriculating student records from admissions to RPS
- document approved transfer credit
- verify records for graduation for the preparation and distribution of diplomas
- provide information about courses, programs, policies, and procedures for the development of institutional publications, websites, and other educational materials
- provide information on academic regulations, policies, and procedures including appeals processes
- certify student enrollment status (e.g., veterans services, rehabilitation services, student loans, insurance, athletic eligibility, residency status)
- provide reports as required (e.g., class rosters, grade rosters, grade reports, transcripts, committee needs)
- provide appropriate institutional access to academic records and information
- prepare statistical reports (as needed for institutional research, enrollment management, assessment, and other purposes, e.g., enrollment projections, retention, attrition, and graduation rates)

If responsibility for other student records, policies, procedures, or regulations is assigned to the RPS, those matters should be handled in accordance with the standards above.

RPS may also be responsible for the academic calendar, coordinate the arrangements for commencement, and provide administrative support to the faculty governance bodies.

RPS should develop appropriate policies and procedures for allowing students to be referenced by a preferred name.

Part 3. ORGANIZATION AND LEADERSHIP

To achieve student and program outcomes, Registrar Programs and Services (RPS) must be structured purposefully and organized effectively. RPS must have

- clearly stated goals
- current and accessible policies and procedures
- written performance expectations for employees
- functional work flow graphics or organizational charts demonstrating clear channels of authority

Leaders with organizational authority for the programs and services must provide strategic planning, supervision, and management; advance the organization; and maintain integrity through the following functions:

Strategic Planning

- articulate a vision and mission that drive short- and long-term planning
- set goals and objectives based on the needs of the population served and desired student learning or development and program outcomes
- facilitate continuous development, implementation, and assessment of goal attainment congruent with institutional mission and strategic plans
- promote environments that provide meaningful opportunities for student learning, development, and engagement
- develop and continuously improve programs and services in response to the changing needs of students served and evolving institutional priorities
- intentionally include diverse perspectives to inform decision making

Supervising

- manage human resource processes including recruitment, selection, development, supervision, performance planning, evaluation, recognition, and reward
- influence others to contribute to the effectiveness and success of the unit
- empower professional, support, and student staff to accept leadership opportunities
- offer appropriate feedback to colleagues and students on skills needed to become more effective leaders
- encourage and support professional development, collaboration with colleagues and departments across the institution, and scholarly contribution to the profession

Managing

- identify and address individual, organizational, and environmental conditions that foster or inhibit mission achievement
- plan, allocate, and monitor the use of fiscal, physical, human, intellectual, and technological resources
- use current and valid evidence to inform decisions
- incorporate sustainability practices in the management and design of programs, services, and facilities
- understand appropriate technologies and integrate them into programs and services
- be knowledgeable about codes and laws relevant to programs and services and ensure that staff members understand their responsibilities through appropriate training
- assess potential risks and take action to mitigate them

Advancing the Organization

- communicate effectively in writing, speaking, and electronic venues
- advocate for programs and services
- advocate for representation in strategic planning initiatives at appropriate divisional and institutional levels
- initiate collaborative interactions with internal and external stakeholders who have legitimate concerns about and interests in the functional area
- facilitate processes to reach consensus where wide support is needed
- inform other areas within the institution about issues affecting practice

Maintaining Integrity

- model ethical behavior and institutional citizenship
- share data used to inform key decisions in transparent and accessible ways
- monitor media used for distributing information about programs and services to ensure the content is current, accurate, appropriately referenced, and accessible

RPS leaders must

- ensure that newly adopted technologies meet standards of data integrity and accuracy
- be sensitive to the special needs of students such as part-time students, non-traditional students, students with disabilities, LGBT students, students of various ethnic and

cultural groups, distance learners, students studying off campus, international students, and students who restrict information access under privacy laws

- **be sensitive to the special needs of faculty members including those teaching abroad and those using distance learning or other alternative delivery systems**

RPS leaders should have

- the skill to motivate and inspire staff members to develop a team atmosphere
- fiscal management skills
- the ability to identify and apply relevant information technology
- strong communication, customer relationship, and service management skills

RPS leaders should

- maintain awareness of changing technology and how it applies to RPS; communicate changes to others and educate them about rationale for adopting technologies
- assess decision-making and problem-solving models and select those most appropriate to the institutional milieu
- incorporate student input in decision-making, as appropriate
- serve as a catalyst in institution-wide partnerships due to the broad scope of RPS responsibilities
- demonstrate a philosophy of service to students and the institution
- maintain awareness of the changing ways people identify and how they name their identities to include references to race, ethnicity, gender identity, and sexual orientation
- provide leadership in institutional compliance with federal, state/provincial, and local regulations

RPS must identify and be responsive to external constraints and requirements that impact unit operation (e.g., implications of local, state/provincial, and federal regulations, governing body policies, union agreements, accreditation, professional associations, athletic conference requirements).

RPS should

- develop an organizational chart that identifies cooperative interrelationships with other institutional units and those outside the institution (e.g., institutions with cooperative programs or agreements, study abroad partnerships)
- coordinate programs and services with other institutional personnel, offices, functions, and activities
- collaborate with other enrollment management offices
- establish clear and concise criteria for decision-

making and define primary responsibility when more than one unit is involved

Part 4. HUMAN RESOURCES

Registrar Programs and Services (RPS) must be staffed adequately by individuals qualified to accomplish mission and goals.

Within institutional guidelines, RPS must

- **establish procedures for staff recruitment and selection, training, performance planning, and evaluation**
- **set expectations for supervision and performance**
- **assess the performance of employees individually and as a team**
- **provide access to continuing and advanced education and appropriate professional development opportunities to improve the leadership ability, competence, and skills of all employees.**

RPS must maintain position descriptions for all staff members.

To create a diverse staff, RPS must institute recruitment and hiring strategies that encourage individuals from under-represented populations to apply for positions.

RPS must develop promotion practices that are fair, inclusive, proactive, and non-discriminatory.

To further the recruitment and retention of staff, RPS must consider work life initiatives, such as compressed work schedules, flextime, job sharing, remote work, or telework.

RPS professional staff members must hold an earned graduate or professional degree in a field relevant to the position they hold or must possess an appropriate combination of educational credentials and related work experience.

RPS professional staff members must engage in continuing professional development activities to keep abreast of the research, theories, legislation, policies, and developments that affect their programs and services.

RPS must have technical and support staff members adequate to accomplish their mission. All members of the staff must be technologically proficient and qualified to perform their job functions, be knowledgeable about ethical and legal uses of technology, and have access to training and resources to support the performance of their assigned responsibilities.

Degree- or credential-seeking interns or graduate

assistants must be qualified by enrollment in an appropriate field of study and by relevant experience. These individuals must be trained and supervised adequately by professional staff members holding educational credentials and related work experience appropriate for supervision. Supervisors must be cognizant of the roles of interns and graduate assistants as both student and employee and closely adhere to all parameters of their job descriptions, work hours, and schedules. Supervisors and the interns or graduate assistants must agree to compensatory time or other appropriate compensation if circumstances necessitate additional hours.

Student employees and volunteers must be carefully selected, trained, supervised, and evaluated. They must be educated on how and when to refer those in need of additional assistance to qualified staff members and must have access to a supervisor for assistance in making these judgments. Student employees and volunteers must be provided clear job descriptions, pre-service training based on assessed needs, and continuing development.

All RPS staff members, including student employees and volunteers, must receive specific training on institutional policies pertaining to functions or activities they support and to privacy and confidentiality policies and laws regarding access to student records and other sensitive institutional information.

All RPS staff members must receive training on policies and procedures related to the use of technology to store or access student records and institutional data.

RPS must ensure that staff members are knowledgeable about and trained in emergency procedures, crisis response, and prevention efforts. Prevention efforts must address identification of threatening conduct or behavior of students, faculty and staff members, and others and must incorporate a system for responding and reporting.

RPS must ensure that staff members are knowledgeable of and trained in safety and emergency procedures for securing and vacating facilities.

Specific titles and reporting structures will vary based on institutional mission, goals, and objectives. RPS should report to a senior officer in academic affairs, student affairs, or enrollment management.

On-going training and staff development should be designed to enhance and broaden understanding of roles and responsibilities within the office and the institution. The support staff should be skilled in interpersonal communications, public relations, knowledge of campus resources, dissemination of information, and the handling of complex and detailed activities. Development for the support staff should include adequate initial training to be able to represent the institution in their office function in a competent, professional, and educational manner.

Part 5. ETHICS

Registrar Programs and Services (RPS) must review relevant professional ethical standards and must adopt or develop and implement appropriate statements of ethical practice.

RPS must publish and adhere to statements of ethical practice and ensure their periodic review by relevant constituencies.

RPS must orient new staff members to relevant ethical standards and statements of ethical practice and related institutional policies.

RPS offices must develop appropriate protocols regarding such disclosure of information and must ensure that all staff members, including students, are trained to understand and follow department policies.

Basic principles of privacy and confidentiality must govern both electronic and paper communications and records. RPS must ensure that the institution has a written policy and published statement regarding confidentiality of records and procedures for access, release, and challenge of educational records, and that the means for enforcement are clearly delineated.

Statements of ethical standards must specify that staff members respect privacy and maintain confidentiality in all communications and records to the extent that such communications and records are protected under relevant privacy laws.

Statements of ethical standards must specify limits on disclosure of information contained in students' educational records as well as requirements to disclose to appropriate authorities.

Statements of ethical standards must address personal and economic conflicts of interest, or appearance thereof, by staff members in the performance of their work.

Statements of ethical standards must reflect the responsibility of staff members to be fair, objective, and impartial in their interactions with others.

Statements of ethical standards must reference management of institutional funds.

Statements of ethical standards must reference

appropriate behavior regarding research and assessment with human participants, confidentiality of research and assessment data, and students' rights and responsibilities.

Statements of ethical standards must include the expectation that RPS staff members confront and hold accountable other staff members who exhibit unethical behavior.

Statements of ethical standards must address issues surrounding scholarly integrity.

As appropriate, RPS staff members must inform users of programs and services of ethical obligations and limitations emanating from codes and laws or from licensure requirements.

RPS staff members must recognize and avoid conflicts of interest that could adversely influence their judgment or objectivity and, when unavoidable, recuse themselves from the situation.

RPS staff members must perform their duties within the limits of their position, training, expertise, and competence.

When these limits are exceeded, individuals in need of further assistance must be referred to persons possessing appropriate qualifications.

Promotional and descriptive information must be accurate and free of deception.

RPS must adhere to institutional policies regarding ethical and legal use of software and technology.

Part 6. LAW, POLICY, AND GOVERNANCE

Registrar Programs and Services (RPS) must be in compliance with laws, regulations, and policies that relate to their respective responsibilities and that pose legal obligations, limitations, risks, and liabilities for the institution as a whole. Examples include constitutional, statutory, regulatory, and case law; relevant law and orders emanating from codes and laws; and the institution's policies.

RPS must inform staff members, appropriate officials, and users of programs and services about existing and changing legal obligations, risks and liabilities, and limitations.

RPS must have written policies on all relevant operations, transactions, or tasks that have legal implications.

RPS must regularly review policies. The revision and creation of policies must be informed by best practices, available evidence, and policy issues in higher education.

RPS staff members must use reasonable and informed practices to limit the liability exposure of the institution and its officers, employees, and agents. Staff members must be informed about institutional policies regarding risk management, personal liability, and related insurance coverage options and must be referred to external sources if the institution does not provide coverage.

The institution must provide access to legal advice for staff members as needed to carry out assigned responsibilities.

RPS must have procedures and guidelines consistent with institutional policy for responding to threats, emergencies, and crisis situations. Systems and procedures must be in place to disseminate timely and accurate information to students, other members of the institutional community, and appropriate external organizations during emergency situations.

RPS staff members must neither participate in nor condone any form of harassment or activity that demeans persons or creates an intimidating, hostile, or offensive environment.

RPS must obtain permission to use copyrighted materials and instruments. RPS must purchase the materials and instruments from legally compliant sources or seek alternative permission from the publisher or owner. References to copyrighted materials and instruments must include appropriate citations.

RPS staff members must be knowledgeable about internal and external governance systems that affect programs and services.

RPS must provide leadership in the development of institutional policies related to educational information and appropriate legal issues, especially privacy laws. RPS must ensure that the institution has written policies on all RPS transactions that may have legal implications.

Relevant areas include privacy laws (e.g., Family Educational Rights and Privacy Act (FERPA) in the USA); affirmative action policies; certification of academic transcript information; academic and disciplinary sanctions and dismissals; parental access to records; refund policies; fraudulent records; name changes; gender transitioning; record-keeping practices; facility scheduling policies; access to student information systems; residency status determination; student enrollment status; policies on applicant and student criminal or judicial history; requests for information from government or law enforcement agencies (e.g., in the USA, those related to Homeland Security or the Solomon Amendment); security procedures; social security number usage; court orders; and subpoenas. RPS leaders should meet with the institution's legal counsel regularly to review all relevant documents for clarity and to determine that current regulations are being followed.

RPS must have procedures to keep staff members informed of all requirements related to the maintenance of academic records. RPS must ensure that procedures and forms used to implement regulations must be developed and regularly reviewed to assure fulfillment of institutional requirements.

RPS staff should meet with the institution's legal counsel periodically to review all relevant documents for clarity and to determine that current regulations are being followed. Some of the relevant areas that should be reviewed include affirmative action policies; certification of academic transcript information; academic and disciplinary sanctions and dismissals; parental access to records; privacy laws; refund policies; fraudulent records; name changes; gender transitioning; record-keeping practices; facility scheduling policies; access to student information systems; residency status determination; student enrollment status; policies on applicant and student criminal or judicial history; requests for information from government or law enforcement agencies (e.g., those related to Homeland Security or the Solomon Amendment in the USA); security procedures; social security number usage; court orders; and subpoenas.

Part 7. DIVERSITY, EQUITY, AND ACCESS

Within the context of each institution's unique mission and in accordance with institutional polices and all applicable codes and laws, Registrar Programs and Services (RPS) must create and maintain educational and work environments that are
- **welcoming, accessible, and inclusive to persons of diverse backgrounds**
- **equitable and non-discriminatory**
- **free from harassment**

RPS must not discriminate on the basis of ability; age; cultural identity; ethnicity; family educational history (e.g., first generation to attend college); gender identity and expression; nationality; political affiliation; race; religious affiliation; sex; sexual orientation; economic, marital, social, or veteran status; or any other basis included in institutional policies and codes and laws.

RPS must
- **advocate for greater sensitivity to multicultural and social justice concerns by the institution and its personnel**
- **modify or remove policies, practices, facilities, structures, systems, and technologies that limit access, discriminate, or produce inequities**
- **include diversity, equity, and access initiatives within their strategic plans**
- **foster communication that deepens**

understanding of identity, culture, self-expression, and heritage
- **promote respect about commonalities and differences among people within their historical and cultural contexts**
- **address the characteristics and needs of a diverse population when establishing and implementing culturally relevant and inclusive programs, services, policies, procedures, and practices**
- **provide staff members with access to multicultural training and hold staff members accountable for integrating the training into their work**
- **respond to the needs of all students and other populations served when establishing hours of operation and developing methods of delivering programs, services, and resources**
- **ensure physical, program, and resource access for persons with disabilities**
- **recognize the needs of distance learning students by providing appropriate and accessible services and resources or by assisting them in gaining access to other appropriate services and resources in their geographic region**

Part 8. INSTITUTIONAL AND EXTERNAL RELATIONS

Registrar Programs and Services (RPS) must reach out to relevant individuals, groups, communities, and organizations internal and external to the institution to
- **establish, maintain, and promote understanding and effective relations with those that have a significant interest in or potential effect on the students or other constituents served by the programs and services**
- **garner support and resources for programs and services as defined by the mission statement**
- **disseminate information about the programs and services**
- **collaborate, where appropriate, to assist in offering or improving programs and services to meet the needs of students and other constituents and to achieve program and student outcomes**
- **engage diverse individuals, groups, communities, and organizations to enrich the educational environment and experiences of students and other constituents**

Relevant constituencies include administrators, faculty members, students, alumni, and the public, as well as other institutions with which there are articulation agreements, cooperative programs, or transfer of students.

RPS must have procedures and guidelines consistent with institutional policy for
- **communicating with the media**
- **contracting with external organizations for delivery of programs and services**
- **cultivating, soliciting, and managing gifts**
- **applying to and managing funds from grants**

RPS must provide leadership to the institution to set standards regarding interpretation of policy and appropriate dissemination of information.

Part 9. FINANCIAL RESOURCES

Registrar Programs and Services (RPS) must have funding to accomplish the mission and goals. In establishing funding priorities and making significant changes, a comprehensive analysis must be conducted to determine the following elements: unmet needs of the unit, relevant expenditures, external and internal resources, and impact on students and the institution.

RPS must demonstrate efficient and effective use and responsible stewardship of fiscal resources consistent with institutional protocols.

RPS leaders must comply with the institution's financial policies that could affect the budget, with required accounting reports that track expenditures, and with policies governing unused funds.

Expenses specific to RPS responsibilities may include purchase and maintenance of customized software systems, adequate security of electronic and hard-copy data, and appropriate back-up systems for all data.

Part 10. TECHNOLOGY

Registrar Programs and Services (RPS) must have adequate technology to support the achievement of their mission and goals. The technology and its use must comply with institutional policies and procedures and be evaluated for compliance with relevant codes and laws.

RPS must use current technology to provide updated information regarding mission, location, staffing, programs, services, and official contacts to students and designated clients.

RPS must explore the use of technology to enhance delivery of programs and services, especially for students at a distance or external constituencies.

When technology is used to facilitate student learning and development, RPS must select technology that reflects intended outcomes.

RPS must

- **maintain policies and procedures that address the security, confidentiality, and backup of data, as well as compliance with privacy laws**
- **have clearly articulated plans in place for protecting confidentiality and security of information when using Internet-based technologies**
- **develop plans for replacing and updating existing hardware and software as well as plans for integrating new technically-based or supported programs, including systems developed internally by the institution, systems available through professional associations, or private vendor-based systems**

Technology, as well as workstations or computer labs maintained by programs and services for student use, must be accessible to all designated clients and must meet established technology standards for delivery to persons with disabilities.

When providing student access to technology, RPS must
- **have policies on the use of technology that are clear, easy to understand, and available to all students**
- **provide assistance, information, or referral to appropriate support services to those needing help accessing or using technology**
- **provide instruction or training on how to use the technology**
- **inform students on the legal and ethical implications of misuse as it pertains to intellectual property, harassment, privacy, and social networks**

Student violations of technology policies must follow established institutional student disciplinary procedures.

Students who experience negative emotional or psychological consequences from the use of technology must be referred to support services provided by the institution.

Backup copies of important documentation such as transcripts, the student data base, and the processes for accessing the back-ups must be stored off site in the event of a natural disaster or damage to the records.

RPS should provide to other offices and departments appropriate access to store or retrieve data on students they serve.

Part 11. FACILITIES AND EQUIPMENT

Registrar Programs and Services (RPS) must have adequate, accessible, and suitably located facilities

and equipment to support the mission and goals. If acquiring capital equipment as defined by the institution, RPS must take into account expenses related to regular maintenance and life cycle costs. Facilities and equipment must be evaluated on an established cycle, including consideration of sustainability, and be in compliance with codes and laws to provide for access, health, safety, and security.

When RPS is responsible for determining facilities usage outside the immediate office, policies and procedures must be developed and disseminated with respect to the assignment of such space.

RPS staff members must have workspace that is well equipped, adequate in size, and designed to support their work and responsibilities. For conversations requiring privacy, staff members must have access to a private space.

RPS staff members who share workspace must be able to secure their own work.

The design of the facilities must guarantee the security and privacy of records and ensure the confidentiality of sensitive information.

The location and layout of the facilities must be sensitive to the needs of persons with disabilities as well as the needs of other constituencies.

Part 12. ASSESSMENT AND EVALUATION

Registrar Programs and Services (RPS) must have a clearly articulated assessment plan to document achievement of stated goals and learning outcomes, demonstrate accountability, provide evidence of improvement, and describe resulting changes in programs and services.

RPS must have adequate fiscal, human, professional development, and technological resources to develop and implement assessment plans.

Assessments must include direct and indirect evaluation and use qualitative and quantitative methodologies and existing evidence, as appropriate, to determine whether and to what degree the stated mission, goals, and intended outcomes are being met as effectively and efficiently as possible. The process must employ sufficient and sound measures to ensure comprehensiveness. Data collected must include responses from students and other constituencies, and aggregated results must be shared with those groups. Results of assessments must be shared appropriately with multiple constituents.

Results of assessments and evaluations must be used to identify needs and interests in revising and improving programs and services, recognizing staff performance, maximizing resource efficiency and effectiveness, improving student achievement of learning and development outcomes, and improving student persistence and success. Changes resulting from the use of assessments and evaluation must be shared with stakeholders.

Student input should be incorporated into program improvement and policy development.

General Standards revised in 2011;
RPS content developed/revised in 1995 & 2008

The Role of Service-Learning Programs
CAS Standards Contextual Statement

Service-learning enables colleges and universities to meet their goals for student learning and development while making unique contributions to addressing community, national, and global needs. Both college students and the communities they serve stand to reap substantial benefits from engaging in service-learning. Among frequently cited benefits to student participants are developing the habit of critical reflection; deepening comprehension of course content; integrating theory with practice; increasing understanding of the issues underlying social problems; strengthening sense of social responsibility; enhancing cognitive, personal, and spiritual development; heightening understanding of human difference and commonality; and sharpening abilities to solve problems creatively and to work collaboratively.

Community benefits include new energy and assistance to broaden delivery of existing services or to begin new ones, fresh approaches to solving problems, access to resources, and opportunities to participate in teaching and learning. Through improved town-gown relationships, colleges and universities also gain additional new learning settings for students and new opportunities for faculty to orient research and teaching to meet human and community needs.

For the purpose of the *CAS Standards for Service-Learning Programs*, service-learning is defined as follows: Service-learning is a form of experiential education in which students engage in activities that address human and community needs together with structured opportunities intentionally designed to promote student learning and development. The hyphen in service-learning is critical in that it symbolizes the symbiotic relationship between the service and the learning. The term community in the definition of service-learning refers to local neighborhoods, the state, the nation, and the world community. Service-learning enables all participants to define their needs and interests (Jacoby, 1996).

Reflection and reciprocity are fundamental concepts of service-learning. As a form of experiential education, service-learning is based on the pedagogical principle that learning and development do not necessarily occur as a result of experience itself. Rather, they occur as a result of reflection intentionally designed to foster learning and development. Service-learning programs emphasize various types of learning goals, including intellectual, civic, ethical, moral, cross-cultural, and spiritual. Programs may highlight different combinations of these goals. Service-learning programs are also explicitly structured to promote learning about the larger social issues behind the needs to which the service is responding. This learning includes a deeper understanding of the historical, sociological, cultural, economic, and political contexts of the needs or issues being addressed. Reflection can take many forms: individual and group, oral and written, and directly related to discipline-based course material or not.

The other essential concept of service-learning is reciprocity between the server and the person or group being served. Service-learning avoids placing students into community settings based solely on desired student-learning outcomes and provision of services that do not meet actual needs or perpetuate a state of need rather than seeking and addressing the causes of need. Through reciprocity, students develop a greater sense of belonging and responsibility as members of a larger community.

Service-learning thus stands in contrast to the traditional, one-way approach to service in which one person or group has resources that they share with a person or group that it is assumed lacks resources. Reciprocity also eschews the concept of service that is based on the idea that a more competent person comes to the aid of a less competent person. Service-learning encourages students to do things *with* others rather than *for* them. Everyone should expect to learn and change in the process.

Although service-learning that is embedded in the curriculum provides opportunities for faculty to enhance students' learning by integrating course content with practical experience in a structured manner intended to meet course objectives, powerful opportunities for student learning and development also occur outside the classroom. Student affairs professionals can and do involve students in co-curricular service-learning programs that contribute to their learning and development. Although service-learning that is connected to faculty research and community involvement can lead to more broad-based and long-term community enhancement, shorter-term service projects also make considerable contributions to communities in both direct and indirect ways. Even one-time experiences that address community needs and that are designed to achieve specific student learning and development outcomes can appropriately be called service-learning.

References, Readings, and Resources

Campus Compact, www.compact.org.

Eyler, J., & Giles, D. (1999). *Where's the learning in service-learning?* San Francisco: Jossey-Bass.

Howard, J. (Ed.). (2001, Summer). *Service-Learning course design workbook.* Ann Arbor, MI: University of Michigan.

Jacoby, B. (Ed.). (2003). *Building partnerships for service-learning.* San Francisco: Jossey-Bass.

Jacoby, B. (Ed.). (1996). *Service-Learning in higher education:*

Concepts and practices. San Francisco: Jossey-Bass.

Kendall, J. (Ed.). (1990). *Combining service and learning: A resource book for community and public service,* Vol. 1. Raleigh, N.C.: National Society for Experiential Education.

Michigan Journal of Community Service Learning, www.umich.edu/~ocsl/MJCSL.

National Service-Learning Clearinghouse, www.servicelearning.org.

Porter Honnet, E., & Poulsen, S. J. (1989). *Principles of good practice for combining service and learning.* Racine, WI: Johnson Foundation.

Contextual Statement Contributors
Current Edition:
Craig Slack, University of Maryland

Previous Editions:
Barbara Jacoby, University of Maryland

Service-Learning Programs
CAS Standards and Guidelines

Part 1. MISSION

The primary mission of Service-Learning Programs (S-LP) is to engage students in experiences that address human and community needs together with structured opportunities for reflection intentionally designed to promote student learning and development.

S-LP must develop, disseminate, implement, and regularly review their missions. The mission must be consistent with the mission of the institution and with professional standards. The mission must be appropriate for the institution's student populations and community settings. Mission statements must reference student learning and development.

Part 2. PROGRAM

The formal education of students, consisting of the curriculum and the co-curriculum, must promote student learning and development outcomes that are purposeful, contribute to students' realization of their potential, and prepare students for satisfying and productive lives.

Service-Learning Programs (S-LP) must collaborate with colleagues and departments across the institution to promote student learning and development, persistence, and success.

Consistent with the institutional mission, S-LP must identify relevant and desirable student learning and development outcomes from among the six domains and related dimensions:

Domain: knowledge acquisition, integration, construction, and application

- Dimensions: understanding knowledge from a range of disciplines; connecting knowledge to other knowledge, ideas, and experiences; constructing knowledge; and relating knowledge to daily life

Domain: cognitive complexity

- Dimensions: critical thinking, reflective thinking, effective reasoning, and creativity

Domain: intrapersonal development

- Dimensions: realistic self-appraisal, self-understanding, and self-respect; identity development; commitment to ethics and integrity; and spiritual awareness

Domain: interpersonal competence

- Dimensions: meaningful relationships, interdependence, collaboration, and effective leadership.

Domain: humanitarianism and civic engagement

- Dimensions: understanding and appreciation of cultural and human differences, social responsibility, global perspective, and sense of civic responsibility

Domain: practical competence

- Dimensions: pursuing goals, communicating effectively, technical competence, managing personal affairs, managing career development, demonstrating professionalism, maintaining health and wellness, and living a purposeful and satisfying life

[LD Outcomes: See *The Council for the Advancement of Standards Learning and Developmental Outcomes* statement for examples of outcomes related to these domains and dimensions.]

S-LP must
- assess relevant and desirable student learning and development
- provide evidence of impact on outcomes
- articulate contributions to or support of student learning and development in the domains not specifically assessed
- articulate contributions to or support of student persistence and success
- use evidence gathered through this process to create strategies for improvement of programs and services

S-LP must be
- intentionally designed
- guided by theories and knowledge of learning and development
- integrated into the life of the institution
- reflective of developmental and demographic profiles of the student population
- responsive to needs of individuals, populations with distinct needs, and relevant constituencies
- delivered using multiple formats, strategies, and contexts

Where institutions provide distance education, S-LP must assist distance learners to achieve their educational goals by providing access to information about programs and services, to staff members who can address questions and concerns, and to counseling, advising, or other forms of assistance.

S-LP must be integrated into and enhance both the academic curriculum and co-curricular programs.

S-LP must

- **allow all participants to define their needs and interests**
- **engage students in responsible and purposeful actions to meet community-defined needs**
- **enable students to understand needs in the context of community assets**
- **articulate clear service and learning goals for everyone involved, including students, faculty and staff members, community agency personnel, and those being served**
- **ensure intellectual rigor**
- **establish criteria for selecting community service sites to ensure productive learning opportunities for everyone involved**
- **educate students regarding the philosophy of service and learning, the particular community service site, the work they will do, and the people they will be serving in the community**
- **establish and implement risk management procedures to protect students, the institution, and the community agencies**
- **offer alternatives to ensure that students are not required to participate in service that violates a religious or moral belief**
- **engage students in reflection designed to enable them to deepen their understanding of themselves, the community, and the complexity of social problems and potential solutions**
- **educate students to differentiate between perpetuating dependence and building capacity within the community**
- **establish mechanisms to assess service and learning outcomes for students and communities**
- **provide on-going professional development and support to faculty and staff members**

When course credit is offered for service-learning, the credit must be for learning, not only for service. Whether service-learning is for academic credit or not, the focus must be on learning and educational objectives, not on hours served.

S-LP must offer a wide range of curricular and co-curricular service-learning experiences appropriate for students at all developmental levels and with a variety of lifestyles and abilities.

Examples may include older students, commuter students, students who are parents, part-time students, fully employed students, and students with disabilities.

S-LP must initiate and maintain collaborative relations among faculty members and departments within the institution for the design and implementation of service-learning experiences. They must also develop partnerships with community-based organizations to meet organizations' service needs and to achieve student learning and development outcomes.

Service-learning experiences should include

- *One-time and short-term experiences.* These can be designed to achieve a variety of student learning outcomes, including introducing students to service-learning as a critical aspect of their college education, enabling students to learn what types of service best suit their interests, familiarizing students with the community in which the institution is located, and understanding the approaches different agencies take to address community problems. These experiences can be co-curricular or part of the academic curriculum, such as first-year seminars.

- *Discipline-based service-learning courses.* Such courses can be designed to enable students to deepen their understanding of course content, apply knowledge to practice, and test theory through practical application. These courses can be designed for students at all levels. Service-learning internships and capstone courses can provide opportunities for students to consider how disciplinary knowledge can be applied in a socially responsible manner in professional settings.

- *Community-based research.* Whether integrated into a course or done on an independent-study basis, students engage in community-based research work with faculty and community partners to design, conduct, analyze, and report research results to serve community purposes.

- *Intensive service-learning experiences.* Service-learning experiences can immerse students intensively in an unfamiliar setting or culture, whether domestically or abroad. They can engage in dialogue and problem solving with the people most affected by the issues and develop a sense of solidarity with people whose lives and perspectives differ from their own. These experiences vary in length from a one-week alternative break to a semester or a year.

The service-learning course syllabus or plan for co-curricular experiences should describe

- needs that the service will address
- desired outcomes of the service and learning for all participants

- assignments that link service and academic content
- opportunities to reflect on one's personal reactions to service and learning experiences
- logistics (e.g., time required, transportation, materials required)
- nature of the service work
- roles and responsibilities of students and community members
- risk management procedures
- evaluation of the service and learning experiences and assessment of the degree to which desired outcomes were achieved

S-LP should foster student leadership through service-learning experiences and should encourage student-initiated and student-led service and learning.

Part 3. ORGANIZATION AND LEADERSHIP

To achieve student and program outcomes, Service-Learning Programs (S-LP) must be structured purposefully and organized effectively. S-LP must have

- **clearly stated goals**
- **current and accessible policies and procedures**
- **written performance expectations for employees**
- **functional work flow graphics or organizational charts demonstrating clear channels of authority**

Leaders with organizational authority for the programs and services must provide strategic planning, supervision, and management; advance the organization; and maintain integrity through the following functions:

Strategic Planning
- **articulate a vision and mission that drive short- and long-term planning**
- **set goals and objectives based on the needs of the population served and desired student learning or development and program outcomes**
- **facilitate continuous development, implementation, and assessment of goal attainment congruent with institutional mission and strategic plans**
- **promote environments that provide meaningful opportunities for student learning, development, and engagement**
- **develop and continuously improve programs and services in response to the changing needs of students served and evolving institutional priorities**
- **intentionally include diverse perspectives to inform decision making**

Supervising

- **manage human resource processes including recruitment, selection, development, supervision, performance planning, evaluation, recognition, and reward**
- **influence others to contribute to the effectiveness and success of the unit**
- **empower professional, support, and student staff to accept leadership opportunities**
- **offer appropriate feedback to colleagues and students on skills needed to become more effective leaders**
- **encourage and support professional development, collaboration with colleagues and departments across the institution, and scholarly contribution to the profession**

Managing
- **identify and address individual, organizational, and environmental conditions that foster or inhibit mission achievement**
- **plan, allocate, and monitor the use of fiscal, physical, human, intellectual, and technological resources**
- **use current and valid evidence to inform decisions**
- **incorporate sustainability practices in the management and design of programs, services, and facilities**
- **understand appropriate technologies and integrate them into programs and services**
- **be knowledgeable about codes and laws relevant to programs and services and ensure that staff members understand their responsibilities through appropriate training**
- **assess potential risks and take action to mitigate them**

Advancing the Organization
- **communicate effectively in writing, speaking, and electronic venues**
- **advocate for programs and services**
- **advocate for representation in strategic planning initiatives at appropriate divisional and institutional levels**
- **initiate collaborative interactions with internal and external stakeholders who have legitimate concerns about and interests in the functional area**
- **facilitate processes to reach consensus where wide support is needed**
- **inform other areas within the institution about issues affecting practice**

Maintaining Integrity
- **model ethical behavior and institutional citizenship**
- **share data used to inform key decisions in**

transparent and accessible ways
- **monitor media used for distributing information about programs and services to ensure the content is current, accurate, appropriately referenced, and accessible**

Part 4. HUMAN RESOURCES

Service-Learning Programs (S-LP) must be staffed adequately by individuals qualified to accomplish mission and goals.

Within institutional guidelines, S-LP must
- **establish procedures for staff recruitment and selection, training, performance planning, and evaluation**
- **set expectations for supervision and performance**
- **assess the performance of employees individually and as a team**
- **provide access to continuing and advanced education and appropriate professional development opportunities to improve the leadership ability, competence, and skills of all employees.**

S-LP must maintain position descriptions for all staff members.

To create a diverse staff, S-LP must institute recruitment and hiring strategies that encourage individuals from under-represented populations to apply for positions.

S-LP must develop promotion practices that are fair, inclusive, proactive, and non-discriminatory.

To further the recruitment and retention of staff, S-LP must consider work life initiatives, such as compressed work schedules, flextime, job sharing, remote work, or telework.

S-LP professional staff members must hold an earned graduate or professional degree in a field relevant to the position they hold or must possess an appropriate combination of educational credentials and related work experience.

Professional development of staff and faculty members engaged in service-learning programs should address how to
- build relationships with community agencies
- establish and maintain collaborative relationships with campus units
- engage students in community action for the common good
- prepare, mentor, and monitor students to deliver services according to legal and risk management policies
- use learning strategies that are effective in achieving learning outcomes
- engage students in structured opportunities for reflection
- develop, implement, and evaluate service and learning goals
- facilitate the process of identifying student and community needs and interests
- clarify the responsibilities of students, the institution, and agencies
- match the unique needs of agencies and students
- sustain genuine and active commitment of students, the institution, and agencies
- educate, train, and support students to facilitate service-learning experiences for their peers
- ensure that the time commitments for service and learning are balanced and appropriate
- foster participation by and with diverse populations
- develop fiscal and other resources for program support

Faculty and staff members who integrate service-learning into their courses should receive institutional support (e.g., reduced course load, mini-grants, or teaching assistants.)

SL-P staff should provide professional development for community partners regarding how to work effectively with students, faculty members, and staff in higher education institutions.

S-LP professional staff members must engage in continuing professional development activities to keep abreast of the research, theories, legislation, policies, and developments that affect their programs and services.

S-LP must have technical and support staff members adequate to accomplish their mission. All members of the staff must be technologically proficient and qualified to perform their job functions, be knowledgeable about ethical and legal uses of technology, and have access to training and resources to support the performance of their assigned responsibilities.

Degree- or credential-seeking interns or graduate assistants must be qualified by enrollment in an appropriate field of study and by relevant experience. These individuals must be trained and supervised adequately by professional staff members holding educational credentials and related work experience appropriate for supervision. Supervisors must be cognizant of the roles of interns and graduate assistants as both student and employee and closely adhere to all parameters of their job descriptions, work hours, and schedules. Supervisors and the interns or graduate assistants must agree to compensatory time or other appropriate compensation if circumstances necessitate additional hours.

Student employees and volunteers must be carefully selected, trained, supervised, and evaluated. They must be educated on how and when to refer those in need of additional assistance to qualified staff members and must have access to a supervisor for assistance in making these judgments. Student employees and volunteers must be provided clear job descriptions, pre-service training based on assessed needs, and continuing development.

All S-LP staff members, including student employees and volunteers, must receive specific training on institutional policies pertaining to functions or activities they support and to privacy and confidentiality policies and laws regarding access to student records and other sensitive institutional information.

All S-LP staff members must receive training on policies and procedures related to the use of technology to store or access student records and institutional data.

S-LP must ensure that staff members are knowledgeable about and trained in emergency procedures, crisis response, and prevention efforts. Prevention efforts must address identification of threatening conduct or behavior of students, faculty and staff members, and others and must incorporate a system for responding and reporting.

S-LP must ensure that staff members are knowledgeable of and trained in safety and emergency procedures for securing and vacating facilities.

Part 5. ETHICS

Service-Learning Programs (S-LP) must review relevant professional ethical standards and must adopt or develop and implement appropriate statements of ethical practice.

S-LP must publish and adhere to statements of ethical practice and ensure their periodic review by relevant constituencies.

The faculty members, staff, and students involved in service-learning must be held to the same ethical standards as the SL-P staff members.

S-LP must orient new staff members to relevant ethical standards and statements of ethical practice and related institutional policies.

Statements of ethical standards must specify that staff members respect privacy and maintain confidentiality in all communications and records to the extent that such communications and records are protected under relevant privacy laws.

Statements of ethical standards must specify limits on disclosure of information contained in students' educational records as well as requirements to disclose to appropriate authorities.

Statements of ethical standards must address personal and economic conflicts of interest, or appearance thereof, by staff members in the performance of their work.

Statements of ethical standards must reflect the responsibility of staff members to be fair, objective, and impartial in their interactions with others.

Statements of ethical standards must reference management of institutional funds.

Statements of ethical standards must reference appropriate behavior regarding research and assessment with human participants, confidentiality of research and assessment data, and students' rights and responsibilities.

Statements of ethical standards must include the expectation that S-LP staff members confront and hold accountable other staff members who exhibit unethical behavior.

Statements of ethical standards must address issues surrounding scholarly integrity.

As appropriate, S-LP staff members must inform users of programs and services of ethical obligations and limitations emanating from codes and laws or from licensure requirements.

S-LP staff members must recognize and avoid conflicts of interest that could adversely influence their judgment or objectivity and, when unavoidable, recuse themselves from the situation.

S-LP staff members must perform their duties within the limits of their position, training, expertise, and competence.

When these limits are exceeded, individuals in need of further assistance must be referred to persons possessing appropriate qualifications.

All faculty and staff members responsible for supervising service-learning activities must monitor student performance based on training expertise and competence and alter placements as needed.

Promotional and descriptive information must be accurate and free of deception.

S-LP must adhere to institutional policies regarding ethical and legal use of software and technology.

Part 6. LAW, POLICY, AND GOVERNANCE

Service-Learning Programs (S-LP) must be in

compliance with laws, regulations, and policies that relate to their respective responsibilities and that pose legal obligations, limitations, risks, and liabilities for the institution as a whole. Examples include constitutional, statutory, regulatory, and case law; relevant law and orders emanating from codes and laws; and the institution's policies.

S-LP must inform staff members, appropriate officials, and users of programs and services about existing and changing legal obligations, risks and liabilities, and limitations.

S-LP must have written policies on all relevant operations, transactions, or tasks that have legal implications.

S-LP must regularly review policies. The revision and creation of policies must be informed by best practices, available evidence, and policy issues in higher education.

S-LP staff members must use reasonable and informed practices to limit the liability exposure of the institution and its officers, employees, and agents. S-LP staff members must be informed about institutional policies regarding risk management, personal liability, and related insurance coverage options and must be referred to external sources if the institution does not provide coverage.

The institution must provide access to legal advice for staff members as needed to carry out assigned responsibilities.

S-LP must have procedures and guidelines consistent with institutional policy for responding to threats, emergencies, and crisis situations. Systems and procedures must be in place to disseminate timely and accurate information to students, other members of the institutional community, and appropriate external organizations during emergency situations.

S-LP staff members must neither participate in nor condone any form of harassment or activity that demeans persons or creates an intimidating, hostile, or offensive environment.

S-LP must obtain permission to use copyrighted materials and instruments. S-LP must purchase the materials and instruments from legally compliant sources or seek alternative permission from the publisher or owner. References to copyrighted materials and instruments must include appropriate citations.

S-LP staff members must be knowledgeable about internal and external governance systems that affect programs and services.

Part 7. DIVERSITY, EQUITY, AND ACCESS

Within the context of each institution's unique mission and in accordance with institutional polices and all applicable codes and laws, Service-Learning Programs (S-LP) must create and maintain educational and work environments that are
- welcoming, accessible, and inclusive to persons of diverse backgrounds
- equitable and non-discriminatory
- free from harassment

S-LP must not discriminate on the basis of ability; age; cultural identity; ethnicity; family educational history (e.g., first generation to attend college); gender identity and expression; nationality; political affiliation; race; religious affiliation; sex; sexual orientation; economic, marital, social, or veteran status; or any other basis included in institutional policies and codes and laws.

S-LP must
- advocate for greater sensitivity to multicultural and social justice concerns by the institution and its personnel
- modify or remove policies, practices, facilities, structures, systems, and technologies that limit access, discriminate, or produce inequities
- include diversity, equity, and access initiatives within their strategic plans
- foster communication that deepens understanding of identity, culture, self-expression, and heritage
- promote respect about commonalities and differences among people within their historical and cultural contexts
- address the characteristics and needs of a diverse population when establishing and implementing culturally relevant and inclusive programs, services, policies, procedures, and practices
- provide staff members with access to multicultural training and hold staff members accountable for integrating the training into their work
- respond to the needs of all students and other populations served when establishing hours of operation and developing methods of delivering programs, services, and resources
- ensure physical, program, and resource access for persons with disabilities
- recognize the needs of distance learning students by providing appropriate and accessible services and resources or by assisting them in gaining access to other appropriate services and resources in their

geographic region

Part 8. INSTITUTIONAL AND EXTERNAL RELATIONS

Service-Learning Programs (S-LP) must reach out to relevant individuals, groups, communities, and organizations internal and external to the institution to

- establish, maintain, and promote understanding and effective relations with those that have a significant interest in or potential effect on the students or other constituents served by the programs and services
- garner support and resources for programs and services as defined by the mission statement
- disseminate information about the programs and services
- collaborate, where appropriate, to assist in offering or improving programs and services to meet the needs of students and other constituents and to achieve program and student outcomes
- engage diverse individuals, groups, communities, and organizations to enrich the educational environment and experiences of students and other constituents

If there is more than one campus unit that facilitates community service and service-learning experiences, those offices should share information and collaborate as appropriate.

S-LP should develop productive working relationships with a wide range of campus agencies, including risk management, transportation, health services, academic departments and colleges, leadership programs, orientation, student activities, and institutional relationships and development.

Service-learning flourishes best when the institution as a whole is engaged as a responsible citizen in its surrounding communities. S-LP professionals should advocate for the institution to share its resources with its community and to develop a wide range of mutually beneficial campus-community partnerships.

S-LP must have procedures and guidelines consistent with institutional policy for

- communicating with the media
- contracting with external organizations for delivery of programs and services
- cultivating, soliciting, and managing gifts
- applying to and managing funds from grants

Part 9. FINANCIAL RESOURCES

Service-Learning Programs (S-LP) must have funding to accomplish the mission and goals. In establishing funding priorities and making significant changes, a comprehensive analysis must be conducted to determine the following elements: unmet needs of the unit, relevant expenditures, external and internal resources, and impact on students and the institution.

S-LP must demonstrate efficient and effective use and responsible stewardship of fiscal resources consistent with institutional protocols.

Part 10. TECHNOLOGY

Service-Learning Programs (S-LP) must have adequate technology to support the achievement of their mission and goals. The technology and its use must comply with institutional policies and procedures and be evaluated for compliance with relevant codes and laws.

S-LP must use current technology to provide updated information regarding mission, location, staffing, programs, services, and official contacts to students and designated clients.

S-LP must explore the use of technology to enhance delivery of programs and services, especially for students at a distance or external constituencies.

When technology is used to facilitate student learning and development, S-LP must select technology that reflects intended outcomes.

S-LP must

- maintain policies and procedures that address the security, confidentiality, and backup of data, as well as compliance with privacy laws
- have clearly articulated plans in place for protecting confidentiality and security of information when using Internet-based technologies
- develop plans for replacing and updating existing hardware and software as well as plans for integrating new technically-based or supported programs, including systems developed internally by the institution, systems available through professional associations, or private vendor-based systems

Technology, as well as workstations or computer labs maintained by programs and services for student use, must be accessible to all designated clients and must meet established technology standards for delivery to persons with disabilities.

When providing student access to technology, S-LP must

- have policies on the use of technology that are clear, easy to understand, and available to all students

- provide assistance, information, or referral to appropriate support services to those needing help accessing or using technology
- provide instruction or training on how to use the technology
- inform students on the legal and ethical implications of misuse as it pertains to intellectual property, harassment, privacy, and social networks

Student violations of technology policies must follow established institutional student disciplinary procedures.

Students who experience negative emotional or psychological consequences from the use of technology must be referred to support services provided by the institution.

Part 11. FACILITIES AND EQUIPMENT

Service-Learning Programs (S-LP) must have adequate, accessible, and suitably located facilities and equipment to support the mission and goals. If acquiring capital equipment as defined by the institution, S-LP must take into account expenses related to regular maintenance and life cycle costs. Facilities and equipment must be evaluated on an established cycle, including consideration of sustainability, and be in compliance with codes and laws to provide for access, health, safety, and security.

S-LP staff members must have workspace that is well equipped, adequate in size, and designed to support their work and responsibilities. For conversations requiring privacy, staff members must have access to a private space.

S-LP staff members who share workspace must be able to secure their own work.

The design of the facilities must guarantee the security and privacy of records and ensure the confidentiality of sensitive information.

The location and layout of the facilities must be sensitive to the needs of persons with disabilities as well as the needs of other constituencies.

Part 12. ASSESSMENT AND EVALUATION

Service-Learning Programs (S-LP) must have a clearly articulated assessment plan to document achievement of stated goals and learning outcomes, demonstrate accountability, provide evidence of improvement, and describe resulting changes in programs and services.

S-LP must have adequate fiscal, human, professional development, and technological resources to develop and implement assessment plans.

Assessments must include direct and indirect evaluation and use qualitative and quantitative methodologies and existing evidence, as appropriate, to determine whether and to what degree the stated mission, goals, and intended outcomes are being met as effectively and efficiently as possible. The process must employ sufficient and sound measures to ensure comprehensiveness. Data collected must include responses from students and other constituencies, and aggregated results must be shared with those groups. Results of assessments must be shared appropriately with multiple constituents.

Results of assessments and evaluations must be used to identify needs and interests in revising and improving programs and services, recognizing staff performance, maximizing resource efficiency and effectiveness, improving student achievement of learning and development outcomes, and improving student persistence and success. Changes resulting from the use of assessments and evaluation must be shared with stakeholders.

General Standards revised in 2011;
S-LP content developed in 2005

The Role of Sexual Assault and Relationship Violence Prevention Programs
CAS Standards Contextual Statement

Introduction

Sexual Assault and Relationship Violence Prevention Programs (SARVPP) operate under the assumption that (a) all students deserve to learn in an environment free from violence and (b) students cannot learn if they do not feel safe. Unfortunately, college campuses often have violence, particularly sexual and relationship violence. Research shows that more than 1 in 3 women (35.6%) and more than 1 in 4 men (28.5%) in the United States have experienced rape, physical violence, and/or stalking by a relationship in their lifetimes (Black, Basile, Breiding, Smith, Walters, Merrick, Chen, & Stevens, 2011), and 28 percent of high school and college students experience dating violence at some point (Brustin, 1995). Clearly there is a need for SARVPP to develop policies and protocols in order to respond to incidents of sexual assault, relationship violence, and stalking but also to educate students and raise awareness in order to prevent and reduce the risk of this type of violence.

History

The movement to address sexual and relationship violence on college campuses came out of the larger anti-rape movement in the United States when college students and staff began to notice an increase in the number of survivors willing to report incidents on campus, not necessarily to police or officials, but to offices such as Residence Life, Health Center, Women's Center, or Counseling Center.

Sexual violence prevention programs, begun on some college campuses in the early 1970s, were frequently located in a health center or women's center. Mostly run by student volunteers, these programs developed their early expertise from students' own experiences and the experiences of their friends. In those early days, research literature to guide sexual violence response practices was scarce; it was not until Burgess and Holmstrom (1974) coined the term Rape Trauma Syndrome that advocates and counselors had a meaningful theoretical framework to understand the experiences of sexual violence victims.

After a number of high-profile cases, many individual institutions began to form their own SARVPP, and legislators became aware of the prevalence of sexual and relationship violence on college campuses. Although many institutions began sexual violence programs in the 1980s, it was not until the mid-1990s that many campuses began to address relationship violence. Some colleges and universities did not provide assistance or programs on domestic violence because of the common misperception that this type of violence only happened in heterosexual marital relationships and not in a dating or casual sex context that better characterized the experiences of the general undergraduate population

(Bogal-Allbritten & Allbritten, 1991).

Federal legislation, in particular the Jeanne Clery Disclosure of Campus Security Policy and Campus Crime Statistics Act (also known as the Campus Security Act), was signed into law in 1990. It required institutions of higher education to annually report incidents of violent crime to the Department of Education. This act was amended in 1992 to include the Campus Sexual Assault Victim's Bill of Rights that requires all colleges and universities that receive federal funding to provide victims with a set of basic rights, such as access to counseling and other services. In 1994, Congress passed the Violence Against Women Act (VAWA), and federal funds were made available five years later through grants to campuses to prevent violence against women. As a result of the increased attention to these crimes on college campuses as well as federal support for programming, more institutions began to respond to incidents of sexual assault, relationship violence, and stalking through the development of offices or programs dedicated to this issue. Recently, the focus of SARVPP has widened to include educational programming and other efforts to prevent the initial occurrence of violence.

Definitions

The following definitions of terms are commonly used to understand and report sexual violence.

Effective Consent. Clear, verbal, sober, affirmative consent must be obtained for each and every sexual activity to constitute effective consent. Consensual sexual conduct is a mutual decision reached by both parties without any hint of force, threat, coercion, pressure, fraud, manipulation, intimidation, or fear of injury. Consent cannot be given if the victim is mentally or physically incapacitated, due to use of alcohol and/or other drugs or due to a temporary or permanent mental or physical condition. Silence, passivity, or lack of active resistance does not imply consent. In addition, previous participation in sexual activity does not indicate current consent to participate. Consent to one form of sexual activity does not imply consent to other forms of sexual activity. Consent can be withdrawn at any point during sexual activity.

Sexual Assault. As defined by the National Center for Victims of Crime, sexual assault includes attacks such as rape or attempted rape, as well as any unwanted sexual act or contact or threats. Types of sexual acts that are considered sexual assault include: forced sexual intercourse (rape), forced oral or anal sex, child molestation, incest, fondling, and attempted rape. Perpetrators use many forms of violence to execute the attack including physical violence, threats, coercion, manipulation, pressure, or tricks.

Relationship Violence. Any acts of physical, psychological, emotional or economic harm, or threats of harm against a current or former relationship are considered relationship violence. This definition includes harm against individuals in same-sex relationships and does not require sexual intimacy between those involved.

- Physical Harm is defined as any act that uses physical force or weapons against another person (can also be other family members including pets) with the potential for causing death, disability, injury, or harm. Physical violence includes, but is not limited to, scratching, pushing, shoving, throwing, grabbing, biting, choking, shaking, slapping, punching, burning, use of a weapon and/or use of restraints, or one's body size or strength.
- Threat of Physical Harm is defined as the act of bullying, threatening, or using words, gestures, or weapons to communicate an intent or desire to cause death, disability, injury, or physical harm upon a current or former relationship.
- Psychological/Emotional Harm is defined as any act, threat, or coercive tactic used to degrade or control a relationship. This can include, but is not limited to, humiliation, controlling what another can and cannot do, withholding information, deliberately doing something to make an individual feel diminished or embarrassed, and isolating someone from friends and family.
- Economic Harm is defined as any acts, threats of acts, or coercive tactics used to degrade or control a relationship by limiting or denying access to money or other basic resources.

Stalking. Any course of harassing, threatening, or intimidating conduct that an individual has willfully and repeatedly (more than once) engaged in that reasonably and seriously alarms, torments, or terrorizes another individual or group of individuals can be defined as stalking. Stalking behaviors may include, but are not limited to, repeated abusive and excessive contact and/or monitoring using telephone calls, voice-mails, emails, instant messaging, text messages, and/or social media to one's home or work; installing spyware on a person's computer or phone without consent; trespassing; following and/or threatening an individual or a person's friends and relatives; driving/walking by a person's home, school, and/or work; or vandalizing property.

Sexual Harassment[1,2]. Unwelcome sexual advances, unwelcome requests for sexual favors, and other verbal or physical behavior of a sexual nature can be defined as sexual harassment when

- submission to or rejection of such conduct or communication is a term or condition of education benefits, academic evaluations, or opportunities;
- submission to or rejection of such conduct or communication has the effect of substantially interfering with a student's education; and
- such conduct is sufficiently severe, pervasive, and objectively offensive as to have the effect of creating an intimidating, hostile, or offensive environment sufficient to deny an individual education benefit of participation in activities.

Primary Prevention. A programmatic approach to preventing sexual violence on campus that includes an understanding of the developmental and social stages of students that allow for shaping future behaviors can be defined as primary prevention. Well-timed prevention efforts can reduce the occurrence of future sexual violence. A comprehensive prevention initiative includes sociopolitical analysis of the anti-rape movement and a multidimensional systematic approach to increasing awareness and promoting healthy behaviors central to public health and safety. The goal of primary prevention is to change the social climate so that sexual violence becomes taboo. These programs include raising awareness of current research on how sexual violence is perpetrated (often by perpetrators who are repeatedly targeting others); training staff and faculty to intervene when they hear rape supportive comments, jokes, or victim blaming; community organizing around gender equality issues; policy creation and revision to reflect gender equity; education on several levels based on healthy relationships; and awareness activities that support healthy relationships and respect.

Risk Reduction. Risk-reduction programs, the most common form of sexual assault education on campuses (O'Donohue, Yeater, & Fanetti, 2003), have a philosophic and programmatic focus on decreasing incidents of sexual violence through activities that focus on steps a person can take to protect themselves, what friends can do to help reduce the risk of sexual violence among their peers, and bystander intervention strategies which try to change attitudes and beliefs about sexual violence. Risk reduction is survivor focused and does not apply to perpetrators.

Summary

Although SARVPP provides expertise on campus sexual assault and relationship violence, this work cannot be successfully undertaken without the active support and participation of a variety of departments across the institution; the Office on Violence Against Women has identified this best practice as a "coordinated campus response team" (CCRT). CCRT should include health and mental health services, women's centers, residence life and housing services, fraternity and sorority life and other student organizations, international programs, athletics, campus police and local law enforcement, judicial affairs, local shelters and community service providers, local Sexual Assault Nurse Examiners (SANE), and Sexual Assault Response Teams (SART). Importantly, CCRT must be visibly supported by senior administrators. Other useful CCRT partners may include academic disciplines that are also concerned with this effort, including the following: gender and women's studies; sociology and anthropology; African American and critical race studies; cultural and ethnic studies; student affairs and higher education administration; student and public health; social work; continuing and adult education; first year experience programs; and professional schools, nursing programs, and counseling programs.

Notes

[1] For the purpose of this standard, CAS adapts the sexual harassment definition promulgated by the Equal Employment Opportunity Commission (EEOC) to the academic setting. Retrieved from http://www.eeoc.gov/laws/types/sexual_harassment.cfm

[2] The CAS standards should use the definitions provided by the Department of Education Office of Civil Rights under Title IX of the Education Amendments of 1972. Retrieved from http://www.dol.gov/oasam/regs/statutes/titleix.htm

References, Readings, and Resources

Black, M. C., Basile, K. C., Breiding, M. J., Smith, S. G., Walters, M. L., Merrick, M. T., Chen, J., & Stevens, M. R. (2011). The national relationship and sexual violence survey (NISVS): 2010 summary report. Atlanta, GA: National Center for Injury Prevention and Control, Centers for Disease Control and Prevention.

Bogal-Allbritten , R. , & Allbritten, W. (1991). Courtship violence on campus: A nationwide survey of student affairs professionals. *NASPA Journal of Student Affairs Practice and Research, 28*, 312-318.

Brustin, S. (1995). Legal response to teen dating violence. *Family Law Quarterly, 29*(2), 331.

Burgess, A. W., & Holmstrom, L. L. (1974). Rape trauma syndrome. *The American Journal of Psychiatry, 131*(9), 981-986.

Knauer, N. (1999) Same-sex domestic violence. *Temple Political & Civil Rights Law Review, 8*, 325-350.

O'Donohue, W., Yeater, E. A., & Fanetti, M. (2003). Rape prevention with college males: The role of rape myth acceptance, victim empathy and outcome expectancies. *Journal of Interpersonal Violence, 18*, 513-531.

Contextual Statement Contributors

Holly Ennis, Rutgers University (primary contributor)
Sara Bendoraitis, American University
Ruth Anne Koenick, Rutgers University
Rebecca Morrow, Idaho State University
Sandra Ortman-Tomlin, Gateway Community and Technical College
Mary-Jeanne Raleigh, St. Mary's College of Maryland
William Smedick, Johns Hopkins University

Sexual Assault and Relationship Violence Prevention Programs
CAS Standards and Guidelines

Part 1. MISSION

The mission of the Sexual Assault and Relationship Violence Prevention Programs (SARVPP) is to support and advocate for survivors of sexual assault and relationship violence and to educate the community in an effort to create an institution free from such violence.

SARVPP must provide, directly or through collaboration, a range of crisis intervention, advocacy, education, training, and prevention programs and services that meet the needs of the students they serve.

Sexual Assault and Relationship Violence Prevention Programs (SARVPP) must develop, disseminate, implement, and regularly review their missions. The mission must be consistent with the mission of the institution and with professional standards. The mission must be appropriate for the institution's student populations and community settings. Mission statements must reference student learning and development.

SARVPP may operate differently at various institutions. Institutions should examine the primary purpose of SARVPP programs and develop the appropriate approach that reflects their institutional needs. SARVPP may offer ongoing direct counseling, crisis intervention and advocacy, and intervention/prevention/response to victims, perpetrators, and the community.

To accomplish this mission SARVPP must
- employ supportive and survivor-centered care that avoids victim-blaming attitudes, practices, and beliefs
- provide information and resources to survivors about the broad range of options available to them, including but not limited to pursuing action in the criminal justice system; pursuing action through the code of conduct; obtaining emergency and follow-up health care; counseling services; and advocacy assistance with living, work, and academic concerns
- provide and/or facilitate access to the range of available services as a way of supporting the choices made by the survivor
- educate the institutional community on issues of violence

Part 2. PROGRAM

The formal education of students, consisting of the curriculum and the co-curriculum, must promote student learning and development outcomes that are purposeful, contribute to students' realization of their potential, and prepare students for satisfying and productive lives.

Sexual Assault and Relationship Violence Prevention Programs (SARVPP) must collaborate with colleagues and departments across the institution to promote student learning and development, persistence, and success.

Consistent with the institutional mission, SARVPP must identify relevant and desirable student learning and development outcomes from among the six domains and related dimensions:

Domain: knowledge acquisition, integration, construction, and application

- Dimensions: understanding knowledge from a range of disciplines; connecting knowledge to other knowledge, ideas, and experiences; constructing knowledge; and relating knowledge to daily life

Domain: cognitive complexity

- Dimensions: critical thinking, reflective thinking, effective reasoning, and creativity

Domain: intrapersonal development

- Dimensions: realistic self-appraisal, self-understanding, and self-respect; identity development; commitment to ethics and integrity; and spiritual awareness

Domain: interpersonal competence

- Dimensions: meaningful relationships, interdependence, collaboration, and effective leadership.

Domain: humanitarianism and civic engagement

- Dimensions: understanding and appreciation of cultural and human differences, social responsibility, global perspective, and sense of civic responsibility

Domain: practical competence

- Dimensions: pursuing goals, communicating effectively, technical competence, managing personal affairs, managing career development, demonstrating professionalism, maintaining health and wellness, and living a

purposeful and satisfying life

[LD Outcomes: See *The Council for the Advancement of Standards Learning and Developmental Outcomes* statement for examples of outcomes related to these domains and dimensions.]

SARVPP must

- **assess relevant and desirable student learning and development**
- **provide evidence of impact on outcomes**
- **articulate contributions to or support of student learning and development in the domains not specifically assessed**
- **articulate contributions to or support of student persistence and success**
- **use evidence gathered through this process to create strategies for improvement of programs and services**

SARVPP must be

- **intentionally designed**
- **guided by theories and knowledge of learning and development**
- **integrated into the life of the institution**
- **reflective of developmental and demographic profiles of the student population**
- **responsive to needs of individuals, populations with distinct needs, and relevant constituencies**
- **delivered using multiple formats, strategies, and contexts**

Where institutions provide distance education, SARVPP must assist distance learners to achieve their educational goals by providing access to information about programs and services, to staff members who can address questions and concerns, and to counseling, advising, or other forms of assistance.

In collaboration with staff members, faculty and students at the institution, SARVPP must

- **implement policies regarding sexual and relationship violence**
- **monitor the use and enforcement of these policies**
- **obtain institutional support for SARVPP during the creation and enforcement of these policies in all departments and offices**

Policies should include but are not limited to sexual assault, relationship violence, sexual harassment and stalking, and rules and regulations for student and faculty and staff members conduct as well as potential sanctions for unacceptable behavior, a victim's bill of rights, and procedures for responding to incidents.

Policies should serve as a statement of the institution's commitment to preventing and responding to acts of violence. Policies should be widely communicated in a variety of methods to staff members, faculty members, and students. Direct training, in-service programs, and updates should be provided on a regular basis.

SARVPP must create and carry out protocols to respond to incidents of sexual assault, relationship violence, stalking, or a related crime.

Protocols should be created so that response to a report is organized, seamless, and survivor-centered in order to ensure that survivors get timely, respectful treatment in a supportive manner.

SARVPP must determine protocols for response and support.

These protocols may also be included in the aforementioned policies and should be distributed to all involved in responding to reports of sexual or relationship violence. Protocols should comply with all laws and regulations. Protocols, like policies, should be widely publicized to all students, faculty members, and staff members at the institution. These protocols should address

- who should be notified and how they should be notified of a report of sexual or relationship violence
- procedures for reporting based on legal requirements, which includes avenues for confidential as well as anonymous reporting
- who is the mandated reporter for purposes of the Campus Security Act compliance, Title IX compliance, or other governmental mandates and what that means
- who keeps records and what should those records include
- who has access to those records
- procedures for special populations such as students who are minors and international students
- disciplinary procedures for those charged with acts of violence, including how the violence will be investigated
- housing policies for on-campus students who need to be relocated
- training requirements for faculty and staff members, especially those in key student contact areas
- campus police involvement and training
- development of a communication plan
- information sharing with outside entities (e.g., media, parents and relatives, campus community)
- the role of external organizations such as local shelters or services, if any
- how to provide services to students who do not wish to report the crime to the police or campus authorities
- collection of forensic and medical evidence and legal support
- availability of mental health services
- use of advocates—how, when, and who must notify advocates

- exceptions to the institutional withdrawal policies to allow flexibility for the victim/survivor

Appropriate institutional authorities should be involved in the enforcement of such policies in an effort to ensure that all departments involved in response are aware of their role and follow the protocols to the best of their ability.

Survivor services must be provided without concern for whether the survivor seeks legal or judicial intervention.

Survivors of sexual and relationship violence experience a broad range of responses that are often dependent on the response they receive from others and the belief system they have about these issues. People respond to trauma differently, and it is imperative that SARVPP provide services that address the diverse responses that survivors experience. Although there are some commonalities among survivors, there are also pronounced differences.

SARVPP must
- **promise confidentiality only if it can be guaranteed**
- **inform individuals of their rights and ensure that they have all the information needed to make an informed decision about what is right for them**
- **provide access to emergency support at all times, even during non-business hours**
- **provide referrals if the individual SARVPP does not provide counseling or other key services for survivors**
- **offer services to all students regardless of sex or gender**

Prevention efforts should be multifaceted and include diverse approaches to issues and learning styles. Although many programs traditionally focused on reduction of risk and raising awareness, recent research suggested that primary prevention is the most effective approach for institutions.

The goal of primary prevention education is to prevent first-time perpetration or victimization by improving knowledge and attitudes that correspond to the origins of sexual violence (such as adherence to societal norms supportive of sexual violence, male superiority, and male sexual entitlement), build skills for respectful interactions, and empower participants to become agents of change. Primary sexual violence prevention education commonly addresses attitudes about sexual assault, the impact of gender roles, healthy relationships, consent, conflict resolution, respect for personal boundaries, and skill building for these topics.

These programs should address (a) the issue of violence against the individual, the relationship, the community, and societal values and (b) the root cause of this violence by challenging attitudes and behaviors that support a culture of violence. This aspect of SARVPP is devoted to proactively

stopping violence before it occurs. One common aspect of prevention programs is an effort to engage men on campus to promote a healthy concept of masculinity as well as to develop allies that stand up against sexual and relationship violence.

SARVPP should provide comprehensive training on all issues related to sexual and relationship violence, including but not limited to sexual assault, domestic violence, stalking, and sexual harassment. Training should cover not only policies and protocols but also information about the nature of these crimes, legal responsibilities, and other important elements of prevention. Training should be available to campus law enforcement, administrators, residence life/housing staff (including undergraduate resident assistants), counseling staff, health services staff, women's center staff, conduct staff, student affairs staff, and faculty members.

Part 3. ORGANIZATION AND LEADERSHIP

To achieve student and program outcomes, Sexual Assault and Relationship Violence Prevention Programs (SARVPP) must be structured purposefully and organized effectively. SARVPP must have
- **clearly stated goals**
- **current and accessible policies and procedures**
- **written performance expectations for employees**
- **functional work flow graphics or organizational charts demonstrating clear channels of authority**

SARVPP is generally housed in some part of student affairs although on occasion, particularly in smaller campuses, it may be part of an academic unit.

Leaders with organizational authority for the programs and services must provide strategic planning, supervision, and management; advance the organization; and maintain integrity through the following functions:

Strategic Planning
- **articulate a vision and mission that drive short- and long-term planning**
- **set goals and objectives based on the needs of the population served and desired student learning or development and program outcomes**
- **facilitate continuous development, implementation, and assessment of goal attainment congruent with institutional mission and strategic plans**
- **promote environments that provide meaningful opportunities for student learning, development, and engagement**
- **develop and continuously improve programs and services in response to the changing needs of students served and evolving**

institutional priorities
- intentionally include diverse perspectives to inform decision making

Supervising
- manage human resource processes including recruitment, selection, development, supervision, performance planning, evaluation, recognition, and reward
- influence others to contribute to the effectiveness and success of the unit
- empower professional, support, and student staff to accept leadership opportunities
- offer appropriate feedback to colleagues and students on skills needed to become more effective leaders
- encourage and support professional development, collaboration with colleagues and departments across the institution, and scholarly contribution to the profession

Managing
- identify and address individual, organizational, and environmental conditions that foster or inhibit mission achievement
- plan, allocate, and monitor the use of fiscal, physical, human, intellectual, and technological resources
- use current and valid evidence to inform decisions
- incorporate sustainability practices in the management and design of programs, services, and facilities
- understand appropriate technologies and integrate them into programs and services
- be knowledgeable about codes and laws relevant to programs and services and ensure that staff members understand their responsibilities through appropriate training
- assess potential risks and take action to mitigate them

Advancing the Organization
- communicate effectively in writing, speaking, and electronic venues
- advocate for programs and services
- advocate for representation in strategic planning initiatives at appropriate divisional and institutional levels
- initiate collaborative interactions with internal and external stakeholders who have legitimate concerns about and interests in the functional area
- facilitate processes to reach consensus where wide support is needed
- inform other areas within the institution about issues affecting practice

Maintaining Integrity
- model ethical behavior and institutional citizenship
- share data used to inform key decisions in transparent and accessible ways
- monitor media used for distributing information about programs and services to ensure the content is current, accurate, appropriately referenced, and accessible

SARVPP leaders must
- promote cooperation from other units in providing services for survivors (e.g., law enforcement and counseling services)
- work with other departments to send a message that violence of any kind is not acceptable, nor are attitudes that contribute to a culture that supports violence (e.g., sexist attitudes)
- model a survivor-centered attitude when responding to incidents of sexual or relationship violence
- encourage the campus administration to be a critical voice in regional issues concerning sexual assault and relationship violence and advocating for survivors

Part 4. HUMAN RESOURCES

Sexual Assault and Relationship Violence Prevention Programs (SARVPP) must be staffed adequately by individuals qualified to accomplish mission and goals.

Within institutional guidelines, SARVPP must
- establish procedures for staff recruitment and selection, training, performance planning, and evaluation
- set expectations for supervision and performance
- assess the performance of employees individually and as a team
- provide access to continuing and advanced education and appropriate professional development opportunities to improve the leadership ability, competence, and skills of all employees.

SARVPP must maintain position descriptions for all staff members.

To create a diverse staff, SARVPP must institute recruitment and hiring strategies that encourage individuals from under-represented populations to apply for positions.

SARVPP must develop promotion practices that are fair, inclusive, proactive, and non-discriminatory.

To further the recruitment and retention of staff,

SARVPP must consider work life initiatives, such as compressed work schedules, flextime, job sharing, remote work, or telework.

SARVPP professional staff members must hold an earned graduate or professional degree in a field relevant to the position they hold or must possess an appropriate combination of educational credentials and related work experience.

SARVPP professional staff members must engage in continuing professional development activities to keep abreast of the research, theories, legislation, policies, and developments that affect their programs and services.

SARVPP must have technical and support staff members adequate to accomplish their mission. All members of the staff must be technologically proficient and qualified to perform their job functions, be knowledgeable about ethical and legal uses of technology, and have access to training and resources to support the performance of their assigned responsibilities.

Degree- or credential-seeking interns or graduate assistants must be qualified by enrollment in an appropriate field of study and by relevant experience. These individuals must be trained and supervised adequately by professional staff members holding educational credentials and related work experience appropriate for supervision. Supervisors must be cognizant of the roles of interns and graduate assistants as both student and employee and closely adhere to all parameters of their job descriptions, work hours, and schedules. Supervisors and the interns or graduate assistants must agree to compensatory time or other appropriate compensation if circumstances necessitate additional hours.

Student employees and volunteers must be carefully selected, trained, supervised, and evaluated. They must be educated on how and when to refer those in need of additional assistance to qualified staff members and must have access to a supervisor for assistance in making these judgments. Student employees and volunteers must be provided clear job descriptions, pre-service training based on assessed needs, and continuing development.

All SARVPP staff members, including student employees and volunteers, must receive specific training on institutional policies pertaining to functions or activities they support and to privacy and confidentiality policies and laws regarding access to student records and other sensitive institutional information.

All SARVPP staff members must receive training on policies and procedures related to the use of technology to store or access student records and institutional data.

SARVPP must ensure that staff members are knowledgeable about and trained in emergency procedures, crisis response, and prevention efforts. Prevention efforts must address identification of threatening conduct or behavior of students, faculty and staff members, and others and must incorporate a system for responding and reporting.

SARVPP must ensure that staff members are knowledgeable of and trained in safety and emergency procedures for securing and vacating facilities.

All employees and volunteers should have sensitivity for all survivors, regardless of their identities, and for their privacy; inform survivors of the limits to their confidentiality; and provide them with information regarding confidential locations on campus.

Some governmental entities also have laws that protect the confidentiality privileges of SARVPP practitioners and may offer a level of required training so that advocates, even those without advanced degrees, are granted that right.

Part 5. ETHICS

Sexual Assault and Relationship Violence Prevention Programs (SARVPP) must review relevant professional ethical standards and must adopt or develop and implement appropriate statements of ethical practice.

SARVPP must publish and adhere to statements of ethical practice and ensure their periodic review by relevant constituencies.

SARVPP must orient new staff members to relevant ethical standards and statements of ethical practice and related institutional policies.

Statements of ethical standards must specify that staff members respect privacy and maintain confidentiality in all communications and records to the extent that such communications and records are protected under relevant privacy laws.

Statements of ethical standards must specify limits on disclosure of information contained in students' educational records as well as requirements to disclose to appropriate authorities.

Statements of ethical standards must address personal and economic conflicts of interest, or appearance thereof, by staff members in the performance of their work.

Statements of ethical standards must reflect the

responsibility of staff members to be fair, objective, and impartial in their interactions with others.

Statements of ethical standards must reference management of institutional funds.

Statements of ethical standards must reference appropriate behavior regarding research and assessment with human participants, confidentiality of research and assessment data, and students' rights and responsibilities.

Statements of ethical standards must include the expectation that SARVPP staff members confront and hold accountable other staff members who exhibit unethical behavior.

Statements of ethical standards must address issues surrounding scholarly integrity.

As appropriate, SARVPP staff members must inform users of programs and services of ethical obligations and limitations emanating from codes and laws or from licensure requirements.

SARVPP staff members must recognize and avoid conflicts of interest that could adversely influence their judgment or objectivity and, when unavoidable, recuse themselves from the situation.

SARVPP staff members must perform their duties within the limits of their position, training, expertise, and competence.

When these limits are exceeded, individuals in need of further assistance must be referred to persons possessing appropriate qualifications.

Promotional and descriptive information must be accurate and free of deception.

SARVPP must adhere to institutional policies regarding ethical and legal use of software and technology.

Part 6. LAW, POLICY, AND GOVERNANCE

Sexual Assault and Relationship Violence Prevention Programs (SARVPP) must be in compliance with laws, regulations, and policies that relate to their respective responsibilities and that pose legal obligations, limitations, risks, and liabilities for the institution as a whole. Examples include constitutional, statutory, regulatory, and case law; relevant law and orders emanating from codes and laws; and the institution's policies.

SARVPP must inform staff members, appropriate officials, and users of programs and services about existing and changing legal obligations, risks and liabilities, and limitations.

SARVPP must have written policies on all relevant operations, transactions, or tasks that have legal implications.

SARVPP must regularly review policies. The revision and creation of policies must be informed by best practices, available evidence, and policy issues in higher education.

SARVPP must determine policies for disclosure of incidents to family members in accordance with relevant laws and practices.

SARVPP staff members must use reasonable and informed practices to limit the liability exposure of the institution and its officers, employees, and agents. Staff members must be informed about institutional policies regarding risk management, personal liability, and related insurance coverage options and must be referred to external sources if the institution does not provide coverage.

The institution must provide access to legal advice for staff members as needed to carry out assigned responsibilities.

SARVPP must have procedures and guidelines consistent with institutional policy for responding to threats, emergencies, and crisis situations. Systems and procedures must be in place to disseminate timely and accurate information to students, other members of the institutional community, and appropriate external organizations during emergency situations.

SARVPP staff members must neither participate in nor condone any form of harassment or activity that demeans persons or creates an intimidating, hostile, or offensive environment.

SARVPP must obtain permission to use copyrighted materials and instruments. SARVPP must purchase the materials and instruments from legally compliant sources or seek alternative permission from the publisher or owner. References to copyrighted materials and instruments must include appropriate citations.

SARVPP staff members must be knowledgeable about internal and external governance systems that affect programs and services.

SARVPP staff must be knowledgeable about changes in relevant laws and practices.

These laws and offices include, but are not limited to, Family Educational Rights and Privacy Act (FERPA), the Jeanne Clery Disclosure of Campus Security Policy and Campus Crime Statistics Act (the Campus Security Act), Title IX of the Education Amendments of 1972, Violence Against Women Act (VAWA) Forensic Compliance 2005 Reauthorization

(42 USCA S. 3796gg-4.b.3.D.d.1) and US Department of Education Office for Civil Rights.

Part 7. DIVERSITY, EQUITY, AND ACCESS

Within the context of each institution's unique mission and in accordance with institutional polices and all applicable codes and laws, Sexual Assault and Relationship Violence Prevention Programs (SARVPP) must create and maintain educational and work environments that are

- welcoming, accessible, and inclusive to persons of diverse backgrounds
- equitable and non-discriminatory
- free from harassment

SARVPP must not discriminate on the basis of ability; age; cultural identity; ethnicity; family educational history (e.g., first generation to attend college); gender identity and expression; nationality; political affiliation; race; religious affiliation; sex; sexual orientation; economic, marital, social, or veteran status; or any other basis included in institutional policies and codes and laws.

SARVPP must

- advocate for greater sensitivity to multicultural and social justice concerns by the institution and its personnel
- modify or remove policies, practices, facilities, structures, systems, and technologies that limit access, discriminate, or produce inequities
- include diversity, equity, and access initiatives within their strategic plans
- foster communication that deepens understanding of identity, culture, self-expression, and heritage
- promote respect about commonalities and differences among people within their historical and cultural contexts
- address the characteristics and needs of a diverse population when establishing and implementing culturally relevant and inclusive programs, services, policies, procedures, and practices
- provide staff members with access to multicultural training and hold staff members accountable for integrating the training into their work
- respond to the needs of all students and other populations served when establishing hours of operation and developing methods of delivering programs, services, and resources
- ensure physical, program, and resource access for persons with disabilities
- recognize the needs of distance learning students by providing appropriate and accessible services and resources or by assisting them in gaining access to other appropriate services and resources in their geographic region

Part 8. INSTITUTIONAL AND EXTERNAL RELATIONS

Sexual Assault and Relationship Violence Prevention Programs (SARVPP) must reach out to relevant individuals, groups, communities, and organizations internal and external to the institution to

- establish, maintain, and promote understanding and effective relations with those that have a significant interest in or potential effect on the students or other constituents served by the programs and services
- garner support and resources for programs and services as defined by the mission statement
- disseminate information about the programs and services
- collaborate, where appropriate, to assist in offering or improving programs and services to meet the needs of students and other constituents and to achieve program and student outcomes
- engage diverse individuals, groups, communities, and organizations to enrich the educational environment and experiences of students and other constituents

SARVPP must have procedures and guidelines consistent with institutional policy for

- communicating with the media
- contracting with external organizations for delivery of programs and services
- cultivating, soliciting, and managing gifts
- applying to and managing funds from grants

SARVPP should recognize that to prevent violence on a college campus, it must be a community-wide effort. Resources and effort should be invested in relationship-building with outside offices and departments in order to strengthen the community's comprehensive response to sexual and relationship violence.

It often takes a number of different departments working in collaboration with one another to provide quality care for survivors. It should be the responsibility of the entire campus community to create an environment intolerant of violence, especially against marginalized groups. No one group, alone, can eradicate sexual assault, domestic violence, or stalking.

Most often, sexual and relationship violence programs work in collaboration with the counseling services department, women's centers and other gender-related departments, health services, student affairs, student conduct, local hospital, response teams (Sexual Assault Response Team-

SART, Domestic Violence Response Team-DVRTO), campus policy or security department, local police, residence life, legal counsel's office, faculty, and other outside entities such as a local sexual assault or domestic violence shelters or broader coalitions.

Part 9. FINANCIAL RESOURCES

Sexual Assault and Relationship Violence Prevention Programs (SARVPP) must have funding to accomplish the mission and goals. In establishing funding priorities and making significant changes, a comprehensive analysis must be conducted to determine the following elements: unmet needs of the unit, relevant expenditures, external and internal resources, and impact on students and the institution.

SARVPP must demonstrate efficient and effective use and responsible stewardship of fiscal resources consistent with institutional protocols.

Although some grant funding may be available from federal and state programs and foundations, this funding is short-term and should not be the primary funding for any program. Using grant funding may be beneficial as it can supplement the institutional funds and allow the program to develop in areas that might not be included in traditional funding.

Part 10. TECHNOLOGY

Sexual Assault and Relationship Violence Prevention Programs (SARVPP) must have adequate technology to support the achievement of their mission and goals. The technology and its use must comply with institutional policies and procedures and be evaluated for compliance with relevant codes and laws.

SARVPP must use current technology to provide updated information regarding mission, location, staffing, programs, services, and official contacts to students and designated clients.

SARVPP must explore the use of technology to enhance delivery of programs and services, especially for students at a distance or external constituencies.

When technology is used to facilitate student learning and development, SARVPP must select technology that reflects intended outcomes.

SARVPP must
- maintain policies and procedures that address the security, confidentiality, and backup of data, as well as compliance with privacy laws
- have clearly articulated plans in place for protecting confidentiality and security of information when using Internet-based technologies
- develop plans for replacing and updating existing hardware and software as well as

plans for integrating new technically-based or supported programs, including systems developed internally by the institution, systems available through professional associations, or private vendor-based systems

Technology, as well as workstations or computer labs maintained by programs and services for student use, must be accessible to all designated clients and must meet established technology standards for delivery to persons with disabilities.

When providing student access to technology, SARVPP must
- have policies on the use of technology that are clear, easy to understand, and available to all students
- provide assistance, information, or referral to appropriate support services to those needing help accessing or using technology
- provide instruction or training on how to use the technology
- inform students on the legal and ethical implications of misuse as it pertains to intellectual property, harassment, privacy, and social networks

Student violations of technology policies must follow established institutional student disciplinary procedures.

Students who experience negative emotional or psychological consequences from the use of technology must be referred to support services provided by the institution.

SARVPP should be aware of methods in which technology can be used by perpetrators to gain control over victims. Examples include unwanted communication via e-mails, text messages, and chat requests; tracking victims via Global Positioning Systems (GPS); installation of spyware on the victim's computer; unauthorized posting of pictures; and information or messages in Internet chat rooms or on websites, including social networking sites.

Because issues of power and control are inherent in relationship violence, perpetrators often keep close watch on the actions and movements of their victims and may do so through such means as monitoring of the victim's email accounts and their online use, including tracking the history of websites that the victim has visited. SARVPP should undertake efforts to maintain the privacy of those who access the program's website. Instructions on how to erase one's Internet history and cookies should be provided to all who visit the SARVPP website, making less likely the perpetrator's ability to discern the sites the victim has visited. If possible, the website should include a quick escape button in the event that the perpetrator should walk in on the victim while accessing the SARVPP Website. Websites should state the limits of confidentiality.

SARVPP staff members should take into account the ability to maintain confidentiality and safety when using technology. Additionally, the use of social networks such as Facebook and other communication methods such as text messaging, Twitter, and blogging should be conducted with privacy in mind. It is recommended that confidential material not be communicated through these social media.

SARVPP should pursue technology applications that increase its ability to provide services to survivors.

Part 11. FACILITIES AND EQUIPMENT

Sexual Assault and Relationship Violence Prevention Programs (SARVPP) must have adequate, accessible, and suitably located facilities and equipment to support the mission and goals. If acquiring capital equipment as defined by the institution, SARVPP must take into account expenses related to regular maintenance and life cycle costs. Facilities and equipment must be evaluated on an established cycle, including consideration of sustainability, and be in compliance with codes and laws to provide for access, health, safety, and security.

SARVPP staff members must have workspace that is well equipped, adequate in size, and designed to support their work and responsibilities. For conversations requiring privacy, staff members must have access to a private space.

SARVPP staff members who share workspace must be able to secure their own work.

The design of the facilities must guarantee the security and privacy of records and ensure the confidentiality of sensitive information.

The location and layout of the facilities must be sensitive to the needs of persons with disabilities as well as the needs of other constituencies.

SARVPP should consider a location and layout that supports multiple purposes, such as support services and educational programming, to protect a survivor's and perpetrator's identity.

SARVPP should be centrally located and visible to increase institutional awareness of the issue of sexual assault and relationship violence.

SARVPP must create and maintain an environment that assures confidentiality, privacy, and trust.

Facilities should be equipped to provide spaces for counseling and other confidential conversations, which might include soundproofing or other efforts to protect confidentiality. A reception area with a private waiting room should also be available if counseling or other private meetings are held regularly.

Ideally SARVPP should also have space for student groups such as peer educators to meet and conduct business. Training facilities, with proper technology, should also be available.

Part 12. ASSESSMENT AND EVALUATION

Sexual Assault and Relationship Violence Prevention Programs (SARVPP) must have a clearly articulated assessment plan to document achievement of stated goals and learning outcomes, demonstrate accountability, provide evidence of improvement, and describe resulting changes in programs and services.

SARVPP must have adequate fiscal, human, professional development, and technological resources to develop and implement assessment plans.

Assessments must include direct and indirect evaluation and use qualitative and quantitative methodologies and existing evidence, as appropriate, to determine whether and to what degree the stated mission, goals, and intended outcomes are being met as effectively and efficiently as possible. The process must employ sufficient and sound measures to ensure comprehensiveness. Data collected must include responses from students and other constituencies, and aggregated results must be shared with those groups. Results of assessments must be shared appropriately with multiple constituents.

Results of assessments and evaluations must be used to identify needs and interests in revising and improving programs and services, recognizing staff performance, maximizing resource efficiency and effectiveness, improving student achievement of learning and development outcomes, and improving student persistence and success. Changes resulting from the use of assessments and evaluation must be shared with stakeholders.

General Standards revised in 2011;
SARVPP content developed in 2012

The Role of Student Conduct Programs
CAS Standards Contextual Statement

Throughout the history of American higher education, colleges have struggled with how to respond to student misconduct. In his letter to Thomas Cooper on November 2, 1822, Thomas Jefferson described the problem of student discipline as "a breaker ahead" that he was not sure that American higher education could weather (Patterson, 1984, p. 1465). In recent years, issues that have come to the forefront are related to student discipline including sexual assault, use and abuse of alcohol and other drugs, as well as the implementation of behavioral intervention teams (BIT)/ behavioral assessment teams (BAT) as a means of providing threat assessment following increased issues surrounding campus safety.

Traditionally, the U.S. courts viewed the administration of student discipline as an internal institutional matter and did not become actively involved in the process through judicial rulings. However, this position changed in 1961, with the landmark case of *Dixon v. Alabama State Board of Education*, 294 F.2d 150 (5th Cir. 1961), the first of an ever-growing modern body of case law related to the administration of student discipline. The courts have held under the 14th Amendment to the U.S. Constitution that public colleges and universities must afford basic due process rights to students accused of violating student conduct codes. However, it is important to note that the rights of due process described in this body of case law differ significantly from those observed in the criminal court system. The limitations placed upon private institutions are substantially less prescriptive. Although the Constitutional rights afforded to students at public institutions are not generally applicable to private institutions, several authors, including Kaplin and Lee (2006), Stoner and Cerminara (1990), and Stoner and Lowery (2004) have encouraged private institutions to bear in mind the restrictions placed upon public institutions and accord their students the same general rights and protections.

In the early American colleges and universities, student discipline was primarily the responsibility of the faculty. As the positions of dean of men and women were established and the field of student affairs evolved, the responsibility for the administration of student discipline shifted. Barry and Wolf (1957) observed, "Despite all of their later disclaimers, most deans of men seem to have been appointed primarily to act as disciplinarians" (p.14). Only in the past twenty-five years has student discipline emerged as a distinct functional area within student affairs. Prior to that time, the responsibility for student discipline was one of a number of duties which fell to an individual or office such as the dean of men or the dean of women and later the dean of students.

In the early 1970s, the American College Personnel Association established Commission XV, Campus Judicial Affairs and Legal Issues, to meet the needs of this emerging profession. In 1988, the Association for Student Judicial Affairs (ASJA) was founded to facilitate the integration of student development concepts with principles of student conduct practice in post-secondary education and to promote, encourage, and support student development professionals responsible for judicial affairs. Reflecting the evolution of the profession, ASJA changed its name in 2008 to the Association for Student Conduct Administration (ASCA).

Over the past fifteen years, the practice of student judicial affairs in the U.S. has been profoundly affected by the passage of federal legislation. Although the Family Educational Rights and Privacy Act of 1974 (FERPA) had implications for judicial affairs, the legislation passed more recently differed significantly in that it directly targeted aspects of the campus student conduct system. For example, the amendments to the Student Right-to-Know and Campus Security Act included in the Higher Education Amendments of 1998 require colleges and universities to include statistics for liquor law violations, drug law violations, and weapons law violations addressed through the student conduct system. The Higher Education Amendments of 1998 also amended FERPA to allow the release of final results of a campus disciplinary proceeding when a student is found responsible of a crime of violence or nonforcible sexual offense and to allow parental notification when the institution determined that a student under the age of 21 had violated alcohol or drug policies. In the years between 1974 and 1998, several pieces of legislation impacting student conduct programs were introduced into Congress annually as well. This increased governmental involvement demands that student conduct professionals remain knowledgeable about legislative developments and actively work to address legislative proposals that would have a negative impact on the fundamental educational mission of the student conduct system. Additionally, a "Dear Colleague Letter" issued by the Office of Civil Rights on April 4, 2011, expanding the requirements of Title IX, pertaining to sexual harassment to apply to acts of sexual violence in American colleges and universities, has also caused many institutions of higher education to more closely examine their student conduct policies and practices.

The Association for Student Conduct Administration established three principles for the administration of student conduct programs, reflecting current thinking in this area:
- The development and enforcement of standards of conduct for students is an educational endeavor that fosters students' personal and social development; students must assume a significant role in developing and enforcing such regulations in order that they might

be better prepared for the responsibilities of citizenship.
- Standards of conduct form the basis for behavioral expectations in the academic community; the enforcement of such standards must protect the rights, health, and safety of members of that community in order that they may pursue their educational goals without undue interference.
- Integrity, wisdom, and empathy are among the characteristics most important to the administration of student conduct standards; officials who have such responsibilities must exercise them impartially and fairly.

The primary role of student conduct administrators is that of educator. The maintenance and enhancement of the ethical climate on campus and the promotion of academic integrity are the primary purposes for enforcing standards of student conduct (ASJA, 1993). The student conduct programs standards and guidelines that follow represent the fundamental criteria by which programs can assess their quality and effectiveness.

References, Readings, and Resources

ACPA – College Student Educators International - Commission for Student Conduct and Legal Issues. One Dupont Circle, Suite 300, Washington, DC 20036, (202) 835-2272. http://www.myacpa.org/comm/judicial/

Association for Student Conduct Administration, P.O. Box 2237, College Station, TX 77841-2237, 979-845-5262. http://asja.tamu.edu/

Association for Student Judicial Affairs. (1993). *Ethical principles and standards of conduct: Preamble.* Retrieved from http://www.theasca.org/en/cms/?60

Dannells, M. (1997). *From discipline to development: Rethinking student conduct in higher education.* ASHE-ERIC Higher Education Report Vol. 25, No. 2. Washington, DC: The George Washington University, Graduate School of Education and Human Development.

Dixon v. Alabama State Board of Education, 294 F.2d 150 (5th Cir. 1961).

Hoekema, D. A. (1994). *Campus rules and moral community: In place of in loco parentis.* Lanham, MD: Rowman & Littlefield.

Kaplin, W. A., & Lee, B. A. (2006). *The law of higher education (4th ed.).* San Francisco: Jossey-Bass.

Letter from Thomas Jefferson to Thomas Cooper (Nov. 2, 1822), in *Thomas Jefferson: Writings 1463, 1465* (M. Patterson, ed., The Library of America) (1984).

Mercer, W. L. (Ed.). (1996). *Critical issues in judicial affairs: Current trends in practice.* San Francisco: Jossey-Bass.

Paterson, G. P., & Kibler, W. L. (Eds.). (1999). *The administration of student discipline: Student, organizational, and community issues.* Asheville, NC: College Administration Publications.

Patterson, M. D. (Ed.) (1984). *Thomas Jefferson: Writings.* New York: The Library of America.

Stoner, E. N., II, & Cerminara, K. L. (1990). Harnessing the "spirit of insubordination": A model student disciplinary code. *Journal of College and University Law, 17,* 89-121.

Stoner, E. N., II, & Lowery, J. W. (2004). Navigating past the "spirit of insubordination": A twenty-first century model student conduct code with a model hearing script. *Journal of College and University Law, 31,* 1-77.

Contextual Statement Contributors
John Wesley Lowrey, Indiana University of Pennsylvania, ASCA
John Zacker, University of Maryland, ASCA
Marc H. Shook, LaGrange College, ASCA

Student Conduct Programs
CAS Standards and Guidelines

Part 1. MISSION

Student Conduct Programs (SCP) develop and enforce standards of conduct, an educational endeavor to foster students' learning and development.

SCP must develop, disseminate, implement, and regularly review their missions. The mission must be consistent with the mission of the institution and with professional standards. The mission must be appropriate for the institution's student populations and community settings. Mission statements must reference student learning and development.

The goals of SCP must address the institution's needs to

- develop, disseminate, interpret, and enforce campus policies and procedures
- protect rights of students in the administration of the student conduct program
- respond to student behavioral problems in a fair and reasonable manner
- facilitate and encourage respect for and involvement in campus governance
- provide learning experiences for students who are found to be responsible for conduct which is determined to be in violation of institutional standards or who participate in the operations of the student conduct system
- initiate and encourage educational activities that serve to reduce violations of campus regulations

SCP should support appropriate individual and group behavior as well as serve the campus community by reducing disruption and harm. The programs should be conducted in ways that will serve to foster the ethical development and personal integrity of students and the promotion of an environment that is consistent with the overall educational goals of the institution.

Part 2. PROGRAM

The formal education of students, consisting of the curriculum and the co-curriculum, must promote student learning and development outcomes that are purposeful, contribute to students' realization of their potential, and prepare students for satisfying and productive lives.

Student Conduct Programs (SCP) must collaborate with colleagues and departments across the institution to promote student learning and development, persistence, and success.

Consistent with the institutional mission, SCP must identify relevant and desirable student learning and development outcomes from among the six domains and related dimensions:

Domain: knowledge acquisition, integration, construction, and application

- Dimensions: understanding knowledge from a range of disciplines; connecting knowledge to other knowledge, ideas, and experiences; constructing knowledge; and relating knowledge to daily life

Domain: cognitive complexity

- Dimensions: critical thinking, reflective thinking, effective reasoning, and creativity

Domain: intrapersonal development

- Dimensions: realistic self-appraisal, self-understanding, and self-respect; identity development; commitment to ethics and integrity; and spiritual awareness

Domain: interpersonal competence

- Dimensions: meaningful relationships, interdependence, collaboration, and effective leadership.

Domain: humanitarianism and civic engagement

- Dimensions: understanding and appreciation of cultural and human differences, social responsibility, global perspective, and sense of civic responsibility

Domain: practical competence

- Dimensions: pursuing goals, communicating effectively, technical competence, managing personal affairs, managing career development, demonstrating professionalism, maintaining health and wellness, and living a purposeful and satisfying life

[LD Outcomes: See *The Council for the Advancement of Standards Learning and Developmental Outcomes* statement for examples of outcomes related to these domains and dimensions.]

SCP must
- assess relevant and desirable student learning and development
- provide evidence of impact on outcomes
- articulate contributions to or support of student learning and development in the

domains not specifically assessed
- articulate contributions to or support of student persistence and success
- use evidence gathered through this process to create strategies for improvement of programs and services

SCP must be
- intentionally designed
- guided by theories and knowledge of learning and development
- integrated into the life of the institution
- reflective of developmental and demographic profiles of the student population
- responsive to needs of individuals, populations with distinct needs, and relevant constituencies
- delivered using multiple formats, strategies, and contexts

Where institutions provide distance education, SCP must assist distance learners to achieve their educational goals by providing access to information about programs and services, to staff members who can address questions and concerns, and to counseling, advising, or other forms of assistance.

SCP must establish the following within the context of its mission and purpose:

Authority
A written statement describing the authority, philosophy, jurisdiction, and procedures of the student conduct programs must be developed and disseminated to all members of the campus community.

This statement should address (a) how student academic or nonacademic misconduct is within the program's jurisdiction, (b) which campus policies and regulations are enforced by these programs, (c) sanctions that may be imposed, (d) a clear description of the relationship between student conduct programs and both campus and external law enforcement agencies, including guidelines regarding when law enforcement authorities will be called in, (e) authority under the policy to address misconduct which occurs off campus including education abroad, and (f) information regarding the impact, if any, of decisions by the criminal courts on the outcome of corresponding student conduct proceedings.

Components
The institution's policies regarding the administration of student discipline must be clearly described in writing. Elements to be addressed in this policy must include prohibited conduct; sanctions; boards and administrators with roles in the adjudication of student misconduct; procedures for the investigation and adjudication of allegations of student misconduct; appeal procedures (if provided); procedures for interim suspension (if provided); and policies regarding student disciplinary records.

Generally, the student conduct system should involve significant roles for students in the adjudication of allegations of misconduct; however, membership on boards need not be limited to students. The system should allow sufficient time for an investigation of all allegations prior to a hearing, while responding to complaints in a timely fashion.

Procedures and processes must be designed to provide for substantive and procedural due process at public institutions of higher education and fundamental fairness at private institutions of higher education.

SCP should provide students with ample opportunity to receive advice about the process, a general time frame for resolution, and a delineation of individual responsibilities in the process.

Institutional disciplinary action against individual students or recognized student organizations must be administered in the context of a coordinated set of regulations and processes in order to ensure fair and reasonable outcomes and the equitable treatment of students and groups. Allegations of improper behavior originating from both instructional and noninstructional components of the institution must be encompassed in a comprehensive student conduct system for students.

Different procedures may be used to address the various forms of misconduct.

The institution must be clear about which board or individual has jurisdiction over specific conduct regulations.

Students should be assisted in understanding the sources and lines of authority.

The sanctions imposed as a result of institutional disciplinary action must be educationally and developmentally appropriate.

SCP must follow up on cases, including enforcement of sanctions, assessing the developmental processes that have been affected, and ensuring that students are directed to appropriate services for assistance.

The institution must be clear about how it defines student status and the jurisdiction of the system to include whether students can be held responsible for behavior that takes place off

campus or between academic sessions.

SCP should maintain written records to serve as referral materials, to document precedents, to provide source material for identifying recurring problems, or to use for appeals.

The institution must clearly state the conduct regulations that apply to student organizations, the procedures that will be followed in the hearing of cases related to student organizations, and the guidelines used to determine if actions of individual members or small groups within an organization constitute action by the organization.

Information to Campus Community
The institution must publish information about the SCP.

Publications should contain (a) campus policies, such as those concerning legal representation, the protection of privacy of student disciplinary records, and the destruction of disciplinary records; (b) campus procedures, such as filing a disciplinary action, gathering information, conducting a hearing, and notifying a student of the hearing or appeal board's decision; (c) the composition, authority, and jurisdiction of all student conduct bodies; (d) the types of advice and assistance that the complainant and others can receive about the process; (e) the types of disciplinary sanctions, including interim suspension procedures; and (f) a general explanation of how and when non-campus law enforcement officials are used.

Publications must be distributed through methods that will reach all students.

Dissemination methods may include electronic media; the institutional catalog; the orientation program; the student handbook; and admissions, registration, and billing materials.

Published information should include not only descriptions about how the system works, but also the results of the system. By publishing the outcomes of student conduct cases in a manner which protects the privacy of those involved, the institution demonstrates that the system does work and encourages an open discussion of issues related to student conduct.

Hearing Authority
In addition to a hearing officer, SCP must include a hearing or appellate board, composed of representatives of the campus community, that is responsible for carrying out student conduct functions delegated by the administration.

Roles and functions of student conduct board members may include (a) reviewing disciplinary referrals and claims; (b) interpreting misconduct allegations and identifying specific charges to be brought against the student(s); (c) conducting preliminary hearings and gathering information pertinent to the charges; (d) advising students on their rights and responsibilities; (e) engaging in substantive discussions with students about relevant ethical issues; (f) scheduling, coordinating, and conducting hearings; (g) reviewing decisions from other hearing bodies, when applicable; (h) notifying the accused in writing about relevant decisions and the board's rationale for such; (i) maintaining accurate written records of the entire proceeding; (j) referring information to an appeal board when applicable; (k) following up on sanctions to ensure they have been implemented; (l) following up with students who have been sanctioned to ensure awareness of available counseling services; (m) establishing and implementing a procedure for maintenance and destruction of disciplinary records; and (n) assessing student conduct procedures, policies, and outcomes.

A student conduct officer may be assigned responsibility for training student conduct board members, scheduling and facilitating evaluations, and informing faculty members, administration, and staff about legal and disciplinary matters.

Student conduct board members should participate on campus government committees associated with student conduct, except when a conflict of interest will result. Student conduct board members may also be involved in the outreach efforts of the SCP.

Training of Student Conduct Board Members
Initial and inservice training of all hearing board members must be provided.

In order for student conduct board members to fulfill their roles and functions, initial training should include (a) an overview of all judicial policies and procedures; (b) an explanation of the operation of the judicial process at all levels including authority and jurisdiction; (c) an overview of the institution's philosophy on student conduct and its role in this process; (d) roles and functions of all student conduct bodies and their members; (e) review of constitutional and other relevant legal individual and institutional rights and responsibilities; (f) an explanation of sanctions; (g) an explanation of pertinent ethics, including particularly the importance of privacy of student disciplinary records and addressing bias and conflict of interest in the student conduct process; (h) a description of available personal counseling programs and referral resources; (i) an outline of conditions and interactions which may involve external enforcement officials, attorneys, witnesses, parents of accused students, and the media; and (j) an overview of developmental and interpersonal issues likely to arise among college students.

Inservice training should include participation in relevant and on-going workshops, seminars, and conferences. A library containing current resources about the student conduct system should be maintained and be accessible to student conduct board members.

Part 3. ORGANIZATION AND LEADERSHIP

To achieve student and program outcomes, Student Conduct Programs (SCP) must be structured purposefully and organized effectively. SCP must have
- clearly stated goals
- current and accessible policies and procedures
- written performance expectations for employees
- functional work flow graphics or organizational charts demonstrating clear channels of authority

Leaders with organizational authority for the programs and services must provide strategic planning, supervision, and management; advance the organization; and maintain integrity through the following functions:

Strategic Planning
- articulate a vision and mission that drive short- and long-term planning
- set goals and objectives based on the needs of the population served and desired student learning or development and program outcomes
- facilitate continuous development, implementation, and assessment of goal attainment congruent with institutional mission and strategic plans
- promote environments that provide meaningful opportunities for student learning, development, and engagement
- develop and continuously improve programs and services in response to the changing needs of students served and evolving institutional priorities
- intentionally include diverse perspectives to inform decision making

Supervising
- manage human resource processes including recruitment, selection, development, supervision, performance planning, evaluation, recognition, and reward
- influence others to contribute to the effectiveness and success of the unit
- empower professional, support, and student staff to accept leadership opportunities
- offer appropriate feedback to colleagues and students on skills needed to become more effective leaders
- encourage and support professional development, collaboration with colleagues and departments across the institution, and scholarly contribution to the profession

Managing
- identify and address individual, organizational, and environmental conditions that foster or inhibit mission achievement
- plan, allocate, and monitor the use of fiscal, physical, human, intellectual, and technological resources
- use current and valid evidence to inform decisions
- incorporate sustainability practices in the management and design of programs, services, and facilities
- understand appropriate technologies and integrate them into programs and services
- be knowledgeable about codes and laws relevant to programs and services and ensure that staff members understand their responsibilities through appropriate training
- assess potential risks and take action to mitigate them

Advancing the Organization
- communicate effectively in writing, speaking, and electronic venues
- advocate for programs and services
- advocate for representation in strategic planning initiatives at appropriate divisional and institutional levels
- initiate collaborative interactions with internal and external stakeholders who have legitimate concerns about and interests in the functional area
- facilitate processes to reach consensus where wide support is needed
- inform other areas within the institution about issues affecting practice

Maintaining Integrity
- model ethical behavior and institutional citizenship
- share data used to inform key decisions in transparent and accessible ways
- monitor media used for distributing information about programs and services to ensure the content is current, accurate, appropriately referenced, and accessible

Part 4. HUMAN RESOURCES

Student Conduct Programs (SCP) must be staffed adequately by individuals qualified to accomplish mission and goals.

Within institutional guidelines, SCP must

- establish procedures for staff recruitment and selection, training, performance planning, and evaluation
- set expectations for supervision and performance
- assess the performance of employees individually and as a team
- provide access to continuing and advanced education and appropriate professional development opportunities to improve the leadership ability, competence, and skills of all employees.

SCP must maintain position descriptions for all staff members.

To create a diverse staff, SCP must institute recruitment and hiring strategies that encourage individuals from under-represented populations to apply for positions.

SCP must develop promotion practices that are fair, inclusive, proactive, and non-discriminatory.

To further the recruitment and retention of staff, SCP must consider work life initiatives, such as compressed work schedules, flextime, job sharing, remote work, or telework.

SCP professional staff members must hold an earned graduate or professional degree in a field relevant to the position they hold or must possess an appropriate combination of educational credentials and related work experience.

SCP professional staff members must engage in continuing professional development activities to keep abreast of the research, theories, legislation, policies, and developments that affect their programs and services.

SCP must have technical and support staff members adequate to accomplish their mission. All members of the staff must be technologically proficient and qualified to perform their job functions, be knowledgeable about ethical and legal uses of technology, and have access to training and resources to support the performance of their assigned responsibilities.

Degree- or credential-seeking interns or graduate assistants must be qualified by enrollment in an appropriate field of study and by relevant experience. These individuals must be trained and supervised adequately by professional staff members holding educational credentials and related work experience appropriate for supervision. Supervisors must be cognizant of the roles of interns and graduate

assistants as both student and employee and closely adhere to all parameters of their job descriptions, work hours, and schedules. Supervisors and the interns or graduate assistants must agree to compensatory time or other appropriate compensation if circumstances necessitate additional hours.

Student employees and volunteers must be carefully selected, trained, supervised, and evaluated. They must be educated on how and when to refer those in need of additional assistance to qualified staff members and must have access to a supervisor for assistance in making these judgments. Student employees and volunteers must be provided clear job descriptions, pre-service training based on assessed needs, and continuing development.

Students from graduate academic programs, particularly in areas such as counseling, student development, higher education administration, law, or criminology, may assist the student conduct programs through practicums, internships, and assistantships.

Students who participate on conduct boards may be awarded academic credit for proper supervision. Clear objectives and assignments should be outlined to ensure that a student's grade for this participation is in no way influenced by his/her decisions on a particular case.

All SCP staff members, including student employees and volunteers, must receive specific training on institutional policies pertaining to functions or activities they support and to privacy and confidentiality policies and laws regarding access to student records and other sensitive institutional information.

All SCP staff members must receive training on policies and procedures related to the use of technology to store or access student records and institutional data.

SCP must ensure that staff members are knowledgeable about and trained in emergency procedures, crisis response, and prevention efforts. Prevention efforts must address identification of threatening conduct or behavior of students, faculty and staff members, and others and must incorporate a system for responding and reporting.

SCP must ensure that staff members are knowledgeable of and trained in safety and emergency procedures for securing and vacating facilities.

A qualified member of the campus community must be designated as the person responsible for student conduct programs.

The designee should have an educational background in the

behavioral sciences (e.g., college student affairs, psychology, sociology, student development including moral and ethical development, higher education administration, counseling, law, criminology, or criminal justice).

The designee and any other professional staff member in the student conduct programs should possess (a) a clear understanding of the legal requirements for substantive and procedural due process; (b) legal knowledge sufficient to confer with attorneys involved in student disciplinary proceedings and other aspects of the student conduct services system; (c) a general interest in and commitment to the welfare and development of students who participate on boards or who are involved in cases; (d) demonstrated skills in working with decision-making processes and conflict resolution; (e) teaching and consulting skills appropriate for the education, advising, and coordination of hearing bodies; (f) the ability to communicate and interact with students regardless of race, sex, disability, sexual orientation, and other personal characteristics; (g) understanding of the requirements relative to confidentiality and security of student conduct programs files; and (h) the ability to create an atmosphere where students feel free to ask questions and obtain assistance.

Part 5. ETHICS

Student Conduct Programs (SCP) must review relevant professional ethical standards and must adopt or develop and implement appropriate statements of ethical practice.

SCP must publish and adhere to statements of ethical practice and ensure their periodic review by relevant constituencies.

SCP must orient new staff members to relevant ethical standards and statements of ethical practice and related institutional policies.

Statements of ethical standards must specify that staff members respect privacy and maintain confidentiality in all communications and records to the extent that such communications and records are protected under relevant privacy laws.

Statements of ethical standards must specify limits on disclosure of information contained in students' educational records as well as requirements to disclose to appropriate authorities.

Statements of ethical standards must address personal and economic conflicts of interest, or appearance thereof, by staff members in the performance of their work.

Statements of ethical standards must reflect the responsibility of staff members to be fair, objective, and impartial in their interactions with others.

Statements of ethical standards must reference management of institutional funds.

Statements of ethical standards must reference appropriate behavior regarding research and assessment with human participants, confidentiality of research and assessment data, and students' rights and responsibilities.

Statements of ethical standards must include the expectation that SCP staff members confront and hold accountable other staff members who exhibit unethical behavior.

Statements of ethical standards must address issues surrounding scholarly integrity.

As appropriate, staff members must inform users of programs and services of ethical obligations and limitations emanating from codes and laws or from licensure requirements.

SCP staff members must recognize and avoid conflicts of interest that could adversely influence their judgment or objectivity and, when unavoidable, recuse themselves from the situation.

SCP staff members must perform their duties within the limits of their position, training, expertise, and competence.

When these limits are exceeded, individuals in need of further assistance must be referred to persons possessing appropriate qualifications.

Promotional and descriptive information must be accurate and free of deception.

SCP must adhere to institutional policies regarding ethical and legal use of software and technology.

Part 6. LAW, POLICY, AND GOVERNANCE

Student Conduct Programs (SCP) must be in compliance with laws, regulations, and policies that relate to their respective responsibilities and that pose legal obligations, limitations, risks, and liabilities for the institution as a whole. Examples include constitutional, statutory, regulatory, and case law; relevant law and orders emanating from codes and laws; and the institution's policies.

SCP must inform staff members, appropriate officials, and users of programs and services about existing and changing legal obligations, risks and liabilities, and limitations.

SCP must have written policies on all relevant operations, transactions, or tasks that have legal implications.

SCP must regularly review policies. The revision

and creation of policies must be informed by best practices, available evidence, and policy issues in higher education.

SCP staff members must use reasonable and informed practices to limit the liability exposure of the institution and its officers, employees, and agents. SCP staff members must be informed about institutional policies regarding risk management, personal liability, and related insurance coverage options and must be referred to external sources if the institution does not provide coverage.

The institution must provide access to legal advice for staff members as needed to carry out assigned responsibilities.

SCP must have procedures and guidelines consistent with institutional policy for responding to threats, emergencies, and crisis situations. Systems and procedures must be in place to disseminate timely and accurate information to students, other members of the institutional community, and appropriate external organizations during emergency situations.

SCP staff members must neither participate in nor condone any form of harassment or activity that demeans persons or creates an intimidating, hostile, or offensive environment.

SCP must obtain permission to use copyrighted materials and instruments. SCP must purchase the materials and instruments from legally compliant sources or seek alternative permission from the publisher or owner. References to copyrighted materials and instruments must include appropriate citations.

SCP staff members must be knowledgeable about internal and external governance systems that affect programs and services.

Appropriate policies and practices to ensure compliance with regulations should include notification to all constituencies of their rights and responsibilities under the student conduct system, a written description, accurate record keeping of all aspects of the student conduct proceedings, and regular reviews of the student conduct policies and practices.

Part 7. DIVERSITY, EQUITY, AND ACCESS

Within the context of each institution's unique mission and in accordance with institutional polices and all applicable codes and laws, Student Conduct Programs (SCP) must create and maintain educational and work environments that are
- welcoming, accessible, and inclusive to persons of diverse backgrounds
- equitable and non-discriminatory
- free from harassment

SCP must not discriminate on the basis of ability; age; cultural identity; ethnicity; family educational history (e.g., first generation to attend college); gender identity and expression; nationality; political affiliation; race; religious affiliation; sex; sexual orientation; economic, marital, social, or veteran status; or any other basis included in institutional policies and codes and laws.

SCP must
- advocate for greater sensitivity to multicultural and social justice concerns by the institution and its personnel
- modify or remove policies, practices, facilities, structures, systems, and technologies that limit access, discriminate, or produce inequities
- include diversity, equity, and access initiatives within their strategic plans
- foster communication that deepens understanding of identity, culture, self-expression, and heritage
- promote respect about commonalities and differences among people within their historical and cultural contexts
- address the characteristics and needs of a diverse population when establishing and implementing culturally relevant and inclusive programs, services, policies, procedures, and practices
- provide staff members with access to multicultural training and hold staff members accountable for integrating the training into their work
- respond to the needs of all students and other populations served when establishing hours of operation and developing methods of delivering programs, services, and resources
- ensure physical, program, and resource access for persons with disabilities
- recognize the needs of distance learning students by providing appropriate and accessible services and resources or by assisting them in gaining access to other appropriate services and resources in their geographic region

Part 8. INSTITUTIONAL AND EXTERNAL RELATIONS

Student Conduct Programs (SCP) must reach out to relevant individuals, groups, communities, and organizations internal and external to the institution to
- establish, maintain, and promote understanding and effective relations with those that have a significant interest in or potential effect on the students or other

- constituents served by the programs and services
- garner support and resources for programs and services as defined by the mission statement
- disseminate information about the programs and services
- collaborate, where appropriate, to assist in offering or improving programs and services to meet the needs of students and other constituents and to achieve program and student outcomes
- engage diverse individuals, groups, communities, and organizations to enrich the educational environment and experiences of students and other constituents

SCP must have procedures and guidelines consistent with institutional policy for
- communicating with the media
- contracting with external organizations for delivery of programs and services
- cultivating, soliciting, and managing gifts
- applying to and managing funds from grants

Representatives of the student conduct system should meet regularly with pertinent campus constituencies (e.g., student government, student development offices, staff, faculty members, academic administrators, public safety, legal counsel) to exchange information concerning their respective operations and to identify ways to work together to prevent behavioral problems and to correct existing ones. Such collaborative efforts might include educational programs and joint publications.

Representatives should also meet periodically with relevant external agencies (e.g., local police, district attorneys, service providers) to ensure understanding about the student conduct programs as well as to address student behavior problems in an effective manner.

Part 9. FINANCIAL RESOURCES

SCP must have funding to accomplish the mission and goals. In establishing funding priorities and making significant changes, a comprehensive analysis must be conducted to determine the following elements: unmet needs of the unit, relevant expenditures, external and internal resources, and impact on students and the institution.

SCP must demonstrate efficient and effective use and responsible stewardship of fiscal resources consistent with institutional protocols.

Part 10. TECHNOLOGY

Student Conduct Programs (SCP) must have adequate technology to support the achievement of their

mission and goals. The technology and its use must comply with institutional policies and procedures and be evaluated for compliance with relevant codes and laws.

SCP must use current technology to provide updated information regarding mission, location, staffing, programs, services, and official contacts to students and designated clients.

SCP must explore the use of technology to enhance delivery of programs and services, especially for students at a distance or external constituencies.

When technology is used to facilitate student learning and development, SCP must select technology that reflects intended outcomes.

SCP must
- maintain policies and procedures that address the security, confidentiality, and backup of data, as well as compliance with privacy laws
- have clearly articulated plans in place for protecting confidentiality and security of information when using Internet-based technologies
- develop plans for replacing and updating existing hardware and software as well as plans for integrating new technically-based or supported programs, including systems developed internally by the institution, systems available through professional associations, or private vendor-based systems

Technology, as well as workstations or computer labs maintained by programs and services for student use, must be accessible to all designated clients and must meet established technology standards for delivery to persons with disabilities.

When providing student access to technology, SCP must
- have policies on the use of technology that are clear, easy to understand, and available to all students
- provide assistance, information, or referral to appropriate support services to those needing help accessing or using technology
- provide instruction or training on how to use the technology
- inform students on the legal and ethical implications of misuse as it pertains to intellectual property, harassment, privacy, and social networks

Student violations of technology policies must follow established institutional student disciplinary procedures.

Students who experience negative emotional or psychological consequences from the use of technology must be referred to support services provided by the institution.

Part 11. FACILITIES AND EQUIPMENT

Student Conduct Programs (SCP) must have adequate, accessible, and suitably located facilities and equipment to support the mission and goals. If acquiring capital equipment as defined by the institution, SCP must take into account expenses related to regular maintenance and life cycle costs. Facilities and equipment must be evaluated on an established cycle, including consideration of sustainability, and be in compliance with codes and laws to provide for access, health, safety, and security.

SCP staff members must have workspace that is well equipped, adequate in size, and designed to support their work and responsibilities. For conversations requiring privacy, staff members must have access to a private space.

SCP staff members who share workspace must be able to secure their own work.

The design of the facilities must guarantee the security and privacy of records and ensure the confidentiality of sensitive information.

The location and layout of the facilities must be sensitive to the needs of persons with disabilities as well as the needs of other constituencies.

SCP must have access to facilities of sufficient size and arrangement to ensure privacy of records, meetings, and interviews.

The facilities should include a private office where individual consultations and pre-hearing conferences with those involved in disciplinary actions may be held, hearing room facilities, a meeting room for small groups, a library or resource area, and a secure location for student disciplinary records. The facilities should also be designed to promote the personal safety of the individuals involved in the SCP (e.g., multiple methods of egress, panic buttons).

Part 12. ASSESSMENT AND EVALUATION

Student Conduct Programs (SCP) must have a clearly articulated assessment plan to document achievement of stated goals and learning outcomes, demonstrate accountability, provide evidence of improvement, and describe resulting changes in programs and services.

SCP must have adequate fiscal, human, professional development, and technological resources to develop and implement assessment plans.

Assessments must include direct and indirect evaluation and use qualitative and quantitative methodologies and existing evidence, as appropriate, to determine whether and to what degree the stated mission, goals, and intended outcomes are being met as effectively and efficiently as possible. The process must employ sufficient and sound measures to ensure comprehensiveness. Data collected must include responses from students and other constituencies, and aggregated results must be shared with those groups. Results of assessments must be shared appropriately with multiple constituents.

Results of assessments and evaluations must be used to identify needs and interests in revising and improving programs and services, recognizing staff performance, maximizing resource efficiency and effectiveness, improving student achievement of learning and development outcomes, and improving student persistence and success. Changes resulting from the use of assessments and evaluation must be shared with stakeholders.

Evaluation of SCP should include
- performance evaluations of all staff members by their supervisors
- periodic performance evaluations of individual hearing boards
- ongoing evaluation of training programs and publications
- periodic review of applicable laws and current case law to ensure compliance

Assessment and evaluation activities may include
- whether student conduct boards accurately follow the institution's procedural guidelines
- general impressions of the student conduct system according to students, faculty members, staff members, and the community
- developmental effects on students and student conduct board members
- annual trends in case load, rates of recidivism, types of offenses, and efficacy of sanctions
- effects of programming designed to prevent behavioral problems
- unique aspects of special function or special population student conduct boards (e.g., student organization, residence hall boards)

General Standards revised in 2011;
SCP content (formerly Judicial Programs and Services) developed/revised in 1986, 1996, & 2005

The Role of Student Leadership Programs
CAS Standards Contextual Statement

Many college mission statements contain commitments to develop citizen leaders or prepare students for professional and community responsibilities in a global context. Throughout the history of higher education, however, leadership development has been targeted primarily toward students holding leadership positions, such as student government officials, officers in fraternities and sororities, and resident assistants. Consequently, only a handful of students had a genuine opportunity for focused experience in leadership development.

During the 1970s, many colleges refocused efforts on leadership development when events such as the Watergate scandal caused institutions to ponder how they taught ethics, leadership, and social responsibility. Subsequent initiatives such as the women's and African-American civil rights movements and adult reentry programs increased access to college. New forms of campus shared governance, coupled with a focus on intentional student development, led to new forms of leadership development through programs such as assertiveness training, emerging leaders' retreats, and leadership targeted toward specific populations.

By the 1970s, professional associations were becoming increasingly interested in broad-based leadership efforts. Several associations, including the American College Personnel Association (ACPA), National Association of Student Personnel Administrators (NASPA), National Association for Campus Activities (NACA), and National Association for Women in Education (NAWE), expanded projects and initiatives with a leadership focus. Burns' seminal book, *Leadership* (1978), brought new energy with its discussion of transformational leadership grounded in values and moral purpose. Thinking about leadership expanded in the 1980s and 1990s to include such perspectives as cultural influences, service learning, social change, and spirituality. Leadership educators focused on developing leadership models with applicability to the college context. Two such models, the Social Change Model of Leadership (SCM) (HERI, 1996) and the Relational Leadership Model (Komives, Lucas, & McMahon, 1996), have been widely adopted.

This shift to colleges developing not just better, but more leaders, has resulted in leadership education efforts directed toward the entire student body. Because students experience leadership in many different settings—in and out of the classroom, on and off campus, through social media, virtually every student engages in some type of activity that involves the practice of leadership. Regardless of differences in academic discipline, organizational affiliation, cultural background, or geographical location, students must be better prepared to serve as citizen-leaders in a global community. The role of student affairs professionals in this arena is to help students understand their experiences and to facilitate their learning so that they become effective contributors to their communities. Comprehensive leadership programs should be based on an active learning pedagogy where learning is situated in students' experiences, where students are validated as knowers, and where there is mutually constructed meaning (Baxter Magolda, 1999).

The Inter-Association Leadership Project brought student affairs leadership educators together in the mid-1980s to create and sustain a leadership agenda. By the end of the decade, higher education's commitment to leadership was clear—with over 600 campuses teaching leadership courses. Special leadership centers were created, such as the Jepson School of Leadership Studies at the University of Richmond and the McDonough Leadership Center at Marietta College, as well as special programs, including the National LeaderShape Institute. In 1992 the National Clearinghouse for Leadership Programs (NCLP) was established at the University of Maryland, and a co-sponsored series of symposia encouraged leadership educators to identify a leadership agenda for the new millennium. Projects funded by the Kellogg, Pew, and Lilly Foundations; FIPSE; and the federal Eisenhower Leadership grant program have also focused broad-based attention on leadership development. By late 1990s, there were over 800 college leadership programs.

The International Leadership Association (ILA) was established in 1999 to bring a global lens to leadership education; ILA developed a set of guiding questions to inform curricular leadership development. The Association of Leadership Educators, largely agricultural and community-based leadership faculty, has a focus on college students. Other leadership institutes serve the leadership educator professional; for example, NCLP and the NACA host the annual summer leadership educators' symposium, and NCLP in partnership with NASPA and ACPA now hosts the Leadership Educators Institute, a bi-annual program for entry and mid-level leadership educators. NCLP and the Association of College Unions International (ACUI) had a webinar series, and NACA developed a set of student leadership competencies. A detailed history of the evolution of leadership education can be found in the *Handbook for Student Leadership Development* (Komives, 2010).

The *CAS Student Leadership Program Standards and Guidelines* can be used to help professionals provide comprehensive leadership programs and enhance students' learning opportunities. Leadership for positional leaders will still occur within specific functional areas such as student activities and residence life; campuses that seek to develop a comprehensive leadership program will recognize the need to make intentional leadership development opportunities available to all students through coordinated campus-wide efforts. Research contains developmental models (e.g., Leadership Identity Development model; Komives, Owen, Longerbeam, Mainella, & Osteen, 2005) that can guide intentional practice. Further, an international Multi-Institutional Study of Leadership has established normative data using the SCM (see www.nclp.umd.edu).

Leadership is an inherently relational process of working with others to accomplish a goal or to promote change. Most leadership programs seek to empower students to enhance their self-efficacy as leaders and understand how they can make a difference, whether as positional leaders or active participants in a group or community process. Leadership development involves self-awareness and understanding of others, values and diverse perspectives, organizations, and change. Leadership also requires competence in establishing purpose, working collaboratively, and managing conflict. Institutions can initiate opportunities to study leadership and to experience a range of leadership-related activities designed to intentionally promote desired outcomes of student leadership learning.

References, Readings, and Resources

Astin, H., & Astin, A., (Eds.). (2000). *Leadership reconsidered: Engaging higher education in social change.* Battle Creek, MI: W.K. Kellogg Foundation.

Baxter Magolda, M. B. (1999). *Creating contexts for learning and self-authorship: Constructive-developmental pedagogy.* Nashville, TN: Vanderbilt University Press.

Boatman, S. (1987). *Student leadership development: Approaches, methods, and models.* Columbia, SC: National Association for Campus Activities.

Boatman, S. (1992). *Supporting student leadership: Selections from the student development series.* Columbia, SC: National Association for Campus Activities.

Brungardt, C. (1996). The making of leaders: A review of the research in leadership development and education. *Journal of Leadership Studies, 3*(3), 81-95.

Center for Creative Leadership, One Leadership Place, P.O. Box 26300, Greensboro, NC 27438-6300. (910) 288-7210. Publisher of periodic sourcebooks.

Concepts & connections: A newsletter for leadership educators. The National Clearinghouse for Leadership Programs, 1135 Stamp Student Union, University of Maryland at College Park, College Park, MD 20742-4631. (301) 314-7174

Guthrie, K. & Osteen, L. (Eds). (2012). *Developing student leadership capacity.* New Directions for Student Services. San Francisco, CA: Jossey-Bass.

HERI_(1996)._*A social change model of leadership development: Guidebook version III.* Los Angeles: University of California Los Angeles Higher Education Research Institute. *(Available from National Clearinghouse for Leadership Programs).*

Journal of Leadership Education, Association for Leadership Education, http://www.leadershipeducators.org/

Komives, S. R., Lucas, N., & McMahon, T. (1998). *Exploring leadership.* San Francisco: Jossey-Bass.

Komives, S. R., Owen, J. E., Longerbeam, S., Mainella, F. C., & Osteen, L. (2005). Developing a leadership identity: A grounded theory. *Journal of College Student Development, 46,* 593-611.

Komives, S. R., Dugan, J., Owen, J. E., Slack, C., & Wagner, W. (Eds). (2011). *Handbook for student leadership development (2nd ed.).* A publication of the National Clearinghouse for Leadership Programs. San Francisco, CA: Jossey-Bass.

Leadership Quarterly. JAI Press, 55 Old Post Road, # 2, P.O. Box 1678, Greenwich, CT 06836-1678. (203) 661-7602

Murray, J. I. (1994). *Training for student leaders.* Dubuque, IA: Kendall/Hunt.

Roberts, D. C. (1981). *Student leadership programs in higher education.* Carbondale, IL: American College Personnel Association.

Zimmerman-Oster, K., & Burkhardt, J. C. (1999). *Leadership in the making: Impact and insights from leadership development programs in U. S. colleges and universities.* Battle Creek, MI: W. K. Kellogg Foundation.

Contextual Statement Contributors

Current Edition:
Susan Komives, University of Maryland, ACPA

Previous Editions:
Jan Arminio, Shippensburg University, NACA
Susan Komives, University of Maryland, ACPA
Julie Owen, George Mason University, NCLP
Craig Slack, University of Maryland, NCLP

Student Leadership Programs
CAS Standards and Guidelines

Part 1. MISSION

The mission of Student Leadership Programs (SLP) must be to prepare students to engage in the process of leadership. To accomplish this mission, the program must
- be grounded in the belief that leadership can be learned
- be based upon clearly stated principles, values, and assumptions
- use multiple leadership theories, models, and approaches
- provide students with opportunities to develop and enhance a personal philosophy of leadership that includes understanding of self, others, and community, and acceptance of responsibilities inherent in community membership
- promote intentional student involvement and learning in varied leadership experiences
- acknowledge effective leadership behaviors and processes
- be inclusive and accessible, by encouraging and seeking out underrepresented populations

SLP must develop, disseminate, implement, and regularly review their missions. The mission must be consistent with the mission of the institution and with professional standards. The mission must be appropriate for the institution's student populations and community settings. Mission statements must reference student learning and development.

Student leadership development must be an integral part of the institution's educational mission.

The SLP mission should be developed in collaboration with appropriate and multiple constituents interested in leadership development.

SLP should seek an institution-wide commitment that transcends the boundaries of the units specifically charged with program delivery.

Part 2. PROGRAM

The formal education of students, consisting of the curriculum and the co-curriculum, must promote student learning and development outcomes that are purposeful, contribute to students' realization of their potential, and prepare students for satisfying and productive lives.

Student Leadership Programs (SLP) must collaborate with colleagues and departments across the institution to promote student learning and development, persistence, and success.

Consistent with the institutional mission, SLP must identify relevant and desirable student learning and development outcomes from among the six domains and related dimensions:

Domain: knowledge acquisition, integration, construction, and application
- Dimensions: understanding knowledge from a range of disciplines; connecting knowledge to other knowledge, ideas, and experiences; constructing knowledge; and relating knowledge to daily life

Domain: cognitive complexity
- Dimensions: critical thinking, reflective thinking, effective reasoning, and creativity

Domain: intrapersonal development
- Dimensions: realistic self-appraisal, self-understanding, and self-respect; identity development; commitment to ethics and integrity; and spiritual awareness

Domain: interpersonal competence
- Dimensions: meaningful relationships, interdependence, collaboration, and effective leadership.

Domain: humanitarianism and civic engagement
- Dimensions: understanding and appreciation of cultural and human differences, social responsibility, global perspective, and sense of civic responsibility

Domain: practical competence
- Dimensions: pursuing goals, communicating effectively, technical competence, managing personal affairs, managing career development, demonstrating professionalism, maintaining health and wellness, and living a purposeful and satisfying life

[LD Outcomes: See The Council for the Advancement of Standards Learning and Developmental Outcomes statement for examples of outcomes related to these domains and dimensions.]

SLP must
- assess relevant and desirable student learning and development

- provide evidence of impact on outcomes
- articulate contributions to or support of student learning and development in the domains not specifically assessed
- articulate contributions to or support of student persistence and success
- use evidence gathered through this process to create strategies for improvement of programs and services

SLP must be
- intentionally designed
- guided by theories and knowledge of learning and development
- integrated into the life of the institution
- reflective of developmental and demographic profiles of the student population
- responsive to needs of individuals, populations with distinct needs, and relevant constituencies
- delivered using multiple formats, strategies, and contexts

Where institutions provide distance education, SLP must assist distance learners to achieve their educational goals by providing access to information about programs and services, to staff members who can address questions and concerns, and to counseling, advising, or other forms of assistance.

SLP must be comprehensive in nature and provide opportunities for students to develop leadership knowledge and skills. SLP staff must design learning environments reflective of the institutional mission, organizational context, learning goals, and intended audience. Programs must have clear theoretical foundations and be based upon well-defined principles, values, and assumptions. Programs must facilitate students' self-awareness, their capacity for collaboration, and their ability to engage within multiple contexts while understanding diverse perspectives.

Key components of SLP must include the following: opportunities for students to develop the competencies required for effective leadership; multiple delivery formats, strategies, and contexts; and collaboration with campus and community partners. These components are described in more detail below.

A. **SLP must provide opportunities for students to develop the competencies required for effective leadership.**

SLP must advance student competencies in the categories of foundations of leadership; personal development; interpersonal development; and the development of groups, organizations,

and systems. Suggested content for each of these categories follows.

Foundations of leadership should include
- historical perspectives on leaders, leadership, and leadership development
- established and evolving theoretical, conceptual, and philosophical frameworks of leadership
- the distinction between management and leadership
- diverse approaches to leadership including positional (leadership-follower dynamics) and non-positional (collaborative-process models)
- theories and strategies of change
- the integrative and interdisciplinary nature of leadership
- cross-cultural and global approaches to leadership

Personal development should include
- an awareness and understanding of various leadership styles and approaches
- exploration of a personal leadership philosophy, including personal values exploration, leadership identity development, and reflective practice
- connection of leadership to social identities and other dimensions of human development, such as psychosocial, cognitive, moral, and spiritual development
- leadership skill development, including accessing and critiquing sources of information, ethical reasoning and decision making, oral and written communication skills, critical thinking and problem-solving, cultural competence, goal setting and visioning, motivation, creativity, and risk-taking

Interpersonal development should include
- movement from dependent or independent to interdependent relationships
- development of self-efficacy for leadership
- recognition of the influences on leadership of multiple aspects of identity, such as race, gender identity and expression, sexual orientation, class, disability, nationality, religion, and ethnicity

Development of groups, organizations, and systems should include
Group competencies:
- team building
- developing trust
- group roles, group dynamics, and group development
- group problem-solving, conflict management, and decision-making

- shared leadership and collaboration

Organizational competencies:
- organizational planning, communication, and development
- organizational culture, values, and principles
- organizational politics and political systems
- organizational lifecycles, sustainability, and stewardship
- methods of assessing and evaluating organizational effectiveness

Systems competencies:
- understanding and critiquing of systems and human behavior within systems including functional and dysfunctional practices
- coalition-building and other methods of systemic change
- civic and community engagement
- leadership across diverse organizations, environments, and contexts

B. **SLP must provide multiple delivery formats, strategies, and contexts. SLP must be intentionally designed to meet the developmental needs of participants across diverse contexts. SLP programs must be based on principles of active learning.**

Examples of delivery formats include retreats, conferences, credit-bearing courses, workshops, internships, panel discussions, case studies, films, lectures, simulations, mentor programs, adventure training, assessment tools, portfolios, and participation in local, regional, and national associations. Consideration should be given to on-line delivery methods.

SLP should provide strategies that may include training, education, and development. SLP *training* refers to activities designed to improve individual performance within specific roles; *education* consists of activities designed to provide improve the overall leadership knowledge of an individual; and *development* involves activities and environments that encourage growth and increasing complexity.

SLP should provide strategies that involve programs and services that are *open* to all students, *targeted* to a specific group of students, and aimed at students with *positional* leadership roles.

SLP should include multiple *contexts* for leadership development, such as diverse academic and career fields, campus organizations and committees, employment and internship settings, community involvement and service-learning, family, international settings, and social and religious organizations.

C. **SLP must collaborate with campus and community partners**

SLP must involve a diverse range of partners in the planning, delivery, and assessment of programs and services.

This group may include faculty members, students, staff members, group advisors, community members, and on- and off-campus organizations.

SLP should consider collaborating with a broad range of campus departments, community groups, schools, and businesses to increase awareness of leadership programs, fiscal and human resources, and access to additional sources of leadership expertise.

Part 3. ORGANIZATION AND LEADERSHIP

To achieve student and program outcomes, Student Leadership Programs (SLP) be structured purposefully and organized effectively. SLP must have
- **clearly stated goals**
- **current and accessible policies and procedures**
- **written performance expectations for employees**
- **functional work flow graphics or organizational charts demonstrating clear channels of authority**

Leaders with organizational authority for the programs and services must provide strategic planning, supervision, and management; advance the organization; and maintain integrity through the following functions:

Strategic Planning
- **articulate a vision and mission that drive short- and long-term planning**
- **set goals and objectives based on the needs of the population served and desired student learning or development and program outcomes**
- **facilitate continuous development, implementation, and assessment of goal attainment congruent with institutional mission and strategic plans**
- **promote environments that provide meaningful opportunities for student learning, development, and engagement**
- **develop and continuously improve programs and services in response to the changing needs of students served and evolving institutional priorities**
- **intentionally include diverse perspectives to inform decision making**

Supervising
- **manage human resource processes including recruitment, selection, development, supervision, performance planning,**

evaluation, recognition, and reward
- influence others to contribute to the effectiveness and success of the unit
- empower professional, support, and student staff to accept leadership opportunities
- offer appropriate feedback to colleagues and students on skills needed to become more effective leaders
- encourage and support professional development, collaboration with colleagues and departments across the institution, and scholarly contribution to the profession

Managing
- identify and address individual, organizational, and environmental conditions that foster or inhibit mission achievement
- plan, allocate, and monitor the use of fiscal, physical, human, intellectual, and technological resources
- use current and valid evidence to inform decisions
- incorporate sustainability practices in the management and design of programs, services, and facilities
- understand appropriate technologies and integrate them into programs and services
- be knowledgeable about codes and laws relevant to programs and services and ensure that staff members understand their responsibilities through appropriate training
- assess potential risks and take action to mitigate them

Advancing the Organization
- communicate effectively in writing, speaking, and electronic venues
- advocate for programs and services
- advocate for representation in strategic planning initiatives at appropriate divisional and institutional levels
- initiate collaborative interactions with internal and external stakeholders who have legitimate concerns about and interests in the functional area
- facilitate processes to reach consensus where wide support is needed
- inform other areas within the institution about issues affecting practice

Maintaining Integrity
- model ethical behavior and institutional citizenship
- share data used to inform key decisions in transparent and accessible ways
- monitor media used for distributing information about programs and services

to ensure the content is current, accurate, appropriately referenced, and accessible

An individual or team should be designated with responsibility for the coordination of the leadership program, including allocation and maintenance of resources and creating leadership opportunities.

SLP are organized in a variety of offices and departments in student and academic affairs, and in other administrative areas. An advisory group with representatives from the involved areas and other relevant campus and community partners should be established for the purpose of communication and consultation.

Part 4. HUMAN RESOURCES

Student Leadership Programs (SLP) must be staffed adequately by individuals qualified to accomplish mission and goals.

Within institutional guidelines, SLP must
- establish procedures for staff recruitment and selection, training, performance planning, and evaluation
- set expectations for supervision and performance
- assess the performance of employees individually and as a team
- provide access to continuing and advanced education and appropriate professional development opportunities to improve the leadership ability, competence, and skills of all employees.

SLP must maintain position descriptions for all staff members.

To create a diverse staff, SLP must institute recruitment and hiring strategies that encourage individuals from under-represented populations to apply for positions.

SLP must develop promotion practices that are fair, inclusive, proactive, and non-discriminatory.

To further the recruitment and retention of staff, SLP must consider work life initiatives, such as compressed work schedules, flextime, job sharing, remote work, or telework.

SLP professional staff members must hold an earned graduate or professional degree in a field relevant to the position they hold or must possess an appropriate combination of educational credentials and related work experience.

Professional staff or faculty involved in leadership programs should possess
- knowledge of the history of and current trends in leadership theories, models, and philosophies

- an understanding of the contextual nature of leadership
- knowledge of organizational development, group dynamics, strategies for change, and principles of community
- knowledge of how social identities and dimensions of diversity influence leadership
- experience in leadership development
- the ability to work with diverse range of students
- the ability to create, implement and evaluate student learning as a result of leadership programs
- the ability to effectively organize learning opportunities that are consistent with students' stages of development
- the ability to use reflection in helping students understand leadership concepts
- the ability to develop and assess student learning outcomes

SLP professional staff members must engage in continuing professional development activities to keep abreast of the research, theories, legislation, policies, and developments that affect their programs and services.

SLP must have technical and support staff members adequate to accomplish their mission. All members of the staff must be technologically proficient and qualified to perform their job functions, be knowledgeable about ethical and legal uses of technology, and have access to training and resources to support the performance of their assigned responsibilities.

Degree- or credential-seeking interns or graduate assistants must be qualified by enrollment in an appropriate field of study and by relevant experience. These individuals must be trained and supervised adequately by professional staff members holding educational credentials and related work experience appropriate for supervision. Supervisors must be cognizant of the roles of interns and graduate assistants as both student and employee and closely adhere to all parameters of their job descriptions, work hours, and schedules. Supervisors and the interns or graduate assistants must agree to compensatory time or other appropriate compensation if circumstances necessitate additional hours.

Student employees and volunteers must be carefully selected, trained, supervised, and evaluated. They must be educated on how and when to refer those in need of additional assistance to qualified staff members and must have access to a supervisor for assistance in making these judgments. Student employees and volunteers must be provided clear job descriptions, pre-service training based on assessed needs, and continuing development.

All SLP staff members, including student employees

and volunteers, must receive specific training on institutional policies pertaining to functions or activities they support and to privacy and confidentiality policies and laws regarding access to student records and other sensitive institutional information.

All SLP staff members must receive training on policies and procedures related to the use of technology to store or access student records and institutional data.

SLP must ensure that staff members are knowledgeable about and trained in emergency procedures, crisis response, and prevention efforts. Prevention efforts must address identification of threatening conduct or behavior of students, faculty and staff members, and others and must incorporate a system for responding and reporting.

SLP must ensure that staff members are knowledgeable of and trained in safety and emergency procedures for securing and vacating facilities.

SLP staff serving as leadership educators must be knowledgeable about learning theories and their implications for student development, program design, and assessment.

Program staff should engage in continuous discovery and understanding of student leadership models, research, theories, and definitions through on-going study and professional development activities.

Part 5. ETHICS

Student Leadership Programs (SLP) must review relevant professional ethical standards and must adopt or develop and implement appropriate statements of ethical practice.

SLP must publish and adhere to statements of ethical practice and ensure their periodic review by relevant constituencies.

SLP must orient new staff members to relevant ethical standards and statements of ethical practice and related institutional policies.

Statements of ethical standards must specify that staff members respect privacy and maintain confidentiality in all communications and records to the extent that such communications and records are protected under relevant privacy laws.

Statements of ethical standards must specify limits on disclosure of information contained in students' educational records as well as requirements to disclose to appropriate authorities.

Statements of ethical standards must address personal and economic conflicts of interest, or appearance thereof, by staff members in the performance of their work.

Statements of ethical standards must reflect the responsibility of staff members to be fair, objective, and impartial in their interactions with others.

Statements of ethical standards must reference management of institutional funds.

Statements of ethical standards must reference appropriate behavior regarding research and assessment with human participants, confidentiality of research and assessment data, and students' rights and responsibilities.

Statements of ethical standards must include the expectation that SLP staff members confront and hold accountable other staff members who exhibit unethical behavior.

Statements of ethical standards must address issues surrounding scholarly integrity.

As appropriate, SLP staff members must inform users of programs and services of ethical obligations and limitations emanating from codes and laws or from licensure requirements.

SLP staff members must recognize and avoid conflicts of interest that could adversely influence their judgment or objectivity and, when unavoidable, recuse themselves from the situation.

SLP staff members must perform their duties within the limits of their position, training, expertise, and competence.

When these limits are exceeded, individuals in need of further assistance must be referred to persons possessing appropriate qualifications.

Promotional and descriptive information must be accurate and free of deception.

SLP must adhere to institutional policies regarding ethical and legal use of software and technology.

SLP staff members must ensure that facilitators have appropriate training, experience, and credentials. Expertise and certification, where appropriate, are essential in the administration and interpretation of personality, developmental, and leadership assessment instruments.

Part 6. LAW, POLICY, AND GOVERNANCE

Student Leadership Programs (SLP) must be in compliance with laws, regulations, and policies that relate to their respective responsibilities and that pose legal obligations, limitations, risks, and liabilities for the institution as a whole. Examples include constitutional, statutory, regulatory, and case law; relevant law and orders emanating from codes and laws; and the institution's policies.

SLP must inform staff members, appropriate officials, and users of programs and services about existing and changing legal obligations, risks and liabilities, and limitations.

SLP must have written policies on all relevant operations, transactions, or tasks that have legal implications.

SLP must regularly review policies. The revision and creation of policies must be informed by best practices, available evidence, and policy issues in higher education.

SLP staff members must use reasonable and informed practices to limit the liability exposure of the institution and its officers, employees, and agents. SLP staff members must be informed about institutional policies regarding risk management, personal liability, and related insurance coverage options and must be referred to external sources if the institution does not provide coverage.

The institution must provide access to legal advice for staff members as needed to carry out assigned responsibilities.

SLP must have procedures and guidelines consistent with institutional policy for responding to threats, emergencies, and crisis situations. Systems and procedures must be in place to disseminate timely and accurate information to students, other members of the institutional community, and appropriate external organizations during emergency situations.

SLP staff members must neither participate in nor condone any form of harassment or activity that demeans persons or creates an intimidating, hostile, or offensive environment.

SLP must obtain permission to use copyrighted materials and instruments. SLP must purchase the materials and instruments from legally compliant sources or seek alternative permission from the publisher or owner. References to copyrighted materials and instruments must include appropriate citations.

SLP staff members must be knowledgeable about internal and external governance systems that affect programs and services.

SLP must advocate for student involvement in institutional governance.

Part 7. DIVERSITY, EQUITY, AND ACCESS

Within the context of each institution's unique mission and in accordance with institutional polices and all applicable codes and laws, Student Leadership Programs (SLP) must create and maintain educational and work environments that are

- welcoming, accessible, and inclusive to persons of diverse backgrounds
- equitable and non-discriminatory
- free from harassment

SLP must not discriminate on the basis of ability; age; cultural identity; ethnicity; family educational history (e.g., first generation to attend college); gender identity and expression; nationality; political affiliation; race; religious affiliation; sex; sexual orientation; economic, marital, social, or veteran status; or any other basis included in institutional policies and codes and laws.

SLP must

- advocate for greater sensitivity to multicultural and social justice concerns by the institution and its personnel
- modify or remove policies, practices, facilities, structures, systems, and technologies that limit access, discriminate, or produce inequities
- include diversity, equity, and access initiatives within their strategic plans
- foster communication that deepens understanding of identity, culture, self-expression, and heritage
- promote respect about commonalities and differences among people within their historical and cultural contexts
- address the characteristics and needs of a diverse population when establishing and implementing culturally relevant and inclusive programs, services, policies, procedures, and practices
- provide staff members with access to multicultural training and hold staff members accountable for integrating the training into their work
- respond to the needs of all students and other populations served when establishing hours of operation and developing methods of delivering programs, services, and resources
- ensure physical, program, and resource access for persons with disabilities
- recognize the needs of distance learning students by providing appropriate and accessible services and resources or by assisting them in gaining access to other appropriate services and resources in their

geographic region

SLP must provide students with the opportunity to

- recognize the influences of aspects of social identity on personal and organizational leadership
- examine social identities, multiple identities, and other aspects of development and how they influence experiences in different contexts
- develop multicultural awareness, knowledge, and skills

Part 8. INSTITUTIONAL AND EXTERNAL RELATIONS

Student Leadership Programs (SLP) must reach out to relevant individuals, groups, communities, and organizations internal and external to the institution to

- establish, maintain, and promote understanding and effective relations with those that have a significant interest in or potential effect on the students or other constituents served by the programs and services
- garner support and resources for programs and services as defined by the mission statement
- disseminate information about the programs and services
- collaborate, where appropriate, to assist in offering or improving programs and services to meet the needs of students and other constituents and to achieve program and student outcomes
- engage diverse individuals, groups, communities, and organizations to enrich the educational environment and experiences of students and other constituents

SLP must have procedures and guidelines consistent with institutional policy for

- communicating with the media
- contracting with external organizations for delivery of programs and services
- cultivating, soliciting, and managing gifts
- applying to and managing funds from grants

Part 9. FINANCIAL RESOURCES

Student Leadership Programs (SLP) must have funding to accomplish the mission and goals. In establishing funding priorities and making significant changes, a comprehensive analysis must be conducted to determine the following elements: unmet needs of the unit, relevant expenditures, external and internal resources, and impact on students and the institution.

SLP must demonstrate efficient and effective use and responsible stewardship of fiscal resources consistent with institutional protocols.

Funding for SLP may come from a variety of sources, including institutional funds, grants, student fees, fees for services, individual donors, academic departments, course fees, and government contracts. Where possible, institutional funding should be allocated regularly and consistently for the operation of leadership programs.

Part 10. TECHNOLOGY

Student Leadership Programs (SLP) must have adequate technology to support the achievement of their mission and goals. The technology and its use must comply with institutional policies and procedures and be evaluated for compliance with relevant codes and laws.

SLP must use current technology to provide updated information regarding mission, location, staffing, programs, services, and official contacts to students and designated clients.

SLP must explore the use of technology to enhance delivery of programs and services, especially for students at a distance or external constituencies.

When technology is used to facilitate student learning and development, SLP must select technology that reflects intended outcomes.

SLP must
- maintain policies and procedures that address the security, confidentiality, and backup of data, as well as compliance with privacy laws
- have clearly articulated plans in place for protecting confidentiality and security of information when using Internet-based technologies
- develop plans for replacing and updating existing hardware and software as well as plans for integrating new technically-based or supported programs, including systems developed internally by the institution, systems available through professional associations, or private vendor-based systems

Technology, as well as workstations or computer labs maintained by programs and services for student use, must be accessible to all designated clients and must meet established technology standards for delivery to persons with disabilities.

When providing student access to technology, SLP must
- have policies on the use of technology that are clear, easy to understand, and available to all students
- provide assistance, information, or referral to appropriate support services to those needing help accessing or using technology
- provide instruction or training on how to use the technology
- inform students on the legal and ethical implications of misuse as it pertains to intellectual property, harassment, privacy, and social networks

Student violations of technology policies must follow established institutional student disciplinary procedures.

Students who experience negative emotional or psychological consequences from the use of technology must be referred to support services provided by the institution.

Part 11. FACILITIES AND EQUIPMENT

Student Leadership Programs (SLP) must have adequate, accessible, and suitably located facilities and equipment to support the mission and goals. If acquiring capital equipment as defined by the institution, programs and services must take into account expenses related to regular maintenance and life cycle costs. Facilities and equipment must be evaluated on an established cycle, including consideration of sustainability, and be in compliance with codes and laws to provide for access, health, safety, and security.

SLP offices and programming space should be conveniently located on campus and designed to facilitate maximum interaction among students, faculty members, and staff.

SLP staff members must have workspace that is well equipped, adequate in size, and designed to support their work and responsibilities. For conversations requiring privacy, staff members must have access to a private space.

SLP staff members who share workspace must be able to secure their own work.

The design of the facilities must guarantee the security and privacy of records and ensure the confidentiality of sensitive information.

The location and layout of the facilities must be sensitive to the needs of persons with disabilities as well as the needs of other constituencies.

Part 12. ASSESSMENT AND EVALUATION

Student Leadership Programs (SLP) must have a clearly articulated assessment plan to document achievement of stated goals and learning outcomes, demonstrate accountability, provide evidence of improvement, and describe resulting changes in programs and services.

SLP must have adequate fiscal, human, professional development, and technological resources to develop and implement assessment plans.

Assessments must include direct and indirect evaluation and use qualitative and quantitative methodologies and existing evidence, as appropriate, to determine whether and to what degree the stated mission, goals, and intended outcomes are being met as effectively and efficiently as possible. The process must employ sufficient and sound measures to ensure comprehensiveness. Data collected must include responses from students and other constituencies, and aggregated results must be shared with those groups. Results of assessments must be shared appropriately with multiple constituents.

Results of assessments and evaluations must be used to identify needs and interests in revising and improving programs and services, recognizing staff performance, maximizing resource efficiency and effectiveness, improving student achievement of learning and development outcomes, and improving student persistence and success. Changes resulting from the use of assessments and evaluation must be shared with stakeholders.

Assessment efforts should include
- student needs
- student satisfaction
- student learning outcomes
- overall program evaluation

Assessment efforts should be linked to strategic planning efforts including the articulation of a clear program mission, vision, and values; theoretical orientation; and short- and long-term goals.

General Standards revised in 2011;
SLP content developed/revised in 1996 & 2009

The Role of Transfer Student Programs and Services

CAS Standards Contextual Statement

The increasing number of students moving between institutions, coupled with national and international attention focused on degree completion, shows the importance of examining higher education programs and services that enhance the success of transfer students. This document establishes guidelines for institutions as they develop and execute policies and procedures related to services for transfer students. Because there is no prototypical transfer student, each institution must determine the approach for providing services that best fits its mission and resources. Therefore, this document is not prescriptive but is intended to define the scope of services needed to create a transfer-friendly culture that meets students' individual goals. The concepts within these standards are applicable for "sending" and "receiving" institutions as well as any transfer scenario.

Transfer includes various pathways, including (a) lateral transfer (transfer to the same type of institution, e.g., 2-year to 2-year, as the one in which a student is currently or previously enrolled); (b) vertical transfer (transferring from a 2-year institution to a four-year institution with the intent of completing a bachelor's degree); or (c) reverse transfer (transfer from a 4-year institution to a 2-year institution) (Poisel & Marling, 2011). It is not uncommon for students to "swirl" between and among institutions taking courses from more than one institution either simultaneously or consecutively as they attempt to achieve their educational goals. The services mentioned within these standards are expected to address all types of transfer students, including those enrolled in online courses.

The numbers of college students in the United States on a transfer track at a community college or as transfer students at a 4-year campus account for one-third of entering students (NACAC, 2010). In California, the number of transfer students moving from 2-year to 4-year institutions is the same as those moving in the reverse direction (Hagedorn, 2010). Nearly 60 percent of college graduates in the U.S. have attended more than one college or university (Adelman, 2009). Although not all of these individuals are considered transfer students, the high percentage underscores the importance of developing sound practices to facilitate transfer student success.

Not only are transfer students a large percentage of the higher education population but postsecondary institutions are also being challenged by legislatures throughout the U.S. and Canada to increase degree completion rates. U.S. President Obama has set a national goal that "America will regain its lost ground and have the highest proportion of students graduating from college in the world by 2020" (http://www.whitehouse.gov/issues/education/). The National Governors Association has urged colleges and universities to produce

improved outcome and progress metrics, including the tracking of transfer students (Reyna, 2010). An emphasis on student mobility is not limited to the U.S., as demonstrated by efforts on behalf of the European Action Scheme for the Mobility of University Students (Erasmus), University Mobility in Asia Pacific (UMAP) (Junor & Usher, 2008), the British Columbia Council on Admissions and Transfer (BCCAT), and other provincial associations (Stewart & Martinello, 2012).

Although moving from a 2-year to 4-year institution is the most prevalent transfer pathway (Handel, 2011), it is important to note that the CAS standards and guidelines for transfer student programs and services are intended to apply to the services available to all transfer students, regardless of their institutions of origin, credential acquisition, or educational goals. For example, it is recommended that community colleges and 4-year institutions collaborate to develop a reverse awarding of degrees process by which students earning enough credits for their associate's degree post-transfer are reverse-awarded their associate's degree by their community college. This is just one example of how the provision of services for transfer students is quite complex. These standards aspire to provide for a range of scenarios about the transfer process.

Understandably, there is an underlying focus on degree completion. Increasing the persistence and graduation rates of transfer students is accomplished by effectively preparing students for planned and unplanned transitions between institutions; helping them anticipate areas where change is more likely to occur; and identifying early in the process their personal, academic, financial, and social goals as well as factors that may inhibit or facilitate success. Early intervention is critical to mitigating the negative effects of transfer shock (Thurmond, 2007), a temporary dip in grade point average during the first and sometimes second semester post transfer (Hills, 1965).

Prior to the last decade, there was a dearth of literature about transfer issues; however, a number of studies since that time have produced valuable information about the migration patterns and success rates of transfer students (Jacobs, Cutright, Niebling, Simon, & Marling, 2010). As a result, transfer student issues have secured a firm place on the national higher education agenda (NACAC, 2010).

Most notably, researchers (Handel, 2009, 2011; Handel & Herrera, 2007; Jain, Herrera, Bernal, & Soloranzo, 2001) have brought into focus the need for community colleges to create a transfer-going culture that respects students' academic goals while creating well-articulated and -communicated pathways for pursuing a baccalaureate degree. Similarly, 4-year colleges and universities are encouraged to provide a transfer-receptive culture that respects students' previous experiences and offers services tailored to their unique needs. All institutions are encouraged to set high expectations for transfer student success and degree completion and ensure that policies and practices lead to positive outcomes. The literature on transfer student success provides good examples of such policies and practices.

To better understand how services for transfer students can be infused into institutional culture, Taylor Smith and Miller (2009) explored the characteristics, practices, and policies of community colleges that contribute to success of students prior to and after transferring to a 4-year institution. Studying six community college campuses, they found programs appearing to contribute to higher-than-expected transfer rates had three common characteristics: structured academic pathway, student-centered culture, and culturally sensitive leadership. Taylor Smith and Miller's recommendations for implementing positive practices and strategies include
- collaborative campus programming
- administrative offices as support and service centers
- data-driven decision making
- faculty engagement in the transfer process
- rewards for personnel who value students
- a culture of performance and accountability

Yet, more must be done to support students' transition between institutions and to strengthen the transfer pathway. Handel (2011) offered three strategies for 4-year institutions: (a) create an institution-wide vision that includes transfer students, (b) value transfers in outreach, admission, and academic and student affairs comparably to first-year students, and (c) understand that the needs of transfer students may be different from those of first-year students. The report (Handel, 2011) also addressed initiating or improving transfer at 4-year colleges and universities through the following recommendations:
- provide explicit institutional leadership and commitment to the transfer pathway
- offer ongoing outreach and preparation for staff and students
- implement user-friendly admission and enrollment processes
- educate on financial aid options
- strengthen the connection of student and academic affairs resources, programs, and services

The successful provision of services for transfer students requires intra- and inter-institutional collaboration among multiple stakeholders across functional lines focused on facilitating transfer student success. It is critical to have a unified and widely communicated institutional approach to providing transfer students services that may result in provision of services directly by a designated department (e.g., a transfer center) or as a function of multiple departments. To facilitate seamless transfer, it is also important to consider creating state/provincial approaches to service delivery and policy. To this end, the CAS standards and guidelines are intended to be aspirational, with the understanding that implementation will vary by state/region/province in response to existing policies, practices, and resources.

References, Readings, and Resources

American Association of Community Colleges (AACC). (2011). *Community college fast facts.* Retrieved from http://www.aacc.nche.edu/AboutCC/Documents/FactSheet2011.pdf

Berger, J. B., & Malaney, G. D. (2003). Assessing the transition of transfer students from community colleges to a university. *NASPA Journal, 40*(4), 1-23. Retrieved from http://www.eric.ed.gov/PDFS/ED453489.pdf

Braxton, J. M. (2003). Student success. In S. R. Komives & D. B. Woodard, Jr., & Associates (Eds.), *Student services: A handbook for the profession* (4th ed., pp. 317-338). San Francisco, CA: Jossey-Bass.

Grites, T. J., & Rondeau, S. (2011). Creating effective transfer initiatives. In T. Brown, M. C. King, & P. Stanley (Eds.), *Fulfilling the promise of the community college: Increasing first-year student engagement and success* (Monograph No. 56, pp. 83-97). Columbia, SC: University of South Carolina, National Resource Center for the First-Year Experience and Students in Transition.

Handel, S. J. (2011). *Improving student transfer from community colleges to four-year institutions—The perspective of leaders from baccalaureate granting institutions.* New York, NY: The College Board.

Handel, S. J. (2009). Transfer and the part-time student: The gulf separating community colleges and selective universities. *Change: The Magazine of Higher Learning, 41*(4), 48-53.

Handel, S. J. (2007). Transfer students apply to college, too. How come we don't help them? *Chronicle of Higher Education, 54*(9), B20.

Handel, S. J., & Herrera, A. (2006, June). *Pursuing higher education access and achievement: Case studies in the development of "transfer-going" cultures.* Prepared for the Jack Kent Cooke National Forum, Washington, DC. Retrieved from http://professionals.collegeboard.com/profdownload/pursuing-higher-education_handel-herrera.pdf

Hills, J. (1965, Spring) Transfer shock: The academic performance of the transfer student. *The Journal of Experimental Education, 33*(3). Retrieved from ERIC database (ED 010 740).

Jacobs, B. C. (2010). Making the case for orientation: A vice president's perspective. In J. Ward (Ed.), *Designing successful transitions: A guide to orienting students to college* (Monograph No. 13, 3rd ed., pp. 29-39). Columbia, SC: University of South Carolina, National Resource Center for the First-Year Experience and Students in Transition.

Jacobs, B. C. (2009). The swirling, whirling world of transfer student orientation. In M. A. Sedotti & M. J. Payne (Eds.), *Orientation planning manual* (pp. 11-16). Minneapolis, MN: National Orientation Directors

Association.

Jacobs, B. C., Cutright, M., Niebling, G. F., Simon, J. F., & Marling, J. L. (Eds.) (2010). Exploring promising practices in transfer student services: A Texas initiative. Denton, TX: University of North Texas, National Institute for the Study of Transfer Students

Jacobs, B. C., Lauren, B., Miller, M., & Nadler, D. (Eds.) (2004). *The college transfer student in America: The forgotten student.* Washington, DC: American Association of Collegiate Registrars and Admissions Officers (AACRAO).

Jain, D., Herrera, A., Bernal, S., & Solorzano, D. (2011). Critical race theory and the transfer function: Introducing a transfer receptive culture. *Community College Journal of Research and Practice, 35,* 252--266.

Junor, S., & Usher, A. (2008). Student mobility and credit transfer: A national and global survey. Educational Policy Institute, Virginia Beach, VA. Retrieved from [http://www.educationalpolicy.org/publications/pubpdf/credit.pdf]

Laanan, F. S. (2007). Studying transfer students. Part II: Dimensions of transfer students' adjustment. *Community College Journal of Research and Practice, 31,* 37-59.

Marling, J., & Jacobs, B. C. (2010). Effective orientation for transfer students. In M. A. Poisel & S. Joseph (Eds.), *Transfer students in higher education: Building a rationale for policies, programs, and services that foster student success* (pp. 71-88). Columbia, SC: University of South Carolina, National Resource Center for the First Year Experience and Students in Transition.

National Association for College Admission Counseling (NACAC). (2010, April). *Special report on the transfer admission process.* Arlington, VA: Author. Retrieved from http://www.nacacnet.org/PublicationsResources/Research/Documents/TransferFactSheet.pdf

National Institute for the Study of Transfer Students (NISTS). (2011).

Poisel, M. A., & Marling, J. L. (2011, October). *Strategies for transition: Facilitating transfer student success.* Pre-Conference workshop presented at the Students in Transition Conference for the National Resource Center for the First Year Experience and Student in Transition, Saint Louis, MO.

Reyna, R. (2010). *Complete to compete: Common college completion metrics.* Washington, DC: National Governors Association. Retrieved from http://www.nga.org/files/live/sites/NGA/files/pdf/1007COMMONCOLLEGEMETRICS.PDF

Stewart, J., & Martinello, F. (2012). Are transfer students different? An examination of first year grades and course withdrawals. *Canadian Journal of Higher Education, 42*(1), pp. 25-42.

Taylor Smith, C., & Miller, A. (2009). Bridging the gaps to success: Promising practices for promoting transfer among low-income and first-generation students. Washington DC: The Pell Institute for the Study of Opportunity in Higher Education. Retrieved from http://www.pellinstitute.org/downloads/publications-Bridging_the_Gaps_to_Success_2009.pdf

Thurmond, K. C. (2007). Transfer shock: Why is a term forty years old still relevant? Retrieved from NACADA Clearinghouse of Academic Advising Resources Website: http://www.nacada.ksu.edu/Clearinghouse/AdvisingIssues/Transfer-Shock.htm

Townsend, B. K., & Wilson, K. (2006). "A hand hold for a little bit": Factors facilitating the success of community college transfer students to a large research university. *Journal of College Student Development, 47,* 439-456. doi:10.1353/csd.2006.0052

Contextual Statement Contributors

Janet L. Marling, University of North Texas, NISTS
Jan Hillman, University of North Texas, NISTS
Bonita C. Jacobs, North Georgia College, NISTS
Marsha Miller, Kansas State University

Transfer Student Programs and Services
CAS Standards and Guidelines

Part 1. MISSION

The mission of Transfer Student Programs and Services (TSPS) is to aid in the successful transfer, persistence, and graduation of transfer students. To accomplish the mission, TSPS must facilitate seamless pathways among and within institutions to support transfer students at all stages of their transitions.

Through the provision of TSPS, the institution's culture becomes one that is supportive and inclusive of transfer students.

TSPS must develop, disseminate, implement, and regularly review their missions. The mission must be consistent with the mission of the institution and with professional standards. The mission must be appropriate for the institution's student populations and community settings. Mission statements must reference student learning and development.

Part 2. PROGRAM

The formal education of students, consisting of the curriculum and the co-curriculum, must promote student learning and development outcomes that are purposeful, contribute to students' realization of their potential, and prepare students for satisfying and productive lives.

Transfer Student Programs and Services (TSPS) must collaborate with colleagues and departments across the institution to promote student learning and development, persistence, and success.

Consistent with the institutional mission, TSPS must identify relevant and desirable student learning and development outcomes from among the six domains and related dimensions:

Domain: knowledge acquisition, integration, construction, and application

- Dimensions: understanding knowledge from a range of disciplines; connecting knowledge to other knowledge, ideas, and experiences; constructing knowledge; and relating knowledge to daily life

Domain: cognitive complexity

- Dimensions: critical thinking, reflective thinking, effective reasoning, and creativity

Domain: intrapersonal development

- Dimensions: realistic self-appraisal, self-understanding, and self-respect; identity development; commitment to ethics and integrity; and spiritual awareness

Domain: interpersonal competence

- Dimensions: meaningful relationships, interdependence, collaboration, and effective leadership.

Domain: humanitarianism and civic engagement

- Dimensions: understanding and appreciation of cultural and human differences, social responsibility, global perspective, and sense of civic responsibility

Domain: practical competence

- Dimensions: pursuing goals, communicating effectively, technical competence, managing personal affairs, managing career development, demonstrating professionalism, maintaining health and wellness, and living a purposeful and satisfying life

[LD Outcomes: See *The Council for the Advancement of Standards Learning and Developmental Outcomes* statement for examples of outcomes related to these domains and dimensions.]

TSPS must
- assess relevant and desirable student learning and development
- provide evidence of impact on outcomes
- articulate contributions to or support of student learning and development in the domains not specifically assessed
- articulate contributions to or support of student persistence and success
- use evidence gathered through this process to create strategies for improvement of programs and services

TSPS must be
- intentionally designed
- guided by theories and knowledge of learning and development
- integrated into the life of the institution
- reflective of developmental and demographic profiles of the student population
- responsive to needs of individuals, populations with distinct needs, and relevant constituencies
- delivered using multiple formats, strategies, and contexts

Where institutions provide distance education, TSPS must assist distance learners to achieve their educational goals by providing access to information about programs and services, to staff members who can address questions and concerns, and to counseling, advising, or other forms of assistance.

TSPS must

- serve as a contact for transfer students throughout the application, acceptance, and transfer processes
- connect students to appropriate institutional academic and behavioral policies and procedures
- facilitate cooperation between institutions to help students align their programs of study to enable a timely and successful transfer
- advocate for improvement of institutional articulation agreements and/or curricular alignment depending on the particular institution's policies
- know how to apply applicable laws, regulations, and policies related to the successful transfer of students
- inform key partners about policies and practices that maximize transfer student success
- provide access to professional advisors, faculty members, counselors, and staff support to help transfer students engage in and develop college and long-term academic, career, and life goals
- advocate for equitable enrollment and flexible class scheduling and delivery methods
- review informational materials for accessible and accurate information about transfer policies, processes, scholarships and affordability, course equivalencies, and programs
- disseminate informational material to transfer students and to institutional personnel supporting transfer students
- participate in recruitment events to communicate with prospective students about transfer and articulation
- collaborate with partners to prioritize programming specific to the needs of transfer students during the first-year and throughout their time at the institution
- collaborate with stakeholders to address transfer student success, retention, and degree completion

TSPS programming should address topics that are pivotal to the successful transfer of students to and from their institution.

Particular attention should be paid to programming specific to the transfer student's first year. Topics could include

- demographics of the institution's transfer students (including first-generation and veteran status)
- institutional academic support services and other learning assistance programs
- eligibility for and promotion of leadership opportunities and awards for students
- student money management, academic resources, financial aid, and scholarships
- living options (both on and off campus), learning communities, and theme halls

TSPS should ensure that the institution provides support for transfer-intending students and current transfers by offering the following opportunities:

- advising regarding the institution's admission process and application for admission
- assistance as needed in orientation and academic advising
- early-alert systems, intrusive advising, academic support, transfer-year seminars and student success courses, peer mentoring, and other transition services

TSPS should provide informal transcript evaluations so that prospective students can gauge their academic standing before committing to an institution.

TSPS should work with Residence Life/Housing to develop opportunities for new residential transfer students to be paired with or mentored by other transfer students

Part 3. ORGANIZATION AND LEADERSHIP

To achieve student and program outcomes, Transfer Student Programs and Services (TSPS) must be structured purposefully and organized effectively. TSPS must have

- clearly stated goals
- current and accessible policies and procedures
- written performance expectations for employees
- functional work flow graphics or organizational charts demonstrating clear channels of authority

TSPS cross-functional and divisional reporting lines must be located in the organizational department or division that can best provide effective programming and services for achievement of the mission.

Leaders with organizational authority for the programs and services must provide strategic planning, supervision, and management; advance the organization; and maintain integrity through the following functions:

Strategic Planning
- articulate a vision and mission that drive

short- and long-term planning

- **set goals and objectives based on the needs of the population served and desired student learning or development and program outcomes**
- **facilitate continuous development, implementation, and assessment of goal attainment congruent with institutional mission and strategic plans**
- **promote environments that provide meaningful opportunities for student learning, development, and engagement**
- **develop and continuously improve programs and services in response to the changing needs of students served and evolving institutional priorities**
- **intentionally include diverse perspectives to inform decision making**

Supervising

- **manage human resource processes including recruitment, selection, development, supervision, performance planning, evaluation, recognition, and reward**
- **influence others to contribute to the effectiveness and success of the unit**
- **empower professional, support, and student staff to accept leadership opportunities**
- **offer appropriate feedback to colleagues and students on skills needed to become more effective leaders**
- **encourage and support professional development, collaboration with colleagues and departments across the institution, and scholarly contribution to the profession**

TSPS leaders should

- be involved in research, publication, presentations, consultation, and relevant professional organizations
- communicate with professional colleagues in the transfer student field and related areas

Managing

- **identify and address individual, organizational, and environmental conditions that foster or inhibit mission achievement**
- **plan, allocate, and monitor the use of fiscal, physical, human, intellectual, and technological resources**
- **use current and valid evidence to inform decisions**
- **incorporate sustainability practices in the management and design of programs, services, and facilities**
- **understand appropriate technologies and integrate them into programs and services**
- **be knowledgeable about codes and laws**

relevant to programs and services and ensure that staff members understand their responsibilities through appropriate training
- **assess potential risks and take action to mitigate them**

TSPS leaders should provide informational resources that are easily accessed and that address the informational needs of transfer students and their families.

Advancing the Organization

- **communicate effectively in writing, speaking, and electronic venues**
- **advocate for programs and services**
- **advocate for representation in strategic planning initiatives at appropriate divisional and institutional levels**
- **initiate collaborative interactions with internal and external stakeholders who have legitimate concerns about and interests in the functional area**
- **facilitate processes to reach consensus where wide support is needed**
- **inform other areas within the institution about issues affecting practice**

TSPS leaders should

- identify examples of successful transfer students, including those who transferred from a community college, and integrate them as able into the operations of TSPS
- work with institutional leaders to plan courses and course sections to accommodate transfer student degree plans
- collaborate with key partners to influence institutional planning, policy, procedural, and fiscal decisions that affect transfer student articulation
- provide a voice for transfer student concerns on institutional committees

Maintaining Integrity

- **model ethical behavior and institutional citizenship**
- **share data used to inform key decisions in transparent and accessible ways**
- **monitor media used for distributing information about programs and services to ensure the content is current, accurate, appropriately referenced, and accessible**

TSPS leaders must serve as role models for transfer student transition to a new institution.

Part 4. HUMAN RESOURCES

Transfer Student Programs and Services (TSPS) must be staffed adequately by individuals qualified to accomplish mission and goals.

TSPS professional staff members must possess the skills and competencies needed to provide assistance to prospective and enrolled transfer students.

TSPS may include, but should not be limited to, the following competencies:

- effective advocacy for prospective and enrolled students
- ethical and objective presentation of the institution's programs and opportunities, including careful and concerned analysis of student goals
- clear understanding of likely student-institution compatibility
- guidance in responsible decision-making in the selection of an institution or degree program
- ability to explain and contextualize relevant academic policies and practices
- ability to articulate relevant cost and financial aid issues, especially since these may differ from policies at the student's current institution
- ability to manage human and fiscal resources, including creative thinking in the augmentation of these resources through strong collaboration skills and fundraising

At least one dedicated institutional employee should be identified as the primary contact and resource for transfer students and their families.

TSPS professional staff should be knowledgeable in the areas of transition issues, barriers to transfer, financial aid, and testing.

TSPS staff members should demonstrate knowledge of and sensitivity to the needs of non-traditional students, traditionally under-represented groups, academically underprepared students, international students, and veterans.

Staff members who provide services for transfer students should have working relationships with advisors, faculty, counselors, and staff as they help students think about academic, career, and life goals.

TSPS should include faculty in the development and delivery of programs for transfer students.

Within institutional guidelines, TSPS must

- **establish procedures for staff recruitment and selection, training, performance planning, and evaluation**
- **set expectations for supervision and performance**
- **assess the performance of employees individually and as a team**
- **provide access to continuing and advanced education and appropriate professional development opportunities to improve the leadership ability, competence, and skills of**

all employees.

TSPS must maintain position descriptions for all staff members.

To create a diverse staff, TSPS must institute recruitment and hiring strategies that encourage individuals from under-represented populations to apply for positions.

TSPS must develop promotion practices that are fair, inclusive, proactive, and non-discriminatory.

To further the recruitment and retention of staff, TSPS must consider work life initiatives, such as compressed work schedules, flextime, job sharing, remote work, or telework.

TSPS professional staff members must hold an earned graduate or professional degree in a field relevant to the position they hold or must possess an appropriate combination of educational credentials and related work experience.

TSPS professional staff should have knowledge of theories of student learning, development, and transition.

TSPS professional staff members must engage in continuing professional development activities to keep abreast of the research, theories, legislation, policies, and developments that affect their programs and services.

TSPS must have technical and support staff members adequate to accomplish their mission. All members of the staff must be technologically proficient and qualified to perform their job functions, be knowledgeable about ethical and legal uses of technology, and have access to training and resources to support the performance of their assigned responsibilities.

Degree- or credential-seeking interns or graduate assistants must be qualified by enrollment in an appropriate field of study and by relevant experience. These individuals must be trained and supervised adequately by professional staff members holding educational credentials and related work experience appropriate for supervision. Supervisors must be cognizant of the roles of interns and graduate assistants as both student and employee and closely adhere to all parameters of their job descriptions, work hours, and schedules. Supervisors and the interns or graduate assistants must agree to compensatory time or other appropriate compensation if circumstances necessitate additional hours.

Student employees and volunteers must be carefully selected, trained, supervised, and evaluated. They must be educated on how and when to refer those

in need of additional assistance to qualified staff members and must have access to a supervisor for assistance in making these judgments. Student employees and volunteers must be provided clear job descriptions, pre-service training based on assessed needs, and continuing development.

All TSPS staff members, including student employees and volunteers, must receive specific training on institutional policies pertaining to functions or activities they support and to privacy and confidentiality policies and laws regarding access to student records and other sensitive institutional information.

All TSPS staff members must receive training on policies and procedures related to the use of technology to store or access student records and institutional data.

TSPS must ensure that staff members are knowledgeable about and trained in emergency procedures, crisis response, and prevention efforts. Prevention efforts must address identification of threatening conduct or behavior of students, faculty and staff members, and others and must incorporate a system for responding and reporting.

TSPS must ensure that staff members are knowledgeable of and trained in safety and emergency procedures for securing and vacating facilities.

Part 5. ETHICS

Transfer Student Programs and Services (TSPS) must review relevant professional ethical standards and must adopt or develop and implement appropriate statements of ethical practice.

TSPS must publish and adhere to statements of ethical practice and ensure their periodic review by relevant constituencies.

TSPS must orient new staff members to relevant ethical standards and statements of ethical practice and related institutional policies.

Statements of ethical standards must specify that staff members respect privacy and maintain confidentiality in all communications and records to the extent that such communications and records are protected under relevant privacy laws.

Statements of ethical standards must specify limits on disclosure of information contained in students' educational records as well as requirements to disclose to appropriate authorities.

Statements of ethical standards must address personal and economic conflicts of interest, or appearance thereof, by staff members in the performance of their work.

Statements of ethical standards must reflect the responsibility of staff members to be fair, objective, and impartial in their interactions with others.

Statements of ethical standards must reference management of institutional funds.

Statements of ethical standards must reference appropriate behavior regarding research and assessment with human participants, confidentiality of research and assessment data, and students' rights and responsibilities.

Statements of ethical standards must include the expectation that TSPS staff members confront and hold accountable other staff members who exhibit unethical behavior.

Statements of ethical standards must address issues surrounding scholarly integrity.

As appropriate, TSPS staff members must inform users of programs and services of ethical obligations and limitations emanating from codes and laws or from licensure requirements.

TSPS staff members must recognize and avoid conflicts of interest that could adversely influence their judgment or objectivity and, when unavoidable, recuse themselves from the situation.

TSPS staff members must perform their duties within the limits of their position, training, expertise, and competence.

When these limits are exceeded, individuals in need of further assistance must be referred to persons possessing appropriate qualifications.

Promotional and descriptive information must be accurate and free of deception.

TSPS must adhere to institutional policies regarding ethical and legal use of software and technology.

TSPS staff members must work to create institutional culture, policies, curriculum, and standards that positively support the success of transfer students

TSPS staff members must
- refrain from challenging another institution's services or information even if those services or information may be different from their own policies or programs
- avoid falsely representing their institution and academic standing for the sole reason of securing the transfer student's admittance

TSPS documents used by admissions, academic

advising and counseling, orientation, housing, personal counseling and testing, the registrar, and international student services must be accurate and handled with confidentiality.

Part 6. LAW, POLICY, AND GOVERNANCE

Transfer Student Programs and Services (TSPS) must be in compliance with laws, regulations, and policies that relate to their respective responsibilities and that pose legal obligations, limitations, risks, and liabilities for the institution as a whole. Examples include constitutional, statutory, regulatory, and case law; relevant law and orders emanating from codes and laws; and the institution's policies.

TSPS staff members must understand and know how to apply appropriate laws, regulations, and policies that are specific to transfer students; including guaranteed admission policies, core curriculum policies, matriculation and articulation agreements, and policies specific to diverse student populations including veterans and first-generation students, and other agreements within and among institutions.

TSPS must inform staff members, appropriate officials, and users of programs and services about existing and changing legal obligations, risks and liabilities, and limitations.

TSPS must have written policies on all relevant operations, transactions, or tasks that have legal implications.

TSPS must regularly review policies. The revision and creation of policies must be informed by best practices, available evidence, and policy issues in higher education.

TSPS staff members must use reasonable and informed practices to limit the liability exposure of the institution and its officers, employees, and agents. Staff members must be informed about institutional policies regarding risk management, personal liability, and related insurance coverage options and must be referred to external sources if the institution does not provide coverage.

The institution must provide access to legal advice for staff members as needed to carry out assigned responsibilities.

TSPS must have procedures and guidelines consistent with institutional policy for responding to threats, emergencies, and crisis situations. Systems and procedures must be in place to disseminate timely and accurate information to students, other members of the institutional community, and appropriate external organizations during emergency situations.

TSPS staff members must neither participate in nor condone any form of harassment or activity that demeans persons or creates an intimidating, hostile, or offensive environment.

TSPS must obtain permission to use copyrighted materials and instruments. TSPS must purchase the materials and instruments from legally compliant sources or seek alternative permission from the publisher or owner. References to copyrighted materials and instruments must include appropriate citations.

TSPS staff members must be knowledgeable about internal and external governance systems that affect programs and services.

TSPS staff members must ensure that all transfer policies, including an appeals process, are publicly available for review prior to the student's commitment to transfer.

TSPS should encourage 2-year and 4-year institutions to collaborate in the development of policies and processes to reverse-award associate degrees to students.

Part 7. DIVERSITY, EQUITY, AND ACCESS

Within the context of each institution's unique mission and in accordance with institutional polices and all applicable codes and laws, Transfer Student Programs and Services (TSPS) must create and maintain educational and work environments that are

- welcoming, accessible, and inclusive to persons of diverse backgrounds
- equitable and non-discriminatory
- free from harassment

TSPS must not discriminate on the basis of ability; age; cultural identity; ethnicity; family educational history (e.g., first generation to attend college); gender identity and expression; nationality; political affiliation; race; religious affiliation; sex; sexual orientation; economic, marital, social, or veteran status; or any other basis included in institutional policies and codes and laws.

TSPS must

- advocate for greater sensitivity to multicultural and social justice concerns by the institution and its personnel
- modify or remove policies, practices, facilities, structures, systems, and technologies that limit access, discriminate, or produce inequities
- include diversity, equity, and access initiatives within their strategic plans
- foster communication that deepens understanding of identity, culture, self-

expression, and heritage
- promote respect about commonalities and differences among people within their historical and cultural contexts
- address the characteristics and needs of a diverse population when establishing and implementing culturally relevant and inclusive programs, services, policies, procedures, and practices
- provide staff members with access to multicultural training and hold staff members accountable for integrating the training into their work
- respond to the needs of all students and other populations served when establishing hours of operation and developing methods of delivering programs, services, and resources
- ensure physical, program, and resource access for persons with disabilities
- recognize the needs of distance learning students by providing appropriate and accessible services and resources or by assisting them in gaining access to other appropriate services and resources in their geographic region

All transfer-related marketing and forms must clearly state student rights and responsibilities in the transfer process. Practices must be congruent with institutional policies on equal opportunity access.

TSPS should respect the diversity of students and their families, acknowledging the many different cultures and backgrounds represented by these individuals, and be prepared to identify resources for support both on campus and locally as needed.

TSPS should provide access to the institution's policies and procedures and resources in multiple language formats, including printed forms for families who do not have informational technology.

Part 8. INSTITUTIONAL AND EXTERNAL RELATIONS

Transfer Student Programs and Services (TSPS) must reach out to relevant individuals, groups, communities, and organizations internal and external to the institution to
- establish, maintain, and promote understanding and effective relations with those that have a significant interest in or potential effect on the students or other constituents served by the programs and services
- garner support and resources for programs and services as defined by the mission statement
- disseminate information about the programs and services
- collaborate, where appropriate, to assist in offering or improving programs and services to meet the needs of students and other constituents and to achieve program and student outcomes
- engage diverse individuals, groups, communities, and organizations to enrich the educational environment and experiences of students and other constituents

TSPS must develop and maintain collaborative relationships between sending and receiving institutions.

TSPS must develop and maintain a relationship with those responsible for the orientation of new students.

TSPS should collaborate with those in charge of new student orientation programs and courses to meet the specific needs of transfer students.

TSPS must be aware of governmental units responsible for laws, policies, and regulations relevant to transfer matriculation and maintain relationships with them.

TSPS should partner with academic unit leadership to develop course acceptance and course applicability plans by major.

TSPS should partner with the academic and enrollment management functions to ensure timely evaluation and application of earned credits.

TSPS should advise prospective and enrolled transfer students about their responsibilities in achieving their goals.

TSPS should work with parent and family programs to inform family members about issues that impact the health, well-being, and success of students through a variety of communication methods.

TSPS should work with parent and family programs to provide a resource guide or handbook to address student-life topics of priority to the institution (e.g., drug and alcohol use, service-learning and study abroad opportunities, research opportunities, financial literacy, health and wellness), resources and benefits available to parents and families, institutional policies and procedures, the academic calendar, and support services.

TSPS must have procedures and guidelines consistent with institutional policy for
- **communicating with the media**
- **contracting with external organizations for delivery of programs and services**
- **cultivating, soliciting, and managing gifts**
- **applying to and managing funds from grants**

Part 9. FINANCIAL RESOURCES

Transfer Student Programs and Services (TSPS) must have funding to accomplish the mission and goals. In establishing funding priorities and making significant changes, a comprehensive analysis must be conducted to determine the following elements: unmet needs of the unit, relevant expenditures, external and internal resources, and impact on students and the institution.

TSPS must demonstrate efficient and effective use and responsible stewardship of fiscal resources consistent with institutional protocols.

TSPS should be funded at the same cost/student ratio as services for the institution's first-time, first-year student population.

TSPS may supplement institutional funding through the development of revenue sources such as fundraising, grants, and fees for services provided.

Part 10. TECHNOLOGY

Transfer Student Programs and Services (TSPS) must have adequate technology to support the achievement of their mission and goals. The technology and its use must comply with institutional policies and procedures and be evaluated for compliance with relevant codes and laws.

TSPS staff members should be trained in transfer specific technologies, including but not limited to digital transcript services.

TSPS must use current technology to provide updated information regarding mission, location, staffing, programs, services, and official contacts to students and designated clients.

TSPS must explore the use of technology to enhance delivery of programs and services, especially for students at a distance or external constituencies.

When technology is used to facilitate student learning and development, TSPS must select technology that reflects intended outcomes.

TSPS must
- maintain policies and procedures that address the security, confidentiality, and backup of data, as well as compliance with privacy laws
- have clearly articulated plans in place for protecting confidentiality and security of information when using Internet-based technologies
- develop plans for replacing and updating existing hardware and software as well as plans for integrating new technically-based or supported programs, including systems developed internally by the institution, systems available through professional associations, or private vendor-based systems

Technology, as well as workstations or computer labs maintained by programs and services for student use, must be accessible to all designated clients and must meet established technology standards for delivery to persons with disabilities.

When providing student access to technology, TSPS must
- have policies on the use of technology that are clear, easy to understand, and available to all students
- provide assistance, information, or referral to appropriate support services to those needing help accessing or using technology
- provide instruction or training on how to use the technology
- inform students on the legal and ethical implications of misuse as it pertains to intellectual property, harassment, privacy, and social networks

If the institution equips first-time first-year students with specific technology, then the institution should provide new transfer students with the same technology.

Student violations of technology policies must follow established institutional student disciplinary procedures.

Students who experience negative emotional or psychological consequences from the use of technology must be referred to support services provided by the institution.

Part 11. FACILITIES AND EQUIPMENT

Transfer Student Programs and Services (TSPS) must have adequate, accessible, and suitably located facilities and equipment to support the mission and goals. If acquiring capital equipment as defined by the institution, TSPS must take into account expenses related to regular maintenance and life cycle costs. Facilities and equipment must be evaluated on an established cycle, including consideration of sustainability, and be in compliance with codes and laws to provide for access, health, safety, and security.

TSPS staff members must have workspace that is well equipped, adequate in size, and designed to support their work and responsibilities. For conversations requiring privacy, staff members must have access to a private space.

TSPS staff members who share workspace must be

able to secure their own work.

The design of the facilities must guarantee the security and privacy of records and ensure the confidentiality of sensitive information.

The location and layout of the facilities must be sensitive to the needs of persons with disabilities as well as the needs of other constituencies.

Part 12. ASSESSMENT AND EVALUATION

Transfer Student Programs and Services (TSPS) must have a clearly articulated assessment plan to document achievement of stated goals and learning outcomes, demonstrate accountability, provide evidence of improvement, and describe resulting changes in programs and services.

TSPS must have adequate fiscal, human, professional development, and technological resources to develop and implement assessment plans.

Assessments must include direct and indirect evaluation and use qualitative and quantitative methodologies and existing evidence, as appropriate, to determine whether and to what degree the stated mission, goals, and intended outcomes are being met as effectively and efficiently as possible. The process must employ sufficient and sound measures to ensure comprehensiveness. Data collected must include responses from students and other constituencies, and aggregated results must be shared with those groups. Results of assessments must be shared appropriately with multiple constituents.

TSPS must collaborate with appropriate partners to conduct research and collect data regarding transfer students. Results must be shared with students, staff, and faculty at both sending and receiving institutions.

TSPS should work to ensure there are processes to monitor and report annual persistence and graduation rates for all types of transfer students, including community college graduates and non graduates as well as those who transfer from 4-year institutions.

TSPS should employ multiple methods to assess program effectiveness in meeting the needs of transfer-intending and current transfer students.

Results of assessments and evaluations must be used to identify needs and interests in revising and improving programs and services, recognizing staff performance, maximizing resource efficiency and effectiveness, improving student achievement of learning and development outcomes, and improving student persistence and success. Changes resulting from the use of assessments and evaluation must be shared with stakeholders.

TSPS should partner with institutional research/assessment personnel to ensure that assessment efforts are tracked.

General Standards revised in 2011;
TSPS content developed in 2012

The Role of TRIO and Other Educational Opportunituy Programs
CAS Standards Contextual Statement

Students from low-income and first-generation (i.e., neither parent has a baccalaureate degree) backgrounds historically have had limited access to higher education. Realizing that the ideal of American higher education includes opportunities for all students, federal and state legislation has been enacted to mitigate some of the inequities to access. Since the 1960s, a variety of educational opportunity programs have been developed at the state and federal levels to increase access, persistence, and success in higher education for students from disadvantaged backgrounds. Additionally, foundation, corporate, and non-profit groups fund scholarship and pre-college preparation programs for these student populations.

The TRIO Programs are federally-funded educational opportunity programs designed to motivate and support students from disadvantaged backgrounds to prepare for, attend, persist in, and graduate from post-secondary education. TRIO includes eight programs that provide academic support for students who are from low-income families and are first-generation. TRIO programs serve students beginning in middle school and provide support through postsecondary education. In addition, TRIO's professional development component provides training opportunities for TRIO staff.

The TRIO programs are authorized under the U. S. Higher Education Act of 1965, Title IV, Part A, Subpart 2. FEDERAL TRIO PROGRAMS and recently reauthorized by the Higher Education Opportunity Act, August 2008. Programs are administered by the U. S. Department of Education, Office of Postsecondary Education (OPE), division of Student Service in Higher Education Programs. TRIO projects are funded through competitive grant applications. In 2012 there were 2,947 TRIO projects hosted by over 1,100 higher education institutions, schools, and community agencies. Annually TRIO programs serve over 800,000 pre-college and postsecondary students.

The initial TRIO programs included Upward Bound, which emerged from the Economic Opportunity Act of 1964 as part of President Johnson's War on Poverty; Talent Search, created in 1965 as part of the Higher Education Act; and Student Support Services, in 1968. The term "TRIO" referred to these three original federal programs. The Higher Education Amendments of 1972 added Educational Opportunity Centers, and the 1986 Amendments authorized the Ronald E. McNair Post-Baccalaureate Achievement Program. The Department of Education established the Upward Bound Math/Science Program as a subset to Upward Bound in 1990.

TRIO Program Descriptions

- Educational Opportunity Centers (EOC) provide counseling and information about college admissions and financial aid with the goal of increasing the number of adult participants who enroll in post-secondary education. Services include advising; counseling; provision of information about educational opportunities and financial assistance; help with completing applications for college admissions; testing and financial aid; coordination with educational institutions and community partnerships; and provision of referrals, tutoring, and mentoring.

- The Ronald E. McNair Post-baccalaureate Achievement program prepares undergraduates to enter doctoral studies. The goal of McNair is to increase graduate degree attainment by students from low-income, first-generation, and designated under-represented groups. Services include faculty mentoring, scholarly activities to prepare students for doctoral study, summer research internships, tutoring, counseling, assistance with securing graduate program admission and financial aid, preparation for GRE exams, and other activities that enhance successful entry to and persistence in doctoral programs.

- The Student Support Services (SSS) program provides academic support for participants, including students with disabilities, to motivate students to complete post-secondary education with the goal of increasing participant college retention and graduation rates and to facilitate two-year college student transition to four-year institutions. Activities include basic skills instruction and tutoring; academic, financial, career and personal counseling; assistance with graduate school admission; mentoring; special services for students with limited English proficiency or are homeless or aged out of foster care systems; cultural activities; and academic accommodations for students with disabilities.

- The Talent Search program identifies, motivates, and assists participants to complete high school and enter and persist in higher education. Talent Search also serves high school dropouts by encouraging them to reenter the educational system. The goal is to increase the number of youth from disadvantaged backgrounds who complete high school and enroll in post-secondary education. Talent Search serves sixth to twelfth grade students with academic, financial, career, and personal counseling; tutoring; information about post-secondary education and college visits; completing college admissions and financial aid applications; preparation for college entrance exams; mentoring; and family involvement activities.

- Upward Bound is comprised of three programs, with intensive college preparatory projects designed to provide high school participants and military veterans with college preparation and skills to complete high school, matriculate to postsecondary, and earn a post-secondary degree. Upward Bound provides academic instruction and enrichment activities throughout the calendar year, including summer academic-year programs at college campuses. Other services include study skills; academic, financial, and personal counseling; tutoring; cultural and social activities; college visits, assistance with college entrance and financial aid applications; and preparation for college entrance exams. The Veterans Upward Bound program serves military veterans who are preparing to enter post-secondary education. The Upward Bound Math/Science program encourages students to pursue post-secondary degrees in math and science through intensive math and science curricula and experiences, computer instruction, and research activities.

Gaining Early Awareness and Readiness for Undergraduate Programs (Gear Up) is also reauthorized through the Higher Education Opportunity Act, 2008, and is administered by the U. S. Department of Education OPE. This discretionary grant program is designed to increase the number of low-income students who are prepared to enter and succeed in postsecondary education. GEAR UP provides six-year grants to states and partnerships for pre-college preparation services to high-poverty middle and high schools. GEAR UP projects serve entire cohorts of students beginning with the seventh grade and following cohorts through high school. GEAR UP funds also provide college scholarships to low-income students and funds both state and partnership grants.

Some states support educational opportunity programs designed to increase access to higher education for lower income, first-generation, and/or students historically underrepresented in higher education. An example is the New Jersey Educational Opportunity Fund created in 1968 "to ensure meaningful access to higher education for those who come from backgrounds of economic and educational disadvantage. The Fund assists low-income New Jersey residents who are capable and motivated but lack adequate preparation for college study." The NJEOF provides supplemental financial aid and campus-based outreach and support services at numerous public and independent New Jersey institutions.

In addition to federal and state educational opportunity programs, numerous foundation, corporate, and non-profit organizations fund scholarship and/or pre-college access and preparation programs. Examples of these include the Lumina Foundation, the I Have a Dream Foundation, Daniels Fund Scholars, Gates Millennium Scholars, National College Access Network programs such as the Ohio College Access Network, Jack Kent Cooke Foundation Scholars, and the Denver Scholarship Foundation, an example of a PromiseNet

organization—a place-based community program located across the U.S. that provides the promise of a scholarship and a network of services to increase college access and success among low-income students and contributes to community economic development by providing access to postsecondary education.

The Council for Opportunity in Education (COE) is the professional association representing over 6,000+ TRIO and Gear Up personnel. COE sponsors professional development activities including national conferences, symposia, workshops, publications, and TRIO and access research through the Pell Institute for the Study of Opportunity in Higher Education; advocates for TRIO programs and students; and acts as liaison to the US Department of Education.

COE provided leadership with CAS in recognizing a need for and developing the first set of TRIO and Other EOP Standards and Guidelines in 1999 and promotes their use for TRIO and other EOP programs. Other professional associations representing educational opportunity programs include the National College Access Network and the Educational Opportunity Fund Association of New Jersey.

References, Readings, and Resources

Council for Opportunity in Education, 1025 Vermont Avenue, N.W. Suite 900, Washington, DC 20005. (202) 347-7430. www.coenet.us

National College Access Network. http://www.collegeaccess.org/

Pathways to College Network. www.pathwaystocollege.net

Pell Institute for the Study of Opportunity in Higher Education. www.pellinstitute.org

U. S. Department of Education Office of Postsecondary Education Gear Up. http://www.ed.gov/gearup

U. S. Department of Education Office of Postsecondary Education TRIO Programs. http://www.ed.gov/about/offices/list/ope/trio/index.htmlprograms/gearup/index.html

Wolanin, T. (April, 1997). The history of TRIO: Three decades of success and counting. NCEOA Journal, pp. 2-4.

Contextual Statement Contributor

Andrea Reeve, Colorado State University, COE

TRIO and Other Educational Opportunity Programs
CAS Standards and Guidelines

Part 1. MISSION

The mission of TRIO and Other Educational Opportunity Programs (TOEOP) is to encourage and assist people who are traditionally under-represented in postsecondary education because of income, family educational background, disability, or other relevant federal, state/provincial, or institutional criteria, in the preparation for, entry to, and completion of a postsecondary degree.

To accomplish this mission, TOEOP must
- serve as advocates for access to higher education
- address the developmental needs of the individuals served
- provide services to assist individuals in developing and achieving educational goals
- assist individuals in acquiring the necessary skills, knowledge, and attributes to enter and complete a postsecondary education
- provide an environment that recognizes the diversity of backgrounds and learning styles of the individuals served
- develop collaborative relationships with institutions, organizations, schools, parents and families, and communities to promote an environment conducive to the completion of a postsecondary degree

TRIO and Other Educational Opportunity Programs (TOEOP) must develop, disseminate, implement, and regularly review their missions. The mission must be consistent with the mission of the institution and with professional standards. The mission must be appropriate for the institution's student populations and community settings. Mission statements must reference student learning and development.

TOEOP mission statements must be consistent with the mission and goals of the relevant governmental or other external grant or funding agency.

Part 2. PROGRAM

The formal education of students, consisting of the curriculum and the co-curriculum, must promote student learning and development outcomes that are purposeful, contribute to students' realization of their potential, and prepare students for satisfying and productive lives.

TRIO and Other Educational Opportunity Programs (TOEOP) must collaborate with colleagues and departments across the institution to promote student learning and development, persistence, and success.

Consistent with the institutional mission, TOEOP must identify relevant and desirable student learning and development outcomes from among the six domains and related dimensions:

Domain: knowledge acquisition, integration, construction, and application

- Dimensions: understanding knowledge from a range of disciplines; connecting knowledge to other knowledge, ideas, and experiences; constructing knowledge; and relating knowledge to daily life

Domain: cognitive complexity

- Dimensions: critical thinking, reflective thinking, effective reasoning, and creativity

Domain: intrapersonal development

- Dimensions: realistic self-appraisal, self-understanding, and self-respect; identity development; commitment to ethics and integrity; and spiritual awareness

Domain: interpersonal competence

- Dimensions: meaningful relationships, interdependence, collaboration, and effective leadership.

Domain: humanitarianism and civic engagement

- Dimensions: understanding and appreciation of cultural and human differences, social responsibility, global perspective, and sense of civic responsibility

Domain: practical competence

- Dimensions: pursuing goals, communicating effectively, technical competence, managing personal affairs, managing career development, demonstrating professionalism, maintaining health and wellness, and living a purposeful and satisfying life

[LD Outcomes: See *The Council for the Advancement of Standards Learning and Developmental Outcomes* statement for examples of outcomes related to these domains and dimensions.]

TOEOP must
- assess relevant and desirable student learning and development

- **provide evidence of impact on outcomes**
- **articulate contributions to or support of student learning and development in the domains not specifically assessed**
- **articulate contributions to or support of student persistence and success**
- **use evidence gathered through this process to create strategies for improvement of programs and services**

TOEOP should write student learning and development outcomes in at least two student learning and development outcome domains specific to their programs.

TOEOP must be
- **intentionally designed**
- **guided by theories and knowledge of learning and development**
- **integrated into the life of the institution**
- **reflective of developmental and demographic profiles of the student population**
- **responsive to needs of individuals, populations with distinct needs, and relevant constituencies**
- **delivered using multiple formats, strategies, and contexts**

Where institutions provide distance education, TOEOP must assist distance learners to achieve their educational goals by providing access to information about programs and services, to staff members who can address questions and concerns, and to counseling, advising, or other forms of assistance.

TOEOP must provide activities that support the matriculation, achievement, persistence, success, and graduation of their students, as relevant to the mission of their specific program.

TOEOP must address their specific learning objectives and the allowable activities of each program.

Programs, services, and activities for students involved in specific TOEOP should be relevant to the demographic profile of individuals served. Programs, services, and activities should provide or ensure access to academic support services such as academic instruction; tutoring; English as a Second Language (ESL) activities; collaborative learning opportunities; Supplemental Instruction; development of oral and written communication skills; assessment of academic needs, skills, and individual plans to provide appropriate interventions; monitoring of academic progress; preparation for proficiency and entrance exams; academic advising; opportunities for national and international study exchange; research internships; and opportunities to present and publish program reports or research.

TOEOP should implement unique programming as well as utilize and coordinate with programming at their institutions,

agencies, schools, or communities.

Part 3. ORGANIZATION AND LEADERSHIP

To achieve student and program outcomes, TRIO and Other Educational Opportunity Programs (TOEOP) must be structured purposefully and organized effectively. TOEOP must have
- **clearly stated goals**
- **current and accessible policies and procedures**
- **written performance expectations for employees**
- **functional work flow graphics or organizational charts demonstrating clear channels of authority**

Leaders with organizational authority for the programs and services must provide strategic planning, supervision, and management; advance the organization; and maintain integrity through the following functions:

Strategic Planning
- **articulate a vision and mission that drive short- and long-term planning**
- **set goals and objectives based on the needs of the population served and desired student learning or development and program outcomes**
- **facilitate continuous development, implementation, and assessment of goal attainment congruent with institutional mission and strategic plans**
- **promote environments that provide meaningful opportunities for student learning, development, and engagement**
- **develop and continuously improve programs and services in response to the changing needs of students served and evolving institutional priorities**
- **intentionally include diverse perspectives to inform decision making**

Supervising
- **manage human resource processes including recruitment, selection, development, supervision, performance planning, evaluation, recognition, and reward**
- **influence others to contribute to the effectiveness and success of the unit**
- **empower professional, support, and student staff to accept leadership opportunities**
- **offer appropriate feedback to colleagues and students on skills needed to become more effective leaders**
- **encourage and support professional development, collaboration with colleagues and departments across the institution, and**

scholarly contribution to the profession

Managing
- **identify and address individual, organizational, and environmental conditions that foster or inhibit mission achievement**
- **plan, allocate, and monitor the use of fiscal, physical, human, intellectual, and technological resources**
- **use current and valid evidence to inform decisions**
- **incorporate sustainability practices in the management and design of programs, services, and facilities**
- **understand appropriate technologies and integrate them into programs and services**
- **be knowledgeable about codes and laws relevant to programs and services and ensure that staff members understand their responsibilities through appropriate training**
- **assess potential risks and take action to mitigate them**

Advancing the Organization
- **communicate effectively in writing, speaking, and electronic venues**
- **advocate for programs and services**
- **advocate for representation in strategic planning initiatives at appropriate divisional and institutional levels**
- **initiate collaborative interactions with internal and external stakeholders who have legitimate concerns about and interests in the functional area**
- **facilitate processes to reach consensus where wide support is needed**
- **inform other areas within the institution about issues affecting practice**

Maintaining Integrity
- **model ethical behavior and institutional citizenship**
- **share data used to inform key decisions in transparent and accessible ways**
- **monitor media used for distributing information about programs and services to ensure the content is current, accurate, appropriately referenced, and accessible**

TOEOP leaders must be knowledgeable about issues, trends, theories, research, and methodologies related to student learning and retention, especially with regard to populations served by their programs.

TOEOP leaders should
- participate in institutional or organizational planning, policy, procedural, and fiscal decisions that affect program and student goal achievement

- seek opportunities for additional funding, resources, and facilities, as needed
- represent the TOEOP on institutional or organizational committees
- promote community environments, where relevant to the program, services, or activities, that result in multiple opportunities for student learning and development
- collaborate with leaders of other programs to address learning needs and persistence of program participants
- educate others within the institution and community about the characteristics, challenges, and persistence of populations served by their programs

TOEOP leaders must collect, understand, and use data to make program decisions as well as to communicate to constituents about the relevance of the program within the context of the institution's or organization's mission, goals, and objectives.

TOEOP leaders should cultivate relationships with colleagues in their own and related professional disciplines. TOEOP leaders should be involved in research, publication, presentations, consultation, and participation in professional development opportunities.

TOEOP must be placed in the institution's organizational structure to ensure visibility, promote cooperative interaction with appropriate campus or community entities, and enlist the support of senior administrators.

Part 4. HUMAN RESOURCES

TRIO and Other Educational Opportunity Programs (TOEOP) must be staffed adequately by individuals qualified to accomplish mission and goals.

Within institutional guidelines, TOEOP must
- **establish procedures for staff recruitment and selection, training, performance planning, and evaluation**
- **set expectations for supervision and performance**
- **assess the performance of employees individually and as a team**
- **provide access to continuing and advanced education and appropriate professional development opportunities to improve the leadership ability, competence, and skills of all employees.**

TOEOP must maintain position descriptions for all staff members.

To create a diverse staff, TOEOP must institute recruitment and hiring strategies that encourage individuals from under-represented populations to

apply for positions.

The size, scope, and role of the program staff depend on the mission of TOEOP and the populations served. Staffing should be based on the needs of the students or participants and the resources available. TOEOP should employ a diverse staff to provide readily identifiable role models for students and to enrich the learning community. When possible, the staff should reflect the characteristics of the population being served.

TOEOP must develop promotion practices that are fair, inclusive, proactive, and non-discriminatory.

To further the recruitment and retention of staff, TOEOP must consider work life initiatives, such as compressed work schedules, flextime, job sharing, remote work, or telework.

TOEOP professional staff members must hold an earned graduate or professional degree in a field relevant to the position they hold or must possess an appropriate combination of educational credentials and related work experience.

TOEOP professional staff members must engage in continuing professional development activities to keep abreast of the research, theories, legislation, policies, and developments that affect their programs and services.

TOEOP must have technical and support staff members adequate to accomplish their mission. All members of the staff must be technologically proficient and qualified to perform their job functions, be knowledgeable about ethical and legal uses of technology, and have access to training and resources to support the performance of their assigned responsibilities.

Degree- or credential-seeking interns or graduate assistants must be qualified by enrollment in an appropriate field of study and by relevant experience. These individuals must be trained and supervised adequately by professional staff members holding educational credentials and related work experience appropriate for supervision. Supervisors must be cognizant of the roles of interns and graduate assistants as both student and employee and closely adhere to all parameters of their job descriptions, work hours, and schedules. Supervisors and the interns or graduate assistants must agree to compensatory time or other appropriate compensation if circumstances necessitate additional hours.

Student employees and volunteers must be carefully selected, trained, supervised, and evaluated. They must be educated on how and when to refer those in need of additional assistance to qualified staff members and must have access to a supervisor for assistance in making these judgments. Student employees and volunteers must be provided clear job descriptions, pre-service training based on assessed needs, and continuing development.

TOEOP should hire student employees and volunteers from groups traditionally under-represented in higher education.

All TOEOP staff members, including student employees and volunteers, must receive specific training on institutional policies pertaining to functions or activities they support and to privacy and confidentiality policies and laws regarding access to student records and other sensitive institutional information.

All TOEOP staff members must receive training on policies and procedures related to the use of technology to store or access student records and institutional data.

TOEOP must ensure that staff members are knowledgeable about and trained in emergency procedures, crisis response, and prevention efforts. Prevention efforts must address identification of threatening conduct or behavior of students, faculty and staff members, and others and must incorporate a system for responding and reporting.

TOEOP must ensure that staff members are knowledgeable of and trained in safety and emergency procedures for securing and vacating facilities.

TOEOP professionals must possess a combination of knowledge and experience applicable to their work with individuals who are traditionally under-represented in postsecondary education.

TOEOP professional staff members should possess
- effective oral and written communication skills
- an understanding of the culture, heritage, social context (e.g., socioeconomic standing, rural vs. urban) and learning styles of the persons served by the program
- leadership, management, organizational, and human relations skills
- ability to work effectively with individuals of diverse backgrounds and ages
- openness to new ideas coupled with flexibility and willingness to change

TOEOP should provide continuing professional development opportunities for staff such as in-service training programs, TRIO professional training seminars, participation in professional conferences, workshops, mentoring, job shadowing, or other continuing education activities.

TOEOP staff should contribute to the knowledge and

practice of the profession through presentations, research, or publications.

Part 5. ETHICS

TRIO and Other Educational Opportunity Programs (TOEOP) must review relevant professional ethical standards and must adopt or develop and implement appropriate statements of ethical practice.

TOEOP must publish and adhere to statements of ethical practice and ensure their periodic review by relevant constituencies.

TOEOP must orient new staff members to relevant ethical standards and statements of ethical practice and related institutional policies.

Statements of ethical standards must specify that staff members respect privacy and maintain confidentiality in all communications and records to the extent that such communications and records are protected under relevant privacy laws.

Statements of ethical standards must specify limits on disclosure of information contained in students' educational records as well as requirements to disclose to appropriate authorities.

Statements of ethical standards must address personal and economic conflicts of interest, or appearance thereof, by staff members in the performance of their work.

Statements of ethical standards must reflect the responsibility of staff members to be fair, objective, and impartial in their interactions with others.

Statements of ethical standards must reference management of institutional funds.

Statements of ethical standards must reference appropriate behavior regarding research and assessment with human participants, confidentiality of research and assessment data, and students' rights and responsibilities.

Statements of ethical standards must include the expectation that TOEOP staff members confront and hold accountable other staff members who exhibit unethical behavior.

Statements of ethical standards must address issues surrounding scholarly integrity.

As appropriate, TOEOP staff members must inform users of programs and services of ethical obligations and limitations emanating from codes and laws or from licensure requirements.

TOEOP staff members must recognize and avoid conflicts of interest that could adversely influence

their judgment or objectivity and, when unavoidable, recuse themselves from the situation.

TOEOP staff members must perform their duties within the limits of their position, training, expertise, and competence.

When these limits are exceeded, individuals in need of further assistance must be referred to persons possessing appropriate qualifications.

Promotional and descriptive information must be accurate and free of deception.

TOEOP must adhere to institutional policies regarding ethical and legal use of software and technology.

Part 6. LAW, POLICY, AND GOVERNANCE

TRIO and Other Educational Opportunity Programs (TOEOP) must be in compliance with laws, regulations, and policies that relate to their respective responsibilities and that pose legal obligations, limitations, risks, and liabilities for the institution as a whole. Examples include constitutional, statutory, regulatory, and case law; relevant law and orders emanating from codes and laws; and the institution's policies.

TOEOP sponsored by community-based agencies or organizations must also adhere to their comparable standards.

TOEOP must inform staff members, appropriate officials, and users of programs and services about existing and changing legal obligations, risks and liabilities, and limitations.

TOEOP must have written policies on all relevant operations, transactions, or tasks that have legal implications.

TOEOP must regularly review policies. The revision and creation of policies must be informed by best practices, available evidence, and policy issues in higher education.

TOEOP staff members must use reasonable and informed practices to limit the liability exposure of the institution and its officers, employees, and agents. TOEOP staff members must be informed about institutional policies regarding risk management, personal liability, and related insurance coverage options and must be referred to external sources if the institution does not provide coverage.

The institution must provide access to legal advice for staff members as needed to carry out assigned responsibilities.

TOEOP must have procedures and guidelines consistent with institutional policy for responding to threats, emergencies, and crisis situations. Systems and procedures must be in place to disseminate timely and accurate information to students, other members of the institutional community, and appropriate external organizations during emergency situations.

TOEOP staff members must neither participate in nor condone any form of harassment or activity that demeans persons or creates an intimidating, hostile, or offensive environment.

TOEOP must obtain permission to use copyrighted materials and nstruments. TOEOP must purchase the materials and instruments from legally compliant sources or seek alternative permission from the publisher or owner. References to copyrighted materials and instruments must include appropriate citations.

TOEOP staff members must be knowledgeable about internal and external governance systems that affect programs and services.

Part 7. DIVERSITY, EQUITY, AND ACCESS

Within the context of each institution's unique mission and in accordance with institutional polices and all applicable codes and laws, TRIO and Other Educational Opportunity Programs (TOEOP) must create and maintain educational and work environments that are
- welcoming, accessible, and inclusive to persons of diverse backgrounds
- equitable and non-discriminatory
- free from harassment

TOEOP must not discriminate on the basis of ability; age; cultural identity; ethnicity; family educational history (e.g., first generation to attend college); gender identity and expression; nationality; political affiliation; race; religious affiliation; sex; sexual orientation; economic, marital, social, or veteran status; or any other basis included in institutional policies and codes and laws.

TOEOP must
- advocate for greater sensitivity to multicultural and social justice concerns by the institution and its personnel
- modify or remove policies, practices, facilities, structures, systems, and technologies that limit access, discriminate, or produce inequities
- include diversity, equity, and access initiatives within their strategic plans
- foster communication that deepens understanding of identity, culture, self-expression, and heritage
- promote respect about commonalities and differences among people within their historical and cultural contexts
- address the characteristics and needs of a diverse population when establishing and implementing culturally relevant and inclusive programs, services, policies, procedures, and practices
- provide staff members with access to multicultural training and hold staff members accountable for integrating the training into their work
- respond to the needs of all students and other populations served when establishing hours of operation and developing methods of delivering programs, services, and resources
- ensure physical, program, and resource access for persons with disabilities
- recognize the needs of distance learning students by providing appropriate and accessible services and resources or by assisting them in gaining access to other appropriate services and resources in their geographic region

TOEOP must adhere to eligibility criteria set by funding sources.

Part 8. INSTITUTIONAL AND EXTERNAL RELATIONS

TRIO and Other Educational Opportunity Programs (TOEOP) must reach out to relevant individuals, groups, communities, and organizations internal and external to the institution to
- establish, maintain, and promote understanding and effective relations with those that have a significant interest in or potential effect on the students or other constituents served by the programs and services
- garner support and resources for programs and services as defined by the mission statement
- disseminate information about the programs and services
- collaborate, where appropriate, to assist in offering or improving programs and services to meet the needs of students and other constituents and to achieve program and student outcomes
- engage diverse individuals, groups, communities, and organizations to enrich the educational environment and experiences of students and other constituents

TOEOP must seek collaborative relations with program area schools, community organizations, government agencies, and students' families.

TOEOP must have procedures and guidelines consistent with institutional policy for

- communicating with the media
- contracting with external organizations for delivery of programs and services
- cultivating, soliciting, and managing gifts
- applying to and managing funds from grants

TOEOP must include a public relations component to regularly inform the institution, communities, agencies, and schools about their missions, services, and outcomes.

Part 9. FINANCIAL RESOURCES

TRIO and Other Educational Opportunity Programs (TOEOP) must have funding to accomplish the mission and goals. In establishing funding priorities and making significant changes, a comprehensive analysis must be conducted to determine the following elements: unmet needs of the unit, relevant expenditures, external and internal resources, and impact on students and the institution.

TOEOP must know and adhere to governmental and agency fiscal regulations regarding funding.

TOEOP must demonstrate efficient and effective use and responsible stewardship of fiscal resources consistent with institutional protocols.

Opportunities for additional funding should be pursued; however, these sources should not be expected to supplant current funding.

TOEOP should negotiate with their institutions to provide additional funding to support areas underfunded by their grants.

Part 10. TECHNOLOGY

TRIO and Other Educational Opportunity Programs (TOEOP) must have adequate technology to support the achievement of their mission and goals. The technology and its use must comply with institutional policies and procedures and be evaluated for compliance with relevant codes and laws.

TOEOP must use current technology to provide updated information regarding mission, location, staffing, programs, services, and official contacts to students and designated clients.

TOEOP must explore the use of technology to enhance delivery of programs and services, especially for students at a distance or external constituencies.

When technology is used to facilitate student learning and development, programs and services must select technology that reflects intended outcomes.

TOEOP must

- maintain policies and procedures that address the security, confidentiality, and backup of data, as well as compliance with privacy laws
- have clearly articulated plans in place for protecting confidentiality and security of information when using Internet-based technologies
- develop plans for replacing and updating existing hardware and software as well as plans for integrating new technically-based or supported programs, including systems developed internally by the institution, systems available through professional associations, or private vendor-based systems

Technology, as well as workstations or computer labs maintained by programs and services for student use, must be accessible to all designated clients and must meet established technology standards for delivery to persons with disabilities.

When providing student access to technology, TOEOP must

- have policies on the use of technology that are clear, easy to understand, and available to all students
- provide assistance, information, or referral to appropriate support services to those needing help accessing or using technology
- provide instruction or training on how to use the technology
- inform students on the legal and ethical implications of misuse as it pertains to intellectual property, harassment, privacy, and social networks

TOEOP must promote alternate access to information in formats accessible for participants and their families, especially when technology is not available to them.

TOEOP should advocate for and facilitate access to technology for program participants and their families. Technology should be employed to promote TOEOP, to provide academic and other student services, to assist participants with career exploration and the processes related to postsecondary transitions (e.g., admissions, financial aid, course registration, housing), and to communicate with students including those at outreach locations. Programs should intentionally model for their students the use of technology.

Student violations of technology policies must follow established institutional student disciplinary procedures.

Students who experience negative emotional or psychological consequences from the use of technology must be referred to support services provided by the institution.

Part 11. FACILITIES AND EQUIPMENT

TRIO and Other Educational Opportunity Programs (TOEOP) must have adequate, accessible, and suitably located facilities and equipment to support the mission and goals. If acquiring capital equipment as defined by the institution, TOEOP must take into account expenses related to regular maintenance and life cycle costs. Facilities and equipment must be evaluated on an established cycle, including consideration of sustainability, and be in compliance with codes and laws to provide for access, health, safety, and security.

TOEOP facilities must be physically located to promote visibility of the programs and to ensure coordination with other campus or organizational programs and services.

TOEOP staff members must have workspace that is well equipped, adequate in size, and designed to support their work and responsibilities. For conversations requiring privacy, staff members must have access to a private space.

TOEOP staff members who share workspace must be able to secure their own work.

The design of the facilities must guarantee the security and privacy of records and ensure the confidentiality of sensitive information.

The location and layout of the facilities must be sensitive to the needs of persons with disabilities as well as the needs of other constituencies.

Part 12. ASSESSMENT AND EVALUATION

TRIO and Other Educational Opportunity Programs (TOEOP) must have a clearly articulated assessment plan to document achievement of stated goals and learning outcomes, demonstrate accountability, provide evidence of improvement, and describe resulting changes in programs and services.

TOEOP must have adequate fiscal, human, professional development, and technological resources to develop and implement assessment plans.

Assessments must include direct and indirect evaluation and use qualitative and quantitative methodologies and existing evidence, as appropriate, to determine whether and to what degree the stated mission, goals, and intended outcomes are being met as effectively and efficiently as possible. The process must employ sufficient and sound measures to ensure comprehensiveness. Data collected must include responses from students and other constituencies,

and aggregated results must be shared with those groups. Results of assessments must be shared appropriately with multiple constituents.

Assessments, evaluations, and annual program performance reports must be conducted in accordance with conditions required by applicable sponsoring agreements.

Results of assessments and evaluations must be used to identify needs and interests in revising and improving programs and services, recognizing staff performance, maximizing resource efficiency and effectiveness, improving student achievement of learning and development outcomes, and improving student persistence and success. Changes resulting from the use of assessments and evaluation must be shared with stakeholders.

Assessments, evaluations, or annual evaluation reports should be made available, when appropriate, to the program's various stakeholders, such as relevant campus offices, external agencies, area schools, community organizations, and program advisory committees and boards.

General Standards revised in 2011;
TOEOP content developed/revised in 1999 & 2008

The Role of Undergraduate Admissions Programs and Services
CAS Standards Contextual Statement

"As the primary linking mechanism between the K-12 and higher education sectors, the college admissions process plays a central role in American education" (Stewart, 1998, p. 3). The process of college admission has in its roots the efforts of the first colonial colleges to recruit and select talented young men to attend their colleges. Although this selection process continued for some time, there were no admissions offices or staff dedicated to the enrollment of qualified applicants into the emerging system of American higher education. In the late 19th century, the financial pressures to enroll enough students to offset the rising costs of faculty resulted in the first organized efforts to recruit larger classes of students. This was the beginning of the need to balance an admissions process that addressed institutional financial solvency with enrolling a class capable of performing well academically (Henderson, 1998).

The increase in high school students in the late 19th and early 20th century led to increased enrollments nationally and to an expansion of the role of the first registrars to include admissions functions (Henderson, 2008). The pressure to recruit prospective students finally led to private institutions hiring admissions officers and then eventually to the creation of the first Office of Admissions in 1915 at Columbia University (Henderson, 2008). The first administration of the Scholastic Aptitude Test by The College Board in 1926 (and its adoption by Harvard and other institutions thereafter) ushered in the era of selective admissions, still in place today (Sparks, 1993).

The emergence of the admission officer as a new role on college campuses led to two significant events in the professionalization of the admission process. The first in 1937 was the establishment of the National Association of College Admissions Counseling (National Association of College Admissions Counselors, 2009). The second in 1949 followed the influx of GIs entering higher education after WWII when the American Association of Collegiate Registrars added "And Admissions Officers" to their name (Constance, 1973). By the 1950s admissions had become institutionalized as a process of "selection and guidance" (Fishman, 1958) and "a theory of administrative action based upon the knowledge of the interaction between a given college environment and various crucial characteristics of the applicant population" (Henderson, 2008).

Today the role of gatekeeper in the admissions office has shifted to include marketing/recruitment and enrollment management. The shift from gatekeeper to recruiter became critical in the 1970s during a decline in enrollment that "led to partially filled residence halls and classrooms, faculty cuts and poorly built buildings" (Johnson, 2000, p.

4). This resulted in the expansion of the role of marketing for admissions offices, the pressure to enroll a more diverse student body, and more competition to recruit academically talented students such as National Merit Scholars.

The scope and responsibilities of an admission professional have expanded to

- provide information and assistance to prospective students, families and secondary and community college counselors on the academic, financial, curricular and co-curricular offerings of their institutions
- evaluate the qualifications of applicants
- develop, implement and coordinate the institutions' strategic marketing or recruitment plans
- work with college faculty and administration to develop, implement, and evaluate enrollment policies and goals for the institution
- establish cooperative relationships with secondary school and community college counselors and other relevant constituencies
- work in concert with other campus offices to ensure that students are not only recruited but retained and eventually graduate

The admissions professional today is faced with many challenges: diverse students and student needs, high college costs, limited financial aid and scholarships, and intense competition for students. They must also apply new technologies in the recruitment, application, and enrollment processes. Admissions professionals must be able to function in a wide range of settings from "open-admissions" to highly selective institutions. Similarly, they must be prepared to work with prospective students with varying academic abilities, academic and career interests, financial concerns, personal challenges, and physical and learning disabilities. Admissions offices must have appropriate and adequate staff policies and skills in human development to manage their important roles.

Although the standards contained herein focus solely on Undergraduate Admissions Programs and Services, it is important to note the larger national trend towards admissions as a part of a larger enrollment management structure. Enrollment management has been defined as a "process that brings together often disparate functions having to do with recruiting, funding, tracking, retaining and replacing students as they move toward, within, and away from the university" (Maguire, p. 16, 1976). Others have added academic and career counseling, academic assistance programs, institutional research, orientation, retention programs, and student services (Henderson,

2008; Kalsbeek, 2006). To manage the complexities of the modern university, enrollment management is seen not as an administrative process, but as a process that involves the entire campus (Hossler, 1986). No matter the organizational structure, it is important to recognize that Undergraduate Admissions Programs and Services may exist in a wide variety of institutional structures.

Clearly today's admissions professionals must continue to engage and counsel students throughout the whole admissions process while also addressing institutional expectations. The Undergraduate Admissions Programs and Services Standards and Guidelines that follow have been written to facilitate the admissions professional's response to these increasingly complex demands.

References, Readings, and Resources

Constance, C. L. (1973). *Historical review of the association.* Washington, DC: American Association of Collegiate Registrars and Admissions Officers.

Fishman, J. A. (1958). Some psychological theory for selecting and guiding college students. In N. Sanford, *The American college: A psychological and social interpretation of higher learning.* New York: John Wiley and Sons.

Henderson, S. E. (2008). Admissions evolving role: From gatekeeper to strategic partner. In B. Lauren, *College admissions officer's guide.* Washington, DC: American Association of Collegiate Registrars and Admissions Officers.

Henderson, S. E. (1998). A historical view of an admissions dilemma: Seeking quantity or quality in the student body. In C. C. Swann & S. E. Henderson, *Handbook for the college admissions profession.* Westport, CT: Greenwood Press.

Hosler, D. (1986). *Creating effective enrollment management systems.* New York: College Entrance Examination Board.

Johnson, A. L. (2000). The evolution of strategic enrollment management: A historical perspective. *Journal of College Admission.* Winter.

Kalsbeek, D. H. (2006). Some reflections on SEM structures and strategies. *College and University Journal. 81*(3).

Maguire, J. (1976). To the organized go the students. *Bridge Magazine, 39*(1): 16-20.

National Association of College Admissions Counselors. (2008). *Fundamentals of college admission counseling (2nd ed.).* Alexandria, VA: National Association of College Admissions Counselors.

National Association of College Admissions Counselors. (2009). *Statement of principles of good practice.* Alexandria, VA: National Association of College Admissions Counselors.

Sparks, L. (1993). *College admissions: A selected bibliography.* Westport, CT: Greenwood Press.

Stewart, D. (1998). Perspectives on educational reform" In C. C. Swann & S. E. Henderson (Eds.), *Handbook for the college admissions profession.* Washington, DC: American Association of Collegiate Registrars and Admissions Officers.

The College Board. (2002). *Best practices in admissions decisions.* New York: College Board Publications.

Contextual Statement Contributors

Kevin Kruger, NASPA
Laura A. Dean, University of Georgia
Eric White, Penn State University
Lori Reesor, University of Kansas
Christine Schneikart-Luebbe, Wichita State University
Joyce Smith, NACAC

Undergraduate Admissions Programs and Services
CAS Standards and Guidelines

Part 1. MISSION

The mission of Undergraduate Admissions Programs and Services (UAPS) is to enroll undergraduate applicants who will, both individually and collectively, benefit from the collegiate learning environment through academic and personal enrichment and development.

UAPS must recruit, admit, and encourage enrollment of applicants whose academic and personal credentials are consistent with the overall priorities and mission of the institution.

This may include applicants who may be underprepared for post-secondary study.

To accomplish this mission UAPS must
- assess and evaluate the abilities, needs, and expectations of prospective students as they move from secondary to postsecondary education, as they move from one postsecondary institution to another, or as they return from a period of non-enrollment
- establish, promulgate, and implement admission criteria that accurately represent the mission, goals, purposes and resources of the institution, and that accommodate the abilities, needs, and interests of potential students
- clearly and accurately present the mission, goals, policies, procedures, facilities, and characteristics of the institution
- develop and regularly review enrollment goals for admission with appropriate individuals within the institution

UAPS must develop, disseminate, implement, and regularly review their missions. The mission must be consistent with the mission of the institution and with professional standards. The mission must be appropriate for the institution's student populations and community settings. Mission statements must reference student learning and development.

Part 2. PROGRAM

The formal education of students, consisting of the curriculum and the co-curriculum, must promote student learning and development outcomes that are purposeful, contribute to students' realization of their potential, and prepare students for satisfying and productive lives.

Undergraduate Admissions Programs and Services (UAPS) must collaborate with colleagues and departments across the institution to promote student learning and development, persistence, and success.

Consistent with the institutional mission, programs and services must identify relevant and desirable student learning and development outcomes from among the six domains and related dimensions:

Domain: knowledge acquisition, integration, construction, and application
- Dimensions: understanding knowledge from a range of disciplines; connecting knowledge to other knowledge, ideas, and experiences; constructing knowledge; and relating knowledge to daily life

Domain: cognitive complexity
- Dimensions: critical thinking, reflective thinking, effective reasoning, and creativity

Domain: intrapersonal development
- Dimensions: realistic self-appraisal, self-understanding, and self-respect; identity development; commitment to ethics and integrity; and spiritual awareness

Domain: interpersonal competence
- Dimensions: meaningful relationships, interdependence, collaboration, and effective leadership.

Domain: humanitarianism and civic engagement
- Dimensions: understanding and appreciation of cultural and human differences, social responsibility, global perspective, and sense of civic responsibility

Domain: practical competence
- Dimensions: pursuing goals, communicating effectively, technical competence, managing personal affairs, managing career development, demonstrating professionalism, maintaining health and wellness, and living a purposeful and satisfying life

[LD Outcomes: See *The Council for the Advancement of Standards Learning and Developmental Outcomes* statement for examples of outcomes related to these domains and dimensions.]

UAPS must
- assess relevant and desirable student

learning and development
- **provide evidence of impact on outcomes**
- **articulate contributions to or support of student learning and development in the domains not specifically assessed**
- **articulate contributions to or support of student persistence and success**
- **use evidence gathered through this process to create strategies for improvement of programs and services**

UAPS must be
- **intentionally designed**
- **guided by theories and knowledge of learning and development**
- **integrated into the life of the institution**
- **reflective of developmental and demographic profiles of the student population**
- **responsive to needs of individuals, populations with distinct needs, and relevant constituencies**
- **delivered using multiple formats, strategies, and contexts**

Where institutions provide distance education, UAPS must assist distance learners to achieve their educational goals by providing access to information about programs and services, to staff members who can address questions and concerns, and to counseling, advising, or other forms of assistance.

UAPS must develop recruitment and admission procedures and strategies designed to establish and meet the institution's enrollment plan and diversity goals.

UAPS should have recruitment plans for targeted groups such as
- first generation
- TRIO-eligible and other underrepresented populations
- veterans
- international

UAPS must accurately represent and promote their institutions by providing current information about academic majors and degree programs. Information must include factual and accurate descriptions of majors, minors, concentrations and/or interdisciplinary offerings, information about bridge programs, dual high school/college enrollment programs, diploma, certificate, and other special admissions programs.

UAPS must clearly articulate the requirements of admission and enrollment processes.

These should include processes for the first-year and transfer students, including secondary school preparation,

standardized testing, financial aid, housing, and notification deadlines and refund procedures.

UAPS should establish procedures to review and admit, as appropriate, applicants with criminal and disciplinary records in compliance with local, state/provincial, and federal law.

UAPS must clearly explain the process by which applicants bring credit to the institution including transfer credit or life experience, if applicable at the institution.

UAPS must be responsible for the accurate representation and promotion of the admission calendar, separate admissions to majors, academic offerings, financial aid and cost of attendance, housing application and deposit deadlines, and other related services.

UAPS must offer recruitment opportunities including community venues for potential adult students.

UAPS should utilize currently enrolled students, alumni, staff, and faculty members in the recruitment process. Examples include ambassador programs, tour guides, student panels, faculty interviews, or other opportunities for prospective students and their families to interact with current students and faculty.

UAPS should use a variety of strategies to introduce postsecondary opportunities to students and their families.

UAPS must provide students, families, and secondary schools with comprehensive information about costs of attendance and opportunities for financial aid.

The cost of attendance should include course materials, fees, and other non-tuition related expenses.

UAPS must include a current and accurate admission calendar in publications and websites. If the institution offers special admission options, the publication must define these programs and state deadlines dates, notification dates, required deposits, and refund policies.

Special admission options may include Early Admission, Early Action, Early Decision, wait lists, or Restrictive Early Admission.

UAPS should provide current wait-listed applicants notification outlining the number of students from the previous year offered admission, the number who accepted spaces, the number of offered places on the wait list, as well as the availability of financial aid and housing.

UAPS must have policies and procedures for managing special admissions requests from politically sensitive constituencies, such as legislators, governing board members, donors, and alumni.

UAPS offices must have policies and procedures for managing applications and communicating to students who do not meet traditional admission criteria.

Part 3. ORGANIZATION AND LEADERSHIP

To achieve student and program outcomes, Undergraduate Admissions Programs and Services (UAPS) must be structured purposefully and organized effectively. UAPS must have
- clearly stated goals
- current and accessible policies and procedures
- written performance expectations for employees
- functional work flow graphics or organizational charts demonstrating clear channels of authority

Leaders with organizational authority for the programs and services must provide strategic planning, supervision, and management; advance the organization; and maintain integrity through the following functions:

Strategic Planning
- articulate a vision and mission that drive short- and long-term planning
- set goals and objectives based on the needs of the population served and desired student learning or development and program outcomes
- facilitate continuous development, implementation, and assessment of goal attainment congruent with institutional mission and strategic plans
- promote environments that provide meaningful opportunities for student learning, development, and engagement
- develop and continuously improve programs and services in response to the changing needs of students served and evolving institutional priorities
- intentionally include diverse perspectives to inform decision making

Supervising
- manage human resource processes including recruitment, selection, development, supervision, performance planning, evaluation, recognition, and reward
- influence others to contribute to the effectiveness and success of the unit
- empower professional, support, and student staff to accept leadership opportunities
- offer appropriate feedback to colleagues and students on skills needed to become more effective leaders
- encourage and support professional

development, collaboration with colleagues and departments across the institution, and scholarly contribution to the profession

Managing
- identify and address individual, organizational, and environmental conditions that foster or inhibit mission achievement
- plan, allocate, and monitor the use of fiscal, physical, human, intellectual, and technological resources
- use current and valid evidence to inform decisions
- incorporate sustainability practices in the management and design of programs, services, and facilities
- understand appropriate technologies and integrate them into programs and services
- be knowledgeable about codes and laws relevant to programs and services and ensure that staff members understand their responsibilities through appropriate training
- assess potential risks and take action to mitigate them

Advancing the Organization
- communicate effectively in writing, speaking, and electronic venues
- advocate for programs and services
- advocate for representation in strategic planning initiatives at appropriate divisional and institutional levels
- initiate collaborative interactions with internal and external stakeholders who have legitimate concerns about and interests in the functional area
- facilitate processes to reach consensus where wide support is needed
- inform other areas within the institution about issues affecting practice

Maintaining Integrity
- model ethical behavior and institutional citizenship
- share data used to inform key decisions in transparent and accessible ways
- monitor media used for distributing information about programs and services to ensure the content is current, accurate, appropriately referenced, and accessible

UAPS leaders should provide training, orientation, and consultation assistance to faculty members, administrators, staff, institution officials (e.g., trustees), and high school and transfer counselors to assist them in responding to the enrollment needs of students and their families.

UAPS must function as an independent unit or

as part of an overall enrollment management structure.

Part 4. HUMAN RESOURCES

Undergraduate Admissions Programs and Services (UAPS) must be staffed adequately by individuals qualified to accomplish mission and goals.

Within institutional guidelines, UAPS must
- **establish procedures for staff recruitment and selection, training, performance planning, and evaluation**
- **set expectations for supervision and performance**
- **assess the performance of employees individually and as a team**
- **provide access to continuing and advanced education and appropriate professional development opportunities to improve the leadership ability, competence, and skills of all employees.**

UAPS must maintain position descriptions for all staff members.

To create a diverse staff, UAPS must institute recruitment and hiring strategies that encourage individuals from under-represented populations to apply for positions.

UAPS must develop promotion practices that are fair, inclusive, proactive, and non-discriminatory.

UAPS staff must recognize and appreciate individual differences among students and integrate an understanding of this information into the recruitment relationship.

Examples of these differences may include aptitude, intelligence, age, interests, first generation, socio-economic status, cultures and cultural identities, and achievements.

To further the recruitment and retention of staff, UAPS must consider work life initiatives, such as compressed work schedules, flextime, job sharing, remote work, or telework.

UAPS professional staff members must hold an earned graduate or professional degree in a field relevant to the position they hold or must possess an appropriate combination of educational credentials and related work experience.

UAPS professional staff members must engage in continuing professional development activities to keep abreast of the research, theories, legislation, policies, and developments that affect their programs and services.

UAPS staff should possess individual and group

communication skills to assist students and their families in the admissions process.

Professional staff in UAPS should have knowledge in the following areas:
- institutional curriculum offerings
- student involvement options
- referrals for appropriate institutional community resources in response to particular needs
- various levels of academic preparation and ability
- life planning
- financial aid opportunities and deadlines
- academic advising and student orientation programs and activities

Professional staff members in UAPS should be competent in providing assistance to prospective students regarding their educational goals, including, but not limited to,
- ethical and objective presentation of the institution's programs and opportunities
- careful and concerned analysis of each student's goals
- responsible decision-making in the selection of an institution
- knowledge of admission issues and concerns

UAPS staff should have an understanding of the psychology of adolescents, young adults, and adult learners, as well as concepts of student development and learning.

UAPS staff must demonstrate an awareness of and sensitivity to the unique social, cultural, and economic circumstances of students including but not limited to age; cultural heritage; disability; ethnicity; gender identity and expression; nationality; political affiliation; race; religious affiliation; sex; sexual orientation; economic, marital, social, or veteran status; and any other bases included in applicable laws.

UAPS staff must have an understanding of the proper administration and uses of standardized tests and be able to interpret test scores and test-related data to students, parents, families, educators, institutions, agencies, and the public.

Examples include, but are not limited to, the following tests: The ACT, ACT PLAN, CLEP, DANTES, GED, Preliminary SAT/ National Merit Scholarship Qualifying Test (PSAT/NMSQT), SAT I and SAT II, and Advanced Placement exams.

UAPS staff must be able to interpret transcripts with honors courses, AP or CLEP credits, when evaluating undergraduate applications.

UAPS staff must have an understanding of the needs of students with unique pre-collegiate experiences when evaluating undergraduate applications.

Examples of experiences and characteristics include

home schooling, foster youth and homeless, international education, GED graduation, veterans, undocumented, and International Baccalaureate programs.

UAPS must provide appropriate training for staff involved with the processing of admission applications, including data integrity, transcript authentication, file management, customer service, and the use of technology in the admission process.

UAPS staff should remain current in emerging recruitment strategies, including the use of call centers, tele-counseling, on-line and social media, and the use of paid and volunteer staff in the recruitment process.

UAPS must have technical and support staff members adequate to accomplish their mission. All members of the staff must be technologically proficient and qualified to perform their job functions, be knowledgeable about ethical and legal uses of technology, and have access to training and resources to support the performance of their assigned responsibilities.

Degree- or credential-seeking interns or graduate assistants must be qualified by enrollment in an appropriate field of study and by relevant experience. These individuals must be trained and supervised adequately by professional staff members holding educational credentials and related work experience appropriate for supervision. Supervisors must be cognizant of the roles of interns and graduate assistants as both student and employee and closely adhere to all parameters of their job descriptions, work hours, and schedules. Supervisors and the interns or graduate assistants must agree to compensatory time or other appropriate compensation if circumstances necessitate additional hours.

Student employees and volunteers must be carefully selected, trained, supervised, and evaluated. They must be educated on how and when to refer those in need of additional assistance to qualified staff members and must have access to a supervisor for assistance in making these judgments. Student employees and volunteers must be provided clear job descriptions, pre-service training based on assessed needs, and continuing development.

All UAPS staff members, including student employees and volunteers, must receive specific training on institutional policies pertaining to functions or activities they support and to privacy and confidentiality policies and laws regarding access to student records and other sensitive institutional information.

All UAPS staff members must receive training on policies and procedures related to the use of technology to store or access student records and institutional data.

UAPS must ensure that staff members are knowledgeable about and trained in emergency procedures, crisis response, and prevention efforts. Prevention efforts must address identification of threatening conduct or behavior of students, faculty and staff members, and others and must incorporate a system for responding and reporting.

UAPS must ensure that staff members are knowledgeable of and trained in safety and emergency procedures for securing and vacating facilities.

Part 5. ETHICS

Undergraduate Admissions Programs and Services (UAPS) must review relevant professional ethical standards and must adopt or develop and implement appropriate statements of ethical practice.

UAPS must publish and adhere to statements of ethical practice and ensure their periodic review by relevant constituencies.

UAPS must orient new staff members to relevant ethical standards and statements of ethical practice and related institutional policies.

UAPS staff and volunteers must not disseminate biased, unflattering, and/or potentially inaccurate information about other secondary or postsecondary institutions, their admission criteria, their curricular offerings, or other related information.

UAPS staff must be compensated in the form of a fixed salary, rather than commissions or bonuses based on the number of students recruited, and must not contract with secondary school personnel for remunerations for referred students.

UAPS staff must not offer or accept any reward or remuneration from a college, university, agency, or organization for placement or recruitment of students.

UAPS must cite the source and year of study when institutional publications and communications reference academic programs, academic rigor or reputations, or athletic rankings.

Except for Early Decision programs, UAPS must not require or ask secondary schools to indicate the order of prospective students' college or university preferences, and must not require or ask candidates to indicate the order of their college or university preferences.

UAPS must not offer exclusive incentives that

provide opportunities for students applying or admitted under Early Decision that are not available to students admitted under other admission options.

Examples of incentive programs include special residence halls, honors programs, full need-based financial aid packages, or special scholarships in addition to any other promise of an advantage in the admission process if student(s) convert from Regular Admission to Early Decision.

Categories might include student athletes, underprepared students, veterans, or those with a unique talent.

UAPS must develop and use notification practices that protect the confidentiality of an applicant's admission or denial status. Specific efforts must be made to protect privacy when using web based technologies or group email announcements.

Statements of ethical standards must specify that staff members respect privacy and maintain confidentiality in all communications and records to the extent that such communications and records are protected under relevant privacy laws.

Statements of ethical standards must specify limits on disclosure of information contained in students' educational records as well as requirements to disclose to appropriate authorities.

Statements of ethical standards must address personal and economic conflicts of interest, or appearance thereof, by staff members in the performance of their work.

Statements of ethical standards must reflect the responsibility of staff members to be fair, objective, and impartial in their interactions with others.

Statements of ethical standards must reference management of institutional funds.

Statements of ethical standards must reference appropriate behavior regarding research and assessment with human participants, confidentiality of research and assessment data, and students' rights and responsibilities.

Statements of ethical standards must include the expectation that UAPS staff members confront and hold accountable other staff members who exhibit unethical behavior.

Statements of ethical standards must address issues surrounding scholarly integrity.

As appropriate, UAPS staff members must inform users of programs and services of ethical obligations and limitations emanating from codes and laws or from licensure requirements.

UAPS staff members must recognize and avoid conflicts of interest that could adversely influence their judgment or objectivity and, when unavoidable, recuse themselves from the situation.

UAPS staff members must perform their duties within the limits of their position, training, expertise, and competence.

When these limits are exceeded, individuals in need of further assistance must be referred to persons possessing appropriate qualifications.

Promotional and descriptive information must be accurate and free of deception.

UAPS must adhere to institutional policies regarding ethical and legal use of software and technology.

Part 6. LAW, POLICY, AND GOVERNANCE

Undergraduate Admissions Programs and Services (UAPS) must be in compliance with laws, regulations, and policies that relate to their respective responsibilities and that pose legal obligations, limitations, risks, and liabilities for the institution as a whole. Examples include constitutional, statutory, regulatory, and case law; relevant law and orders emanating from codes and laws; and the institution's policies.

UAPS staff members must establish policies with respect to the release of student names during the admission process. Any policy that authorizes the release of students' names must indicate that the release be made only with the students' permission and be consistent with applicable laws and regulations.

UAPS must abide by regulations in the *Family Educational Rights and Privacy Act* (FERPA), or other applicable privacy laws when developing policies that authorize the release of student names during the admission process.

UAPS must inform staff members, appropriate officials, and users of programs and services about existing and changing legal obligations, risks and liabilities, and limitations.

UAPS must have written policies on all relevant operations, transactions, or tasks that have legal implications.

UAPS must regularly review policies. The revision and creation of policies must be informed by best practices, available evidence, and policy issues in higher education.

UAPS staff members must use reasonable and informed practices to limit the liability exposure

of the institution and its officers, employees, and agents. UAPS staff members must be informed about institutional policies regarding risk management, personal liability, and related insurance coverage options and must be referred to external sources if the institution does not provide coverage.

The institution must provide access to legal advice for staff members as needed to carry out assigned responsibilities.

UAPS must have procedures and guidelines consistent with institutional policy for responding to threats, emergencies, and crisis situations. Systems and procedures must be in place to disseminate timely and accurate information to students, other members of the institutional community, and appropriate external organizations during emergency situations.

UAPS staff members must neither participate in nor condone any form of harassment or activity that demeans persons or creates an intimidating, hostile, or offensive environment.

UAPS must obtain permission to use copyrighted materials and instruments. UAPS must purchase the materials and instruments from legally compliant sources or seek alternative permission from the publisher or owner. References to copyrighted materials and instruments must include appropriate citations.

UAPS staff members must be knowledgeable about internal and external governance systems that affect programs and services.

Part 7. DIVERSITY, EQUITY, AND ACCESS

Within the context of each institution's unique mission and in accordance with institutional polices and all applicable codes and laws, Undergraduate Admissions Programs and Services (UAPS) must create and maintain educational and work environments that are
- welcoming, accessible, and inclusive to persons of diverse backgrounds
- equitable and non-discriminatory
- free from harassment

UAPS must not discriminate on the basis of ability; age; cultural identity; ethnicity; family educational history (e.g., first generation to attend college); gender identity and expression; nationality; political affiliation; race; religious affiliation; sex; sexual orientation; economic, marital, social, or veteran status; or any other basis included in institutional policies and codes and laws.

UAPS must
- advocate for greater sensitivity to

multicultural and social justice concerns by the institution and its personnel
- modify or remove policies, practices, facilities, structures, systems, and technologies that limit access, discriminate, or produce inequities
- include diversity, equity, and access initiatives within their strategic plans
- foster communication that deepens understanding of identity, culture, self-expression, and heritage
- promote respect about commonalities and differences among people within their historical and cultural contexts
- address the characteristics and needs of a diverse population when establishing and implementing culturally relevant and inclusive programs, services, policies, procedures, and practices
- provide staff members with access to multicultural training and hold staff members accountable for integrating the training into their work
- respond to the needs of all students and other populations served when establishing hours of operation and developing methods of delivering programs, services, and resources
- ensure physical, program, and resource access for persons with disabilities
- recognize the needs of distance learning students by providing appropriate and accessible services and resources or by assisting them in gaining access to other appropriate services and resources in their geographic region

Students inquiring about disability services accommodations must be referred to the appropriate institution staff and resources.

UAPS must accurately describe and depict images of the diversity of the institution in admission material and media.

Part 8. INSTITUTIONAL AND EXTERNAL RELATIONS

Undergraduate Admissions Programs and Services (UAPS) must reach out to relevant individuals, groups, communities, and organizations internal and external to the institution to
- establish, maintain, and promote understanding and effective relations with those that have a significant interest in or potential effect on the students or other constituents served by the programs and services
- garner support and resources for programs

and services as defined by the mission statement

- disseminate information about the programs and services
- collaborate, where appropriate, to assist in offering or improving programs and services to meet the needs of students and other constituents and to achieve program and student outcomes
- engage diverse individuals, groups, communities, and organizations to enrich the educational environment and experiences of students and other constituents

UAPS must work collaboratively with institutional marketing and communications departments in developing publications, websites, video, and other related media that accurately represent the institution to prospective students and their families.

UAPS must work collaboratively with academic departments throughout the recruitment and enrollment process. UAPS staff must provide appropriate training to faculty and campus administrators about the admissions process and their role in the recruitment process.

UAPS must provide appropriate training to alumni and other volunteers who participate in the recruitment process to delineate their role in representing the institution with prospective students and their families.

UAPS must work collaboratively with the registrar and institutional research staff when analyzing yield and conversion rates and other related data for admitted students.

UAPS should coordinate and provide linkages to other campus units such as housing and residential life, campus and visitor information services, financial aid, orientation, registrar, student activities, athletics, academic advising, campus bookstore, student accounts, academic support, disability services, counseling, and career services.

UAPS should identify students deficient in required academic skills and preparation and refer to the appropriate campus units.

UAPS must have procedures and guidelines consistent with institutional policy for
- communicating with the media
- contracting with external organizations for delivery of programs and services
- cultivating, soliciting, and managing gifts
- applying to and managing funds from grants

Part 9. FINANCIAL RESOURCES

Undergraduate Admissions Programs and Services

(UAPS) must have funding to accomplish the mission and goals. In establishing funding priorities and making significant changes, a comprehensive analysis must be conducted to determine the following elements: unmet needs of the unit, relevant expenditures, external and internal resources, and impact on students and the institution.

UAPS must demonstrate efficient and effective use and responsible stewardship of fiscal resources consistent with institutional protocols.

UAPS should have processes to waive admission application fees for prospective students who meet institutionally defined criteria.

Part 10. TECHNOLOGY

Undergraduate Admissions Programs and Services (UAPS) must have adequate technology to support the achievement of their mission and goals. The technology and its use must comply with institutional policies and procedures and be evaluated for compliance with relevant codes and laws.

UAPS must use current technology to provide updated information regarding mission, location, staffing, programs, services, and official contacts to students and designated clients.

UAPS must explore the use of technology to enhance delivery of programs and services, especially for students at a distance or external constituencies.

UAPS staff should have expertise in utilizing appropriate technologies in recruiting students, including, but not limited to, social networking, broadcast text messages, instant messaging, electronic financial aid resources, and student record-keeping.

When technology is used to facilitate student learning and development, UAPS must select technology that reflects intended outcomes.

UAPS must
- maintain policies and procedures that address the security, confidentiality, and backup of data, as well as compliance with privacy laws
- have clearly articulated plans in place for protecting confidentiality and security of information when using Internet-based technologies
- develop plans for replacing and updating existing hardware and software as well as plans for integrating new technically-based or supported programs, including systems developed internally by the institution, systems available through professional associations, or private vendor-based systems

Technology, as well as workstations or computer labs maintained by programs and services for student use, must be accessible to all designated clients and must meet established technology standards for delivery to persons with disabilities.

When providing student access to technology, UAPS must:

- have policies on the use of technology that are clear, easy to understand, and available to all students
- provide assistance, information, or referral to appropriate support services to those needing help accessing or using technology
- provide instruction or training on how to use the technology
- inform students on the legal and ethical implications of misuse as it pertains to intellectual property, harassment, privacy, and social networks

Student violations of technology policies must follow established institutional student disciplinary procedures.

Students who experience negative emotional or psychological consequences from the use of technology must be referred to support services provided by the institution.

Part 11. FACILITIES AND EQUIPMENT

Undergraduate Admissions Programs and Services (UAPS) must have adequate, accessible, and suitably located facilities and equipment to support the mission and goals. If acquiring capital equipment as defined by the institution, UAPS must take into account expenses related to regular maintenance and life cycle costs. Facilities and equipment must be evaluated on an established cycle, including consideration of sustainability, and be in compliance with codes and laws to provide for access, health, safety, and security.

UAPS staff members must have workspace that is well equipped, adequate in size, and designed to support their work and responsibilities. For conversations requiring privacy, staff members must have access to a private space.

UAPS staff members who share workspace must be able to secure their own work.

The design of the facilities must guarantee the security and privacy of records and ensure the confidentiality of sensitive information.

The location and layout of the facilities must be sensitive to the needs of persons with disabilities as well as the needs of other constituencies.

UAPS should encourage the maintenance of attractive and appealing campus facilities that complement the recruitment and admissions process as well as a welcome facility that provides appropriate first stop information and greeting service to all visitors.

Part 12. ASSESSMENT AND EVALUATION

Undergraduate Admissions Programs and Services (UAPS) must have a clearly articulated assessment plan to document achievement of stated goals and learning outcomes, demonstrate accountability, provide evidence of improvement, and describe resulting changes in programs and services.

UAPS must have adequate fiscal, human, professional development, and technological resources to develop and implement assessment plans.

Assessments must include direct and indirect evaluation and use qualitative and quantitative methodologies and existing evidence, as appropriate, to determine whether and to what degree the stated mission, goals, and intended outcomes are being met as effectively and efficiently as possible. The process must employ sufficient and sound measures to ensure comprehensiveness. Data collected must include responses from students and other constituencies, and aggregated results must be shared with those groups. Results of assessments must be shared appropriately with multiple constituents.

Results of assessments and evaluations must be used to identify needs and interests in revising and improving programs and services, recognizing staff performance, maximizing resource efficiency and effectiveness, improving student achievement of learning and development outcomes, and improving student persistence and success. Changes resulting from the use of assessments and evaluation must be shared with stakeholders.

UAPS must employ data-based strategic enrollment management principles when identifying prospective students.

Predictive modeling should be used to identify prospective students and yield data when evaluating the effectiveness of specific recruitment programs and admissions strategies.

Feedback about admission processes should be sought from relevant participants including prospective students, faculty members, staff, and families.

General Standards revised in 2011;
AP content developed/revised in 1987, 1997, & 2010

The Role of Undergraduate Research Programs
CAS Standards Contextual Statement

Colleges and universities have long recognized the value of student scholarship as the culminating hallmark of an engaged and successful undergraduate career. Research experiences and creative practice projects—conducted in collaboration with and/or under the mentorship of concerned and dedicated faculty—have the potential to be transformative, moving our undergraduates to deeper understanding of and engagement with the world around them. Undergraduate research and creative practice also provide an important measure of cumulative student learning. (AAC&U, 2007)

This position of the Association of American Colleges and Universities crystallizes the value of undergraduate research programs. All too often these activities are loosely connected to the overall academic program and are implemented as boutique opportunities. The CAS undergraduate research program standards are designed to integrate undergraduate research across the institution and implement a vision of undergraduate education that offers students the opportunity to emphasize their identities as learners and scholars.

Although the origins of the undergraduate research concept are not clear, it is likely that credit for this phenomenon of American higher education resides in the undergraduate liberal arts college. In 1958 the US was awakened to deficiencies in science education by the launching of Sputnik by the USSR. In the early 1960s the National Science Foundation created its Undergraduate Research Program to encourage faculty-student science research. Credit needs to be given to two organizations that have been instrumental in promoting undergraduate research.

The Council on Undergraduate Research (CUR), founded in 1978, is a national organization of individual and institutional members representing over 900 colleges and universities. CUR and its affiliated colleges, universities, and individuals share a focus on providing undergraduate research opportunities for faculty and students at predominantly undergraduate institutions. CUR believes that faculty members enhance their teaching and contribution to society by remaining active in research and by involving undergraduates in research. CUR's leadership works with agencies and foundations to enhance research opportunities for faculty and students. CUR provides support for faculty development (http://www.cur.org).

The National Conferences on Undergraduate Research (NCUR), established in 1987, is dedicated to promoting undergraduate research, scholarship, and creative activity in all fields of study by sponsoring an annual conference for students. Unlike meetings of academic professional organizations, this gathering of young scholars welcomes presenters from all institutions of higher learning and from all corners of the academic curriculum. Through this annual conference, NCUR creates a unique environment for the celebration and promotion of undergraduate student achievement, provides models of exemplary research and scholarship, and helps to improve the state of undergraduate education (http://www.ncur.org).

The National Collegiate Honors Council (NCHC) has contributed to the undergraduate research movement through its influence on honors programs and colleges. Although there is not a standard requirement for research projects and theses, most programs offer that track for interested students.

There is a rich tradition of highly developed college and university undergraduate research programs, awards and grants, symposia, workshops, research presentations, poster sessions, and journals (print and online). Student organizations, particularly honor societies, also offer regional and national conferences that feature oral reports, poster sessions, and awards. Mercyhurst College maintains a directory of undergraduate journals and conferences (http://upd.mercyhurst.edu). About 30 institutions have formed the Undergraduate Research Community for the Human Sciences (URC) that seeks to develop a dynamic and pervasive culture of the human sciences for developing the next generation of scholars (http://www.kon.org/urc/undergrad_research.html). All of these initiatives advance undergraduate learning and development.

The undergraduate research standards and guidelines provide a basis for institutional self-assessment and program development. In addition, because a comprehensive assessment of student outcomes has not had a high priority in undergraduate research, the student learning and development outcomes can be instrumental in raising the bar for assessment.

References, Readings, and Resources

AAC&U. (2007). The student as scholar: Undergraduate research and creative practice. www.aacu.org.

Undergraduate Journals & Conferences Directory. http://upd.mercyhurst.edu

Council on Undergraduate Research. http://www.cur.org

Undergraduate Research Journal for the Human Sciences, http://www.kon.org/urc/undergradresearch.html

National Conferences on Undergraduate Research. http://www.ncur.org

Contextual Statement Contributor
Dorothy I. Mitstifer, ACHS

Undergraduate Research Programs
CAS Standards and Guidelines

Part 1. MISSION

The primary mission of Undergraduate Research Programs (URP) is to engage students in investigative and creative activity to experience firsthand the processes of scholarly exploration and discovery. Undergraduate research is an inquiry or investigation conducted by an undergraduate student to examine, create, and share new knowledge in the context of disciplinary and interdisciplinary traditions.

URP must develop, disseminate, implement, and regularly review their missions. The mission must be consistent with the mission of the institution and with professional standards. The mission must be appropriate for the institution's student populations and community settings. Mission statements must reference student learning and development.

Part 2. PROGRAM

The formal education of students, consisting of the curriculum and the co-curriculum, must promote student learning and development outcomes that are purposeful, contribute to students' realization of their potential, and prepare students for satisfying and productive lives.

Undergraduate Research Programs (URP) must collaborate with colleagues and departments across the institution to promote student learning and development, persistence, and success.

Consistent with the institutional mission, URP must identify relevant and desirable student learning and development outcomes from among the six domains and related dimensions:

Domain: knowledge acquisition, integration, construction, and application

- Dimensions: understanding knowledge from a range of disciplines; connecting knowledge to other knowledge, ideas, and experiences; constructing knowledge; and relating knowledge to daily life

Domain: cognitive complexity

- Dimensions: critical thinking, reflective thinking, effective reasoning, and creativity

Domain: intrapersonal development

- Dimensions: realistic self-appraisal, self-understanding, and self-respect; identity development; commitment to ethics and

integrity; and spiritual awareness

Domain: interpersonal competence

- Dimensions: meaningful relationships, interdependence, collaboration, and effective leadership.

Domain: humanitarianism and civic engagement

- Dimensions: understanding and appreciation of cultural and human differences, social responsibility, global perspective, and sense of civic responsibility

Domain: practical competence

- Dimensions: pursuing goals, communicating effectively, technical competence, managing personal affairs, managing career development, demonstrating professionalism, maintaining health and wellness, and living a purposeful and satisfying life

[LD Outcomes: See *The Council for the Advancement of Standards Learning and Developmental Outcomes* statement for examples of outcomes related to these domains and dimensions.]

URP must
- assess relevant and desirable student learning and development
- provide evidence of impact on outcomes
- articulate contributions to or support of student learning and development in the domains not specifically assessed
- articulate contributions to or support of student persistence and success
- use evidence gathered through this process to create strategies for improvement of programs and services

URP must be
- intentionally designed
- guided by theories and knowledge of learning and development
- integrated into the life of the institution
- reflective of developmental and demographic profiles of the student population
- responsive to needs of individuals, populations with distinct needs, and relevant constituencies
- delivered using multiple formats, strategies, and contexts

Where institutions provide distance education, URP must assist distance learners to achieve their

educational goals by providing access to information about programs and services, to staff members who can address questions and concerns, and to counseling, advising, or other forms of assistance.

URP must
- create an active learning environment supportive of scholarship and research
- integrate research activities with professional and liberal education
- create an infrastructure to recognize and reward research excellence and successful completion of research
- create a collegial climate in which to conduct research
- allow students to define their interests within the context of the research activity
- promote intellectual rigor and student intellectual growth and development
- require an appropriate report of the student's completed work
- provide opportunities for research dissemination

URP must encourage research that is commensurate with practice in the disciplines and enables students to recognize work that is original, current, and significant.

URP must establish mechanisms for individual or small-group mentoring on a regular basis that is based on the intellectual readiness of students. Mentoring must address research design; appropriate forms of data collection, verification, and analysis; information retrieval; oversight of research on human subjects; and appropriate forms of written and oral scholarly communication.

URP must ensure that students are made aware that disciplines and publications have specific authorship policies and ethical standards and are provided resources to identify those relevant to their research.

URP should provide opportunities for undergraduate students to present their research to peers, faculty members, professionals, and appropriate others and to participate in undergraduate and disciplinary research conferences. These may include institutional, local, regional, national, and international meetings.

URP should offer opportunities for academic credit for research activity where applicable.

URP should offer a range of research experiences appropriate for students at various developmental levels, abilities, and with various life circumstances.

Because a particular research activity may not be appropriate for every student, a range of options should be provided

so that all students may find appropriate opportunities. Examples of such opportunities may include first-year experiences, living-learning programs, honors programs, graduation requirements, general education courses, major requirements, capstone courses, and community-based research. These illustrative examples are not mutually exclusive. An undergraduate research activity may involve two or more of these. Activities may be initiated by students, faculty members, programs, or institutions.

Part 3. ORGANIZATION AND LEADERSHIP

To achieve student and program outcomes, Undergraduate Research Programs (URP) must be structured purposefully and organized effectively. URP must have
- clearly stated goals
- current and accessible policies and procedures
- written performance expectations for employees
- functional work flow graphics or organizational charts demonstrating clear channels of authority

Leaders with organizational authority for URP must provide strategic planning, supervision, and management; advance the organization; and maintain integrity through the following functions:

Strategic Planning
- articulate a vision and mission that drive short- and long-term planning
- set goals and objectives based on the needs of the population served and desired student learning or development and program outcomes
- facilitate continuous development, implementation, and assessment of goal attainment congruent with institutional mission and strategic plans
- promote environments that provide meaningful opportunities for student learning, development, and engagement
- develop and continuously improve programs and services in response to the changing needs of students served and evolving institutional priorities
- intentionally include diverse perspectives to inform decision making

Supervising
- manage human resource processes including recruitment, selection, development, supervision, performance planning, evaluation, recognition, and reward
- influence others to contribute to the effectiveness and success of the unit
- empower professional, support, and student

staff to accept leadership opportunities
- offer appropriate feedback to colleagues and students on skills needed to become more effective leaders
- encourage and support professional development, collaboration with colleagues and departments across the institution, and scholarly contribution to the profession

Managing
- identify and address individual, organizational, and environmental conditions that foster or inhibit mission achievement
- plan, allocate, and monitor the use of fiscal, physical, human, intellectual, and technological resources
- use current and valid evidence to inform decisions
- incorporate sustainability practices in the management and design of programs, services, and facilities
- understand appropriate technologies and integrate them into programs and services
- be knowledgeable about codes and laws relevant to programs and services and ensure that staff members understand their responsibilities through appropriate training
- assess potential risks and take action to mitigate them

Advancing the Organization
- communicate effectively in writing, speaking, and electronic venues
- advocate for programs and services
- advocate for representation in strategic planning initiatives at appropriate divisional and institutional levels
- initiate collaborative interactions with internal and external stakeholders who have legitimate concerns about and interests in the functional area
- facilitate processes to reach consensus where wide support is needed
- inform other areas within the institution about issues affecting practice

Maintaining Integrity
- model ethical behavior and institutional citizenship
- share data used to inform key decisions in transparent and accessible ways
- monitor media used for distributing information about programs and services to ensure the content is current, accurate, appropriately referenced, and accessible

URP leaders must promote a research environment that recognizes and respects all aspects of diversity.

This includes research topics and the recruitment, access, and full participation of diverse students in research activity.

Part 4. HUMAN RESOURCES

Undergraduate Research Programs (URP) must be staffed adequately by individuals qualified to accomplish mission and goals.

Within institutional guidelines, URP must
- establish procedures for staff recruitment and selection, training, performance planning, and evaluation
- set expectations for supervision and performance
- assess the performance of employees individually and as a team
- provide access to continuing and advanced education and appropriate professional development opportunities to improve the leadership ability, competence, and skills of all employees.

URP should offer training for individuals who mentor undergraduate researchers about research policies and procedures, URP goals and opportunities, and the diversity of student learning styles.

URP must maintain position descriptions for all staff members.

To create a diverse staff, URP must institute recruitment and hiring strategies that encourage individuals from under-represented populations to apply for positions.

URP must develop promotion practices that are fair, inclusive, proactive, and non-discriminatory.

To further the recruitment and retention of staff, URP must consider work life initiatives, such as compressed work schedules, flextime, job sharing, remote work, or telework.

URP professional staff members must hold an earned graduate or professional degree in a field relevant to the position they hold or must possess an appropriate combination of educational credentials and related work experience.

The professional development of staff and faculty members engaged in URP should address
- identification of the compatibility between research activities and student interests
- establishment and maintenance of relationships with academic and other units on campus
- development, implementation, and assessment of learning goals
- preparation, mentoring, and monitoring of students

- involved in research experiences
- use of active learning strategies
- education and support of students to apply learning from research experiences to future endeavors

URP professional staff members must engage in continuing professional development activities to keep abreast of the research, theories, legislation, policies, and developments that affect their programs and services.

URP must have technical and support staff members adequate to accomplish their mission. All members of the staff must be technologically proficient and qualified to perform their job functions, be knowledgeable about ethical and legal uses of technology, and have access to training and resources to support the performance of their assigned responsibilities.

Degree- or credential-seeking interns or graduate assistants must be qualified by enrollment in an appropriate field of study and by relevant experience. These individuals must be trained and supervised adequately by professional staff members holding educational credentials and related work experience appropriate for supervision. Supervisors must be cognizant of the roles of interns and graduate assistants as both student and employee and closely adhere to all parameters of their job descriptions, work hours, and schedules. Supervisors and the interns or graduate assistants must agree to compensatory time or other appropriate compensation if circumstances necessitate additional hours.

Student employees and volunteers must be carefully selected, trained, supervised, and evaluated. They must be educated on how and when to refer those in need of additional assistance to qualified staff members and must have access to a supervisor for assistance in making these judgments. Student employees and volunteers must be provided clear job descriptions, pre-service training based on assessed needs, and continuing development.

All URP staff members, including student employees and volunteers, must receive specific training on institutional policies pertaining to functions or activities they support and to privacy and confidentiality policies and laws regarding access to student records and other sensitive institutional information.

All URP staff members must receive training on policies and procedures related to the use of technology to store or access student records and institutional data.

URP must ensure that staff members are knowledgeable about and trained in emergency procedures, crisis response, and prevention efforts. Prevention efforts must address identification of threatening conduct or behavior of students, faculty and staff members, and others and must incorporate a system for responding and reporting.

URP must ensure that staff members are knowledgeable of and trained in safety and emergency procedures for securing and vacating facilities.

Part 5. ETHICS

Undergraduate Research Programs (URP) must review relevant professional ethical standards and must adopt or develop and implement appropriate statements of ethical practice.

URP must publish and adhere to statements of ethical practice and ensure their periodic review by relevant constituencies.

URP must orient new staff members to relevant ethical standards and statements of ethical practice and related institutional policies.

Statements of ethical standards must specify that staff members respect privacy and maintain confidentiality in all communications and records to the extent that such communications and records are protected under relevant privacy laws.

Statements of ethical standards must specify limits on disclosure of information contained in students' educational records as well as requirements to disclose to appropriate authorities.

Statements of ethical standards must address personal and economic conflicts of interest, or appearance thereof, by staff members in the performance of their work.

Statements of ethical standards must reflect the responsibility of staff members to be fair, objective, and impartial in their interactions with others.

Statements of ethical standards must reference management of institutional funds.

Statements of ethical standards must reference appropriate behavior regarding research and assessment with human participants, confidentiality of research and assessment data, and students' rights and responsibilities.

These policies and procedures must guard against potential physical and psychological harm to human subjects of research.

Statements of ethical standards must include the expectation that URP staff members confront and hold accountable other staff members who exhibit unethical behavior.

Statements of ethical standards must address issues surrounding scholarly integrity.

As appropriate, URP staff members must inform users of programs and services of ethical obligations and limitations emanating from codes and laws or from licensure requirements.

URP staff members must recognize and avoid conflicts of interest that could adversely influence their judgment or objectivity and, when unavoidable, recuse themselves from the situation.

URP staff members must perform their duties within the limits of their position, training, expertise, and competence.

When these limits are exceeded, individuals in need of further assistance must be referred to persons possessing appropriate qualifications.

Promotional and descriptive information must be accurate and free of deception.

URP must adhere to institutional policies regarding ethical and legal use of software and technology.

URP staff members must acknowledge authorship based on disciplinary guidelines and practices.

Part 6. LAW, POLICY, AND GOVERNANCE

Undergraduate Research Programs (URP) must be in compliance with laws, regulations, and policies that relate to their respective responsibilities and that pose legal obligations, limitations, risks, and liabilities for the institution as a whole. Examples include constitutional, statutory, regulatory, and case law; relevant law and orders emanating from codes and laws; and the institution's policies.

URP must inform staff members, appropriate officials, and users of programs and services about existing and changing legal obligations, risks and liabilities, and limitations.

URP must have written policies on all relevant operations, transactions, or tasks that have legal implications.

URP must regularly review policies. The revision and creation of policies must be informed by best practices, available evidence, and policy issues in higher education.

URP staff members must use reasonable and informed practices to limit the liability exposure of the institution and its officers, employees, and agents. URP staff members must be informed about institutional policies regarding risk management, personal liability, and related insurance coverage options and must be referred to external sources if the institution does not provide coverage.

The institution must provide access to legal advice for staff members as needed to carry out assigned responsibilities.

URP must have procedures and guidelines consistent with institutional policy for responding to threats, emergencies, and crisis situations. Systems and procedures must be in place to disseminate timely and accurate information to students, other members of the institutional community, and appropriate external organizations during emergency situations.

URP staff members must neither participate in nor condone any form of harassment or activity that demeans persons or creates an intimidating, hostile, or offensive environment.

URP must obtain permission to use copyrighted materials and instruments. URP must purchase the materials and instruments from legally compliant sources or seek alternative permission from the publisher or owner. References to copyrighted materials and instruments must include appropriate citations.

URP staff members must be knowledgeable about internal and external governance systems that affect programs and services.

Part 7. DIVERSITY, EQUITY, AND ACCESS

Within the context of each institution's unique mission and in accordance with institutional polices and all applicable codes and laws, Undergraduate Research Programs (URP) must create and maintain educational and work environments that are
- welcoming, accessible, and inclusive to persons of diverse backgrounds
- equitable and non-discriminatory
- free from harassment

URP must not discriminate on the basis of ability; age; cultural identity; ethnicity; family educational history (e.g., first generation to attend college); gender identity and expression; nationality; political affiliation; race; religious affiliation; sex; sexual orientation; economic, marital, social, or veteran status; or any other basis included in institutional policies and codes and laws.

URP must
- advocate for greater sensitivity to multicultural and social justice concerns by the institution and its personnel
- modify or remove policies, practices, facilities,

structures, systems, and technologies that limit access, discriminate, or produce inequities
- include diversity, equity, and access initiatives within their strategic plans
- foster communication that deepens understanding of identity, culture, self-expression, and heritage
- promote respect about commonalities and differences among people within their historical and cultural contexts
- address the characteristics and needs of a diverse population when establishing and implementing culturally relevant and inclusive programs, services, policies, procedures, and practices
- provide staff members with access to multicultural training and hold staff members accountable for integrating the training into their work
- respond to the needs of all students and other populations served when establishing hours of operation and developing methods of delivering programs, services, and resources
- ensure physical, program, and resource access for persons with disabilities
- recognize the needs of distance learning students by providing appropriate and accessible services and resources or by assisting them in gaining access to other appropriate services and resources in their geographic region

Part 8. INSTITUTIONAL AND EXTERNAL RELATIONS

Undergraduate Research Programs (URP) must reach out to relevant individuals, groups, communities, and organizations internal and external to the institution to
- establish, maintain, and promote understanding and effective relations with those that have a significant interest in or potential effect on the students or other constituents served by the programs and services
- garner support and resources for programs and services as defined by the mission statement
- disseminate information about the programs and services
- collaborate, where appropriate, to assist in offering or improving programs and services to meet the needs of students and other constituents and to achieve program and student outcomes
- engage diverse individuals, groups, communities, and organizations to enrich the educational environment and experiences of students and other constituents

URP must have procedures and guidelines consistent with institutional policy for
- communicating with the media
- contracting with external organizations for delivery of programs and services
- cultivating, soliciting, and managing gifts
- applying to and managing funds from grants

Part 9. FINANCIAL RESOURCES

Undergraduate Research Programs (URP) must have funding to accomplish the mission and goals. In establishing funding priorities and making significant changes, a comprehensive analysis must be conducted to determine the following elements: unmet needs of the unit, relevant expenditures, external and internal resources, and impact on students and the institution.

URP should seek funding to increase undergraduate research activities that involve a wide range of students and disciplines.

URP must demonstrate efficient and effective use and responsible stewardship of fiscal resources consistent with institutional protocols.

Part 10. TECHNOLOGY

Undergraduate Research Programs (URP) must have adequate technology to support the achievement of their mission and goals. The technology and its use must comply with institutional policies and procedures and be evaluated for compliance with relevant codes and laws.

URP must use current technology to provide updated information regarding mission, location, staffing, programs, services, and official contacts to students and designated clients.

URP must explore the use of technology to enhance delivery of programs and services, especially for students at a distance or external constituencies.

When technology is used to facilitate student learning and development, URP must select technology that reflects intended outcomes.

URP must
- maintain policies and procedures that address the security, confidentiality, and backup of data, as well as compliance with privacy laws
- have clearly articulated plans in place for protecting confidentiality and security of information when using Internet-based technologies
- develop plans for replacing and updating

existing hardware and software as well as plans for integrating new technically-based or supported programs, including systems developed internally by the institution, systems available through professional associations, or private vendor-based systems

Technology, as well as workstations or computer labs maintained by URP for student use, must be accessible to all designated clients and must meet established technology standards for delivery to persons with disabilities.

When providing student access to technology, URP must

- have policies on the use of technology that are clear, easy to understand, and available to all students
- provide assistance, information, or referral to appropriate support services to those needing help accessing or using technology
- provide instruction or training on how to use the technology
- inform students on the legal and ethical implications of misuse as it pertains to intellectual property, harassment, privacy, and social networks

Student violations of technology policies must follow established institutional student disciplinary procedures.

Students who experience negative emotional or psychological consequences from the use of technology must be referred to support services provided by the institution.

Part 11. FACILITIES AND EQUIPMENT

Undergraduate Research Programs (URP) must have adequate, accessible, and suitably located facilities and equipment to support the mission and goals. If acquiring capital equipment as defined by the institution, URP must take into account expenses related to regular maintenance and life cycle costs. Facilities and equipment must be evaluated on an established cycle, including consideration of sustainability, and be in compliance with codes and laws to provide for access, health, safety, and security.

URP staff members must have workspace that is well equipped, adequate in size, and designed to support their work and responsibilities. For conversations requiring privacy, staff members must have access to a private space.

URP staff members who share workspace must be able to secure their own work.

The design of the facilities must guarantee the security and privacy of records and ensure the confidentiality of sensitive information.

The location and layout of the facilities must be sensitive to the needs of persons with disabilities as well as the needs of other constituencies.

Part 12. ASSESSMENT AND EVALUATION

Undergraduate Research Programs (URP) must have a clearly articulated assessment plan to document achievement of stated goals and learning outcomes, demonstrate accountability, provide evidence of improvement, and describe resulting changes in programs and services.

URP must have adequate fiscal, human, professional development, and technological resources to develop and implement assessment plans.

Assessments must include direct and indirect evaluation and use qualitative and quantitative methodologies and existing evidence, as appropriate, to determine whether and to what degree the stated mission, goals, and intended outcomes are being met as effectively and efficiently as possible. The process must employ sufficient and sound measures to ensure comprehensiveness. Data collected must include responses from students and other constituencies, and aggregated results must be shared with those groups. Results of assessments must be shared appropriately with multiple constituents.

Results of assessments and evaluations must be used to identify needs and interests in revising and improving programs and services, recognizing staff performance, maximizing resource efficiency and effectiveness, improving student achievement of learning and development outcomes, and improving student persistence and success. Changes resulting from the use of assessments and evaluation must be shared with stakeholders.

General Standards revised in 2011;
URP content developed in 2007

The Role of Veterans and Military Programs and Services
CAS Standards Contextual Statement

The purpose of Veterans and Military Programs and Services (VMPS) is to provide support for student veterans, military personnel, military family members, and family members receiving veterans' benefits through the GI Bill (and similar programs in Canada) that are affiliated with an institution of higher education. The need for such support is evidenced by the experiences of personnel impacted by their involvement in the Global War on Terrorism (GWOT), Operation Enduring Freedom (OEF), Operation Iraqi Freedom (OIF), and other service-related actions, who have been subject to sudden mobilization and demobilization. The VMPS standards and guidelines were developed to be as inclusive as possible without being prescriptive and are designed to provide the greatest latitude for VMPS providers to serve clientele.

Although VMPS is relatively new to higher education, colleges have had a relationship with military service since the founding of the United States. Thomas Jefferson indicated, "[we] must train and classify the whole of our male citizens, and make military instruction a regular part of collegiate education. We can never be safe till this is done" (University of Virginia, 2010). Jefferson believed education and military service to be key elements of a democratic society and signed legislation establishing the United States Military Academy in 1802. In the Rockfish Gap Report, Jefferson outlined plans for the University of Virginia and identified the need for military training in geometry and architecture (1818). In 1824, the Board of Visitors authorized the institution's faculty to hire a military instructor to drill and train the students (Bruce, 1917, p. 117). Other state-based colleges with military training programs included Virginia Military Institute (1839) and The Citadel in South Carolina (1842). Formalizing military training on college campuses was established with the Morrill Act of 1862, which brought about the development of the land-grant university systems and with it the placement of military training programs, the precursor to the modern Reserve Officer Training Programs or ROTC.

After World War I, Canada created the Department of Soldiers' Civil Re-establishment and provided subsistence allowances and educational grants (Mosch, 1975), and the United States provided educational benefits for disabled veterans as part of the Rehabilitation law of 1919 (Olson, 1974). Several states, including Arkansas, California, Colorado, Illinois, Minnesota, New York, North Dakota, Oregon, and Wisconsin offered free or reduced tuition and other education benefits to World War I veterans (Mosch, 1975).

In 1944 US President Franklin D. Roosevelt signed into law the Servicemen's Readjustment Act (1944). This legislation, known as the GI Bill, provided tuition assistance and subsistence to support educational pursuits for returning WWII veterans. Considered a grand experiment in education (Olson, 1973), the GI Bill is one of the most influential acts to impact education and society (Wolfe, 2001) and served as the catalyst for mass education in the United States. In 1946, James Bryant Conant, Harvard President, stated the GI Bill was "a heartening sign that the democratic process of social mobility is energetically at work, piercing the class barriers that, even in America, have tended to keep a college education the prerogative of the few" (Altschuler & Blumin, 2009, p. 95). The Veteran's Rehabilitation Act (VRA) or Canadian GI Bill was administered unevenly by provinces but had similar effects for Canadian veterans (Lemieux & Card, 1998). A key outcome of the GI Bill was the development of student advisement centers to support veterans (Altschuler & Blumin, 2009). GI bills have followed each conflict since World War II, including specific bills for the Korean and Vietnam Wars, and are now staples to military service.

In 1973 the US Army adopted the Total Force Concept (TFC), increasing the reliance on reserve components for both combat and combat support and making reservists and guardsmen more susceptible to recall. Also in 1973 the draft ended for US males and an all-volunteer military was established. The volunteer military created an increased focus on recruitment incentives such as Voluntary Education Programs (VEP), which offer tuition assistance, counseling, classroom facilities, and other systems to support voluntary education; the Student Loan Repayment (SLR), which offers loan repayment for service to both active and reserve military service personnel; and the Simultaneous Membership Program (SMP), which allows guard and reserve enlisted personnel to join college and university Reserve Officer Training Corps (ROTC) programs.

Colleges and universities, eager to demonstrate their accessibility to military personnel and their families, sought alignment with Servicemembers Opportunity Colleges (SOC). SOC is affiliated with the American Association of State Colleges and Universities (AASCU) in partnership with the Department of Defense (DOD) and active and reserve components of the military services to increase and enhance postsecondary education opportunities for military service members. To be SOC eligible an institution must develop a system for reasonable transfer of credit, reduce academic residency requirements, provide credit for military training and experience, and give credit for nationally-recognized testing programs.

Recent wars in Iraq and Afghanistan have raised the visibility of veterans, military personnel, and their families on college campuses. The numbers of veterans from these conflicts (now the third longest in US history), the educational benefits of the Montgomery and Post 9-11 GI bills, and the use of VEP and SLR as recruitment incentives will continue to have major impacts on higher education.

Professional associations have been established to assist in the professional development of administrators providing services to veterans, military service members, and their families matriculating through higher education:

- The National Association of Veteran Program Administrators (NAVPA) serves individuals working in the growing field of veterans' educational support and has been instrumental in the development of the CAS Standards and Guidelines for Veterans and Military Programs and Services. NAVPA members are service providers and VCOs on US campuses seeking to promote professional competency and efficiency in veterans educational programs.
- The National Association of Veterans Upward Bound Project Personnel (NAVUBPP) is the professional association for personnel associated with these programs. Veterans Upward Bound projects are funded by the US Department of Education and serve eligible veterans across the nation.
- Founded in 2008, the Student Veterans Association (SVA) works to develop new student groups, coordinate between existing student groups, and advocate on behalf of student veterans at the local, state, and national levels. SVA consists of an executive staff and campus-based student veterans groups that coordinate programs, enhance networking, and assist in the transition to higher education. The SVA published a *Veterans Center Handbook*, available from the association's website, which identifies concerns, provides resources, and outlines steps for developing a center.
- The NASPA Veterans Knowledge Community identifies and advances best practices for veterans' programs.

References, Readings, and Resources

Ackerman, R.T. & DiRamio, D. (Eds.). (2009). *Creating a veteran-friendly campus: Strategies for transition and success. New Directions for Student Services, No. 126.* San Francisco, CA: Jossey-Bass.

Altschuler, G. C., & Blumin, S. M. (2009). *The GI Bill: A new deal for veterans.* Oxford, UK: Oxford University Press.

Bruce, P. A. (1920). *History of the University of Virginia: The lengthened shadow of one man. Vol. II.* New York, NY: The MacMillan Company.

Cook, B. J., & Kim, Y. (2009). *From soldier to student: Easing the transition of service members on campus.* Washington, DC: ACE, SOC, AASCU, NASPA, NAVPA.

Lemieux, T., & Card, D. (1998). *Working paper: Education, earnings, and the Canadian GI Bill.* Cambridge, MA: National Bureau of Economic Research.

McMurray, A. J. (2007). College students, the GI Bill, and the proliferation of online learning: A history of learning and contemporary challenges. *The Internet and Higher Education, 10,* pp. 143-150.

Mosch, T. R. (1975). *The GI Bill: A breakthrough in educational and social policy in the United States.* Hicksville, NY: Exposition Press.

Olson, K. W. (1974). The GI Bill, the veterans, and the colleges. Lexington, KY: University Press of Kentucky.

Olson, K. W. (1973). The GI Bill and higher education: Success and surprise. *American Quarterly, 25,* pp. 596-610.

University of Virginia. (2010). *Thomas Jefferson on politics and government: 47. The military and the militia.* Retrieved from http://etext.virginia.edu/jefferson/quotations/jeff1480.htm

Wolfe, M. P. (2001). Reflections on the most important educational developments of the 20th century: Kappa Delta Pi laureates. *Educational Forum, 65,* pp. 146-163.

Organizations and Websites

National Association of Student Personnel Administrators, Veterans Knowledge Community, http://www.naspa.org/kc/veterans/

National Association of Veterans Personnel Administrators, http://www.navpa.org/index.htm

Servicemembers Opportunity Colleges, http://www.soc.aascu.org/

Student Veterans Association, http://www.studentveterans.org/about/

United States Military Academy, http://www.usma.edu/history.asp

Veterans Upward Bound, http://navub.org/article/index.php?article_id=8&mainmenu_id=7

Contextual Statement Contributor

Douglas Franklin, Ohio University

Veterans and Military Programs and Services
CAS Standards and Guidelines

Part 1. MISSION

The primary mission of Veterans and Military Programs and Services (VMPS) must be to provide, facilitate, or coordinate programs and services for student veterans, military service members, and their family members. VMPS must identify student veterans and military service members and establish a community that connects and supports this population.

Family members include veterans' and service members' spouses/partners and children as well as survivors of veterans.

VMPS must develop, disseminate, implement, and regularly review their missions. The mission must be consistent with the mission of the institution and with professional standards. The mission must be appropriate for the institution's student populations and community settings. Mission statements must reference student learning and development.

Part 2. PROGRAM

Veterans and Military Programs (VMPS) must assist student veterans, military service members, and their family members with
- transitions from military service to higher education
- issues related to deployment of active duty students or call up for students affiliated with National Guard and Reserve Units
- integration into institutions and campus life
- reintegration following activation
- establishment of procedures to facilitate progress toward educational goals

VMPS should include admissions support, orientation, financial aid, housing and logistics, advising and mentoring, and learning communities.

VMPS should develop systems to establish and maintain communications between the institution and deployed students.

VMPS must collaborate with key departments to streamline campus administrative procedures for student veterans and military service members, particularly those preparing for or returning from deployments.

VMPS must provide support and advisement for student veteran organizations and veteran advisory groups on campus.

The VMPS should establish an advisory group to assist in developing a campus responsiveness plan for returning veterans and their family members. Membership of veteran advisory groups may include representatives from the offices of admissions, financial aid, registrar, counseling services, disability services, and health services.

VMPS should facilitate the development of a campus-wide community of student veterans, military service members, and their family members to provide opportunities to connect with their peers.

VMPS must provide, directly or in collaboration with other institutional units, education and training for faculty and staff on issues relevant to student veterans, military service members, and their family members.

VMPS should facilitate workshops and seminars for the campus community regarding the needs and issues facing student veterans, military service members, and their family members.

VMPS must obtain, distribute, and provide referrals to current information on educational benefits for veterans.

VMPS must work with the veteran certifying official and make available certifying paperwork for student veterans, military service members, and their family members for all applicable educational benefits.

The formal education of students, consisting of the curriculum and the co-curriculum, must promote student learning and development outcomes that are purposeful, contribute to students' realization of their potential, and prepare students for satisfying and productive lives.

VMPS must collaborate with colleagues and departments across the institution to promote student learning and development, persistence, and success.

Consistent with the institutional mission, VMPS must identify relevant and desirable student learning and development outcomes from among the six domains and related dimensions:

Domain: knowledge acquisition, integration, construction, and application

- Dimensions: understanding knowledge from a range of disciplines; connecting knowledge to other knowledge, ideas, and experiences; constructing knowledge; and relating knowledge to daily life

Domain: cognitive complexity

- **Dimensions: critical thinking, reflective thinking, effective reasoning, and creativity**

Domain: intrapersonal development

- **Dimensions: realistic self-appraisal, self-understanding, and self-respect; identity development; commitment to ethics and integrity; and spiritual awareness**

Domain: interpersonal competence

- **Dimensions: meaningful relationships, interdependence, collaboration, and effective leadership.**

Domain: humanitarianism and civic engagement

- **Dimensions: understanding and appreciation of cultural and human differences, social responsibility, global perspective, and sense of civic responsibility**

Domain: practical competence

- **Dimensions: pursuing goals, communicating effectively, technical competence, managing personal affairs, managing career development, demonstrating professionalism, maintaining health and wellness, and living a purposeful and satisfying life**

[LD Outcomes: See *The Council for the Advancement of Standards Learning and Developmental Outcomes* statement for examples of outcomes related to these domains and dimensions.]

VMPS must
- **assess relevant and desirable student learning and development**
- **provide evidence of impact on outcomes**
- **articulate contributions to or support of student learning and development in the domains not specifically assessed**
- **articulate contributions to or support of student persistence and success**
- **use evidence gathered through this process to create strategies for improvement of programs and services**

VMPS must be
- **intentionally designed**
- **guided by theories and knowledge of learning and development**
- **integrated into the life of the institution**
- **reflective of developmental and demographic profiles of the student population**
- **responsive to needs of individuals, populations with distinct needs, and relevant**

constituencies
- **delivered using multiple formats, strategies, and contexts**

Where institutions provide distance education, VMPS must assist distance learners to achieve their educational goals by providing access to information about programs and services, to staff members who can address questions and concerns, and to counseling, advising, or other forms of assistance.

Part 3. ORGANIZATION AND LEADERSHIP

Veterans and Military Programs and Services (VMPS) leaders must be knowledgeable about and responsive to the needs and experiences of student veterans, military service members, and their family members. VMPS must advise decision-makers and advocate for institutional policies and procedures that address these issues.

VMPS leaders should have a working knowledge of relevant governmental organizational structures and processes to advocate for student veterans, military service members, and their families.

To achieve student and program outcomes, VMPS must be structured purposefully and organized effectively. VMPS must have
- **clearly stated goals**
- **current and accessible policies and procedures**
- **written performance expectations for employees**
- **functional work flow graphics or organizational charts demonstrating clear channels of authority**

Leaders with organizational authority for the programs and services must provide strategic planning, supervision, and management; advance the organization; and maintain integrity through the following functions:

Strategic Planning
- **articulate a vision and mission that drive short- and long-term planning**
- **set goals and objectives based on the needs of the population served and desired student learning or development and program outcomes**
- **facilitate continuous development, implementation, and assessment of goal attainment congruent with institutional mission and strategic plans**
- **promote environments that provide meaningful opportunities for student learning, development, and engagement**
- **develop and continuously improve programs and services in response to the changing**

needs of students served and evolving institutional priorities
- intentionally include diverse perspectives to inform decision making

Supervising
- manage human resource processes including recruitment, selection, development, supervision, performance planning, evaluation, recognition, and reward
- influence others to contribute to the effectiveness and success of the unit
- empower professional, support, and student staff to accept leadership opportunities
- offer appropriate feedback to colleagues and students on skills needed to become more effective leaders
- encourage and support professional development, collaboration with colleagues and departments across the institution, and scholarly contribution to the profession

Managing
- identify and address individual, organizational, and environmental conditions that foster or inhibit mission achievement
- plan, allocate, and monitor the use of fiscal, physical, human, intellectual, and technological resources
- use current and valid evidence to inform decisions
- incorporate sustainability practices in the management and design of programs, services, and facilities
- understand appropriate technologies and integrate them into programs and services
- be knowledgeable about codes and laws relevant to programs and services and ensure that staff members understand their responsibilities through appropriate training
- assess potential risks and take action to mitigate them

Advancing the Organization
- communicate effectively in writing, speaking, and electronic venues
- advocate for programs and services
- advocate for representation in strategic planning initiatives at appropriate divisional and institutional levels
- initiate collaborative interactions with internal and external stakeholders who have legitimate concerns about and interests in the functional area
- facilitate processes to reach consensus where wide support is needed
- inform other areas within the institution

about issues affecting practice

Maintaining Integrity
- model ethical behavior and institutional citizenship
- share data used to inform key decisions in transparent and accessible ways
- monitor media used for distributing information about programs and services to ensure the content is current, accurate, appropriately referenced, and accessible

VMPS must serve as a primary point of contact to serve student veterans, military service members, and their family members. In institutions with multiple service providers, the VMPS must collaborate to ensure resources and support.

Institutions with small numbers of military members and veterans should maximize services by collaborating with other post-secondary institutions and community agencies.

Part 4. HUMAN RESOURCES

Veterans and Military Programs and Services (VMPS) must be highly visible to student veterans, military service members, and their family members with at least one staff member to serve as an institutional single point of contact to coordinate services, provide advice, and advocate for students with issues related to their military experiences and student status.

VMPS must be staffed adequately by individuals qualified to accomplish mission and goals.

VMPS staff must possess the knowledge and skills to assist student veterans, military service members, and their family members with transition and orientation to campus and to address the needs of veterans with disabilities.

VMPS staff should have experience with issues related to student veterans, military service members, and their family members.

VMPS should identify and promote student employment opportunities and career transition opportunities to support student veterans, military service members, and their family members. When possible, VMPS should identify and hire students eligible for work-study programs for veterans.

Within institutional guidelines, VMPS must
- establish procedures for staff recruitment and selection, training, performance planning, and evaluation
- set expectations for supervision and performance
- assess the performance of employees individually and as a team
- provide access to continuing and advanced

education and appropriate professional development opportunities to improve the leadership ability, competence, and skills of all employees.

VMPS must maintain position descriptions for all staff members.

To create a diverse staff, VMPS must institute recruitment and hiring strategies that encourage individuals from under-represented populations to apply for positions.

VMPS must develop promotion practices that are fair, inclusive, proactive, and non-discriminatory.

To further the recruitment and retention of staff, VMPS must consider work life initiatives, such as compressed work schedules, flextime, job sharing, remote work, or telework.

VMPS professional staff members must hold an earned graduate or professional degree in a field relevant to the position they hold or must possess an appropriate combination of educational credentials and related work experience.

VMPS professional staff members must engage in continuing professional development activities to keep abreast of the research, theories, legislation, policies, and developments that affect their programs and services.

VMPS must have technical and support staff members adequate to accomplish their mission. All members of the staff must be technologically proficient and qualified to perform their job functions, be knowledgeable about ethical and legal uses of technology, and have access to training and resources to support the performance of their assigned responsibilities.

Degree- or credential-seeking interns or graduate assistants must be qualified by enrollment in an appropriate field of study and by relevant experience. These individuals must be trained and supervised adequately by professional staff members holding educational credentials and related work experience appropriate for supervision. Supervisors must be cognizant of the roles of interns and graduate assistants as both student and employee and closely adhere to all parameters of their job descriptions, work hours, and schedules. Supervisors and the interns or graduate assistants must agree to compensatory time or other appropriate compensation if circumstances necessitate additional hours.

Student employees and volunteers must be carefully selected, trained, supervised, and evaluated. They must be educated on how and when to refer those in need of additional assistance to qualified staff members and must have access to a supervisor for assistance in making these judgments. Student employees and volunteers must be provided clear job descriptions, pre-service training based on assessed needs, and continuing development.

All VMPS staff members, including student employees and volunteers, must receive specific training on institutional policies pertaining to functions or activities they support and to privacy and confidentiality policies and laws regarding access to student records and other sensitive institutional information.

All VMPS staff members must receive training on policies and procedures related to the use of technology to store or access student records and institutional data.

VMPS must ensure that staff members are knowledgeable about and trained in emergency procedures, crisis response, and prevention efforts. Prevention efforts must address identification of threatening conduct or behavior of students, faculty and staff members, and others and must incorporate a system for responding and reporting.

VMPS must ensure that staff members are knowledgeable of and trained in safety and emergency procedures for securing and vacating facilities.

Part 5. ETHICS

Veterans and Military Programs and Services (VMPS) must review relevant professional ethical standards and must adopt or develop and implement appropriate statements of ethical practice.

VMPS must publish and adhere to statements of ethical practice and ensure their periodic review by relevant constituencies.

VMPS must orient new staff members to relevant ethical standards and statements of ethical practice and related institutional policies.

Statements of ethical standards must specify that staff members respect privacy and maintain confidentiality in all communications and records to the extent that such communications and records are protected under relevant privacy laws.

Statements of ethical standards must specify limits on disclosure of information contained in students' educational records as well as requirements to disclose to appropriate authorities.

Statements of ethical standards must address personal and economic conflicts of interest, or appearance thereof, by staff members in the performance of their work.

Statements of ethical standards must reflect the responsibility of staff members to be fair, objective, and impartial in their interactions with others.

Statements of ethical standards must reference management of institutional funds.

Statements of ethical standards must reference appropriate behavior regarding research and assessment with human participants, confidentiality of research and assessment data, and students' rights and responsibilities.

Statements of ethical standards must include the expectation that VMPS staff members confront and hold accountable other staff members who exhibit unethical behavior.

Statements of ethical standards must address issues surrounding scholarly integrity.

As appropriate, VMPS staff members must inform users of programs and services of ethical obligations and limitations emanating from codes and laws or from licensure requirements.

VMPS staff members must recognize and avoid conflicts of interest that could adversely influence their judgment or objectivity and, when unavoidable, recuse themselves from the situation.

VMPS staff members must perform their duties within the limits of their position, training, expertise, and competence.

When these limits are exceeded, individuals in need of further assistance must be referred to persons possessing appropriate qualifications.

Promotional and descriptive information must be accurate and free of deception.

VMPS must adhere to institutional policies regarding ethical and legal use of software and technology.

Part 6. LAW, POLICY, AND GOVERNANCE

Veterans and Military Programs and Services (VMPS) must be aware of applicable laws affecting student veterans, military service members, and their family members, including educational benefits. VMPS must refer student veterans to the institution's veterans benefits certifying official for application and certification of benefits.

VMPS should maintain awareness of changes to entitlement programs and statute-based tuition discounting such as tuition benefits and communicate these to student veterans, military service members, and their family members.

VMPS must be in compliance with laws, regulations, and policies that relate to their respective responsibilities and that pose legal obligations, limitations, risks, and liabilities for the institution as a whole. Examples include constitutional, statutory, regulatory, and case law; relevant law and orders emanating from codes and laws; and the institution's policies.

VMPS must inform staff members, appropriate officials, and users of programs and services about existing and changing legal obligations, risks and liabilities, and limitations.

VMPS must have written policies on all relevant operations, transactions, or tasks that have legal implications.

VMPS must regularly review policies. The revision and creation of policies must be informed by best practices, available evidence, and policy issues in higher education.

VMPS staff members must use reasonable and informed practices to limit the liability exposure of the institution and its officers, employees, and agents. VMPS staff members must be informed about institutional policies regarding risk management, personal liability, and related insurance coverage options and must be referred to external sources if the institution does not provide coverage.

The institution must provide access to legal advice for staff members as needed to carry out assigned responsibilities.

VMPS must have procedures and guidelines consistent with institutional policy for responding to threats, emergencies, and crisis situations. Systems and procedures must be in place to disseminate timely and accurate information to students, other members of the institutional community, and appropriate external organizations during emergency situations.

VMPS staff members must neither participate in nor condone any form of harassment or activity that demeans persons or creates an intimidating, hostile, or offensive environment.

VMPS must obtain permission to use copyrighted materials and instruments. VMPS must purchase the materials and instruments from legally compliant sources or seek alternative permission from the publisher or owner. References to copyrighted materials and instruments must include appropriate citations.

VMPS staff members must be knowledgeable about internal and external governance systems that affect programs and services.

Part 7. DIVERSITY, EQUITY, AND ACCESS

Veterans and Military Programs and Services (VMPS) must coordinate with units providing disability related services to ensure access to relevant programs and services for veterans with disabilities.

VMPS should coordinate with units providing disability related services about the use of services by veterans and military service members assumed to have a disability but lacking documentation.

VMPS should work with students to obtain required disability documentation in accordance with the institution's documentation guidelines for students with disabilities.

Within the context of each institution's unique mission and in accordance with institutional polices and all applicable codes and laws, VMPS must create and maintain educational and work environments that are
- **welcoming, accessible, and inclusive to persons of diverse backgrounds**
- **equitable and non-discriminatory**
- **free from harassment**

VMPS must not discriminate on the basis of ability; age; cultural identity; ethnicity; family educational history (e.g., first generation to attend college); gender identity and expression; nationality; political affiliation; race; religious affiliation; sex; sexual orientation; economic, marital, social, or veteran status; or any other basis included in institutional policies and codes and laws.

VMPS must
- **advocate for greater sensitivity to multicultural and social justice concerns by the institution and its personnel**
- **modify or remove policies, practices, facilities, structures, systems, and technologies that limit access, discriminate, or produce inequities**
- **include diversity, equity, and access initiatives within their strategic plans**
- **foster communication that deepens understanding of identity, culture, self-expression, and heritage**
- **promote respect about commonalities and differences among people within their historical and cultural contexts**
- **address the characteristics and needs of a diverse population when establishing and implementing culturally relevant and inclusive programs, services, policies, procedures, and practices**
- **provide staff members with access to multicultural training and hold staff members accountable for integrating the training into**

their work
- **respond to the needs of all students and other populations served when establishing hours of operation and developing methods of delivering programs, services, and resources**
- **ensure physical, program, and resource access for persons with disabilities**
- **recognize the needs of distance learning students by providing appropriate and accessible services and resources or by assisting them in gaining access to other appropriate services and resources in their geographic region**

In this context, diverse groups include partners of disabled and deceased service members and single parents. VMPS should coordinate provision of services to diverse military service members with various organizations, centers, and other appropriate venues on campus that serve those populations.

Part 8. INSTITUTIONAL AND EXTERNAL RELATIONS

Veterans and Military Programs and Services (VMPS) must reach out to relevant individuals, groups, communities, and organizations internal and external to the institution to
- **establish, maintain, and promote understanding and effective relations with those that have a significant interest in or potential effect on the students or other constituents served by the programs and services**
- **garner support and resources for programs and services as defined by the mission statement**
- **disseminate information about the programs and services**
- **collaborate, where appropriate, to assist in offering or improving programs and services to meet the needs of students and other constituents and to achieve program and student outcomes**
- **engage diverse individuals, groups, communities, and organizations to enrich the educational environment and experiences of students and other constituents**

VMPS must have procedures and guidelines consistent with institutional policy for
- **communicating with the media**
- **contracting with external organizations for delivery of programs and services**
- **cultivating, soliciting, and managing gifts**
- **applying to and managing funds from grants**

VMPS must work with the office of admissions to coordinate and address the needs and issues

of student veterans, military members, and their matriculated family members.

VMPS should advocate for the inclusion of questions on the admission application regarding anticipated status at the time of enrollment – active duty, veteran, member of the Guard or reserve, or military dependent.

VMPS should advocate for consideration of military experience and training in admissions decisions.

VMPS must advocate for flexible policies to deal with the deployment of military service members and work with the institutional registrar to ensure the effectiveness of withdrawal and course-completion procedures, including withdrawals, incomplete grades, and awarding of partial credit.

VMPS must work with academic services to facilitate advising, tutoring assistance, and supplemental instruction for student veterans, military service members, and their matriculated family members.

VMPS must advocate for awarding credit for previous military training and experience.

Articulation agreements should use documents similar to the American Council of Education Guide to the Evaluation of Educational Experiences in the Armed Services.

VMPS should be aware of national testing programs such as College Level Examination Program (CLEP), DANTES Subject Standardized Tests (DSST), and Excelsior College Examinations (ECE).

VMPS must advocate for clear and facilitative articulation agreements between home institutions and colleges and universities providing education to military members serving on active duty.

Articulation agreements should avoid both excessive loss of previously earned credit and duplication of coursework.

VMPS should advocate for policies that consider and recognize civilian courses taken and formal training obtained while in the military.

VMPS should coordinate with various institutional departments to facilitate the resolution of grades from students' final semesters and the potential posthumous awarding of degrees for students who die while in military service.

VMPS must work with the campus career services and other units to identify or develop specific programs and opportunities that support career planning and employment.

VMPS must work with campus units to encourage student veterans, military service members, and their family members in campus-wide social and cultural events, academic programs, orientation programs, and other activities designed to ease the transition to campus life.

VMPS should work with student affairs and other co-curricular units to tailor some programs to meet the specific needs of student veterans, military service members, and their family members.

VMPS must assist student veterans, military service members, and their family members to find appropriate on- and off-campus psychological counseling and mental health care service providers and advocate for specialized training for campus providers dealing with mental health issues affecting this population.

VMPS should advocate for institutional counseling resources to be knowledgeable of veterans' issues, e.g., Post-Traumatic Stress Disorder (PTSD), Combat Stress Reaction (CSR), and Traumatic Brain Injury (TBI), and post deployment transition challenges.

VMPS must advocate for and work with the bursar to ensure deferment of tuition and fees for students when education benefits are delayed beyond normal payment due dates or for military withdrawals due to activation.

VMPS may advocate for tuition discounting for student veterans, military service, members, and their matriculated family members.

VMPS should assist in addressing the financial aid needs and issues of student veterans, military service members, and their family matriculated members.

VMPS should collaborate with the institution's foundation and development offices to identify or establish scholarships for veterans and other financial support pools and establish procedures for their disbursement to qualified students.

When an institution has determined that it can provide the necessary services, VMPS must participate in institutional recruitment efforts, including establishment of marketing and outreach strategies to enroll student veterans, military service members, and their family members.

VMPS should work with institutional outreach services such as lifelong learning and distance education units to bring academic programs to mobilized and deployed military service members.

VMPS may advocate for reducing academic residency requirements by eliminating on-campus degree requirements, supporting 100 percent on-line degrees and eliminating final-year or semester-in-residence requirements for student veterans, military service members, and matriculated family members.

VMPS staff must establish a working relationship with the institutional veterans benefits certifying

official, if this position is separate from VMPS.

VMPS must work with the Veterans Affairs offices and serve as liaisons between the campus and the Veterans Affairs education office in providing services for student veterans.

VMPS should coordinate opportunities for recruitment, academic advising, and admissions counseling with military bases and National Guard units in the area.

VMPS should communicate with programs and services at peer institutions to develop and implement additional best practices to serve veterans, military service members, and their families.

Part 9. FINANCIAL RESOURCES

Veterans and Military Programs and Services (VMPS) must have funding to accomplish the mission and goals. In establishing funding priorities and making significant changes, a comprehensive analysis must be conducted to determine the following elements: unmet needs of the unit, relevant expenditures, external and internal resources, and impact on students and the institution.

VMPS must demonstrate efficient and effective use and responsible stewardship of fiscal resources consistent with institutional protocols.

Adequate funds should be provided for the following budget categories: staff and student salaries, general office functions, student assessment activities, data management and program evaluation processes, staff training and professional development activities, instructional materials and media, information technology, and office technology.

VMPS should explore state/provincial or federal funding sources or write grant proposals to support the service. In the event the VMPS receives a start-up grant, a financial plan should be developed to sustain the operation after the term of the grant.

External funding sources should not be expected to supplant institutional funding.

Part 10. TECHNOLOGY

Veterans and Military Programs (VMPS) must have adequate technology to support the achievement of their mission and goals. The technology and its use must comply with institutional policies and procedures and be evaluated for compliance with relevant codes and laws.

VMPS must use current technology to provide updated information regarding mission, location, staffing, programs, services, and official contacts to students and designated clients.

VMPS must explore the use of technology to enhance

delivery of programs and services, especially for students at a distance or external constituencies.

When technology is used to facilitate student learning and development, VMPS must select technology that reflects intended outcomes.

VMPS must

- maintain policies and procedures that address the security, confidentiality, and backup of data, as well as compliance with privacy laws
- have clearly articulated plans in place for protecting confidentiality and security of information when using Internet-based technologies
- develop plans for replacing and updating existing hardware and software as well as plans for integrating new technically-based or supported programs, including systems developed internally by the institution, systems available through professional associations, or private vendor-based systems

Technology, as well as workstations or computer labs maintained by programs and services for student use, must be accessible to all designated clients and must meet established technology standards for delivery to persons with disabilities.

When providing student access to technology, VMPS must

- have policies on the use of technology that are clear, easy to understand, and available to all students
- provide assistance, information, or referral to appropriate support services to those needing help accessing or using technology
- provide instruction or training on how to use the technology
- inform students on the legal and ethical implications of misuse as it pertains to intellectual property, harassment, privacy, and social networks

Student violations of technology policies must follow established institutional student disciplinary procedures.

Students who experience negative emotional or psychological consequences from the use of technology must be referred to support services provided by the institution.

VMPS must maintain an Internet presence with information to ease the transition of student veterans, military service members, and their families into higher education. VMPS web pages must provide timely and accurate information regarding programs and services offered by the institution and must connect the student to external resources for veterans.

Communication must be accurate in describing program requirements and pre-requisites, costs, payment and refund policies, partnerships with military or government agencies, and occupational opportunities for program graduates.

VMPS web information should include links to governmental veterans administration agencies and institutional web links with services for student veterans, military service members, and their families.

VMPS should advocate for technology that supports distance learning for mobilized or deployed students.

Part 11. FACILITIES AND EQUIPMENT

Veterans and Military Programs and Services (VMPS) must have adequate, accessible, and suitably located facilities and equipment to support the mission and goals. If acquiring capital equipment as defined by the institution, VMPS must take into account expenses related to regular maintenance and life cycle costs. Facilities and equipment must be evaluated on an established cycle, including consideration of sustainability, and be in compliance with codes and laws to provide for access, health, safety, and security.

VMPS staff members must have workspace that is well equipped, adequate in size, and designed to support their work and responsibilities. For conversations requiring privacy, staff members must have access to a private space.

VMPS staff members who share workspace must be able to secure their own work.

The design of the facilities must guarantee the security and privacy of records and ensure the confidentiality of sensitive information.

The location and layout of the facilities must be sensitive to the needs of persons with disabilities as well as the needs of other constituencies.

The VMPS center should be centrally located and in proximity to institutional student support services.

VMPS should establish a dedicated physical space where student veterans military service members and their family members can congregate, seek academic support services, and complete assigned coursework. The space should be safe, with easily identifiable and accessible exits, and located near the VMPS center and other student organization offices.

Part 12. ASSESSMENT AND EVALUATION

Veterans and Military Programs and Services (VMPS) must have a clearly articulated assessment plan to document achievement of stated goals and learning outcomes, demonstrate accountability, provide evidence of improvement, and describe resulting changes in programs and services.

VMPS must have adequate fiscal, human, professional development, and technological resources to develop and implement assessment plans.

Assessments must include direct and indirect evaluation and use qualitative and quantitative methodologies and existing evidence, as appropriate, to determine whether and to what degree the stated mission, goals, and intended outcomes are being met as effectively and efficiently as possible. The process must employ sufficient and sound measures to ensure comprehensiveness. Data collected must include responses from students and other constituencies, and aggregated results must be shared with those groups. Results of assessments must be shared appropriately with multiple constituents.

Results of assessments and evaluations must be used to identify needs and interests in revising and improving programs and services, recognizing staff performance, maximizing resource efficiency and effectiveness, improving student achievement of learning and development outcomes, and improving student persistence and success. Changes resulting from the use of assessments and evaluation must be shared with stakeholders.

General Standards revised in 2011;
VMPS content developed/approved in 2010

The Role of Women Student Programs and Services
CAS Standards Contextual Statement

History

Women Student Programs and Services (WSPS) refer to campus offices that support women and advance gender equity, including women's centers, offices for women, and other units. In 2009, there were over 490 such programs housed within colleges and universities across the U.S., including public and private institutions, two-year and four-year schools, historically black colleges and universities, tribal institutions, Hispanic-serving institutions, Asian American- and Pacific Islander-serving institutions, and institutions serving deaf and blind students (National Women's Studies Association, n.d.). The first women's center was established in 1960 at the University of Minnesota ("About Us," 2009) at the cusp of an era of tremendous change in higher education, and these centers continue to serve as catalysts and leaders of positive institutional change.

Women Studies Program and Services were established on campuses as a result of concerns about gender equity raised by students, administrators, faculty, staff, alumnae/alumni, and community members. Informed by women's; lesbian, gay, bisexual, transgender, queer, and intersex (LGBTQI); African American; and other civil rights movements, they were developed to respond to individual and institutional needs to support women in achieving their educational goals, encouraging them to think more broadly about fields of study and leadership positions, and advancing women in higher education. Reporting lines for Women Student Programs and Services differ among institutions, with some embedded in the missions and services of divisions of student affairs and others with reporting lines reflecting other institutional organizational structures. In recent decades, scholars and practitioners have debated the use of the term women in both the field of women's and gender studies as well as in naming campus centers, offices, and programs that address gender issues. Some argue that the term women (as in women's center) reproduces an essentialist framework that privileges a monolithic category of women and that the term gender (as in gender studies and gender equity center) is more inclusive of individuals and their diverse experiences of gender and of gender-based inequity and discrimination. For some, gender also more explicitly encompasses masculinities and services for men, which women's centers have provided to varying degrees. Others worry that replacing the term women with gender erases the history of the struggle to put women's lives and experiences at the center of attention as well as opens the door to co-opting the goals of that movement and shifting resources, energy, and attention away from addressing the status of women (Berger & Radeloff, 2011).

Important Tenets

Women Studies Programs and Services have varied missions that express the unique cultures and goals of the institutions within which they reside. Most of them include in their mission the need to address equity, including institutional change; education, including equal access, affordability, recruitment, retention, and professional development; support and advocacy; personal safety; and community development (Davie, 2002; Kunkel, 1994, 2002). Some provide services to students only, while others also provide services to faculty and staff, alumnae, and community members (Davie, 2002). Supporting the success of women-identified students involves working with individuals of all gender identities to raise awareness about and contribute to cultural change relating to gender issues more broadly, addressing concerns that affect all members of a campus community and beyond.

The unique experiences of women-identified college and university students require that the programs—regardless of its reporting structure—engage with every element of campus life, including collaboration with all sectors of student affairs, health and mental health services, residence life and housing services, campus safety and law enforcement, student conduct, campus Title IX coordinators, athletics, human resources, and other cultural and identity-based areas, including LGBTQI centers, academic and co-curricular units, and student organizations. Ultimately, the WSPS is dedicated to advancing knowledge of how historical and current imbalances of power between genders impact equity issues, both on campus and in society, with the goal of helping all people to reach their full potential. Women Studies Programs and Services are informed by academic disciplines and professions such as women's and gender studies, queer studies, African American and critical race studies, cultural and ethnic studies, student affairs and higher education administration, student and public health, social work, continuing and adult education, among others.

Current Issues

When Women Studies Programs and Services were first founded, they tended to focus on questions of access (i.e., assisting women in gaining entrance into academic institutions). Given that for the past 40 years the majority of students in higher education have been women (Allen, Dean, & Bracken, 2008), the focus has evolved to include

- supporting access for specific subsets of women who remain underrepresented in higher education
- fostering the full integration of women students once they are on campus;
- continuing to advocate for equity and change in the seemingly intractable area of traditional sex and

- gender roles
- challenging the explicit and implicit biases and stereotypes that continue to hinder women's progress in male-dominated fields of study such as science, technology, engineering and math (Hill, 2010).

The WSPS assumed leadership roles on campuses in conducting campus climate assessments and advocating for policy change at the institutional level and in forming collaborations to accelerate institutional changes so that campus climates reflect sensitive and inclusive policies. The programs and services demonstrate success in reaching traditionally underserved and underrepresented populations, including students of color, LGBTQI students, students with disabilities, nontraditional students, student parents, immigrant students, and international students.

Women Studies Programs and Services operate in the context of historical roots in social justice, community activism, and social change efforts, as well as in student development theory and administrative leadership practice. Acknowledging the immense potential of higher education to improve the lives of people of all gender identities, they translate the richness of feminist and womanist community organization- and movement-based work to college and university settings, demonstrating the relevance of women to all aspects of higher education. Through support, advocacy, and education, the programs and services address sexual assault and other forms of power-based personal violence, sexual harassment, gender discrimination, sexism, and other barriers to student academic achievement that disproportionally impact women student success. With a commitment to the continuous examination of power, privilege, and the intersection of gender with other identities, the WSPS seeks to support and advocate for the positive educational experiences of all members of college and university communities, while simultaneously maintaining a specific focus on gender and women. With increasingly limited resources, like other functional areas, the programs and services are creatively responding to increased demand for services through collaboration and the use of technology. In light of women comprising the majority of students enrolled in colleges and universities in the U.S., obtaining and sustaining funding and resources sufficient to fully actualize the missions of Women Student Programs and Services remains one of the most significant challenges facing them. These standards have been updated over time to reflect the changing focus and missions of women's centers and WSPS offices.

References, Readings, and Resources

About Us. (2009, July). University of Minnesota Women's Center. Retrieved from http://www1.umn.edu/women/about.html

ACPA - College Student Educators International
Standing Committee for Women: http://www2.myacpa.org/what-is-scw
American Association of University Women: http://www.aauw.org
Campus Women Lead: http://www.aacu.org/campuswomenlead
College and University Professional Association for Human Resources (CUPA-HR)
http://www.cupahr.org/surveys

Allen, J. K., Dean, D. R., & Bracken, S. J. (2008). *Most college students are women: Implications for teaching, learning, and policy.* Sterling, VA: Stylus.

Bengiveno, T. A. (2000). Feminist consciousness and the potential for change in campus based student staffed women's centers. *Journal of International Women's Studies, 1*(1). Retrieved from http://www.bridgew.edu/SoAS/JIWS/index.htm

Berger, M. T., Radeloff, C. (2011). *Transforming scholarship: Why women's and gender studies students are changing themselves and the world.* New York, NY: Routledge.

Curry, C. H. (2008). *Understanding the empowerment phenomenon: Effects of a pilot women's empowerment program on female college students.* Saarbrücken, Germany: Verlag.

Davie, S. L. (Ed.). (2002). *University and college women's centers: A journey toward equity.* Westport, CT: Greenwood Press.

Gould, J. S. (1989). Women's centers as agents of change. In C. S. Pearson, D. L. Shavlik, & J. G. Touchton (Eds.), *Educating the majority: Women challenge tradition in higher education* (pp. 219-229). New York, NY: American Council on Education & Macmillan.

Hill, C., et. al. (2010). Why so few? Women in science, technology, engineering and math. Washington, D.C.: American Association of University Women.

Kasper, B. (2004). Campus-based women's centers: A review of problems and practices. *Affilia, 19*(2), 185-198.

Keller, M. J., & Rogers, J. L. (1983). The awareness, impressions, and use of a campus women's center by traditional and nontraditional women students. *Journal of College Student Personnel, 24,* 550-556.

Kunkel, C. A. (1994). Women's needs on campus: How universities meet them. *Initiatives, 56*(2),15-28.

Kunkel, C. A. (2002). Starting a women's center. Key issues. In S. L. Davie (Ed.), *University and college women's centers: A journey toward equity* (pp. 65-78). Westport, CT: Greenwood Press.

Marine, S. (2011). Reflections from "professional feminists" in higher education: Women's and gender centers at the start of the twenty-first century. In P. A. Pasque & S. Errington Nicholson (Eds.), *Empowering women in higher education and student affairs: Theory, research, narratives, and practice from feminist perspectives* (pp. 15-31). Sterling, VA: Stylus Publishing.

NASPA - Student Affairs Administrators in Higher Education
Center for Women:
http://www.naspa.org/divctr/women/default.cfm
Women in Student Affairs Knowledge Community (WISA):

http://www.naspa.org/kc/wisa/default.cfm

National Association of Women Deans, Administrators, and Counselors (NAWDAC) (1988, Summer) (Eds.). *Initiatives* (Vol. 51) [Special issue: Women's centers]. Washington, D.C.: Author.

National Council for Research on Women (NCRW): http://www.ncrw.org

National Women's Studies Association (NWSA) Women's Centers Steering Committee: http://www.nwsa.org/centers/index.php

NWSA Women's Centers Resources: http://www.nwsa.org/centers/resources

WRAC-L: The Women's Resource and Action Centers Group: http://www.nwsa.org/centers/resources

National Women's Studies Association (n.d.). NWSA Campus Women's Centers Database. Retrieved from http://nwsa.org/research/centerguide/index.php

National Women's Studies Association (2005, Fall). Women's Centers at Work. *NWSAction, 17*(1).

Parker, J., & Freedman, J. (1999). Women's centers/women's studies programs: Collaborating for feminist activism. *Women's Studies Quarterly, 27*(3/4), 114-121.

Santovec, M. (2009, August). Strategies to confront privilege in women's centers. *Women in Higher Education, 18*(8), 15.

Stineman F. C. (1984). Women's centers in public higher education: Evolving structure and function (retention, comparable worth, managerial style, feminism). Retrieved from ProQuest Digital Dissertations database. (Publication No. AAT 8511085).

Wies, J. R. (2011). The campus women's center as classroom: A model for thinking and action. In P. A. Pasque & S. Errington Nicholson (Eds.), *Empowering women in higher education and student affairs: Theory, research, narratives, and practice from feminist perspectives* (pp. 255-269). Sterling, VA: Stylus Publishing.

Zaytoun Byrne, K. (2000). The role of campus-based women's centers. *Feminist Teacher, 13*(1), 48-60.

Contextual Statement Contributors

Current Edition:

Corrie Martin, University of the Pacific
Rebecca Morrow, Idaho State University
Claire K. Robbins, University of Maryland
Nora Spencer, Vanderbilt University
Amber L. Vlasnik, Wright State University

Previous Editions:

Brenda Bethman, Texas A&M University (2006)
Ellen Plummer, Virginia Tech (2006)
Beth Rietveld, Oregon State University (2006)
Chimi Boyd, North Carolina Central University (2009)
Janine Cavicchia, Western Illinois University (2009)
Peg Lonnquist, University of Minnesota (2009)
Rebecca Morrow, Idaho State University (2009)
Claire K. Robbins, University of Maryland (2009)
Cathy Seasholes, University of Wisconsin - Milwaukee (2009)
Jennifer Wies, Xavier University (2009)

Women Student Programs and Services
CAS Standards and Guidelines

Part 1. MISSION

The purpose of Women Student Programs and Services (WSPS) is to promote a supportive, equitable, and safe environment for women.

WSPS must develop, disseminate, implement, and regularly review their missions. The mission must be consistent with the mission of the institution and with professional standards. The mission must be appropriate for the institution's student populations and community settings. Mission statements must reference student learning and development.

The mission is accomplished by
- empowering students to create a campus culture that values all women and their diverse identities and experiences
- providing, coordinating, or participating in comprehensive sexual violence risk reduction programs and services for survivors of sexual violence
- educating all students on the ways in which gender is constructed and shapes social structures and individual experiences
- assessing the climate for women and advocating for the diverse needs of women
- providing information and referrals about issues that disproportionately affect women, such as sexual harassment, relationship violence, rape, and disordered eating
- sponsoring speakers, performers, events, and activities that address gender issues
- creating opportunities for women's voices to be heard

Part 2. PROGRAM

The formal education of students, consisting of the curriculum and the co-curriculum, must promote student learning and development outcomes that are purposeful, contribute to students' realization of their potential, and prepare students for satisfying and productive lives.

Women Student Programs and Services (WSPS) must collaborate with colleagues and departments across the institution to promote student learning and development, persistence, and success.

Consistent with the institutional mission, WSPS must identify relevant and desirable student learning and development outcomes from among the six domains and related dimensions:

Domain: knowledge acquisition, integration, construction, and application

- Dimensions: understanding knowledge from a range of disciplines; connecting knowledge to other knowledge, ideas, and experiences; constructing knowledge; and relating knowledge to daily life

Domain: cognitive complexity

- Dimensions: critical thinking, reflective thinking, effective reasoning, and creativity

Domain: intrapersonal development

- Dimensions: realistic self-appraisal, self-understanding, and self-respect; identity development; commitment to ethics and integrity; and spiritual awareness

Domain: interpersonal competence

- Dimensions: meaningful relationships, interdependence, collaboration, and effective leadership.

Domain: humanitarianism and civic engagement

- Dimensions: understanding and appreciation of cultural and human differences, social responsibility, global perspective, and sense of civic responsibility

Domain: practical competence

- Dimensions: pursuing goals, communicating effectively, technical competence, managing personal affairs, managing career development, demonstrating professionalism, maintaining health and wellness, and living a purposeful and satisfying life

[LD Outcomes: See *The Council for the Advancement of Standards Learning and Developmental Outcomes* statement for examples of outcomes related to these domains and dimensions.]

WSPS must
- assess relevant and desirable student learning and development
- provide evidence of impact on outcomes
- articulate contributions to or support of student learning and development in the domains not specifically assessed
- articulate contributions to or support of student persistence and success
- use evidence gathered through this process to create strategies for improvement of

programs and services

WSPS must be
- intentionally designed
- guided by theories and knowledge of learning and development
- integrated into the life of the institution
- reflective of developmental and demographic profiles of the student population
- responsive to needs of individuals, populations with distinct needs, and relevant constituencies
- delivered using multiple formats, strategies, and contexts

Where institutions provide distance education, WSPS must assist distance learners to achieve their educational goals by providing access to information about programs and services, to staff members who can address questions and concerns, and to counseling, advising, or other forms of assistance.

WSPS staff must address the needs of undergraduate and graduate women students by incorporating the dimensions of ethnicity, race, religion, ability, sexual orientation, age, socioeconomic status, and other aspects of identity through programs and services. WSPS must promote unrestricted access for full involvement of women in all aspects of the collegiate experience.

WSPS must provide programs and services that address institutional environment, social justice, campus support services, networking opportunities, and other educational issues of significance to women.

WSPS may address issues of equity for staff members, faculty members, and women in the surrounding community.

To address the institutional environment, WSPS must
- advocate for a campus culture that eliminates barriers, prejudice, and bigotry, and creates a hospitable climate for all women
- assess and monitor the campus climate for women in areas of sexual harassment and sexual violence, and collaborate with on- and off-campus partners to create institutional policies, education, and programs to work toward the elimination of violence against women
- advocate for assessment of the campus environment for the presence of gender bias in areas including but not limited to employment, educational opportunities, and classroom climate
- advocate for the elimination of institutional policies and practices that result in an inequitable impact on women as students or employees
- promote awareness in ways in which gender bias intersects with racism, classism, and homophobia
- serve as a resource in helping campus constituencies identify and create equitable practices

WSPS must advance social justice through opportunities for involvement in global, national, state/provincial, and local action initiatives related to improving women's lives.

WSPS should provide models of non-hierarchical and collaborative leadership.

WSPS should provide social activism opportunities that allow for the integration of theory with practice.

WSPS must address the provision of campus support services including
- advocacy, resources, and referrals related to sexual assault, sexual harassment, cyber-harassment, stalking, and relationship violence
- academic support that addresses concerns such as flexible scheduling, the environment for women students in traditionally male-dominated disciplines, and gender equity in the classroom
- resources and referrals for prevention, counseling, medical services, healthcare, disordered eating, physical and mental health, and equitable access to wellness, fitness, and health services
- resources and referrals for under-represented or under-served communities
- the need for adequate, accessible, affordable, and flexible child and family care

WSPS must facilitate networking opportunities that
- create support systems and communication networks for women students
- identify role models by recognizing and celebrating the accomplishments of women on and off campus
- encourage liaisons between global, national, state/provincial, and local women's organizations and campus-based women student programs and services

WSPS must provide educational programs that promote awareness of the way in which gender is constructed and shapes social structures and individual experiences. WSPS must offer experiential opportunities that explore oppression, privilege, and racism to increase students' understanding of the intersections of sexism with racism, classism, homophobia, and other forms of oppression.

WSPS should support the promotion of scholarship and research on women and gender in collaboration with a women studies program, if available, as well as with other departments.

Educational programs should focus on women's physical and mental health, personal safety, sexual assault and relationship violence, healthy relationships, leadership, spirituality, current events, and global issues.

WSPS should provide service-learning and internship opportunities.

WSPS should advocate curricular change to include women's issues and contribution to society.

Part 3. ORGANIZATION AND LEADERSHIP

To achieve student and program outcomes, Women Student Programs and Services (WSPS) must be structured purposefully and organized effectively. WSPS must have
- clearly stated goals
- current and accessible policies and procedures
- written performance expectations for employees
- functional work flow graphics or organizational charts demonstrating clear channels of authority

Leaders with organizational authority for the programs and services must provide strategic planning, supervision, and management; advance the organization; and maintain integrity through the following functions:

Strategic Planning
- articulate a vision and mission that drive short- and long-term planning
- set goals and objectives based on the needs of the population served and desired student learning or development and program outcomes
- facilitate continuous development, implementation, and assessment of goal attainment congruent with institutional mission and strategic plans
- promote environments that provide meaningful opportunities for student learning, development, and engagement
- develop and continuously improve programs and services in response to the changing needs of students served and evolving institutional priorities
- intentionally include diverse perspectives to inform decision making

Supervising
- manage human resource processes including recruitment, selection, development, supervision, performance planning, evaluation, recognition, and reward
- influence others to contribute to the effectiveness and success of the unit
- empower professional, support, and student staff to accept leadership opportunities
- offer appropriate feedback to colleagues and students on skills needed to become more effective leaders
- encourage and support professional development, collaboration with colleagues and departments across the institution, and scholarly contribution to the profession

Managing
- identify and address individual, organizational, and environmental conditions that foster or inhibit mission achievement
- plan, allocate, and monitor the use of fiscal, physical, human, intellectual, and technological resources
- use current and valid evidence to inform decisions
- incorporate sustainability practices in the management and design of programs, services, and facilities
- understand appropriate technologies and integrate them into programs and services
- be knowledgeable about codes and laws relevant to programs and services and ensure that staff members understand their responsibilities through appropriate training
- assess potential risks and take action to mitigate them

Advancing the Organization
- communicate effectively in writing, speaking, and electronic venues
- advocate for programs and services
- advocate for representation in strategic planning initiatives at appropriate divisional and institutional levels
- initiate collaborative interactions with internal and external stakeholders who have legitimate concerns about and interests in the functional area
- facilitate processes to reach consensus where wide support is needed
- inform other areas within the institution about issues affecting practice

Maintaining Integrity
- model ethical behavior and institutional citizenship

- share data used to inform key decisions in transparent and accessible ways
- monitor media used for distributing information about programs and services to ensure the content is current, accurate, appropriately referenced, and accessible

In response to the assessed needs of women students, WSPS must play a principal role in creating and implementing institutional policies and programs developed.

In the case of student-run women's programs, student leaders should have access to policy and decision makers of the institution.

Emphasis should be placed on achieving an organizational placement so that activities of WSPS are not limited to a specific group of women students (e.g., solely undergraduate women) or specific service (e.g., solely counseling services).

WSPS should function as an autonomous unit rather than be housed as a component of other units on campus.

Individual units should be afforded the opportunity to organize in a manner that is efficient and best promotes equity.

Part 4. HUMAN RESOURCES

Women Student Programs and Services (WSPS) must be staffed adequately by individuals qualified to accomplish mission and goals.

Within institutional guidelines, WSPS must
- **establish procedures for staff recruitment and selection, training, performance planning, and evaluation**
- **set expectations for supervision and performance**
- **assess the performance of employees individually and as a team**
- **provide access to continuing and advanced education and appropriate professional development opportunities to improve the leadership ability, competence, and skills of all employees.**

WSPS should be staffed by persons with the credentials and ability to forge gender equity on campus to promote the integrity of the unit.

WSPS staff positions must be classified and compensated on a level commensurate with equivalent positions in other units.

WSPS must maintain position descriptions for all staff members.

To create a diverse staff, WSPS must institute recruitment and hiring strategies that encourage individuals from under-represented populations to apply for positions.

WSPS must develop promotion practices that are fair, inclusive, proactive, and non-discriminatory.

To further the recruitment and retention of staff, WSPS must consider work life initiatives, such as compressed work schedules, flextime, job sharing, remote work, or telework.

WSPS professional staff members must hold an earned graduate or professional degree in a field relevant to the position they hold or must possess an appropriate combination of educational credentials and related work experience.

The leadership must have knowledge of and preferably experience with gender issues and their impact on learning and development.

The professional staff should possess the academic preparation, experience, professional interests, and competencies essential for the efficient operation of the office as charged, as well as the ability to identify additional areas of concern for women. Staff members should have coursework in women's studies or demonstrated experience in advocacy on women's issues. Specific coursework may include organization development, counseling theory and practice, group dynamics, leadership development, human development, and research and evaluation.

Professional staff should demonstrate a commitment to improving women's lives and a respect for the diversity of women's identities and experiences.

Professional staff should (a) develop and implement programs and services; (b) conduct assessment, research, and evaluation; (c) advocate for the improvement of the quality of life for women as students, faculty members, and staff members; and (d) participate in institutional policy and governance efforts to ensure that policies and practices take into account the unique experiences of women.

WSPS professional staff members must engage in continuing professional development activities to keep abreast of the research, theories, legislation, policies, and developments that affect their programs and services.

WSPS must have technical and support staff members adequate to accomplish their mission. All members of the staff must be technologically proficient and qualified to perform their job functions, be knowledgeable about ethical and legal uses of technology, and have access to training and resources to support the performance of their assigned responsibilities.

Technical and support staff should be sufficient to perform

office and administrative functions, including welcoming, sharing resources, problem identification, and referral. In the selection and training of technical and support staff members, special emphasis should be placed on skills in the areas of crisis response and management, public relations, information dissemination, problem identification, and referral. A thorough knowledge of the institution, its various offices, and relevant community resources is important.

Degree- or credential-seeking interns or graduate assistants must be qualified by enrollment in an appropriate field of study and by relevant experience. These individuals must be trained and supervised adequately by professional staff members holding educational credentials and related work experience appropriate for supervision. Supervisors must be cognizant of the roles of interns and graduate assistants as both student and employee and closely adhere to all parameters of their job descriptions, work hours, and schedules. Supervisors and the interns or graduate assistants must agree to compensatory time or other appropriate compensation if circumstances necessitate additional hours.

Student employees and volunteers must be carefully selected, trained, supervised, and evaluated. They must be educated on how and when to refer those in need of additional assistance to qualified staff members and must have access to a supervisor for assistance in making these judgments. Student employees and volunteers must be provided clear job descriptions, pre-service training based on assessed needs, and continuing development.

WSPS should provide student staff with training and development that fosters an understanding of gender, race, class, sexual orientation, religion, ability, and other identity formations. Wherever possible, efforts should be made to ensure that student staff reflects the diversity of women students.

All WSPS staff members, including student employees and volunteers, must receive specific training on institutional policies pertaining to functions or activities they support and to privacy and confidentiality policies and laws regarding access to student records and other sensitive institutional information.

All WSPS staff members must receive training on policies and procedures related to the use of technology to store or access student records and institutional data.

WSPS must ensure that staff members are knowledgeable about and trained in emergency procedures, crisis response, and prevention efforts. Prevention efforts must address identification of threatening conduct or behavior of students, faculty

and staff members, and others and must incorporate a system for responding and reporting.

WSPS must ensure that staff members are knowledgeable of and trained in safety and emergency procedures for securing and vacating facilities.

To remain current and effective in understanding and addressing needs of women students, staff members should be encouraged to enroll in credit courses and seminars and be given access to published research, opinion, and relevant other media.

Part 5. ETHICS

Women Student Programs and Services (WSPS) must review relevant professional ethical standards and must adopt or develop and implement appropriate statements of ethical practice.

WSPS must publish and adhere to statements of ethical practice and ensure their periodic review by relevant constituencies.

WSPS must orient new staff members to relevant ethical standards and statements of ethical practice and related institutional policies.

Statements of ethical standards must specify that staff members respect privacy and maintain confidentiality in all communications and records to the extent that such communications and records are protected under relevant privacy laws.

Statements of ethical standards must specify limits on disclosure of information contained in students' educational records as well as requirements to disclose to appropriate authorities.

Statements of ethical standards must address personal and economic conflicts of interest, or appearance thereof, by staff members in the performance of their work.

Statements of ethical standards must reflect the responsibility of staff members to be fair, objective, and impartial in their interactions with others.

Statements of ethical standards must reference management of institutional funds.

Statements of ethical standards must reference appropriate behavior regarding research and assessment with human participants, confidentiality of research and assessment data, and students' rights and responsibilities.

Statements of ethical standards must include the expectation that WSPS staff members confront and hold accountable other staff members who exhibit unethical behavior.

Statements of ethical standards must address issues surrounding scholarly integrity.

As appropriate, WSPS staff members must inform users of programs and services of ethical obligations and limitations emanating from codes and laws or from licensure requirements.

WSPS staff members must recognize and avoid conflicts of interest that could adversely influence their judgment or objectivity and, when unavoidable, recuse themselves from the situation.

WSPS staff members must perform their duties within the limits of their position, training, expertise, and competence.

When these limits are exceeded, individuals in need of further assistance must be referred to persons possessing appropriate qualifications.

Promotional and descriptive information must be accurate and free of deception.

WSPS must adhere to institutional policies regarding ethical and legal use of software and technology.

Part 6. LAW, POLICY, AND GOVERNANCE

Women Student Programs and Services (WSPS) must be in compliance with laws, regulations, and policies that relate to their respective responsibilities and that pose legal obligations, limitations, risks, and liabilities for the institution as a whole. Examples include constitutional, statutory, regulatory, and case law; relevant law and orders emanating from codes and laws; and the institution's policies.

WSPS must inform staff members, appropriate officials, and users of programs and services about existing and changing legal obligations, risks and liabilities, and limitations.

WSPS must have written policies on all relevant operations, transactions, or tasks that have legal implications.

WSPS must regularly review policies. The revision and creation of policies must be informed by best practices, available evidence, and policy issues in higher education.

WSPS staff members must use reasonable and informed practices to limit the liability exposure of the institution and its officers, employees, and agents. WSPS staff members must be informed about institutional policies regarding risk management, personal liability, and related insurance coverage options and must be referred to external sources if the institution does not provide coverage.

The institution must provide access to legal advice

for staff members as needed to carry out assigned responsibilities.

WSPS must have procedures and guidelines consistent with institutional policy for responding to threats, emergencies, and crisis situations. Systems and procedures must be in place to disseminate timely and accurate information to students, other members of the institutional community, and appropriate external organizations during emergency situations.

WSPS staff members must neither participate in nor condone any form of harassment or activity that demeans persons or creates an intimidating, hostile, or offensive environment.

WSPS must obtain permission to use copyrighted materials and instruments. WSPS must purchase the materials and instruments from legally compliant sources or seek alternative permission from the publisher or owner. References to copyrighted materials and instruments must include appropriate citations.

WSPS staff members must be knowledgeable about internal and external governance systems that affect programs and services.

WSPS should serve as a resource to individuals and the institution on legal issues, institutional policy, applicable laws related to FERPA or Canadian Freedom Of Information and Protection of Privacy (FOIPP), the Clery Act (the Campus Security Act), sexual harassment and discrimination, Title IX, and the rights and responsibilities associated with confidentiality.

Part 7. DIVERSITY, EQUITY, AND ACCESS

Within the context of each institution's unique mission and in accordance with institutional polices and all applicable codes and laws, Women Student Programs and Services (WSPS) must create and maintain educational and work environments that are
- welcoming, accessible, and inclusive to persons of diverse backgrounds
- equitable and non-discriminatory
- free from harassment

WSPS must not discriminate on the basis of ability; age; cultural identity; ethnicity; family educational history (e.g., first generation to attend college); gender identity and expression; nationality; political affiliation; race; religious affiliation; sex; sexual orientation; economic, marital, social, or veteran status; or any other basis included in institutional policies and codes and laws.

WSPS must
- advocate   for   greater   sensitivity   to

multicultural and social justice concerns by the institution and its personnel

- modify or remove policies, practices, facilities, structures, systems, and technologies that limit access, discriminate, or produce inequities
- include diversity, equity, and access initiatives within their strategic plans
- foster communication that deepens understanding of identity, culture, self-expression, and heritage
- promote respect about commonalities and differences among people within their historical and cultural contexts
- address the characteristics and needs of a diverse population when establishing and implementing culturally relevant and inclusive programs, services, policies, procedures, and practices
- provide staff members with access to multicultural training and hold staff members accountable for integrating the training into their work
- respond to the needs of all students and other populations served when establishing hours of operation and developing methods of delivering programs, services, and resources
- ensure physical, program, and resource access for persons with disabilities
- recognize the needs of distance learning students by providing appropriate and accessible services and resources or by assisting them in gaining access to other appropriate services and resources in their geographic region

WSPS should be intentional about addressing race, ethnicity, class, sex, religion, sexual orientation, ability, and other aspects of identity in WSPS educational programs and services as well as in institutional policies and practices.

Part 8. INSTITUTIONAL AND EXTERNAL RELATIONS

Women Student Programs and Services (WSPS) must reach out to relevant individuals, groups, communities, and organizations internal and external to the institution to

- establish, maintain, and promote understanding and effective relations with those that have a significant interest in or potential effect on the students or other constituents served by the programs and services
- garner support and resources for programs and services as defined by the mission statement
- disseminate information about the programs and services
- collaborate, where appropriate, to assist in offering or improving programs and services to meet the needs of students and other constituents and to achieve program and student outcomes
- engage diverse individuals, groups, communities, and organizations to enrich the educational environment and experiences of students and other constituents

WSPS should maintain good working relationships with agencies such as counseling, financial aid, clinical health services, health promotion services, career services, recreational sports, athletics, residential life, multicultural affairs, and public safety. WSPS should maintain a high degree of visibility with academic units through direct promotion and delivery of services, involvement with co-curricular programs, and staff efforts to increase understanding of the needs of women students.

Program staff should be an integral part of appropriate campus networks to participate effectively in the establishment of institution-wide policy and practices and to collaborate effectively with other staff and faculty members in providing services.

WSPS should build effective partnerships with the community to articulate common concerns and share resources.

WSPS must have procedures and guidelines consistent with institutional policy for

- communicating with the media
- contracting with external organizations for delivery of programs and services
- cultivating, soliciting, and managing gifts
- applying to and managing funds from grants

Part 9. FINANCIAL RESOURCES

Women Student Programs and Services (WSPS) must have funding to accomplish the mission and goals. In establishing funding priorities and making significant changes, a comprehensive analysis must be conducted to determine the following elements: unmet needs of the unit, relevant expenditures, external and internal resources, and impact on students and the institution.

WSPS must demonstrate efficient and effective use and responsible stewardship of fiscal resources consistent with institutional protocols.

Although initial funding for WSPS may come from a combination of institutional funds, grant money, student government funds, fees for services, and government contracts, permanent institutional funding should be allocated for the continuing operation of WSPS.

Part 10. TECHNOLOGY

Women Student Programs and Services (WSPS) must have adequate technology to support the achievement of their mission and goals. The technology and its use must comply with institutional policies and procedures and be evaluated for compliance with relevant codes and laws.

WSPS must use current technology to provide updated information regarding mission, location, staffing, programs, services, and official contacts to students and designated clients.

WSPS must explore the use of technology to enhance delivery of programs and services, especially for students at a distance or external constituencies.

When technology is used to facilitate student learning and development, WSPS must select technology that reflects intended outcomes.

WSPS must

- maintain policies and procedures that address the security, confidentiality, and backup of data, as well as compliance with privacy laws
- have clearly articulated plans in place for protecting confidentiality and security of information when using Internet-based technologies
- develop plans for replacing and updating existing hardware and software as well as plans for integrating new technically-based or supported programs, including systems developed internally by the institution, systems available through professional associations, or private vendor-based systems

Technology, as well as workstations or computer labs maintained by programs and services for student use, must be accessible to all designated clients and must meet established technology standards for delivery to persons with disabilities.

When providing student access to technology, WSPS must

- have policies on the use of technology that are clear, easy to understand, and available to all students
- provide assistance, information, or referral to appropriate support services to those needing help accessing or using technology
- provide instruction or training on how to use the technology
- inform students on the legal and ethical implications of misuse as it pertains to intellectual property, harassment, privacy, and social networks

Student violations of technology policies must follow established institutional student disciplinary procedures.

Students who experience negative emotional or psychological consequences from the use of technology must be referred to support services provided by the institution.

Part 11. FACILITIES AND EQUIPMENT

Women Student Programs and Services (WSPS) must have adequate, accessible, and suitably located facilities and equipment to support the mission and goals. If acquiring capital equipment as defined by the institution, WSPS must take into account expenses related to regular maintenance and life cycle costs. Facilities and equipment must be evaluated on an established cycle, including consideration of sustainability, and be in compliance with codes and laws to provide for access, health, safety, and security.

WSPS staff members must have workspace that is well equipped, adequate in size, and designed to support their work and responsibilities. For conversations requiring privacy, staff members must have access to a private space.

WSPS staff members who share workspace must be able to secure their own work.

The design of the facilities must guarantee the security and privacy of records and ensure the confidentiality of sensitive information.

The location and layout of the facilities must be sensitive to the needs of persons with disabilities as well as the needs of other constituencies.

Facilities may be located in prominent, visible areas to visually demonstrate the institution's commitment to WSPS. Facilities should include private meeting areas and welcoming communal space. Facilities should be staffed beyond traditional business hours to ensure access for non-traditional students and other community members.

Part 12. ASSESSMENT AND EVALUATION

Women Student Programs and Services (WSPS) must have a clearly articulated assessment plan to document achievement of stated goals and learning outcomes, demonstrate accountability, provide evidence of improvement, and describe resulting changes in programs and services.

WSPS must have adequate fiscal, human, professional development, and technological resources to develop and implement assessment plans.

Assessments must include direct and indirect

evaluation and use qualitative and quantitative methodologies and existing evidence, as appropriate, to determine whether and to what degree the stated mission, goals, and intended outcomes are being met as effectively and efficiently as possible. The process must employ sufficient and sound measures to ensure comprehensiveness. Data collected must include responses from students and other constituencies, and aggregated results must be shared with those groups. Results of assessments must be shared appropriately with multiple constituents.

A comprehensive evaluation of the on-going program should be carried out in accordance with the general practice of program review for other units of the institution. To assist staff in planning and program formation, WSPS should establish an on-going evaluation process.

Results of assessments and evaluations must be used to identify needs and interests in revising and improving programs and services, recognizing staff performance, maximizing resource efficiency and effectiveness, improving student achievement of learning and development outcomes, and improving student persistence and success. Changes resulting from the use of assessments and evaluation must be shared with stakeholders.

WSPS should inform constituencies and the institution of the results of assessment and evaluation. WSPS should engage the institution in climate-related research that addresses issues that might have a disparate effect on women.

General Standards revised in 2011;
WSPS content developed/revised in 1992, 1997, & 2005

Appendix A
CAS Member Associations - June 2012

Association	Member Since
ACPA: College Student Educators International (ACPA)	1979
American Association for Employment in Education (AAEE)	1979
American College Counseling Association (ACCA)	1993
American College Health Association (ACHA)	1995
Association for Student Conduct Administration (ASCA, formerly ASJA)	1990
Association of College and University Housing Officers-International ACUHO-I)	1979
Association of College Honor Societies (ACHS)	2004
Association of College Unions International (ACUI)	1979
Association of Collegiate Conference and Events Directors-International (ACCED-I)	1999
Association of Fraternity/Sorority Advisors (AFA)	1981
Association of Higher Education Parent/Family Program Professionals (AHEPPP)	2010
Association on Higher Education and Disability (AHEAD)	1981
Canadian Association of College and University Student Services (CACUSS)	1994
College Media Advisers (CMA)	2011
College Reading and Learning Association (CRLA)	1993
Collegiate Information and Visitor Services Association (CiVSA)	1998
Consortium of Higher Education LGBT Resource Professionals (Consortium)	1999
Cooperative Education and Internship Association (CEIA)	2009
Council for Opportunity in Education (COE)	1994
International Association of Campus Law Enforcement Administrators (IACLEA)	2009
NACADA: National Academic Advising Association (NACADA)	1981
NAFSA: Association of International Educators (NAFSA)	1989
NASPA: Student Affairs Administrators in Higher Education (NASPA)	1979
National Association for Campus Activities (NACA)	1979
National Association for Developmental Educators (NADE)	1992
National Association of College and University Food Services (NACUFS)	2004
National Association of College Auxiliary Services (NACAS)	1998
National Association of Colleges and Employers (NACE)	1979
National Association of College Stores (NACS)	2005
National Association of Student Affairs Professionals (NASAP)	2004
National Association of Student Financial Aid Administrators (NASFAA)	1991
National Clearinghouse for Commuter Programs (NCCP)	1980
National Clearinghouse for Leadership Programs (NCLP)	2004
National Council on Student Development (NCSD)	1979
National Institute for the Transfer Students (NISTS)	2010
National Intramural-Recreational Sports Association (NIRSA)	1981
National Orientation Directors Association (NODA)	1979
National Society for Experiential Education (NSEE)	2004
National Women's Studies Association (NWSA)	2006
Southern Association for College Student Affairs (SACSA)	1982
The Network - Addressing Collegiate Alcohol and Other Drug Issues (The Network)	1999

Appendix B
Protocol for Developing New CAS Standards and Guidelines

The protocol for developing new standards has been developed as a broad-based and inclusive process. It encompasses an internal-external-internal drafting procedure that is outlined below.

Identify the Functional Area. The CAS Executive Committee with the approval of the CAS Board of Directors identifies and defines the functional area for which a CAS standard is to be written. New standards may be proposed by individuals, professional entities, or a group of concerned professional practitioners by considering the following list of CAS Evaluation Questions for Selecting New Standards:

1. Is there a trend toward a distinct functional area?
2. Is there consistency in practice across multiple institutions?
3. Is there a clear need for these standards within higher education?
4. Would creating these standards match the CAS mission and purpose to enhance student learning?
5. Are there policies, practices, and structures that are increasingly unique?
6. Is there a body of literature?
7. Would new standards be different enough from existing standards?
8. Would an expansion of existing standards address this need?
9. Are additions to the general standards more appropriate as an approach to address this need?
10. Are there professionals interested in supporting the development of the standards?
11. Is there a group of professionals working to support the functional area?
12. Is there a professional association related to the proposed standard?

CAS should identify standards created by one or more organizations outside of CAS and seek involvement and cooperation in developing new CAS standards and guidelines for that functional area. If such organizations decide not to join, CAS will move forward. The CAS Board of Directors must agree by majority vote to sponsor development of a new professional standard.

Charge a Development Committee for New Standards Creation. Once the CAS Board of Directors has approved the development of a new CAS functional area standard, a Development Committee of three to five CAS directors (or alternate directors) will be appointed and charged by the CAS president to guide the development process. If further help is needed, committee members with functional area expertise from outside of CAS can be added. The chair cannot be a representative of a professional association that has significant interest in the new standard. However, at least one person on the committee must be connected with the functional area to serve as an expert and play a significant role in ensuring that the standards demonstrate contemporary quality practices. Development Committee appointments should be made after the spring CAS Board of Directors meeting and be followed by a New Committee Chair Training Program. The Development Committee members will work with the CAS Executive Committee Member-at-Large for Standards Development to establish online reference materials and the editing environment. Copies of existing CAS standards with similarity to the new functional area can be requested by the Development Committee to be placed online along with a copy of the current CAS General Standards.

Develop Initial Draft. Usually the initial draft is developed by the chair and area expert with feedback and suggestions from Development Committee members. If a professional association connected with the functional area has already written a standard, it should be used in the creation of the first draft. The CAS General Standards will be used as the foundation for newly developed functional area standards.

Solicit Internal Review and Comment. The CAS Development Committee should identify all CAS member associations that have a significant interest in the new functional area standard. The first draft of the standards should be sent to CAS directors of identified organizations with the request that they provide timely and substantive recommendations and feedback. The Development Committee then creates a second draft based on feedback from these CAS directors. A minimum of two months should be allowed for the writing of the second draft.

Solicit External Expert Review and Comment. The CAS Development Committee must identify expert functional area professionals for their review of the second draft of the new standards. To achieve diversification, the committee should consider institution size, location, and type (e.g., 4 year/2 year, public/private, historically underrepresented, etc.). In addition, the Development Committee should consider soliciting feedback from practitioners through online professional lists, organizational web pages, and the database of users collected from purchasers of CAS materials. CAS directors can be consulted for names of those who are currently filling positions with connections and interest in the new standards under development. It should be the goal to receive feedback from at least five experts within two months.

Incorporate comments into a third draft document. The Development Committee will evaluate all substantive feedback and recommendations from experts (compiled either electronically or with the assistance of the CAS Intern) and provide its own well-considered ideas for the development of the third draft of the functional area standards and guidelines. This draft should be prepared within one year after the beginning of the development process.

Executive Committee Review and Approve. Submission of the CAS Development Committee's final standards draft along with an updated version of the contextual statement should be made to the CAS Editor approximately six weeks prior to the next CAS Executive Committee meeting. The proposed new standards and contextual statement are checked by the CAS Editor for accuracy and completeness and then forwarded to the CAS Executive Committee for review at least two weeks before the meeting. The Development Committee chair and/or area expert will present the draft to the Executive Committee in person or by electronic conference. The CAS Executive Committee reviews the draft and can either return it for further work by the Development Committee or formulate a penultimate draft to be sent to the CAS Board of Directors for final review and approval. This penultimate draft should be sent to the CAS directors no later than 45 days before the board meeting.

Full CAS Board of Directors Review, Consider, and Approve. The CAS Board of Directors will be asked to review the penultimate draft of the new standards and contextual statement and provide substantive feedback and suggestions to the Development Committee at least two weeks prior to the CAS Board of Directors meeting. The Development Committee will meet to review and discuss this feedback and prepare alternate language and/or feedback and answers to questions prior to the board meeting. The chair of the Development Committee will submit all materials, including a summary of any areas of substantive feedback, to the Executive Committee for review prior to presentation of the new standards and contextual statement to the CAS Board of Directors. The chair of the Development Committee along with the functional area expert will formally present the new standards to the CAS directors following a facilitation-training program that explains and clarifies the process and specific roles at the meeting. Following final review and discussion, the CAS Board of Directors will vote to adopt the new standards and guidelines. This process should be completed within eighteen months after beginning the development process.

Publish. The new Standards and Guidelines, upon adoption by the Board of Directors and final review by the Development Committee chair, are then submitted to the Editor to format the CAS Self-Assessment Guide for distribution to the profession at large. Upon completion, the Standards and Guidelines and contextual statement will be published in the next Book of Standards, along with the appropriate contextual statement. The standards will be made available as a separate publication on the CAS Website and/or directly linked to appropriate CAS member associations' websites. The completion of the new Standards and Guidelines from the beginning of the process through publication should take no longer than two years. The committee chair will also be asked to provide guidance for marketing, including interested professional association information and potential quotes for press releases. If during final editing and review there are any substantial changes, this document should be returned to the Board of Directors for approval. The CAS secretary maintains the official version of the final approved standards and guideline.

Development Process Timeline

Event Chronology	Time Allotted	Total Time
Evaluate potential new function area standard	3 months	3 months
Development Committee chair and committee members identified and trained	2 months	5 months
Initial draft created	3 months	8 months
Solicit internal CAS review and comment	2 months	10 months
Create a second draft	2 months	12 months
Solicit external expert review and comment	2 months	14 months
Create a third draft	2 months	16 months
Draft is submitted for review to the Executive Committee	1 month	17 months
Executive Committee approved draft is distributed to Directors for review. Initial feedback from directors received by Development Committee and Executive Committee	1 months	18 months
Substantial items reviewed by Development Committee and reported to the Executive Committee and prepared for discussion at Board Meeting	0.5 month	19 months

Appendix B - continued
Protocol for Revising Existing CAS Standards and Guidelines

The CAS Board of Directors will systematically review approximately four or more CAS Functional Area Standards and Guidelines per year within a projected eleven-year planning cycle. The standards revision protocol is developed as a broad based and inclusive process. It encompasses an internal-external-internal drafting procedure that is outlined below. Member associations with interest in the functional area(s) under review will be called upon to provide functional area expert committee members and reviewers.

Initial Review: When it becomes necessary to consider standards for revision, the president will appoint and charge a Revision Committee. The revision process includes the following actions:

1. The composition of the committee will consist of a chair, to guide the revision process, and at least two other CAS directors or alternate directors.
2. The chair cannot be a representative of a professional association that has significant interest in the standard.
3. At least one person on the committee must be connected with the functional area to serve as an area expert and play a considerable role in ensuring that the revised standards demonstrate contemporary language and quality practices.
4. Revision Committee appointments are made following the spring Board of Directors meeting and should be followed with a training program for new committee chairs.
5. The Revision Committee will work with the CAS Executive Committee Member-at-Large for Standards Development to establish an Internet-based reference collection related to the functional area and editing environment.
6. A copy of the existing standards, updated to reflect the current CAS General Standards, will be made available to the Revision Committee through the CAS secretary.
7. The chair will work with the functional area expert to identify an initial list of experts in the field for a high level review of the existing standards.
8. The Revision Committee will circulate the existing standards with general standards updates to its members and identified experts to determine if a substantial revision is necessary or whether an editorial revision will be adequate.

Editorial Standards Revision: An editorial revision of existing standards includes

1. basic word, punctuation, and grammatical corrections
2. alteration of phrases for purposes of improved clarity
3. modification required by changes in general standards
4. presentation/format changes
5. non-substantive word changes

After deciding that an editorial revision would be appropriate, the Revision Committee should begin work on creating a first draft that will be distributed to the identified functional area experts for review. The use of other experts in the field usually will not be necessary.

1. Following expert feedback and final updates by committee members, the revised standards and updated contextual statement should be submitted to the CAS Executive Committee.
2. The Revision Committee chair and/or functional area expert will present the draft to the Executive Committee in person or by an electronic conference as needed.
3. The CAS Executive Committee will review the revised draft, formulate a penultimate draft, and either return the standards and contextual statement to the Revision Committee for further work (including undertaking a substantial standards revision) or forward it on to the full CAS Board of Directors for review and possible approval at a regular meeting.
4. The penultimate draft, clearly identifying changes from the original version of the standards and contextual statement, must be sent to the Board of Directors no later than 45 days before a board meeting.
5. The directors must return any substantive feedback or suggestions at least two weeks before the Board of Director's meeting so that the Revision Committee will have time to consider and prepare any responses or alternate suggestions.
6. The chair of the Revision Committee will submit all materials, including a summary of any areas of substantive feedback, to the Executive Committee for review prior to presentation of the revised standards to the CAS Board of Directors.
7. The chair of the Revision Committee, along with the functional area expert, will formally present the revised standards to the CAS Board of Directors.

8. A short training program prior to the meeting will explain and clarify the facilitation process.
9. An editorial revision should take approximately six months to complete from the beginning of the review process.

Substantial Standards Revision: After deciding that a substantial revision is required, the Revision Committee should begin work on creating an initial draft. The revision process includes the following actions:

1. Usually the creation of the initial draft is lead by the chair and functional area expert with feedback and suggestions from other committee members.
2. The Revision Committee will poll all CAS member associations to determine those that have a significant interest in the standard under revision and contact those CAS directors for review and feedback of the initial draft.
3. The chair and functional area expert should also take the lead in identifying an expanded and diverse list of experts who can be asked to review and provide feedback about the initial draft. To achieve diversification, they should consider institutional size, location, and type (e.g., 4year/2year, public/private, historically underrepresented, etc.).
4. The chair of the Revision Committee should contact non-member professional associations, who have a significant interest in the standards under revision, to seek their involvement and review of the revised standards. It is also recommended that feedback be gathered from practitioners through online professional lists, organizational web pages, and the database of users collected from purchasers of CAS materials.
5. Once a list of experts and interested parties is completed, the Chair should request that those individuals review the initial draft of the revised standard and give feedback and suggestions.
6. Ten external or internal experts are suggested for review and comment. The CAS Intern can assist in compiling this material into a useful format for the committee.
7. The Revision Committee should use feedback and suggestions to prepare a second draft of the revised standards.
8. Once the committee is comfortable with the second draft, the revised standards and updated/revised contextual statement should be submitted to the Editor to forward to the CAS Executive Committee.
9. The Revision Committee chair and/or functional area expert will present the draft to the Executive Committee in person or by electronic conference.
10. The CAS Executive Committee will review the draft and formulate a penultimate draft to either return to the Revision Committee for further work or send to the full board for review and possible approval at a regular meeting.
11. The penultimate draft clearly identifying all substantive changes from the original version of the standards must be sent to the Board of Directors no later than 45 days before a board meeting. The directors must return any substantive feedback or suggestions to the Revision Committee Chair and CAS Executive Committee at least two weeks before the Board of Directors meeting so that the Revision Committee will have time to consider and prepare any responses or alternate suggestions.
12. The chair of the Revision Committee will submit all materials, including a summary of any areas of substantive feedback, to the Executive Committee for review prior to presentation of the revised standards to the CAS Board of Directors.
13. A short training program prior to the meeting will explain and clarify the facilitation process.
14. The chair of the Revision Committee along with the functional area expert will present the revised standards to the CAS Board of Directors.
15. This revision process should be completed within one year.

Publication: The newly revised standards and contextual statement, upon adoption by the CAS Board of Directors, will be sent by the CAS secretary to the Editor for final editing and formatting the *CAS Self Assessment Guide*. Upon completion, the revised standard will be published in the next *Book of Standards* along with the appropriate contextual statement. In addition, it will be made available as a separate publication on the CAS Website and/or directly linked to appropriate CAS member association Websites. If during final editing and review there are any substantial proposed changes, this document should be returned to the Board of Directors for approval. A substantial standards revision should take approximately 12 months. The CAS secretary maintains the official version of the final approved standards and guidelines.

Revision Process Timeline – Editorial Review

Event Chronology	Time Allotted	Total Time
Revision Committee chair and committee members identified and trained	2 months	2 months
Decision made as to substantial or editorial review	1 month	3 months
First draft completed by Revision Committee	2 months	5 months
Experts identified and first draft distributed for feedback	1 month	6 months
Draft is submitted for review to the Executive Committee	1 month	7 months
Executive Committee approved draft is distributed to Directors for review. Initial feedback from directors received by Development Committee and Executive Committee	1 month	8 months
Substantial items reviewed by Development Committee and reported to the Executive Committee and prepared for discussion at Board Meeting	0.5 month	8.5 months

Revision Process Timeline – Substantial Review

Event Chronology	Time Allotted	Total Time
Revision Committee chair and committee members identified and trained	2 months	2 months
Decision made as to substantial or editorial review	1 month	3 months
First draft completed by Revision Committee	2 months	5 months
Experts identified and first draft distributed for feedback	1 month	6 months
Experts return feedback and second draft is written by Revision Committee	3 months	9 months
Draft is submitted for review to the Executive Committee	1 month	10 months
Executive Committee approved draft is distributed to Directors for review. Initial feedback from directors received by Development Committee and Executive Committee	1 months	11 months
Substantial items reviewed by Development Committee and reported to the Executive Committee and prepared for discussion at Board Meeting	0.5 months	11.5 months

Appendix C
Glossary of Terms

accreditation. A voluntary process conducted by peers through non-governmental agencies for purposes of improving educational quality and assuring the public that programs and services meet established standards. In higher education, accreditation is divided into two types—institutional and specialized. Although both are designed to assure fundamental levels of quality, the former focuses on the institution as a whole while the latter focuses on academic pre-professional or specialty professional programs such as law, business, psychology, and education, or services such as counseling centers within the institution. Although the CAS Standards have utility for accreditation self-study, CAS is not an accrediting body.

affirmative action. Policies and/or programs designed to redress historic injustices committed against racial minorities and other specified groups by making special efforts to provide members of these groups with access to educational and employment opportunities. This may apply to students as well as to faculty and staff members. Legality varies by state in the U.S.

best practice. A level of professional conduct or practice identified as being necessary for college and university personnel to exhibit in their daily work for the host program or service to be judged satisfactory, sufficient, and of acceptable quality. By this definition, CAS Standards and Guidelines represent best practice; however, it is more accurate to say that they represent good practice, a level that can be achieved regardless of institutional or resource differences.

CAS. The Council for the Advancement of Standards in Higher Education. A consortium of professional associations founded in 1979 and concerned with the development and promulgation of professional standards and guidelines for student support programs and services in institutions of higher learning. The CAS Board of Directors is composed of representatives from member associations and meets semiannually in the spring and fall. Prior to 1992, the consortium's name was the Council for the Advancement of Standards for Student Services/Development Programs.

CAS Blue Book. The informal name of the publication entitled CAS Professional Standards for Higher Education (previous editions were "The CAS Book of Professional Standards for Higher Education") that presents the CAS standards and guidelines. The first iteration of the CAS standards was published in 1986. Revised editions were published in 1997, 1999, 2001, 2003, 2006, 2009, and the current 2012 edition. CAS policy calls for an updated revision to be published regularly.

CAS Board of Directors. A body of representatives from professional higher education associations in the U.S. and Canada that have joined the CAS consortium, pay annual dues, and keep their memberships informed about CAS standards and related initiatives. Each member association may designate two official representatives (Director and Alternate) to act on its behalf at CAS Board meetings; each association has one vote on the Council.

CAS Executive Committee. A body of elected CAS officers, including president, secretary, treasurer, members at large, and others elected at the discretion of the Board of Directors. This body meets periodically to deal with CAS governance issues and to review penultimate standard statements prior to final review and adoption by the Board of Directors.

CAS Internet URL. http://www.cas.edu The CAS web site at which various CAS initiatives and resources are described, publications may be ordered, and links to CAS member associations are listed.

CAS member association. One of the higher education professional associations that has joined the CAS consortium and is committed to the development and promulgation of professional standards for college student learning and development programs and services.

CAS preparation program standards. A set of professional standards developed and promulgated for purposes of providing student affairs administration master's level programs with criteria to guide the professional education and preparation of entry-level practitioners in student affairs.

CAS Public Director. An individual appointed to the CAS Board of Directors to represent the public at large. CAS by-laws call for the appointment of public directors who do not represent a specific functional area or professional association.

CAS Standards and Guidelines. Published criteria and related statements designed to provide college and university support service providers with established measures against which to evaluate programs and services. A standard uses the auxiliary verbs "must" and "shall," while a guideline uses the verbs "should" and "may." Standards are essentials, guidelines are not.

certification. Official recognition by a governmental or professional body attesting that an individual practitioner meets established standards or criteria. Criteria usually include formal academic preparation in prescribed content areas and a period of supervised practice and may also include a systematic evaluation (e.g., standardized test) of the practitioner's knowledge.

compliance. Adherence to a standard of practice or preparation. Compliance with the CAS standards implies that an institution or program meets or exceeds the fundamental essential criteria established for a given functional area program and service or for an academic student affairs administration preparation program.

dimension. A subcategory of learning and development outcome domains. See *outcomes* below.

domain. A broad category of learning and development outcomes. See *outcomes* below.

FALDOs. Frameworks for Assessing Learning and Development Outcomes. A companion publication to the CAS Professional Standards for Higher Education (2006), the FALDOs are designed to assist practitioners in designing and implementing assessment of outcomes. The FALDOs are out of print but available as an electronic download.

functional area standard. A statement that presents criteria describing the fundamental essential expectations of practice agreed upon by the profession at large for a given institutional function. Standards are presented in bold type and use auxiliary verbs "must" and "shall." Currently there are 43 sets of CAS functional area standards (see Table of Contents).

general standards. Statements presenting criteria that represent the most fundamental essential expectations agreed upon by the profession at large for all higher education support programs and services. The general standards are contained within every set of functional area standards; they apply to every area. These "boilerplate" criteria are presented in bold type and use the auxiliary verbs "must" and "shall" as do all CAS standards. The most recent revision of the General Standards was adopted in 2011.

guideline. A statement that clarifies or amplifies professional standards. Although not required for acceptable practice, a guideline is designed to provide institutions with suggestions and illustrations that can assist in establishing programs and services that more fully address the needs of students than those mandated by a standard. Guidelines may be thought of as providing guidance in ways to exceed fundamental requirements, to approach excellence, or to function at a more optimal level. CAS Guidelines use the auxiliary verbs "should" and "may."

in-service (or inservice) education. Educational skill-building activities provided by an institution to staff members within the context of their work responsibilities. This is a form of staff development designed to strengthen the ability of practitioners to carry out their duties more effectively.

licensure. Official recognition, usually by a government entity, that authorizes practice in the public arena. A license is usually granted only upon the presentation of compelling evidence that the individual is well qualified to practice in a given profession. Granting of a professional license typically authorizes holders to announce their qualifications to provide selected services to the public and attach professional titles to their names. Insurance companies often require individuals to be licensed to qualify for third-party payments.

outcomes. Changes occurring in students as a direct result of their interaction with an educational institution and its programs and services. Often referred to as learning outcomes, or learning and development outcomes, they represent the intended change prior to the intervention or interaction, as well as the change that is determined to have occurred afterward. Part 2 of the CAS standards identifies six broad outcome *domains* in which students should experience growth as a result of their higher education experiences. The standards also outline a number of *dimensions*, or subcategories, of the outcome domains to provide practitioners with assistance in developing intended outcomes.

personal development. Closely related to student development, this term refers to the processes associated with human maturation, especially those concerned with evolving psychosocial, moral, relational, and self-concept changes that influence an individual's quality of life.

pre-professional. An individual who is in the process of obtaining professional education that will qualify her or him for professional practice (e.g., graduate student, intern).

program. Refers to one of two types: a) organizational, a departmental level administrative unit or sub-unit; b) activity, an institutional support service such as an invited lecture, a workshop, a social event, or a series of organized presentations over time (e.g., a "lunch and learn" program).

quality assurance. The raison d'être for the CAS standards and virtually all types of credentialing activities devised to assure the public that educational institutions, programs, and services and those providing them exhibit high levels of competence leading to excellence. Quality assurance initiatives are intended to ensure that those accessing available programs and services will truly benefit from them.

registry. An official record of the names and qualifications of individuals who meet pre-established criteria to function as professional practitioners. The names of professionally licensed and/or certified practitioners are typically listed in a registry. In some instances a professional "register" may be maintained for purposes of providing individuals, institutions, and organizations with the names of those who meet an established level of competence for employment or other activity such as consulting or lecturing. A registry may also be used to identify those judged to possess relevant knowledge or skill outside the context of licensure.

Self-Assessment Guide (SAG). An operational version of the CAS Standards and Guidelines designed to provide users with an assessment tool that can be used for self-study or self-assessment purposes. A SAG is available for each functional area for which a CAS standard exists.

self-study. An internal process by which institutions and programs evaluate their quality and effectiveness in reference to established criteria such as the CAS standards. This process, often used for institutional and specialty accreditation purposes, results in a formal report presenting the findings of the internal evaluation implemented by institutional employees. For accreditation purposes, this report is then validated by a visiting, external committee of peers from comparable institutions or programs. CAS SAGs have great utility for this purpose.

self-regulation. The recommended process by which the CAS Standards and Guidelines can best be used to evaluate and assess institutional support programs and services. This approach calls for institutions and programs to establish, maintain, and enhance the quality of their offerings and environments by using the standards to evaluate themselves. From the CAS perspective, each institution and its programs can and should seek to identify and regulate its own practices rather than relying on external agencies to do so.

staff development. Refers to the programs, workshops, conferences, and other training related activities offered by institutions, professional associations, and corporate entities for purposes of increasing effectiveness in accomplishing work responsibilities of staff members.

standard. A statement framed within the context of a professional arena designed to provide practitioners with criteria against which to judge the quality of the programs and services offered. A standard reflects an essential level of practice that, when met, represents quality performance. CAS standards use auxiliary verbs "must" and "shall" presented in bold print.

student development. Refers to those outcomes that occur as a result of students being exposed to higher education environments designed to enhance academic, intellectual, psychosocial, psychomotor, moral, and, for some institutions, spiritual development. This concept is based on applying human development theories within the context of higher education. In some instances, the term has also been applied to administrative units (e.g., center for student development).

student learning and development. Refers to the outcomes students realize when exposed to new experiences, concepts, information, and ideas; the knowledge and understanding gleaned from interactions with higher education learning environments. Learning means acquiring knowledge and applying it to life, appreciating human differences, and approaching an integrated sense of self.

Appendix D
FAQ: Frequently Asked Questions about CAS and Its Initiatives

1. Why does CAS write standards?
One criterion for the existence of a profession is a set of professional standards to guide and judge practice. Without standards there would be few if any criteria established that institutions and their programs and services could use to judge their quality. CAS was established to develop and promulgate the standards necessary to achieve educational excellence.

2. How many CAS Standards and Guidelines are currently in place? Where can I find the list?
As of July 2012, CAS had developed 42 sets of functional area standards and guidelines and one set of student affairs master's level preparation standards. They are listed in the Table of Contents of CAS Professional Standards for Higher Education and on the CAS website at www.cas.edu.

3. Why does CAS call them "functional areas" instead of using a more common term?
The areas for which CAS publishes standards represent functions on campuses; in some cases, these are commonly organized in departments or offices (e.g., housing and residential life, counseling), but in other cases, the function may be distributed across multiple offices or only one part of a department's total scope (e.g., assessment services, internships). The term "functional area" is used as an inclusive term to encompass the wide range of functions on campus.

4. What is the difference between a CAS standard and a CAS guideline?
A CAS standard, which is printed in BOLD type, is considered to be essential to successful professional practice and uses the auxiliary verbs "must" and "shall." Compliance with the CAS standards indicates that a program meets essential criteria as described in each standard statement and that there is tangible evidence available to support that fact. A CAS guideline, printed in light-face type, is a statement that clarifies or amplifies a CAS standard. Although not required for achieving compliance, CAS guidelines are designed to offer suggestions and illustrations that can assist programs and services to more fully address the learning and development needs of students. CAS guidelines use the auxiliary verbs "should" and "may."

5. Are institutions in jeopardy if they fail to meet the CAS Standards and Guidelines?
CAS Standards are provided primarily for institutions to use within the context of a "self-regulation" process. That is, although compliance with the standards evidences "good practice" that is recognized profession-wide, there are no external sanctions for non-compliance. However, institutions that do not meet the CAS standards will likely discover that their programs and services fail to function effectively or to meet the needs of their students. Further, institutions that evidence compliance with the CAS standards are virtually assured of receiving "high grades" from regional or specialized accrediting bodies.

6. What utility do the CAS Standards and Guidelines have for practitioners?
The CAS standards are multi-purpose in nature. They can be used to study and evaluate institutional divisions of student affairs and the various student-oriented functional areas common across institutions. Likewise, they can be used for professional development purposes to ensure that staff members comprehend their roles and functions and develop the level of knowledge and skill essential for good practice. Also, the CAS standards can be used to guide the development of new or enhanced functional areas designed to provide students with additional learning and development opportunities.

7. Where will I find the CAS Standards and Guidelines?
CAS publishes two versions of its standards, one in text format and another in workbook format. CAS Professional Standards for Higher Education (2012, sometimes known as the "CAS Blue Book") provides an introduction to CAS, its mission, initiatives, and the principles upon which it was founded. Individual functional area standards accompanied by introductory contextual statements are included, along with the CAS Learning and Development Outcomes, the CAS Characteristics of Individual Excellence, and the CAS Statement of Shared Ethical Principles. In addition, for use in programmatic self-studies, there is a CAS Self-Assessment Guide (SAG) for each set of standards. These assessment workbooks include the standards and guidelines along with a series of "criterion measure" statements used to judge the level of program compliance with the standard. The CAS SAGs are available electronically via the CAS web site and also in CD-ROM format.

8. How can I obtain the CAS publications and what are their costs?
All available CAS publications, along with current costs and payment options, are listed on the CAS internet web site, www.cas.edu; they may also be purchased from the CAS national office, One Dupont Circle, NW, Suite 300, Washington, DC 20036-1188. Current publications include the CAS Professional Standards and the SAGs, and packaged sets are available. The FALDOs are available only as an electronic download. . Questions can be addressed to the CAS Executive Director at executive_director@cas.edu, or (202) 862-1400.

9. Where will I find information about using the CAS Standards and Guidelines?
An outline of how to put the CAS standards to work is included in the Blue Book, and each functional area SAG has an

introductory section that describes how to apply the SAG for self-study purposes. The SAG CD also contains a PowerPoint presentation and E-learning course to help train users. PowerPoint presentations are also available on the CAS website.

10. Can a partial program self-study using less than a full functional area standard be implemented?
Each CAS standard is organized into 12 parts. These individual program components can be used on stand-alone bases for program self-studies or for program development purposes. That is, a partial self-study using selected components may be desirable for some programs to consider. Likewise, each component has utility for staff development purposes. One recommended training approach is to hold a series of training sessions in which individual parts are examined in detail. It should be understood, however, that a full program assessment cannot be accomplished using less than the complete functional area standard, and a functional area cannot be considered to be in compliance with CAS standards if all the component parts are not evaluated.

11. How long does a typical division or individual program self-study take to complete?
The time required to complete the self-study process varies greatly with size and complexity of institutions and programs. In most instances, it will take from 6 to 9 months to complete a comprehensive division or campus-wide self-study, while a single administrative unit functional area program self-study may well be completed in approximately 3 to 6 months. One of the major time-consuming factors of any self-study is the data collection process in which documentary evidence is obtained and organized into a usable format. More time will be required if the documentary evidence has not already been collected and analyzed.

12. Does CAS offer certification or accreditation?
CAS does not function as a certification or accreditation agency. Rather, CAS encourages institutions and their functional area programs to follow a "self-regulation" approach wherein program evaluation self-studies are implemented for internal assessment purposes.

13. Do the CAS Standards have utility for regional or other accreditation purposes?
Institutions undergoing accreditation self-studies will find the CAS standards most useful. Because CAS functional area standards are invariably more comprehensive than regional accreditation criteria, a self-study using the CAS standards will provide ample documentation that can be used as evidence of compliance with accreditation criteria.

14. How does one become a member of CAS?
Because CAS is a consortium of professional organizations, there are no individual memberships currently available. The CAS Board of Directors is composed of representatives from member organizations, and each member association has one vote on CAS business. Organizational membership information is available from the CAS national office. [Isn't this something we might be changing? Should we hedge and say "there are currently no individual memberships available.."

15. Does CAS have a presence at national association meetings?
Because CAS is a consortium of professional associations, each member association is responsible for providing its membership with information about the nature and availability of CAS standards. Most member associations include CAS-related presentations at their conventions. Several CAS officers and directors are available upon request to provide CAS workshops or programs sponsored by professional organizations. CAS-oriented programs have been offered at numerous national and international conferences in recent years.

16. Does CAS provide institutional staff training programs and workshops?
The CAS national office can provide information about CAS officers and board members who are well qualified to provide staff development training workshops and programs for institutions, or to consult about use of the CAS materials.

17. How often are CAS functional area standards and guidelines revised?
CAS policy calls for every functional area standard to be reviewed regularly for purposes of determining whether a revision is needed. Individuals or organizations who believe a given standard is in need of revision are invited to contact CAS to make such recommendations.

18. My association has already written professional standards. What can CAS provide that we don't already have?
Several professional associations have established standards for their constituent members, some of which are quite comparable to CAS standards. In general, CAS standards are designed to be used in every type and size of higher educational institution and were created for this broad user base. A primary benefit of the CAS standards is the fact that CAS represents a profession-wide effort to develop, promulgate, and encourage use of its professional standards. Consequently, the professional credibility of the CAS Standards and Guidelines tends to exceed those proffered by a single organization. If an institution or division uses the CAS standards to study more than one functional area, use of CAS ensures that the areas to be examined and the criteria will be consistent across areas.

19. How are CAS projects funded?

CAS membership dues have been maintained at a low annual fee since the Council's inception in 1979. Consequently, CAS has come to rely upon sale of professional publications as its primary source of funding. As a non-profit organization, CAS can accept tax-exempt contributions from individuals as well as grants from philanthropic foundations.

20. Who uses the CAS Standards and how are they typically put to use?

This important question has been studied through a comprehensive, CAS sponsored nation-wide research project. Results, including publication citation, are included in Part I of the CAS Blue Book. A bibliography of articles is also available on the website.

21. Why use CAS standards to evaluate my program rather than using another process (e.g., benchmarks)?

The CAS standards were developed and adopted by knowledgeable representatives from a wide range of higher education organizations. They represent a profession-wide perspective about what constitutes good practice.

22. What is the appropriate citation format for referencing the CAS Professional Standards in Higher Education?

APA format citation for the Blue Book (subsections should follow the citation format for chapters in a book): Council for the Advancement of Standards in Higher Education. (2012). *CAS professional standards for higher education* (8th ed.). Washington, DC: Author.

Appendix E
CAS Publications Ordering and Website Information

Current Publications:

CAS Professional Standards for Higher Education (8th ed.), 2012

CAS Professional Standards for Higher Education is now in its 8th edition. It contains the complete set of 43 functional area standards and guidelines, including standards and guidelines for Masters Degree Student Affairs Preparation Programs. Recent additions include standards and guidelines for a) Parent and Family Programs, b) Veterans and Military Programs and Services, c) Sexual Assault and Relationship Violence Prevention Programs, d) Campus Police and Security Programs (e) Transfer Student Programs and f) a complete review of the General Standards that appear in functional area standards and guidelines.

The following functional area standards and guidelines have been updated from the previous edition of the Standards book: a) Campus Information and Visitor Services, b) Career Services, c) Lesbian, Gay, Bisexual, and Transgender Programs and Services, d) Undergraduate Admissions Programs and Services, e) Counseling Services, and f) Conference and Event Programs.

Each functional area has been updated to address technology programs and services and distance education services to students. Both sections will help institutions make effective decisions as they continue to address the rapidly and ever-changing student technology services and programs.

In addition, CAS has authored a "Statement of Shared Ethical Principles" and the "Characteristics of Individual Excellence for Professional Practice in Higher Education."

CAS Self-Assessment Guides – interactive CD (version 5.0)

Self-Assessment Guides (SAGs) are tools to help you conduct self-assessment activities. They provide the operational view to the standards and guidelines. Each functional area standard has an accompanying SAG. The SAG is in a form that guides you through collecting appropriate information, evaluating how strongly the program or service meets the standards, and finally, developing an appropriate action plan for improvement or for recognizing strong achievement of student learning. The CD contains all SAGS for the functional area standards and guidelines, contextual statements, an e-learning course to learn how to conduct self-assessment, and a PowerPoint presentation that you can download to your computer and use for training purposes.

Frameworks for Assessing Learning and Development Outcomes, 2006 (FALDOs Book/PDF Only)

The FALDOs are complete with a theoretical description of the learning outcome domain, assessment examples, list of possible instruments, and additional resources. This publication is available as electronic download only; domains reflect the structure of *CAS Professional Standards* (2006), which has since been revised.

Packaged sets, quantity discounts, international shipping, and expedited shipping are available. All CAS publications are available for purchase via the CAS website, www.cas.edu, or by contacting the CAS office:

One Dupont Circle, NW, Suite 300
Washington, DC 20036-1188
Phone orders: (202) 862-1400; Fax: (202) 296-3286; CAS website – www.cas.edu

For additional CAS information, Contact – ExecutiveDirector@cas.edu